Clad in Iron

Clad in Iron

The American Civil War and the
Challenge of British Naval Power

Howard J. Fuller

Foreword by Robert J. Schneller, Jr.

Westport, Connecticut
London

Library of Congress Cataloging-in-Publication Data

Fuller, Howard J., 1968–
  Clad in iron : the American Civil War and the challenge of British naval power /
Howard J. Fuller.
      p. cm.
  Includes bibliographical references and index.
  ISBN-13: 978-0-313-34590-6 (alk. paper)
  1. United States. Navy—History—Civil War, 1861-1865. 2. Great Britain. Royal
Navy—History—19th century. 3. Armored vessels—United States—History—19th
century. 4. Armored vessels—Great Britain—History—19th century. 5. Sea-power—
United States—History—19th century. 6. Sea-power—Great Britain—History—19th
century. 7. Trent Affair, 1861. 8. Hampton Roads, Battle of, Va., 1862. 9. United
States—Foreign relations—Great Britain. 10. Great Britain—Foreign relations—United
States. I. Title.
  E591.F88 2008
  973.7'5—dc22   2007035408

British Library Cataloguing in Publication Data is available.

Library of Congress Catalog Card Number: 2007035408
ISBN: 978-0-313-34590-6

First published in 2008

Praeger Publishers, 88 Post Road West, Westport, CT 06881
An imprint of Greenwood Publishing Group, Inc.
www.praeger.com

Printed in the United States of America

The paper used in this book complies with the
Permanent Paper Standard issued by the National
Information Standards Organization (Z39.48-1984).

10 9 8 7 6 5 4 3 2 1

To John F. Fuller
—*Thanks Dad.*

Contents

PART TWO: The Fulcrum of Hampton Roads

PART THREE: Deterring Britannia: The *Trent* Affair Reversed

A photo essay follows page 158.

Foreword

Books about ironclad warships fill shelf after shelf in libraries across Europe and the United States. Most of the historical literature on the subject falls into two categories: technological studies and battle narratives. Writings in the latter category deal overwhelmingly with the American Civil War and began to appear as aging veterans refought their battles in print. Since then historians have continued fighting the same battles, all too often in execrable popular histories that add nothing new to our understanding. One such recurring argument is that the battle of Hampton Roads, the war's most storied naval engagement, sparked a revolution in naval architecture that culminated by 1906 in armored steel battleships armed with large-bore rifled cannon. Whatever their quality, most such books on American ironclads look to the North or South rather than across the Atlantic. James P. Baxter III launched the technological genre in 1933 with *The Introduction of the Ironclad Warship*, which established that the battle of Hampton Roads did not initiate the nineteenth-century revolution in naval architecture, but rather symbolized a revolution that had already been occurring in Europe. Since then scholars working along these lines have examined the development of the ironclad in terms of technological determinism, social construction, and social history.

In *Clad in Iron*, historian Howard Fuller explores a barely scratched corner of an otherwise well-plowed field. Fuller's book examines the development of ironclad warships during the mid-nineteenth century from the diplomatic and high-level strategic perspective of Anglo-American rivalry. Rather than a social constructionist study or a Union versus Confederate battle narrative, his approach is comparative, arguing that Union ironclad development was aimed at Britain as well as the Confederacy, and that British ironclad development eventually had to meet the American threat as well as the original French threat. Fuller bases his argument on prodigious primary-source research and a mastery of the secondary literature on the subject. The result reveals new truths about the introduction and development of ironclad men-of-war.

Howard Fuller is a brilliant, energetic, young scholar who has already compiled an impressive curriculum vitae and who promises to fill many more pages. I met him during his 2002–2003 Rear Admiral John D. Hayes Predoctoral Fellowship at the U.S. Naval Historical Center in Washington, D.C. At that time he was doing dissertation research on the western side of the Atlantic, gathering mountains of material from various American archives after having gathered mountains of material on the eastern side of the Atlantic from various British archives. Since then he has finished his dissertation, received a D. Phil. from King's College, London, landed a job as Senior Lecturer in War Studies at the University of Wolverhampton, and published articles in *The Mariner's Mirror*, *The American Neptune*, *The Northern Mariner/Le Marine du nord*, and *The Journal for Maritime Research*. He also has several other books and articles waiting in the wings to follow *Clad in Iron*, his first book, one sure to have a long shelf life as the standard work on mid-nineteenth-century ironclad development as an Anglo-American strategic phenomenon.

Robert J. Schneller, Jr.
U.S. Naval Historical Center
Washington, D.C.
July 2007

Acknowledgments

I've learned that writing a book is very much like constructing a ship: a process of collaboration. My thanks begin with the unqualified support of the professional staffs at the British National Archives (formerly the "Public Record Office") at Kew, London; the U.S. National Archives in Washington, D.C.; the British Library; the Library of Congress, Manuscript Division; the library of the British National Maritime Museum at Greenwich; the New York Public Library; the library of the Royal United Services Institute (London); the library of the U.S. Naval Historical Center (Washington, D.C.); and the Tekniska Museet (National Museum of Science and Technology), Stockholm. Added to this was the very necessary assistance provided by the Buckinghamshire Record Office; the Nimitz Library at the U.S. Naval Academy (Annapolis); the West Sussex Record Office; the New York Historical Society (New York); the Royal Naval Museum Archives (Portsmouth); Durham University Library; the University of Southampton's archives; the Carlisle Army Archive; the American-Swedish Historical Foundation at Philadelphia; and the John Ericsson Societies of Stockholm and New York.

Funding for this "transatlantic" research was crucial. The Department of War Studies at King's College, London, provided me with several grants to get me out of the country (smile); while the U.S. Naval Historical Center welcomed me back to the States with first an internship and then the Rear Admiral John D. Hayes Fellowship in U.S. Naval History, which allowed me to return to the United Kingdom—and stay there until I finally produced my doctoral thesis, upon which much of this book is based. The University of Wolverhampton and its History and Governance Research Institute (HAGRI) have since taken up much of the burden.

In addition to research, I have enjoyed enthusiastic support in seminars for both Military and British Maritime History at the Institute of Historical Research (the School of Advanced Study at the University of London, in affiliation with the National Maritime Museum); the International Commission for Maritime History at King's College, London; the wonderful "Battle of Hampton Roads Weekend" conferences sponsored by the Mariners' Museum at Newport News, Virginia; the American Historical Association's Annual Meeting of 2004; the National Defence College of Sweden; and the New Researchers in Maritime History-conferences—sponsored by the Society for Nautical Research and the British Commission for Maritime History—where it all began. The Royal Historical Society gave me another, much-needed boost in its Alexander Prize competition of 2002. To the *International Journal of Naval History* and the Canadian Nautical Research Society, I owe a debt of gratitude for allowing me to use extracts from previously published essays. The *IJNH*, in particular, has given me the opportunity of publicly "testing the water" with many ideas that have found there way in here.

Of course, the most important contributions have been personal. Both Professors Brian Holden Reid and Andrew Lambert graciously took me under their wing at the Department of War Studies, and have supplied their scholarly and moral support ever since. William N. Still Jr. and Susan-Mary Grant very liberally endorsed my efforts at the Ph.D. viva examination. Iain Hamilton responded to my inquiries with all the professionalism and sensitivity I hoped for and more, supplying me with useful edits to the manuscript when I needed them most. The crew at the U.S. Naval Foundation and Historical Center (Contemporary History Branch) have quite simply been lifesavers, especially Bob Schneller—who characteristically overwhelmed me with his Foreword—Gary Weir (the "Skipper"), Edward J. Marolda, Randy Papadopoulos, and John Darrell Sherwood, who taught me the finer workings of the American naval historical profession. Praeger Security International's Adam Kane has been a good friend—ever since our adventurous West Point Summer Fellowship in Teaching Military History—as well as editor. John Buckley at the University of Wolverhampton has been a perfect colleague and academic role model. Finally, it almost goes without saying that my family has always been there for me, along with Jonathan ("Sam") Sander, Bethan Lant—the best of the British—the invincible Warwick Brown, and Adèle Cardonnel—*la belle âme de la France.*

Despite all the efforts of all these good people, the responsibility for any mistakes "in design" is entirely my own.

Introduction

Ding, Clash, Dong, BANG,
Boom, Rattle, Clash, BANG,
Clink, BANG, Dong, BANG,
Clatter, BANG BANG BANG!
What on earth is this! This is, or
soon will be, the Achilles, iron
armour-plated ship. Twelve
hundred men are working at her
now; twelve hundred men
working on stages over her sides,
over her bows, over her stern,
under her keel, between her
decks, down in her hold, within
her and without, crawling and
creeping into the finest curves of
her lines wherever it is possible
for men to twist. Twelve hundred
hammerers, measurers, caulkers,
armourers, forgers, smiths,
shipwrights; twelve hundred
dingers, clashers, dongers,
rattlers, clinkers, bangers bangers
bangers! Yet all this stupendous
uproar around the rising Achilles

Plain be the phrase, yet apt the
     verse,
More ponderous than nimble;
For since grimed War here laid
     aside
His Orient pomp, 'twould ill
     befit
Overmuch to ply
The rhyme's barbaric cymbal.
Hail to victory without the gaud
Of glory; zeal that needs no fans
Of banners; plain mechanic
     power
Plied cogently in War now
     placed—
Where War belongs—
Among the trades and artisans.
Yet this was battle, and
     intense—
Beyond the strife of fleets heroic;
Deadlier, closer, calm 'mid
     storm;
No passion; all went on by
     crank,

is as nothing to the
reverberations with which the
perfected Achilles *shall resound*
upon the dreadful day when the
full work is in hand for which
this is but note of preparation—
the day when the scuppers that
are now fitting like great, dry,
thirsty conduit-pipes, shall run
red. All these busy figures
between decks, dimly seen
bending at their work in smoke
and fire, are as nothing to the
figures that shall do work here of
another kind in smoke and fire,
that day.

> —Charles Dickens, *The*
> *Uncommercial Traveller*

Pivot, and screw,
And calculations of caloric.
Needless to dwell; the story's
  known.
The ringing of those plates on
  plates
Still ringeth round the world—
The clangor of that blacksmiths'
  fray.
The anvil-din
Resounds this message from the
  Fates:
War shall yet be, and to the end;
But war-paint shows the streaks
  of weather;
War yet shall be, but warriors
Are now but operatives; War's
  made
Less grand than Peace,
And a singe runs through lace
  and feather.
> —Herman Melville, *A Utilitar-*
> *ian View of the Monitor's Fight*

Although historian Stanley Sandler writes that "few exercises are more
difficult than an evaluation of the comparative strength of the warships
of different nations,"[1] this book will examine the correlative development and significance of British and Union ironclad programs during the
American Civil War "era" (roughly 1860–1866), concentrating on the
pivotal, decision-making years of 1861 and 1862. The principal reason for
this focus rests on three consequentially related conditions:

1. Great Britain was engaged in an ironclad naval arms race against
   Imperial France, but her most likely antagonist during this period
   was unquestionably the United States of America.
2. Such a war between the two greatest maritime nations in the world
   would be primarily a *naval* one,[2] fought for "command of the sea,"
   especially the coastal waters of the Northern States themselves.
3. Strategic "sea power"[3] is often based on the tactical supremacy of
   warships—in this case, the physical ability of individual armor-
   plated men-of-war to command the seas in question.

Great Britain and the United States faced common technological challenges to their naval power while often teetering on the brink of hostilities with each other throughout the Civil War era. The combination of rapid industry-based changes in naval warfare and heightened diplomatic tension yielded contrasting solutions that reflected each nation's unique perspective on—and predicament with—foreign affairs. While the Federal Union was from first to last concerned with subduing the rebellion of Southern states, it also took clear steps both to prepare for and to deter any foreign interference in the conflict, starting with its Navy. Britain's Navy, meanwhile, faced a wide range of peacetime problems both foreign and domestic. "Economising the Empire" while also consolidating its security worldwide, maintaining battle fleet parity (if not superiority) over France, and determining the most effective ironclad warships for these seemingly contradictory roles caused the British Admiralty to be frequently drawn to the American struggle for examples in modern naval warfare, in addition to the strategic implications of an ironclad U.S. Navy. These, in turn, provoked intense discussion of great importance (as they did in the United States) both of tactics and of strategy. The "tactical" debate over ironclad programs—including the limits and roles of the latest naval technology—led directly to larger issues of national policy. Moreover, the controversies that evolved on both sides of the Atlantic were not isolated; they originated with and continued to affect one another, American and British, in a precise relationship during a mutually decisive phase of a common history. This book, therefore, is not intended to be a technical exposition of ships per se, but a chiefly manuscript-based chronicle of the men behind their design, construction, and deployment, and the larger technological, political, and even social forces affecting these ultimately personal decisions of national—and imperial—defense. In this story, the documents will speak for themselves.

It is curious that there have been no comparative studies of this precise *naval* relationship before. A general review of American Civil War historiography suggests that the conflict itself is given almost supreme importance in national and supranational terms. James McPherson notes in the preface of his Pulitzer Prize–winning *Battle Cry of Freedom: The Civil War Era* that the "crucible" of the American Civil War "fused the several states bound loosely in a federal *Union* under a weak central government into a new *Nation* forged by the fires of a war in which more Americans lost their lives than in all of the country's other wars combined."[4] In Ken Burns's celebrated television documentary *The Civil War* (1991), the late historian Shelby Foote describes the event as "the crossroads of our being," which "defined us a nation." Even a British historian who recently compared the "Wars of the Industrial Revolution" observes that "the American Civil War was the greatest struggle of the nineteenth century—the most destructive conflict between the Napoleonic Wars (1798–1815) and the First World War (1914–1918)," and that "Europeans are inclined to forget that the rise of the United States to world power is the greatest historical event of the nineteenth century."[5]

Although the Civil War is the most published historical topic in the United States, and is still increasing in popularity, its study remains primarily devoted to the role of the contending armies and leaders in deciding the fate of the American republic. Note the many books analyzing Gettysburg and its consequences as a "decisive battle," or the effective military command of Confederate General Robert E. Lee, or the unwavering leadership of President Abraham Lincoln as the guiding political force behind the eventual triumph of the Union. Yet, as McPherson points out, "although naval personnel constituted only 5 percent of the Union armed forces, their contribution to the outcome of the war was much larger."[6]

At the same time, the overall focus of most works relating to the Civil War is acutely *domestic.* After all, one might reason, it was a *civil* war, fought on American soil. But along with a general revitalization of popular interest in the 1960s, including Bruce Catton's very readable, three-volume *Centennial History of the Civil War,* an inevitable trickle-down of greater historical attention to this naval "5 percent" has occurred. Likewise, more historians have sought to understand the American conflict in relation to foreign powers, mainly those of Europe; for that matter, some historians have delved into the question of how European relations affected the destiny of the American nation-state.[7] As a result, many more works have appeared that examine solely *either* the naval history of the war *or* its international, diplomatic side.[8] These subdividing lines are as perceptible as those that distinguish studies treating the American Civil War as an event in modern history from others that exclusively belabor its military narrative.

C. I. Hamilton, perhaps, has recently come closest to striking a balance in coverage with his superlative *Anglo-French Naval Rivalry, 1840–1870* (1993). This book significantly addresses an important, relatively unexplored subject—neglected in naval histories probably because no shots were actually fired in anger during this period; nor did the naval arms race end with (or indeed help initiate) a great war like the subsequent Anglo-German one. Hamilton was able to shed light on the character of both the British and French navies at a time when technologies born during the Industrial Revolution threatened to destabilize the European balance of power at sea.[9] Nevertheless, as A. J. P. Taylor noted, "between 1861 and 1865 . . . when British statesmen thought of war in these years it was with the United States, not with any continental Power."[10] In this vein, Kenneth Bourne's *Britain and the Balance of Power in North America, 1815–1908* (1967) briefly discusses the ongoing Anglo-*American* naval (if not maritime) rivalry, but only as part of the larger diplomatic relations between the two countries. It therefore offered little insight into how the formulation of national policy crucially affects national warship design and vice versa— even though Bourne's three-part work clearly hinges on the American Civil War years, specifically the *Trent* affair (November–December 1861), which he regards as "the most dangerous single incident of the Civil War and perhaps in the whole course of Anglo-American relations since 1815."[11]

The following three-part analysis also concentrates on the *Trent* affair, but in direct contrast to the battle of Hampton Roads (March 8–9, 1862). Somehow in the span of these three months, the Anglo-American naval balance of power was completely upset; though Bourne classically derides the Union's force of ironclad monitors as "unseaworthy"— taking contemporary assessments at face value only—he admits "there were still from the British point of view periods of awkward disparity between the two fleets."[12]

An even more comprehensive comparative naval history is James Phinney Baxter's *Introduction of the Ironclad Warship*, published in 1933, which plumbed British, French, *and* American archival sources, but which also ends, rather than starts, with Hampton Roads. This was because Baxter's purpose, as stated in the introduction to his book, was to debunk American claims that the famous naval battle sounded "the death knell of the wooden walls" and that the mastless, turreted U.S.S. *Monitor* was the forerunner of the modern battleship.[13] Instead, "Hampton Roads demonstrated and emphasized the foresight of the French," who from 1858 had laid down an entire fleet of broadside-and-sail ironclads, while British Navy Captain Cowper Phipps Coles at least insisted on multiple turrets for his fully rigged (though ill-fated) experiments.[14]

Deliberately picking up where Baxter left off, Sandler's *Emergence of the Modern Capital Ship* (1979) dropped all pretense of a comparative naval history and sought to give full credit not to Dupuy de Lôme (the brilliant French innovator), Coles, or the *Monitor*'s inventor, John Ericsson, but to Edward J. Reed, the Chief Constructor of the Royal Navy. Though Reed's solution to the vexing paradox of how to reconcile the strategic strengths ideally represented by H.M.S. *Warrior* with the tactical advantages posed by the *Monitor* was the "central battery" ironclad, there is a clear break from his (concentrated) broadside-and-sail H.M.S. *Hercules*, for example, and his mastless, double-turreted H.M.S. *Devastation* (which Sandler and most naval historians—British and

American—recognize as the first modern battleship). Even British naval authority Oscar Parkes fleetingly observed that "mention must be made of these ships [the monitors of the American Civil War] as they had a certain bearing upon subsequent British designs, to the extent that the *Miantonomoh* idea was behind the *Cerberus* and through her the *Devastation*, while the [Admiralty] Board must have had the *Puritan* in mind when specifying the design of the *Glatton*."[15] Yet Sandler proved unwilling to more fully explore this important connection. "Whether the monitors were a failure," he wrote, "is not so important here as the fact that the reports from America, by both British and American authorities [especially Rear Admiral Samuel F. Du Pont], almost uniformly wrote off the Ericsson monitor as practically useless, particularly for sea service. Such reports could only strengthen the resolve of the controller and the chief constructor and most of the board against any precipitate oceanic turret-ship program. Coles himself termed the federal monitors *wretched vessels*."[16]

Indeed, it was difficult in the early 1860s to see exactly *how* a small coastal defense ironclad of a relatively "provincial" continental power like the United States could ever hope to compare with the large imperial ironclads of England and France—though the comparison was certainly made—and post-"Mahanian" naval historians and bluewater advocates today seem to find it still more perplexing. Examples abound on both sides of the Atlantic. For many revisionist British naval historians, there is a somewhat defensive tendency to ridicule obviously "inferior" "foreign" navies that may have had "a certain bearing" on Whitehall decision making, let alone policymaking at Westminster. In *Battleships in Transition: The Creation of the Steam Battlefleet, 1815–1860* (1984) Andrew Lambert writes of the "block obsolescence of [France's] wooden-hulled [though fully armored] ironclads," which "left the Royal Navy pre-eminent." Navies of "The Rest of the World" in the same volume are reduced to pithy paragraphs occupying about two and a half pages.[17] David K. Brown, in *Warrior to Dreadnought: Warship Development, 1860–1905* (1997), is even more succinct: "From 1860 to 1905 British warships, with few exceptions, were the best in the world." Like Lambert, however, he cites no supportive evidence, and there is no foreign research actually conducted off the British Isles. The main agenda instead is to debunk the notion that the "nineteenth-century Navy, and to some extent the Admiralty as a whole, [was] reactionary . . . the Admiralty was usually the leader and in the few cases when it was not the leader there were usually good reasons and it was not far behind."[18]

This treatment, however, only replaces a threatened American chauvinism with a "Rule Britannia" one. Meanwhile, "though the subject remains ideologically charged, the passions aroused by British imperialism have so lessened that we are now better placed than ever before to see the course of the Empire steadily and see it whole."[19] Even a recent volume of the *Oxford History of the British Empire* primarily ventures "to explain how varying conditions in Britain interacted with those in many other parts of the world to create both a constantly changing territorial Empire and ever-shifting patterns of *social and economic relations.*" Missing here is a sense of how the "Pax Britannica" was dependent upon the ascendancy—or not—of the Royal Navy. "Fundamentally, the British Empire was concerned with power,"[20] notes Peter Burroughs in one essay of this anthology; in another, titled "Defence and Imperial Disunity," he maintains that "warships restrained the expansionist designs of France and Russia, especially in the crucial Mediterranean corridor; gunboats occasionally backed British diplomatic or commercial ventures with a show of force, as in South America and China; naval squadrons suppressed piracy and African slave trading and guaranteed the openness of the seas." If Great Britain was the "world policeman" of the nineteenth century, it was this predominating naval presence that gave it real power, if not authority, and supplied the Empire with its ultimate sense of defensive unity. Even current historiographical issues of British "informal" imperialism must take into account an equally informal naval hegemony that reflected changes in social and economic relations (constituting essentially a maritime empire) as well as technological, if not political, pressures.

In many histories of the period, however, this reality is either assumed or ignored altogether, though "in the nineteenth century it began to appear possible," Michael Howard points out, "for the nation which most effectively applied in its naval building programmes the developing techniques of marine engineering, metallurgy, and artillery construction to pulverize any opposing fleet without its victim being able to land a single shot on its assailant."[21] Burroughs's excellent assessment of the central role played by the Royal Navy might thus also benefit from a more thorough understanding of how mid-Victorian naval policy was possibly also the *victim* of an "Imperial Defence" strategy, if one in fact existed in the early 1860s. Where British ironclads could reach but make no impression upon rival, local naval powers, the apparatus of world supremacy was lost.[22]

Nowhere was this dilemma manifest more acutely than in the American Civil War crisis in international relations. Winston Churchill, in his illustrious *History of the English-Speaking Peoples,* regarded the nineteenth century as characterized not only by Victorian Britain but also by the other "Great Democracy": America. Nor did he entertain any serious conflict of interests between the two rising powers—later to be the closest of wartime allies. Indeed, the formulation of the anti-monarchical, anti-European Monroe Doctrine in 1823 "depended on the friendly vigilance of the 'British man-of-war,' but this fact was seldom openly acknowledged. For the best part of a century the Royal Navy remained the strongest guarantee of freedom in the Americas. Thus shielded by the British bulwark, the American continent was able to work out its own unhindered destiny."[23] During the Civil War, this presence was regarded differently. British interests in keeping "Continental despots" out of Latin America, for example, propounded by earlier aggressive foreign secretaries like George Canning, could turn a sense of protection into mortal intrusion itself when those interests saw fit to change. In an 1851 speech on the Royal Navy's campaign against the slave trade, Foreign Secretary Lord Palmerston extolled England's "proud position among the nations of the earth," exercising "a great influence upon the destinies of mankind":

> That influence is owing, in the first place, to our great wealth, to our unbounded resources, to our military and naval strength. But it is owing still more, if possible, to the moral dignity which marks the character and conduct of the British people. . . . Those who desire to see the principles of liberty thrive and extended throughout the world, should cherish, with an almost religious veneration, the prosperity and greatness of England. So long as England shall ride preeminent on the ocean of human affairs, there be can none whose fortunes shall be so shipwrecked—there can be none whose condition shall be so desperate and forlorn—that they may not cast a look of hope towards the light that beams from hence. . . .[24]

Yet as long as America's development as a united republic was also "dependent" upon the naval supremacy of an imperial, non-republican democracy, she was also a hostage to fate. Consequently, the Union Navy's first concern in the rapid buildup of U.S. naval might was the *exclusion* of influence in American affairs exercised by the Royal Navy; though this historical phenomenon remains relatively unappreciated and unexplored.

Indeed, American naval historians have all too often measured the "success" or "failure" of the Union's ironclad program from a determinist perspective. After all, how could a coastal defense warship be powerful if it was not yet part of an *imperial* navy? For Harold and Margaret Sprout, in their *Rise of American Naval Power, 1776–1918*, published in 1939, the "Continental" naval strategy of the early United States was a violation of good Mahanian "maritime" sense:

By unqualifiedly endorsing the shallow draft, unseaworthy monitor-type to the exclusion of sea-going ironclads, not merely as a temporary wartime expedient, but also as a permanent policy, the United States was perpetuating the strategy of passive coast and harbor defense, which had contributed so largely to the disasters of the War of 1812, and which was now failing to save the Confederate seaboard either from blockade or occupation by the Union forces.[25]

But if the real issue was the *type of ironclad,* insofar as this determined which far-reaching *strategy* was best for the survival of the nation, the Sprouts entirely omit any actual explanation of these ironclads' varying characteristics. Instead, it is virtually assumed that recent tactical developments in naval warfare, such as armor plating and super-heavy mounted naval ordnance, made no difference in strategic principle compared with the earliest days of wooden fighting ships. Bernard Brodie's *Seapower in the Machine Age,* also published on the eve of America's entry into the Second World War, similarly argued, "[T]here is no use in rejoicing about an invention which enables the United States, for example, better to withstand the blows of an enemy if it also disables us from retaliating when he strikes at our vital interests abroad." This was the very definition of "sea power," or "command of the sea": "retain seaborne communications for oneself and to deny them to the enemy" while also relying upon the "concentrated strength of a battle force."[26]

Implicit in these works is not how the monitors helped the Union achieve victory in the Civil War, but how they almost prevented it. A very recent study of Samuel Du Pont's ironclad repulse before Charleston (April 7, 1863) by Robert M. Browning Jr. ultimately takes the Union admiral's view of events: it was the tools at his disposal that were to blame for the failure, not his leadership.[27] At the same time, William H. Roberts's treatment of the only sea-going broadside ironclad constructed for the Union Navy before the end of the Civil War, U.S.S. *New Ironsides,* ultimately misses the point of *why* monitor ironclads were favored over possible sisters of her. Unarguably, the broadside was more effective in shore bombardment, where number of guns and a "suppressing fire" were more important than individual caliber. This, in combination with *New Ironsides'* 4½-inch–thick iron armor, and especially her light draft in comparison with the sea-going ironclads of European powers, made her the most respected ironclad to Confederates huddled in forts. But only the more heavily armored, rotating turret could handle the 15-inch Dahlgren, and this was the weapon most feared by Confederate sailors in their own ironclads.[28] Was there more to the attraction of mounting such heavier, if fewer, guns—in smaller, less expensive, more quickly constructed, and better-protected vessels of even lighter draft—than subduing domestic opposition to the blockade? Roberts does not ask this question, nor does Browning, and relies in its place upon a conspiratorial theory that "politics, desire for commercial advantage, and 'monitor mania,' rather than any innate technological superiority, allowed the monitor type of ship to dominate the Union ironclad program."[29] Added to this is his obvious disappointment that "the vessels needed immediately took precedence: many shallow-draft armored ships that could operate in the shallow harbors and rivers of the Confederacy, instead of a few expensive ocean-going ships to meet the European ironclads on equal terms at sea," though he later admits—but fails to explain—that the end result of the Union Civil War ironclad program was that "within a strictly limited sphere (i.e., the coastal waters of the United States), the U.S. Navy was superior to any possible invader."[30]

What these works share is the lack of a deliberate comparative approach, which—especially concerning Union and British ironclad programs of the Civil War era—must address the roots of naval power itself, as well as decision making in ship design and national policy. Mahan himself wrote that "the natural tendency of the extreme effort for protection undoubtedly is to obscure the fundamental truth . . . that the best protection is to injure the enemy," but this did not necessarily answer the question of how the United States was potentially clad in iron—by either the Union Navy or the British Navy—during this crucial interval of technological, political, and social upheaval.[31]

Hence, in neither case (the naval or diplomatic histories of the Civil War) has the vital connection between the two approaches been adequately explored. This gap in the literature may exist simply because no naval conflict occurred between Great Britain and the United States, as it did between American "North" and "South." Yet the entire question of *how* and *why* these two powers avoided a confrontation, which many considered inevitable at the time, is answered only to the point that such a war was considered unnecessary—ignoring the equally important concern of whether it was winnable.[32] Even in his 2004 Presidential Address of the American Historical Association, James McPherson signally ignored the role of the Union Navy's "5 percent" in the British Cabinet's fateful deliberations over intervention in the fall of 1862.[33] Howard Jones, in his *Union in Peril: The Crisis over British Intervention in the Civil War* (1992), for example, makes the same general omission, though he does at least provide a clue:

> Northerners believed that the *Monitor*'s activities revealed British concern about the Union's strength at the end of the war. . . . [Charles Francis Adams, the U.S. minister to Britain] noted that the Union Navy's

new prowess exhibited at Hampton Roads had caused a sensation in England and would probably force a build-up in its own navy and fortifications. He also believed that the Union's military power had neutralized British interest in intervention. That same evening, puffed up by the day's good news, Adams attended a reception held by Lady Palmerston and engaged in a brief conversation with [Secretary for War Sir George Cornewall] Lewis, who uncharacteristically lost self-control and lashed out at the North for seeking to subjugate the South. Reconstruction of the Union was impossible, Lewis exclaimed. Adams cut short the heated exchange by remarking that British desire to see the United States divided was the most compelling argument against allowing that event to take place.[34]

Concentrating on the front line of this peacekeeping process is Regis A. Courtemanche's *No Need of Glory: The British Navy in American Waters, 1860–1864* (Annapolis, MD: U.S. Naval Institute Press, 1977), a deferential study of Vice Admiral Sir Alexander Milne's command of the North American and West Indian Station. Milne was in a position of tremendous responsibility during the Civil War. Queen Victoria's Proclamation of Neutrality of May 13, 1861, meant that British subjects had to refrain from materially aiding either American belligerent. The officers of Milne's command were especially warned not to commit acts that would immediately lead to a diplomatic incident.[35] One such act, perpetrated by U.S. naval Captain Charles Wilkes against the Royal packet steamer *Trent*, triggered British national outrage and very nearly led to a collision between Britain and the United States. Milne was thus responsible for measures against any violations of British neutrality committed by Americans as well. When the *Trent* crisis quickly escalated into British military and naval preparations for war, Milne made plans for naval operations against the Union. Afterward, and for the remainder of his assignment, he was under increasing pressure from Lord Lyons, the British Minister in Washington, and Earl Russell, the Foreign Secretary in London, to maintain the peace. As Lyons wrote to Milne a year after the *Trent* crisis, "I have no reason to expect any alteration in our relations here, which are, so far as this Government and myself are concerned, friendly and cordial—but the times are dangerous, and one cannot ever be entirely free from disquiet."[36] Diplomacy was, in this case, a delicate balance between firmness and forbearance, luckily in the hands of a prudent British flag officer.

But Milne's specially commended service was not above disapproval, as Courtemanche paraphrases from a Feb. 13, 1864, article in the English *Saturday Review:*

The essential difference between Milne and his successor [Vice Admiral Sir James Hope] was that Hope "is a fighting man" and "he is more of a warrior than of a diplomatist and of more proved capacity for firing on an enemy than for negotiating a compromise or smoothing a difficulty." Of Milne it said, "He has been, we suspect, the Admiral of the Foreign Office than of the Admiralty. He was selected for his tact, patience, temperate demeanour and courteous bearing." His orders, the article continued, might have been: "cooperate with Lord Lyons to preserve peace by all means in your power. Don't be irritated into a quarrel." . . . The writer of the article believed that possibly peace between England and the Union "was purchased very dearly . . . by a temporary abdication of national self-respect and a temporary abdication of national honour."[37]

Was this criticism from the press, not so much of Milne's skillfulness but of his superiors' guidelines, well founded? Two years earlier, at the culmination of the *Trent* affair—with Lincoln's government accepting British demands for the surrender of the captured Confederate envoys James Mason and John Slidell—Lyons wrote to Milne:

> There is of course no chance of this Government's deliberately resorting to hostilities while things remain in their present condition. After the great sacrifice of pride which they have made to preserve peace, they are not likely to resort wantonly to hostilities. I suppose too that there is rather less than more chance of some 'heroic' Naval Officer committing an aggression upon us, on his own account. In fact the only present danger seems to lie in the surrender's causing so violent an outburst of public wrath, as to drive the Government to some left handed proceeding in order to satisfy the American populace. This, I hope, is not likely. Both Government and people are, I hope, more likely to profit by the lesson which has been given them, and to mend their manners.[38]

What happened, therefore, in the following two years, when "British" could perhaps substitute for "American" in the above statement? The *Saturday Review*'s assessment of later British foreign policy to the United States was "to have refused to take offence when it was deliberately offered; to have disregarded impertinence, and not to have resented insolence . . . to have been indifferent not only to personal slights but even to affronts heaped upon their flag. . . ."[39] Indeed, many more "insults" to British prestige would be made after the *Trent* affair.

The issue was both politically complex and brutally simple, for U.S. anger over British violations of their self-proclaimed neutrality also rose following the *Trent* affair. Even Milne, toward the end of his command, felt "the advisability of considering the policy of allowing notorious Blockade Runners to be repaired in Her Majesty's Yards," especially when

> it is to be borne in mind that the United States Government and People not unnaturally consider that the unhappy strife in which they are

engaged would long since have been brought to an end, had it not been for the activity of the Blockade Runners . . . and although I am well aware that it is not any part of our duty as Neutral to stop this Trade, it may yet be found that the Federal Government is only waiting a good opportunity of drawing the distinction between merely permitting such a Trade, and actually aiding in it, by repairing in Her Majesty's Naval yards, Vessels openly, notoriously and regularly engaged in this Fraudulent Trade, in direct defiance of Her Majesty's Proclamation and thus enabling the Vessels, when disabled, to resume with greater expedition their adventurous and profitable traffic, and work the more injury to the Federal cause.

At the heart of this practice by many British shipbuilders, captains, and crews were simple calculations of gain or loss, irrespective of how private enterprise was seriously irritating the diplomatic relations of the two powers. As long as the Royal Navy seemed unbeatable, with frigates and fortifications lining the wharves at Bermuda, for example, British subjects were most likely emboldened to inflame a smoldering peace as much as possible. Milne continued, "I cannot but think that had the French Government, in the old days when smuggling was so rife, been in the habit of repairing well known Smugglers in their Dockyards, we should have deemed it an unfriendly proceeding on their part; if so, how much more may the Federals in this case, when the interests involved are so much more vast and important."[40] Misgivings crept in at even higher levels, for Russell replied to the First Lord of the Admiralty, the Duke of Somerset, "You hardly cannot mean to say that if the American merchants in Japan did what the Liverpool Merchants have been doing with impunity we should be obliged to go to war with America, for this would be urging that we are at this moment giving America just cause of War. This of course would be a strong condemnation of ourselves, and one which we could never admit."[41]

Courtemanche shows, moreover, a growing British appreciation for Northern anger combined with a heightened sense of respect for what that implied—especially as the full scale of damage to the Yankee merchant marine around the globe, committed by only a few steam raiders such as the British-built C.S.S. *Alabama*, became widely known. Great Britain was also keenly interested in the rapid armored growth of the U.S. Navy. Because Milne was the highest-ranking naval officer at the scene, he was promptly instructed to gather as much intelligence as practicable, relaying these orders to the ship captains under his command off American ports. Although he strongly objected to Union monitors as a model for the Royal Navy in general, he recognized that their value for harbor and coast defense had completely upset the balance of power. Following news of the naval action in Hampton Roads, Milne, surveying the most powerful British fleet ever assembled at Bermuda, wrote privately to an Admiralty Board member: "[I]f these ships of the line now here were cut up into small vessels, they would be of use to me, but except for Demonstrations clear of *Merrimac* and *Monitor*, they are no use. . . ."[42]

The fleet that Milne commanded in early 1862 served as political leverage against the U.S. Government. By 1862 only a few British ironclads were ready for trials, and comparative naval power was still measured by overall numbers of wooden steamships, as opposing numbers of guns were counted between warships themselves. Whether that blunt instrument of "Palmerstonian diplomacy" was taken away by the Union's Civil War ironclad program will be also be examined.

No Need of Glory is a valuable and instructive testament to a British naval officer's good diplomatic sense, and for that matter, Milne stands as an interesting contrast to Wilkes of the Union Navy. But the increasing pressure on Milne *to act diplomatically* was the result of a perceptible and fundamental change in British confidence, which Courtemanche does not wholly identify. Nor was this change strictly political, for technology played an important role in strategy, which contemporary reviewers were even less inclined to acknowledge. By the close of Milne's command in early 1864, the London *Times* would conclude only that British foreign influence, based upon status, respect, and fear of the Royal Navy in America as well as Europe, was directly undermined by domestic labors for economy (if not peace). With Liberal advocates like William Gladstone, the Chancellor of the Exchequer, pushing for naval and military reductions against the old arguments of Prime Minister Palmerston and Russell, England seemed bound to suffer abroad:

We could sweep the seas with our fleets. At an hour's notice we could close the Mediterranean and the Baltic, and blockade any port of any maritime country. We could throw 30,000 men on any point of any coast, and subsidize ten times as many more. . . .But, though this may be a proud position to occupy, it should be clearly understand at what cost it is held. If we wish to stand as France stands, we must pay as France pays for the privilege;—that is to say, we must prepare ourselves for largely increased taxations, and deficits after all. Twenty millions would not cover our Navy Estimates on these principles of foreign policy, nor would any amount of armaments answer the purpose without actual war now and then. . . .We must be ready at any minute and on any provocation to go to war with anybody, and as a necessary consequence our forces must be always in a state of perfect efficiency and strength. . . .When a man who will not fight except under irresistible pressure interferes in a quarrel, and wishes the combatants to accept his judgment, we know what words he is likely to get. But this "humiliation," such as it is, is the inevitable incident of such a policy as we have chosen.[43]

Here, the emphasis on cost, on quantity if not quality of naval armaments, is blamed for the change of policy. The following work will focus on the implicit relationship between British decision making in the areas of economy, politics, technology, and foreign policy. Previous studies of the influence of the Royal Navy during the American Civil War have not fully accomplished this.

The fact remains—though inexplicably dormant—that in 1862 U.S. Secretary of the Navy Gideon Welles could write, "[W]e are not, it is true, in a condition for war with Great Britain just at this time, but England is in scarcely a better condition for a war with us."[44] Historical comparisons between American and European navies should therefore not stop for the years 1861–1865 when one is examining the Union Navy; they should intensify. Nor should histories of America's role as a naval power assume that this great struggle for national identity was entirely domestic in scope, or that the technologically sophisticated weapon systems devised by the Union Navy— the most advanced ironclad steamers of their kind in the world—indicated a preoccupation solely in that direction. Whether "world naval power" began or ended at one's own shores is a question that needs reconsidering.[45] Even studies of Union Civil War ironclads themselves tend to be nearsighted. The *Monitor* did more than save the blockade from a devastating Confederate challenge, and thereby restore international belief that Federal power was ascendant. In the high-stakes game of Civil War diplomacy, it offered Lincoln's administration a unique and valuable playing card with which to counter the recent menace of a British counter-blockade of the North. As Bourne made clear, this had become Britain's ultimate strategic guarantee for the security of her Canadian provinces. The British North America Act of 1867, establishing the "Dominion of Canada"—not to mention the Colonial Naval Defence Act of 1865 (providing for the self-protection of Australia)—was therefore hardly a coincidence. As Gladstone expressed in a Cabinet Memo, "It appears to me that the time is now come for us to show whether all that has recently been said about our calling on the Colonies to bear their full share of military burdens has a meaning or not, and whether we do or do not mean to alter our system of Colonial defence with reference to altered circumstances of capability, power, and privilege. . . . It is not the simple matter of money that is in view; it is the peril of committing the honour of this country to the assumption of an attitude, which it may be unable or unwilling permanently to maintain."[46]

Perhaps not ironically, one of the few naval histories to stress this correlation was also the first. Reverend Charles B. Boynton, with the official approval of the U.S. Navy toward the close of the Civil War, began compiling a two-volume *History of the Navy during the*

Rebellion, which laid particular stress on the influence of British sea power upon American history. Completed three years after hostilities ended, Boynton, Chaplain of the U.S. House of Representatives and Assistant Professor at the U.S. Naval Academy, saw fit to make the following remarkable observation: "While our Army has done a work beyond all praise, and has settled the question of our ability to defend our territory against any force which could be brought here, the Navy has saved us from foreign intervention that could not have been otherwise avoided, while at the same time its labors in putting down the rebellion have been far greater than has been generally supposed." Clearly, the emphasis Boynton makes is on the *foreign*—not the domestic—potency of the Union Navy during the Civil War. Where is that discernment now?

Indeed, the entire purpose of the Union Navy, as Boynton saw it, was to guarantee national sovereignty against foreign enemies first, insofar as the Union army dealt primarily with the domestic rebellion of the Southern states. "With England and France," Boynton observed, "the most interesting question connected with our affairs has been, whether we could create a truly formidable Navy":

> Our naval strength was the standard by which they measured their power to attack, and ours to defend. They did not believe it possible for us to produce a Navy in a few months which could both seal up our long line of sea-coast and defy their most formidable ships, and this mistaken judgment was the main influence in deciding their policy in regard to American affairs. A history of the Navy, then, is a history of that power by which Europe gauges our national importance, and by which our rank among nations is assigned.[47]

History of the Navy during the Rebellion thus regarded the American Civil War as a contest of "American" versus "European" political and social values, and "more than all else, the Navy has been an original creation, a true outgrowth of distinctive American thought . . . the embodying of truly American ideas; and whatever question there may be in regard to any other feature of our civilization, no one will deny that there are American ships, American cannon, and an American Navy." National identity in this sense, its ironclads, "should be studied by the people," Boynton maintained, "because they show the originating and independent power of the American mind, when operating on a large scale, and competing with the whole of Europe." Invaluable for its long-forgotten insight, Boynton's obsequious (and perhaps ingratiating) portrayal of the U.S. Navy nevertheless suffers from partial resources, severe patriotic bias, and the still-widespread Anglophobia of the day. England, Boynton was sure, "desired, with an earnestness not exceeded by that of Jefferson Davis himself, the humbling of the North, and the separation of the Union."[48]

As a result, many questions remain. Had Britain fully "desired the separation of the Union," would the course of her naval construction been altered? What effect did the ironclad naval race with France—before the outbreak of the war in America—have on British policy? If national protection and deterrence of foreign intervention in the Civil War, if not outright preparations for a worldwide maritime war against the British Empire, were guiding principles behind the rapidly mobilizing United States Navy, what was the basis for British national and imperial doctrine?[49] These questions were frequently asked by opposing members of Parliament, for they were deterministic of what "naval power" meant. The Admiralty spokesman, Lord Clarence Paget, replied by stating that, in determining Britain's ironclad shipbuilding policy, "one could not advert to the subject without more or less dealing with foreign nations, and especially with France."[50] In other words, power was a relative concept. The United States had *re-nationalized* itself during the Civil War; this was something Great Britain was not prepared to do. Rival "ironclad" systems exposed conflicting Anglo-American priorities. Of course, to meet the Yankees on their own terms was possible, but not probable, to mid-Victorians unconcerned by "American" issues of slavery, if not popular democracy, and unaffected by a great new military and naval power an ocean away. Boynton's comparison of Union and British naval means (surprisingly limited, given his main argument) would therefore have benefited by also examining the evolution of Britain's ironclad program, instead of proceeding with an already straightforward history of the American Civil War. Subsequently, it might have contributed much more satisfactorily to an appreciation of American, if not British, predominance even in the absence of actual campaigns and battles. As such, this comparative narrative picks up where Boynton, not Baxter, left off.

Part One

Deterring Columbia: British Naval Supremacy

Chapter 1

An Ironclad Race with France

The British ironclad program began purely as a response to the establishment of the French ironclad fleet of Napoleon III. Until 1858 Great Britain held a precarious edge in the international competition over the screw-propelled, steam-powered, wooden-hulled ship of the line.[1] Then, as the advantage appeared to be decisively in favor of the Royal Navy once more, the French ironclad *Gloire* seemed to claim the lead for France again.[2] Following the evident success of the *Gloire* design—and concept—the French added to the ironclad's sisters still under construction with an announcement of a program for an entire fleet of oceangoing, iron-plated warships. The sheer scale of the program, so quickly engineered by the talented naval architect and chief constructor Dupuy de Lôme and decisively endorsed by the Emperor himself, suddenly made the British response of the *Warrior*-class vessels—superior in virtually every aspect of sea-keeping, powerfully armed and strongly protected—seem inadequate.[3] The Board of Admiralty, headed by the Duke of Somerset, under Lord Palmerston's new "Liberal Coalition" government (1859), met in early 1861 to discuss the urgency of a full-scale response.[4]

The immediate threat to British security was apparently invasion. This threat, coupled with the massive fortification and modernization of the strategic port of Cherbourg, made it obvious to the naval members of the Board that "immediate steps should be taken to meet so formidable a force—otherwise the spring of 1862 might see the French in possession of such a fleet of iron-cased ships as could give them the command of the Channel." This was not a politically calculated alarmist sentiment, but a cool appraisal of fact.[5] To the professional Navy such a prospect was embarrassing and unthinkable.[6]

In January the Controller (formerly "Surveyor"), Admiral Sir Baldwin W. Walker, presented designs to the Board for what was to be the new *Valiant* class of broadside ironclad. Taking into account the public as well as professional criticisms[7] of the *Warrior* class, and of the two successor broadside ironclads of considerably smaller dimensions, *Defence* and *Resistance* (length 280 feet, speed 11.2 knots for *Defence*), the new ship was "proposed to place 30 of the guns on the Main Deck, which is to be protected by Armour Plating from end to end."[8] This would give the new *Valiant* and *Hector* substantially more protection than the unarmored ends of the first four broadside ironclads—*Warrior, Black Prince, Defence,* and *Resistance*—whose limited armor belts protected barely half their long batteries.[9] Yet, even while the battery itself was now to be fully protected, the waterline protection was still less than complete, being "within 30 ft of the Stem, and 35 ft of the Stern Post," 5 feet below the load waterline.[10] If the ships heeled or rolled during action and suffered a penetrative hit in this unprotected stretch of 65 feet, the consequences could be instantly disastrous. If they did not sink, they could be seriously crippled.

This was not the only disadvantage with increased armor protection of the first four broadside ironclads. Walker warned that "it will scarcely be questioned that this amount of security against injury from Shot and Shell is not to be obtained without compromising important qualities of sea-going ships." The added weight toward the ends of the ships would contribute to heavy pitching at sea and thus make them "unsuited for general service" (as was yet to be tested for the *Warrior*). Furthermore, "from their comparatively larger amount of Armour Plating, they will approximate much more nearly to that of the 'Warrior' class than their relative tonnage would appear to indicate."[11] This was considered a move more toward coastal defense than otherwise, despite the immediate tactical improvements in design. The *Gloire*, however, already incorporated a fully protected battery and was as fast as the *Valiant* class, which in turn was slower than *Warrior*'s 14-knot maximum under steam by 2 knots.[12]

If the challenge to British naval supremacy began with the waters separating England from France, if not from Europe in general, *Warrior* was intended at the same time to operate anywhere in the world, if need be. Defending her design at the Institution of Naval Architects, Sir John Pakington (the former First Lord, and President of the Institution) remarked:

> Shall I not be correct if I say that in constructing a man-of-war it is most important to combine in these days great speed with good seagoing

qualities? . . . Now, the *Warrior* and other vessels of that class were designed with the express intention of securing these two great qualities, even at the expense of total protection. It was the desire of the Admiralty in trying that experiment that these ships should not be mere floating batteries, but fit to encounter the worst seas, and to go to India, America, or wherever the exigencies of the country might render their presence desirable. . . .[13]

This initial distinction, apparently special to British interests, also led to a unique and fundamental confusion over what these armorclads were intended to accomplish. If the strategic command of the Channel was really at stake, long-range "cruisers," partially protected, were not the clear and obvious solution to a manifestly local threat. The French conception of a fully armored frigate thus held an important tactical advantage.[14] Captain E. P. Halsted, R. N., condemned the *Warrior* as "unworthy to be called a warship at all," a remark that drew Pakington's response.[15] But even Palmerston had his misgivings, repeatedly pressuring Somerset that it would be "impossible to strengthen the Stem and Stern of the *Warrior* and her Companions without materially impairing her Sea going qualities. She is at present, there is no denying it, a fine yacht, but not an efficient Ship of War."[16]

If the Board expressed alarm at the French ironclad program in January 1861, it is significant that these statements came *after* the designer of the *Warrior*, Chief Constructor Isaac Watts, provided the Admiralty with improved Warriors in the form of the *Achilles*, and only two weeks after the *Valiant*-class submission was approved. Some of the original problems with the first four ironclads were solved in the new design. An iron ship—and the first to be constructed in a Royal Dockyard (at the newly refacilitated Chatham)[17]—the *Achilles* was armored entirely along the waterline, with modifications that saw to the protection of the rudder and steering gear, dangerously exposed on the preceding ironclads.[18] As with the first ships, little more than half her bulwarks and battery were covered by armor plating at first; within a year, all the unprotected guns were removed. But the *Achilles'* full armor protection (4½ inches of wrought-iron plating on 18 inches of teak, identical to *Warrior*'s), combined with the need for speed and seaworthiness, again produced an ironclad as long as the *Warrior*, with a gigantic spread of sail 30,133 square feet carried in four masts and a bowsprit (later reduced to three masts). Speed was comparable, yet the draft exceeded *Warrior*'s, at 27½ feet. This stupendous warship was a Victorian overkill. If the original concern of the Board was better actual protection for this most expensive naval investment (especially considering the length of time involved in its construction, and given the unforeseen problems occurring with the other ships), then Britain herself was still vulnerable at sea. When an ironclad of these dimensions was finally produced, its armor was no longer superlative but inferior, and the problem of where to station these ships, even in home ports, remained a significant one. Nor did the new broadside monster solve the problem of sheer handiness in combat, especially in close quarters such as harbors and inlets. If the issue of armor and armament was in the front of the mind of the Controller, as was sea-keeping, the capacity for coastal defense was growing by comparative leaps and bounds. But under Walker's direction, at least, the emphasis was more on sea-keeping than on full protection and powerful armament. His resignation shortly afterward did little to encourage the Board or the British public that the French threat was properly met.

On May 2, 1861, the new Controller, Rear Admiral Robert Spencer Robinson, recommended the testing of armor plates, using the plan of Charles Lancaster, who had boasted of his ability "to deliver any quantities of such Plates so manufactured, of any thickness up to ten inches."[19] The following day Robinson wrote to the Admiralty that "it would be very advantageous to erect the Frames of such of these [line-of-battle] ships as are nearly completed, with a view of preparing them for 50 Gun Frigates to be covered with Armour plating. . . ." Surplus wood supplies in the dockyards could thus be taken care of, and "If from any cause a pressing necessity should arise for a Force of this description, a great proportion of the work will be already done . . . and time will have been gained for any further experiments on the combination of wood and Iron which it may be desirable to make." This next step, the introduction of the wooden-hulled conversions of the *Royal Oak* class, was regarded as an improvement on the *Valiant*, with a fully protected battery (and along the waterline), but not so much in terms of range as the *Warrior*, for his submission added only that "she would be a sufficiently good Sea Boat to go to the Mediterranean if required. . . ."[20]

However, with wooden hulls, the ships of this class could be seen as more free ranging because there was no worry of the excess marine fouling that was endemic to iron hulls (which could not be coppered because of the corrosive electrolytic reaction). Although the main theater of naval operations for France was more likely to be the Mediterranean, hull design was also a factor in the French decision to proceed with Dupuy de Lôme's first ironclads—which capitalized more on French strengths and relied less on comparative French weaknesses, such as iron ship manufacture.[21] What did it matter that wooden-hulled ships would not last as long as iron-hulled ones, when advances in armor, ordnance, and engineering made it painfully obvious that the new warships would be obsolete within years, not decades? The Controller toughened his proposal by remarking, "[I]t is needless to call their Lordships' attention to the fact that every maritime power in Europe is advancing in this direction, and that unprotected wooden ships cannot contend with success against their iron-coated rivals, and I confidently submit for their Lordships' consideration that we should not neglect this means of preparing for a conflict, which though we may not seek it, may yet against our will be forced upon us."[22] Thus the decision to initiate the *Royal Oak* class of broadside ironclads was influenced more by the need to use existing wooden ships still under construction from the previous government's building program—increasingly regarded as a liability in a naval action against French ironclads. Conversions saved time and money.[23] They likewise made the most of government resources while the private firms struggled with the iron-hulled ironclads already on order.

Rear Admiral Robinson increased the pressure for these conversions (which also satisfied the earlier need of the Board) as a means simply to increase numbers. His "Table of French iron-plated Ships," dated May 21, 1861,[24] identified 16 French ironclads built, launched, or under construction, in addition to 11 floating batteries (including the 5 constructed for coastal operations in 1855, during the Crimean War).[25] Though the 5 Royal Oaks ships would be "in every way inferior for all the purposes for which we require a Ship of War, to Ships of the 'Achilles' class, built of Iron and with those modifications in Plating &c. which we are prepared to make," nevertheless it was "so important . . . to have some Ships constructed to meet the Navies of other Powers at least on equal terms, that, rather than be without such Ships . . . not as the wisest, nor as the most economical, nor as the safest way of meeting the exigencies of the case, but because . . . other considerations make this plan the only practicable one at the present moment. . . ."[26]

These comments were directed at the cautious policy of experimenting with the new technologies carefully before fully committing to one design. Somehow, superiority in individual ship design was gained (with the *Warrior* class, and the improved *Achilles*), but the collective ironclad force soon to be at Britain's disposal was markedly less than that of France. The issue was more complex than which sea-going ironclads would best counter the French ones, or how many ironclads of what degree of greater or lesser armor protection or speed would be required. Intertwined with these deliberations was the growing certainty that strategic superiority, more representative of the *Achilles* and the *Warrior* class, did not necessarily equate with the tactical advantages innate to smaller, more numerous ironclads—even wooden-hulled conversions such as the *Royal Oak* class—or the grander imperative that the best use be made of the nation's existing industrial and maritime resources. The proper balance still had not been reached, and the Royal Navy seemed to be losing the race.

The Admiralty again considered its options. Along with Robinson's *Royal Oak*–class expedient, the growing concerns of armor protection and armament still rested on the one principle linking the two. The best armor scheme was the *Warrior*'s, which, at 4½ inches, was equal to the first-generation French ironclads.[27] In regard to armor, therefore, it was a question not so much of thickness, but of *coverage*—protecting more of the ship's armament with nothing less than the prescribed arrangement, an increase in area rather than volume. Similarly, the 68-pounder muzzle-loading smoothbores and the breech-loading 110-pounder rifled Armstrong guns were seen in the spring of 1861 as the heaviest naval ordnance available. Greater armament still implied weight of broadside. To increase this aggregate sense of firepower, improved ironclads had to mount more guns—not fewer guns of heavier caliber. The logical consequence of this principle would be the *Minotaur*-class ironclads, "the longest and largest single-screw fighting ships ever built, and the heaviest in the Navy for the next ten years, uniquely favored in a rig which comprised the spectacular array of five masts. . . ."[28] These ships represented the "second generation" phase of the British ironclad program and would quickly prove the most problematic in terms of construction, cost, practicality, and obsolescence. Referring back to the Jan. 13 minute that the Lords Commissioners of the Board of Admiralty recited to the Government on May 23, 1861, on the progress of French ironclads:

> . . . Fifteen Iron cased sea going Frigates of the First Class including two, rated as ships of the line which are either in commission afloat or plating, in process of building or ordered to be commenced immediately.

> | | |
> |---|---|
> | 1 | in Commission |
> | 1 | afloat-plating |
> | 1 | afloat, engines finished |
> | 1 | ready for launching |
> | 2 | nearly ready for launching |
> | 8 | laid down this year |
> | 1 | *named-not laid down* |
> | 15 | total[29] |

Against this the Board of Admiralty could offer only "two Frigates of the First Class afloat and plating. [in margins: *Warrior, Black Prince,* 46 guns each] . . . Two of an inferior class afloat and plating. [*Resistance, Defence,* 22 guns each] . . . Two of a superior class the tender of which was accepted in the end of January last [*Hector, Valiant,* 32 guns each]. . . . And one of the First class the keel of which is not yet laid [*Achilles,* 50 guns], making a total of seven afloat building and ordered." It was therefore a matter "of urging on Her Majesty's

Government the necessity of adopting immediate measures for the construction of iron plated vessels of the first class with such improvements as experience has suggested," and "to ask for authority to call for tenders for new iron-cased ships from the private trade as well as to employ additional hands in building and converting wooden ships to carry armour, being convinced that none but the most vigorous and energetic measures will prevent the command of the Channel at an early date falling into the hands of the French Emperor."[30] The pressure behind this minute appears to have come from the First Naval (or "Sea") Lord, Vice Admiral Sir Richard Dundas, who, in one of the minutes, confessed a degree of uncertainty between strategic and tactical range and protection that did not seem to hamper the French:

> . . . [A]t present [we have] not more than four ships of classes with which we are perhaps less well contented, and of which two only can be considered as well adapted for seagoing purposes indispensable to the defence of this country. Considering therefore that under these circumstances we are in a great measure forced to a decision, and that even a wrong decision and certain progress may tend to postpone a rupture, while evident superiority might tempt France to encroachments, it seems advisable to yield to the necessities of the case and determine to construct not less than 10 new Ships [6 of them built of iron by private contract] of the best description which we can devise.

However, it was the First Lord's candid and direct analysis of the "best plan" on the same day that correctly observed: "One great difficulty in deciding upon the best mode of effecting this increase [in numbers of ironclads] has arisen from the uncertainty in which we still remain as to the construction which should be adopted." Three choices now presented themselves. The first was to cut down existing screw ships of the line or frigates and cover their sides with 4½-inch armor plates. It was the fastest and cheapest plan. Nevertheless, "these vessels would . . . not be sea-going ships, they would be equal to the floating batteries building in France, but inferior to the frigates now laid down," and Somerset immediately concluded that "unless therefore there should be the apprehension of an immediate necessity for defensive preparations, this course appears to be unadvisable." The next possibility was that of the *Royal Oak* class—proceeding with existing frames in Royal Dockyards, which would allow for greater control during completion (including lengthening) and a more integrative finished product. Less expensive than new iron ships, they would "probably be equal to the French plated ships," but their wooden hulls would not last. Ever mindful of public criticism, the First Lord noted that "they will be inferior to the *Warrior* type, and will be justly considered as indicating a retrograde movement rather than an advance in ship-building."

The third alternative was "to apply to the Treasury and propose a supplementary vote to Parliament with the intention of constructing five or six iron-ships to be plated according to the system which the Controller and the practical officers of his department now approve." This was to be an improved *Achilles* class, the *Minotaur*. But exclusive to the *Minotaur* class was the introduction of a new armor scheme that called for thicker plates, now 5½ inches, backed by only 10 inches of teak (versus the *Warrior*'s 18 inches) to compensate for the greater weight in iron. As serious as the fact that the new combination was untested was the implication that all previous armor protection arrangements were inadequate:

> The objections to this course are chiefly financial and political. While the navy estimates amount to twelve millions it would be necessary to review carefully every source of expenditure before applying for an increased outlay under the head of iron-ships. It would reasonably be said that until the *Warrior* had been tried at sea, such a demand was pre-posterous, and that if we condemn the construction of the *Warrior* before this vessel has even been tried, Parliament may fairly refuse to entrust the board with means of making new experiments at such a cost. The political objection would be equally strong as such an application to Parliament would be ascribed to some new distrust, at a moment when a good understanding with France may most usefully tend to the removal of difficulties in our relations with the United States.[31]

Somerset's political message was overlooked.[32] The Board's minute reemphasized the danger of French naval power, not the potential diplomatic manipulation of it. Thus, despite the initiation of two smaller improvements of the first four partially protected broadside ironclads, a more protected version of the *Warrior* that was to lose none of its essential sea-going qualities, particularly its speed, and four immediate wooden-hulled conversions (to be named *Royal Oak, Prince Consort, Ocean,* and *Caledonia*)—and despite growing uncertainty over the private shipyards' ability to cope with this peacetime drive—the Admiralty insisted upon the construction of three (rather than six) more large iron-hulled broadside ironclads as a response to the perceived threat from France.

The British ironclad program was a mixed choice. Four of the ironclads were slower than the rest, and two of these, the *Defence* and the *Resistance*, had been considered "inferior" before completion. By March 1862, the Controller would report: "[T]he sum that the Firm [Westwood and Baillie] may be considered as having paid exactly out of Pocket for building the *Resistance* amounts to £157,972.11.02," and the Admiralty "will have paid . . . a sum of ten thousand pounds beyond what they were strictly entitled to by the terms of the Contract."[33] Of the 14 ironclads built, under construction, or approved to be contracted for by the summer of 1861, 10 were iron hulled, but these were broken down into five different classes—two of them smaller and slower than the other three, and each with its own armament and armor configuration—making a comparative representation of their fighting abilities tedious. As a result, confusion surrounded the intended purposes of these ships: were they to be used as coastal defense vessels, ships to operate in an open-sea line of battle, or simply to "command the Channel"? It may well be argued that this variety of ironclads *built within the same period of naval ordnance and armor advances* was in fact an asset to the Royal Navy, whose duties stretched from the global arena to the immediate vicinity of the British Isles. In hindsight, however, there is no indication that this would be anything other than an exercise of justification because there is very little discussion concerning exactly *how* vessels other than ironclads built expressly for coastal defense were actually to defend the country. Because the French ironclads were intended to dominate any wooden warship they might encounter at home or abroad, it can only be assumed that the British ironclads were projected to overwhelm those of the French, wherever they may be encountered. If the *Defence* was a failure at sea, its ability to fight in more sheltered waters was no less, and probably more, than that of the *Warrior.* If the primary concern was the defense of the Channel—or Mediterranean trade routes to India—then transoceanic ironclads were a violation of the principle of consolidation of force. The heart of the problem was that the proper ironclad simply was not found in either the first- or second-generation response, first, to the French threat; second, to armor-plated challenges emerging from the rest of Europe; and finally, to the danger of entanglement in the American Civil War. There is no other way to explain the *Defence* and *Resistance* without referring to cost-effectiveness and to the *limited,* not extended, operational range of the *Warrior* and *Black Prince;* the *Valiant* and the *Hector* perpetuated this criticism by adding more armor protection in place of speed. To regain speed and range while adding more protection, the *Achilles* returned the Royal Navy to a state where some of its ironclads were better than any existing French design in all these respects.

Even so, this did not solve the initial problem of superior numbers, and by gambling more, not less, in the taxing production of a few "super" broadside ironclads, the Admiralty committed itself to the hope that well before these vessels were even launched, potential enemies would not develop guns powerful enough to pierce their long, thin sides or armor thick enough to make the fire of so many guns as meaningless as the broadsides that were poured into the C.S.S. *Virginia* in March 1862 by heavily armed Union warships. Because the *Achilles* was not launched until December 1863—the same month as the *Minotaur* (the first of the class of the same name), which was not commissioned, however, until April 1867—this calculation proved to be unrealistic within months. It was the need for a practical solution to the immediate if not geostrategically proximate threat posed by Napoleon III's decision that motivated Spencer Robinson to suggest the "retrograde" *Royal Oak* conversions, all of which were launched before the *Achilles*. At a stroke, the continued production of vulnerable first-class wooden men-of-war was replaced with such vessels clad in iron, without exceeding the naval estimates. Indeed, it was the new First Naval Lord Sir Frederick Grey's opinion, in a letter written to the Commander in Chief of the Atlantic Station, Vice Admiral Sir Alexander Milne, shortly after the ship's completion, that "the *Royal Oak* is the best of the whole. . . ."[34] This was fortunate because the race with France left the British Empire partially protected.

Chapter 2

Industry and Conversion Problems

Work on the next generation of British ironclads proceeded with all available resources at hand. Great Britain's economy was strong, yet a growing number of critics were crying out for reform, which naturally would interfere with large naval and military outlays.[1] While much of the populace supported the notion of unquestioned naval mastery over France or any other power—indeed, the lore of the older generation demanded it—the price involved was such that "wooden ships and hearts of oak" could not suffice in the Industrial Age without additional costs. Taxation was, for every household income, more real, generally, than patriotism and world prestige.[2] It therefore appeared to be an inconvenient time, with the Empire "happily at Peace with all Sovereigns, Powers, and States," for an expensive, technologically perplexing naval arms race with Britain's nearest and most dynamic continental neighbor.[3] For every ironclad the French emperor was prepared to lay down, the Admiralty felt compelled to answer with its own.[4] Furthermore, if the threat took the form of oceangoing ironclads, the British response was effectively decided as well.[5] Already the Royal Dockyards were filled to capacity, with work being done on the completion of the unarmored steamships insisted upon in the previous administration (in an attempt to decisively outnumber French steam ships of the line and thus reach a "two-power standard"), in addition to the new ironclads.[6] When Radical Leader Richard Cobden complained to the Foreign Secretary about rising national defense expenditures, which undermined the goodwill of the commercial treaty with France that he had recently brokered, Russell replied with crisp irritation:

> The Emperor wishes to defend France, he completes Cherbourg, he adopts a peace army of 600,000 men. Not a word of complaint. We add to our Navy, and propose to fortify the arsenals where they are built and repaired. We are accused immediately of warlike intentions. Is it to be deliberately said that France may be armed, but that we should be unarmed? Belgium, Antwerp, Dover and Portsmouth would in that case soon fall into French possession. I am anxious for the completion of the commercial treaty. But I cannot consent to place my country at the mercy of France.[7]

Cobden regarded Russell's views as "lamentable." According to him, "a liberal government [was] made the instrument for laying unparalleled burdens on the taxpayers to guard against dangers, which, if a full investigation were entered into, would be found to have no existence."[8]

There can be no denying that the pace and scale of industry were high. Although Lord Lyons informed Vice-Admiral Milne of the hostile reaction in Washington, DC, to the Queen's Proclamation of Neutrality in the expanding war between the Northern and Southern states and warned him that the Federal government was unlikely to "abstain from provoking language or even aggressive conduct," the Admiralty Controller was approving 10-hour days, starting at 6 A.M. for workmen, Monday through Saturday, in the Deptford yard. Two days later, on June 14, 1861, Robinson objected to the request to assign steam gunboats for the training of Royal Navy volunteers and the crews of Coast Guard ships, pointing out that "no serious interruption of all the proposed works in the Dock Yards and factories will be occasioned."[9]

The need for consolidating resources was understandable, even given the size and demands of the existing Royal Navy. Perhaps in response to Lyons's letter to Milne, forwarded by the Foreign Office, the Admiralty directed the Controller the following day (June 12) to comment on their historic memorandum abolishing the historic "Sailing Ordinary" as it merged into the new "Steam Reserve." Robinson prescribed "in the First Division of Steam Ordinary at each Port a Line of Battle Ship, a Frigate, a Corvette, a Sloop, a small vessel, and a Paddle Wheel Steamer"—a considerable force, with three other divisions behind it, in addition to the vessels actually in commission.[10] In March 1862 he counted 39 corvettes afloat alone, with the Royal Navy categorized into line-of-battle ships, frigates, corvettes, sloops, and gun vessels and gunboats of the first and second class, whereas "the Paddlewheel Steam Ships should be divided into Frigates, Sloops, Despatch Vessels, and Small Vessels."[11] Iron-clad warships were not mentioned, but they were, in fact, at the top of the list in power and priority. The Parliamentary *Expense of Ships in 1861–1862*[12] recorded a labor and materials total of £932,323 for "Ships and Vessels built or building by contract, or purchased," in comparison to the £1,003,047 paid for all "Steam ships and vessels fitting out, refitting, repairs and maintenance in commission and reserve." Of the 25 ships of private construction subsequently registered, only 18 were armed, and of those, 9 were ironclads:

Name of Ship + Contractor	Guns	Tonnage	Where Built or Building	When Laid Down	Total Expenditure on Each Ship to 31-3-1862	Remarks
Agincourt J. Laird, Sons & Co.	50	6,621	Birkenhead	30-10-1861	12,352	
Black Prince Napier & Sons	40	6,109	Glasgow	12-10-1859	322,239	Launched 27-2-1861
Defence Palmer, Brothers & Co.	16	3,720	Jarrow, Newcastle	14-12-1859	209,075	Launched 24-4-1861
Hector Napier & Sons	32	4,063	Glasgow	8-3-1861	157,285	
Minotaur Thames Iron Ship Building Co.	50	6,621	Blackwall	12-9-1861	18,847	
Northumberland C. J. Mare & Co.	50	6,621	Millwall	10-10-1861	8,905	
Resistance Westwood, Baillie, Campbell & Co.	16	3,710	Poplar	21-12-1859	213,047	Launched 11-4-1861
Valiant Westwood, Baillie, Campbell & Co. + Thames Iron Ship Building	32	4,063	Poplar	1-2-1861 and then 24-2-1862	119,911	
Warrior Thames Iron Ship Building Co.	40	6,109	Blackwall	25-5-1859	328,453	Launched 29-12-1860
Total					**1,627,198**	

Listed separately from "Ships and Vessels building in Her Majesty's Dockyards" were those "Ships, commenced as wooden ships, converted into iron cased vessels while building," the five emergency expedients of the *Royal Oak* class:

Name of Ship + Contractor	Guns	Tonnage	Where Built or Building	When Laid Down	Total Expenditure on Each Ship to 31-3-1862
Caledonia	34	4,125	Woolwich	1-10-1860; conversion 6-6-1861	70,248
Ocean	34	4,045	Devonport	23-8-1860; 3-6-1861	74,999
Prince Consort (late Triumph)	34	4,045	Pembroke	13-8-1860; 6-6-1861	103,969
Royal Alfred	34	4,045	Portsmouth	1-12-1859; 22-6-1861	94,113
Royal Oak	34	4,056	Chatham	1-5-1860; 3-6-1861	112,166
Total					**455,495**

Perhaps more indicative of the level of dependency upon private contractors in which the Royal Navy found itself during the beginning of its ironclad program was that, of the 68 ships listed under construction in Royal Navy yards, only the *Achilles* was armor plated.

Name of Ship	Guns	Tonnage	Where Built or Building	When Laid Down	Total Expenditure on Each Ship to 31-3-1862	Remarks
Achilles	30	6,079	Chatham	1-8-1861	62,921	Building in a dock

The remaining £2,761,198 expended on ships being constructed in Her Majesty's Dockyards included 10 of 89 guns or more (such as H.M.S. *Howe*, 121 guns, laid down in Pembroke, March 10, 1856, and launched March 7, 1860), 9 of 51 guns, 3 of 36 guns, 4 of 22 guns, and 2 of 21 guns. At this juncture, the total cost was still a considerable £1,371,084 more than what had been paid to private contractors for ironclads; but it is essential to keep in mind that this outlay was for 67 warships, as opposed to 9, whose costs, in most cases, were increasing well beyond their contracts.[13]

The contract tenders for the three broadside frigates, of what was to be the *Minotaur* class—originally the *Alexander, Dictator,* and *Invincible* (awarded to Thames Iron Shipbuilding Co., C. J. Mare & Co., and J. Laird, Sons & Co., respectively)—specified a £5,000 penalty if the ships were not completed for the Navy in time. None of the estimates for the construction of the six new iron-hulled ironclads submitted to the Controller on the last day of August 1861 exceeded 24 months, and in the case of Thames Iron, in addition to its estimated cost of an extra three months' work, the price per ton of £48.10 would rise to £50, but only if Thames opted to have the armor plates made elsewhere. The Board did not necessarily accept the cheapest estimate, for in addition to quality of construction and completion time was the factor of the actual likelihood of firms already committed to government, commercial, and foreign orders meeting their obligations successfully. Previous experience with ironclad ships cast growing doubt on the prospect of the busiest companies meeting their deadlines. Although Robinson ranked the south London Mare & Co. fifth on the list of "character and experience of the Parties and therefore their fitness to be employed in building Ships of this Class, irrespective of price," and Glasgow's Napier & Sons third, the Admiralty did not "consider it advisable to give another contract at present to Messr. Napier until the *Hector* is further advanced."[14] The Admiralty made this decision despite the enclosed letter from Napier, which explained that "although the completion of the *Black Prince* has occupied considerably more time than was anticipated—in consequence of the details of that Vessel being of an unusual nature and new to us & and also to your Inspectors—who often could not give us the information we required, when wanted to continue the progress of the work uninterruptedly, and thereby, besides the delay, leading us into much extra expense—yet, from the experience Inspectors and ourselves have now acquired, we feel confident that, with the proposed new Vessel, we should be able to make rapid progress. . . ."[15]

The lack of confidence also worked the other way. Aside from noting the presence of government inspectors in their shipyards, Napier (and Wigram & Sons of Blackwall) acknowledged Robinson's item 4 proviso of his Aug. 5 bid for tenders, which stipulated that "the Admiralty are to be at liberty to alter the arrangement of the Plating within three months from the date of the Contract without additional charge."[16] It was, after all, the business of these major firms to know of the Navy's growing predilection for modifying the construction of its new iron ships up until the last possible moment, in keeping with any ordnance advances or armor plate tests. On Sept. 5 the Admiralty reconsidered the names of the ships themselves in browsing through the Navy Signal Books. *Dictator,* recalled as the ship that received

Napoleon I in 1815, became *Northumberland; Invincible* was changed to *Captain* and then to the more politically explicit *Agincourt*. Meanwhile, *Alexander* became *Audacious*, because it was criticized for "always [being] used in a bad sense," and then the *Elephant*—a name that suggested not so much great size and power as clumsiness—later to be changed to *Minotaur*.[17]

Even as Thames Iron accepted the challenge for its second great ironclad construction, it petitioned the Admiralty for the financial losses incurred "two years and a half to the production of so noble a specimen of iron shipbuilding," H.M.S. *Warrior*.[18] At first Robinson took a lenient approach. Even though the company could legally be asked to reimburse the government £8,000 for its own work in completing the first ironclad, the costs per ton for the *Resistance* and *Defence* were higher. He advised the Admiralty that "the liberal conduct they will have adopted with regard to this Company, will I think prove in the end of great advantage, as it will encourage private Firms to tax their resources to the utmost to answer any extraordinary demands which the Government may find if necessary to make upon them." Thames's letter to the Secretary of the Admiralty, William Romaine, was especially important because it described the real problems facing Britain's shipbuilding industry. The question was not just changes in design, multiple orders, and rapid production rates; the firm required all extra costs plus "the moderate addition of twelve and a half per cent profit."[19]

Meanwhile, the *Resistance* herself, though launched in April, was still in the Victoria Docks, waiting for Admiralty possession. Owing to the state of the tides, the 6,000-ton broadside ironclad would now not be available until Dec. 3. She was far from complete and ready for service. Her propeller was "still in a barge on the docks"; "[t]here are no Anchors or Cables on board," and "the Steering Gear is not completed, but temporary Steering Gear might be fitted by Wednesday next. . . . There are no coals at present on board the Ship."[20] Though £50,000 was set aside in the estimates for any unknown costs incurred during the building of the first four ironclads, Robinson was careful to mention that "their Lordships would be perfectly justified in authorizing [*sic*] the payment of £5,000 . . . on account of extras on the *Resistance*, though not on account of the terms of the contract. . . ."

During the war scare with the United States over the *Trent*, from the end of November until the New Year, the Controller's attitude toward private contractors soured a great deal. The same company that had launched the *Resistance* nearly a year before—Westwood, Baillie, Campbell & Co.—was also responsible for the new ironclad, *Valiant*, and informed the Admiralty, "[W]e have a claim of £12,000 for Extras, etc., which we are satisfied could not be reduced to £8,000 if disputed. . . ."[21]

Robinson had objected to these claims three weeks earlier, observing that "in dealing with the *Warrior*'s case their Lordships were induced to consider it as favourably as possible for the Firm employed in building that Ship, for reasons which were obvious, and which must be so fresh in Their memories that they need not be repeated." Though the *Resistance* was as new a ship in design and structure to its builders as the *Warrior* was to Thames Iron Shipbuilding, "the Firm had ample means of judging of the nature of the work required of them, and of their resources for executing it." By taking on the *Valiant* at £42 per ton after 12 months of construction on the former ironclad, at £44 per ton, the contractors signaled their confidence in enjoying a profit from extra work, and Robinson coolly remarked, "[I]t certainly is not the province of the Admiralty to take care that no loss should fall on the Parties who, as Men of Business, had every means of knowing how best to conduct their own affairs." At this point, the *Resistance* was delivered far later than hoped, the *Valiant*'s progress was in jeopardy, and the final bill calculated by the Controller's Department was £157,972.11.02—a figure that put the Admiralty "ten thousand pounds beyond what they were strictly entitled to by the terms of the Contract." Robinson accused them of gross carelessness in accepting what he considered too heavy a burden. Furthermore, in his opinion the builders were simply "wasteful" and "negligent." The issue of added cost was, if anything, a justifiable complaint by the Admiralty, whose own proposal, Robinson noted, "appears to me to be as liberal . . . as possible, unless manifest injustice were done to other Contractors."[22]

Problems continued to emerge from every corner, however, which must have eroded Robinson's original optimism, even when private contractors did feel obliged to "tax their resources to the utmost." On May 5, 1862, Robert Napier & Sons wrote to Romaine that "the precedence of the *Warrior* was of no practical assistance to us, but was in many respects, and more particularly in the details of finishing the *Black Prince* after her launch, seriously detrimental from having to receive very often our instructions at second hand from the *Warrior*'s Inspector." The company pointed out that the situation was regrettable, especially considering that work was being performed day and night, "employing on the *Black Prince* in the Building Yard alone fully 1600 men. . . ."[23] In addition to noting cost overruns of £8,463, Napier claimed it was actually making zero profit in building *Warrior*'s sister ship, echoing the point made by Thames Iron the previous November. But Robinson disputed the figures as erroneous and was suspicious of what he saw as possible client jealousy. In actuality, "neither of the contractors received the whole command named for their respective Ships, each of them failed to deliver the Ship complete, and from the sum of £255,164 which the *Warrior* cost, £3,578 was deducted on account of works done in the Dock Yard; and from the sum of £251,071 which the *Black Prince* cost, £10,818 was deducted for work done in the Dock Yard to complete the Ship."[24]

Nor was the problem restricted to the dockyards. The relatively sudden, large-scale manufacture of iron armor plates appeared to have caught most everyone unprepared. Between the delays occasioned by the ships themselves and the delays caused by the Admiralty's hesitancy in committing fully to designs from inception to actual completion, the rigid standards set by government examiners for 4½-inch slabs of uniformly welded iron proved to be impediments. Coincidentally, on the same day Napier was writing to Romaine, Robinson was obliged to report to the Board that "the supply of Armour Plates is in an unsatisfactory state":

> Nine Firms at the beginning of this year were after survey of their Premises considered to be capable of supplying Armour Plates of [solid] 4½" thickness. . . .
>
> Tenders have been accepted for the supply of Armour Plates, dependent on their due resistance to the effects of shot, from five Manufacturers for 6 Ships:
>
> | | |
> |---|---|
> | *Achilles* | W. Sanderson |
> | *Royal Oak* | The Thames Company |
> | *Royal Alfred* | Mess. Brown & Co. |
> | *Ocean* | The Butterley Company |
> | *Prince Consort* | W. Sanderson |
> | *Caledonia* | Lancefield Forge Company |
>
> Of the nine manufacturers above named four only up to this time have succeeded in making Plates which successfully resist the trials:
>
> The Thames Company
> Mess. Brown & Co.
> W. Sanderson
> Mess. Hill & Smith
> [not accepted for contract]

The other firms though some of them are undoubtedly capable of manufacturing these Plates have failed to do so hitherto, the quality of the Plates having proved inferior, and unsuitable for the purpose.

In November last a Tender was accepted for Armour Plating for the *Caledonia* from the Lancefield Forge Co. The Plates to be delivered in six months from the date of the order.

No Plate that this firm has manufactured has stood the test, and five months have elapsed.

In the month of January last a Tender was accepted from the Butterley Co. for Armour Plating for the *Ocean*. The Plates to be delivered in six months. No plate has yet been completed and consequently none have been tested.

Robinson then recommended that the 5½-inch plate contract for the experimental turret ship conversion *Royal Sovereign* be given to Brown & Co. As he confidently expressed, "I may add that there is no doubt of Mess. Brown's capability to fulfil any Contract they may enter into, or of the excellency of the work they turn out; and that the prices named in their letter are reasonable."[25] Like some of his others, this would prove to be a completely ingenuous prediction.

On March 12, 1862, Robinson reminded the Admiralty that "the *Warrior* having 4½-inches of iron Plating over 18-inches of Teak and the *Minotaur* and her class having 5½-inches of Iron Plating over 9-inches of Teak," the new armor scheme for the *Minotaur*-class broadside iron-clads was still uncertain until the Iron Plate Committee, which seemed "to be rather doubtful whether 5½-inch iron plates of good quality can be manufactured, though the Contractors for building these ships do not doubt that they can easily be procured," actually conducted its tests.[26] By May 15 nothing had been accomplished, and again the Controller submitted an urgent request for a target to be fired upon at the testing grounds at Shoeburyness.[27]

When the results of the firing were evaluated, they were disappointing. Using the new Armstrong 12-ton gun (with cast-iron spherical 150-pound shot and a 50-pound charge) at a combat range of 200 yards, "the *general damage* was much greater than in the *Warrior* Target, although the latter was subjected to much more severe fire." After only four heavy shots, the target itself was battered beyond service. The first shot alone "hit the centre plate . . . and made a hole through the plate 12.5" × 12.2", and about 13" deep," while the second hit struck the bottom plate and passed clean through, making a hole "13" × 12.5". . . ." The test proved the comparative inferiority of the *Minotaur*'s defense; the crucial differences in iron plate manufacture (some plates submitted by different firms reacted better or worse than others); the inadequacy of the fastenings of the through bolts of the first-generation ironclads (less than 2" in diameter); and the power of the heavier gun (the vaunted, traditional 68-pounder smoothbore that was fired immediately afterward produced serious dents but no penetration).[28] The Committee's findings included the following:

The advantage of the *Warrior* wood-backing is fourfold.

1. It *stops* small fragments of iron from entering the ship.
2. If large pieces of the plate are broken off, it *holds them in their places*, and makes them still useful, to a certain extent.
3. It *deadens the jar*, and so preserves the fastenings and the structure generally.
4. It *distributes* the effect of the blow over a *larger area* of the skin and frame of the ship.

We do not attach importance to wood as a *support* to the plate. In this respect we conceive it is inferior to more rigid material.[29]

With regard to the specific deficiencies of the iron-forging of certain private firms, even for those ironclads of the same class, the Iron Plate Committee remarked in September 1862 that in testing the new "120-pounder Whitworth gun . . . fired from a 600 yards range, at a target representing the side of the *Warrior*," the plates were of a "very inferior character of the 4½-inch plates of which this *Warrior* target was composed. They were from Parkhead forge, near Glasgow, and are said to be of the number of those made for the *Black Prince*."[30]

By now the situation seemed to be getting worse rather than better, with British iron shipbuilding in the hands of private industry. The Controller noted five firms in particular—Napier, Thames, Laird, Samuda, and Mare—as being unacceptably delinquent with their orders:

Ship	Contractor	Contract Price
Minotaur	Thames Iron Ship Building Co.	£321,117
Northumberland	C. J. Mare & Co.	£295,295
Agincourt	J. Laird, Sons & Co.	£329,393
Hector	Napier & Sons	£172,677
Valiant	Westwood, Baillie, Campbell & Co.	£207,212
Orestes (troopship)	J. Laird, Sons & Co.	£73,109
Tamar (troopship)	J. Samuda & Co.	£68,188

The situation with the *Minotaur*-class *Northumberland* was the worst. "The Contractors have been repeatedly written to and urged to expedite this Ship, but without effect. She should be launched in February 1863, but there is no prospect now of her being launched earlier than April 1864." The advice of the Admiralty Solicitor, moreover, was that the contract could not be withdrawn and handed to another builder for no other reason than "slow progress," as this was not a specific clause in the contract.[31] A letter to Thames Iron regarding the "backward state" of the *Minotaur* met with a list of numbered complaints, which included the alterations to the ship's design and construction ordered subsequently by the Admiralty. These involved the changing of a screw that could be raised while under sail, as with the first-generation ships, to a fixed one, requiring the reworking of the complicated stern posts, and changes in the armor itself in proportion to its wood backing. Robinson addressed these points one at a time "in order to prevent the Board of Admiralty from being placed at a disadvantage at any future time, if the Company should become remiss and fail to complete the Contract within the stipulated time."[32]

Even so, Robinson must have felt that Thames Iron was not alone: "[T]he case of the *Valiant* has been already reported on, and the progress of that Ship has been far less satisfactory than that of the *Minotaur*."[33]

Part of the problem was organizational, for even within the Admiralty, misunderstanding, indecision, and delay were likely if changes were not constantly made to meet the new demands. A revealing report on bureaucratic stiffness was made on Nov. 19, 1862, entitled "Ships in Commission—Alterations & Additions, Mode of Processing." This report described "the present roundabout practice" as follows:

> The Captain writes a letter containing the suggestion to his Commander-in-Chief who forwards it to the Secretary of the Admiralty, who sends it to the Lord in whose department the matter is supposed to be, who orders the Controller to report, who sends it back to the Dock Yard Officers for the necessary explanations and reports, who send it back to the Controller, who sends the report with any observations he may think requisite to the Secretary of the Admiralty, who places it in the hands of the Lord to whose department it relates, who gives the requisite authority, which is communicated to the Controller.[34]

In December 1862 Rear Admiral Robinson offered a summary analysis of the needs of the Royal Navy.[35] The issue at stake, though superficially one of government decreases in dockyard wages, was nothing less than the ability of private industry to adequately provide for the needs of the nation. "The number of Men, Seamen, and Marines voted for the service of the Navy," the Controller began, "tells directly on the number of men required in the Dock Yards." As it was, for every man afloat, there could be expected a rise in dockyard wages of £10 over the next three years, and the proportion was a reliable indicator of the manpower needed, as the number of Men, Seamen, and Marines voted for each year rose or declined. Whatever the total, it represented a ratio of 40 percent devoted to new ships, wood, and iron, and the burden upon the Navy was only increasing as the number and tonnage of steam ships grew each year—which meant rising costs for maintenance and fitting as a whole. Furthermore, "it may . . . be taken as a rule that one fourth of the whole Force afloat requires to be renewed every year, that is, that if 300 Ships are in Commission in any given year, 75 will be paid off and require repair and refit." The number of ships in commission by the end of 1862 was such that nearly all of those ships paid off and requiring repair and refit "must be carried over to the ensuing year," whereas in the previous year, already half of those paid off were necessarily carried over.[36] However, the number of new ships under construction was *decreasing*, which possibly meant they were breaking even in the estimates. In fact, Robinson calculated, "it is just possible to keep pace with the wants of the service with slight reductions in the Force of the Dock Yards. . . . As far as can be foreseen there will be a saving on Vote 8 of between thirty and forty thousand pounds."[37]

Year	Number of Ships	Tons
1859	15	37,364
1860	23	40,519
1861	15	21,482
1862	9	16,616

But the issue before Parliament of a "total abandonment of Ships building in our Dock Yards would be a dangerous measure to adopt in the present transition state of our Military Navy," and here the Controller ran through the main considerations, requirements, and objectives for Britain's ironclad program as he saw them. First, the issue between wood and iron ships was suggested as one between the "present large force afloat" and its maintenance, and the ability of Royal Navy yards to adapt to the utter necessity in naval warfare for armor-cladding ships.

Robinson's unequivocal belief that "the ordinary wooden Ship is sure to be immediately destroyed by the ordinary artillery of all nations, and the larger the Ship the more certain the destruction" probably refers to the only such engagement known by 1863: the destruction of the U.S.S. *Cumberland* and the U.S.S. *Congress* by the ironclad-ram C.S.S. *Virginia.* Not just France, Robinson said, but "every maritime power, according to its means, has considered it indispensable to clothe its Military navy in Iron Armour," yet because the greatest of these (and the nearest to England) had "perfected and prepared a large number of [seagoing] Ships," Robinson recapitulated the basic decision of the Admiralty that such ironclads "can only be met on equal terms by a similar description of Force . . . a certain number of Ships which can contend on equal terms with our neighbours"—hence the determination to employ numerous commercial iron shipbuilders, a recourse of little alternative when the Royal Navy itself was obliged to maintain in its own facilities such a "large force afloat" for the protection of British interests worldwide.[38]

Nevertheless, this solution had only led to problems: "[T]he work is slow, very expensive, requires an immense amount of inspection as to Workmanship and materials and in no case has such a ship been perfected without large expenditure of time and money in the Dock Yards." Even if iron shipbuilding was found to be unquestionably better than wooden conversions, Robinson was severe in his judgment that "our past experience teaches us that no reliance whatever can be placed on private Shipbuilders keeping any engagements they may enter into with the Admiralty."

Because the Controller maintained "that our present large force afloat, and the reliefs that it requires, are insuperable objections to any considerable reductions in the expenditure of Wages in our Dock

Yards," the natural conclusion would be to favor wooden conversions into ironclads in the government facilities. It was the second plan adopted by the Admiralty in May 1861, with the first concerning the privately built iron-hulled ironclads, and it was bound to mitigate any "new discovery of the power of Artillery," which "disturbs all foregone conclusions" (and therefore suggested that time-consuming iron-hulled ventures were short-lived in any case). This plan would both modernize the Navy and protect it from any commercial exploitation or failures. It would also give the Controller, the Navy, and the Government much more direct and encompassing control over the means of ironclad construction. After all, Robinson made sure to point out to the Admiralty that "whatever may be said as to Iron Ships Armour Plated it is to be remembered that we have not yet afloat one Ship of that description plated from end to end, while several powers have actually sent to Sea wooden Ships so protected."[39]

This decision marked a personal preference by the Controller for more fully protected ironclads, more quickly produced, at less cost, and perhaps handier as well, if limited to some degree in range—although range was defined inevitably as the ability to match the French examples.[40] It was a discussion of these very principles, which suited the Royal Navy best in the mind of its Controller, that contributed to the debates with Captain Coles. Likewise, it was the preference of Rear Admiral Robinson for ships of the *Royal Oak* class that eliminated the possibility for any major introduction of turret ships based on Coles's designs. By the time the Admiralty was seriously willing to reconsider the inventor's claims—in the wake of the public furor that accompanied the news of the American ironclads—the nation's dockyards were already occupied with wooden conversions and standard repair and fitting of wooden steam vessels on the one hand, and massive iron-hulled constructions on the other, which were consuming the full attention of those contractors whom they did not force out altogether.

Chapter 3

Enter Captain Coles

The two trends in the British ironclad program—the move by Coles for turret ships as opposed to broadside ironclads and the desire of Robinson to shed the unprotected wooden bulk of the navy in favor of sea-going ironclads—began their convergence at the beginning of 1861.[1] If the initial decisions of the Board of Admiralty were designed to answer the French challenge ship to ship, then the list of Louis-Napoleon's new ironclad navy included a preponderance of floating batteries for coastal and harbor defense.[2] The program, which included the *Valiant* and *Hector*, the five *Royal Oak* wooden conversions, the improved *Warrior* ship *Achilles*, and the even larger *Minotaur*-class iron broadside ships, left no room for coastal defense, as discussed previously. As with the *Warrior*, the first instinct in filling in this strategic layer was to design a ship intrinsically superior to its French counterpart in every way. This included its ability to carry the war to the other side of the English Channel, overseeing an assault on heavily fortified naval bases such as Cherbourg. The original armored floating batteries, if not the earlier "block ships" (cut-down steam ships of the line), were constructed during the Crimean War against the Russians, and not against Cherbourg.[3] Their success in October 1855 during the bombardment of the forts at Kinburn (which protected the enemy supply lines en route to Sevastopol at the mouth of the Dnieper) had proven their effectiveness in penetrating closer to shore under heavy fire to deliver at close range the firepower that more vulnerable, deeper-draft wooden screw-liners dared not. In that sense—and this is significant—the first coastal ironclads acted almost as classical siege engines. It was this stigma of steam "batteries" that clung to the perception of these types of ironclads in mid–nineteenth-century naval warfare and contributed to the prejudice against more traditional types of men-of-war, namely the graceful sailing broadside vessels. Coastal ironclads were "infernal machines"; sea-going ones were "armored ships."

Present at the Kinburn bombardments was Commander Cowper Coles, who three months before had devised a raft to carry a 32-pounder and its crew into shallow water to attack the guns at Taganrog in the Sea of Azov. The plan worked, but the inherent deficiencies of the French broadside batteries at Kinburn, namely the large and vulnerable gun ports needed to permit the training of the guns on either axis, compelled him to seek an improvement. With the endorsement of his uncle, the Black Sea theater's second-in-command, Admiral Sir Edmund Lyons, Coles's idea for a steam-powered raft of extremely light draft (5-feet on average) mounting a single 68-pounder cannon in a hemispherical—though non-revolving—turret was sent to the Admiralty for consideration in November 1855.[4] It was this occasion that the inventor would refer to on first receiving news of the U.S.S. *Monitor* six and a half years later. One crucial difference was that the ship itself was expected to maneuver to bring its single gun to bear. Furthermore, because of the ship's qualities as a close-shore vessel, both the Surveyor, Admiral Walker, and his Chief Constructor, Isaac Watts, rejected the design on Jan. 22, 1856, for its obvious poor seaworthiness and its lack of full armor protection.

After several years Coles returned with a new submission, evidently taking into account many of the previous objections. He had reversed his opinion that turning the ship itself was acceptable, once he discovered that the armor-protected guns themselves could be mounted on a turntable. With the Admiralty's order on May 11, 1859, to build the *Warrior*, in response to France's *Gloire*, Coles applied to mount several such "shotproof hemispherical screens" on similar vessels. The improvement over a partially protected fixed battery to him was obvious. But Coles's seemingly omnipresent foe, Walker, the Surveyor, was the first to make the important observation (which was to harry Coles to the very end of his life) that

> as these guns with their screens are to be ranged at the mid-ship fore and aft line of the deck they could only occupy the intervals of space between the masts and funnel and other necessary middle line fittings of the vessel, while the spread of the shrouds for the support of the masts would very considerably restrict the degree of training of several of the guns, either therefore the guns must be small or the ship must have great length. . . .[5]

There was a fundamental incompatibility between turrets and seagoing ironclads reliant upon sails as their secondary, and even sometimes primary, means of propulsion. Remarkably, Coles seems to have forgotten the tactical origins of armored ships to begin with, focusing his attention instead on their armament. Revolving turrets on light-draft ironclads had merits other than engaging fortifications on land, and the inventor, Coles, seemed obsessed with the conviction that revolving turrets held many advantages over the traditional, somewhat unimaginative broadside type. What he failed to grasp were the practical limitations of turret ships on the high seas. If only the *Warrior* class could be relied upon to employ full sail for long-distance cruising or engage in fleet actions on the high seas, and if turrets were superior to broadsides, then the strategic limitations of turret ships suggested tactical limitations to the class. If the latter were to engage fortifications from any distance, they would be prey to the former, whose zone of operation ironclads such as the *Warrior* had overlapped. If the latter were denied the power to attack fortifications—or to conduct close blockades over ports defended by the latter—of what use were they? They were superior to any wooden vessels on the high seas through their imperviousness at least to explosive shell fire. This made them extremely potent as commerce raiders or protectors. Moreover, a squadron of such ships would be superior to a single ironclad of comparable strength. It was therefore the original threat from France, that greatest of continental powers who had often employed a *guerre de course* naval strategy against (Britain's) commerce, that drew attention away from the unique primacy of coastal defense implicit in Coles's turrets, while at the same time convincing the Admiralty that an oceangoing ironclad fleet was the only way to check French aggression in a naval war. It was an expensive hypothesis, and even Coles bought into it. As it turned out, he would spend the remainder of his life in an obsessive though fruitless attempt to combine successfully the best of both extremes in ironclad design.

The Admiralty did manage to recognize the potential value of turrets themselves, particularly for coast defense purposes. Shortly after Coles's submission in 1859, private shipbuilder John Scott Russell was commissioned to construct an experimental turret using Coles's plans. This turn of events proved ironic, given Russell's claim to fame for contributing to the *Warrior* concept.[6] In the meantime Coles prepared new specifications for a turret ship, which he finally patented on June 15, 1860. His specifications included several revolving turrets mounted along the middle line, and undoubtedly played a key role in pointing the way toward the steel battleships of the future. In Coles's design, the ship platform itself was fully armor protected;

the sides inclined 40° from the water's edge to a point above the inclined and truncated cone of the turrets themselves, which were thus partially sunk below the edge of the "upper deck." In essence, the iron-clad, had it been constructed, might very well have resembled one of the subsequently built Confederate casemate ironclads, but with the additional superior feature of a turret armament. Only in the U.S.S. *Dunderberg* was this general scheme put into action, but before the massive armored casemate was completed (and fitted also for broadside ports), Coles's turrets, as described here, were left out.[7] Coles also introduced the measure of "a flying bulwark . . . capable of being turned down either inwards or outwards in order to allow the gun to be fired over all from beneath the shield," which would become a significant feature, with future low-freeboard turret ships rigged for sail, as "this flying bulwark would mask the battery until fire is opened, and shelter the crew in bad weather from wind and sea. . . ." Coles's plan, however, did not specify whether the ship was intended for coastal or deep-sea operations. Judging from the design, it seemed better suited for brown-water operations. There were no details of sail configuration provided; the patent was sought only for the turret and the armored shell. Yet, as Baxter pointed out, Coles alluded to 15 such vessels, each armed with 9 turrets carrying 18 guns, at the Royal United Services Institution on June 29, 1860:

> An enormously strong ship is thus obtained—not weakened, as are ordinary ships, by numerous portholes, but having a continuous side, with the weights placed amidships instead of at the sides. . . . three of these shield ships would be equal to ten 3-deckers. . . . In future our fleets must fight in armour; and supremacy afloat must depend henceforth on superior ability to produce the new ships required.[8]

Here the reference to ironclad construction was telling, for the efficiency of the ships, considering their armor and size, would make them generally less expensive than the controversial *Warrior.* Also significant was a reference not to tackling fortifications or enemy ironclads, but to taking on wooden ships of the line. The replacement of broadside ironclads or "3-deckers" with turret ships was never intended by Coles to cause the British to forfeit command of the sea.

Nevertheless, as in earlier cases, the oversights inherent in the design's seaworthiness did not escape the attention of the Admiralty constructors, even as publicity surrounding the concept heated up. It was, in fact, a peculiar feature of the public debate eventually encompassing Captain Coles and his turret ship inventions that the issue was looked at from completely different viewpoints. To the public at large, the superiority of a turret ship over a fixed row of guns was easy to comprehend. So was the concept of an ironclad itself—even though in all previous cases, the emphasis was just as much on superior numbers of ships of the line or seamanship as on the pattern of the armament or the physical protection of the vessel itself. The situation had changed dramatically. In the Age of Sail (and then also Steam), the best means of defense lay in superior firepower alone. Wooden walls could deflect some shot, but that was not necessarily their purpose. The key to preventing a great deal of damage to one's own vessel was simply to inflict more on the opponent's first, usually by maneuver (raking) or heavier weight of broadside at the closest effective range, and at a superior rate of fire. Coles's inventions challenged this point of view in several fundamental respects. The key to a superior offense was now in the superior *defensive* qualities of the armored cupola. Coles did not mention weight of broadside or firepower because, as Spencer Robinson would reassert, "two guns in a ship that cannot be sunk and where the battery is protected will prove more than a match for twenty, in an ordinary wooden Ship."[9] In an armored man-of-war, range counted for little, except for the actual likelihood of hitting the target, as with broadside fire. Meanwhile, the need for finding the proper tack or lee in combat was mitigated—even without the use of steam-driven screws—by the maneuvering of the armament itself; by forward or aft fire, regardless of the position of the ship; and in the tracking of the enemy. In addition, the success of the design in affording superior shelter made it a better form of warship altogether. To a growing audience outside the Admiralty, it was difficult to see why the professionals were hesitant to accept the obvious.

On the opposite end of this debate, however, were arguments about the practical limitations in applying the principles of an armored cupola to every purpose a man-of-war in the Royal Navy might require. In early 1861 the new Controller, Spencer Robinson, relayed to the Board of Admiralty the opinions of the "professional officers of [his] department," Isaac Watts and his assistants, Joseph Large and Richard Abethall. Even "vessels of the size of the Gun Boats are much too small to carry Captain Coles' revolving platform and iron shield or any adaptation of it (as recommended by Captain [Sherard] Osborn) without losing the advantage of light draught of water, and a great deal of stability." Furthermore, "the propositions to armour plate the sides for the protection of the boilers; to place the Boilers within a dome of wrought iron, or to make the outer side of the wing boilers of increased thickness to resist shot; to employ wrought iron plates instead of wood more generally in the construction of Gun Boats; and to fit transverse watertight compartments in them, appear to us impossible to be carried out in such small vessels." Osborn's original submission, dated Nov. 17, 1860, also made the often-overlooked observation that "from the day rifled cannon came into use, ship armour and the introduction of vessels offering less larger area than our present line of battle ships, has become an absolute necessity for success in naval warfare."[10]

According to observers, there was no indication that a broadside ironclad would prove inferior to a turret ironclad in close combat. While the turret ship could aim its armament more freely, the broadside ship had twice the guns and could engage simultaneous enemies in a sea battle. A similar espousal of the broadside argument began when Henry Hubbard, a gunner on H.M.S. *Gannet* at Constantinople, wrote to his commander on March 15, 1861, of changes in armament "that will change this Ship into a good Fighting Sloop, capable of not only holding our own against, but proving very destructive to, an enemy of even superior numbers." Hubbard argued for fewer guns (the new rifled, heavier ordnance of Sir William Armstrong) positioned on pivots that could deliver more overwhelming fire at a much longer range over a greater arc. The smaller number of guns would require a relatively smaller vessel, which was an advantage in combat. Captain Richard S. Hewlett, of the gunnery training ship H.M.S. *Excellent* at Portsmouth, disagreed. As he saw it, the problem was the slower speed of the *Gannet,* which would not allow her to choose the range. "Now it is in close Action that every Engagement will be brought to an issue," Hewlett said, "and although a Vessel with powerful long range Guns may no doubt annoy another from a distance of 1500 or 2000 yards, experience has shown us that a very large quantity of Ammunition may, under these circumstances, be fired away at a small object (constantly on the move) with little or no effect."[11]

This time the Board sided with the lower rank. On July 18 Robinson acknowledged "the established armament of the present sloops of 17 and 11 guns being in many respects, and especially with reference to the more powerful nature of modern artillery, very inefficient." It was decided that reducing the number of 17-gunned sloops to 6 guns with mobile guns would be an improvement. According to Robinson, "The weight of shot thrown at a broadside by the proposed Armament will exceed that now delivered; the range will be far greater, and the angle of training of the guns on the broadside will be 100° as compared with 69° on the old plan."[12] On Sept. 2 Grey confirmed the change in armament for the new steam sloops under construction.[13]

Though the double armament added to the weight, length, draft, and cost of the broadside ironclad, the actual weight, proportion, and cost of any turret ships were yet to be discussed; and as long as the

Warrior carried the heaviest guns available, in a larger quantity than the *Gloire* and behind armor thick enough to withstand most fire, she was herself "Mistress of the Seas." Still, the ideas of Captain Coles— even before the news of the *Monitor* and the *Virginia* escalated the public debate into a national one (in March 1862)—whispered the latent contemporary appeal of "Progress" that experiments, if they were conducted, seemed bound to be justified.

Such an opportunity did not come until mid-September 1861, by which time, in addition to the first four broadside ironclads—two large and two small—the British Admiralty had committed itself to 11 modified ironclads of the more customary design. Coles's prototype turret, whose armor arrangement matched the *Warrior*'s, was transferred to the Crimean War ironclad battery H.M.S. *Trusty* for testing under severe fire. The trial was a complete success; the turret took 33 hits from 68-pounder smoothbores and 110-pounder Armstrong rifled guns and yet proved capable of firing at moving targets without complication as the vessel itself turned. Another success was the loading of the guns, which proved more efficient than was the case in cramped broadside quarters. Interest in the highly publicized experiment went all the way to the top. Prime Minister Palmerston wrote with evident approval to Lord Russell on Sept. 24, 1861, "Somerset thinks that comparatively small iron-cased ships armed in this way with all their guns, perhaps 16 on deck, and without any portholes and therefore low in the water, will prove formidable ships of war."[14]

Shortly afterward, the Admiralty directed Robinson to report on Coles's proposals for a new ironclad warship. The Controller noted the following: "[T]he protection afforded by the Cupola to the guns' crews is complete, and far more effective against vertical as well as horizontal fire than that obtained by iron plating applied to the general form of ships sides; and the offensive power of guns in these shields is also considerably greater than that possessed by guns mounted in the ordinary way and fired through Port holes." However, the Controller seemed to have come away from the interview with the captain-inventor somewhat confused.[15] First, he declared it likely that the design for "a Flush-deck vessel to carry two cupolas with four Armstrong guns" was in fact a modification of Coles's original June 1860 patent turret vessel. He also said that better protection from "vertical as well as horizontal fire" must refer to the angled turret ("shield") design, sloped at right-angle fire from another ship, and from plunging fire. In addition, he remarked that "up to this time [Coles] has not clearly determined whether an inclined or vertical side is to be part of his plan." This comment referred again not to the form of the turrets but to the angled casemate of the ship itself. Robinson's comment was corroborated in the enclosed "Remarks on the proposed

Designs for a vessel to carry two of Capt. Coles' shields," from the Chief Constructor, the day *before* the date of the Controller's report. Here the Constructor noted two plans; in one "the iron on the inclined side is . . . too thin to offer effectual resistance to shot, being only equivalent to 4½-inches vertical plates <u>without backing</u>."[16] As specified in Coles's 1860 patent, "the outer side is to be of iron and should be constructed as lightly as is consistent with the required strength."[17] Both plans seemed sensible on paper:

> But I cannot understand from anything that has been described to me by Captain Coles that the ship which is to carry these Cupolas stands less in need of Armour Plating than any other ship so that if their Lordships have decided, and decided wisely in my opinion, that every part of a ship must be protected in that manner, it will be necessary that Captain Cole's ship should be plated all round as heavily as any other ship, and carry in addition the weight of the cupolas. To do this, and to obtain a tolerable degree of speed, larger dimensions per gun will be required than have yet been given in any ship, and consequently the expense per gun will be infinitely greater.

If the ship in question was similar to Coles's 1860 patent, according to the opinion of the Constructor, and also of Robinson, the whole concept of the angled sides was inadequate and they would require thicker support. As with the 1860 design, the armored vertical side beginning at the waterline from the casemate had "the important defect that in consequence of not having sufficient displacement to allow of the Armour on the transverse bulkheads being carried more than 2ft 6ins below the waterline, the Engines, Boilers, and Magazines are greatly exposed to a raking fire." According to the Constructor, if "sufficient security" was the issue, "a much larger ship would be required." Whether there was an element of professional bias involved—for Coles's ship was in every way a public challenge to his own—the Controller's hesitancy only increased after he promised the Board of Admiralty improved designs correcting the various flaws "as soon as I can get exactly from Captain Coles what is considered requisite for the proper adaptation of his shield to a sea-going ship." The precise calculations never came.

Although events were finally under way that would lead to the order for both the *Prince Albert* and the *Royal Sovereign*—Britain's first turret ironclads—Coles himself must have come away from the October meeting somewhat disappointed. His inclined-armor plan was clearly disapproved, and his lack of technical familiarity with specific issues was exposed on several points. The most discomfiting of these, again, was the issue of seaworthiness. Robinson preferred to abandon the inclined casemate. But because the vessel would still require extra armor protection below the waterline, with a much larger hull required to carry the added weight—and with more powerful engines and finer lines—why not add more turrets? Robinson addressed the main issue directly when he remarked "that probably the most disadvantageous mode possible of applying Captain Coles' shields to a ship is limiting the number of shields to two."[18]

Chapter 4

The Specter of Modern Coastal Defense and Assault

During the time when Coles's scheme of armament was gaining acceptance, though the conundrum of how to actually exploit its qualities was surfacing, events abroad reminded British naval thinkers of the traditional character of sea power. As warships of the Royal Navy were about to operate with a French squadron off the coast of Mexico, ostensibly to collect on defaulted loans, the Foreign Office inquired of the Board of Admiralty "the probable success of a combined military and naval attack on Vera Cruz."[1] The two main concerns were the effectiveness of an assault on the improved fortifications protecting the harbor, and the "facilities or difficulties of a blockade of Vera Cruz and Tampico." The Admiralty replied that because the forts were "built of a sort of coral rock which receives a shot without suffering much damage" and were armed with 68-pounder smoothbores of English or Belgian make, "a force of two line of battle ships and three frigates or corvettes with four gun vessels armed with 100 pdr. Armstrong guns, would be the least that could be sent with the prospect of having to encounter a serious resistance on the part of the Mexicans. Looking to the probable composition of a Mexican garrison and the probable defective organisation of the defence my Lords believe that a well arranged attack by the above detailed force would have a good probability of success."[2] This composition meant a sea-to-land ratio of almost 2 to 1 in guns, with the heaviest guns available necessary to demolish the Mexican ramparts. Most likely, a covering barrage would be laid down from a protective, though ineffective, distance by the ships of the line and frigates, while the shallow gunboats moved in to deliver a precise, devastating fire. But it was important to keep in mind that this attack would be led against a bankrupt "non-Power" without a navy or the resources to fully develop one.

A much more serious and complicated operation threatened in the following months during the _Trent_ crisis, when the United States, although engaged in a continental-scale civil war, managed to present the Royal Navy with the gravest challenge it could imagine. A British assault upon French harbors or the maintenance of an effective block-ade of France's Atlantic and Mediterranean coasts was one thing; the logistics alone of a war against the vast American eastern seaboard—on the opposite side of the Atlantic Ocean—was even more compli-cated in an age of steam-powered warships than in the wars of 1812 or the American Revolution. Fuel was now a major factor, and it had to be supplied from the greatest of distances, along open-ocean routes subject to attack.[3] Effective convoy protection meant fewer ships available for blockade duty or the line of battle, let alone coastal defense for Britain against American privateers. The ravages of fast, heavily armed Confederate cruisers (built and being built in Great Britain) were about to demonstrate that steam power offered greater flexibility to commerce raiding. Coal might be taken from captured ships, purchased with confiscated goods, or seized from the many unprotected depots of the British Empire around the world. Naval resources would be stretched far thinner against Civil War America than in a war against France (which was more prepared but also much more proximate) or even undeveloped though extremely distant China and Mexico. A December 14, 1861, circular from Colonial Secretary, the Duke of Newcastle, "to the Governors of West India Colonies" thus warned that it would be "impossible to increase the Land Forces now in the West Indies . . . for repelling any attack of a predatory kind from which no disposition of H.M.'s Naval Forces can give them absolute security." Local forces that could be scraped together by colo-nial administrators would probably have to fend for themselves.[4] The old defenses of Bermuda itself—Milne's chosen central base of operations—the British admiral found by the beginning of January 1862 to be "unstable and unsatisfactory . . . still mounting 24 pdrs. instead of those of the heaviest calibre." Although it "may be said to be no busi-ness of mine," Milne wrote to his superiors in London, "the Navy is looked to for the defence of the Island[;] indeed in its present state it would be impossible to leave it without Ships of War."[5] On the other hand, Russell specified to Somerset a "first anxiety" of safely reinforc-ing Canada "without being intercepted" and then securing British trade with large numbers of protective cruisers well before "we may consider aggressive operations."[6] Somerset for his part was concerned that "some disaster" in Canada was "not impossible in the event of war." Openly consulting the best authorities for its defense, he wrote to Lewis, would at least preempt a likely public inquiry afterward, "as we shall have abundant advice after the event, telling us what we ought to have done."[7] The bitter Crimean experience was still fresh in everyone's mind.

Yet the biggest problem facing British politicians and naval thinkers at the end of 1861 was not the defense of Canada, the maritime colonies, or the protection of trade, but rather laying down an offensive against the American coastline itself. If a maritime war with a continental power could be lost by England on the open sea lanes, it could only be won against the shores of the enemy.[8] Earlier that year a confidential printed report had been circulated describing what would be required for such a campaign. This was the *List of the Chief Ports on the Federal Coast of the United States, showing the Shipping, Population, Dockyards and Defences as far as known; also how far accessible or vulnerable to an Attack, as far as can be gathered from the Charts. With an approximate Estimate of the Number of Vessels required to blockade the several Ports and Rivers*—a valuable exposé of the British conception of blockade and assault as of 1861.[9] It began with the geographical setting: "The length of the seaboard of the United States, not including bays and rivers, from the eastern frontier in the Bay of Fundy to Cape Hatteras, south of the Chesapeake, is about 1,300 miles." By breaking down this imposing stretch, the report optimistically denotes "seven principal ports and five secondary places, which it might be considered right to blockade." But in addition to the scope of the task involved, there was the factor of time. Every day, the resources of the North were being mobilized, and the defenses of each locale were being improved. In Portland, Maine, for example, the entrance to the principal channel leading to within three-quarters of a mile of the city itself was listed as protected by two forts on either end of the approach, 1,000 yards apart, with a third fort being built deeper in the center, forming a triple cross fire. It was a typical harbor defense leftover from the previous national coastal fortification program (which had confronted so many Union planners throughout the Civil War), augmented by modern ordnance.[10]

If the channel was obstructed, however, making the passage of deep-draft ironclads difficult, or sown with torpedoes (mines), the attack could quickly be stalled under fire.[11] Perhaps it was for this reason that Milne "would rather have avoided or . . . felt my way at Portland, than at once adopting any active operations against that Town and State," and this was supplemented by unrealistic British hopes that Maine would contemplate secession if Union leaders foolishly allowed the Civil War to escalate into a world war.[12]

Natural obstruction by ice was also a factor that had to be considered, and the greatest concern in the report was, of course, depth of water. Milne, for example, was alarmed to observe U.S. warships taking soundings at Bermuda and stressed the need for British ships to do the same in American ports while peace still existed.[13] In the case of Boston, *The List of Chief Ports* noted that "the harbour is spacious and safe when once inside, but the entrances are intricate, with a depth of only 18 feet in some parts at low water, or 27 feet at high water." Furthermore, "all the forts looked new and in good order when seen last autumn. Fort Warren on George island is a double tier of casemates, probably with the American or small embrasure, faced with 8-inch wrought iron." Given this, the report was forced to conclude that "it is probable that Boston could not be attacked with any hope of success," although a blockade of the entrances to the city from the sea was possible with "at least . . . one line-of-battle ship, two frigates, two sloops, and two gunboats."[14] Indeed, it seems more likely that Milne preferred counter-blockade and a disruption of Union "communications" rather than "to make war felt" by carrying it out "against the Enemy with Energy, and every place made to feel what War really is."[15] This type of operational strategy was simply less risky than direct assault because it allowed the British to fight on "chosen ground" of their own: the open sea. Here, factors such as vessels' draft and natural or man-made obstructions could be safely and conveniently ignored, as could even "maneuverability" to a far greater extent.

The primary case in point in any proposed offensive operation against the United States was New York City, which the report labeled "the commercial capital of the United States, [with] a population of 600,000 [and] near one million tons of shipping." The city's defenses were listed in the survey as "10 or more forts and batteries," some of which carry "every modern improvement; the guns, too, no doubt are of heavy calibre." As for the "practicability or policy of an attack on the city of New York," the report continued, "there are so many circumstances to be considered that it might appear presumptuous, at present to offer any remark." But in a breathtaking scenario, the attack is indeed played out in the *List* ("which is by no means recommended"):

> There is the great advantage of deep water, as 10, 12, and 14 fathoms, just in the Narrows, where the principal forts are placed. The channel here likewise . . . is 1,500 yards wide, and quite straight for upwards of four miles, so that a squadron might steam rapidly past the forts. But for wood ships to be stationary and engage at close quarters casemated forts armed with guns throwing 11-inch shells, is most strongly to be deprecated. If an armour-plated frigate, one on each side, could place herself within two hundred yards of the forts, and take off the fire while the squadron passed

up between, it would be a great protection. Doubtless earthworks and heavy guns would be brought down and planted on the shores above on either side, but as they are nearly two miles apart, their fire against ships in rapid motion would not much signify; they would, however, have the effect of preventing the squadron from anchoring off Robin Reef. It must dash on, run the gauntlet of the very strong forts on Governor Island, passing at a distance of 1200 yards, and so up the Hudson river abreast the quays of New York and out of range of the forts.

The great obstacle to such a dash would be that the Federals, if they had time would resort to the plan of sinking ships in the channel. . . . At three miles higher up off Robin Reef the water is shallower, and the channel only half a mile wide, it might therefore, be blocked by sinking some 10 or 12 vessels, but hardly so completely that a steam ram might not cut her way through the barrier and form a channel for other ships to follow, especially as this part is out of the reach of any shore batteries.

But, supposing a powerful squadron to have overcome all obstacles and to have anchored in Hudson's river off New York, what further steps could be taken. To go up the East river and burn the Navy Yard and the few U.S. ships of war which, probably, would have taken refuge there, would be impracticable, the channel is too intricate to attempt it unless with the best local pilots and every gun silenced. All that could be done then, would be to hold out the threat of bombarding the city unless the ships of war were surrendered and the Navy Yard destroyed. This measure might have the effect of putting an end to the war, and if so it might be worth the risk. But the risk would be too great if the intention transpired and time were allowed the enemy to make preparations. The only hope of success would be to obtain good local pilots beforehand, to appear off Sandy Hook by day-break, at half-flood tide, and to make a bold dash for 16 miles from sea to the quays of New York.[16]

There were weaknesses in the conception of the report itself. Laced with references to the deployments of the War of 1812, it often noted an effective blockade of a major port maintained by a single wooden man-of-war. As one naval authority on that struggle concluded, "Weather had less to do with the ability of the U.S. Navy to sortie and to return than did British strategic and operational warship allocations, conflicting objectives, and even the actions of individual ship captains. . . ."[17] Nor did the *List* seem to take steam-powered blockade runners into consideration, operating regardless of the wind. On Admiral Milne's copy of the *List*, the Commander in Chief of any probable naval war against the Union remarked that the proposed total number of warships outlined in the report ("6 Line-of-Battle, 11 Frigates, 23 Sloops, and 20 Gunboats") was "entirely inadequate." Reflecting on the situation after the immediate danger posed by the *Trent* affair had passed, Milne wrote to Somerset that even the renowned steam frigates of the *Orlando* class—the British response to the pre–Civil War threat posed by the American Navy's slow but powerfully armed *Merrimack*-class steam-frigates—would "prove unsatisfactory to the service as Sea Boats, and will work themselves to pieces, nor can the rudder exert its power over them, the Leverage is too great and they fall off into the trough of the Sea." For littoral warfare, if not also blockade, the greater need was for paddle-steamers, the "most efficient and useful vessels for every service."[18]

Meanwhile, the British admiral regarded the presence of steam-and-sail ships of the line in American waters as a positive drawback. His opinion was dramatically underscored on Dec. 29, 1861, when the 27-foot draft steam ship of the line H.M.S. *Conqueror* ran aground and was destroyed at Rum Cay, Jamaica.[19] By early March, Milne's opinions against these ships of the line had crystallized. In a highly significant letter to Sir Frederick Grey, he reflected:

> If it had been war the great want would have been Frigates and Corvettes. By my letter to the Duke you would see the large service I had in view, and the Line of Battle ships would never have stood the gales and sea off the American coast. Every one of them would have been disabled, in fact I don't see of what service I could have employed them. As to attacking Forts it must never be done by anchoring ships but by ships passing and repassing in rotation so as not to allow a steady object to the Enemy. Ships with larger draft of water are unfit for this mode of attack you need not build any more. Their days are numbered except [against] France . . . if she ever gets up a Navy.[20]

With frequent references to modern, heavy, shell-firing guns in networks of fortifications, the *List* relied in no small degree upon iron-plated frigates to make coastal assaults, let alone blockades, truly successful. The presence of "iron," as such, protected traditional "wood" against modern ordnance. Whether this concern was well founded is another matter, because at least American Civil War combat experience went both ways; some vessels were quickly devastated by close-range shell fire, while others absorbed surprising amounts of punishment. What is certain, however, is that the added tactical risk of facing American ordnance necessitated the strategic presence of British ironclads. Even Palmerston was quick to point out to Somerset the desirability of sending either the old Crimean War ironclad batteries or the new armored frigates (most of which were still under construction): "the Americans put large Shell throwing Guns into all their Ships of War and our Ironsides would check mate such assailants."

"It seems to me," the Prime Minister added at the height of the *Trent* crisis, "that the only Danger we can have to apprehend from the American Navy would arise from their having armed their vessels with very heavy guns throwing large Shells, and being therefore Gun for Gun probably stronger than ours of similar classes." Two days later, Grey confirmed this opinion.[21]

Notably missing from the late 1861, British plans for assaulting or even blockading the Northern States was a consideration of the possibility of ironclad vessels emerging from the harbors or inlets to challenge enemy ships, wood or iron, although *The List of the Chief Ports* did mention a large broadside ironclad (U.S.S. *New Ironsides*) being built at "the private shipyard of Messrs. Cramp & Son . . . for the use of the United States Government" and to be "ready for sea by the middle of July 1862."[22] On Dec. 3, 1861, the Foreign Office also transmitted to the Admiralty a copy of the *New York Herald* (dated Nov. 11), which noted the second of the three ironclad prototypes approved by the Union Navy's Ironclad Board of 1861, the *Galena*, an important token of "the many improvements and the ideas that will be gained by experience" that would allow the Union Navy "to cope with any" of the boasted navies of Europe."[23] But how would the Royal Navy in turn cope with Federal ironclads?

Another important reference that the *List* made in discussing the armament of Fortress Monroe, but did not weigh accordingly, is of "a 15-inch gun, named Rodman's gun, cast at Pittsburg, on the Ohio, (300 miles west of Philadelphia) which throws a solid shot of 420 lbs. weight, and the bursting charge of its shell is 16 lbs. of powder. Weight of gun nearly 22 tons."[24] For the next four years this massive-caliber weapon, the main armament for most of the U.S. monitors constructed during the Civil War, would earn a reputation for smashing 4- to 6-inch laminated (though inclined), rolled armor plating. It was the nightmare of wooden warships falling prey to shell-firing guns writ large for early British ironclads.

SUMMARY

It was difficult to establish, first, what Britain's overall strategic objectives were concerning the role of the Royal Navy by the 1860s and, second, how those objectives were to be met by various—and opposing—types of armor-plated warships. Its traditional response to French challenges was to outbuild them, ship for ship, perhaps also achieving a qualitative as well as a quantitative edge. Yet the advent of ironclad frigates complicated this formula. It was not seen as possible to reconcile full armor protection with the greatest tactical speed and strategic range in one design. There would have to be some compromise. The *Royal Oaks* thus represented an acknowledgment that regional supremacy, based on more fully protected ironclads of at least equal numbers to French varieties, was more important than high-seas or imperial supremacy. Meanwhile, a Colonial Office memo observed that "the Colonies, especially the lesser Colonies which most call for assistance, are not separate nations; they are members of one immensely powerful and wealthy nation, from which they believe that they are entitled to some share of general protection. The question is what that share should be."[25]

Even when the Board of Admiralty decided to push ahead with super iron-hulled *Warriors* in the form of the *Achilles* and then the *Minotaur*-class ironclads, it became doubtful whether British private industry and shipbuilding would be able to meet the new demands of the Royal Navy. Somerset complained that a Committee on Dockyard Economy unfairly concluded "that the Dockyards will not bear comparison with the private establishments of the day."[26] If anything, the need for more comprehensive strategic protection and tactical protection in the shape and form of ironclads themselves required equally greater consolidation of modern shipbuilding in the dockyards, under tighter government control, than otherwise. This consolidation would be an expensive undertaking and did not sit well with Liberal drives for retrenchment—hence, the appeal of Coles in providing the "most economical ship," which would also be the "most invulnerable and the most durable," though his system of turret ship conversions of steam ships of the line could really offer only "National," as opposed to Imperial, defense.[27]

What caught the British Empire in the proverbial flank—obsessed as it was with the recent French challenges to its naval supremacy—was the prospect of hostilities against the Northern States at the beginning of the American Civil War. By then it was already questionable whether steam power entailed a greater economy of resources for modern naval operations or had in fact made them much more difficult and expensive. Added to this was the relative efficiency of blue-water, battle fleet warships for close blockade work against the treacherous American coastline. Admiral Milne discounted as too risky coastal or harbor assault itself, depending as it did upon Union defenses not being ready in time. Though the naval and military buildup during the *Trent* crisis would succeed in convincing Washington that the Union was indeed not prepared by the end of 1861 for a hostile dose of British seapower, it also stressed to British authorities just how perilously transitional that force had become.

Chapter 5

Two Ironclad Adversaries: The Confederacy and Great Britain

The creation of the ironclad navy of the United States was a response directed against two adversaries, one actual and one potential: the Confederate States and Great Britain. Before the Civil War erupted in America, beginning with the bombardment of Fort Sumter in Charleston Harbor, South Carolina (April 12, 1861), few U.S. naval authorities gave the matter serious thought. As 1860 rolled around, *Scientific American* bemoaned the fact that "at present we have not a single first class war steamer—one that can compete with the most recently built French and British ones, and we regret that the Secretary of the Navy has not paid attention to these—we mean the iron-cased war wolves."[1] Indeed, Secretary Isaac Toucey's Annual Report, published on Dec. 1, 1860, stated that "to arm a ship of war without a modern patented invention would give great advantage to the enemy" but nowhere mentioned the phenomenon of armor-plating men-of-war that was occurring across the Atlantic. Instead, he "earnestly" recommended "the policy of a gradual, substantial, and permanent increase of the Navy, accompanied by the universal introduction into it of the motive power of steam." The policy that Toucey recommended, however, was dependent on the resolution of a number of important contemporary issues that took precedence over any plans the Navy sought to implement. Because the U.S. Constitution prohibited individual states from developing navies of their own—thus antagonizing advocates of "states' rights"—it was even more imperative for Congress "to provide and maintain a naval force adequate to our [national] protection."[2]

Probably no other American naval officer was better qualified to offer an opinion on the topic of ironclads than Commander John A. Dahlgren. Already famous for the Navy's widespread adoption of his shell-firing, "bottle-shaped," heavy smoothbore cannon, Dahlgren had also established himself as an authority on contemporary naval strategy and tactics with his treatise on *Shells and Shell-Guns,* published in 1857. His methodical argument included a detailed analysis of the Crimean War, which Dahlgren suggested pointed to the superiority of the steam-powered vessel over forts, especially when running gauntlets of fire. His book also also demonstrated, at Kinburn, the value of impregnable floating batteries, at least as "auxiliaries in attacking shore works."[3]

Dahlgren was systematic in his advocacy of heavy-caliber smoothbore guns (based and built on his pattern), which could fire both solid balls and exploding shell at practicable combat ranges under 2,000 yards. To better ensure accuracy, he explained, spherical shot could also be used for valuable ricochet firing. Against this system of naval ordnance stood William Armstrong's rifled breechloaders, which Dahlgren criticized as too complicated. He noted that elongated shells still tended to topple in flight, which compromised their accuracy and hitting power precisely at the point where their added range and velocity were supposed to outclass smoothbores. He also bristled at inferior rifling, which he said became easily jammed or fouled. "Windage," meanwhile, the space between the shell and the gun barrel, became an even more serious issue, according to Dahlgren. Their "liability to derangement," Dahlgren noted to Captain George A. Magruder, the Chief of the Bureau of Ordnance and Hydrography, "has rendered it necessary to accompany them with a corps of Artificers or 'battery Armorers,' as the official order styles them." This, he said, also applied to the Royal Army's Armstrongs; the 40-pounder naval versions "have not done so well under proof . . . and the recoil is excessive."[4]

On Dec. 10, 1860, Dahlgren, as Commander in charge of the Ordnance Department at the Washington Navy Yard, wrote to Magruder that "the earnest attention now given by naval authorities to the armature of ships-of-war, and the enormous expenditure which England and France are incurring in building ships of this description, induce me to recall the attention of the bureau to the suggestions made by me on this subject several years ago." Dahlgren reminded Magruder of his recognition after successful tests of his 9-inch shells against wooden targets in 1852 that "the sides of a vessel may be protected by iron frames or plates as to make it nearly certain that shells will break by impinging them." But permission was not granted by his superiors at this time to conduct his armor plate tests.[5]

The question Dahlgren now addressed was how to reconcile the French *Gloire's*—and, even more important, the gigantic British *Warrior's*—proportion of armor protection with "the capacity of the vessel to carry ordnance, coals, &c., upon which depends the power of attack, and to keep the sea for any length of time. . . ." Could an iron-clad, in effect, combine the qualities of a turtle and a shark? "Now, without sailing power and relying only on steam, it is obvious that they cannot go but a few days from their depots of coal, therefore can only be used in coast defense or cruising along shore." Dahlgren's proposed solution would use "an iron ribbing *externally*, with such stowage of coal *within* as the ship permits; using also an interior arrangement of thin plates, calculated to give a harmless direction to projectiles, that is, from vital parts." How the armor might cope with solid shot was another problem, not to mention how the rapid deple-tion of coal would affect matters. "But these more lightly clad steam-ers, carrying more coal and rising with greater buoyancy on the waves," Dahlgren maintained, "will go further, and may even, accom-panied by squadrons of screw coal-ships, pass to distant seas and there, by their speed, harass commerce, blockade harbors, and engage the heaviest ships that will venture to assail them." Though laid down far earlier than the French or British varieties, the "Stevens Battery," in the meantime, remained an incomplete experiment in armor-plating ships.[6]

By Feb. 2, 1861, Dahlgren was writing to Senator James Grimes of Iowa, Chairman of the U.S. Senate Naval Committee, maintaining it was "advisable that the construction of some armored Gun Boats should be proceeded with." But, he emphasized, this should not be "to the exclusion of at least the one heavy frigate," which Dahlgren specified as a ship "of 5000 to 6000 Tons" and that "may cost 1¾ to 2 millions which is the estimated expense of the English Plated frigate *Warrior*, just launched—$500,000 will do to begin with." Time was of the essence, he added, "for with all effort it would not be possible to get a ship ready for service in less than two years." This tight timeline was unusual, especially considering that the previous month he had informed the House Chairman of Naval Affairs that "Gun Sloops [were] a class of vessel more needed in the Navy than any other"—if an ironclad were to be considered—suggesting the recent *Iroquois* class as a model to be plated.[7] One might ask why there was an immediate need for a long-range, oceangoing ironclad. In fact, why was there a need for one at all? The ordnance expert did not specify his source, but noted instead an inquiry "from one of our most eminent private Ship Builders" [Donald McKay of Boston] on armament schemes for various classes of ironclads. "Unless Government acts promptly," Dahlgren cautioned, "[the need] will be anticipated by private enterprise."

Presumably, then, this would be a fate worse than falling behind England or France. Nevertheless, in response to Donald McKay's inquiry, Dahlgren had to "regret to perceive that this Congress is not likely to make any appropriation for constructing an Iron plated ship."[8]

With a civil war looming, it was difficult to determine exactly what kind of naval force would be needed to protect, if not preserve, the Union. The U.S. Navy's instincts were blue-water; the disposition of its existing warships, protecting far-flung American commercial interests, was proof of that. The initial public and professional reaction to European ironclad programs was to meet them on similar terms, differences in broadside armament notwithstanding. John Lenthall, Chief of the Bureau of Ship Construction and Repair, therefore rejected many early proposals flowing into the Navy Department, typically because "the necessarily large size, the cost and the time required for building an iron cased steam vessel is such that [the Navy] is not recommended to adopt any plan at present."[9]

Opinion across the Atlantic was not so clearly united. "We cannot, with our wide-spread dominions, or colonies and commerce dotted all over the surface of the globe, expect to be superior at every assailable point," argued *Blackwood's* in March 1861, "and we should utterly fail if, in the event of war with a great maritime power, we attempted to be everywhere in force at the same time—a strategy which seems to be indicated by the powerful efforts made to produce that marine impossibility, great fighting-power and great speed." Instead, *Blackwood's* proposed, Britain should have "a number of iron-clad vessels for the defense of our coast and narrow seas. Let them be capable of going as far as Brest or Cherbourg on the one hand, and Antwerp, Rotterdam, or Copenhagen on the other."[10]

Besides, as events would dictate, within the next year these instincts would have to adapt to radically altered circumstances. Blockade would be waged against the American coastline; American forts would be challenged and gauntlets run, with battles ranging up and down American rivers. At the same time, the threat of war with foreign naval powers would actually intensify with the commencement of the Civil War. "Americans saw before them the danger of a national humiliation, the depth of which it is perhaps necessary to be an American to understand," described a British historian at the close of World War I:

In no country in the Old World are sentiments of national pride and patriotism so intimately bound up with the political constitution of the nation as in the United States. In Europe such feelings gather round the traditions, literary, artistic and historic, of the past; in America, to a far greater extent, they are bound up with the future. The American Constitution is felt to be, not a heritage of the past, but a model for the future; a thing to which it will be the pride of Americans to see the Old World gradually conform. . . . If it failed, if it were broken by disruption, everything failed.[11]

Queen Victoria's Proclamation of Neutrality (May 13, 1861) thus angered the North by implicitly granting the newly forming Southern Confederacy of States, which Lincoln would only acknowledge as "insurgents," and which the Northern press regarded as "traitors," legitimate belligerent status. Both North and South saw this as the first step toward Europe's formal political recognition of Confederate sovereignty. On the other hand, British policymakers regarded Lincoln's proclamation of a naval "blockade" of the Southern States— and not simply a Federal declaration that such ports in the South were "closed"—as further indicating the real truth of the matter: the United States was in a state of war, practically against a foreign power, rather than merely "suppressing an insurrection." The British viewpoint therefore coincided all too closely with that of the rebellious states. Indeed, it supplied the new Confederate cause with important political validation and moral support from abroad—perhaps, the South could hope, to be followed by material assistance. Any further move in that direction would therefore present those in favor of the Union with an additional enemy. Thus, as the *New York Herald* relayed in May 1861, "the diplomatic corps has also been notified that if any Commissioner, or Minister, from the seceded States be received by any European Power the government will not hesitate to break off all diplomatic relations with such power—will recall the United States Minister at such Court, and will dismiss the representative of that Power resident in Washington."[12]

This tense and chilly animosity worked two ways. By June, both the Northern and the British press were hotly engaged—not against the South or France, respectively, but against one another. *Punch* magazine's depiction of "Naughty Jonathan" was that of a spoiled child throwing a tantrum before a cool and indifferent "Mother" England. Edward Dicey, after his six-month swing through the North as a foreign journalist, reported "how very liable Americans are to make mistakes in judging England from our press, and how much more liable, for special reasons, we are to make like mistakes in taking the American press as the standard of America."[13] *Harper's Weekly* was already speculating on the costs of a war with England:

If [an embargo against British goods] led to war it could not injure us much more than active British sympathy with the rebels would. England has not men enough to effect a landing on our coast. In the Crimean War she could not raise an army of 50,000 men. New York alone could take care of any army she might send out. She would of course blockade many, if not all of our ports. But the same result will practically be reached if privateers are fitted out in England; already our insurance companies have raised the war risk to a point which absorbs the profit of shippers. . . . On the other hand, a war with England would this time insure the annexation of Canada—no mean gain to us in view of the future.

. . . [A] war with England would not injure us more than such British sympathy with the rebels as is foreshadowed in the Queen's proclamation, the declarations of the Ministry, and the tone of the London press.[14]

Yet even U.S. Secretary of State William H. Seward's publicized scheme of keeping the nation united (or compensating for the loss of the South)—by wresting control of Canada, the West Indies, Mexico, and Central America from European monarchies[15]—was fortunately giving way to Lincoln's sense of Union and foreign policy. In truth, according to some, neither man was fit to address these important issues. The newly appointed minister to Great Britain, Charles Francis Adams (whose lineage included President John Quincy Adams and early Federalist President John Adams), noted after the Civil War that "in the history of our Government down to this hour, no experiment so rash has ever been made as that of elevating to the head of affairs a man with so little previous preparation for his task as Mr. Lincoln." "Mr. Seward himself came into the State Department with no acquaintance with the forms of business other than that obtained incidentally through his service in the Senate."[16]

Nevertheless, Congress was informed by the President upon special assembly on the Fourth of July 1861 that "this illegal organization, in the character of confederate States, was already invoking recognition, aid, and intervention, from foreign Powers." U.S. national power or expansion was not the issue of the Civil War, which instead presented "to the whole family of man the question, whether a constitutional republic, or democracy—a government of the people, by the same people, can, or cannot, maintain its territorial integrity against its own domestic foes. . . . It forces us to ask: 'Is there, in all republics, this inherent and fatal weakness? Must a government, of necessity, be too *strong* for the liberties of its own people, or too *weak* to maintain its own existence?'" Heading off potential Congressional criticism of his actions as Executive in the opening stages of the Civil War—including the calling out of militia volunteers, additions to the Federal Army and Navy, and even the suspension of habeas corpus in some cases— Lincoln noted that, indeed, "the forbearance of this government had been so extraordinary, and so long continued, as to lead some foreign nations to shape their action as if they supposed the early destruction of our National Union was probable." While he was now "happy to say that the sovereignty and rights of the United States are now everywhere practically respected by foreign powers; and a general sympathy with the country is manifested throughout the world," Lincoln nevertheless required Congressional approval for 400,000 more men and an appropriation of $400 million "for making this contest" of rival ideologies in the mid-Victorian era "a short and decisive one. . . ." "A right result, at this time," Lincoln pointedly added, "will be worth more to the world than ten times the men, and ten times the money."[17]

For Gideon Welles, the new Secretary of the Navy, who came to office during the Civil War, "the necessity of an augmentation of our navy in order to meet the crisis. . . was immediately felt, and a class of vessels different in some respects from any that were in service, to act as sentinels on the coast, was required."[18] These 23 purpose-built, wooden-hulled, screw-driven steamships were later nicknamed the "90-Day Gunboats," for their speed of construction. They could operate in shallow draft and mounted a heavy 11-inch Dahlgren smoothbore pivot. Already, the naval appropriations total that was approved till the end of the fiscal year (June 30, 1862) had jumped during the secession crisis—before Congress could approve—from $13,168,675 to $30,609,520, including the purchase or charter of 21 steam and 3 sailing merchant vessels. Although "much attention has been given within the last few years to the subject of floating batteries, or iron-clad steamers," however, Welles doubted whether "the period is perhaps not one best adapted to heavy expenditures by way of experiment and the time and attention of some of those who are most competent to investigate and form correct conclusions on this subject are otherwise employed." Still, he recommended the appointment of a special board to report on "a measure so important."[19]

Within weeks, at least two important contenders for contracts for ironclads, Donald McKay and Cornelius Bushnell, were writing to Commodore Joseph Smith, the head of the Bureau of Yards and Docks, regarding any decisions on a Union program for their construction.[20] Finally, on Aug. 3, 1861, and by an Act of Congress, Welles was directed "to appoint a board of three skilful naval officers to investigate the plans and specifications that may be submitted for the construction or completing of iron-clad steamships or floating batteries to be built," $1.5 million having been appropriated for the purpose. At the time, this was equivalent to £300,000, roughly the price of a single British *Warrior*.

Whether the Union would invest in such an "iron-clad steamship" *or* "floating batteries," however, was unclear. As J. P. Baxter noted, simply pushing Welles's proposal for an Ironclad Board through Congress was not easy, despite the grandiose vision (and therefore naval requirements) of the well-publicized "Anaconda Plan"[21] and the emerging reports that the rebels at Norfolk had salvaged the scuttled wreck of the U.S.S. *Merrimack*—to convert her into a powerful ironclad of their own. A House amendment to Senator Grimes's July 19 bill for an Ironclad Board nearly made completion of the abortive Stevens Battery a condition for the special $1.5 million appropriation since the Senate opposed this portion of the bill. Referring back to the Navy's strategic requirements, Grimes argued that "it was supposed to be possible that a conflict with some foreign Power might grow out of our present complications. . . ." Moreover, "in that event it might be important to provide armored batteries, floating steam batteries, for the defense of the various harbors along our sea-coast." These statements more clearly reflected the national resentment at England's neutrality—the threat of recognition of the Confederacy and an ensuing Anglo-American maritime war—Lincoln's perception of the global political and social significance of the Civil War, and Welles's "immediately felt" need for a brown-water naval force. "The sole purpose of this bill," Grimes acknowledged, was "to enable the Secretary of the Navy to construct some floating steam batteries that can take position on either side of a harbor, or in the center of a harbor, to resist the ingress of vessels of war."[22]

The story of how civilian engineer-inventor John Ericsson entered the picture at this point has been well told many times before. During the Crimean War, Ericsson submitted plans for an "Iron-Clad Steam Battery, with Revolving Cupola" to Napoleon III. It was essentially a monitor. In his proposal to the French Emperor, dated Sept. 26, 1854, Ericsson declared that "the present system of *long* range is abortive" in naval combat tactics and technology. Smaller, rifled projectiles lacked sufficient weight and, consequently, hitting power, while "accurate aim at long range becomes absolutely impossible in practice." What was needed , it was found, was a "complete system of *naval attack*" with a "self-moving vessel capable of passing within range of guns and forts, and of moving at pleasure in defiance of the fire of broadsides." Despite its amazing inherent defensive powers (low freeboard and "semi-globular turret of plate iron 6 inches thick") and the concentrated, all-powerful armament scheme—what torpedoes would be for submarines in the following century—Ericsson's dream-ironclad lacked auxiliary sail power, extra coal bunkers, or some equally revolutionary form of super-efficient steam engine. Though it would "place an entire fleet of sailing vessels, during calms and light winds, at the mercy of a single craft," this was implicitly a *coastal* system of naval attack.[23]

Ericsson was originally called upon by Bushnell to inspect the latter's own plans for an ironclad, which he intended to submit to the

Ironclad Board of 1861 (consisting of Commodore Smith, Commodore Hiram Paulding, and Commander Charles H. Davis). This vessel, later to bear the name the U.S.S. *Galena*, was largely approved by Ericsson, who then revealed to Bushnell in the form of plans and a cardboard model complete with a revolving turret his own conception of a "perfect ironclad." Bushnell, immediately intrigued, pressed Ericsson to submit the design to the Board and then gained the stubborn and doubtful inventor's permission to bring it to Washington for him. On Aug. 29, 1861, Ericsson drafted a letter to Lincoln seeking "no private advantage or emolument of any kind" for his ironclad proposals because a thousand of his caloric engines already provided him with enough personal means. "Attachment to the Union alone," he declared, "impels me to offer my services—my life if need be—in the great cause which Providence has called you to defend." His battery, he averred, could within 10 weeks "take up position under the rebel guns at Norfolk and . . . within a few hours the stolen ships would be sunk and the harbor purged of traitors." Ericsson concluded by drawing the President's attention to the "now well established fact that steel clad vessels cannot be arrested in their course by land batteries." New York was therefore "quite at the mercy of such intruders, and may at any moment be laid in ruins"—unless the Union possessed ironclads impervious to Britain's "Armstrong Guns" and was furnished in turn with armor-crushing ordnance.[24] Meanwhile, on Sept. 3, Merrick & Sons of Philadelphia proposed to Welles "an iron plated steamer" taking nine months to build, at a cost of $780,000. The steamer would eventually be accepted as the U.S.S. *New Ironsides*, the Union Navy's only active sea-going broadside ironclad.

Welles also saw merit in Ericsson's model, which Bushnell displayed for the Secretary at his home in Hartford, Connecticut, directly after his meeting with Ericsson. Encouraged by this response, Bushnell hurriedly solicited the backing of New York iron industrialists John F. Winslow and John A. Griswold, who also had influential connections with the former state governor William H. Seward, now the influential Secretary of State. By Sept. 7 Bushnell was writing from Willard's Hotel in Washington to Cornelius Delamater of the Novelty Iron Works of New York (who had originally referred Bushnell to Ericsson for professional scrutiny of the *Galena*'s stability) with good news. Ericsson's plan "was formally laid before the President last Evening—on an introductory letter from Mr. Seward." Lincoln, he reported, was "much pleased"—even so far as to make an appointment to accompany Bushnell and the "Ericsson Battery" before the Ironclad Board.[25]

Perhaps the involvement of so much civilian authority made the naval professionals intransigent. Ericsson's name also evoked bad memories of the U.S.S. *Princeton*'s "Peacemaker" gun disaster of

Feb. 28, 1844. The *Princeton* was the world's first screw-propelled frigate, designed and engineered by Ericsson, but the "Peacemaker" was that of his Navy advocate, Captain Robert F. Stockton. When the gun exploded in a celebrated trial, killing the Secretary of State, the Secretary of the Navy, and others, as well as wounding several more (including Stockton himself), Ericsson found his own professional reputation tarnished. Worse still, his subsequent labor bill to the Navy of $15,000 for work on the *Princeton* was flatly rejected by Stockton, as was Ericsson's connection with the vessel as being on anything but a "volunteer" basis. In Stockton's version of events, Ericsson had come uninvited to America from England and then built the *Princeton* for free. His bill was never paid.[26] At any rate, all of the Board members saw Ericsson's model as a dangerously radical departure from conventional ship design. Commander Davis contemptuously advised Bushnell to "take the little thing home and worship it, as it would not be idolatry, because it was in the image of nothing in the heaven above or on the earth beneath or in the waters under the earth."[27]

Dismayed but not dispirited, Bushnell returned home to New Haven, informing Ericsson on Sept. 11 that Welles would "be pleased to see your plans and have the same adopted at once if you can secure the approval of the Board," which Ericsson would—keeping to Davis's own religious allegory—need to "convert."[28] Accordingly, Ericsson proceeded to Washington, where he heard with indignation the naval officers' doubts about his proposed vessel's stability. In a superb display of instructional presentation and salesmanship, Ericsson proceeded to convince the Board of his extraordinary grasp of the laws of physics and his equally stunning ability to translate them into sound mechanical principles. Science was Ericsson's religion, and none of the Board members could deny that modern warfare was headed in that direction. "Gentlemen, after what I have said," Ericsson concluded, "I deem it your duty to the country to give me an order to build the vessel before I leave the room."[29]

When the Ironclad Board of 1861 at last reported its findings to Gideon Welles on Sept. 16, the Secretary of the Navy must have found their opening remarks discouraging. The "three skilful naval officers" doubted their own ability to address such a novel topic, "having no experience and but scanty knowledge in this branch of naval architecture."[30] Indeed, iron armor properties, experimental ordnance, and steam power seemed to be areas reserved for engineers and inventors as opposed to professional sailors. Though an application "was made to the department for a naval constructor . . . with whom we might consult . . . it appears that they are all so employed on important service that none could be assigned to this duty." One thing, however, was certain, almost to the point of understatement: "Opinions differ amongst naval and scientific men as to the policy of adopting the iron armature for ships-of-war." Specifically, was it better to invest in "ships" or "batteries"? The Board's response to this central question was momentous:

> The enormous load of iron, as so much additional weight to the vessel; the great breadth of beam necessary to give her stability; the short supply of coal she will be able to stow in bunkers; the greater power required to propel her; and the largely increased cost of construction, are objections to this class of vessel as cruisers which we believe it is difficult successfully to overcome. For river and harbor service we consider ironclad vessels of light draught, or floating batteries thus shielded, as very important; and we feel at this moment the necessity of them on some of our rivers and inlets to enforce obedience to the laws.

Already the Union Navy was turning away from a blue-water conception of naval power toward a brown-water one.[31] But there were limits here as well. The Board felt that "no ship or floating battery, however heavily she may be plated, can cope successfully with a properly constructed fortification of masonry."[32] This, too, would prove to be an important observation. "Armored ships or batteries may be employed advantageously to pass fortifications on land for ulterior objects of attack, to run a blockade, or to reduce temporary batteries on the shores of rivers and the approaches to our harbors."

The focus of these statements was ambiguous. Did they outline the limits of Union ironclads attacking Confederate defenses, or Union defenses against foreign ironclads? New York might be as weakly or strongly defended by forts as Charleston; the blockade might be run from two sides. For that matter, the issue of which type of ironclad might be best against another is not mentioned in the Board's report, though "wooden ships may be said to be but coffins for their crews when brought in conflict with iron-clad vessels. . . ."[33] There were no ironclad versus ironclad engagements during the Crimean War to serve as reference.

As for ironclad ordnance, the Board acknowledged the great range of rifled guns, but "as yet we know of nothing superior to the large and heavy spherical shot in its destructive effects on vessels, whether plated or not." Though rifled guns enjoyed greater range, "the conical shot does not produce the *crushing* effect of spherical shot." This point obviously echoed Dahlgren's conclusions. Armor plate itself should be "of tough iron, and rolled in large, long pieces" and probably backed by "some elastic substance (soft wood, perhaps, is the best)" that "might relieve the frame of the ship somewhat from the terrible shock of a heavy projectile, though the plate should not be fractured." Since there were no facilities in America for rolling (rather than hammering) plates in the 4½-inch thickness standard in Europe, the Board considered the possibility of contracting for ironclads in England. Yet "a difficulty might arise with the British government, in case we should undertake to construct ships-of-war in that country, which might complicate their delivery; and, moreover, we are of opinion that every people or nation who can maintain a navy should be capable of constructing it themselves."[34] Either the Union would find the means— and the time—to invest in machinery and infrastructure to produce such armor on an equal scale, or another scheme would have to be found that made the best of the nation's existing resources.

In the meantime, the Ironclad Board concluded, "our immediate demands seem to require, first, so far as practicable, vessels invulnerable to shot, of light draught of water, to penetrate our shoal harbors, rivers, and bayous. . . . The amount now appropriated is not sufficient to build both classes of vessels to any great extent."[35] As a result, three contracts were awarded: to Bushnell, for the *Galena*; to Merrick & Sons, for the *New Ironsides*; and to Ericsson, for the *Monitor*, which seemed even at this stage in the Union Navy's ironclad program to meet the needs for coastal and river operations. That such a turreted, coastal-defense ironclad could make headway at all with the U.S. Navy in 1861 perhaps is more a reflection on the contingency of the Civil War itself than a rejection of the Navy's blue-water instincts. There was no guarantee, indeed, that Congress would be willing to invest in a wide-ranging ironclad force to "compete" with England or France after the war. Given past tendencies, in fact, such an investment must have seemed highly unlikely. But in 1861, especially after the defeat of the hastily assembled Union Army at the first Battle of Bull Run (July 21), there was no guarantee that the war could be won. By the end of the year, it would be doubtful whether it could even be contained.

What is often overlooked in this story, however, is the implicit role of Ericsson's ironclad battery, the famous *Monitor*, in relation to British—not Confederate—naval power. Already the overriding need was for light-draft, steam-powered men-of-war during the Civil War. The European ironclad examples could not be taken seriously until at least coastal hegemony was assured. But, in addition to enforcing the blockade from within, there was the need to protect it from intervening, outside naval forces. Europe, especially Britain, had a vested interest in the failure of the Union blockade of the South. The failure of the blockade was, in fact, the Confederacy's greatest hope and best chance for national independence, just at it was for the original Thirteen Colonies struggling against England during the Revolutionary War. On May 21, 1861, Seward wrote unofficially to Adams in London that "British recognition would be British intervention, to create within our territory a hostile state by overthrowing this Republic itself." The result would be a world war "between the European and the American branches of the British race." Secretary of War Sir George Cornewall Lewis found it "incredible" "that any Government of ordinary prudence should at the moment of civil war gratuitously increase the number of its enemies, and, moreover, incur the hostility of so formidable a power as England. The first effect would be that we should raise the siege of the Southern ports and ourselves blockade the Northern ports." Seward later informed Adams that Union leadership understood and accepted the precautionary measures undertaken by Britain to protect its interests in North America, namely the dispatch of three regiments to Canada and additional warships to the British West Indies and North American Station. Indeed, Seward continued, "On our part the possibility of foreign intervention, sooner or later, in this domestic disturbance is never absent from the thoughts of this government." It was precisely because of this fear that Seward was adamant about the danger of British recognition of the Confederacy. An Anglo-American war, necessarily a maritime one, would involve "scenes of devastation and desolation which will leave no roots remaining out of which trade between the United States and Great Britain, as it has hitherto flourished, can ever again spring up."[36]

Hence, when Cornelius Bushnell, Ericsson's earliest backer, first exhibited the *Monitor* plans to Secretary Welles in early September 1861, he announced that an anxious President Lincoln "need not further worry about foreign interference; I [have] discovered the means of perfect protection."[37]

Chapter 6

Building the *Monitor*

Ericsson was officially notified of the *Monitor*'s acceptance by the Ironclad Board on Sept. 21, 1861. The contract itself was not agreed upon, however, until Oct. 4. Still not completely satisfied with its decision, the Ironclad Board members demanded Ericsson's battery prove itself in combat before its full price was reimbursed to the contractors. Though his partners—Bushnell, Winslow, and Griswold—thought this irregular and offensive, Ericsson himself found it "perfectly reasonable and proper." Writing to Smith, he confidently stated, "If the structure cannot stand this test, then it is indeed worthless."[1] Bushnell wanted the promised date of completion modified to include "such time as she can be fairly tested under the enemy's fire." This was not asking for much, he argued. In terms of "National defense, the whole vessel with her equipment will cost no more than to maintain one regiment in the field 12 months, and each are experiments to be used to save the Government and Union; should ours prove what we warrant it, will it not be of infinitely more service than 100 regiments?"[2] Winslow in turn was optimistic about completing the vessel in the promised "100 days," though in the winter shipbuilding season these would be necessarily "short ones—and few enough to do all that is to be done. . . ."[3]

But this was only the beginning of Ericsson's problems. On Sept. 25 Commodore Smith was already expressing worry that "the concussion in the Turret will be so great that men cannot remain in it and work the guns after a few fires with shot." Ericsson replied that his "long drilling in the army" made him "perfectly familiar with the effect produced by firing heavy ordnance in close chambers." If the turret were in a semi-globular form, the gunners "would be stunned as if struck by lightning." But the *Monitor's* cylindrical turret was perforated on top, 9 feet high, and "so thick it will not vibrate." The vessel's forced air draft and positive air pressure from steam-powered blowers would also alleviate this concern. Indeed, "it will be comparatively a luxury for gunners to stand on the open grating of my turret, to standing on the gun deck of a frigate during action: more air, less smoke and greatly diminished vibration overhead."[4] Not that Ericsson was prepared to submit finished designs for the battery in question. The genius-inventor was, in essence, making it up as he went along; building by day, planning by night, adapting to varying circumstances often beyond his control.

The armor scheme for the *Monitor's* turret was—and perhaps remains—a controversial case in point. Widely publicized British tests had determined that thin layers of iron plate did not offer the same resistance to shot and shell as a single, homogeneous plate of equal overall thickness. Furthermore, plates backed by an "elastic" substance, which helped to absorb shock waves generated by the impact of projectiles, were less prone to penetration or fracturing. Well versed in the latest published theories, and having a keen understanding of physics, chemistry, and engineering, Ericsson originally proscribed a single rolled 4-inch plate, backed by four layers of 1-inch plates to act as a cushion. These were all carefully overlapped to "break-joint," since the junctures of armor-plates were definite weak points. On Oct. 4 Ericsson wrote to Smith of his "expectation of obtaining rolled plate 4 inches thick to form the outer half of the turret, the inner half being composed of lighter plate riveted together. . . ." But within a week he wanted to amend the contract to grant him "the authority to select either of the two modes specified of plating turret and the vessel's sides" because "Mr. Abbott of Baltimore states he will require full two months preparation to roll 4 inch thick plates," and "other establishments have not given a positive reply." Expediency of the precious contract, as well as the urgency of the Civil War, led him to adopt eight layers of 1-inch plates, since these he could have "at once, 5 feet square, at the rate of 140 tons per week."[5] Ericsson was, for the moment, satisfied with this concession. "We are not going to fight the steel clad vessels of Europe at present, and for home use the four inch plating sustained by 40 feet of deck, and the end of 10 inch deck beams of oak, will be more than sufficient."[6]

Another concern was the system of armament that would be used. Not only did Ericsson, like Dahlgren and other American ordnance experts, prefer the smashing power of heavy smoothbores at close ranges, but "the carriage as well as the slides" would be redesigned to work in the turret. This was not a concern for Ericsson. "You will not doubt my ability to handle the [XI-inch] gun," he assured Commodore Smith, "if you call to mind the facility with which the 12 inch guns of the *Princeton* were worked with my carriages and friction gear."[7] In fact, the weapons determined the size of the turret, and consequently the entire structure of the ship.[8] This underlying principle, fundamental in the evolution of the modern warship, marked a crucial difference from British practice. Following the Civil War, the British Ordnance Select Committee observed the U.S. Navy's "policy of considering the armament of a ship more particularly before designing her, with a view to obviate the difficulty and inconvenience frequently experienced in placing suitable guns on board a given ship, for the want of sufficient room, is a question for the consideration of the Admiralty—but it appears to the Committee to be well worthy of their attention." Admiral Robinson, the Controller, could only "entirely concur in the remarks made both by the Ordnance Select Committee and Captain [Astley Cooper] Key on the necessity of considering the Armament of a Ship before designing her, and on the importance of considering a Ship as mainly designed to carry Guns. . . ." But heavy guns for the Royal Navy were the responsibility of the War Office, which in turn relied largely upon private inventors; the leading British guns were still on the testing grounds and few in number. The Admiralty was increasingly frustrated; Robinson had "often pointed out the difficulties of designing a Ship without minute information as to the Armament proposed to be carried" and noted with his usual touch of complaint "that at this very moment there are more Ships fitted to carry large guns than there are guns ready to put into them."[9]

On Oct. 8, 1861, therefore, when Ericsson requested specs for the 11-inch Dahlgren, Smith was quick to inform Captain A. A. Harwood, the new Chief of the Bureau of Ordnance, that in addition to the specs, two of the guns themselves would need to be "supplied at New York for the use of said Vessel." On Oct. 13, Ericsson wrote Smith he could not "proceed with the work on the battery turret until the receipt of drawing of the Dahlgren gun," but by then it was already en route. Smith, in the meantime, was sure to remind Secretary Welles that the Dahlgrens "should be prepared soon, as in case they are not ready when demanded by the Contractor, advantage may be taken of that clause in the contract which provides that the test shall be made by the Department within ninety days after the time stipulated for her completion." The Navy's own bureaus had to cooperate fully and quickly amongst themselves. Increasing tension between the private contractor and the naval professionals meant increased efforts to ensure that such an arrangement was not "impaired in any manner on our part." This relationship was probably more one of mutual "respect" than of mutual trust. "If the guns are not furnished and the vessel should prove a failure," Smith warned, "the contract may be vitiated and the Government suffer."[10]

The building of the original *Monitor* was highly indicative of how this relationship evolved in the Union Navy's ironclad program. Smith may have wanted to trust Ericsson during the early stages of the *Monitor*'s construction but frequently did not. He did, however, make sincere efforts to learn and was relentless in this pursuit with the irritable inventor. "I understand computations have been made by expert Naval Architects of the displacement of your vessel," Smith wrote to Ericsson on Oct. 11, "and . . . she will not float with the load you propose to put upon her and if she would she could not stand upright for want of stability, nor attain a speed of 4 knots." The Navy Chief also disapproved of the abrupt overhang where the *Monitor*'s upper raft hull was fastened to the lower hull and actually advised Ericsson to consult published British reports on Coles's shield design. Yet he was "extremely anxious about the success of this battery" for good reason: "the Govt. want some Dozen of them if they prove successful."[11] Feeling challenged, tempted, though nonetheless annoyed, Ericsson replied "to these absurd statements made in relation to the battery" with full calculations of displacement and buoyancy that Smith could examine for himself. Ericsson promised to send a diagram/lecture on stability the following day, adding "there is no living man who has tripped me in calculation or proved my figures wrong in a single instance in matters relating to theoretical computation."[12] At some point the established authorities would simply have to trust him. "Monitor converts," or "Ericsson's disciples," would have to be made one at a time, at least at first. These uses of these terms—often derogatory—only emphasized that an entire reordering of thought was occurring—a scientific rather than a religious affair. This entire process marked a naval paradigm in the making.

Nor was there, given the circumstances, any margin for failure. Smith tried to explain to Ericsson how he had "taken for granted" the latter's confident and energetic arguments, thereby assuming "a great responsibility in recommending in haste, to meet the demands of the service, your plan."[13] At stake were not just the Navy and the Government's reputations, but his own as well. Skepticism prevailed. The "knowing ones" at the Ordnance Bureau, for example, doubted he would receive the highly coveted 11-inch Dahlgrens, saying they "will never be used on *her*." Though slightly more at ease, thanks to Ericsson's essays on displacement and stability, Smith then doubted the *Monitor*'s ventilation system. Surely, carbonic acid gas would afflict the crew, especially the firemen. The only obvious solution to him was "that a temporary house must be constructed on deck, to be knocked away by shot if it so happens, for the officers."[14] Ericsson responded that "the magnitude of the work I have to do exceeds anything I have ever before undertaken because there is not sufficient time left for planning, everything must be put in hand at once, a condition truly difficult." Yet he begged Smith "to rest tranquil as to the result; success cannot fail to crown the undertaking." This was precisely because the vessel in question was more of a "machine," the product of an engineer and a traditional shipbuilder. "Nothing is attempted not already well tried," Ericsson wrote, "or of so strictly a mechanical a nature as to be susceptible of previous determination."[15] At the height of the Industrial Age, Ericsson was banking on the idea that the *Monitor* could be designed as a matter of universal calculation rather than as an outcome of personal experience. An engineer, like a shipbuilder, could design an ironclad. But the more potential problems were theoretically solved by mechanical means (in this instance, the "sub-aquatic" *Monitor's* necessarily artificial system of ventilation[16]), the more important became the role of the engineer, and the more a steam-powered, iron-armored warship became a device rather than a tool. Significantly, after the battle of Hampton Roads, the *National Intelligencer* wrote that Ericsson had "placed the people and the Government under incalculable obligations to his scientific attainments," the *Monitor.*[17]

There was another dimension involved. On Oct. 17, when Ericsson finally received the Department's own calculations of his battery's displacement, it did not take him long to report them "erroneous from beginning to end." Lenthall had calculated for freshwater, not saltwater, and either way, the difference, according to Ericsson, was only 2 inches of extra immersion—a positive advantage in combat. In fact, it proved relatively easy for the ironclad inventor to dismantle an "observer's" calculations of the weight of his ship. "There are several dimensions that have been changed in laying out the work," he noted, and "the substances particularly are varied." As an example, the "1-inch" armor plates were really "15/16ths-inch thick." Though the difference in weight (and therefore cost) would be readily adjusted on the Government's bill, Ericsson assured Smith, it was clearly impossible to double-check vital factors like displacement since these could only be based on details missing in the original contract specifications or free from constant, practically daily, modifications.[18] The Government was thus perpetually one step behind the contractor in the design evolution of such a vessel, who could also move to counter-question professional authority. What did the Navy know about ironclads, let alone iron-hulled steamships? "A builder of iron vessels alone can correctly estimate what his vessel will weigh. In the present instance," Ericsson bluntly asserted, "the writer is the builder and knows all about the matter." Furthermore, because the Navy had "thrown the entire responsibility, as to practical success, on the contractor, you will I respectfully submit permit him to exercise freely his own judgment in carrying out the mechanical part of the work."[19]

Both sides, however, recognized the value of cooperation. Neither the contractors nor the Navy could afford to alienate one another. "Captain Ericsson is at work day and night to drive the work along," Bushnell assured Smith on Oct. 21, "and is confident that it is impossible to improve in any particular upon his plan; but I am much pleased to have you keep him supplied with suggestions, for I know of two instances in which he has, in my judgment, greatly improved the vessel by adopting your suggestions: one by lining the inside of the turret with felt, and the other by making the bottom of [the] lower vessel wider." Though Smith wrote to Ericsson that "the more I reflect upon your battery, the more fearful am I of her efficiency," he was nevertheless willing to assign Chief Engineer Alban C. Stimers to assist Ericsson, as requested, and on Oct. 26 he made the remarkable gesture of humbly apologizing to the civilian he had hired. "You are the last man I desire to contest engineering questions with. I am fully aware of your scientific knowledge, skill & experience" The old Admiral was, however, understandably anxious about the Union Navy's experimental warships, upon whose success so much depended:

> I make suggestions, offer objections which are only intended for your consideration but is nowise to control your action. The responsibility rests with you and I would not change it if I could. Excuse my interference thus far if I have annoyed you, & I will be silent in future.[20]

Chapter 7

Effect of the *Trent* Affair

It was in the midst of this complex and frenzied state of affairs in New York that news of the capture of James Mason and John Slidell from the British mail packet steamer *Trent* reached Washington. The following day, Nov. 16, 1861, Ericsson forwarded to Smith an account of his battery in the latest *Scientific American,* which he found "admirably clear." "In view of its bearing on the harbor defenses of the country," he noted, "I respectfully suggest to the promoters of the enterprise to present a copy to the Secretary of State." Smith was not pleased, regretting "to see a description of the vessel in print before she shall have been tested." Wariness of publicity "damaging alike to the enterprise and the navy," however, is what prompted Ericsson to supply the press with an accurate description. "We are closely watched by hundreds, and the work has now progressed so far that many *imagined* they saw enough to judge of the result," he explained. This was not an effort on the part of the inventor merely to preserve his own reputation. The all-important sense of Northern morale, in relation to national security, was at stake.[1] Not without ominous irony, the same article leads with a description of the *Warrior.* "She has proved herself to be the fastest large war vessel afloat," as reported in the British press, "as she is no doubt the most powerful." Including the "new iron-clad gunboat" building at the Continental Works, Greenpoint, the United States "had no less than five iron-clad ocean war vessels in progress of construction, besides several iron-plated river steamboats on the Mississippi."

We are therefore making considerable progress toward securing an iron-clad navy, although, with but one exception, perhaps, none of these vessels will be first-class; still they may prove very efficient, and answer all the purposes demanded by the exigencies of the times.[2]

By the end of 1861 these naval requirements of the Union were distinctly double-edged. Reflecting after the immediate crisis over the *Trent* had passed, *Blackwood's* spelled out very clearly what dangers perpetually threatened the United States during the Civil War—from the other side of the blockade; from possible offensive actions conducted by the Royal Navy:

> The Americans have been coerced into an act of justice, which they performed with the worst possible grace; and we are frankly assured that a time is coming, when they mean to take ample vengeance for present humiliations. It appears, then, that a war with the Federal States of America is only deferred. If not imminent, it is pretty sure to come sooner or later. . . . How shall we prepare for such a contingency and conduct the war when it comes?
>
> There are two modes of carrying on war with America—one aggressive, the other defensive. We shall probably adopt both. We shall assail their harbours, burn their fleets, destroy their commerce, and keep their whole seaboard in a state of constant alarm; and we shall give employment by these means to no inconsiderable portion of the half million of men whom they boast to have under arms. But we shall have a defensive war likewise to provide for, on the side of Canada.[3]

On Oct. 19, 1861, *Harper's Weekly* noted sarcastically that "John Bull is a practical man" who "should scornfully trample and toss all other nations, provided always that they are weak or that calamity has befallen them. . . ." In its issue two weeks later (whose cover also featured an artist's conception of "the Rebel Steamer '*Merrimac*,' Razeed, and Iron-Clad"), Seward was depicted in a cartoon as ready to extract the teeth of the British Lion over the legal issue of arresting British subjects during the national crisis, his forbidding surgical instrument clutching a published letter to the governor of New York calling for improved coastal defenses.[4] Yet the crisis over the *Trent* came before the "operation," as such, even started. *Punch* recognized the Union's predicament with typically explicit relish. Its Dec. 7 issue alone featured two cartoons: of a gentlemanly "Mr. Bull" threatening Abraham Lincoln in a buffoonish admiral's attire of "no shuffling—an ample apology—or I put the matter into the hands of my lawyers Messrs. Whitworth and Armstrong," and an oversized Jack Bull–sailor warning a diminutive Uncle Sam (dressed as a buccaneer and obviously too small for his boots) to "do what's right, my son, or I'll blow you out of the water."[5]

The issues of the Civil War, indeed, were openly discussed in terms of how they related to the rival political constitutions and social systems not of the American North and South, but of the United States and Great Britain. *Blackwood's* happily endorsed the declaration by William Howard Russell of the London *Times* that the domestic conflict in America really demonstrated the weaknesses of "[o]ur own agitators, in their clamour for reform, [who] are descending towards universal suffrage. Universal suffrage means the government of a numerical majority, which means oppression—which means civil war."[6] Russell himself confided in his diary that "[t]here is after all great satisfaction among the representative property men & tories [*sic*] in England with the rupture in America & I confess for one that I agree in thinking this war if it be merely a lesson will be of use":

> Had there been a possibility in human nature to make laws without faction & interest & to employ popular institutions without intrigue & miserable self seeking the condition of parts of the U.S. does no doubt cause regret that it did not occur here, but the strength of the U.S. employed by passion interest self seeking became dangerous to other nations & therefore there is an utter want of sympathy with them in their time of trouble & England regards the North without fear favour or affection & in spite of liberty rather favours the South.[7]

On the other hand, the *New York Herald*, for example, stated that the recent Federal naval victory at Port Royal (Nov. 7, 1861) "would fall like a bombshell in the midst of the British aristocracy and government, who have been secretly intriguing for the last thirty years for the disruption of the republic and the destruction of democratic government." The American Civil War was nothing less than "the third revolutionary war upon which we have entered with the English aristocracy, and the hearts and hopes of the English democracy are all embarked in the unity and success of the American republic." If the Government could not suppress the Rebellion soon, England's commercial industry would surely collapse, leading to a mass uprising of the unemployed working classes. If the Government succeeded, the same revolutionary movement might occur anyway, emboldened—as were the French in 1789—by the American example.[8]

The danger was that these widely circulated words and images, in the new age of a free press and mass consumption, would so influence and inflame public opinion that political leaders would follow suit, if only to maintain their own political base of support. The *Times* was convinced Lincoln's administration was controlled by "the Mob." Two years before the outbreak of hostilities in America, the newly appointed British minister to the United States, Lord Lyons, reported to Foreign Secretary Lord Malmesbury his belief that "the People are irritable, excitable, and have a great longing to play the part of a first-rate power." Weak U.S. (democratic) governments regularly pandered to "the Mob" while "the upper classes keep aloof from political life, and have little influence in public affairs." Two years later, following the rout of the Union Army at First Bull Run (July 21, 1861), a minute by Prime Minister Palmerston asserted, "The Truth is, the North are fighting for an Idea chiefly entertained by professional politicians, while the South are fighting for what they consider rightly or wrongly vital interests."[9]

Conversely, an American visitor "in the House of Commons" astutely noted in the *Atlantic Monthly* that even the apex of British political power—in the rather unquestionably popular figure of Lord Palmerston—was "guided by . . . a need to follow the nation."[10] The office of Prime Minister itself was not formally recognized by the British Constitution until the early 20th century, and though it was not fixed by terms the Government could be dramatically forced to resign on a vote of "No Confidence" by Parliament (as happened to Lord North's Ministry in 1782 as a result of defeat in the American Revolutionary War). Failure to win over the House of Commons on crucial votes might "oblige" a Government to resign—a proposed inquiry into the conduct of the Crimean War saw to the fall of Lord Aberdeen's Ministry—unless a general election could be counted on to restore the Prime Minister's sense of command. In less than seven years a string of governments led by Aberdeen, Palmerston, Lord Derby, and Palmerston again had left a general feeling of instability repeated only after Palmerston died in office in October 1865—followed by Russell, Derby, Disraeli, and Gladstone in the span of three years. "The success or failure of a Ministry, whether in legislation or administration," wrote one authority, "depended largely upon the Prime Minister."[11] Palmerston's popular strength lay in his ability to maintain an impression of righteous national power and prestige in Britain's foreign relations, starting with the Navy. Addressing an audience in 1873 on the "Life, Character and Services of William Henry Seward," Charles Francis Adams recounted that during the *Trent* crisis "[w]ar was considered inevitable; hence provision was promptly made by many to remove American property out of the risk of confiscation, the dock-yards resounded by night as well as by day with the ring of hammers, fitting out the largest iron-clads, and order went forth to assemble the most available troops for immediate embarkation to the points in America closest upon our northern border":

> Looking at these proceedings as calmly as I can from our present point of view, it seems impossible for me to doubt that the issue of this peremptory demand had been already prejudged by her Majesty's ministers. They

did not themselves believe that the men would be restored. Hence what seems to me the needless offensiveness of these preliminaries prompted, no doubt, by the violence of the popular feeling, which would insist upon an immediate display of what would be called a "proper spirit."[12]

It was therefore difficult to establish where official policy began and public influence ended. The *National Intelligencer* reflected this back to the American public in early March 1862, for example, by reporting John Bright's condemnation of the £973,000 bill for the *Trent* affair's mobilization of British army and naval units. "He refuted the idea that the American Government was influenced by a mob, and argued that the interests of England were so bound up with America that it was in every respect inadvisable to inflict a sting that it would take centuries to remove." But accompanying this stance on the issue was that of Palmerston, who "contended that there was every reason to justify England in backing up her demand in the manner she did. . . ." "He thought the course taken deserved commendation, and believed it was calculated to insure the continuance of peace."[13] The manifestation of the *Trent* crisis was thus a perfect and terrifying example of the political force of naval power in international diplomacy. "If we had not shewn that we were ready to fight," Palmerston confided to lifelong friend Laurence Sulivan, "that low-minded fellow Seward would not have eat the leek as he has done." And while the Prime Minister later recommended to Queen Victoria that Lord Lyons be decorated with a Knight Grand Cross of the Civil Order of the Bath, Lyons himself observed to Lord Russell that the ultimate reason the captured Southern emissaries were given up "was nothing more nor less than the military preparations made in England." He had been "sure from the first that [the Americans] would give in, if it were possible to convince them that *war* was really the only alternative." It was left to him only to present such an ultimatum politely.[14]

It was surprising, therefore, for the *New York Herald* to announce on Nov. 23, 1861, and before news of the British public reaction to the *Trent*'s seizure reached America, that "we anticipate no conflict with Great Britain, nor do we believe that any serious trouble will grow out of Messrs. Slidell and Mason's arrest."[15] Active Midshipman Oliver Ambrose Batcheller, serving aboard the U.S.S. *Vincennes* off the mouth of the Mississippi River, wrote to his mother that he, too, could "not believe" there would be war; rumors of a British ultimatum were "nonsense." "Trust Johnny Bull for any thing but so bold a move as that! It is not his nature." Even if it was, he confidently assured his mother "that our Government will refuse to comply with the demand and that every possible means be employed to prepare for the war and when it comes fight until there are just men enough left to hang

Mason and Slidell. . . ."[16] Some members of the public felt otherwise. "I do not feel at all sure that we shall not get into a serious complication with England," a friend of Secretary Welles wrote. "England is terribly touchy about her flag, & does not feel any too good natured to us to begin with." An Anglo-American war "would be death to us just now." Another informed Welles that "the tone of feeling among capitalists & merchants" in Boston was to refuse any unconditional demand for surrendering the captives. Instead the Administration should offer to submit the matter to "an impartial & neutrally chosen umpire." If the British government rejected this, national, world, and even a large portion of British public opinion would therefore be united against it. "The interests involved are too large & important to allow either nation to go into a war unless it can be shown to be an inevitable necessity."[17]

Instead, when the Lincoln Administration decided a month later to restore the Confederate emissaries on their way to England, the *Herald* coolly pledged "as Rome remembered Carthage from the invasion of Hannibal, and as France remembers St. Helena, so will the people of the United States remember and treasure up for the future this little affair of the *Trent*." A poem by Herman Melville described "The bitter cup / Of that hard countermand / Which gave the Envoys up" as "wormwood in the mouth." Midshipman Batcheller was also dismayed, noting that "[a] foreign war just at this time is much to be dreaded," but nevertheless calling for a "war to the last breath but never dishonor."[18]

Be that as it may, the Union, in the meantime, remained acutely vulnerable to British seapower. This fact made embarrassingly obvious the price in national prestige for "depriving the rebels of much strength which they would certainly have acquired in case of a war with England and France. . . ."[19] Here *Scientific American* anticipated a vast, mutually destructive commerce war carried out mostly by private "swarms of rovers." Of the 15 million tons of total world shipping, 5 million belonged to Britain and 5 million to the United States. An Anglo-American holocaust would leave both nations "degraded from their proud preeminence," leaving France as "the leading commercial nation of the world."[20] A direct comparison of both navies at the beginning of 1862 overwhelmingly favored Great Britain. This left the Royal Navy largely free to act against Northern port-cities, either by blockade or by direct assault. The Union Navy could not possibly attempt a similar offensive against the British Isles. Could it even mount an effective defense? Though it mentioned Congress's passing a new bill for 20 more ironclad gunboats, *Scientific American* suggestively recounted losses inflicted against English convoys during the War for Independence, and the famed exploits of American naval commanders in the War of 1812. The defense of New York harbor was therefore left to the forts guarding its entrance. "But the introduction of iron-plated ships exposes us to attacks for which these forts were not provided," explained *Scientific American.* Only with the immediate mass production of U.S. Army Captain Thomas J. Rodman's 15-inch guns could the prized city hope to "bid defiance to the ironclad navies of the world." Nothing else was mentioned, or in sight.[21] The cold months between November 1861 and March 1862 were thus the darkest of the Union Navy, and possibly the Union itself, throughout the American Civil War.

Against this backdrop, work on the *Monitor* continued at a fever pitch. "I wish we had your vessel now," Smith wrote to Ericsson, three days after the U.S.S. *San Jacinto* removed Mason and Slidell from the *Trent.* "The Govt. must create a fleet of plated Gun Boats. They will cost much less & will be more effective than the Army." Lincoln knew that with General George B. McClellan still sitting with his newly reformed "Grand Army of the Potomac," the conspicuous absence of Northern military victories, or even offensive operations against the South, further tempted European powers to intervene in what they regarded as a hopeless and unnecessary struggle, damaging to all. This only transferred demands for success to the Union Navy. On Nov. 7 an expedition under Commodore Samuel F. Du Pont succeeded in overwhelming the fortifications defending Port Royal. Now the controversial blockade of the southern Atlantic ports would be strengthened with a valuable Union base halfway between Savannah and Charleston. The presence of an entire flotilla of light-draft ironclad batteries might therefore lead to even more ambitious projects against the Confederacy, while at the same time acting in the capacity of harbor and coast defense. Smith tantalized Ericsson. "Already I think the Department contemplates augmenting this description of force," he indicated, though the decision would not be in his hands. Furthermore, "all the mistakes we may make I suppose may turn to the advantage of others."[22] Smith had doubts about the *Galena* as well. To Bushnell he expressed his "fear that in your eagerness to build an armored vessel, you did not reflect sufficiently on the many obstacles to be encountered, and which we now have to overcome as best we can."[23]

In combination with the initially well-received news of Mason and Slidell's capture, Welles could write to his son that "this last week has been a pretty eventful one for the Navy Department, or rather the news of great events have been highly interesting."[24] Twelve years later, the former Secretary wrote that the capture of Port Royal was in fact "eclipsed by the startling news that the two rebel leaders, who had recently abandoned their seats in the Senate, and been selected by the

Confederate organization to represent it abroad, and enlist foreign governments in its behalf, had been intercepted and were prisoners." While this was initially accepted as a victory for the Union cause, considering that the Confederate mission to secure national recognition and material assistance was dramatically blocked before it began, Lincoln, Welles recalled, quickly realized that the prisoners "would be elephants on our hands, that we could not easily dispose of." Patriotic citizens might wrathfully demand their formal execution for treason. What message would this send to the people of the South? Lincoln's grand hopes for national reunification might be shattered.[25] A more immediate and palpable danger, however, came from an enraged British government and public. This served to sharply refocus the North's attention back to its own weaknesses, never mind its need for ironclad gunboats to spearhead further naval attacks against the Confederate States. As Captain John Rodgers wrote to his wife, Anne, from the Union flagship at Port Royal, "[W]e are unready and overmatched with the South, England, France, and Canada—all at once." Washington might have to acknowledge the Confederacy. "The blockade I apprehend must be stopped whether we fight or apologize—certainly if we fight."[26] It was a cruel reminder of the international strategic disposition of the United States at the end of 1861. As Welles later recounted, "our country was then crippled, and Palmerston and Russell well knew it. The Administration felt that we were in no condition to embark in a foreign war, whatever might be the justification of our cause."[27]

The exact purpose of the 20 new ironclad gunboats was, however, still a matter of debate in Congress. Could private contractors be relied upon to produce them in time, and without extravagant price? How would the inability of either the Navy Yards or commercial firms to produce the necessary quantity of iron armor plates complicate these concerns? What ironclad designs were best for the Union? Arch-Democrat Clement L. Vallandigham of Ohio stressed that the ironclads "should be constructed as soon as possible," considering that "they will be needed in case of the occurrence with a foreign Power of the war which seems impending over us. . . ." The House Chairman of Naval Affairs, Charles B. Sedgwick, disagreed—or at least misunderstood the implication. The vessels in question were "not required for any such purpose" and in fact "it did not enter into the design of the Department in recommending them. They are required at home, for use here. . . ."[28] Two days previously he described them as "intended to be of such draught and built in such a way that they will be able to enter any harbor in the United States where there is over twelve feet of water upon the bar . . . to be so protected as to be able, without injury, to run past any forts or defenses of any such harbors. . . ."[29]

Undoubtedly these were the "Bureau" turret ships designed by Lenthall and chief of the new Bureau of Steam Engineering Benjamin F. Isherwood, as discussed by J. P. Baxter.[30] Any interference in the contracting of these Departmental designs, Sedgwick, argued, "utterly embarrassed [the Department's] plan of overthrowing this rebellion and seizing the cities in the southern States by means of these armed vessels." But the Bureau's design had inherent drawbacks. Although Navy Yards and existing private contractors might be relied upon to produce engines, boilers, and hulls, the armor plates themselves were to be in solid 4½-inch thicknesses, "very large, of the best quality hammered iron, and so bent as to fit the model of a vessel." Because such plates could not currently be manufactured in America extensively or quickly, they would have to be procured in England or France.[31] All this dependence on foreign help was fraught with added expense, delay, and political complications—especially at the height of the serious crisis over the capture of Mason and Slidell.

Charles W. Whitney also tried to persuade Commodore Smith that the company he represented, H. Abbott & Son of Baltimore, was indeed capable of rolling 4½-inch plates. Hammered, or "forged," plates were proven by recent English experiments "to be brittle, unreliable, and incapable of resisting heavy shot. . . ." With "our American charcoal iron" Abbott could ensure superiority over any plates contracted abroad. Three of their mills were already "in full operation day and night" with a fourth mill, even larger, having been under construction for the past six months. Within a month this nearly completed mill "could commence rolling the 4½-inch plates at once." The 1-inch plates for Ericsson's battery were already being supplied by them. Smith noted that "Mr. Ericsson . . . endeavored to get Plates (4-inch thickness) from Mr. Abbott of Baltimore, for his battery, but in vain." He believed "the Navy Department is now about to build some iron-clad vessels, to be plated of 4½-inch iron"; perhaps now Abbott's offers could be taken more seriously than in early October. But Smith had "no control and no knowledge" of the Construction Bureau's plan for ironclads.[32] Insistence by the Department upon hammered plates might save time and avoid complication compared with formally encouraging private firms to invest in new rolling machines, planers, cranes, etc.[33] The *New Ironsides* was already committed to hammered armor plates of 4½-inch thickness. Twenty turret-ironclads, however, would require more such forged iron than time permitted, let alone a large-scale industrial upgrade for rolling even thicker armor than Ericsson's battery required.

Meanwhile, the *Trent* affair also had the effect of redoubling Washington's efforts to improve the North's coastal fortifications.[34] Seward had already addressed the Governors "of all the States on the seaboard and lakes" on Oct. 14, 1861. Even though the likelihood of European intervention was "less serious than it has been at any previous period during the course of the insurrection," Southern agents were working hard to capitalize on "the embarrassments of agriculture, manufactures, and commerce in foreign countries" as a result of the blockade. A controversy might suddenly add "the evils of a foreign war . . . upon those of civil commotion which we are endeavoring to cure." By neglecting the defense of its ports and harbors, the Union would "voluntarily incur danger in tempestuous seasons when it fails to show that it has sheltered itself on every side from which the storm might possibly come." Preoccupied with the immediate needs of the Army and Navy, the Federal Government needed the states to assess their own defenses and submit the matter to Congress when it next convened.

The Governor of Maine responded that his state was particularly subject to attack, as it had been in the War of 1812. Portland's strategic importance was immense. "Its geographical position commands Canada on the north, and the lower provinces on the east, if properly fortified, as lines of railway, completed or in process of construction, radiate from it to Quebec and Montreal, and to St. John and Halifax." If occupied by Great Britain, American commerce on the Great Lakes and the ocean would be driven away; if properly fortified, it could serve as a main base of operations by the U.S. Navy. Lincoln and the War Department agreed. Officers would be sent to make official estimates, but Maine would have to pay the bill "in the first instance, advanced to the general government in the nature of a loan for the general defense of the country at large," which there was "every reason to believe" Congress would approve. This would be paid back "within a reasonable period," later specified on Dec. 17, in the form of U.S. bonds "twenty years after date, bearing six per cent. interest, payable semi-annually."[35] Because it was by no means clear whether the Union would actually survive the Civil War, the government's warning of possible hostilities with foreign powers, and the willingness of Northern states to risk the expense of greater defenses, was both realistic and brave. Preserving the sovereignty of the United States required an enormous act of faith.

Chapter 8

Congress Debates the "20 Ironclad Gunboats"

On Jan. 8, 1862, the U.S. Senate debated whether to amend House Bill No. 153, which authorized Gideon Welles to construct "twenty iron-clad steam gunboats." The proposal would replace the words "Secretary of the Navy" with "the President" and would make the Chief Executive directly responsible for the contracting—and therefore also for the designs, and the success or failure—of the Union's new ironclads. Welles was, at the time, under suspicion for some of the New York–based contracting of the early converted merchant ships purchased for the service on the blockade.[1] Much of this mistrust stemmed from disaffected contractors wielding powerful newspaper connections in revenge, and from rumor and innuendo. But worse than the implication that the Secretary was incompetent or corrupt (perhaps even "treasonous") was the attempt to spotlight and possibly blame Lincoln if he retained Welles in his Cabinet.[2] The failure of a single ironclad in the midst of the Civil War might conceivably sink the entire Administration, not just one of its departments, or one of its department's bureaus.

Coincidentally, on the same day, John Griswold wrote to Ericsson that their business partner John F. Winslow had returned from Washington, after a "thorough & very satisfactory interview with Secretaries Welles & Seward; also with the Pres. & Asst. Fox." The issue, of course, was which pattern the new fleet of armored gunboats would take. Bureau chiefs Lenthall and Isherwood enjoyed the obvious inside track, with their scheme for Coles-type turret ironclads. But inasmuch as the Navy professionals asserted that their own design would best match the complex strategic needs of the country, the New York contractors already had a rival prototype nearing completion. Ericsson's *Monitor* had finally managed to gain the respect of Commodore Smith, another Bureau Chief, and was fast becoming a technological icon for young, ambitious engineers like Alban Stimers.[3] "We can have things our own way," Griswold related to Ericsson, but only "if the Battery proves Equal to our expectation." The Government, while in a desperate hurry to obtain ironclads, was nonetheless willing to wait; "nothing, to any extent, will be contracted for till she has been tested."[4]

As time passed, events came to have sometimes dire effects on the Union. For instance, alarming reports reached the North of the steady progress of the rebel conversion of the *Merrimac* at Norfolk. Such an ironclad in the hands of Confederate Captain Franklin Buchanan (recent commandant of the Washington Navy Yard and first superintendent of the U.S. Naval Academy in 1845) would surely be used for more than just the protection of Norfolk or the James River, the latter leading to the Confederate capital of Richmond. The entire control of Hampton Roads, the anchor of the Union blockade itself, would be challenged. Wooden steamships would face an armored one. Fortress Monroe might even be compelled to surrender—a loss more devastating than that of the North's Fort Sumter nearly a year earlier—because the backdoor to Washington would be exposed to Confederate naval power. The offensive aims of the Union Army were also converging on this vital strategic crossroads, North and South. Although "his" Army of the Potomac was now properly trained and equipped following the disaster of Bull Run, General McClellan was not eager to risk its destruction in another frontal assault against the reinforced Confederate Army blocking the same route to Richmond. Instead, he contemplated a massive flanking thrust toward Richmond via the York and James Peninsula, using—and thus depending on—Union naval power. It became increasingly likely, therefore, that—in a battle for control of Hampton Roads—a showdown would take place between the *Merrimac* and the only Union ironclad that could possibly be ready in time for such a crucial match-up: the *Monitor*. A struggle of this magnitude would be the latter vessel's contractual "test of fire."[5] Yet Ericsson and his associates held a distinct advantage. As Griswold pointed out, "[T]hey were amazed at Washington to learn that within the hundred days the Battery would be completed. . . ." Under these circumstances, "they [Lenthall and Isherwood] <u>dare not</u> override us, & the 'arrangement' so nicely made is knocked into the future, if not killed."[6]

According to Baxter, the status of the Bureau's ironclad proposal was by then already uncertain. The reason was that one man in particular, Captain Gustavus Fox, the Assistant Secretary of the Navy, was now uncertain about at least the timeliness of the Bureau's design against Ericsson's. It had been his insistence that the Bureau press ahead, and the concept was as much his own as it was Lenthall and Isherwood's.[7] But when Ericsson and his associates learned of this ambitious move on the part of the Navy, they moved quickly to question the expediency of Fox's choice, if not also the implicit purpose of the intended ironclads. On Dec. 23 Ericsson wrote to Welles, offering to build six more ironclads and noting that Coles's turrets were ill designed, unable to withstand the shock of impact from heavy shot because of their reliance on short segments of wood backing and their use of cogs for rotation near the vulnerable inside base of the turret.[8]

At any rate, these technical objections coincided with Welles's own aversion to procuring ironclads or armor plates abroad—in fact, to relying upon foreign powers at all during the Civil War, and especially in the malodorous climate before, during, and especially as a result of the *Trent* crisis. On January 31, prominent engineer Daniel B. Martin reported to Lenthall from Liverpool. After he visited all the major armor plate manufacturers and iron shipbuilders of the United Kingdom, and "invited bids for the Armor and Towers [of the Bureau's proposed turret ship] to be sent to me at this place by the 20th inst.," he had still not received "one direct offer." Violating British neutrality was a concern. The North's financial credit was as dubious as the South's. "None of the parties would be willing to make a Contract until advices [sic] was received about the payments." Finally, "all of the parties capable of doing this kind of work are full of orders, there is I understand orders for Armor plates from the French, Spanish, Russian, Austrian, and Italian Governments, beside what is being done for this Government which appears to be doing considerable in that line." At any rate, the actual bending of plates, Martin noted, "has been done by the Ship Builders," not the manufacturers.[9] The seed of doubt was thus effectively planted. A hasty commitment entirely to one class of ironclads might prove disastrous—and Congress was already indicating just how far the repercussions might reach.

Concurrently, time, if not technical certainty, again favored the construction of Ericsson's monitor ironclads. Fox was soliciting the advice of experts in preparation for a naval attack—and capture—of New Orleans, the Confederacy's largest port city. To pass Forts Jackson and St. Philip would require ironclad batteries, specified Major General and Chief Engineer George Barnard to Fox. It was decided that these ironclads should be armed with as many 11-inch guns as possible, firing canister on the forts' waterfront and barbette batteries—suppressing Confederate fire while the rest of the squadron ran the gauntlet up the Mississippi River. What form the batteries themselves should take was not as important as when they could be available. As

Barnard concluded, no delay should be made in their preparation.[10] This warning would take on powerful meaning a year later, when Fox planned another great Union naval attack—this time against Charleston, South Carolina.

These factors actually combined to place more pressure on the original battery to "penetrate Southern barriers," "withstand shore batteries fire," and check the *Merrimac*. On Jan. 14, Smith crisply notified Ericsson that "the time for the completion of the shot-proof battery, according to the stipulations of your contract, expired on the 12th instant." Ten days previously Ericsson had grumbled that, although $200,000 of private funds had already been expended in construction of the vessel, "only $37,500 have as yet been paid by the navy agent, and that amount was not obtained until five weeks after the presentation of your order." Because of this tardiness, his "contemplated organization and operation by what is called night gangs, has been to some extent frustrated." Stimers, also feeling frustrated, noted on Jan. 21 that the two 11-inch Dahlgrens now needed for the "Ericsson Battery"' were nowhere to be seen. "I believe, however," he wrote to Smith, "that there are now two of these guns afloat in the gunboats at the navy yard, and it therefore resolves itself into a choice between whether the Ericsson Battery or two wooden gunboats should be delayed." One can imagine the Commodore's anger upon receiving this news. It was exactly the sort of bureaucratic obfuscation that he had feared since October might humiliate the Department in its dealings with private contractors, while depriving the Government of its right to enforce deadlines. Few professionals within the Department seemed to take the experimental ironclad seriously. "I took pains to have two 11-inch guns ready for the Erricsson [*sic*]," Smith complained to Secretary Welles, "but it seems they have been taken for other vessels."[11] At least the *Monitor*'s newly appointed commanding officer, Lieutenant John L. Worden, "after a hasty examination of her," was "induced to believe that she may prove a success."[12] By Jan. 24, Stimers had offered his estimate for a revised launching date for the *Monitor* of five days, "if the tide does not serve badly on that day." Along with the missing Dahlgrens, the last armor plates ordered for this completely "prefabricated" iron warship were behind delivery.[13] As Stimers poignantly observed, "[T]he more nearly completed each part becomes, the more practicable it looks."[14] Ericsson's long-held, radical vision was becoming a clear-cut reality. But would this reality successfully conform to the multiple (and often contradictory) requirements of the Union Navy?

The following day, the Chairman of the Committee on Naval Affairs, Senator John P. Hale, was obliged to ask the Navy Department exactly what its plans for an ironclad flotilla were: purpose and form.[15]

Welles's reply of Feb. 7, 1862, was, at this juncture, absolutely crucial. The Department could "probably build ten or twelve ironclad gunboats in the next six months," he wrote, "and probably double or three times that number within a year." As for any specific model, Welles relayed that his Department did not "propose to confine itself exclusively to any particular plan yet offered," but would indeed "avail itself of the experience which will be gained in the construction of those now going forward, one of which will soon be tested in actual conflict." Clearly, Welles was referring to the *Monitor*. Ericsson's proposal, to dispel any doubts, was mentioned by name; and the "ten or twelve gun-boats" are in fact his own. The Bureau turret ship scheme had already lost its inside advantage, primarily because of its inherent design drawbacks rather than the "political" influence of Ericsson and his financial backers, as some historians have suggested.[16] Facts spoke louder than words at the time; if the Bureau turret ships could have been produced as cheaply, easily, and quickly as Ericsson's monitor ironclads, they might have stood a better chance with the primary decision-makers involved, namely Fox and Welles, and probably to some extent, Abraham Lincoln himself. The actual tactical superiority of the monitor design over the Fox-Lenthall scheme was another matter. Issues of laminated armor versus solid plate (and rolled iron over hammered), Coles "cupolas" versus Ericsson "towers" (two turrets with one gun or one turret with two), and low freeboard versus even lower freeboard were all largely conjectural. They remain so today. But laminated 1-inch plating, bent into turrets, could be had; rolled 4½-inch plates could not. A working model of an Ericsson turret vessel at least now existed for testing and improvement; Coles's prototype was still years away from completion. Ericsson's arguments for maximum concentration of weight, armor protection, and firepower *were* better realized in the single turret of even thicker iron plating and greater guns than multiple turrets weakly protecting weaker armaments. Higher freeboard, at the same time, meant more area to be plated—or less area protected overall.[17] Given the fact that the Bureau turret ships were not intended for cruising purposes, any arguments for partial protection lost their meaning, while a monitor's freeboard capitalized on even greater economy of national resources needed for its construction and the consolidation of defensive force.

There are at least two important features of Welles's response to Hale, the Navy's response to the Senate, and the Administration's response to Congress. First, the *Monitor* had all but established itself as the prototypical coastal defense ironclad of the Civil War at least a month *before* the battle of Hampton Roads, not as a result of its famous duel with the C.S.S. *Virginia*. Recurring arguments that *"Monitor* Mania," as a result of the events of March 8–9, 1862, somehow "blinded" Assistant Secretary Fox and the Navy Department as a whole neglect this fact.[18] To be sure, the enormous and unprecedented national excitement and enthusiasm for Ericsson's strikingly futuristic warships did wonders for the Navy's public relations and gave the White House an ever-welcome boost of support. If the Navy had half-committed itself to monitors before Hampton Roads, it was certainly bound to them afterward. But any efforts made by the "powerful Ericsson Lobby," or "clique," were far from conspiratorial in nature. They were wide open to professional scrutiny.[19] Indeed, it was Ericsson's near-invincibility on technical issues that all but guaranteed his design an advantage over many rival designs for ironclads submitted to the Navy throughout the American Civil War. As Hale later commented to Congress, "[T]hese boats are considered by the Department, and by practical men who have the best means of judging, as the very best, and in fact the only means of coast defense that is now known to the military science."[20]

Second, to Hale's inquiry of the *purpose* of the (monitor) ironclad gunboats proposed by the Navy, Welles said they were "to reduce all the fortified sea ports of the enemy and open their harbors to the Union Army." Upon close examination, this was a significant caveat not mentioned by Ericsson. Even the 1856 proposal to Napoleon III was for vessels intended to attack ships, not forts. His private letter to Lincoln of August 1861 maintained this distinction, adding only that his floating batteries would help protect Northern ports from attack by European ironclads. Even in naming the *Monitor*, Ericsson specified:

> The impregnable and aggressive character of this structure will admonish the leaders of the Southern Rebellion that the batteries on the banks of their rivers will no longer present *barriers to the entrance* of the Union forces.
>
> The iron-clad intruder will thus prove a severe monitor to those leaders. But there are other leaders who will also be startled and admonished by the booming of the guns from the impregnable iron turret: "Downing Street" will hardly view with indifference this last "Yankee notion," this monitor. To the Lords of the Admiralty the new craft will be a monitor, suggesting doubts as to the propriety of completing those four steel ships at three and a half million apiece.
>
> On these and many similar grounds, I propose to name the new battery *Monitor*.[21]

Yet, when Hale recommended Ericsson's "boats" to Congress, he, too, added that "stone forts can be battered down by these batteries."[22]

Welles's reply bears the hallmark influence of Fox, whose own thinking retained the original concept that the gunboats were to run Confederate gauntlets and engage Confederate forts, not Grimes's assertion that they were to solve the nation's coastal defense problems in the face of foreign—particularly British—naval intervention.[23] This contradiction between coastal assault and coastal defense, between attacking the Confederacy and defending against the British Empire, would manifest itself more clearly when the *Passaic*-class monitors saw action a year later. Furthermore, their obvious failure to reduce or destroy forts—at least without direct support from the Army—would outweigh their intrinsically less obvious success in deterring foreign intervention. It would be much easier for political opponents of the Lincoln Administration to point to blatant battlefield defeats, or at least "repulses," than to subtle diplomatic victories. The ironclads might topple the Executive after all.

At any rate, the Union's naval resources were perpetually split between the Navy's need to maintain its command of the sea, or at least the protection of its commerce worldwide, and the objective of striking at the Confederacy. On the eve of the battle of Hampton Roads, Assistant Secretary Fox apologized to Flag-Officer Louis M. Goldsborough, commanding the North Atlantic Blockading Squadron, for the short supply of the new double-ender gunboats. "I presume you are aware that we are about to undertake the biggest job of the war," he wrote, referring to the forthcoming operation against New Orleans, "and that we are straining every nerve to concentrate a force to accomplish it successfully; this is why we have no boats." Meanwhile, the Confederate commerce raiders *Nashville* and *Sumter* were having their own way against Northern shipping, Fox said, "when we ought to have a dozen boats after them." Still, the Navy was "immensely popular and will remain so if we continue successful," Fox concluded.[24] In addition to victories off the North Carolina coast, the Union had seen Forts Henry and Donelson fall in the West (Feb. 6 and Feb. 16, 1862, respectively), thanks to the combined operations of Union land forces under General Ulysses S. Grant and partially armored steam-gunboats led by Commodore Andrew H. Foote.

Victories at home served two types of political purposes. In debating the Naval Appropriations Bill on Feb. 12, including the supplementary appropriation of $15 million for an improved class of double-ender gunboats, Navy supporters could easily point to their own usefulness in suppressing the rebellion. Sedgwick recapitulated: "Mr. Speaker, Congress has appropriated money for the Navy with great liberality. It has hitherto ordered to be built twenty-three gunboats, twelve side-wheel vessels, and three ironclad vessels." Already the Navy has "got something to show for the money expended on it. It has got Hatteras, and Port Royal, and Roanoke Island, and it will have taken every fortified place on the rebel coast within the next four months if liberal appropriations are continued to be made for it." Yet, "on the other side of the Atlantic to-day, nothing can be pointed to as having been achieved by the Army that looks to the suppression of the rebellion," remarked one congressman. "The governing classes of England, with Palmerston at their head," were "willing if not anxious to go to war. . . ." Subsequently, "the one power which we can create to resist them, is just the power to the creation of which these $15,000,000 are to be set apart; and I am, therefore, large as the sum is, in favor of putting it at the disposal of the Secretary of the Navy for this purpose."

A disaster at New Orleans, on the other hand, Fox wrote to Commander David D. Porter, would be "fatal to everything and overwhelms the Navy and everybody connected with it in everlasting disgrace." Taunting foreign and domestic eyes were watching, too. "The French and Russian both said to me today 'Recollect that you are to have New Orleans on the 10th of March, but we will give you till the 20th.'"[25]

All this said nothing for any Confederate naval initiative, however. On Feb. 21, Captain John Marston of the steam frigate *Roanoke*—lying at Hampton Roads with her engine disabled and a crew short by 180 men—related to Welles the disturbing local intelligence that "the *Merrimack* will positively attack Newport News within five days. . . ."[26]

SUMMARY

The *Trent* affair suddenly upset the Union's offensive strategic initiative against the Confederacy, forcing a defensive one instead against Great Britain. This led to subsequent confusion over what type of ironclads should be built, and what their ultimate purpose would be—offensive or defensive. Such a tactical-level dichotomy reflected the larger strategic debate over how the Union would successfully crush the Rebellion. It obviously could not win the war on the defensive, and in the absence of aggressive action on the part of the Army of the Potomac under General McClellan, relatively quick strikes by the Navy, feasibly taking out one Southern port-city after another, seemed a logical alternative. Nevertheless, the war could neither be won if it involved foreign powers operating against one Northern port city after another. In this sense it was always held as more important to secure the Union against possible interference first and last, before any efforts to subdue the domestic enemy could reasonably be expected to succeed. Great Britain was the bigger potential threat to the survival of the United States, even if—and especially if—the Union was already at war with the Confederate States.

This was not a universal opinion, however. In the final Senate debate of Feb. 12, 1862—a debate over House Bill No. 165, concerning coastal fortifications—Senator Hale objected that it had "nothing to do with the present war. It is prospective. It looks to other things than the prosecution of this war or the defense of the country in it; and it appropriates $7,000,000, when we need every dollar we can beg and borrow, and I had almost said steal, but the stealing is the other way." A string of fortifications along the northern frontier, he added, would provoke a similar British response and a spiraling arms race. Nevertheless, the bill passed the Senate by a vote of 28 to 10.[27] Evidently, the majority had no difficulty believing that it was better to be safe than sorry. However, by 1862 the U.S. Navy, the Lincoln Administration, and the Northern public alike found themselves thoroughly humiliated by the very real and likely threat of British intervention—British sea power—and were determined that this type of political influence could never again be wielded against the Union. In the mordant words of a Confederate War Department clerk, the *Trent* affair had brought "the Eagle cowering to the feet of the Lion."[28]

The shift toward a brown-water naval force even before the issue of ironclad "boats" or "batteries" arose also reflected the overriding strategic requirements of the United States in comparison with those of the British Empire at the same time. Dahlgren, meanwhile, had expressed a willingness to forgo a measure of strategic range, if not sea keeping, in favor of a tactically superior, mastless ironclad entirely reliant upon her supply of coal to determine the extent of her operations. The foreign threat only added to this concern for regional, if not coastal, supremacy—even as the Admiralty committed itself to a program of deep-draft, iron-hulled ironclads mounting the largest array of mast, sails, and rigging ever seen. Did the British commitment to imperial defense imply an inability to operate against an enemy's coastline? On Feb. 8, 1861, Vice-Admiral Sir Richard Dundas wrote to the Secretary of the Defence Commission, for the attention of the Duke of Cambridge and Sidney Herbert, the Secretary for War, that "to prevent the passage of iron-cased ships" ("as exemplified in the French ship 'La Gloire'") into Portsmouth harbor, floating batteries could be readily devised by converting ships of the line. Though it would "not be desirable that they should [be] fitted for permanent service at sea . . . they should be so adapted as to render it inexpedient that they should be detached to a distance. . . ." The Defence Committee (again) disagreed. Such vessels would not be as effective as fixed forts, it defensively declared, and "the proposal to devote so large a portion of our naval resources to a special purpose . . . so far from increasing our security, will tend to weaken our strength by dividing our means of resistance." Indeed, it was not clear how ironclads might be used for coastal defense or assault. "It certainly appears to us a strange argument that, because by the introduction of iron-cased vessels, bombardment has become comparatively easy, and consequently, that iron-cased ships are required for protection, therefore, the defending vessels are to be deprived of the support of forts, and are to be put on an equality with an equal number, or on an inferiority with a greater number of a similarly equipped squadron of the enemy."[29]

By this reasoning, it was perhaps fallacious for the Union Navy to concentrate on armored batteries as well, whether for coastal assault or defense—with the important distinction, not mentioned by the British Committee, that it was not so much about "equal numbers" of ironclads as about their individual character, based on their strategic function. All things not being equal in ironclad design, between coastal and global operational parameters, it remained to be seen whether a mastless ironclad "battery" would by its nature be superior to "iron-cased ships," if not also forts. On Dec. 23, 1861, the height of the *Trent* crisis, Ericsson insisted to Welles that "our gun boats or floating batteries, since they lack speed, size, and many other potent elements of the large European iron clad war ships will be worthless unless absolutely impregnable and capable of carrying the heaviest ordnance." The original *Monitor,* still under construction, possessed "the properties called for, requiring only increased substance of turret plate and to be armed with 15 inch guns to bid defiance to any war ship afloat."[30] This was a promise the Bureau of Construction could not make with a Coles-type "shield ship." But for the

U.S. Navy, it also remained to be seen whether its hasty reliance upon coastal defense, and therefore a superior ironclad battery, could be fully entrusted to the abilities of private contractors such as John Ericsson. Deprived of much of their practical seafaring experience in this unique situation, professional Union sailors were naturally dubious of "weapons platforms," much less "machines," as warships.[31]

Part Two

The Fulcrum of Hampton Roads

Chapter 9

Hampton Roads and Its Consequences

When the Confederate ironclad *Virginia* finally did attack, on Saturday, March 8, 1862, the Union Navy was, surprisingly, fairly surprised. Not only were the frigates and sloops at Hampton Roads caught helpless, disabled, or aground, but repeated broadsides of 9-inch solid shot against the ironclad's 38° sloping armored casemate proved futile in preventing the vessel—moving at 4 knots—from ramming the *Cumberland* and then leisurely setting the *Congress* on fire. The vital crossroads between Fortress Monroe, Norfolk, and the mouth of the James River, in fact, consisted of mostly disabled Union vessels, all wooden, many of which were sail only. The oaken heart of Union sea power was literally pierced with iron. Two powerfully armed Federal warships were destroyed in a matter of minutes, suffering more than 250 casualties in the process.[1] Even worse, the enemy was virtually untouched and prepared to finish off the rest of the Union fleet. It sought to bombard Fortress Monroe—perhaps into surrender—along with surrounding Union positions. In fact, it looked as though the *Virginia* might dominate the strategic nexus of the war.

Welles famously recounted in his diary how Lincoln's Cabinet panicked at the news. Secretary of War Edwin Stanton feared the *Virginia* would steam up the Potomac and shell the White House. Even though the Secretary of the Navy assured him the *Merrimack*'s old hull drew too much water and therefore could not possibly ascend the Potomac to Washington, Stanton was doubtful. Welles informed him that the *Monitor* was en route to Hampton Roads and should already be there, and doubt turned to scorn when Welles noted that the Union's ironclad champion had only two guns.[2]

Almost incredibly, this was the performance of a single converted ironclad on its first day of operation.[3] For the Union Navy in early March 1862, it was a disaster of the greatest magnitude. Furthermore, it was well known that other rebel "rams" were under construction throughout the South: at New Orleans, at Mobile, at Savannah, at Charleston, and on the Mississippi. The rapid mobilization of the North's maritime and industrial resources had produced a credible blockade covering roughly 3,500 miles of enemy coastline. Wooden gunboats had already launched successful strikes against the Confederacy's exposed seaboard flanks. At Richmond, Confederate Secretary of War Judah P. Benjamin had dispatched his best soldier, General Robert E. Lee, to oversee the coastal defenses of the Carolinas and Georgia.[4] Lee knew that Union sea power could pressure Richmond to divert precious manpower resources away from its defense or operations in the West. Suddenly the situation appeared to be reversed. Still, though, the rebels' technological "wonder weapons" might yet outweigh the numerical superiority of the Federal fleet.[5]

Into this already historic maelstrom of naval warfare steamed the U.S.S. *Monitor* later that night. News of her arrival, it was telegrammed to Brigadier-General John E. Wool, commanding some 10,000 Union troops at the scene, "infused new life into the men."[6] The next morning, the two iron-plated steam warships dueled for the immediate fate of the stricken Union steam frigate *Minnesota* and the control of Hampton Roads. Among the thousands of Northern and Southern spectators crowded along opposite shores who witnessed this dramatic encounter was Gustavus Fox. He had come down from Washington to see for himself the contentious *Monitor*, scheduled to arrive from New York. There is little doubt that the experience fully "converted" the Assistant Secretary of the Navy to Ericsson's claims as well. In a telegram to Welles, Fox briefly relayed the events:

HEADQUARTERS, *Fortress Monroe—6:45 p.m.*

(Received March 9, 1862.)

The *Monitor* arrived at 10 p.m. last night and went immediately to the protection of the *Minnesota*, lying, aground just below Newport News.

7 a.m. to-day the *Merrimack*, accompanied by two wooden steamers and several tugs, stood out toward the *Minnesota* and opened fire.

The *Monitor* met them at once and opened her fire, when all the enemy's vessels retired, excepting the *Merrimack*. These two ironclad vessels fought part of the time touching each other, from 8 a.m. to noon, when the *Merrimack* retired. Whether she is injured or not it is impossible to say. Lieutenant J. L. Worden, who commanded the *Monitor*, handled her with great skill, assisted by Chief Engineer Stimers. Lieutenant Worden was injured by the cement from the pilot house being driven into his eyes, but I trust not seriously. The *Minnesota* kept up a continuous fire and is herself somewhat injured.

She was moved considerably to-day, and will probably be off to-night. The *Monitor* is uninjured and ready at any moment to repel another attack.

G. V. FOX,
Assistant Secretary

G. WELLES,
Secretary Navy[7]

Fifteen minutes later, Fox telegrammed John Ericsson in New York that his "noble boat" had "performed with perfect success." In the unprecedented, critical relationship between man and machine in naval warfare, the officers and crew of 58 men (including Stimers) had handled their own wonder-weapon "with great skill."[8]

The *Monitor* was indeed shot-proof—but so was the *Virginia*. The rebel ironclad remained a serious threat. "I was the nearest person to her outside of the *Monitor*," Fox wrote to Welles, "and I am of the opinion she is not seriously injured." Any of the 11-inch gunboats still available Fox wanted sent to Hampton Roads.[9] It was now painfully obvious that only the biggest Union guns on hand might succeed in overcoming such armor protection.[10] In addition to the superiority of "iron over wood," the "revolution" in naval warfare manifested at the battle of Hampton Roads was that concentrated broadsides of lighter cannon were useless in comparison with single, overwhelming blasts.[11] In two consecutive days of firing against the *Virginia*, the *Minnesota* alone expended 78 10-inch and 169 9-inch solid shot, without result.[12] The first action between ironclad ships was thus a famously frustrating one, with neither antagonist able to wield a decisive advantage over the other.[13] The stage was immediately set for new ordnance, ship design, and tactics in the age of steam.

On March 10 the *Minnesota* finally got off ground and resumed position back at the entrance of the Roads, off Fortress Monroe. The *Monitor* followed her. That day Fox and General Wool inspected the battle-scarred ironclad and conferred with her officers. Wool had already been telegraphed by General George B. McClellan to prepare to evacuate the Union position at Newport News, if the Navy lost control of the Roads, and fall back on Fortress Monroe, taking care of the valuable 12-inch "Union Gun"—the only one of its kind in existence.[14] Undoubtedly, Fox was shown the Army's massive, experimental rifled gun and its companion 15-inch caliber smoothbore, as they were both prepared to assist in the defense of the fort.[15] Two of his telegrams from the following day confirm that the Assistant Secretary had made the important connection between the corporeal events of recent days and the Union ironclad program's course for the future. The first, to Lieutenant Henry Wise, Assistant Inspector of Ordnance at the Navy Department, requested Dahlgren to assist Brigadier-General J. W. Ripley (the Army's Chief of Ordnance) in the casting of "some projectiles for the Union gun here."[16] The second one, to Dahlgren, clearly reflected Stimers's frustration in not being allowed to fire the wrought-iron shot specially cast for the *Monitor*'s 11-inch guns because of Dahlgren's fear that the guns would be overstrained. "It is the only thing that will settle the *Merrimack*," Fox persisted. Additionally, "We must have more of these boats with 15-inch guns, and you must go ahead with your furnaces at once to make them to stand solid shot."[17]

Dahlgren replied that the risk of an 11-inch gun burst within the *Monitor*'s turret—as a result of firing wrought-iron shot—outweighed their strategic value. "I am only awaiting the action of the Senate and then for as large guns as you want with solid shot."[18] The day before the *Virginia*'s attack, Dahlgren wielded his authority in ordnance matters in response to Fox's "proposition to build a vessel like the 'Lancaster' so as to carry 20 guns of XI in. on the Gun deck, in lieu of 22 of IX in., and to retain the two XI in. on the Spar deck." The increase, he calculated, would add 170 to 280 tons to the vessel's weight and nearly 80 men to the crew. Only twelve 11-inch guns therefore could be contemplated, six to a broadside. Whether these should be on a regular broadside-carriage on an enclosed gun deck or an open-deck pivot was another matter, especially since such large guns would have to be stowed at sea "in two line fore and aft on each side of the middle line of the deck," parallel to the ship's side. "You may safely rely on one thing," he concluded to Fox: "that the <u>power of a ship of War may always be in proportion to her capacity</u>, And that the <u>largest</u> ship can always be made the <u>most powerful</u> in <u>offense</u> as well as in <u>defense</u>."[19]

The events at Hampton Roads had Dahlgren eating his words later. Ericsson's published remarks on the ironclad duel—that the *Monitor*'s 11-inch guns should have been aimed more at the *Virginia*'s waterline—Dahlgren argued, only proved his point: the lack of wrought-iron shot would not have made any positive difference in the battle's outcome. "That the use of but one XI in. gun at a time should have effected so much against a vessel 4 times the size with perhaps 6 or 8 times the Ordnance power, presenting an entire oblique surface to the *Monitor*'s aim is so good a result that it seems to me the excess of hypercriticism even to suggest that more might have been done. . . ."[20] Here was both veiled disapproval of Ericsson, the now wildly popular civilian inventor, and an acknowledgment by Dahlgren that Ericsson's principles—embodied in the *Monitor*—had somehow overturned his own.[21] The smaller, lighter-draft turret vessel had succeeded in driving away the large, deep-draft, broadside-armed opponent. Various proposals submitted by Dahlgren before the battle emphasized either converting shallow-draft gunboats into armored central-battery ironclads or lightly protecting the new double-ender gunboats with their open-deck pivots.[22] Now Ericsson and Fox were rushing forward with plans of even more heavily armored turret-mounted guns, of even heavier caliber—designed to inflict singular mortal blows against ostensibly "more powerful" ironclads.

In this regard Ericsson's proposal to Welles of Dec. 23, 1861, to build six improved monitors held an important advantage over rival designs—particularly the Bureau's—since arming them with 15-inch guns was a specific feature. "The *Monitor* was not half completed before I saw clearly what <u>might</u> be done," Ericsson wrote to Fox. He had been perfecting them since early that December at least, anticipating many of the suggested improvements Stimers offered following the *Monitor*'s trial by fire. Foremost among these was the placing of the pilothouse on top of the turret, as an alternative to the isolated, vulnerable box-like structure on the *Monitor*'s forward deck. It would be cylindrical too, made of 8 inches of laminated 1-inch plates, and would remain fixed in position when the turret revolved. But "on account of the most unexpected march which Mr. Isherwood stole upon me in relation to my cylindrical, impregnable, steam revolving turret," Ericsson explained, "I have kept my own counsel."[23]

In the meantime, the North reacted to news of the two-day naval battle at Hampton Roads with mixed feelings of shock, amazement, and joy. After relating his own account of the *Monitor*'s performance, Stimers congratulated Ericsson on his "great success":

> Thousands have this day blessed you. I have heard whole crews cheer you. Every man feels that you have saved this place to the nation by furnishing us with the means to whip an ironclad frigate that was, until our arrival, having it all her own way with our most powerful vessels.[24]

To Commodore Smith, a man nearly as responsible for the *Monitor*'s completion as her builder, Stimers had to express his condolences. The Bureau Chief's son, Joseph, was among those killed in action. "I knew him well; indeed, we were shipmates in that same *Merrimack* when she sailed under an honorable flag—by people who did not steal her." At sea the *Monitor* needed higher ventilation pipes, but otherwise he considered "the form and strength of the vessel equal to any weather I ever saw at sea." Waves rolled smoothly uninterrupted "right across her deck; it looks to the sailor as if his ship was altogether under water, and it is only the man who has studied the philosophical laws which govern floatation and stability who feels exactly comfortable in her during a gale of wind." The Chief Engineer also considered laminated armor plating better than "solid forged plates."[25]

The battle of Hampton Roads also gave John Lenthall of the Bureau of Ship Construction & Repair new hope for his own scheme of turreted ironclads. One of the chief objections the previous winter was their requirement for (foreign-built) slab armor plates. Now, "in justice to the Bureau," Lenthall wrote to Welles, the Department would reconsider "a vessel built on the principles of the plan then prepared." The Novelty Iron Works, which built the *Monitor*'s laminated iron turret, was offering to build a Bureau turret ship in "5½ months for the sum of Five hundred and thirty thousand dollars, suggesting a modification in the plating which recent experience will justify. . . ."[26] But this would either undermine the sudden popularity of the *Monitor*'s inventor, and his own proposal for six improved sister-ships of the same basic design, or introduce a rival turret ship system with higher freeboard and Coles cupolas.

At any rate, Lenthall's proposals were again too reactionary, too slow to effectively compare with Ericsson's. Nothing was mentioned of increasing the firepower of the former's turret ship, from one 11-inch gun per turret (similar to Coles's idea of only one 110-pdr Armstrong per turret on the *Royal Sovereign* conversion and the purpose-built *Prince Albert*) to two, or more important, of substituting 15-inch guns for the 11-inch, especially after the indecision of the *Monitor*'s guns against the *Virginia*'s armor protection. Nor was the other drawback of the Bureau's turret vessel prototype, its relatively higher freeboard and therefore greater hull area needing protection—and therefore also increased expense, difficulty, and delay of construction—addressed by the Union Navy's chief of ship construction.[27]

On the same day Lenthall wrote to Welles, Ericsson wrote to Fox of his delight that the proactive Assistant Secretary, fully converted from the Bureau's vision to his own, seriously considered 20-inch caliber guns for the "swift, impregnable turret carrier" that Ericsson was already busy designing. The concept of alternative "visions" here is crucial: whereas the Bureau (and its advocates) had its eye more on deploying turret ships for coastal assault—attacking Charleston, for example—Ericsson, Fox, and their supporters were focusing ever more on the problem of strategic coastal defense: deterring foreign intervention. This strategy included the construction of even larger monitors with oceangoing pretensions. "With all my heart," Ericsson wrote Fox, "if you can make the guns I [will] most willingly supply the gear for supporting, working and housing the same. Enforce your plan of employing such heavy ordnance and in twelve months we can say to England and France, leave the Gulf! We do not want your Kings and monarchical institutions on this continent."[28]

Chapter 10

Super-Monitors, Super-Guns

On the morning of March 15, 1862, Fox met with Ericsson in New York. Their conference all but hammered out the future shape of the Union's ironclad Navy for the rest of the Civil War and beyond. Ericsson wrote soon after the Assistant Secretary's departure that he was "much gratified . . . to find how fully you appreciate the advantage of drawing the supply of air, in the intended swift turret carrier, through pilot house and turret." With a projected 5,000-horsepower engine, there would be more than enough artificial ventilation available through a separate, armored vent-pipe above deck "when chasing an enemy with full power" at sea. This ample power promised to resolve any doubts about the habitability of new monitors. The second main concern, low freeboard, was closely connected to the first, and therefore the solution of the former implied the acceptance of the latter. Ericsson was jubilant: "Your support in relation to the <u>flush deck only 18 inches out of water</u> is most encouraging and will be a tower of strength in the battle with prejudice, which must be waged, before the good cause is triumphant."[1]

Much of the credit for the acceptance of the monitor system of ironclads belongs to Fox, whose ideas often proved to be as farsighted and free from convention as Ericsson's. Such a kindred spirit was nothing new for the Swedish engineer-inventor, however, who must have recalled his initial friendship with Stockton some 20 years before. Whereas Ericsson was new to the country and vulnerable, his status since Hampton Roads seemed more secure than the country's. But this did not prevent Fox from honestly confronting him with proposed modifications to his plans. "When I spoke to you last Summer of a vessel of extraordinary speed and one 20-inch gun, invulnerable, so far as the tower was concerned, as a fit match for the *Warrior*," Fox wrote on his return to Washington, "I did not think you would take the *Monitor* as a type." Events since then had compelled him "to consent fully in the plans which you showed me in New York Saturday." He therefore trusted that Ericsson would take his "suggestions of detail" "in the kind spirit which prompted them." These included the specific incorporation of a ram; a 12-foot height for the ventilation pipe of the seagoing monitor, forward of the stack; an iron cage around the propellers to prevent fouling; "a nice iron gallery . . . abaft the smoke pipe for promenade," 8 feet high; and a staggering 25-inch–thick iron turret. Always prone to optimism, however grim the situation, Fox regarded the Navy's losses at Hampton Roads as useful in "awakening" the public mind (and opening the purse strings of Congress). "Most fortunately we have met with a disaster—this is the Almighty's teachings always—success never gives a lesson."[2]

Far from feeling insulted, Ericsson regarded Fox's suggestions as "genius." He was in a good mood, to be sure, and it never hurt to flatter equally enthusiastic patrons. Fox being "a perfect master of the subject," Ericsson pledged that "we shall now have a navy that will place the United States at the head of Naval powers." Fox rightly suspected that this might prove easier said than done, even with the full backing of Congress. Yet Ericsson assured him that "the building of a dozen Monitors is a mere trifle with the enormous engineering capabilities of the United States at this moment."[3]

There were, however, major qualifiers to this statement. If "a dozen Monitors" meant simple reproductions of the original, including its guns, building them might have indeed been fairly painless. If more were needed, and of a more complicated design and demanding armament, there would be difficulties. The fixed price of materials and availability of skilled labor were also requisite. But in the early spring of 1862 there was still every reason to expect an early end to the war; Federal forces were poised in both the eastern and western theaters to deliver simultaneous crushing blows against the Confederacy. Fox replied he wanted "25 inches for the fast boats that will cross to the enemy's country," because he foresaw "that the most enormous caliber of ordnance must immediately come into use, and we must prepare for them, not for anything in existence at this time."[4] Fox knew it would take at least a year before such fearsome naval weapons were ready for use. Maybe by then it would be England's turn to yield to the spread of Lincoln's American democracy.

Almost immediately the qualifiers set in. On March 22 Fox wrote Ericsson he preferred two turrets in his "three hundred & fifty feet vessel." Two days later he added twin screws. In this he "would risk a voyage around the world, and a battle with the whole iron fleet of England."[5] Though Ericsson wrote he found his patron's "boldness in the matter . . . a source of gratification," he had to stress the importance of keeping Dahlgren's new 15-inch gun to Ericsson's exacting proportions to fit his 20-foot–diameter turret. In the meantime he was settling for 11-inch–thick laminated turrets for the six improved monitors under way, capable of an additional outer plate of solid 4-inch thickness, as soon as northern mills could readily produce them.[6] But on the same day that Dahlgren complained to Fox of delays in finishing the specifications for the 15-inch gun—due to constant wartime demands and a shortage of staff—Ericsson wrote Fox that his requirements of twin turrets and screws "have depressed me in spirit more than any occurrence. . . ." While before he "had supposed we were on the same track," Fox's new ideas, he exclaimed, "convince me that our ideas are as opposite as the poles." The topic was "too vast" to go into at present; for now he enclosed a plan for a 26-foot–diameter turret housing a massive 20-inch–caliber gun of prescribed length. He was, finally, "very curious to see Captain Dahlgren's guns and fear greatly he will require more width than the turrets will admit of."[7]

It was impossible to reconcile so much in a single person. Even if Fox agreed completely and always with Ericsson's vision, that agreement alone was in growing danger from other interested parties who shared common ends but opposing means. As reported by *Scientific American*, on March 18 the New York City Chamber of Commerce, along with industrialist Peter Cooper "and delegations from the Philadelphia and Boston Boards of Trade," solicited Ericsson's advice. Forts were considered ineffective next to "several light iron-clad vessels to carry 15-inch guns . . . to resist such a vessel as the *Warrior*."[8] This sort of alarm was a good thing, Du Pont wrote to his wife, Sophie, "[f]or the *Warrior* could run up and shell New York all day and retire comfortably at night and finish the Navy Yard before breakfast in the morning."[9] Meanwhile, various state governments of the North were busy preparing information for Congress on the series of nationally strategic canals under proposal. "You will much oblige many parties here, amongst our prominent merchants in particular if you will favor me," Richard P. Morgan of Chicago wrote Ericsson, "with a statement as to the least draft of water admissible for vessels like the *Monitor* designed to cope with such craft as might be brought into the Lakes by the British Government through their Canals in Canada."[10]

The Department itself was under extraordinary pressure. Welles found himself writing his son a week after the ironclad duel at Hampton Roads that "instead of giving me credit for my months of labor and care to get that vessel [the *Monitor*] built and ready, I am abused for not having built more." Yet "few believed that the experiment, for she was until last Sunday an experiment, would be successful and the malcontents were prepared to ridicule and denounce us for her failure."[11] According to an indignant letter in the *National Intelligencer* penned by the Navy Department's Chief Clerk, William Faxon, the public's misconception stemmed from a lecture given by Wendell Phillips at the Smithsonian on March 14. This described the *Monitor* as "conceived, built, fitted out, and sent by the people themselves, in opposition to all former official ideas" and threatened to open yet another rift in civil-military relations during the Civil War. Compared with the roles of other Navy professionals, Commodore Smith's role as superintendent of the *Monitor*'s construction, Faxon pointed out, was all but ignored. "Day and night it occupied his thoughts, and his well-matured suggestions have proved of great value."[12] Ericsson, too, leapt to the Navy's defense. "Our newspapers are crazy," he assured Smith, "and by their extraordinary comments and propositions are not only hurting but murdering every body and every thing connected with the ironclad navy."[13] Part of the problem was political. Admiral Hiram Paulding regarded Senate Naval Affairs Chairman John Hale as more of "a Harlequin than Statesman—a person without merit & whose claim to principles will scarcely be admitted by anyone who has observed his course in public life." Because Hale "aspired to the [Navy] Department . . . his disappointment in not being able to make an impression on the Administration will not have lessened his hostility." Welles could therefore expect only continued opposition in every conceivable fashion, and this was par for the course: "No prominent man in this country can escape from injustice & defamation."[14]

Even after the *Monitor* restored the blockade at Hampton Roads, if not also the Union's strategic initiative, doubts existed. "I would not trust [Washington] and the fleet you see coming down into the river to the strength of a single screw bolt in the *Monitor*'s new machinery[;] if one (1) breaks, the *Merrimac* beats her," telegrammed M. C. Meigs, the Army's brilliant Quartermaster-General, to Dahlgren.[15] Yet could not the same be said for a bolt in the *Virginia*'s (old) machinery? Was the *Monitor* more vulnerable because of her greater technical sophistication—her reliance upon machinery—than the *Virginia*, or more powerful? To Ericsson there was no question, but to others concerned in the spring of 1862, it was not implicit that machines and power were so synonymous.[16] "Oversophistication" could be an equally implicit weakness.[17]

Lenthall and Isherwood were also dismayed with the larger strategic direction the Navy's undeniable and growing reliance upon Ericsson represented. Monitors, according to the professionals, could not possibly "constitute a navy or perform its proper functions." Sea-going iron-clads of the largest possible dimensions, built in expanded Government dockyards equipped for iron shipbuilding and large-scale, heavy armor-plate manufacture, would be better suited to America's long-term interests. "Wealth, victory and empire are to those who command the Ocean, the toll gate as well as the highway of Nations; and if ever assailed by a powerful maritime for, we shall find to our prosperity, if ready, how much better it is to fight at the threshold than upon the hearthstone."[18] Yet the question remained for Welles and the Government whether or not the United States during the Civil War could rightly afford such a strategy.

Another practical qualifier was the bureau chiefs' own abilities to actually put words into action. Two days after writing the Secretary, Lenthall and Isherwood acknowledged "it may be proper economy in the government to plate its larger wooden vessels, as practiced by England and France. . . ." The Union Navy's own steam frigates, they asserted, "can be made efficient sea-going iron clad vessels in the least possible time and at the least cost," and they recommended that the U.S.S. *Roanoke* be converted by cutting her down and arming her with "eight 12 or 15 inch guns in four 'Cole' [*sic*] towers. . . ." The entire broadside, expected to be 6 feet above the waterline, would have to be armored with laminated 4½-inch iron plates, covering the exposed 6-foot freeboard to "4 feet below the water-line amidships and 3 feet at the ends"—an enormous undertaking for a vessel that they calculated would draw nearly 23 feet, and carrying no sails for long-range cruising.[19] The *Roanoke* would serve as the bureau chief's own model ironclad, and upon her success would depend their own in shaping the Union's ironclad program while they still could.

Before the fateful month of March 1862 was out, this was far from settled or free of complications. Fox may, in fact, have been trying to reconcile the best of the old Bureau design features (twin screws and turrets) with Ericsson's own (low freeboard; a steam-rotated turret mounting the heaviest possible guns). At any rate, Welles tried to sum up the immediate lessons of Hampton Roads—and capitalize on them—in his March 25 appeal to the House and Senate Naval Committees. Drawing upon the recent arguments from both the bureau chiefs and his own assistant, he asserted that "[t]he navy, as it exists at present, cannot successfully contend against a power employing iron-clad vessels, and consequently cannot meet the requirements of the country." It was therefore time to initiate the "construction of armored vessels on a scale commensurate with the great interests at stake." Another public advertisement, dated Feb. 20, called for submissions of plans "which are now being received, developing the ingenuity and skill of our countrymen," and the Secretary had "faith they will produce models for a class of vessels for home defense and for sea-service. . . ." This statement already suggested a predisposition to Ericsson's own efforts rather than the Bureau's; it also served to confirm politically that the Navy was indeed fully supportive "of the people themselves." Additionally, Welles called for $500,000 for improved gun-making facilities at the Washington Navy Yard (and assistance for Dahlgren); and a new (monitor) program of light-draft ironclads for river service, a 15-inch gun class for harbor defense and coastal operations, and a 20-inch gun class for oceangoing purposes. Curiously, he also noted the need for "mechanical" obstructions for full harbor defense against a concentrated, superior naval force, not just forts and a few harbor defense floating batteries. Finally, it was necessary for a $100,000 appropriation for iron target tests, Dahlgren's old request—around $30 million for all of the above.[20] Significantly, this was the price tag for getting the nation ready for a major naval war with one or more European powers, not for simply winning the war against the Confederacy.

This preparation was also a matter of some debate in Congress. Powerful supporters of the Stevens family, including Senator Hale, were in favor of appropriating over $750,000 to complete their own battery, apparently much improved from more than 20 years' unfulfilled development costing previous governments $500,000, with another $228,435 advanced by the Stevens family itself. Others preferred a pair of improved monitors for the same price. How could politicians decide which design was best? For that matter, how could the professionals? "We have got to depend on ironclad steamers; we have got to go without the light of experience," declared Hale. "If you had judged and determined by the reports of these experts—I have myself got sick of the name; I am glad it is not an old Saxon word—we never would have had the *Monitor*; we should have had nothing but a horse laugh from learned pundits over the very idea, instead of having what we now have." For all they knew, the Stevens Battery might prove as surprisingly successful in meeting any foreign threat—and Edwin Stevens as much of a genius as John Ericsson, another "private individual, having no connection with your Government or any of its Departments." Senator Grimes disagreed. The *Monitor*, at least, was tried and tested; the improved versions would mount 15-inch guns that could sink the deep-draft Stevens Battery, with her exposed deck guns.[21] Samuel C. Fessenden of Maine also favored the monitors for national defense:

> I undertake to say that when we have those finished, they will be good against any navy in the world that can be sent here, without Stevens's battery. No force of ironclad vessels can be sent across the Atlantic that

could beat it, because these vessels are not made to cross the Atlantic. Iron vessels are for home defense. They are not made to navigate the ocean; that is to say, on these long voyages. They cannot, as everybody says, carry coal enough without having tenders alongside of them to supply them. We are, therefore, in no danger of attack from iron vessels abroad.

But this last assertion played into the hands of the proponents of the Stevens Battery. No one could forget the *Trent* affair, and even a million dollars seemed a small price to pay for the added protection of at least New York City.[22] A proposed amendment the next day offered to resolve the problem by making the satisfaction of the Secretary of the Navy a prerequisite for the vessel's acceptance, and "the payment of said sum shall be contingent upon the success of said vessel as an ironclad steamer, to be determined by the President. . . ." Though members of Congress objected to burdening the Executive with such details, political opponents of Lincoln saw this as another chance to make him directly responsible for any specific military or naval failure. Hale was more furious that a proviso made the Secretary of the Navy's opinion the deciding factor. "It seems to me it is time that this Congress vindicated its right to some opinion in regard to their own action in reference to the war in which we are engaged." Left to its own devices, the Army (and also the Government) had clearly mismanaged the war. Would the Navy be given the same freedom from restraint? The Secretary, he charged, had "no more peculiar knowledge, no more peculiar experience, to fit him to form a judicious opinion on this subject than very many gentlemen on this floor. . . ." The members of Congress "have uniformly reserved to themselves the right of saying what kind of vessel shall be built, and have not left it to the Department; and whenever the Department have undertaken to act upon it, they have acted in derogation and usurpation of the rights of Congress. . . . Congress get[s] the information that they think necessary, and then they judge, and judge of the character of the vessels. . . ."[23]

The day after Welles wrote to Congress, he appointed Smith, Lenthall, Isherwood, and civilian naval architect Edward Hart to form a new Ironclad Board to review the advertised ironclad proposals; Dahlgren finally sent his plans for a naval 15-inch gun to Fox; and Ericsson addressed the Assistant Secretary's preferences for twin screws and turrets.[24] "I cannot give up the idea, which I have cherished for some time," Ericsson wrote, "of building a war vessel under your auspices, as I cannot entertain a doubt that you will after carefully looking into the subject, abandon the double propeller system as well as your last proposition of employing two turrets." Fully confident of his own expertise, the builder of the *Monitor* reminded Fox it was a mistake to always defer to British customs, which were often founded on erroneous principles. Indeed, everyone was new in the ironclad game. "The English are now on the wrong track," he asserted. "Put the weight of Coles' 6 turrets and 12 guns into one turret with two guns and you will defeat him in two rounds." Nor was Ericsson afraid of critiquing Fox's "argument in favor of two propellers," which he believed was "not strong enough." The principle of maximum concentration could also be applied in this regard, since a single shaft would be stronger than two smaller ones in the same hull, and could be more fully protected. "In relation to the superiority of a single turret I would have published a statement long ago," he added, "but for the fact that our enemies would be taught how to beat us. As long as England builds many-turreted vessels we can defy her, for our single vessel such as I have sent you a model of, with your two 20 inch guns and 2 feet thick turrets, can destroy the whole English navy in open water." It was a simple matter of calculation. [25]

By April 1, 1862, Ericsson was under exceptional strain to furbish the six *Passaic*-class ironclads to ensure "impregnability" for the Union, and to finish off plans for a veritable super-monitor that could end British naval supremacy. The task of designing the latter, however, which Ericsson proposed to name the *Dictator*, required specs for a 20-inch gun, which Dahlgren was loath to provide.[26] Even after finally submitting amended plans (with their trunnions) for a 15-inch gun to fit within Ericsson's 26-foot–diameter turrets, Dahlgren could not resist protecting himself by formally notifying Harwood "that this can only be considered as an experiment on a large scale, unsupported by any of the data usually considered important to the introduction of new ordnance, and, for a piece of this size, indispensable." In Dahlgren's opinion, the safety of the gun was now dependent upon its proper forging, and was therefore the responsibility of the original 15-inch Rodman's *manufacturer*—"the same kind of iron . . . the same grades of that iron, the same process of casting . . . the same tensile strength, density and other characteristics"—not his own modified version of it.[27] Ericsson, at the same time, was worried about the contractors—and the Navy—providing the adequate number of 15-inch guns even for the Passaics. "I fear these will not be done in time," he wrote to Fox, "and if so our impregnable fleet will not amount to much."[28]

Even young Oliver Batcheller realized the significance and potential of the new Yankee invention; "I trust now," he wrote to his father on April 3, "that all our harbors will be protected by iron clad 'Monitors' after which we can look for some form of 'iron machines' which will place us on an equal footing with France & England in foreign waters."[29] Ericsson's close confidant, Boston attorney John O. Sargent, went still further. The success of the *Monitor* ensured that "you will enjoy something a little earlier than the posthumous reputation which you were always sure of." The London *Times* was in a state of panic, and "if North and South would leave off fighting each other [and] get into a war with France and England," Sargent wrote, "you would have a better field for your operations and I should feel a little easier in mind and body." Saving the Union was one thing, but if Ericsson "could add to it the title of the Conqueror of England and France" his "ambition would probably be full."[30]

In the meantime, the Civil War itself could not wait. "The *Galena* is wanted for service immediately," Smith wrote to the vessel's supervisor, Henry Dunham. "She is at best only an experiment, and it is not deemed advisable to incur further expense or risk of delay preparing her for service."[31] "As to charges for extras," he threatened Bushnell, "you will find the government's claim for damages more than an offset to the account even if the vessel shall prove satisfactory."[32] The Whitney ironclad (the *Keokuk*) was also in a state of frightening uncertainty. Smith was not sure which form of fixed turret would be best, and preferred two thicknesses of armor plating to three. Her projected bellcrank engines would not be sufficient "to propel her at a continued speed of ten sea miles," nor were they as efficient as direct-action, back-acting ones. The days were ticking away, and Smith exasperatingly "supposed the ribs of the vessel were all up ere this."[33]

Nor was Ericsson immune. Smith was waiting for his full schematics for the *Passaic* monitors, "as the contract embodies a large amount of work as well as money, and in this transitory world, no one is safe until the bargain and instrument of indenture has been sealed, signed and delivered."[34] But as weapons platforms, or "Carriers," as Ericsson was prone to describe them, the monitors were dependent upon the types of weapons themselves. Smith wrote to Welles of his concerns. The *New Ironsides* would need 16 heavy broadside guns as well as two rifled pivots on deck. The monitors should have 12-inch guns and those for river service 11-inch.[35]

Yet the findings of the Ironclad Board for even Mississippi River war steamers seemed to support the monitor concept. There was a fundamental difficulty, Smith reported to Welles, in designing "Shot & Shell proof boats with so light a draught of water—from three to five feet—as stated in your letter of the 4th inst." Forward fire would be essential. Turret vessels alone would have to incorporate those of Ericsson's *Monitor* design.[36] Likewise, Ericsson reported with confidence to the Chairman of the Lake Defense Committee of the New York Chamber of Commerce that "an impregnable iron vessel 200 feet long and 25 feet wide, constructed on the general plan of the *Monitor*, will have sufficient buoyancy to carry a shot-proof iron turret carrying a gun of 15-inch caliber, with a ball of 450 pounds, and capable of destroying any hostile vessel that could be put upon the Lakes." At a price of $200,000, such a monitor ironclad would draw 6½ feet without coal, ammunition, and stores, and 8 feet with enough of these to attain her fighting trim.[37]

Smith was not satisfied with Ericsson's specifications when they did arrive on April 9. The scale appeared off, and the 5-inch keel made the depth of hull nearly 13 feet rather than 12½ feet. Furthermore, the government could not guarantee supply of Treasury note payments within the 30 days specified by the contract. Stimers's own modifications to the *Monitor* were not included or expected until Stimers could first make a copy. Smith therefore advised Ericsson that "you are not safe in going ahead too rapidly until your plans and specifications are perfected, and the contract consummated. The Department will not ratify the contract until it is in complete in all its parts."[38]

The Bureau of Ordnance, meanwhile, responded to Smith's concerns about the ironclads' various armaments by recommending a Board to examine the ironclads in question, both those already under construction and still under consideration. Harwood candidly informed Welles he found "the sudden introduction of so many different calibers objectionable," and he could not "perceive . . . any good reason exists for adopting XII inch cast iron guns for the iron-clad vessels."[39] Indeed, as Fox wrote to Ericsson the same day, Dahlgren was already busy with the "big guns. . . . we must stand to that."[40] Far from ignoring the habitability of the new monitors, the Assistant Secretary was deeply concerned. "It was blowing a gale during my whole visit and the little *Monitor* was rather uncomfortable being pretty well under water. Her deck leaks some and as the iron cannot be removed, this point should be looked to in others." Simple additions such as light deck platforms and "a tarpaulin tent to enable Jack to take his segar [*sic*] would render him more comfortable and contented.

"As I wrote you before," Fox stressed, "these low craft must be made perfectly comfortable for all hands in all weathers if we wish to succeed in them as regular cruisers, a point I desire to obtain." Perhaps testing a mock-up turret against a 15-inch gun would shed light on other issues as well. Ericsson replied, "What we are now building will be tight. Jack will also be made comfortable this time. Yet let me say that when actually face to face with the enemy awaiting action any moment, the hatches must be closed excepting on turret." A target test, Ericsson also agreed, might be useful. "Of course if we do not like to look at the scars we produce, we can put on new plates to hide our bruises." More significant for Ericsson, at least, news was coming back of England's reaction to the battle of Hampton Roads and the *Monitor*. "They imagine their Warriors impregnable. Why, our new Monitors with their 450 pound balls, will sink the boasted Ironsides in two rounds, nor will their applying also 15-inch guns help the matter. <u>We can stand that pill, but they will perish under its operation.</u>"[41]

Finally, in regard to wood versus iron hulls for the new ironclads, Ericsson disagreed with Fox's assertion that "[w]ood under water does not rot." The Assistant Secretary had "only to carry out the plan" that Ericsson "urged on the Department some 16 years ago, to build sheds under which to place your Iron Gun boats, on dry land, with a convenient inclined machinery for putting your fighting craft in and out of water at pleasure." Stimers was "much struck" by the idea when Ericsson repeated it the previous day. "A dozen gun boats under houses" might thus be kept in "good working order for 50 years at less annual expense than a single gun boat" otherwise. "In times of trouble a fleet may on this system be launched at a day's notice." Previously this scheme was regarded as "quite 'visionary'"; if only Fox would "give the subject a deliberate consideration" he would "find the idea not so stupid as it was once pronounced." Likewise, the notion of fitting the new monitors with permanent deck vents, perhaps even a superstructure—to facilitate better living conditions, especially for long-distance cruising—Ericsson strongly opposed. Even an elevating hatch would be better, he thought. "Let us take care not to fritter away the grand principle of a perfectly <u>flush</u> deck within 18 to 20 inches of the water's edge and absolute success will attend our labors." Again, Ericsson specifically promised what this "absolute success" would mean, for by "[a]dhering to this idea we are masters of the sea within a year."[42]

There could be no doubt who the real adversary was in this pursuit of naval power. Two days later, Ericsson took the bold step of addressing William Seward, the U.S. Secretary of State, with one of the most revealing declarations of Union ironclad policy during the American Civil War. "The state of the naval defenses of the country being so intimately connected with its inter-national relations," he wrote,

> I deem it my duty to report to you that under orders from the Secretary of the Navy, keels for 6 vessels of the Monitor class of increased size and speed have already been laid. . . . The amount of mechanical force now concentrated on the work is quite unprecedented.
>
> The speech of the Duke of Somerset in the House of Lords on the 4th instant and the news from England to-day in relation to the expedients now adopted by the Admiralty to avert the dangers to England suggested by the recent developments in naval warfare, tend to prove that this country now occupies the vantage ground. The six vessels above alluded to will be absolutely impregnable against even the last "14-ton gun" of Armstrong, in consequence of their sides being only 18 inches above water, a circumstance which converts their decks into bulwarks supporting the armor plate with resistless force. Our turrets, too, are

absolutely impregnable as we now make the same 11¾ thick—all iron. Our guns of 15-inch caliber will throw 450-pound shot. To this enormous projectile the *Warrior, Black Prince* and the razeed line-of-battle ships, will present only a five-inch iron plating. This thin armor may be said to afford no resistance to our 450-pound Shot. Under its terrific impact, the sides will be actually crushed in. England is now committing the serious blunder of attending to the protection of her guns alone by the so-called cupolas. She overlooks the safety of the vessel intended to carry her guns.

The British Admiralty, it would appear, can only see in the *Monitor* a revolving turret (erroneously supposed to be of English origin), forgetting that without the peculiarly constructed hull of the *Monitor*, her cupola Ships will stand no chance in a conflict with this country.[43]

Nothing gave more impetus to Ericsson and the Union's preference for monitor-type ironclads than England's own reaction to the battle of Hampton Roads, and the controversy between Coles and the British Government over turret-ship ironclads for the Royal Navy. "To save time, and repetition" Ericsson enclosed a copy of his letter to Seward to Fox. Perhaps the inventor was circumventing the Navy's authority, if not pre-empting its freedom of choice in terms of ironclad policy? It did not seem to matter. After all, Ericsson was delighted to point out to the Assistant Secretary how "[t]he English government are all adrift on the question of naval defense." Armstrong's latest gun test "only confirms what all the world knows, that England is now without a fleet."[44] Nothing sealed the case for coast defense monitor-ironclads more than the recent *Trent* affair, Anglo-American tensions, and the threat of foreign intervention in the Civil War. As official committee reports came back to Congress in April 1862, the largely accepted wisdom was that "[g]ood armor and upright dealing united are well calculated to make nations friends."[45] While the Northern States were becoming, "by the pressure of domestic rebellion, more able to take care of our interests at sea, with the aid of gunboats and steamers and a marine of armed cruisers and privateers, ever ready," England had "lowered her tone and altered her policy to conform to the changed relations which her navy bears to the rest of the world."[46]

Chapter 11

Ericsson, the Navy, and Control of the Union Ironclad Program

Even as this new profile of British naval power became rapidly more distinct, Fox was less than sanguine about the proper course for the Union's ironclad program, and Stimers had his own ideas about the shape of the new ironclads themselves. "Putting in for only 9 knots is a most serious mistake and one that I blame myself for not insisting upon," Fox wrote to Stimers on April 20, 1862, "but I found nobody to back me, not even Ericsson who would leave us nothing to hope or wish for, if the speed was put at twelve knots." Faced with sheer technical limitations in the multitude of often conflicting warship qualities such as speed, range (sea keeping), maneuverability, draft, cost, production time, and offensive and defensive power, Fox noted that Ericsson "gives us powerful ordnance, invulnerability, but not speed." Even then the monitors as machines were inherently vulnerable. "You must look out for the details which are definite, but important," the Assistant Secretary instructed Stimers, "and above all recollect that the turret must stand a fifteen inch shot."[1] If the machinery broke, the ironclad, as a man-of-war, could suddenly be rendered useless. Impregnability was essential, unlike the case with a more traditional, less complicated broadside vessel. It would be up to Stimers to keep a practical, technical eye on Ericsson, cajoling him at the same time with Fox's concerns.[2] Ericsson's sense of professional pride, suddenly wounded, might jeopardize the entire program. The Union clearly needed him, but also needed to maintain its control over him.

Maintaining control over Ericsson was feasible because Ericsson was hardly the only skillful mechanic in the country. The Navy fortunately had many talented, enthusiastic engineers already at its disposal. On the same day Ericsson wrote to Seward, and Fox to Stimers, U.S. Navy Engineer Isaac Newton responded to Ericsson's earlier request "to state what defects I have discovered in the steam machinery of the *Monitor*" with precision and respect. Some steam pipes could be rerouted more efficiently, while working parts of increasingly vital aspects of the machinery, such as the blower engines and pumps, "should be made very heavy, so as not to require frequent keeping up, &c. . . . [N]o pains should be spared so as to make them <u>impossible to give out</u>."[3] This account said nothing about whether they would be affected by actual combat. Simple mechanical failure alone for a ship largely below the surface of the water could prove fatal. "All radical changes in the construction of the vessel" that had occurred to Newton were already conveyed to Stimers,[4] except a plan to add a layer of heavy angle iron along the exterior edge of the upper hull's armor shelf, to prevent the thin deck plates from curling up from the side plates and exposing the wood when struck from (ricochet) shots along the waterline. This idea was not adopted.[5] In the meantime, Newton succeeded in depressing the *Monitor*'s 11-inch Dahlgrens 1.5°. A penetrative solid shot against the *Virginia*'s waterline, the next time she appeared in Hampton Roads, might be quickly followed by an exploding shell. As the *Monitor* did not have "sails and ropes," Newton added that "the spare time this deficiency gives the first Lieut. causes me very great annoyance." More in the Navy were beginning to understand the implications. "The *Monitor* is a <u>machine</u>[,] the creation of an Engineer."[6]

Added to the role of the monitors as British ironclad-killing machines (practically devices in themselves) was the task of defying Confederate gun emplacements as "barriers to the entrance of the Union forces." Ericsson's originally proposed names for the six improved monitors of the *Passaic* class demonstrates this clearly: *Impenetrable, Palladium, Agitator,* and *Parado*—likely stressing the "Monitor Riddle" effect on Great Britain, for American coastal defense—*Penetrator* and *Gauntlet,* for coast assault operations during the Civil War. John Rodgers wrote to his wife, Anne, that even the presence of the comparatively lightly armored U.S.S. *Galena* on the York River was "worth some two millions a day." He was ready to risk passing the batteries erected on the James River to protect Richmond from yet another grand naval coup by the U.S. Navy. The current operation against Forts Jackson and St. Philip (guarding the Mississippi delta approach to New Orleans) was on everyone's mind. If the *Galena*'s plates proved to be too thin, "so much the worse for the plates."[7] Smith wrote to Whitney the same day of his decision "not to increase the cost of your vessel [the *Keokuk*] by making the proposed addition to her length, or by putting one inch more of plating on her turrets."[8] Both of these ironclads would attempt to run gauntlets and suffer brutally. The *Galena* finally ascended the James as far as Drewry's Bluff on May 15, 1862, with the *Monitor* and three wooden escorts. There, plunging fire from Fort Darling tore holes through the *Galena*'s armor. Well before the repulse, Rodgers wrote, "I do not think [the *Galena*] fully comes up to the idea of an iron plated craft," though she was unarguably safer than most others. "One is apt to fancy that fighting in a perfect iron plated vessel is to be without risk," he reflected, "which is simply an absurdity."[9]

In response to Welles's request for assistance in nearly every aspect associated with Union turret ironclads, coastal or (Western) river—and at the lowest possible price—Ericsson wrote, "There cannot be the slightest objection to your ordering copies to be made and distributed of the plans and specifications which I have presented to the Department. No change whatever has been contemplated on my part for those plans and specifications."[10] If ever there was a chance for the Swedish-American inventor-engineer to "make a killing," this was it. Yet Ericsson seems to have been much more interested in fame than fortune. It was more important to him that he be proved—rather than paid—right in the face of years of official rejection and what he regarded as professional prejudice. The unforeseen circumstances of the American Civil War had completely changed the nature of this relationship, placing the "Individual" over the "System," and the Navy rather at the mercy of a civilian inventor, let alone an engineer. Consequently, magnanimity, if not patriotism, to the American Union was probably worth more to John Ericsson at this moment in his life than mere royalties.[11] When Stimers responded to Fox's concerns of May 23, he had to agree "about the importance of <u>time</u> in getting out new vessels." No one else could promise—and deliver—ironclads meeting so many of the Union's urgent requirements than Captain Ericsson. Furthermore, Stimers was not above admitting he found Ericsson's "new plans so superior to any thing I had expected, that it appears to me it will be better for the Government to depend mainly on him for some time to come, at least until the subject is fully and satisfactorily developed." The two navy professionals, one an engineer, the other a leading voice in the Department, recognized how to handle the nineteenth century's quintessential irascible genius. As Stimers wrote:

> I think now that our best course is to permit him to take the lead and then influence him by such kindly, respectful treatment that we shall retain his friendship and consequently his services. I suppose, that this course will enable him to make a fortune, but I am satisfied that every intelligent man in the country would be glad to hear that such was the case. As for myself I think the country would be disgraced if it permitted

him to remain poor. Just look at it! England had a thousand Ships of war, we had a hundred, Ericsson has made our effective Navy equal to that of England—the greatest in the world! If he had been an Englishman and had benefited England as he has us they would have knighted him and voted him at least two hundred thousand pounds sterling.

He is quite sensitive about professional matters and I perceive that if we went on and built upon my specifications he would consider that it was because the Government thought me superior to him in his own invention and he would do no more for us than to complete his present contracts, leaving us to go back ward again, as we did twenty years ago, when the Navy Department would not even copy him. In this way we shall have to put up with some things we don't like, some things that we consider inferior, but as a whole, we shall do much better, have much better vessels and get them out quicker than if we looked upon him as we ordinarily do on contractors. For myself, I am willing to forego the reputation it would give me to have superior vessels built after my plans and specifications, rather than the Government shall lose his great genius, skill and experience at this critical time.[12]

Ericsson wrote to Fox shortly afterward that Stimers's (and thus also Newton's) proposed modifications for the *Monitor* were "head, body and tail the same and yet a different animal." Struggling to be accommodating, Ericsson found them "so utterly defective that I cannot without serious injury to my excellent friend report to the Department as I intended. To speak the truth there is not a redeeming feature in the whole production." Stimers would be better employed, Ericsson advised, superintending the construction of his new monitors and staying out of the design business.[13] Fox could avoid hurting Stimers's feelings because it was obviously impossible to both superintend construction and design. Even Ericsson could not successfully cope with that burden for long. If, however, the Department wanted a "candid report without fear or favor" to be made, Ericsson would do it, though he could not refrain from adding, with a touch of threat, "It was a great breach of professional courtesy in Mr. Stimers to put forth plans under my invention":

It may well be asked if the inventor is incompetent since the matter is taken out of his hands. I should like to administer a little caution to my young friend, but I do not wish to hurt him and therefore request of you to adopt some course that will prevent the necessity of my making a formal report as it will, if made, contain an utter condemnation of the plan and reflect great discredit on the progenitor.

If the Assistant Secretary wanted "four more similar vessels of 12 mile speed," Ericsson was "ready to take the matter in hand"—as opposed to continuing with the design of the much larger, faster, oceangoing monitor. Already he suspected that "Captain Dahlgren hesitates about the 20 inch gun."[14] In Ericsson's opinion it would be much better to push the existing technology to its limit—quality over quantity. Yet "the construction of the larger swift vessel will require full four times more labor in point of planning than the four smaller vessels. Would it not be better to have the latter than the former? Then as to time, the big Ship requires twice that of the smaller craft."[15]

The prospect of humbling England was also an irresistible part of the bargain, and that, too, probably drove Ericsson to dictate ironclad policy "for free" during this crucial interval rather than demand his fair share of the actual price of an ironclad navy predominantly of his design. Besides, Ericsson was still pressing Fox and Welles for a squadron of huge oceangoing monitors, and Fox clearly shared this preference, which Ericsson wrote "came just in time to give proper direction to my labors":

> Armstrong's last boast also stimulates to exertions in the same direction. The national contest for supremacy is now inaugurated. Sir William may do his best, but we will make floating targets which he cannot demolish, and guns that will sink any thing that his country has yet out to sea.[16]

Fox's timely reassurance that the biggest possible monitors and guns were still in favor ironed out other remaining wrinkles with Ericsson. Although he might "question the propriety" of parting with the plans of the *Passaic* class as a diplomatic gift to Russia, Ericsson was willing to recognize that the ancient enemy of his native Sweden was currently the only apparent friend of his adopted home, the United States. Stimers also could be safely left "working out the arrangements for officers, crew, stores, ammunition, &c. of the Impregnables." The young naval engineer, Ericsson wrote, "knows all about the wants of a vessel of war. I therefore cheerfully defer to his judgment and feel greatly obliged to him for his efficient assistance."[17]

Generosity with his designs and patents now could mean greater opportunities for Ericsson in the near future. Over 120 engines were already in demand, "counting upwards of 10,000 written dimensions" for which he was preparing to charge 5 percent. But "if you deem this too high," Ericsson informed Welles, "I beg that you will fix a lower rate." He would not charge for the use of the specifications he supplied. All he asked was compensation for the "actual cost of preparing the plans.

"In the mean time any contractor who presents . . . me a contract duly ratified by the Department will at once be supplied with plans and full instructions."[18] Given that Commodore Smith was pushing the Secretary for an armament upgrade of 9-inch to 11-inch Dahlgrens for the broadsides of the *New Ironsides*—and was himself dependent on Ericsson for the carriage and slide designs to make it possible—this might have added to Ericsson's extraordinary influence at this time.[19] These were solid, practical factors affecting Union naval policy rather than matters of "public hysteria" or "monitor fever" following the battle of Hampton Roads.

Welles himself gently pushed for more. Could not Ericsson have the new monitor specifications photographed for faster distribution to contractors nationwide? Was it possible to increase the monitors' speed? Ericsson replied that using photography was, surprisingly, not practical. "The plans I furnish are of that accurate and detailed character that they may at once be put into the engineer's hand. Engineers well know that obtaining such plans is in the present case equal to putting the work six months ahead." The speed of the Federal ironclads was a relative affair—and this, of course, meant their superiority to "the average rate of European war vessels." Because of the Union's overriding need to operate along its own coast, with ironclads therefore of comparatively light tonnage, Ericsson assured the Secretary of the Navy that "we are building exactly what we most need." The new monitors' finer lines combined with a more moderate length would "admit of very rapid evolutions," while the "large class (the *Warrior* class) and the steam rams" could not "affect anything against our small turret vessels." In close combat it was better to turn quickly, to "present our stems to assailants," while the monitors were well designed to act as rams as well. A vessel that tried to ram a monitor would do more damage to itself. Ericsson was adamant with respect to both the suitability of his ironclads and their purpose. "You will find on careful examination that there are no vessels yet produced in Europe that could sustain an encounter with the fleet of turret vessels now building under your orders."[20]

Even on the discussion of laminated armor plating, Ericsson was confident. Fox had conversed with several witnesses of British target tests, and "not one was to be found who entertained any doubt as to the superiority of solid plate. The subject is considered to be disposed of."[21] Yet to Welles two days later, Ericsson observed that "Sir William Armstrong has just proved practically what theory long since pointed out . . . that if the shot moves with sufficient velocity, it will readily pass through the rigid thick plate." The solution, he wrote, was "not an unyielding substance" that brought "the whole momentum to bear on the plate at the instant of contact—we want a yielding structure that checks the force of the shot by degrees." Numerous convex plates, he assured the Secretary, "offer just the kind of gradual resistance or yielding which will exhaust the force of impact and entirely prevent penetration. We can well afford to go out of a naval conflict marked with numerous unsightly indentations (honorable scars) provided we succeed in keeping the balls out." British tests had crucially been conducted on vertical targets only; "a convex turret target is quite a different structure."[22] There was more at issue than just the overall structure of the target itself. The fastening bolts for the plates were prone to snap if the shock of impact was not better absorbed, while the joints between plates were their most vulnerable point. Hence, when Ericsson wrote to Fox a month later on the subject, he was willing to admit that "one 3 inch plate is fully equal to five 1 inch plates." Moreover, "but for our ability readily to float the great number, not to mention our inability to obtain thick plates," Ericsson "never would have employed the thin plates." Yet "two thicknesses of 1 inch plates, placed under the thick side armor plates" he would "always recommend, to give support under the joints of the latter."[23]

The inventor-engineer was more specific in his essay on "Impregnable Armor," dated Jan. 18, 1863. "The enormous dynamic force lodged in the shot, compared with the inadequate cohesive force of the metal at the place struck, together with the incompressible nature of the material, furnishes a ready explanation of the cause of the fractures which have resulted from heavy charges of powder at short range with the solid English target." Ericsson had deduced that "applying a laminated protection" would "exhaust the <u>vis viva</u> of the shot by degrees before reaching the solid core intended as the real armor."[24]

At any rate, Dahlgren brought his scholarly experience to bear on the subject by pointing out discrepancies in the British reports, which suggested rolled (as opposed to hammered) iron plates still suffered from inferior welds. This was only "to bring to the attention of the Navy Department that the British Experience must be taken with large qualifications":

> Throughout their whole course of several years, there appears a total want of proper direction or what Captain Halsted terms "true experiment." And yet the authorities do not seem to have noticed this defect, but to have followed the last result implicitly.
>
> As a necessary consequence there has been the greatest irregularity in the Government proceedings, and sometimes direct contradictions.
>
> Some persons have supposed this to be premeditated in order to deceive, which is entirely unwarranted when we consider that millions of dollars have been expended by England in constructing ships upon the same plan as that which has so recently been demonstrated to be insufficient by their last trial.[25]

Scientific American, for its part, wanted as much detail of U.S. target tests published. "We shall then soon display a bold and threatening front which will do more toward averting foreign intervention than all the diplomatic double-dealing of both hemispheres combined."[26] Nor was it difficult in the spring of 1862 for Northerners to imagine a war with England. Rodgers wrote to his wife of an "English captain [who] was on board" the *Galena:*

> I thought his feelings were on the other side. This may have been fancy but is possibly to be expected that they should be with the Rebels. The Rebels are <u>the weaker</u> and the unfortunate. The English bear us no particularly good will and look at our horrid war as at a bull fight not caring particularly whether the man or the bull gets the fatal blow.[27]

Responding to a Congressional inquiry over the British Consul at Charleston's report to London that "armed troop ships of the Confederate States carrying munitions of war have been allowed to go in and out of Charleston and no attempt made to stop them," Welles could only express his "surprise . . . under the difficulties and embarrassments of the service," including "the contrivances and assistance rendered by certain foreign agents," that "the violations have not been vastly more numerous."[28] A petition made to Congress shortly afterward, for the enlargement of the Illinois and Michigan Canal, stated it was "not extravagant to assert that, if the proposed work were accomplished, no attempt would be made to wrest control of the Great Lakes from our National Government." If not, "A long line of flourishing cities and villages" could be "laid under contribution or be destroyed, while a commerce, exceeding in value the foreign trade of the Nation, is either suspended or falls prey to our ambitious rival."[29] A subsequent report on the "Enlargement of the Locks of the Erie and Oswego Canals," made by Francis P. Blair Jr. of the Committee on Military Affairs, agreed that Great Britain was an imminent threat, quoting the London *Times* at the height of the *Trent* crisis.[30]

Dealing with this potential threat, however, was still "a difficult and delicate task," Smith privately relayed to Welles on May 10, "to decide between the plans submitted, varying as they do in model and general character." Furthermore, "much delay" was experienced because of "the constant and indispensable office duties of the Bureau Members of the [Ironclad] Board." Smith, in his role as Chairman, expressed his own "opinion that vessels or Floating Batteries for harbor and coast defense, should first claim attention to protect our Ports from foreign or rebel aggression. . . ." Most of the money appropriated by Congress for more ironclads should be allocated for this particular class and the rest invested in two large oceangoing types—one wooden hulled, the other iron hulled—for experimental purposes. On the other hand, Smith was not convinced that turret ships should fully dominate the Union's ironclad program. "For obvious reasons," he maintained, "case-mated batteries affording more guns for broadside action than turrets, should also be tested." Monitors were "no doubt efficient for harbor defense," but in his estimation they were "not the safest or of the most approved plans for Ocean or coast-service." He offered as proof the original *Monitor's* stormy passage to Hampton Roads. It was therefore disturbing to him that the other Board members had disregarded their full responsibility "of expressing an opinion upon each case presented for consideration," and had in fact recommended "the adoption of but one of the plans presented, and that is nearly identical in form and appointments with the plan prepared and advertised for by the Bureau of Construction &c, except that the material of the vessel is to be of iron." The Commodore also promised his comments in the forthcoming report on the various proposals would be brief, finding it irresistible to add that they "should not, perhaps, be entitled to the weight due those expressed by other members of the Board who are presumed to be experts in the matters treated of."

Consequently, the Ironclad Board's report three days later was again prepared to call out Ericsson's low-freeboard, single-turret, single-screw, laminated turret ship ideal against the design of the Bureau of Ship Construction & Repair, "the thick plated iron-clad wooden vessel of the usual form, with two revolving towers, and two propellers, of which the complete printed specifications of hull, plating, towers and machinery, accompanied by photographic working drawings— prepared by order of the Department—have been for long time widely circulated." There was more than a hint of resentment present. All of the submissions seemed mere modifications, the Board stated, of these two types, which "seem thus far to cover the entire field on this subject and . . . whatever may originally have been a matter of opinion as to relative merits an actual experiment with the *Monitor* has given a result satisfactory to the Department." No one had solved the problem of combining the best qualities of an ironclad with those of a cruiser. Wooden steamships would "still be found useful, especially in times of general peace for the protection of commerce in distant seas, and for war purposes against half civilized or barbarian nations, and others not having the means of obtaining armored vessels." It might therefore "be sound economy" to follow the British example and apply iron plating to some of the larger steam frigates, which alone could "carry iron plates of the thickness required to resist the artillery now in use." The Department's experimental refitting of the *Roanoke* would "determine the question of the practicability and economy of the conversion of vessels of this class." If the *Roanoke* proved a success, the Navy might invest more of its resources into wooden-hulled, sea-going conversions, but seasoned white oak and yellow pine were in short supply, both for the government and for private industry. To avoid the wastes associated with building warships with green timber, only iron-hulled ventures ought to be considered in the future: "Only the most pressing necessity can justify constructions from such materials, and in the event of less time being required." Laminated armor plate schemes were also to be considered "a make shift justified by the impossibility of obtaining solid plates in the time allowed." What the Board was looking for was an iron-hulled, twin-screwed, double-turreted ironclad, with "rudder, screws, and anchor . . . protected by overhanging portions of the hull, the deck of which need not exceed two feet above the water level": a monitor. Of all the proposals recently submitted, that of G. W. Quintard's Morgan Iron Works of New York City best met these preferred qualities.[31] This would become the U.S. Navy's first twin-turret monitor ironclad, the *Onondaga.*[32]

Perhaps most important, the Ironclad Board was determined not to forfeit all control over Union ironclad policy and construction to private inventors and firms. The Department would begin designing a new class of double-turreted monitor-type ironclads for harbor defense that would "best suit its purposes."[33] Relying upon departmental plans—and control over "distribution of resources" among other factors—would ensure greater uniformity in designs to various contractors, avoid confusion, and keep down costs.[34] Furthermore, the Board was averse to any designs for oceangoing ironclads. "The cost of such vessels is so enormous, and the interests to be confided to their protection are so great that the most mature consideration should precede the adoption of any design or system of construction." Though this in itself implied an experimental process that could take years, similar perhaps to great efforts under way in Europe, the "most judicious course" for the Union ironclad program would be "for the Department to have plans and specifications prepared by a Board of Naval Officers, with which might be associated, if the Department deems necessary, other persons of reputation and experience in the building of iron vessels, and upon such plans and specifications advantageous offers to construct will be proposed by contractors in competition on equal terms."[35] Ericsson's role would thus become that of an "associate"—possibly, but unlikely. Though the Navy had no experience building iron ships, it should now assume direct command of the Department's design and lease their construction at its own professional discretion. But, of course, terms like "professional" and "Navy" really meant individuals—in this case, Lenthall and Isherwood, who would replace Ericsson's influence over Fox and Welles with their own: the old war.

Finally, the members of the Ironclad Board expressed their "doubt as to the efficiency of these or any small vessel for the defense of harbors, as it is obvious they could not prevent the entrance of a large sea going iron plated steamer." This was a flat contradiction to Ericsson's motives behind the *Monitor* and, especially, her successors. To the Board, however, ironclads like the *Warrior* "need not reply to the fire of the harbor vessel, but could receive it with impunity and retire unharmed after accomplishing the destruction of all the wooden vessels and land property within its reach." This statement might have assumed a relative stalemate between ordnance and armor, as occurred between the *Monitor* and the *Virginia* at Hampton Roads; assumptions similar to those opposing Coles's harbor defense cupola vessels in Britain. But the *Monitor* had prevented the destruction of further wooden vessels against the *Virginia*, a more fully armored and less vulnerable opponent than the *Warrior*.[36] Nevertheless, the Board stated, with at least some degree of foresight, "The successful defense of harbors will, probably, consist in a combination of forts with a temporary obstruction in the channel commanded by their guns and removable at will."[37]

At the same time, Ericsson and Dahlgren continued to wrangle over the heavy guns for the new proposed monitors. Without the heaviest possible ironclad-killing armament, the oceangoing monitors would be useless. Ericsson pushed Welles, through Stimers and Fox, in an effort to gain as much as possible before the momentum from his success with the *Monitor* was lost.[38] When that occurred, it seemed, so would the last, best chance for any more leaps forward in warship and ordnance design. Dahlgren, for his part, resisted, preferring to initiate a whole series of American target tests that would free professional and public opinion from the influence of British experiments—as well as potentially demonstrate that his existing 11-inch guns were sufficient for winning the war.[39] Simply enlarging smoothbores and the monitor turrets (with their laminated plates) to accommodate them was a hasty expedient. Truly establishing American superiority over British practices would require more time, money, and patient deliberation than circumstances—or Fox and Ericsson—allowed; this was a pressure Dahlgren resented.[40] After all, whose authority was going to influence the major decisions regarding the Navy's ordnance, if not ironclad warships—his or Ericsson's?

This issue became manifest with Ericsson's surprising answer to Dahlgren's reservations: "I am glad that the Ordnance Department at last admits that the gun which has required so long a time to plan is a mere experiment." He also wrote to Fox:

> This candid confession now authorizes me to step forward with an offer to build the guns as well as the vessel. With your permission I will relieve you of all responsibility and make the guns under guaranty [*sic*]. I will however change the material and give you wrought iron pieces. Sir William Armstrong has just shown what the writer demonstrated

twenty years ago, viz: that wrought iron may be so combined as to produce the most reliable material for ordnance.

The subject is a mere engineering question that can be best settled by
those who know most about iron.[41]

Dahlgren's role could thus be completely eliminated. Ericsson's
dexterous maneuver also implied that another Navy Bureau would be
bypassed in the process of constructing ironclads. The Bureau of Ship
Construction & Repair would not design or build them; private
contractors would. The Bureau of Yards & Docks would not supervise
their construction; their designer would have the final say. Nor would
the Bureau of Ordnance be responsible for designing or building their
armaments.[42] It was consolidation of power in the hands of the private
shipbuilding industry, under John Ericsson's direction. But could Fox
and Welles maintain their direction of Ericsson? Could they afford not
to? The following day, May 15, Fox wrote to Harwood, assuring him
the Department appreciated the "difficulties which the Bureau of
Ordnance is called upon to surmount in the fabrication of guns of
enormous caliber." But the duel between the *Monitor* and the *Virginia*
demonstrated the inadequacy of the Navy's existing guns to combat
ironclads. Dahlgren's insistence that his smoothbores could not—or
should not—be fired with greater charges only meant that "we are
called upon to produce larger calibers and a great initial velocity." The
question was then whether the cast-iron guns of Rodman, or
Dahlgren's design and manufacture could be used. Perhaps testing a
20-inch prototype would be in order. At stake was nothing less than
the survival of the Union against rival foreign technologies:

> The United States Naval Ordnance has to its very great credit, led all
> nations in the perfection of its smooth bore guns. It devolves upon it to
> keep pace, and lead, if possible, in the production of smooth bore and
> rifled guns of such calibers and velocities as shall be irresistible against
> anything possible to construct which will cross the ocean.[43]

"Most everybody doubt [*sic*] the strength of such large masses of cast
iron to resist the tremendous discharge which the new condition of
things impose," Fox meanwhile admitted to Ericsson: "I think we shall
have to come to hooped guns—not a single shot of the *Monitor* penetrated the *Merrimac*—of this I have the most positive information."[44]

The tide had definitely turned against the 20-inch smoothbore, but
the 15-inch was left intact, probably because of the simple existence of
at least one working model—as with the original *Monitor* herself.
Even Ericsson was astonished at Dahlgren's 20-inch specifications,
"64 inches in diameter!"[45] He was willing to "demonstrate that such
a mass of metal will be so much compressed by the internal force

under heavy charges as inevitably to cause fissures in the chamber and hence bursting."

At least the plans for the oceangoing monitor were ready, to be sent to the Department within days "with a definite offer to construct Ship and guns forthwith." Ericsson reminded Fox that "what we are undertaking is vast and ahead of any thing else in the world—Guns consuming 75 lbs. of powder as a regular charge, a wrought iron Turret 24 inches thick, Side armor 10 inches thick (above water), Pistons 100 inches in diameter moving at the rate of 560 feet per minute, means by which 1000 tons of coal may be consumed without changing the draught of water a single inch and sundry other properties. . . ." All this power and advancement would not come cheap. In order not to scare Fox "by stating the sum in dollars," Ericsson would give it in English pounds-sterling. This would also enable the Assistant Secretary to "compare the figure with English prices for Iron Clad ships": £230,000 (or roughly $1,150,000).[46]

Stimers himself thought Fox's choice of Ericsson's "great ocean steamer" over "Harbor defense vessels to go twelve knots an hour" a mistake—until he saw Ericsson's finished, though preliminary, specifications. "That vessel will astonish the world fully as much as the *Monitor* did," he wrote to Fox. Again, Ericsson's sublime ambitions combined with his very obvious ability to carry them out converted another skeptical disbeliever, even one as closely affiliated as Stimers. "Now if we can build this vessel and send her to sea without having any description of her published and let her make her first appearance in an English port, it would absolutely frighten them, with no boasting account having preceded her, to have a Yankee ship come right into their port, which the merest inspection would show was impregnable to Sir William Armstrong's experimental achievements; would do more to keep Mr. Bull on his good behavior toward us than any one thing it is possible to do."[47] Ericsson, Fox, and Stimers constituted a triumvirate, with the usurpation of British naval power its stated goal.

But would Gideon Welles join in, too? Ericsson's cursory designs were for a par deluxe monitor with a single, 30-foot–outside diameter turret, which he promised to build for the Secretary "within nine months from the date of receiving your orders to proceed, for . . . $1,150,000." It would be the fastest war vessel afloat. Side armor would consist of six layers of 1-inch iron plate, backed by 4½-inch–thick iron stringers and 3 feet 9 inches of wood. The turret itself would consist of 10-inch–deep rolled-iron bars sandwiched between layers of 1-inch plates, making a total thickness of 24 inches. As a result, "the balls from the powerful new Armstrong gun will prove harmless against this impenetrable mass of wrought iron." The description of guns,

CHRISTOPHER / RONALD MR
PREMIER
UA 0306219193289

UA 411   APR 25
FROM   CHARLOTTE
TO   CHICAGO/OHARE

GATE   A4
DEPARTS AT   5:04 PM

GIVE FEEDBACK - WWW.UALSURVEY.COM

SEAT 23E

.: CABIN
.6 2106902962 C.P

Earn **20,000** Bonus Miles after first purchase.

First year free.

VISA

CHASE

4417 1234 5678 9112

MEMBER SINCE

MileagePlus

however, was ambiguous. They would not be 20-inch Dahlgrens but "constructed of wrought iron" and "warranted to stand twice the charge and carry three times the weight of ball compared with the boasted English gun."[48] Even as a ram, "she will be far more formidable than anything that Europe has yet produced." Ericsson calculated that moving his monitor at 17 knots would inflict a staggering 32 million pounds of force "acting through a space of one foot"—and pointed, significantly, across the Atlantic.[49] Despite the fantastical qualities of Ericsson's proposed super-monitor, one thing was certain: this was high-pressure salesmanship at work.

Yet Fox could guarantee Ericsson only that his plan would be "immediately considered." He wrote, "It seems a powerful vessel, worthy of your brains." The Assistant Secretary wanted four, perhaps for a round million dollars per ship. Did Ericsson believe they could be built simultaneously, "two at New York, one at Boston, and one at Philadelphia"? Regardless, Fox would now officially cancel the order for the over-large, cast-iron 20-inch gun.[50] Remarkably, on the same day (May 21), Commodore Smith expressed to Welles his whole-hearted disapproval of a rival proposal for an oceangoing turret ship, mounting 20-inch guns, from "Messrs. Pervil and Howes." The turrets were too large, "and the 20 inch guns too big for working at sea, even if they can be made, which, under the present system of casting, I consider impracticable," Welles said. Laminated armor he also objected to, and the "gun deck will be too near the water, it should be at least six feet above the line of flotation." This assessment did not bode well for Ericsson's own version, which Welles on the same day instructed Smith, John Lenthall, and Benjamin Isherwood to evaluate.[51] Worse still, Ericsson responded to Fox's inquiries that the cost of his super-monitor was simply beyond negotiation, given practical engineering requirements. Building four would not decrease their price (or completion time) but possibly the opposite, given the competition over limited labor and resources.[52] Perhaps not surprisingly, Fox informed prominent Boston shipbuilder Robert B. Forbes soon afterward that the Department had "given out about a dozen harbor defense craft" and needed "a class of vessels to go out and meet the enemy, not to receive him in our harbors." To date, Fox was still fishing around and open to suggestions. "We have not a single proposition for a cruising vessel and most of the sea steamers proposed must probably hover on the coast."[53]

As could also be expected, Smith's first impression of Ericsson's new monitor ironclad was not favorable. To the Bureau Chief it was nothing more than a proportionately larger version of the original, obviously therefore "well adapted for harbor defense, but not calculated for Ocean service." As such, many of the objections he made of the original were revived, especially the upper hull overhang. For harbors would it not be better to construct for the same price "three batteries," "each bearing guns and iron armature equal to this, though with less speed"? Yet, the Commodore noted to Welles, "We have already under contract ten vessel of the class of the *Monitor* of increased size and dimensions, besides nine others with the *Monitor* Turret for river service." Smith also objected to relying upon new ordnance without a lengthy and meticulous series of tests.[54] The entire principle, in fact, of a sea-going monitor was incongruous to the same U.S. naval professional who supervised the already historic *Monitor's* construction.[55]

Lenthall and Isherwood, meanwhile, cast doubt on Ericsson's calculations over speed. Fox grew worried. "As we sacrifice every thing for speed this is of the most vital importance":

> The old *Monitor* can only be called a six knot boat, and the new ones have the same engine but more boiler, which will give them about 8 knots. I opposed this but gave way. I wished 12 knots, and now will never consent to the large vessels unless our engineers will say that the speed will be 15 knots per hour.[56]

On the same day, Ericsson anticipated other potential objections by writing Fox of his willingness to employ solid 4½-inch hammered, or forged, plates. "Some six months ago I advised certain iron works in Massachusetts to turn their attention to producing hammered plate for armor." Now he had a sample of one of their 6-foot slabs bent 27 inches by a 1,200-pound hammer without fracture. These he would readily substitute for "the thin rolled plates proposed for the intended large turret ship."[57] He also wrote Smith of his willingness to produce heavy wrought-iron guns for the monitors, if need be. But time would prevent Ericsson from conducting the necessary proofs, in addition to all his other projects, already under contract, the Commodore observed. "The prestige of your name carries great weight throughout the country in matters of invention and science," he added, "& I always yield to you (tho my opinion is of little value in such things) except on the sea qualities of ships." Here, Joseph Smith felt more qualified, as an old seaman, to make a stand. "Your Sea-going turret ship will have great speed but will not, in my opinion, answer the requirements of an Ocean Steamer." Stimers, he could see now, was "completely indoctrinated" by Ericsson's beliefs in the perfect seaworthiness of a watertight, low-freeboard craft. "If we possessed the secret of breathing under water I admit she would be more safe with some modifications," he added sardonically, perhaps revealing his own indoctrination. "We seem to be behind," he wrote as a final touch, "or lag astern of John Bull in the matter of speed."[58]

At this point it seems Ericsson's confidence in the full acceptance of his ideas wavered. "I learn, not without regret," he wrote to Fox, "that my plans of the large turret ship are being 'thoroughly examined and will be reported upon.'" These were "but a <u>sketch</u> intended as a basis for a contract." Whatever the "Engineer in Chief" (his Bureau Chief rival Benjamin Isherwood) might report, Ericsson assumed he could "consider it as an instruction conveying the wishes of the Department rather than a criticism on my plan and proposition." If the Department wanted more details he could easily supply them. First, were they intrigued by the ship's *potential?* Did they trust Ericsson, as they finally did in the autumn of 1861 with the original *Monitor?* Did they trust him any more, or less, since the battle of Hampton Roads?

Already he was willing to give in on the idea of twin turrets "for two of the proposed four vessels," as much as "the ship can sustain." Smaller guns and improved armor-plate manufacture might indeed facilitate such an option. For less than $100,000 Ericsson was willing to provide the former, of 15- or 16-inch caliber, promising they would "mark an era in the history of artillery and naval warfare." Concerning Isherwood's preliminary memo on the super-monitor's speed, however (which Fox had forwarded), Ericsson could not "refrain from recording [his] dissent."[59] Stimers's own calculations tended to favor Ericsson's. All other mechanical and structural factors for the proposed vessel being fixed, the grate surface of the boilers was, in the Chief Engineer's experience, where "the shoe always pinches when we are trying to make our ship go fast and I find in this instance that [Ericsson] has been (as engineers usually are) more liberal with his engine power than he has in the extent of his fire." Furthermore, while "no one admires the talents of Isherwood more than I do," Stimers ventured his opinion to Fox, "if you will examine his professional writings during the past twelve years, you will perceive that for some reason he is greatly prejudiced against Ericsson. Commodore Smith will tell you the speed he predicted for the *Monitor.*"[60]

The Assistant Secretary in turn could only relay to Ericsson, "If you and Isherwood differ with regard to the grate surface, other engineers had better look over the figures. All I ask is to be convinced that 16 knots can be obtained the first day." There was no need for his prize inventor to take alarm. "Whatever responsibility attaches to the recommendation of the plan I assume." Double-checking Ericsson's figures, rough as they were, was "of course very necessary before making the large contract that I desire."[61] Concessions worked both ways, for Ericsson could not refuse to consider the thicker hull plate, more solid-plated turret armor, and different boilers that Fox (and Stimers) desired if he wanted the "large contract," too.[62] Whether this sort of compromise was best was another matter; giving ground to get approval,

Ericsson might critically disfigure his original specifications with outside suggestions and modifications that were better than his own in some cases, worse in others. In any case, Stimers tried to reassure his mentor: "You will not be interfered with in your arrangements. The Secretary and Mr. Fox have the greatest confidence in your skill and uprightness. . . . " But Ericsson had to keep in mind the extraordinary demands he was placing on them, for Stimers considered "they take as much responsibility as could be expected from them when they decide in favor of your plans *in direct opposition* to the views of the Bureau officers."[63]

This opposition arrived the following day in the form of Lenthall and Isherwood's report to Welles on Ericsson's oceangoing monitor proposal—a referendum on who should direct the Union's ironclad program. According to their calculations, Ericsson's ship would draw 19 feet 5 inches, with 2 feet 7 inches above the waterline amidships and her extremities only "just awash." Perhaps more damaging, the Bureau chiefs estimated the ship's material value at $883,000, "which by adding five (5) per centum for omissions" became $927,000—over $220,000 less than Ericsson's asking price. Comparing the dimensions of the proposed ironclad with other (commercial) vessels, and her engines and boilers, "under the most favorable conditions and for short periods a maximum speed of 13¾ knots per hour may be attained." Burning 158 tons of coal every 25 hours, such a monitor could carry only enough fuel "sufficient for 6⅓ days consumption," hardly making her an oceanic steamer. The upper hull overhang inhibited greater speed and distance (though how they were able to make such a determination, especially if "based on the performance of coppered vessels of the usual form," is not mentioned). Consequently, her draft prohibited her use for efficient harbor, if not coast, defense, while the vessel had no masts and sails, relying upon engines that could offer little speed or strategic range.[64] Ericsson's super-monitor was all but worthless. This also said little for her actual seaworthiness, which Lenthall and Isherwood regarded "under all conditions of weather is extremely problematical: the small height of her deck above the water and the form and position of her projecting hips are opposed to the requirements of an efficient sea going vessel, if the past experience of most Seamen can be applied to vessels of this kind."

Perhaps that was the point. Ericsson's naval and maritime technology was so radical that few, if anyone, could properly assess its likelihood of success. Truly, the Swedish-American inventor-engineer was taking the Union Navy off into uncharted waters. Ericsson's assertions that low freeboard did not necessarily imply a lack of seaworthiness could be counterbalanced by Lenthall and Isherwood's equally convincing arguments that semi-submersion acted as a drag upon the projected speed of monitors at sea. Furthermore, it seemed logical that "rafts" were more vulnerable to ramming than higher-freeboard warships; and who could say whether turret guns could be operated in open seas? Ericsson's recent conceded preference for thicker plates for the side hull armor only coincided "with the views we have given on this subject on several occasions."[65] What did this imply with regard to Ericsson's credibility?

In a draft of a letter to Fox dated June 11, 1862, Ericsson stated his intention to "meet your wishes" to "greatly reduce the proportion of the armor timbers at the bow, in other regards, the length of the ram." Apparently this alteration "came just in time—to a day almost." The "manner in which the said overhang is now being secured is such that the entire weight of the ship would not have power enough to endanger the security of the junction." In other words, the super-monitor would not feature an overhang at the bow.[66] Fox also wanted Ericsson to "try and make the bottom of the big ships 1/16 [13/16 inch in thickness] and the frames in proportion, and the grate and heating surface as expressed in my note." These modifications, too, would radically affect the ironclad's weight, but Fox still encouraged Ericsson to write "an official letter to the Secretary of the Navy proposing to build four vessels of the speed of 16 knots and according to other points herein talked of. Two of one turret each, and two of two turrets each. . . . The Secretary will answer your proposition at once."[67] It was not exactly what Ericsson wanted, but Fox would continue to allow him to argue his case to Welles, in direct opposition to the Bureau chiefs. Assuming Ericsson was willing to bend to his (and to some extent, the Bureau chiefs') wishes, the Assistant Secretary would also continue to personally advocate Ericsson's plans. This way Ericsson would get his contracts, and the Department would get more of the *type* of ironclad it preferred.

Here, however, Chief Engineer Stimers played the middleman, assuring Fox that "Capt. Ericsson appears to be willing to comply with our wishes with regard to putting in the 1000 square feet of grate surface to the <u>Monitor Cruisers</u> and to add to the thickness of the bottom." In the process, Stimers would attempt to insert changes of his own (such as angle-ironed floor plates and double riveting of all the seams), yet with a touch of complaint because the Master's specifications "ought also to describe more fully than they do—the beams supporting the Berth deck, the Berth deck itself, the thickness of iron in boilers, number and size of stays, etc." The power to make changes was the power of personal influences, skillfully managed by a third party:

These specifications furnish a guide to the superintending engineers who labor in the dark when they are not sufficiently explicit. He is a little jealous of my interference in any such matters which could be construed by his sensitive mind into defects but he fully appreciates the boldness of the stand you have taken in favor of this class of vessels and is very anxious to relieve you from as much cavil on the part of those who are opposed it as he possibly can, a request from you therefore that he would introduce the foregoing into his specifications would be all sufficient without argument.[68]

Though Ericsson remonstrated against using iron deck beams rather than wood, which he felt added to the deck- and side-armor's resisting powers,[69] nevertheless, on June 16 he sent to Welles a list of modifications to his original proposal "for building Iron Clad Ships of War" of the previous month, taking into account the "requirements in certain particulars" of the various naval professionals. These "particulars" included especially the preference for twin turrets, which would involve lengthening the ships. High speed would be attained "without resorting to excessive blast, the boilers of each ship [being] made of such capacity as to present one thousand square feet of grate surface and thirty thousand feet of heating surface." The wrought-iron framework of the engines and the hull itself would all be made thicker.[70] Ericsson would generously supply the gun carriages—fortunate, since no one else could tackle the problem of how to handle guns heavier than the 11-inch Dahlgren on board ship—but not the guns because several competitors would be given a chance to submit designs of their own as well. Moreover, the laminated turrets would be "lined on the outside with hammered wrought-iron plates or broad bars of great strength." How thick these would be would depend on the tests conducted by the Ordnance Department.[71] Nine months would be needed for the first single-turret version, 10 for the second, and 12 months each for two with double turrets. Finally, Ericsson had to "respectfully observe that but for the want of plate iron these ships might be constructed in much shorter time."[72]

Two days later Fox wrote to Ericsson, "The [Secretary] has to day decided to let you build two vessels of the big class—one of 1 turret and 1 of two turrets." He was sorry that an entire squadron had not been approved—the original dream—"but if no new plans are presented within a few months," he promised, "it may be considered by him desirable to build two more."[73] Clearly, the Union Navy was not about to go as far as Ericsson wanted. There was still—and likely would always be—enough opposition to prevent a technological overhaul so radical in nature, with such a sweeping professional reliance upon one man. Even the extraordinary and tumultuous circumstances of the American Civil War—especially the overriding threat of war with the British Empire—could not justify giving Ericsson carte blanche.

As Donald Canney notes, it was around this time, therefore, that Welles considered different options from other reputable ship-builders.[74] The navy yards were too "crowded."[75] Though William H. Webb of New York was already building a fully armored, broadside steam frigate for newly nationalized Italy (at a cost of $1,500,000), he was more than willing to offer a design that might better suit the wishes of Commodore Smith, at least.[76] Webb proposed a casemated ram that would operate as a cruiser and make 15 knots. In addition to broadside and pivot 11-inch Dahlgrens, the huge sea-going ironclad would mount two revolving turrets on top of the citadel, each armed with a pair of 15-inch guns. Truly, this would be the champion battle-ship of the U.S. Navy.[77] Though the vessel would be necessarily wooden hulled, its chance of obtaining the high speeds Fox demanded might be provided by the higher freeboard that Smith and the other Bureau Chiefs expected of any cruising ironclad. Its sloping, 60° case-mate and the hull above and just below the waterline would be protected with solid 4½- and 3½-inch plates, respectively—which would also satisfy critics of Ericsson's monitors.[78]

But Ericsson also recognized that the Civil War at least gave him recurring chances to prove himself. If the first two monster-monitors succeeded, followed by an imminent duel with the Royal Navy, the Union would surely call upon him again, and again. Opportunity was sufficient. Hence, far from showing disappointment or resentment, Ericsson wrote to the Assistant Secretary:

> The receipt of your brief note of yesterday is an event in my life. I might say the event—as it conveys the intelligence that you are going to open to me a full, fair field where I can concentrate, in one focus, the result of all the experience gained and knowledge acquired during a long and arduous mechanical career. I will not detain you by complimentary expressions, but simply say all my energies will be exerted to merit, as far as possible, the extraordinary confidence you place in me in relation to your war ships.[79]

One side effect, however, of Ericsson's focus upon his most formida-ble monitor ironclads was the lack of time and attention he could invest in, first, the *Passaic*-class follow-ons to the original *Monitor*—the upcoming third-generation, "harbor and river" monitors of the *Canonicus* class—and, second, the critically needed light-draft monitors, much less any miscellaneous projects and improvements in naval tech-nology that Fox was continually placing before him. Ideally, there would be four or five "John Ericssons" to manage all these responsibilities of varying, and perhaps equal, value. Yet it made sense for the one and only Ericsson to apply himself to the biggest technical challenge that prom-ised the biggest payoffs in terms of both personal and national prestige.

The grandiose magnitude of this objective—maximum concentration of force—all but eclipsed that of subduing the South—though not that of over-powering any future ironclads crudely fashioned by the South. Indeed, wiping out the threat of the converted *Virginia* and her rough-and-ready sisters would be a logical side effect of the investment in monitors that could handle the more formidable ironclads under construction in Europe (rather than vice versa). At any rate, the spring of 1862 saw the Union in an excellent position, it seemed, to end the war within months. New Orleans was captured, Vicksburg was next (thereby completing Union control of the Mississippi River and cutting the South in two), and the Army of the Potomac was closing in on the Confederate capital of Richmond. The events at Hampton Roads, meanwhile, served to give Britain pause, as well as to ensure the survival of the Union blockade. A single Confederate ironclad had suddenly upset the balance of power; a single Union one restored it. Another obvious lesson was the need for singularly heavy guns to smash iron more than wood.

It was this growing obsession for maximum concentration of force—to undo the outcome of the *Trent* crisis—that again favored John Ericsson's schemes over those of the Navy bureaus. Lenthall and Isherwood could only respond that the United States had to confront British naval supremacy on similar terms. Instead of consolidating the technological powers of individual warships, the power of the Federal government itself over national technologies—in iron shipbuilding, armor manufacture, engine production and gun making—should be consolidated to produce a wide-ranging, first-class ironclad Navy second to none. This said little for the actual design of the ironclads themselves, basing their innate superiority more, as was the case with the Royal Navy, upon incremental increases of armor thickness, firepower, and overall numbers of such warships—a supremacy of mass production in the modern Industrial Age between rival national resources, one continental based and the other maritime based.[80] It also ignored the circumstances of the United States at the time, desperately fighting, as it was, for a continental-scale government.

Aside from the pervasive threat of a war with Great Britain, which Ericsson and Fox exploited to the fullest, the enormous popularity of the *Monitor* after her duel with the *Virginia* paradoxically risked the military alienation of her civilian inventor. The press and Congress both proved willing to twist Hampton Roads as a means of challenging the authority of the Navy, if not also the White House, in a variety of competing political agendas. Only the close working relationship and personal trust between

Fox, Ericsson, and Stimers managed to preserve the monitor system, though Ericsson was never able to secure the total faith he expected from others in his radical vision of the Union's ironclad program. Nor was he free to concentrate his own formidable talents and energies upon the lone *Dictator*. Unparalleled personal success brought Ericsson equally unparalleled responsibilities, and these would only intensify as the fortunes of the American Civil War changed yet again.

Chapter 12

British Reactions to Hampton Roads and the "*Monitor* Riddle"

What an ironclad duel might actually involve for the British, following the *Trent* affair at the end of 1861, was demonstrated soon enough, when the Union *Monitor* confronted the Confederate *Virginia* at Hampton Roads on March 9, 1862. More dramatic for British interests, perhaps, was the one-sided engagement between the heavy sloop U.S.S. *Cumberland* and the frigate U.S.S. *Congress* against the *Virginia* the previous day. In a letter to "The Peace Society" (which it frequently ridiculed), *Punch* rejoiced in "imagining the havoc which one *Warrior* would create amongst a whole fleet of timber vessels crowded with invaders," though with ironclads "there really does seem some ground for hoping that, ships being rendered practically invulnerable, any two vessels of war belonging to hostile nations, will, hereafter, meeting on the high seas, each find herself unable to injure the other, and therefore be obliged to part in peace. . . ."[1] The London *Times* likewise commented on the obvious "efficiency of a single iron-cased frigate against any number of wooden vessels," adding, however, "the fact that nine-tenths of the British Navy have been rendered comparatively useless":

> Now, suppose these two vessels had encountered a division of the magnificent fleet under Admiral Milne; what would have been the result? Would our Ariadnes or Orlandos have fared any better than the Cumberland and Congress against an invulnerable enemy? True, they might have availed themselves of their speed and escaped destruction; but if they had chosen, as they, no doubt, would have done, to fight, what would have been the end of the battle?[2]

The *Illustrated London News*, meanwhile, depicted "The Naval Revolution" on its cover page of April 5 with the "Merrimac" spectacularly ramming the *Cumberland*. But whereas the *Times*, in its relentless campaign of anti-U.S. sarcasm, wrote that "the Warrior and her escorts" would have expressed "our naval supremacy . . . as decidedly, though more compendiously than ever" against "turreted Monitors," the *I.L.N.* was "not sure, indeed, that the case is not worse than the *Times* believes":

> Is the Warrior itself a match for the Monitor? It is useless now to talk of speed and magnificence. We don't want our war ships to run away successfully, or to be looked at admiringly, but to fight. How would the Monitor deal with the Warrior? The guns of the first send shot of 170lb.; the guns of the second, shots of 100lb. . . . Again, the Monitor is practically invulnerable to existing artillery: is the Warrior the same?[3]

What should England do? The "Revolution" of Hampton Roads suggested that the Royal Navy's ironclads could indeed prove decisive against an enemy's wooden fleet—whether on the defense or on the attack—but the same applied to British wooden ships constituting the bulk of Britain's naval force in early 1862 against even the hastily built ironclads of a resourceful potential antagonist. An Admiralty memo on the "Royal Navy Classification of Ships," dated March 17, 1862, fine-tuned its definition of sloops and gun-vessels but conspicuously did not mention ironclad warships at all, revealing perhaps the still "experimental" status they carried.[4] News of the American action at Hampton Roads, combined with the growing doubts of exactly how a war against the Northern States could be prosecuted successfully,[5] forced an end to this. Furthermore, the actual type and *character* of ironclads themselves was suddenly a public as well as a professional topic of concern. The radically opposed designs of the Americans, North and South—the slanted-casemate *Virginia* and the raft-like, turreted *Monitor*—could now be contrasted with the concept of a fully rigged armored frigate. The fate of imperial Britain's "national" security and its ability to extend or project its naval power beyond its own coasts was no longer as straightforward or traditional a question as it was against Vera Cruz. Bold new technological challenges required equally bold responses, but which ones?

For the *I.L.N.*, the answer began with treating "Captain Coles as our cousins are treating Captain Ericsson—that is, put the right man into the right place, and give him hearty support when there." Britain was now "entering a race in which success will no longer be achieved by wealth or material resources, under merely ordinary conditions of skilful development," since "men of inventive genius," men of "skill, science and individual energy" were clearly able to devise and produce high-tech weapons systems that might abruptly change the face of naval warfare, and more.[6] Somehow, in little more than three months, the Yankees seemed to have reversed the entire strategic balance enjoyed by Great Britain during the *Trent* affair—stealing a march in ironclad design as well. Uncomfortable about its effects on already strained Anglo-American relations, Russell hoped Palmerston would "stir up the slow and steady Admiralty to some vigour about Iron Ships":

> The French have long been before us and in six months the United States will be far ahead of us unless our builders in the Navy Department exert themselves.
>
> I would willingly pay the additional per centage on assessed taxes which Gladstone suggested if it was to give us at least some acceleration of our iron ship building.
>
> Only think of our position if in case of the Yankees turning upon us they should by means of iron ships they should renew the triumphs they achieved in 1812–13 by means of superior size and weight of metal.[7]

It was therefore obvious to the *I.L.N.* that the expensive land-based fortifications insisted on by Palmerston's government should be temporarily suspended, while existing wooden steam-powered warships should be cut down and refitted as "cupola vessels." In addition to the vulnerability of wooden ships against ironclads, and the shape and function of ironclads themselves, the sensational American ironclad duel thus constituted a third serious challenge to Britain's existing— and proposed—defenses. A timely letter from Coles led the attack on Monday, March 31, in the *Times*. Although the "various experiments upon every sort of iron-clad targets, sections of ships, sections of forts, even old floating batteries, and, lastly, with shields or revolving towers on them" were very judicious and valuable, "the one on the other side of the water that has taken place in the natural course of events is of more value than all" since it solved the question of "how are we in future to protect our harbours from iron marauders and our dockyards from being destroyed?" Some twenty "of our screw and now useless line of battle ships could now be converted into most efficient iron blockships"—coast defense "shield ships" of Coles's design—which he vowed would be much cheaper and constructed more rapidly than forts or *Warrior*-type ironclads, and yet be deadlier against invading (broadside) ironclads than either.[8]

Acceptance of these more radical ironclad concepts exemplified by private inventors like Coles and Ericsson, British and American, tapped into the latent Victorian romantic imagery on both sides of the Atlantic of the "misunderstood genius" or individual hero whose vision alone could save his country from immediate peril—or at least a loss of prestige.[9] "Let it not be said by history, as it has already been suggested in Parliament," the *I.L.N.* concluded, that "it is harder to work a conversion in our Government than among our ships."[10] Any discussion, any debate, over individual classes of ironclads was set to be one over individuals themselves, a war of wills—hence, Ericsson's endless personal struggles against Lenthall and Isherwood of the U.S. Navy Bureaus for commanding influence in the Union's ironclad program, and Coles's even more publicized challenges against Robinson the Controller and Edward Reed the soon-to-be new Chief Constructor of the Royal Navy.

As was to be expected, the anxieties of the British press quickly extended to the Houses of Parliament. The same day Coles's proposed solution to the riddle of the *Monitor's* implications for Imperial Britain was published in the *Times,* Sir Frederic Smith noted in the Commons that the "great question of iron-plated ships against wooden vessels had been brought to an issue," adding "happily, without any action on our part." While he was formerly willing to accept the proposed massive island towers at Spithead, guarding the approaches to Portsmouth (objecting, on the other hand, to the ring of landward-facing forts designed to hold off a besieging army), the recent spectacle of ironclad steamers impervious to even close-range heavy cannon fire changed this. Armored batteries—carrying "both heavier guns and much more impenetrable armour plating than any sea-going vessel"—could run the gauntlet of forts and protect commercial ports and naval dockyards more effectively than fixed defenses. Another member added that "if the *Warrior* had met the *Merrimac*, it was a matter of grave doubt whether the angular-sided vessel would not have overcome her vertical-sided antagonist; but if the *Warrior* and the *Monitor* had met, there was little doubt that the smaller vessel would have plunged her shot into the unprotected parts of the *Warrior*, and would, in fact, have overcome the pride of the British navy."[11]

In response, Sir George Lewis referred to the 1861 Report of the Defence Commission, which concluded that fortifications and floating batteries combined would be the best plan. Was the House therefore prepared to vote for "a Supplementary Estimate of some £10,000,000 or £15,000,000" for the latter? Noting even the Union Army's experimental Rodman guns, Lewis was confident ironclads would ultimately prove vulnerable to ever-heavier ordnance—itself always easier to mount and man on land. In this sense the greater cost associated with forts was still a safer investment to the Government than "to rush into a series of costly changes" associated with naval defenses that technology was more prone to affect adversely.[12] John Bright, however, felt "the man must be particularly stupid who does not see the importance" of the latest events in America. The current question was "whether the batteries which we are about to erect at a vast cost in the neighbourhood of Portsmouth harbour are capable of resting the entrance of iron-plated vessels, such as the *Monitor.*" For the moment no one could say yes, so the construction of such fortifications should be temporarily suspended and public money saved, while his Birmingham constituents, at least, coped with the expected deprivations rising from the blockade of southern cotton. *Punch,* for once, agreed with Bright:

> If Sir George Lewis is going to play the Old Fogy, and resist all improve-
> ments, the sooner he retires to some sequestered spot, and studies his
> Greek authors without interruption by public affairs the better. Mean-
> time we beg to remind the learned man, that neither the Pyrrhic [*sic*]
> phalanx nor Greek fire was invented by parties who declined to advance
> with the military spirit of the time. Will that consideration move him—
> or must *we* move him?[13]

Nor was the reply of Lord Clarence Paget, the Admiralty spokesman, that the Navy generally accepted Coles's principle of "shield-ships," entirely satisfactory—for he also had to condemn, along with the *Monitor,* their relative lack of strategic range and seaworthiness.[14] Either the entire conception of British national and imperial defense was going to be upset by the American example, it seemed, or it was not.[15]

For that matter, how radical were Britain's leaders truly prepared to be? Politically, there was little doubt that mid-Victorian society was basking in something of a Pax Britannica—or "Age of Equipoise"—under "Old Pam's" Whiggish, yet undeniably conservative, steward-ship. Closely linked with this sense of social and even political security (since Palmerston's coalition government had indeed managed to keep the Liberals intact, the Tories content, and the Radicals at bay) was the commonly expressed desire for potent military and naval symbols of national prestige; anything else would be construed by the popular press as foolishness. As caricatured in *Punch,* Lord Palmerston, the "Old Guard," would "slap" naïve Radicals such as Richard Cobden and Bright, who believed peace could be maintained by anything other than fortress walls or an Armstrong Gun.[16] Occasional "Panics" of rising continental armaments and intentions—the old suspicion of a French desire for revenge for Trafalgar and Waterloo—were fueled by a latent xenophobia and classically stoked by politicians for a multitude of pri-vate or "public" reasons. "It was Palmerston who discovered the art of managing the Commons," wrote historian Asa Briggs, "thereby impos-ing some sort of order and continuity on half-reformed English politics. And it was by inducing sympathy for his foreign policy rather than by offering new doses of parliamentary reform that Palmerston was to cast his spell."[17] In this sense, therefore, realism coincided more closely with conservatism on issues of defense. "The whole of this scheme of inland fortifications is the offspring of these old men's brains whose united ages amounted to about 240 years, viz. Palmerston, Howard Douglas, and [John] Burgoyne," wrote an exasperated Cobden to Coles in 1864:

> A moment's thought from a <u>modern point of view</u> would shew the absolute uselessness and waste of any such contrivances. . . . If an enemy is our Master at Sea, so as to be enabled to land an army and keep open his communications, he is capable of blockading us and starving us into subjection. He would therefore be a fool to land an army at all. We are like a garrison afloat and our existence depends on our communications by sea being kept open. But the people who by birth divine govern us do not trouble their heads about such matters.[18]

Yet Britain's industrial and financial resources, though recognized as the most developed in the world, were not by any means limitless. Few speakers in Parliament would dare to suggest that it was not better to be safe than sorry, but many could appeal to equally prevalent Victorian values of thrift, efficiency, and progress. It was thus in early 1862 that Palmerston's nemesis, Cobden, argued for essentially strategic (naval) arms limitations talks with France, to negotiate a mutual reduction at least in wooden ships of the line, now universally recognized as obsolescent.[19] Somerset, however, disagreed with Cobden's gloomy forecast of endless rival naval expenditures, even with the advent of iron and armored ships, which prevented "any exclusive advantage from the augmentation." Improved armaments would likely lead to improved economy. "In a few years it seems probable that, instead of a large fleet of two deckers at sea, we shall keep a smaller number of iron-plated frigates ready in our ports and harbours, from which one or two will occasionally go out for a cruise, but that the general duties of the navy will be performed by a smaller class of vessels such as corvettes sloops and gun-vessels." The current increase was due to the state of transition only, the First Lord argued. Indeed, it was his conviction that "our large naval force has not however incited us to war, but has been on the contrary instrumental in maintaining peace. Our hostile passions have not been inflamed, but on the contrary this country has shown a temper and forbearance which Mr. Cobden as well as every lover of peace must approve and admire."[20]

Of all other nations in the world, it was the United States that many Englishmen were in the habit of pointing to, the "other" Victorian society—the English-speaking republic—that always seemed to move forward as fast, if not faster, than Britain herself.[21] "The whole spirit of modern warfare," one Parliamentary critic declared, was now obviously one of "mobility against permanence."[22] As such, Somerset had to warn Palmerston [on April 1] that "under present excitement the

Government will be beat" on the issue of forts or floating batteries, especially since it was unclear "how far the Government is committed to the [fort] contractors and no statement on this point was made to the House of Commons."[23] Lewis wanted the First Lord to attend a meeting at the War Office on April 4 to discuss the issue of ironclads versus fortifications.[24]

But before this chance for the Government to regroup, Somerset was compelled to answer criticism in the House of Lords on April 3. The Earl of Hardwicke referred to "the late events on the American coast and in the James River," which "had brought about a sort of crisis in the state of public opinion":

> It had evinced the world that in contest between iron and wooden vessels the latter were utterly valueless. It was, therefore, for the Government to consider whether they would any longer nibble at this matter, but whether they should not rather open their jaws wide and swallow the whole, let the cost be what it might, and persevere in the construction of an iron-plated navy. As the question now stood before the country, it was as much one of common sense as of science. The duty of a navy was to secure the coasts of the country inviolate, to protect the coasts and harbours of our colonies, to blockade the enemy in his own ports, and to supply an adequate number of cruising ships for service at home and abroad.[25]

As most of the Royal Navy was wooden, it stood to reason that it could not deal with coastal defense ironclads. The same, however, applied to a potential adversary. Two types of vessels should therefore comprise the navy of the future: mastless steam-powered turret vessels like the *Monitor*—limited, however, by the fact that they "could not keep the sea long for want of coal"—and sail-and-steam ironclads of good speed that should at any rate be of smaller dimensions for greater maneuverability and lighter draft for general dockyard accommodation than the *Warrior*-class ironclads; "in fighting ships it was necessary to combine the qualities of sea-going vessels with those of a man-of-war, and to abandon a portion of each for the sake of the whole."[26]

Somerset replied that the current Government, on taking power in the summer of 1859, was merely fulfilling the wishes of the House then and the previous Government to "possess a powerful fleet of line-of-battle ships, and that we should add to the strength of our naval reserve" in addition to laying down two experimental iron-cased steamers. Though the new First Lord apparently considered altering *Warrior*'s sister ship, *Black Prince* (on what basis he did not say), he "found it would be necessary to have the whole details calculated over again and the lines re-drawn, which would have taken three or four months; and as there was a feeling throughout the country that it was desirable to proceed, I ordered her to be completed on the same lines as the *Warrior*":

> But I was not quite satisfied with those vessels. I admit, with the noble Earl, that great length and great draught of water, although characteristic of powerful vessels, and enabling them to make rapid passages, are also attended with inconveniences. I therefore caused the Department to reconsider the question, and to suggest plans for two vessels of a smaller class, which were accordingly prepared at the close of the autumn. Those two were *Defence* and *Resistance.*

Yet Somerset admitted he was also "not satisfied with these"— none of the first four ironclads, large and small, were "sufficiently protected." The *Valiant* class was a third attempt to produce Hardwicke's well-balanced, armored "fighting ship." All of the vessels were at the mercy of contractors, who "find more difficulties than they had calculated upon; so much time is required in forging enormous pieces of iron, and the quality of iron is so carefully examined by us that contractors complain of the heavy obligations under which they labour in meeting our requirements, and we have a great deal of trouble in some cases to get them to continue the work." Four more fast, iron-hulled, sail-and-steam ironclads were ordered, yet on the basis that the 100-pounder Armstrong and 68-pounder gun were still the heaviest serviceable British ordnance, and "that if both the armaments and the iron plates which vessels carried were greatly increased in weight, the vessels would be very ill adapted for service at sea." These were therefore ever longer and deeper than the *Warrior* but at least more fully protected, carrying a heavier armament overall: the *Achilles* and the three vessels of the *Minotaur* class. Conversions of wooden ships of the line were also under way (the *Royal Oak* class). Finally, guns mounted in revolving shields on Captain Coles's plan were tested the previous year with good results; Somerset "was at once satisfied that we had got a vessel which would be most useful for the protection of our harbours. But as there was no pressure for defence, and no alarm about the safety of our harbours, I did not think it necessary to apply to the Treasury for authority to commence that vessel at once." To ward off Parliament's alarm over fortifications as an efficient means of harbor defense, as well as justify the Admiralty's investment in super broadside ironclads rather than a turret-ship flotilla—given the current pressure generated by news of the American ironclad action—the First Lord now had to belittle its actual "importance." Hence, the *Monitor* was "something between a raft and a diving bell," barely seaworthy, of poor (laminated) armor configuration, and armed with shell-firing

Dahlgren guns, which nevertheless had lower velocity than the 68-pounder. Though "these conflicts, viewed solely as matters of scientific experiment," were "highly interesting" to the Admiralty, they were, at most, only that.[27]

Meanwhile, intelligence reports were coming in that even the French were now taking "Captain Cowper Coles' plan of constructing iron plated vessels" under "serious consideration. . . ." Although one authority suggested that smaller-caliber rifled guns on either American ironclad, fired with higher velocity, would have proven more decisive, and that ironclads would ever be vulnerable to improved ordnance, Dupuy de Lôme told the British naval attaché in Paris, Captain Edward Hore, that he was "equally confident that he can always obtain more power of resistance than the means of penetration brought against him can overcome, and that these cannot be pushed beyond a certain limit, at least on board of ships, for not only would the handling of the guns and shot become too difficult, but also the ships' decks would [not] stand the recoil and the strain."[28] If the French lead was to be followed in ironclads, therefore, it seemed likely that the broadside of lighter, though feasibly more powerful, guns was the way of the future—not American turrets and heavy guns.

Chapter 13

Enter E. J. Reed, Naval Architect

These considerations from various sources further served to complicate relations between the Admiralty and Coles. Encouraged by the debate in Parliament, the inventor-captain wrote to Paget, claiming, first of all, priority of the "Shot proof Steam Raft" concept over Ericsson's *Monitor*. His Crimean War proposals were of even lighter draft and smaller dimensions, though his hemispherical turret was fixed rather than being a rotating cylinder. Responding to Somerset's request to Grey for more details, Robinson declared, however, that "no trace" could be found "of any report" in the Surveyor's department. Coles could also not "withhold from their Lordships the deep mortification" he felt "at the Americans' taking away the Palm of the invention from this country. . . ." By giving "further publicity" to his "inventions and views to the Defences of Great Britain," Coles suggested he was saving England's honor—if not his own:

> I wish to point out to their Lordships how admirably those Steam Rafts could be adopted for the defence of our dockyards, Mercantile Ports, and Rivers. If in Peace time we only constructed a few as a pattern, and stationed them at the principal ports, when in case of being threatened with war, our rivers would swarm with them in an incredibly short time; they could be manned by our Dockyard men, pensioners, Coast Volunteers, and sea board population, giving an incentive to Voluntary services, and a specific understanding as to how, and what they were to fight in, when I believe no Vessel dare ventures near our Coast.
>
> If necessary to have a little more speed a few feet more length, draught of water, and more power would give it, it must be remembered

that the great superiority which these Vessels have over larger ones which have to cross the Channel, or Atlantic to attack us is from their smallness, lowness in the water, rapidity in turning and light draught.[1]

But added publicity was exactly what the Admiralty and the Government did *not* want, and there was more than a trace of extortion in Coles's exuberant "offer." The Admiralty would not be patriotically drawn into a private dispute between rival inventors; the two turret ships, the *Prince Albert* and the *Royal Sovereign* conversion, were already committed for the purpose of "trying" his plan; and "the whole question" of smaller ironclads for coastal defense had been "for some months under the consideration of the Board," which would "not fail to take advantage of Capt. Coles' services should the adoption of his plan of arming small vessels be found desirable."[2]

Back in the House of Commons, the *Monitor,* the *Virginia,* and Coles's proposed turret vessels spearheaded a renewed attack on the Spithead fortifications on April 4. The opposition noted that although Coles's Crimean War ironclad plans were virtually on hold—while the Admiralty endlessly deliberated its merits—the new forts received no-expense-spared treatment. Yet "while we have been thinking, the Americans have been acting":

> They have been satisfied by the experiment, which is doubted upon the Treasury bench here, in the same way as the efficiency of the matchlock was doubted when it speeded the crossbow; of "Brown Bess," when it superseded the matchlock; and of the Enfield rifle, when it superseded Brown Bess. Our great men are very slow to be convinced; and unless the House of Commons urges them on—unless a lesson is taught us on our own shores by the burning of some of our own ships—they will be as slow as the men of former times were.[3]

Mr. Bentinck added, however, that the criticism of the House should not "at all be construed into an irritating or party feeling. . . ." The Government "could not have dealt with this question before, because it had not arisen," but it was obliged by recent events to make some bold decision, regardless. Though the *Monitor* was a "comparatively small vessel, a shapeless monstrosity," it was also virtually invulnerable— and John Ericsson, according to American newspapers, was now already busy designing improved, larger versions. Though the *Monitor* might not be able to cross the Atlantic, "it is perfectly easy to construct vessels quite as invulnerable—and therefore quite as invincible as the *Monitor,* and yet possessing all the requisite sea-going qualities for making a passage to any part of the world."[4]

Palmerston's personal dislike for the *Warrior* and her "pasteboard sisters" would now have to be put on hold.[5] If conservative policy was mid-Victorian policy, the aging Prime Minister would have to publicly defend his Admiralty's decision to invest in broadside ironclads, though they were not, in fact, as fully armor-protected as their French counterparts. He was "not surprised," therefore, that "the public at large should have their eyes opened, and their minds struck, by the conclusions naturally derived from the event which has taken place." But, as the First Lord of the Admiralty had demonstrated the previous day, the Government had indeed undertaken experiments of its own that already suggested the relative invulnerability of armored vessels against wooden ones. Moreover, the recent encounter in American waters served as a warning of "what kind of vessel will not do for the general service which we require of our ships"; the crews of both American ironclads were stifled by their low freeboard, which also threatened their seaworthiness, except in smooth waters. "Therefore it will not do to take these vessels as your model and when the House is told that they cost comparatively but a small sum, and were completed in a short space of time, I must say that is no ground sufficient for us to go on with respect to the ships we may construct." Tenders were being sent out for constructing a ship on Coles's plan; "whether it can be made capable of going to sea is another thing, but for purposes of coast defence we are of opinion that the construction of that vessel will turn out most effectual." By the year 1864, Britain should have "16 iron ships, of different sizes, but all of a very respectable and formidable character." As for the man-made island-forts at Spithead, only contracts for the foundations were made; the actual design of the forts to rest upon them was not yet settled by experiment.[6] Terminable annuities were planned to pay for their cost, which seemed reasonable, because forts, unlike floating batteries, were considered long-term investments. If, however, the House wanted the Government to suspend those contracts until a new Commission reexamined the question of batteries or forts, or batteries and forts combined for national defense, then it would be done. For now, it was obvious that "floating defences can be constructed more rapidly than forts" and that "so long as those floating defences were not sent elsewhere—so long as they were available, and had their machinery in order, they would, in all probability, be as effectual . . . as forts." But it also stood to reason that future improvements in heavy guns would favor their being mounted on land rather than floating at sea.[7] In fact, Palmerston was trying to defer any decision that might kill the fortifications scheme altogether until after the Easter recess of Parliament, waiting for events to cool down and for the British public to have its attention diverted once more.

Sir John Pakington, on the opposite side of the House, was not satisfied with the Prime Minster's explanation. As Palmerston noted,

£1,000,000 was recommended for the construction of floating batteries by the 1860 Defence Commission, in addition to the £9 million estimated for fixed fortifications. Even if long-term forts might be paid by terminable annuities, and batteries could not, why was nothing for the construction of the latter put into the annual estimates? Indeed, "up to this moment the Government have taken no measures whatever to carry out that portion of the recommendations of the Royal Commission." There was thus no need to wait for yet another Commission; let the million pounds be voted now for iron-plated "gunboats" before the French assumed too great a lead in both frigates and coastal defense/assault ironclads. Paget countered by suggesting that the five line-of-battle ship conversions (the *Royal Oaks*) were "to be plated as floating defences," a partial truth inasmuch as they were *not* intended to operate as Ericsson's *Monitor* or Coles's proposed flotilla of cupola ships. Thus another three-decker (the *Royal Sovereign*) was to be converted on Coles's plan "for Channel defence" as opposed to "harbour defence." Their draft would still be around 26 feet—hardly suitable for the defense of most harbors—but, as Paget challenged, "it is said that the Americans in the course of a few months plated the marvellous *Monitor,* and we in this country are behindhand; but supposing we were at war to-morrow, do you suppose we could not put forward our energies and create *Monitor*s by the dozen in a few months?" This was a sensible point, for the Americans were at war; Britain was engaged in an arms race with France, and in such a contest the maintenance of long-range power projection was perhaps more vital for international relations and a secure peace than even immediate defense closer to home, for purposes of deterrence, if not practicality. How this strategy affected the forts was another matter. As Sir Frederic Smith observed, it was "all moonshine to suppose that a vessel passing [fixed forts] could be destroyed by heavy guns." Monitors were also, simply, much cheaper than forts, even if they were paid for immediately.[8]

But inasmuch as forts were part of the United Kingdom's overall vision of strategic defense mixed with offensive deterrence, or hitting power—indeed, what else could explain the obvious preference being given to deep-draft, long-range ironclads?—coastal ironclads were not, even if light-draft turret ships proved deadlier against broadside ironclads than forts. In this sense, perhaps, the new technology represented by Ericsson and Coles was destabilizing. Forts were classic elements of strategic defense, which veteran statesmen such as Palmerston understood and respected as well. Would reliance on an "invention" prove sufficient at the negotiating table or merely laughable? Writing to his son, U.S. minister Charles Francis Adams said he thought "the effect is to diminish the confidence in the result of hostilities with us":

In December we were told that we should be swept from the ocean in a moment, and all our ports would be taken. They do not talk so now. So far as this may have a good effect to secure peace on both sides it is good. . . .[9]

The extraordinary lessons from the battle of Hampton Roads could not yet outweigh the larger history of conflict in Europe, where ships of the line and forts were acknowledged playing pieces in the high-stakes game of international diplomacy. A Cabinet Memo from Sir George Grey acknowledged there was "a good deal of truth" in Coles's arguments, "but it is a truth no one denies. Every one admits that we ought to retain our maritime superiority and to render an invasion impossible if we can by our first line of defence—the Navy":

> . . . but Captain Coles appears to me to overrate the power [turret vessels] would give us of defeating an attempted invasion, if, as in the case he assumes, "Our fleet should be ordered or called away for the protection of our colonies and commerce." His 20 iron ships might be concentrated rapidly at a given point, but what is the French fleet doing all the time?[10]

Somerset later added in the House of Lords that forts served another psychological purpose: to defend the country "against panic attacks at home."[11] At any rate, the final vote of 74 to 13 successfully suspended "the construction of the proposed Forts at Spithead until the value of iron-roofed gunboats for the defence of our Ports and Roadsteads shall have been fully considered. . . ." A new Committee would convene May 1, 1862, to consider diverting any money set aside for fortifications to construct or convert coast defense ironclads instead.[12] The possibility of Royal Navy monitors was therefore also put on hold, despite Hampton Roads.

During this time, Edward J. Reed, described by Robinson to the Board of Admiralty as a naval architect by profession, "educated at the central Mathematical School at Portsmouth," was hired to build a small ironclad of "novel description" for the Navy. The Controller was looking for alternatives to the wooden conversions and the big iron-hulled broadside ironclads—ships with greater handiness and armor protection, with less demanding construction and perhaps also lighter draft.[13] Thus far "no plan that has yet been proposed, for partially Armour Plating small ships, has apparently presented the same prospect of success as this Design of Mr. Reed's," wrote Robinson.[14] The new "Armour Plated Corvette," H.M.S. *Enterprise,* had a fully armored waterline belt, with thicker armor concentrated in a central "box" housing a small but heavier battery, with traversing guns that would permit fore and aft fire. In essence, the vessel was similar to Confederate casemate-rams, though the casemate itself was not angled and was part of a larger, traditional topside which would facilitate the use of masts.

At once the "central-battery" system posed a challenge to Coles's proposals for lighter, sea-going ironclads, which also concentrated armament into fewer but heavier guns, though mounted in turrets to permit wide fields of fire rather than traversing through alternate ports. However, whereas Coles was still finalizing even the shape of his turrets, from truncated cones to cylinders like the *Monitor*'s turret, and perceptibly failing to provide actual schematics for a vessel ready to build, Reed was having an easier time of it. The reason was that he was a trained professional, a skilled engineer, creative, and at least as eager as Coles to mold Britain's new ironclads. An editor of *Mechanics' Magazine*, Reed had already published a book, *On the Modifications which the Ships of the Royal Navy Have Undergone During the Present Century* (1859), in which he asserted that "there never was a period when the art of naval warfare was more susceptible of change than it is at this moment."[15]

Robinson was prepared to offer Coles £20,000 "to surrender absolutely to the Admiralty all his Patent rights so far as they relate to Guns in Cupolas or Shields to be carried on board ship," with an obligation to "furnish such plans and drawings to the Admiralty connected with his patent as they from time to time may require of him, receiving while so employed a remuneration to be fixed by them on a fair and liberal scale." The Admiralty attorneys thought this "inconvenient for many reasons and objectionable as a precedent," drafting instead a proposal to the Treasury for a down-payment sum of £5,000 "and also a royalty of £100 for every Cupola built in a ship or fort during the time of his patent," which would expire in 1864. Again, the turret system was considered an "uncertainty" at best, though "an element which must be paid for. . . ." Armstrong guns, another product of a private inventor, were by now an accepted component of Her Majesty's fleet; but Coles's system was "hardly . . . a parallel" case, and was already inspiring "resentment" from authorities. This resentment was underscored when Coles pointed out to Romaine on April 16 that "Foreign Governments" were willing to pay him handsomely for his shield ships, that the British Government owed him money after the successful trial of his system in the *Trusty* six months previous, and that his plan was "pronounced by the United Voice of the Nation through both Houses of Parliament to be eminently successful and of the greatest value to the Country."[16] Coles was making a nuisance of himself and, worse, becoming a focal point of political embarrassment to the Navy and the Government.

When Reed offered to carry out the construction of the *Enterprise*, for which he would have to give up his regular work, Robinson suggested a fee up to £600.[17] This was a far cheaper (and much quieter) alternative to giving in to Coles and his supporters. The less radical central-battery concept was perhaps also less overtly "American" than coastal-defense turret ships—vessels that strayed too close to the cutting edge of British naval strategy, policy, and economy by bringing national defense much closer to home shores than imperial interests required. The issue broadened when the Duke of Newcastle, the Colonial Secretary, argued against Somerset's remarkable proposal "to enable such Colonies as may be willing to establish a naval force of their own defence to do so," while William Gladstone, the Minister of Exchequer, was publicly challenging the expediency of increased military and naval expenditures—and infuriating Palmerston in the process.[18] Significantly, therefore, the London *Mechanics' Magazine* reported the laying down of the *Enterprise* at Deptford dockyard, comparing her not to *Warrior* or even Coles's "cupola vessels" but to "the American *Monitor*, of which the world has lately heard so much." The new type of British ironclad could be "sent to any part of the world" and was "the first which has rendered the application of extremely thick and heavy armour to our larger ships possible."[19]

This last factor was demonstrated as especially important on April 8, when a new, experimental 12-ton gun designed by the ever-innovative William Armstrong pierced the *Warrior* target at Shoeburyness with a 156-pound projectile, firing an increased charge of 40 pounds. The gun was smoothbore only, but Armstrong assured observers that, if modified with rifling, a 10-inch–caliber "300-pounder" could pierce the target at an even greater range. The American spectacle of ironclads firing away at one another, with apparently no effect, was clearly short-lived.[20] So was the concept of merely extending armor protection to greater and larger broadside batteries.[21] Partial protection was once again mandatory—not on a point of seaworthiness, as with the *Warrior*, but because of its likelihood of surviving in combat against heavier, more powerful ordnance. Armor must henceforth be thicker, just as existing guns were previously deemed "useless" in Parliament against iron sides. Though Somerset was complaining to Palmerston of all the crank proposals flooding in to him every day as a result of the Hampton Roads sensation, only two classes of future ironclads stood a chance against the gun makers of the testing grounds, if not also against potential foreign antagonists, namely France and especially the United States.[22] The *Scientific American* was reprinting U.S. Army Captain Rodman's letter to the War Department, dated a year before, explaining there was "no doubt of our ability to make reliable" monster smoothbores of 20-inch caliber, capable of firing solid shot of 1,000 pounds. With their "whole crushing force being brought to bear upon a single point at the same time, while that of the smaller shot would be unavoidably dispersed, as regards both time and point of impact," it was "not deemed probable that any naval structure, proof against that caliber, will soon if ever be built. . . ." In the meantime, some fifty 15-inch caliber smoothbore guns, designed by Dahlgren, were already ordered by the Navy Department of the U.S. Government to be cast at the Fort Pitt Works in Pittsburgh. These would act as the new monitors' primary weapons.[23]

The infamous debate between Coles and the Admiralty, and then between himself and Reed, intensified over the next few months. The victory of Armstrong's "150-pounder" over the *Warrior* target prompted the Admiralty to test its powers against the trial Coles turret on *Trusty*. Coles objected that the turret in question was obsolete in comparison with the new gun, unlike the improved ones intended for the *Royal Sovereign*. The Board assured him, however, that "the result of their intended experiments 'will involve no condemnation of the principle of the Shield.'"[24] Indeed, *Punch* considered "floating iron shot-towers to constitute our fleet" something of a foregone conclusion; henceforth, sailors would be "frozen out" by "flat-irons with neither masts nor spars. . . ."[25] Yet Coles's patent was itself still under negotiation, and the matter was now hopelessly entangled with his status as either a full- or half-pay serving officer. On May 3 Coles wrote to the Admiralty claiming travel and subsistence expenses of £1 per day. When the Admiralty questioned why a full-pay officer should be granted these as well, Coles requested on April 10 that he be put on half-pay, "as I believe that it will enable me more fully to develop the advantages which I think may be derived from placing guns in revolving shields."[26] This was important, since half-pay status also technically allowed him to publish criticism of Admiralty ironclad policy—and promote his own scheme—without necessarily jeopardizing his position with the Admiralty to supervise the construction of trial cupola vessels. Already Coles was privately writing to the editor of *Blackwood's* that "official prejudice is working hard against me. . . ."[27] It was likely he also knew of Reed's increasing influence. When Coles considered offering the Admiralty a license to use his cupolas, rather than purchase his patent, so that he could retain the right to sell them to other (including foreign) parties, Sir Frederick Grey and Paget confronted Coles over his resort to the *Times* while he was still on full-pay, and even proved willing to publicly retaliate against him in Parliament—much to Coles's horror. On May 16 Coles and his attorney thus decided to accept the Admiralty offer of £5,000 with a £100 royalty for his turrets extending to 14 years from the date of his original patent, "for the benefit of the Government and the Country," though Coles added he would probably "suffer pecuniarily by doing so." The Admiralty in turn considered Coles's request for half-pay dropped, but Coles may have waited too long. The following day

Robinson suggested that Reed "proceed to Portsmouth, Devonport, and Pembroke, to prepare drawings" for "Plating small Ships of War." Master Shipwrights and draftsmen were to be placed at his disposal as well. "From the great amount of work in this Office," Robinson argued, "much delay would be avoided" by accepting his request, which the Board subsequently did.[28]

The Controller's attitude toward Coles's patent changed. He argued that the inventor should retain his patent rights but not be allowed to extend his services to other parties. Assigning them to the Board of Admiralty would not "practically do what the Board wants."[29] With Reed on board, the Admiralty could better afford to do without Coles if need be. Could Coles do better without the Admiralty? What would the public think if he sold his cupolas abroad but refused to benefit his own country for pecuniary reasons? Keeping Coles's turrets tied to the British Isles would prevent their spread to potential rivals, and by keeping free of commitments to Coles, the Admiralty would be kept free from private or public manipulation of the development of the British ironclad program.

Chapter 14

Palmerston's Policy

The threat was real enough. On May 19, the entire history of the program and its expenses up to that point was subjected to a blistering attack in Parliament by Conservative Lord Robert Montagu. Once more the Admiralty was accused of allowing dust to collect on "plans of a better form" of ironclad, "which would also not be regarded until they had already done execution in the hands of the Americans." Worse still, Montagu motioned the Government to "appoint a Committee of scientific men, who would investigate the subject of ship-building with a desire to obtain a real knowledge of facts, instead of relying upon empty opinions." This would clearly take decision-making out of the hands of the professionals, the Navy, and especially the Surveyor (Controller). Earlier evidence before an Admiralty Committee stated:

> Generally speaking, if it is a matter connected with ship building or fitting, it is submitted to the Surveyor of the Navy, and, in common language, he pooh-poohs it. . . . I very much question whether you will find one single instance in which an inventor has gone to the surveyor's office and received an acknowledgement of his invention having been good. . . .

The House now called for a return of "the number of proposals, or plans, for the purposes of shot-proof ships, which have been received at the Admiralty during the last three years . . . and if any such proposals or plans have been referred to a Committee. . . ." Paget demurred, since "inventions in reference to iron-cased ships come to us at the rate of about 100 a month. . . ." It was also advisable not to move "too fast," though "we have no less than seven different classes of ships in progress of the iron-cased family, by various inventors, some of which are plated right round, and others plated only amidships."[1]

At any rate, the motion was prefatory to a much wider offensive in Parliament against the Government's "National Expenditure." The public, much less the politicians, was still not satisfied by the answers given by the professionals. Foreign powers still seemed "ahead" of Britain, while Coles was seemingly still unsupported by the Admiralty. Instead, the Government was spending more money than was needed on outdated forms of defense; the fortifications and its choice of iron-clads were increasingly suspect. Palmerston, the consummate politician, braced himself for yet another struggle. On May 23 Somerset replied to Palmerston's request for details on French naval armaments. "The Revue Contemporaire of 30 April 1862 gives 6 iron-plated afloat, 10 iron-plated building, also 10 new floating batteries building in addition to the former batteries. The French iron-plated ships building are not progressing fast at present. If we go on steadily, we shall be equal if not above them by next spring. It is difficult to speak on the subject, as some are anxious to stop our progress, others wish to excite unnecessary alarm."[2] Exaggerating the French threat might lead to criticism of the Government; ignoring it would do the same.

The same was true concerning the United States. A letter from an American informant providing firsthand details of the *Monitor* and the *Virginia* warned that "the Americans are a most impulsive people, and just now everybody wants iron clad ships and I doubt not that in a year from this time, America will have at least 30 afloat, I have no idea that they will be all good ones, but in all probability they will all of them be more than a match for any ship not so protected, and should they get the largest number or have in any way the advantage, a War with England is as certain as the rising of tomorrow's sun."[3]

Four days later Palmerston thus wrote to Gladstone there was no foreseeable "Change of Circumstances likely to take Place between this Time and next February which would justify any considerable Reduction either of Army or Navy. . . ." It was fundamentally a matter of national security versus economy, and Palmerston was willing to gamble that the nation would support his own conception of a Government's primary duty: defense. Fear, or at least caution, was always more suggestive in people's minds than the Free-Trade, penny-counting, Liberal optimism of his opponents. An appeal to the lowest common denominator was one not necessarily to enlightened reason but to the public mind—which Palmerston was highly skilled at manipulating. "But these anticipatory Resolutions are nothing but a Trap for a government," Palmerston explained to his less experienced colleague—and dubious political ally. "They tend either to expose a Government to the imputation of breaking Faith with Parliament" (too much was being spent by the Government, and spent unwisely, regardless of Parliament's concerns) "or to compel them to provide inadequately for the proper Demands of the public service" (economy at the expense of security, for which the Government could also be accused later). "I am unwilling to place myself in either of those Conditions."[4] How much could the Naval Estimates be reduced, Palmerston inquired of Somerset, "supposing always that our Friends in France and our Cousins in America should be well behaved and peaceable"? The First Lord replied that "for the last two years I have kept steadily in view the measures which may assist the Government towards a reduction of expenditure without any great decrease of naval efficiency":

> For example in May 1861 we had in commission 306 vessels of all rates. In May 1862 we have 282 in commission. Again in May 1861 we had line of battle 1st rates, 2nd rates, and 3rd rates 30 ships. We have now of these expensive ships 21 in commission.
>
> We have constantly replaced on distant stations ships-of-the-line by frigates and larger by smaller vessels.

But the French had 11 serviceable ships of the line in the Mediterranean as well as 2 ironclad-frigates ready at Toulon; Britain had 7 ships of the line and might be able to send an ironclad of her own there "before the Autumn." This was "the great difficulty" in regard to reductions, "our position in regard to iron-plated ships." Foreign powers could not be allowed to gain any decisive lead, "yet the iron-plates add enormously to the cost of a ship":

> If France had not a large wooden navy in addition to their iron-plated ships we could easily cut down some of our two deckers and plate them; by which means they would soon be ready, and the cost of engines would be avoided. But it would not in my opinion be prudent to adopt this course except with a few ships, and those chiefly for mere coast defence.
>
> The degree of speed with which we should advance in preparing iron-plated ships is a question of such importance politically as well as financially, that I should be glad if some members of the Cabinet would agree to meet here when the matter could be brought before them with the information requisite to enable them to decide on the course to be pursued.[5]

The following day, however, Somerset wrote he could bring the current naval Estimate of £11,794,305 "below 11 millions" because the cost of current ironclads under construction by private contract would be reduced for 1863–1864 to £1 million, a savings of £450,000 from the current year's payments. The vote for timber might be reduced but counterbalanced by an increased vote for iron plates; those "for one of the wooden frigates now to be plated will cost about £40,000. This is a direct addition to the cost of a frigate as there is no saving on other materials to compensate for this."[6]

The tumultuous debate in the crowded House of Commons on June 3, 1862, represented one of the most serious challenges to Palmerston's leadership ever—a debate revolving around the fortifications, the threat from France—instigated by the news of the Battle of Hampton Roads, the issue of turret ironclads, the state of the Royal Navy, and Coles. Palmerston objected to even the *point* of the various proposed resolutions and openly reduced them as politically motivated, "whether the Gentlemen who sit on these benches or the Gentlemen who sit on the opposite benches are best entitled to the confidence of the House and of the country." If all parties agreed the nation's defenses needed improving, there was no real need for debate. If, however, economy was considered a more pressing issue than defense, Palmerston declared it "better for the House to go at once to the question fraught with serious important consequences, instead of wasting time in discussing the comparative value of the Amendments which have been proposed."

This aggressive move immediately put the opposition, rather than the Government, on the defensive. Here, too, was an implied logic that "the proper Demands of the Public service," or "naval efficiency" was by definition incompatible with any significant reductions in naval or military expenditure. Though Montagu held "a sincere and honest desire to promote economy in the financial arrangements of the country," he was shocked the Prime Minister had converted the question "into the stalking-horse of ambition, and the prostitute of our claims to power." Nevertheless, as Spencer Horatio Walpole admitted, no one really wanted the Liberal Coalition Government to resign. Indeed, political stability in the wake of the Crimean War, and in the face of rising social, economic, and strategic worries, was a positive necessity. Palmerston's indignation was an ultimatum to the House, reduced to expressing opinions on defense, but not to the point of denying his Administration, or "the Nation," of its demands. Not surprisingly, John Bright, speaking through the uproar, dared to call Palmerston's bluff. Questioning the matter in the House was not, after all, politically "dangerous or subversive"; "if we are all in favour of economy, and so much in favour of it that we do not object to any definite statement with regard to it—I should like to know why we should have any party contest at all?"

If the House is disposed for a debate, let us have a debate. But I ask the House—especially those sixty or seventy gentlemen who, a year ago, requested the noble Lord, in very civil and humble terms, to condescend in a little degree to diminish the expenditure of the country—Whether they now intend to set up the noble Lord as dictator absolute upon this subject?[7]

"The truth is, that the amount of the Military and Naval Estimates," Stansfeld declared, "is decided by general views of policy, which cannot be discussed in Committee. . . ." Taken for granted, such policy always allowed the Estimates to "pass almost as a matter of course." Humiliated by "the early disasters of the Crimean war, the temporary collapse of our military system, on its first trial after a long peace, before the eyes of Europe, and by the side of France," the popular cry for "the efficiency and sufficiency of our armaments" was to be met by the House "as a representative and deliberative assembly—not parrot-like, to repeat the public cry and leave all to the Government of the day, but to consider something of greater importance than any individual Votes in Committee . . . the great questions of the cost, the policy, and method of those armaments that may be deemed necessary for the purposes of the country." Were such armaments necessary in a time of peace, with taxes on the British population to pay for them? There was a contradiction at work, even in terms of "defense," between England's determination "to be safe and to feel safe, and at the same time to hold her own before the world. . . ." The former was "above suspicion," but the latter was "much more within the range of discretion, and within the limits of which . . . large economies are possible—it is the possession of the means of aggressive warfare, and the preparation for the possibility of external warfare."[8] This struck at the heart of the mid-Victorian British Empire, between strategic concepts of national defense, imperial inviolability, and worldwide power projection, or "deterrence." Coastal or harbor defense ironclads, on Coles's model—monitors—might deter attacks defensively but not provide for the deterrent threat of counter-attack. If such ironclads were designed first for coastal assault (in the British case, at least for trans-Channel operations), and then for longer-range strikes or blockades, early 1860s technology required ironclads of an altogether different fashion—*Warriors* rather than *Monitors*. It was a question of policy after all; and Stansfeld was a Member for Halifax.

That such a policy was "justly called for by the country, wisely sanctioned by Parliament, and legitimately proposed and carried into effect by successive Administrations," as opposed to the product of his own will, Palmerston declared he had no doubt:

> . . . It is part of the duty of Parliament to enable the Government of this country to hold a proper position with regard to the affairs of the world,

and, without interfering by force of arms, at all events to exert a moral and, I will not say, preponderating, but at all events a powerful influence in favour of the principles which this great nation so heartily and cordially approves. But to do this, it is essential that we should be in a position of perfect self-defence; and by self-defence I mean not merely self-defence upon the shores of these islands; we have interests all over the world; we have possessions in every part; and the perfect defence of the country means that we should . . . have the means not merely of defending our shores, but also of protecting those vast interests, commercial and political, which we have in every part of the world.[9]

The Prime Minister therefore proposed an Amendment of his own, noting that "any Government that came down to this House to make a reduction simply as a claptrap attempt to gain momentary favour with the public, would soon find that they lost a great deal more than they gained." The House might state instead that economy would be studied and practiced by the Government, but it would "not lose sight of its duty to provide adequately for the defence of the country, and"—this was an important caveat—"for the maintenance of our interests abroad."[10]

Implied here was that a string of coastal fortifications, leaving the Army in charge of directly defending against naval assault, let alone invasion, would allow the Navy to "defend" interests abroad—protecting commerce and colonies, but also conducting blockades and coastal assaults of its own. Economy may not have been incompatible with defense, but it was a difficult proposition to reconcile with *offense*, or perhaps "strategic defense."[11] The amount of money invested in Britain's ironclad program reflected this dilemma, but certainly the offensive character of the ironclads themselves suggested that Coles's scheme for a coastal defense flotilla was fundamentally at odds with Palmerston's strategic thinking. Any challenge to this would therefore be regarded by the popular Prime Minister as a political one as well; and so, amid desperate shouts of protest, Walpole's Resolution was accused of omitting "altogether the protection of the interests of the country abroad. His Resolution would confine the attention of the House to the defence of our shores."

Again, Palmerston was not speaking to the House so much as he was consciously, bluntly addressing the press reporting the debate and the educated, interested classes of the public. Would the "man in the street" be willing to sacrifice the wealth and honor of the Empire just to save a few pennies? How important was "position" to mid-Victorians after all? Palmerston knew better than most of his well-meaning, though frustrated, contemporaries. If they wanted "by the force of reason and the expression of opinion, backed by the moral weight of the country, to endeavour to influence in a liberal spirit the course of events" in foreign countries, for example, Italy—or perhaps also the United States—then the House should not attempt to restrain the Government from spending whatever it felt was necessary to achieve this. Any proposed "humiliation" of the Government by Parliament would be a humiliation of "public opinion." "I do say," Palmerston taunted, "that we possess the confidence of the country."

The Tory Leader, Benjamin Disraeli, had been "trying to give some meaning to a phrase so vague" as "the protection of our interests abroad." Strong garrisons, fortifications, and naval squadrons "in every clime" defending commerce were no doubt "sources of respect for us with foreign Courts and countries." But England's real strength and influence had always been her moral resolve and "financial reserve," which enabled her to sustain war efforts longer than most of her enemies. Economy, in this sense, was strength, not weakness. Where there was "financial embarrassment the results are certain, and comparatively speaking immediate, and a Minister may be a most popular Minister—he may have a majority of 200 in this House; but if his policy is that two and two make five, the time will come when all his majorities will not be able to maintain him in his pride of place." It was also difficult to convince the man in the street "of the necessity of extravagant armaments" when Britain was in fact at peace, and Europe exhausted from wars and revolutions.

Richard Cobden, a legendary though unpopular Free-Trade "Radical"' since the Crimean War, could likewise dismiss visions of French "Command of the Channel" or even invasion in favor of "a great gulf yawning which none of us has the courage to look into or fathom": the state of the economy. The real strength of a nation rested not "upon armaments so much as upon its resources," and Cobden pointed to the difficulties Britain experienced with overbearing, expansionist America before the Civil War. There was a country which "was never armed," but which was now "manifesting a power such as I have no hesitation in saying no nation of the same population ever manifested in the same time." This was because debilitating prewar taxation was kept to a bare minimum. Nor were the French such a threat to warrant expenditure in the name of "defense." "The noble Lord [Palmerston], indeed, scarcely ever speaks but it is to produce some apprehension, some disquietude, with reference to French preparations." Of the "thirty-six iron-cased [French] ships— he always speaks of 'ships'—built or building," only 16 of them were sea-going frigates; the rest were batteries, "and of these five are actually lying in the warehouse at Toulon, having been built to be carried by railway to Lake Guarda to be used in the siege of Peschiera." What, indeed, was the point of an *entente cordiale* with France, including the trade agreement he himself had recently negotiated, when the object of the Prime Minister "was first to frighten people into the apprehension of danger of attack, and then find an excuse for a large expenditure of money, and at the same time to get for himself the credit of being a spirited Minister, enable to protect the people by all his forethought and preparation"?

But Palmerston, "with that adroitness of which he is so great a master," Sir William Heathcote bitterly admitted, had successfully confused and diffused the House enough for now. Members were aware "how far the noble Lord's Government has gained in character by the course pursued to-night" and yet that the "financial subject" remained open, unresolved, delayed.[12] Stansfeld withdrew his resolution, unwilling to accept the sudden and unexpected responsibility of a vote of confidence that might topple the Government—or irreparably disgrace himself and his supporters any more than Palmerston had already done. Palmerston, writing in his diary later that night, declared a great "triumph" for his Cabinet, which earlier that day at his house had "determined to oppose all the Resolutions but our own."[13]

The political confidence of Britain's Prime Minister did not have to wait long for an opportunity to "exert a moral . . . and powerful influence" on foreign governments. When U.S. General Benjamin Butler issued his infamous Order of May 15, which threatened to treat the women of recently captured and occupied New Orleans as "women of the town, plying their vocation" if they continued to harass Federal officers and soldiers, Palmerston angrily wrote the U.S. minister to Britain, Charles Francis Adams, that "no example can be found in the History of Civilized Nations till the publication of this order of a General guilty in cold Blood of so infamous an act, as deliberately to hand over the female inhabitants of a Conquered City to the unbridled License of an unrestrained soldiery." His opinion of Union "mob"-conscripts, or American soldiers in general, was less than flattering. But "if the Federal Government chooses to be served by men capable of such revolting outrages," he concluded with a veiled threat, "they must submit to abide by the deserved opinion which Mankind will form of their conduct."[14] "Adams," Russell wrote to Palmerston two days later, was "in a dreadful state" about the letter over Butler. The Order was misinterpreted, and probably did not reflect the full wishes of President Lincoln. "If you would withdraw the letter altogether it would be best," Russell cautioned, "but this you may not like to do."[15]

Even the debate over fortifications was far from over. On June 23 Sir George Lewis told the House Committee on Fortifications and Works that construction on the Spithead forts was suspended until the following year, thanks to misleading public reaction to the battle of Hampton Roads, rather than the results of British ordnance tests, which suggested instead the vulnerability of ironclads—but urged a resolution "to serve for a foundation to a Bill for continuing the Act" from 1860, adding that military "efficiency" was "only another term for increased expense." This remark drew a sharp response from Bernal Osborne, a previous Secretary to the Admiralty. The House was definitely "not pledged" to the scheme of fortifications for defense. Though the May 20, 1862, report of the Commissioners on National Defences was willing largely to dismiss the significance of Hampton Roads, wooden Union steamships had since run the gauntlet of 200 guns from two Confederate forts at short range to capture New Orleans. The Armstrong 150-pounder, moreover, was tried under only ideal circumstances to establish its superiority over the *Warrior*'s armor protection (a target previously fired upon) and was, at any rate, an experimental prototype. Now the Government had ordered 20 more 300-pounders and authorized Armstrong to come up with a 600-pounder rifled (muzzle-loading) gun, which would still have difficulty hitting a moving target 1,000 yards away—all at an exorbitant price. "With a man like Sir William Armstrong going on regardless of expense, backed by the Government as his sleeping partner, I am afraid we may take further steps until we run up a bill large enough to require the addition of another penny to the income tax." There was more:

> If we are always assuming a pugnacious attitude, and initiating what is called a spirited foreign policy, the result of which has been to increase our taxation to something like £70,000,000—if we are one day drawing Reform Bills for Sardinia, another day lecturing America, and always pointing the finger of suspicion at France, the natural consequence must be that we shall have the income tax saddled upon us forever. . . .

Osborne noted that the Chancellor of the Exchequer, Gladstone, himself disapproved of Palmerston's "spirit of interference" and Francophobia. These were "neither the traditions of the Liberal party, nor are they the traditions of that Whig party once great and flourishing." All this said nothing for the other Liberal platform (other than Peace and Retrenchment): Reform, which was "courted and caressed and adopted by both sides of the House in the palmy days of its Parliamentary prosperity; but now it is treated like an indigent and disagreeable connection, and not suffered to come into the House. Such, Sir, is the state of the Liberal party."[16] An attack on the Government over state-centered national expenditures in mid-Victorian Britain was a direct attack on political and class structures themselves.

Again, Palmerston's response deserves study as a definition of British foreign, if not naval, policy in this period under examination. The Government would not use part of the loan for fortifications for the construction of floating batteries, though they were the other vital ingredient for defense prescribed by the Report of the Commissioners. The thinking was that forts were long-term investments and therefore "it was fair to throw the burden upon some years to come by providing terminable annuities of thirty years . . . a burden we thought was too great to ask the House and country to submit to in the current year"—whereas "floating defences were in their nature temporary, and could last only for a limited time." They ought to be paid for by a vote in the annual estimates. If Parliament was willing to pay extra for these types of ironclads, in addition to armored frigates and fortifications, then so be it. But that, of course, would spoil any Liberal argument for economic retrenchment or "restraint" on the part of the Government. It was incontestable that forts were needed, even assuming the Navy was to be regarded as the nation's ultimate guardian. "Go to Pembroke, go to Plymouth, go to Portland, go to Portsmouth, go to Sheerness, go to Medway—all these fortifications are expressly intended for the protection of our arsenals and dockyards, without which you cannot have a navy at all. You might as well expect to have a good dinner without a kitchen, as a good navy without dockyards; and you cannot have good dockyards unless they are securely defended." This policy conveniently sidetracked the issue of whether the Royal Navy could defend its own dockyards, in the form of ironclad batteries (or the traditional "block ships"), rather than vastly more expensive fortifications (which also took years rather than months to construct). The public's reaction to the apparent invulnerability of the *Monitor* and the *Merrimack* at the battle of Hampton Roads Palmerston derided in Cobden's direction as another "Panic," which Cobden himself had often attributed to Palmerston's Francophobia and manipulation of the British public's fears. Though his Government had agreed to suspend construction of the forts, "we did not think the contest decisive." Gunnery experts had since promised to deliver ordnance that would restore the "general principle that forts as opposed to ships must have the advantage, because they may have a gun of any size you can manage, whereas a floating battery cannot sustain more than a certain weight." How this applied to armored ships running a gauntlet of forts rather than fighting a fixed artillery duel with them was another matter not mentioned by Palmerston.

More fundamentally, the tiresome debates in Parliament only served to question, confuse, and weaken the resolve of Britain's ruling elite and therefore the political character of the nation itself. "If all these opinions were acted upon," Palmerston complained, "the result would be that the country would have neither fleet, nor army, nor a dockyard, and that we should have to rely entirely on the goodwill, kindness, and forbearance of our neighbours to protect us in all possible contingencies against any difficulties in which we might be involved. I do not think that this is the feeling of the British nation." As to the charge that Britain's increased "defences" were in fact provocative and jeopardized peaceful relations with other (and especially comparatively defenseless) nations, Palmerston argued that a strong self-defense gained respect from potential enemies. "So long as nations are equal, they are likely to be friends." The *Trent* affair demonstrated how even long-term "Friends," or at least close trading partners, could quickly become enemies—and the value "of those means of defence which every nation is bound to provide for itself." That "peace" in this instance was preserved not by the military and naval equality of the Northern States with Great Britain but by Palmerston's ultimatum was, again, another matter. Unilateral domination seemed to serve peace as well. Yet "these works, when complete," he assured the House, "will not be a menace to any country whatever, nor will they in any way increase the liability to war; but they will be a security for the continuance of peace."[17] Missing here, too, was a comparison with France's recent modernizing of the defenses of Cherbourg, opposite Portsmouth, an event that famously alarmed Prince Albert and the Queen after their visit there in August 1858, and that originally served as one of the strongest reasons Palmerston employed for counter-fortifying the south coast of England.[18] It was not, in fact, the "defensive" quality of the forts that maintained peace, but the continued ability of the Royal Navy to counter-attack France, if need be. If the forts were to securely protect the dockyards, and good dockyards were essential for a strong navy, the purpose of a navy was to act offensively, not necessarily in the direct defense of its own dockyards. The Royal Navy would better defend its own bases by attacking those of France or any other enemy. As Palmerston asked of the House a year later, "But even if our fleet should be superior, can we always keep it in the Channel? Can we keep it simply for the defence of our shores? Have we no interests in other parts of the world which may be attacked by iron-clad ships?"[19] Fortifications, even more necessary if other naval powers fortified themselves for similar reasons, simply restored a longer leash for the British Lion.

SUMMARY

The Battle of Hampton Roads had a profound impact on both the British and the Union ironclad programs, though in remarkably different ways. For the U.S. Navy, attention was drawn seaward; improved monitors with improved guns might successfully contest British naval supremacy on the open ocean as well as along the American coastline. By August 1862, *Harper's Weekly* went so far as to "take for granted that, if it became necessary, the large iron-clads which Captain Ericsson and Mr. Rowland are constructing could sail up the Thames to London Bridge with perfect impunity, sinking every war-vessel they found in their way, and could dictate terms to the British over the ruins of the House of Lords."[20] Though probably not for a purpose that extravagant, Assistant Secretary Fox was still more willing to rely upon civilian contractor Ericsson than his own Bureau of Ship Construction & Repair. Indeed, Ericsson's *Monitor* was regarded as a much-needed boost in Northern morale and confidence in Lincoln's administration of the war. *Scientific American* observed, "Had the Navy Department undertaken last August to construct a vessel like the *Warrior*, the huge frame would be now standing on the stocks, with a prospect of being finished in the latter part of 1863, and the destructive course of the *Merrimac* would have gone on unchecked."[21]

For Palmerston's Government, however, the example of the American ironclads, and especially Ericsson's taunting *Monitor*, was politically destabilizing—ultimately forcing the popular Prime Minister to call the bluff of Parliament in a way Lincoln could have never dreamed of—even though, as *Blackwood's* remarked, "The debates of the present session . . . have been absolutely unparalleled for the absence of party spirit and party contests. . . . to impute to selfish ambition the telling exposures of Ministerial incapacity which have of late proceeded from the front benches of the Left."[22] This was because news of Hampton Roads focused British attention inward, to critically reexamine the character of England's own national shore defenses—and the political, if not social, disposition of its expenditures. Ironclad batteries, whether of Coles's pattern or Ericsson's *Monitor*, were clearly cheaper and faster to produce than fortifications—and probably more efficient in checking the attacks of ironclad frigates. This sense of economy strongly appealed to the mid-Victorian Liberal ideal, as well as the romanticized image of the highly pragmatic, highly inventive "Man of the Future" struggling against government red-tape and conservative "Old Fogies." Ericsson managed to escape this dangerous association, cultivating even closer ties with the most powerful elements within the Navy Department in order to secure future contracts. Coles, on the other hand, was quickly alienating himself from the Controller of the Royal Navy and allowing his ideas to be publicly used as weapons against the Government.

Part of the problem for Coles, unlike Ericsson, was his simple lack of professional shipbuilding experience and engineering skill. In actuality, both Robinson and Fox increasingly relied upon Reed and Ericsson, respectively, neither of whom was a naval officer but both of whom were nevertheless capable of supplying the types of ironclads their superiors demanded and willing to do so without fundamentally questioning their authority. Facts spoke louder than words in convincing each navy which model of ironclad was best for each nation; and both Ericsson and Reed were able to supply ironclad facts that Coles, in turn, could only allude to with editorials, lectures, and colorful sketches.[23]

A couple of other factors weighing against Coles were his insistence upon oceangoing "shield ships" and his lack of technical expertise. If turret batteries threw the Government on the defensive in Parliament, it was the allusion to dubious sea-going versions that allowed Admiralty spokesmen and Palmerston to charge that Coles and his supporters jeopardized the safety of the Empire for mere Liberal economy. As the ultra-Conservative *Blackwood's* further remarked:

> There may be a difference of opinion as to the aspect of foreign affairs. Some may think that we could reduce our armaments if we were to cultivate a still closer alliance with France, and abnegate our own views and interests wherever a difference of policy arose with our Imperial ally. Others, like Messrs. Cobden and Bright, may go further, and believe it possible to dispense with all armaments, and establish a millennium of peace. The latter opinion is absurd; the former is untenable. England, in our opinion, is not one whit overarmed—we would almost say that we cannot be too well armed, considering the state of affairs abroad.[24]

In truth, Armstrong's new 150-pounder gun had suddenly done as much as the *Monitor* did to demonstrate to the British, as Henry Adams wrote from the American Legation in London, that "their wooden navy, their iron navy, and their costly guns, [are] all utterly antiquated and useless."[25] It remained to be seen how each ironclad navy would adapt to ever-changing technological, strategic, and political circumstances.

The magnificently restored H.M.S. *Warrior*, now at Portsmouth (UK). She was the world's most revolutionary warship as of 1861; only against her can the *Monitor*'s radical innovations be appreciated. Note the extreme length and exposed rudder head. (Photo courtesy of the *Warrior* Preservation Trust.)

The christening ceremony for the full-scale U.S.S. *Monitor* replica (June 11, 2006) at the Mariners' Museum, Newport News, Virginia. The state-of-the-art, $30 million American warship museum is devoted to "the history of the famous Civil War ironclad warship that revolutionized naval warfare." (Photo courtesy of the U.S.S. *Monitor* Center.)

Henry John Temple, 3rd Viscount Palmerston, during his last ministry (1859–1865). (Photo from Jasper Ridley, *Lord Palmerston* (1970), courtesy of Ridley estate.)

John Ericsson in 1862, age 59. (U.S. Naval Historical Foundation.)

PAT ON THE MASON AND SLIDELL AFFAIR.

PAT. "Whist, JONATHAN, will ye Plaze to jist go on *Crushin' the Rebellion,* an' lave the Starvin' Ould Curmudgeon to Me?"

Illustration from *Harper's Weekly,* Jan. 11, 1862.

AN ADVOCATE OF MORAL FORCE.

BRITISH LION (*solus*) "This hain't the hattitude we used to take—hem! but 'Circumstances halter Cases.' Those Hiron Vessels of the Yankees — hem! — yes! We must try the '*Peaceable Remonstrance*' Dodge."

Illustration from *Harper's Weekly,* May 31, 1862. Note again the background "actor."

THE NATIONAL CRINOLINE.

Mr. Punch. "TELL YOU WHAT IT IS, MARM, ALL YOUR GUARDS WON'T KEEP YOU OUT OF THE FIRE, UNLESS YOU REDUCE SOME OF *THAT*."

Illustration from *Punch, or the London Charivari*, Feb. 7, 1863. Just as there was a domestic/foreign dichotomy at work in Union naval strategy, mid-Victorian British society found itself torn between conflicting desires for peace, whether through strong national defenses or in spite of them. Coastal-defense turret iron-clads offered an alternative to fixed fortifications—but were ultimately rejected as tying down rather than freeing the Royal Navy.

Illustration from *Harper's Weekly,* Aug. 9, 1862. Both British and Northern presses fanned the flames of an Anglo-American "Cold War" at the heart of the Civil War with explicit national insults and threats. Tensions between the two countries continued until the "Great Rapprochement" of the early twentieth century.

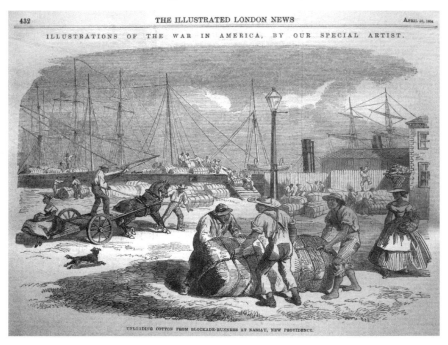

Illustration from *The Illustrated London News,* 30 April 1864, "Unloading cotton from Blockade-Runners at Nassau, New Providence." As long as the Royal Navy was considered "supreme" British entrepreneurs were willing to risk an Anglo-American war by running the Union blockade and sheltering in imperial bases, like Nassau, despite formal neutrality.

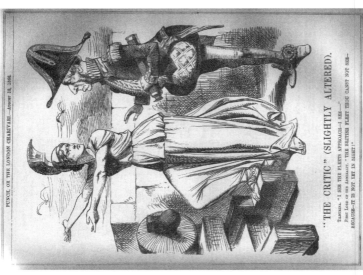

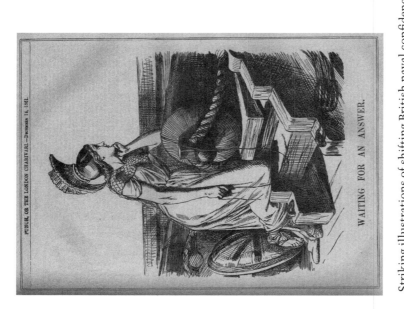

Striking illustrations of shifting British naval confidence, from *Punch,* Dec. 14, 1861, during the *Trent* crisis (*left*), and Aug. 18, 1866, following the visit of the monitor U.S.S. *Miantonomoh* to England (*right*).

Part Three

Deterring Britannia: The *Trent* Affair Reversed

Chapter 15

Coles Loses Ground

Disraeli was quick to note that "the noble Lord's plan of defending our arsenals seaward by forts" had, in fact, "really been demolished by the general opinion of the country"; defense in itself was not being questioned.[1] This was where Coles rested his hopes; after all, the public was fascinated by the American high-tech *Monitor* as an alternative means of national defense as opposed to Palmerston's "Follies." But the Government was not obviously going to abandon the forts—just as the public was unwilling to lose Palmerston—to the *Monitor*. Coles therefore largely gave up his attack against fixed land defenses with light-draft, cupola-armed coastal defense ironclads and switched to a campaign against broadside-armed ironclads in favor of turret ships. The more official opposition he encountered, the more he relied upon political connections and the media. The events of the American Civil War, however, which originally tended to support his system, later turned against him. Coles now had to distance himself from both Ericsson's achievements and apparent failures with the monitor-class of ironclads.

But Coles's turret ship ventures were managing only to stutter forward. Impressed with the new Armstrong 150-pounder guns, and insisting that the *Royal Sovereign*'s turret carry the heaviest guns practicable as part of the system's principle, Coles had to redesign the turret's larger than 22'8" diameter to accommodate at least a single gun—rather than 110-pounder rifled Armstrongs or 68-pounders. This required computations from the Controller's Department for "the total weight allowed for the 5 shields, their fittings and iron rings as proposed on the deck around them."[2] Robinson was impatient with the changes and irritated by Coles's insinuations to the Board that the Controller's Office was in some way responsible for the delay.

An Admiralty Return ordered by Parliament on June 30, 1862, "of all Iron-Cased Ships and Floating Batteries Building or Afloat," noted (as of July 17, 1862):

Iron-hulled (built):	*Warrior, Black Prince, Defence, Resistance*
Wooden-hulled (built):	*Prince Consort*
Iron-hulled Floating Batteries:	*Erebus, Terror, Thunderbolt*
Wooden-hulled Floating Batteries:	*Trusty, Thunder, Glatton, Aetna*
Iron-hulled (building):	*Hector, Valiant, Achilles, Minotaur, Agincourt, Northumberland, Prince Albert*
Wooden-hulled (building):	*Royal Oak, Caledonia, Ocean, Royal Alfred, Enterprise, Favorite*

Under "Wood Built, Converting" was the *Royal Sovereign.*[3] Added to this, Robinson wanted to convert the 91-gun *Zealous,* "in frame at Pembroke," into a central-battery ironclad of 4½-inch iron armor protecting 16 guns up to 120 cwt (6½ tons) each, "with doors of sufficient size to admit of a Gun being taken from the battery on each side to a Port forward or aft which will enable the Guns to fire in a line with the ship's keel."[4] This conversion was distinctly not another turret vessel.

Robinson had already proposed an armor test-target for another Reed design, the *Favorite*—on the same day he was advising against any further test of Coles's turret on the *Trusty,* which was so battered in the recent firing that five of the truncated cone's eleven 4½-inch plates, in Coles's words, "do not fit at the joints with that accuracy which they formerly did, and which the strength of the cone so much depended upon."[5] Five days later, a report from the Controller on whether to accept a Coles offer for two privately built, iron-hulled ironclads, each "to carry two Shields on Capt. Coles' plan," did even more damage. There was no provision in the Estimates for these. "The great question therefore is," Robinson noted, "can any saving be made in the building of other ships in the Dockyards which shall counterbalance the expense of building such a ship by Contract"? Only barring other wooden conversions (the five *Royal Oaks,* the *Royal Sovereign,* and now the *Enterprise*), and thus the need to pay for more engines, could £130,000 be saved and the necessary shipwrights freed from employment by the Admiralty, possibly in the autumn. The savings in wooden materials would be counterbalanced by the added cost of armor plates. Though it was "possible to build these two Ships by contract if it is so desired," Robinson did not "recommend that course" because it would be "dangerous, to effect such large reductions in our dockyards and thus throw ourselves completely into the hands of Contractors and private builders. . . ." Furthermore, this "class of vessel for which this sacrifice would have to be made, though admirable for the defence of the Channel and its Ports, would not be one adapted for general service at Sea, and this consideration would of itself influence their Lordships in not abandoning in the manner referred to the Construction of Ships of War in the Dockyards." If the wants of the country were pressing enough, the ships might be constructed at Pembroke and Sheerness, although those dockyards were not properly equipped or experienced for the building of ironclads:

> But considering how far behind our neighbours we are in the number of iron plated Ships of all classes, I would submit whether it is not necessary not only to build these two Ships for Channel Service by Contract but also to convert such of our Ships now on the Slips and in France, to partially Iron plated Ships with few but heavy Guns, their batteries and water line being wholly protected by 4½-inch Armour Plates. In all our Dockyards, there are Ships in a state to admit of this proceeding.

This possible alteration referred to Reed's central-battery concept applied to corvettes, which would "require considerable strengthening"; frigates, which could be "altered with greater ease, but with rather more waste of material"; and even the line-of-battle ships such as the *Royal Oaks*, "involving however a still larger proportionate loss of work already done." Were turret ironclads even necessary? "The objections to altering Ships designed for one purpose and adapting them to another are obvious; but the objections to throwing away all that has been already done for the purpose of beginning an entirely new system, seem to be still more conclusive, against the latter course." Only if the Navy was willing to apply for a greater Vote should the cupola ships be built by contract, while the dockyards continued to convert the frames of existing wooden steamships, first on the *Royal Oak* pattern and then on Reed's. As far as Robinson was concerned, with various foreign powers now investing in armor-plated ships, it was "impossible to put ourselves on an equality with our rivals without incurring an excess of naval expenditure."[6]

Despite the Admiralty's previous assurances, Coles anticipated their hesitation over his turret ship principle and suggested improvements to the *Royal Sovereign* (and *Prince Albert*) designed to make the ship itself not only much more formidable against an enemy, but impressive to the Board. Instead of four hand-revolved turrets with one 68-pounder and a fifth turret with two, the ironclad conversion should carry either four or three larger (26'-diameter), steam-powered turrets, each with a pair of the forthcoming Armstrong 150-pounders. This echoed the U.S. Navy's proposal to convert the steam frigate *Roanoke* following the battle of Hampton Roads.[7] Whether or not Coles was aware of the details of the *Roanoke*, possibly through New York newspapers, he insisted masts were "of the very greatest importance . . . circumstances might occur when the want of them would paralyse all beneficial advantages of the Shields":

> Consider this Vessel sent outside the Isle of Wight to grapple with an enemy in a sea way, something, although for a short time, goes wrong with the Engines, and she has no head sails, or means of getting her head the right way, lying in the trough of the Sea, she would be at the mercy of her antagonist. Again, when she has but a narrow space to turn in, and a good breeze blowing, her head Sails would be invaluable. If she is caught in a gale going across the Channel, or from Portsmouth to Plymouth, thick weather comes on, and she cannot run into Port, I believe she would roll herself, shields, and all to pieces, for it must be remembered that this Vessel having her weights low, and great beam, will be very quick in her rolling motion.

Therefore Coles wished "to record that if these Ships are tried without Masts, it may vitiate the whole principle of Shield Ships." Robinson, however, told the Board he saw not much advantage of a single 150-pounder over two 68-pounders, and that "considering the possibility of totally disabling a shield, which an unforeseen accident might bring to pass, it would not be wise" to reduce the number of shields in order to carry heavier ordnance "even if it were practicable." The larger number of smaller shields, with their lighter guns, should remain. It was already too late to convert their rotating power to steam, and time was a factor. Rather than wait for a possibly improved prototype turret conversion based on Coles's plan, Robinson argued it was instead "extremely desirable to show with what rapidity this work can be executed and to turn out of hand promptly what must prove a most formidable engine of war, deferring some possible improvements until further experience has been acquired, and until the construction or alteration of another vessel may afford the means of adopting them with facility and economy."[8] By the middle of 1862 this was becoming extremely unlikely, and a lightly armed turret ship unable to sink the *Warrior*, as Coles had promised for years, would hardly be regarded as the new model ironclad for the Royal Navy. In the meantime, Robinson was complaining to the Board how "the greatest possible inconvenience is felt both as regards the *Royal Sovereign* and the *Prince Albert*, from the want of the Drawings of the Shields which Captain Coles was requested to furnish in April and May last."[9]

In England, matters were complicated by Coles's application for half-pay status, finally granted by the Board, but not until the issue was paraded through the Commons—in connection with the fortifications debate—on July 16.[10] Now, Coles was technically free to further publicly express his opinions "not as a Naval Officer serving in the Fleet, but as a Patentee protecting a valuable invention." The implication was that Coles could "do more good for the Navy" outside of his strict professional obligations (and the chain of command) and in the capacity of a civilian-inventor. He promised, in turn, "I shall not relax in my exertions to carry out the details and adjuncts connected with the application of my inventions in any way [the Admiralty] may be pleased to order."[11] But whatever ground Coles gained politically from his ability to join the debate on national defenses by promoting his cupola-ship system as an officer on half-pay, he lost professionally. What he needed were powerful friends on the Board of Admiralty who might counter the increasing influence of Admiral Spencer Robinson and Edward Reed on the issue of turrets versus broadsides—or versus central-battery ironclads. The matter therefore became a question of which force would determine the Admiralty's ironclad-building policy: external political and public pressure or the Controller's Department?

For the record, battle lines had yet to be clearly drawn. On July 26 Robinson reversed his opposition to Coles's proposal for a single cylindrical turret of 25' diameter (rather than two of 22'6") to house the new 12-ton gun on the *Royal Sovereign*, even adding, "on the whole I think Captain Coles' plan preferable to the design made in this Office, and would recommend its adoption."[12] It was also still undetermined as to what form sail-and-steam broadside ironclads themselves should take. On Aug. 7 Russell privately communicated to the Duke of Somerset his own ideas "about the distribution of the Navy, so far as foreign stations were concerned." Only in the Mediterranean and "Home," (or Channel) stations were line-of-battle ships still required, but in numbers equaling those of France, Italy, and Russia, respectively—"large frigates and smaller ships" to best protect trade in North America, as well as light-draft swift steamers to help suppress the slave trade off the coasts of Cuba and Africa. Somerset in turn forwarded the Foreign Secretary's views to Palmerston, noting his hopefulness that with the *Defence* then in the Baltic, the *Warrior*, the *Black Prince*, and the *Resistance* would be ready for Channel service "by the end of August." Considering that these ironclads—the only ones in commission in the Royal Navy—were "at least equivalent to ships-of-the-line," there was little need to commission more wooden liners as replacements. Instead, wooden-hulled conversions of the *Royal Oak* class should be ready by the spring of 1863, "and we shall wish to try these as a guide to future construction." Indeed, many naval officers already preferred the *Royal Oak* class to the *Warrior* class.[13] When the Board issued orders to Rear Admiral Sydney Dacres, in command of the Channel Squadron, to proceed to Malta in mid-September, he was also informed that he was "at liberty to order the *Black Prince* and *Warrior* to return to England previous to his arrival at Gibraltar should he deem it advisable"—caution and uncertainty about the huge armorclads' sailing qualities were still clearly prevailing.[14]

At the same time, the First Lord was startled by the recent test results of Whitworth's rifled 70-pounder, which put a shell through 4-inch plate with 8 inches of oak backing at 200 yards. "I wish Sir W. Armstrong had been there to see it," he wrote to Lewis. By contrast, the experimental "Horsfall Gun," a monster 13-inch smoothbore weighing 24 tons, blasted a jagged 4-foot square hole through a full *Warrior* target. This marked an important divergence of practice in naval ordnance: high-velocity rifled guns "punching" clean holes through armor, as opposed to lower-velocity, heavy smoothbores crushing large sections of plate, or "racking" the entire structure. Either way, "iron-ships are rather down again," Somerset concluded, "and fighting at sea will not be the harmless amusement imagined lately." The Secretary for War agreed: "[T]he history of scientific warfare has hitherto been a history of the power of attack on the power of defence. The iron plated ships seemed a move in the other direction but this superiority has been much reduced by the late experiment."[15] Inasmuch as guns had defeated armor on the British testing fields of Shoeburyness in Essex, ironclads had also lost ground in the politically charged attack against fortifications, and no longer was it thought that invulnerable steamships could act decisively on the offensive. In that sense, guns were to defense what armor was to offense. In a matter of months, the precarious equilibrium of modern warfare had changed again.

Chapter 16

The Practical Concerns against British Intervention

By the end of September 1862, Britain's international relations had proved to be equally as unstable as her weapons technology and associative defense policy. Although the Government fought hard over the spring and summer to protect the fortifications bill and the Navy's ironclad program, on the basis that it was certainly not the time for liberal efficiency and retrenchment, Lewis could also confide to Somerset that a reduction in at least the number of men and stores voted seemed feasible.[1] News from the American Civil War again upset this forecast, in unpredictable ways. The repulse of Confederate General Robert E. Lee's invasion of the North, at Antietam Creek (or Sharpsburg) on Sept. 17 finally encouraged President Lincoln to issue a preliminary Emancipation Proclamation. This tack, he hoped, would help convince London and Paris of Washington's moral high ground over Richmond—the physical liberation of the slave, not the political triumph of his master. Yet bowing to the strategic threat of alienating the Border States, Lincoln proposed to free only those slaves in the Confederacy. Already, the British public was appalled by the relentless character of the war; McClellan and the Union Army of the Potomac could not take the rebel capital that summer after all, and even under a different commander, Northern arms were disgraced at the second battle of Bull Run (August 28–30). Secession was alive and well. Furthermore, it was on the counterattack.

The policy of the Union had, in the words of the London *Times*, "produced enormous bloodshed, enormous waste of treasure, created an unparalleled amount of private suffering and public debt, and

widened an originally small—and perhaps bridgeable—gulf into a yawning chasm, on each side of which stands a separate nation . . . never again
to be reunited." *Punch* represented Lincoln and Confederate President
Jefferson Davis as two exhausted boxers, propped up by amused slaves,
with the French and British looking on. "Interference would be very
Welcome."[2] Now the North seemed deliberately willing to incite a massive slave uprising in the South, a grisly servile war all too reminiscent
of the ferocious Indian Sepoy Mutiny of 1857. The London *Times* cynically denounced emancipation as nothing more than an effort to incite
"the Negroes of the Southern plantations to murder the families of
their masters while these are engaged in the war. The conception of
such a crime is horrible."[3] *Punch* considered this, in a deadly game
of "Rouge-et-Noir" between the two American presidents, to be
"Abe Lincoln's Last Card."[4] Foreign Secretary Lord Russell agreed.
Even though Seward advised Lincoln to forestall an announcement of the
Proclamation until Union arms could produce a victory—so that it
would not be regarded as an act of "desperation"—the bloodiness of
Antietam and the lack of any foreseeable end to the war nevertheless
failed to convince the bulk of European opinion otherwise.[5] On Oct. 27
Napoleon III thus proposed to Lord Cowley, the British ambassador in
Paris, a joint mediation before the American conflict became even worse.
The proposed six-month armistice would include, above all, a suspension of the Northern blockade of the South.[6] But mediation might lead
to formal recognition of the Confederacy; and this would most likely
lead to war with an already irritated Union.

Palmerston was unusually cautious in the affair. Only "great success of the South against the North," he wrote to Russell weeks earlier, might convince the Yankees to consider foreign mediation.
Antietam deprived them of this opportunity, "but we do not yet know
the real course of recent events, and still less can we foresee what is
about to follow." More important for British interests, "as regards possible resentment on the part of the Northerns following upon our
acknowledgement of the Independence of the South, it is quite true
that we should have less to care about that resentment in the Spring
when communication with Canada was open and when our Naval
force could more easily operate upon the American Coast, than in winter when we are cut off from Canada and the American coast is not so
safe." As long as England, France, and possibly other Great Powers
could act together, "the Yankees would probably not seek a quarrel
with us alone and would not like one against a European Confedera-
tion." Russell believed—or rather hoped—that Napoleon's commitments in Mexico made him vulnerable to British demands in Europe,
namely over the French protectorate in Rome, as a condition for comediation. But Russia would not back any diplomatic alliance at odds

with Washington. Indeed, Russia was one of the few friends the United States had during the Civil War, a natural strategic partner in a world still dominated by the nations of Western Europe.[7]

At any rate, the British Cabinet had already convened on Oct. 16 to deliberate intervention in wake of the news of Antietam and the Emancipation Proclamation. Russell felt that "unless some miracle takes place this will be the very time for offering mediation," and he had drafted a memo that ridiculed in altruistic rather than practical terms Lincoln's reasons in freeing some, but not yet all, of the slaves.[8] Gladstone, politically embarrassed as a result of a speech in Newcastle on Oct. 7 (where he announced there was "no doubt that Jefferson Davis and other leaders of the South have made an army; they are making, it appears, a navy; and they have made what is more than either—they have made a nation"), also favored intervention.[9] The American Civil War was "the most gigantic" and likely "the most purposeless of all great civil wars that have ever been waged" because it seemed incapable of any (domestic) military or political resolution. "Secondly," he wrote in his own Cabinet memo, "it is certainly the one which has inflicted, beyond all comparison, the severest suffering on the other countries of the civilized world, and has given them the best title to be heard, if they shall think fit to speak, on the question of its continuance."[10] For once, Palmerston and Gladstone seemed of like mind.

But the military and naval leaders of the Cabinet, perhaps crucially, felt otherwise. "[The Foreign Office] wishes to do something before Parliament meets, and there is great risk of doing mischief," Somerset wrote to Lewis. Intertwined with the idea of recognizing the Confederacy was the political, if not moral, issue of slavery and its probable expansion into new territories. It was highly unlikely that the North was ready for foreign mediation. If they refused, what then? "The French having sent an iron-plated ship [the *Normandie*] to Vera Cruz," Somerset observed, "could hardly have done this against Mexico, which has no fleet and no fort to be taken. If they mean to recognise the South, it is well to have such a vessel in those waters, otherwise the ship is ill-suited to that climate and station." Lewis stated he could "understand effective assistance, in money and men, to the South," and could "understand sending our fleet to break the blockade." Had not France done this against Britain during the Revolutionary War? "But a request to them to be good boys and not to give one another black eyes and bloody noses, does seem to me the weakest and most hopeless course which could be conceived."[11]

Was Britain, in fact, ready to go to war with the United States? Writing to his Foreign Secretary, Palmerston again uncharacteristically stated his preference to wait a little longer for events to decide themselves.

"The Love of quarrelling and fighting is inherent in Man and to prevent its Indulgence is to impose Restraint on Natural Liberty; a State may so shackle its own subjects but it is an Infringement on national Independence to restrain other Nations." Underlying this philosophy were practical military and strategic concerns. "A Rupture with the United States would at all Times be an evil but it would be more inconvenient to us in Winter than in Summer," he explained, "because our Communications with Canada would be cut off, and we have not there a Garrison sufficient for War Time. The French are more at ease in this Respect— they have no Point of Contact with the Americans, and their Naval Force is stronger than that of the Americans while they have less commercial navy to protect or to lose."[12] By Oct. 24, Russell, not convinced that the North would be willing to fight Britain if it could not maintain the Union, was nevertheless willing to concede that "if Russia agreed Prussia would, and if France and England agreed Austria would," and that "less than the whole five would not do." Such a coalition, he must have known, was unlikely, and the following day he wrote, "[I]t should not take place till May or June next year, when circumstances may shew pretty clearly whether Gladstone was right."[13]

In response to the recent French proposal, Lewis also modified his views. "Assuming . . . the right to intervene," he asked in another printed memo, dated Nov. 7, 1862, "would such an intervention be expedient?"

> Greece and Belgium were small circumscribed districts, lying at the feet of the Great Powers of Europe, which the latter could manipulate at their will, so long as they were willing to act together. But the Northern States, even weakened by the Secession, are a great Power, and the intervention of European fleets and armies on the Potomac is very different from their intervention at Navarino or Antwerp. It is difficult and expensive to send large armies across the Atlantic, and the wooden ships of Europe would encounter the small iron-cased steamers of America, which, though not sea-going ships, would prove destructive in the ports and rivers.[14]

Here was a decisive admission. Whatever the moral, political, or even economic justification for accepting the French proposal for comediation, Britain was as unprepared to act against the Northern States now as it was ready to do so over the comparatively trivial affair of the *Trent* less than a year earlier. The *Atlantic Monthly* later speculated that "two circumstances . . . were a restraint upon [Palmerston], and appealed with controlling force to his caution. He was not only an aristocrat and a hater of republics, he was also the Prime Minister of all England." Most of the British working classes seemed to support the Union, and their political power was inexorably rising. Palmerston owed his own position to his remarkably skillful appreciation—or manipulation—of "the public," if not also the press (much to the consternation of his opponents). "His love of place is too strong to succumb either to personal prejudice or national jealousy; and the long habit has made the self-denial more easy." Furthermore, "while Lord Palmerston and Lord Russell are very apt to stalk about and threaten and talk very loudly at nations whose weakness causes them not to be feared, and by bullying whom some power or money may slide into British hands, they are slow to provoke nations whose resentment either is or may become formidable."[15]

Though this assessment was partisan enough, "the small iron-cased steamers of America," Ericsson's monitors, had clearly made a historic difference in Britain's foreign policy. Indeed, this was at least half their intention. "If the condition of our relations with other nations is less gratifying than it has usually been at former periods," Lincoln deftly understated to Congress, in his Annual Message of Dec. 1, 1862, "it is certainly more satisfying than a nation so unhappily distracted as we are, might reasonably have apprehended." The accompanying report of the U.S. Secretary of the Navy was more explicit. From a prewar (March 1861) force of 76 men-of-war, Union naval power had jumped to 264 vessels by December 1861—136 of them converted merchant vessels—and to 437 by the end of the following year. Of these, 123 were purpose-built warships, "completed and under construction," and 44 of them—more than a third—were armored. According to Gideon Welles, before the events of Hampton Roads (in fact, at the height of the *Trent* crisis), he had determined that Ericsson's model of ironclad "was particularly adapted to our harbor and coast defense, and service on the shallow waters of our sea-board. . . ." Their purpose was clear. "Whatever success may attend the large and costly armored ships of the *Warrior* class, which are being constructed by some of the maritime Powers of Europe, cruising in deep waters," his report continued, "they can scarcely cause alarm here, for we have within the United States few harbors that are accessible to them, and of those few the Government can always be prepared whenever a foreign war is imminent."[16]

After the diplomatic wrangling over intervention in the fall of 1862, Palmerston himself was noticeably frustrated. Though he was unquestionably popular at home, he could not bargain the French out of Rome, cynically complaining to the King of the Belgians on Nov. 18 of the Emperor's stated reason that withdrawal would alienate the priesthood. "With his immense army devoted to him and a nation the great mass of which look up to him, and to nobody else, he might well do what is right and just without caring for fanatical Priests, sentimental Ladies, or intriguing Politicians. A Fait accompli would silence them all." This was an apparent freedom of action the British Prime Minister did not enjoy. Four days later *Punch,* in a similar vein, retreated from its earlier stance on the intervention issue with a cartoon entitled "One Head Better Than Two." Pointing to a scene of American battle-field commotion, a fully uniformed Napoleon III asks, "Hadn't we better tell our friend there to leave off making a fool of himself?" "H'm, well," replies a civilian-dressed Palmerston with a knowing smile, "suppose you talk to him yourself. He's a great admirer of yours, you know."[17]

At the same time, local intelligence from British naval officers on the North American Station was arriving in London to confirm the boastings of the Northern press made that summer.[18] "I have lived long enough in this atmosphere of puffing not to be blinded by its smoke," wrote the *Times* correspondent from San Francisco on July 29. But reports of an improved Ericsson monitor to be constructed there, and possibly more, "must not be overlooked by our Government. They are suggestive at best; perhaps ominous." Mr. Ericsson had promised that "'applications of mechanical science will put an end to the power of England over the seas, and render the United States impregnable against the navies of the world.'"[19] From Sept. 4 to Oct. 8 Captain John Bythesea, an important figure in the history of British assessments of the Union's ironclad program during the American Civil War, toured U.S. naval dockyards and commercial establishments along the Great Lakes and the eastern seaboard, after participating in the Royal Defence Commission of Canada. Between Chicago, Detroit, Newport, Cleveland, and Buffalo he found some 6,000 shipwrights employed; "foundries and machine work shops of every description" could be found in "all the important places, many of which, now employed in the manufacture of Agricultural implements and Railway rolling stock, could, in the event of hostilities, be employed in the construction of Marine Engines and iron cased Vessels." The Federal navy yards, however, were "inadequate to either the construction or maintenance of a large fleet. Private yards partially supply the defect." This must have sounded familiar to the Admiralty, especially the remark that "the work done by contract is reported to be unsatisfactory and the expense to Government much greater than it would be if the public yards were on a more extended scale."

Still, Bythesea listed 14 ironclads (mostly armored gunboats of the Western river flotilla) afloat, as of Sept. 1, 1862, "mounting 153 guns and representing 14,375 Tons," with another 38 under construction in both government and private yards.[20] Aside from the sea-going broad-side battery U.S.S. *New Ironsides,* "nearly the whole of the Iron clad Vessels building are to be armed with heavy guns in turrets and to be protected with layers of inch iron plates on Mr. Ericsson's plan."[21]

While at Boston, the British naval officer got a close look at one of these, the *Passaic*-class monitor U.S.S. *Nahant*, and provided details of her mode of construction. It was unlikely that the monitors would be sent to sea, yet they were "fairly adopted for river and harbour defenses [*sic*]." Persons inside the turret could withstand the concussion of shot, he was informed by an experienced, though unidentified Union naval officer, as long as they were not in contact with the turret walls at the time, and "no inconvenience was felt by the firing of their own guns."

What made the Union turret truly ships ominous *was* their armament, which would be either 15-inch Dahlgren-designed smoothbores or 300-pounder Parrott rifles. Dahlgren himself, Bythesea wrote, "stated to me at Washington in April last that he did not think favourably of rifled guns larger than 40 pdrs. or of the range of any guns beyond 2,000 yards." The Chief of the Navy's Bureau of Ordnance was busily designing a gun "to carry a projectile of 20 inches diameter and spoke of adopting a plan which has been submitted to him of a gun with 36 inch bore." Perhaps Dahlgren was indulging in his own boasts calculated to impress foreign minds. More important, "he was of opinion that for the protection of rivers and harbours the gun would soon be the principal part and the vessel only its carriage."[22]

SUMMARY

On Dec. 15, 1858, Edward J. Reed delivered a paper to the Society of Arts on "The Ships of the Royal Navy." With the onset of the recent Crimean War, he noted that "the fleets of England, though well adapted for battles by sea, and sufficient to drive the enemy from the open waters, were almost totally deficient of the class of vessels which were essential to the putting forth of our full power against his fleets and coasts. Nor was the want supplied with anything like that promptitude which the occasion demanded." By December 1862, it was still questionable whether the Royal Navy could cope with the American Union's newfound capacity for self-defense, contrasting sharply with the Secretary of War's promise a year before (during the *Trent* crisis) to "iron the smile out of their face." The Civil War had undeniably become a unique source of strength as well as weakness for the United States. Federal defeats were more spectacular as the war evolved and the North mobilized its vastly superior resources, while Confederate victories for the same reason carried with them an increasingly noticeable edge of desperation. But on the sea, the Union Navy remained an undefeated force, developing at an even more impressive rate—and with an iron backbone. Times had changed quickly indeed, and no one knew what to expect. Even Reed, in his 1858 paper, asserted, with all the confidence befitting the Editor *of Mechanics' Magazine,* that the "attempt to build ships which shall be proof to solid shot—at least, to wrought-iron solid shot—is an altogether illusory one; and such ships are not urgently required."[23]

Captain Cowper Phipps Coles also found himself grappling with events apparently beyond his control. The attempt to introduce his cupola vessels at the cost of fortifications on a wave of popular support only confirmed instead that national pride was in fact imperial pride. Though doubts lingered about the seaworthiness of the experimental broadside ironclads, these would hardly be dispelled by assaulting, in the press, as a half-pay naval officer, the broadside principle itself in favor of masted turret ships—especially when the Controller of the Navy found what he was looking for in Reed's central-battery concept. "It is no merit whatever in such ships to have a large proportion of weight to steam power, obtained by means of excessive length and size," Reed, as Chief Constructor, recounted to a new First Lord of the Admiralty in 1868. "The merit of an armoured fighting ship consists in having a large weight of guns and of armour, carried by a short, cheap, and handy hull; and, judged in this way, the Bellerophon is much superior to the Achilles."[24] Because Coles critically delayed the completion of his trial turret ship, the *Royal Sovereign*, in order to incorporate the almost daily changes occurring in heavy ordnance (and thereby decisively defeat the broadside), any initiative he may have enjoyed by the spring of 1862 was lost by the summer. Instead of representing an even greater economy of force, sea-going "shield ships" were therefore relegated by the Admiralty as expensive, untried luxuries the public would have to pay extra for. This outcome was further ensured by his own refusal to build a mere "battery" first.[25] Even Ericsson in a wartime Navy had to address and overcome many of the original *Monitor's* deficiencies—in habitability, ventilation, seaworthiness, speed, armor protection, and armament—before his own version of a free-ranging capital ship found some acceptance with the powers-that-be.

Chapter 17

Summer of 1862: The Tide Turns against the Union

While the evolution of ironclads as weapons platforms intrigued British naval observer Captain Bythesea, the issue of laminated armor plating versus solid armor plating was also occupying serious attention in Washington. In early June, Fox "mentioned the general idea prevailing here and in England for the thick plates" and wrote to Ericsson, "[N]evertheless the advantages of thin plates in stiffening the armor, and breaking joints, is very great, and your plan allows the increase of thickness which is objectionable in vessels like the *Warrior* already overloaded."[1] Actually testing armor plate schemes was quickly becoming a manifest drain of time and resources for the Americans. "We asked Congress for $100,000 to experiment with," Fox explained to Robert Forbes, "and they gave us $25,000 which will not test one 10th of the really meritorious plans presented." Dahlgren's initial test with his 11-inch smoothbore, fired with an increased charge of 30 pounds against a forged 4½-inch iron target backed by 20 inches of oak and secured against a clay bank, succeeded in merely cracking the plate—at a distance of 20 yards.[2] Fox speculated to Ericsson that contemporary English theory ranked a 3-inch solid plate equal to five 1-inch layers.[3] Ericsson agreed: "But for our ability readily to float the greater number, not to mention our inability to obtain thick plates, I never would have employed the thin plates." Still, he would always recommend employing thin layers behind a thicker front "to give support under the joints of the latter."[4]

Yet, when Dahlgren tried the same test against "Target No. 6," composed of four 1-inch–thick wrought-iron plates, one ½-inch wrought plate, and again backed by 20 inches of oak and an inner-skin plate 1 inch thick, the results were mixed. An 11-inch Dahlgren, its muzzle "83¾ feet from target, firing 30 lbs. charge, powder 1862, cored wrought iron Shot of 160 lbs.," cleanly penetrated the five laminated plates, and penetrated another four inches into the wood backing. However, the official report significantly noted, "No cracks were observed in the plates while the heat was much less than in the solid Iron plates."[5] Instead, rippling shock waves broke several of the 1¼-inch–diameter through-bolts. Dahlgren added that "the plate[s] is not bent inward so as to throw the ends, as the solid plate is, but retains its general planeness." Furthermore, the Union navy's ordnance expert distrusted "those results which have misled the English." His own preliminary tests indicated that the results were "entirely too limited yet to furnish a general rule even as regards flat plates" and even when this had been achieved there would be "nothing to indicate whether it holds good in the formation of a tower as it does in the flat side."[6]

The Union capture of New Orleans likewise drew confusing lessons. Flag Officer David G. Farragut's squadron did not include a single ironclad and faced potentially three, including the huge casemate-rams *Louisiana* and *Mississippi*. Though both of these leviathans were blown up by the Confederates to prevent their capture, *Louisiana* had been sufficiently intact to act as a moored floating battery near Fort Jackson. Porter drew up close-range, desperate plans for how to deal with her armored broadside.[7] The diminutive C.S.S. *Manassas*, a poorly armored, semi-submerged ram armed with a single 32-pounder, made valiant efforts to check the progress of passing Union warships, but a few broadsides from the U.S.S. *Mississippi* were enough to overwhelm her thin plating and drive her ashore. The forts themselves were bypassed, but only after the barrier blocking the river was removed days before, never mind the prefatory bombardment from Porter's mortar flotilla.[8] In an official report to Secretary of War Stanton, printed for Congress, Brevet Brigadier General and Colonel of Engineers Joseph G. Totten also declared that "while it is true that floating batteries will be useful auxiliaries in many cases, and in some cases our only safe resort, it is equally true that their expensiveness, to build and maintain, and their certainty of decay, exact that we rely in general upon works ashore, where, for the same outlay, ten times the amount of artillery may be arranged, with imperishable cover, impenetrable to guns afloat." Ships would always be at the mercy of forts.[9] Welles, however, was already informing Du Pont, commanding the South Atlantic Blockading Squadron, of the Department's intention "to capture Charleston so soon as Richmond falls, which will relieve the iron boats *Galena* and *Monitor*." These could then be used in the same manner as Farragut on the lower Mississippi. "The glorious achievements of our Navy inaugurated by yourself give every reason to hope for a successful issue at this point, where rebellion first lighted the flames of civil war."[10]

Yet within 48 hours the prospects for a fairly straightforward, if not easy, victory were mitigated by the Navy's repulse at Drewry's Bluff on the James River (May 15). Most of the damage to the *Galena* was inflicted by 8-inch solid shot that stripped her decks of fittings and numerous gun crews.[11] "I have seen the elephant in the fighting line," Rodgers wrote to his wife. "I ran up within eight miles of Richmond and there found three separate barriers formed of piles and sunken vessels[,] the channel only as wide as the vessels length[,] the banks lined with rifle pits and sharp shooters and a battery of heavy guns on a hill some 200 feet high to protect the barrier." It was a formula for combined defense that would also prove effective at Charleston a year later. Unable to move forward as Farragut had before New Orleans, the formidable Union ironclads were suddenly rendered sitting ducks. Significantly, no one was hurt aboard the *Monitor,* where Anne Rodgers assumed her husband would be, "and therefore perfectly free from personal danger. . . ."[12]

Stimers, too, was surprised that the *Galena* led the attack. "It seems to me that that is the position for the *Monitor.* She draws the least water and has the most impregnable armor." Yet the Chief Engineer could only suggest piling rocks "upon the deck of the *Monitor* at the side farthest from the elevated battery and give her a list" so that the turret guns "could then reach the enemy."[13] The *Monitor*'s new commander, Lt. William N. Jeffers, was not so hopeful. He could recall trying to force river barricades under fire, in command of a flotilla of gunboats at the capture of Roanoke Island and the occupation of Albemarle Sound, in early February 1862.[14] Operations up the James River in a monitor proved to be even more complicated. Already Flag Officer Goldsborough was furious at Jeffers for failing to silence all the batteries he passed to join Rodgers in the *Galena,* thus forcing wooden supply steamers to run gauntlets each way.[15] The Army of the Potomac was close behind. At any rate, Goldsborough was exceedingly anxious that the lighter-draft *Monitor* "should push on up to Richmond, if possible, without any unnecessary delay, and shell the place into a surrender." This would no doubt have saved General McClellan a lot of trouble. "Should Richmond fall into our possession, inform me of the fact at the earliest possible moment," wrote the Flag-Officer somewhat optimistically. "Send off a special messenger with the intelligence, if she can get here sooner than a letter by mail."[16]

Jeffers's subsequent report of the repulse that same day would dash these hopes. Obstructions blocked the way to the Confederate capital.

The *Monitor*'s guns could not be elevated to reply against heavy gun emplacements on bluffs 200 feet high. Obliged to anchor farther down-river, the *Monitor*'s two 11-inch Dahlgrens were thus handicapped by greater distance and therefore reduced accuracy, "with the usual effect against earthworks."[17] On the basis of his previous experience against Roanoke Island, Jeffers told Rodgers it was "impossible to reduce such works except by the aid of a land force."[18] Perhaps anticipating the enormous disappointment from his superiors, if not the nation, the *Monitor*'s commanding officer soon compiled an official list of "defects" of his vessel. This list would be the first in a long line of similar compilations of complaints, made for similar reasons, against these ironclads. The complaints would bear an unmistakable uniformity: the machines were at fault, not the men who were forced to fight with them. To Jeffers, the Navy's solution to the *Monitor*'s and the other ironclads' perpetual problems was facile: give its naval officers and crews better tools, and the Union could reasonably expect better results. Jeffers wrote that he would have made a special report earlier, but "most of [the *Monitor*'s] prominent defects have been pointed out to or discovered by Chief Engineer Stimers, the Government inspector, and provided for in the contract for the new [ironclads]."[19] Likewise, he did not "consider it expedient in our then state of constant readiness for a naval battle to supply information which, by some accident becoming known [to] the enemy, might be used to our detriment." Among the chief defects of the *Monitor* was the position of the isolated pilothouse near the bow, which made fire control almost impossible and prevented forward fire within 30° of the line of keel. Firing within 50° directly astern, Jeffers believed, "would undoubtedly set [the boilers] leaking, if nothing worse happened." Ventilation in the summer heat, however, was more of a problem:

> When the weather was cool it was quite warm below, but no inconvenience was felt other than the impurity of the air passing up through the turret. But with the heat of the last ten days, the air stood at 140° in the turret when in action, which, when added to the gases of the gunpowder and smoke, gases from the fire room, smoke and heat of the illuminating lamps, and emanations from the large number of persons stationed below, produced a most fetid atmosphere, causing an alarming degree of exhaustion and prostration of the crew. In the action at Drewry's Bluff I was obliged to discontinue the action for a quarter of an hour and take the men below to the forward part of the ship for purer air.[20]

Occupying a hostile river, with sharpshooters keeping the men below deck, hatches closed, severely limited the *Monitor*'s effectiveness. Once again, there was the issue of seaworthiness. This problem was inextricably linked to the *Monitor* as a "machine"—her Achilles' heel, as far as Jeffers was concerned—because whether "in action or at sea the loss of the vessel might readily be caused by the failure of a leather belt."

There were other concerns. "The opportune arrival of this vessel at Hampton Roads, and her success in staying the career of the *Merrimack,* principally by the moral effect of her commander's gallant interposition between that vessel and the *Minnesota,* caused an exaggerated confidence to be entertained by the public in the powers of the *Monitor,* which it was not good policy to check." It was his duty, Jeffers wrote, "to put on record my deliberate opinion of her powers." His conclusions were striking: "Notwithstanding the recent battle in Hampton Roads and the exploits of the plated gunboats in the Western rivers, I am of the opinion that protecting the guns and gunners does not, except in special cases, compensate for the greatly diminished quantity of artillery, slow speed, and inferior accuracy of fire; and that for general purposes wooden ships, shell guns, and forts, whether for offense or defense, have not yet been superseded."[21]

This level of defiance, coming from a naval veteran in command of the nation's most celebrated engine of war, was sure to provoke an equally virulent response, touching as it did upon so many nerves. The White House still had every reason to believe that the "operations against Richmond may close favorably at any moment." Therefore the Department of the Navy ordered Goldsborough to prepare for "a sudden naval demonstration against Fort Caswell . . . without a moment's delay so soon as Richmond falls."[22] The *Monitor* was to be edged as close as possible to rebel works up the James, to conduct reconnaissance. But on June 2 the *Monitor*'s engines broke down. Taking into consideration the previous combat damage to the *Galena,* Goldsborough could write his superiors only that he was "less confident of success" and that the "principal work is now, perhaps, more formidable than the Department is aware."[23] Meanwhile, the commanding officer of the *Monitor* was pointedly "much chagrined at the necessity of forwarding the accompanying report of the senior engineer relative to an accident to the engine."[24] Jeffers was apparently as irritated by his reliance upon the *Monitor*'s mechanic as he was by the *Monitor* herself.[25]

Equally irritated was the *Monitor*'s designer. In quick response to Jeffers's report of May 22, Ericsson wrote to Welles that it did not "convey a single new idea, nor does it develop a single new fact . . . relative to the construction of the *Monitor* not previously known to the constructor." Presently forgoing a point-by-point "analysis of the subject"—for he had precious little time for this—Ericsson could only assure the Secretary that the new monitors, "being pushed towards completion by all means that funds and mechanical energy have at command," were free from any previous oversights in the original prototype. "Lieut. Jeffers's assumption that the *Monitor's* reputation is based on fictitious grounds," however, demanded "immediate refutation":

> The advocates of the new system so far from admitting that too much is claimed for it deplored the circumstances that *Monitor* was not supplied with powerful guns. How different the result, they say, if the impregnable turret had contained guns of proper calibre [*sic*] and strength. . . .[26]

Having given Jeffers's report more thought, Ericsson returned to his counterattack the following day. He had "no hesitation in saying that is a pernicious document, coming as it does at the very moment when you are called upon to decide the question of Iron Clad vessels." Nothing the *Monitor's* own commanding officer wrote overturned "the success, of every essential feature, claimed for the new system, and yet Lieut. Jeffers clings to 'wooden vessel and shell guns for general purposes.'" As usual, when defending his monitors, Ericsson took to the high ground. "The commander of the *Monitor* evidently is not aware of the extraordinary—unprecedented— activity of the European dock yards in fitting out whole fleets of Iron Clad vessels at this moment, or he would not advise his government to rely on 'wooden vessels and shell gun,' rather than impregnable iron vessels carrying solid-shot-guns protected by impregnable iron turrets."[27] Ericsson could fairly be described as aghast. After all, what was the *point* of such reports, given their negative, unconstructive, almost insubordinate tone?

Perhaps the underlying issue of correct "attitude" was behind the Department's May 7 decision to appoint Rear Admiral Francis H. Gregory, U.S.N., as General Superintendent of the new ironclads' troublesome construction—rather than Commodore Smith.[28] Indeed, there was no time for interminable debates on ironclad policy. Fundamentally defective ironclads, such as the *Galena*, Fox was not interested in even repairing. Gregory underscored the heavy work already being done on the monitors when he wrote to Smith (in transmitting the latest installment-payment bills for the monitors) that "Mr. Ericsson has over eight hundred men now employed at Green Point, working extra time and progressing energetically."[29] In Congress, suspicion still lingered over private contractors and the role of the Navy Department, culminating in an Act of June 2 "to prevent and punish fraud on the part of officers intrusted with making of contracts for the Government." Welles responded to Senator Hale of the Committee on Naval Affairs that the passage of this act would "render necessary increased clerical force in the several bureaus of this Department" and therefore an additional appropriation of $12,500 for staff and additional office space. Already the Navy, apart from its agents, dealt with some 400 contracts annually. "The writing for a single bureau is estimated to be equal to fifteen hundred foolscap pages, relating to contracts alone." And this ignored the "very voluminous" copies required of all the unaccepted bids.[30] At any rate, the Act of June 2 was superfluous to the detailed annual reports produced by the Secretary to Congress, and even dangerous. The Assistant Secretary of the Navy, Hale relayed, had safety-related concerns regarding increased copies of contracts "for new and improved projectiles, guns, gunboats, and iron-clad boats, the models of which they have refused, upon application, to allow to be inspected by the agents of foreign Governments, and . . . in some instances, by foreign ministers." Senator John Sherman of Ohio was embarrassed that such an act could even be passed by Congress—and might now have to be repealed as quickly.[31] It was obviously too easy for the national legislature and Government to "confuse"—or second-guess—one another. In peacetime this was discomfiting, even humiliating; in war it could be disastrous.

Yet Senators Grimes and Fessenden still fiercely debated the wisdom of even more dockyards, let alone naval expansion, in June 1862. At stake was the establishment of League Island, off the existing Navy Yard at Philadelphia, as a base for ironclad construction, including the manufacture of armor plates.[32] Was the American Civil War an occasion to initiate all this or not? "Does anybody imagine this thing is going to last always," challenged Fessenden, "that we are going to have a necessity for three or four hundred vessels when this war is over, and that we ought to provide for that?"[33]

Even in consideration of the House of Representatives' Bill No. 364, on the building of a transcontinental railroad and telegraph line from the Missouri River to the Pacific Ocean, issues of American national growth, security, and naval power intertwined. For Senator Milton S. Latham of California, this was a simple matter of history—or manifest destiny. Steam, industry, and science had made the world much smaller, much faster, and the United States as a nation much greater by proportion than any that had come before it. The only question now was, who would dominate the rest of the planet, the British or the Americans? "The restless Anglo-Saxon race, under its newborn Government of freedom, soon spread itself over the great valley of the Mississippi, and new on the Pacific shores confronts the millions of Asia, and is preparing to dispute supremacy with the commercial rivals of the Union." California gold, like that of Australia, required frank acknowledgment of national strategy in its highest—and perhaps basest—sense. Just as Britain's maritime possessions around the globe required a strong navy to protect such tenuous commercial links, the security of pan-American interests demanded well-defended lines of communication and supply:

> The growth of our commercial power has brought us into superiority over the greatest maritime people of the eastern hemisphere, our tonnage being five millions five hundred thousand, or an excess over them in tonnage of half a million. The popular nature of our institutions is a standing cause of disquiet to the feudal aristocracy of the Old World. Their leading reviews, journals, and parliamentary discussions, breathe a tone almost of animosity toward us, and indicate their yearning hope that this intestine war may end in overthrow and ruin as a great nation . . . We are competitors for a fair division of [world] trade, and in the ratio in which we lessen [England's] share by increasing our own, we weaken her power, and advance to that position in the family of nations which we feel is the destiny of a great and free people. . . . A recent political event growing out of our belligerent rights has brought to our shores a hostile fleet with all the equipments of war, threatening to strike upon the instant, while a formidable and well-appointed army in the Canadas even now keeps watch upon the long line of our lake frontier. We are living in an age when the political elements of the Old and New World are in commotion.[34]

The Civil War was therefore, in one sense, a fortuitous opportunity for the American republic. It had "developed new ideas in respect to military and naval strength in the United States, furnishing examples which tell upon the policy and bearing of nations." The Union was demonstrating just how powerful it had become by the mid-nineteenth century. For "the protection of our firesides and altars" against any foreign challenge, its capacity for military force would swell even more. Meanwhile, "we have launched upon the deep steel-clad warriors of such model and power as to mock and defy those 'wooden walls' once the boast and glory of proud maritime Powers. The ability of our Government for the rapid construction and multiplication of these new iron engines of naval strength is such as to enable us to place invincible sentinels at the doors of our harbors in the Atlantic, the Gulf, the great lakes [*sic*], and in the Pacific." The golden promise that followed Union victory in the Civil War was the demonstration of "the entire competency of this Government to maintain and further, in a spirit of justice, all the varied interests committed to its charge. . . ." Secure again internally, and from coast to coast, the United States would ultimately triumph in a much wider war, already under way, for nothing less than prevailing world influence. On this score, even Queen Victoria was advised by her trusted Uncle Leopold, the King of the Belgians, that the "point of most importance to England is, that there should be two great Republics instead of one, the more so as the South can never be manufacturing, and the North, on the contrary, is so already to a great extent, and actually in many markets a rival. . . ."[35]

This sentiment was repeated in the fervent debate of June 30, 1862, in the House of Representatives—over the proposals for a consolidated national network of essentially anti-British ship canals. To Francis P. Blair of Missouri, Chairman of the Committee on Military Affairs, "it becomes the honor of the United States to arouse from the lethargy which has held us so long, and not longer to be blinded to the dangers which threaten us from the boundless ambition of Great Britain, our political and commercial rival. . . . " Britain's own canals along the northern frontier were clearly meant to facilitate invasion of the Union if need be, naval control of the Great Lakes at least.[36] Alfred Ely of New York agreed. The combination of *potential* British naval power on the Great Lakes, and the boastings to that effect of the London *Times*, at least, was justification enough to take appropriate action. "The paw of the British lion," he added dramatically, "is rather too plainly in sight on these peaceful lakes."[37]

For Samuel C. Pomeroy of Kansas, national security and union were inseparable factors of American identity—"stupidity alone would have failed to exercise the power thereby acquired to attain by all honorable means the continental proportions indicated to [the United States] by the geography of the country":

> Nature had already designed what man has accomplished. Our mission, almost divine, is to bind together this great empire which has been committed to us, so that its protected frontiers shall henceforth offer no inducement to foreign aggression, and its social and material interests no bribe to individual ambition or domestic insurrection.

For Pomeroy, "the embarrassments of the time only enhance the necessity of action," not the reverse. The Napoleonic Wars, he argued, had in fact been good for England. While her sacrifices were undoubtedly extreme, the eventual peace saw "her credit unimpaired, her resources expanded in proportion to her liabilities, and her position first among the nations of the earth." Thus the Civil War in America, despite its deplorable apocalyptic qualities, offered dazzling prospects for action, change, and growth. The United States as a nation must either assume far greater responsibilities, adapting to its own demographic as well as international realities, or diminish.[38]

Even the controversial Morrill Tariff, enacted by Congress during the Secession Crisis of 1860–1861, had been a step in this direction—though it further alienated powerful British manufacturing interests, as cheap British imports were about to give way to an era of renewed American protectionism and industrialization.[39] This eventually did wonders for the Union's ability to mobilize its own national resources against the South—but at a price carrying the threat that the war, while self-sustained, would not be self-contained. "We, of course, must condemn the Protective Tariff of the Union as oppressive and benighted folly—silly and suicidal in itself, iniquitous towards the West, and hostile to ourselves," declared the *Economist* in September 1861. Such sentiment was justified "as at once natural, statesmanlike, and righteous," and "we do not see why we should hesitate to declare our belief that the dissolution of the Union will prove good to the world, to Great Britain, and probably in the end to America herself. . . ." The cutting-down-to-size of Britain's rising competitor was therefore regarded as a golden opportunity, and possibly a further incentive for intervention. If the North demonstrated it would "not be able to subdue the South," Palmerston wrote the Parliamentary Under-Secretary for Foreign Affairs that an independent, Confederate nation "would afford a valuable and extensive Market for British Manufactures. . . ."[40] Less than a month later, the *Trent* crisis only seemed to further vindicate U.S. policy fears. As the Secretary of the Treasury, Salmon P. Chase, observed, "[W]hile other nations look with indifferent or unfriendly eyes . . . sound policy would seem to suggest, not the extension of foreign trade, but a more absolute reliance . . . upon American labor, American skill, and American soil. Freedom of commerce is, indeed, a wise and noble policy; but to be wise and noble, it must be the policy of concordant and fraternal nations."[41]

But all this depended upon the real probability, or not, of a great naval war with Great Britain. "We are sure there will be a war," quipped Thaddeus Stevens of Pennsylvania, "because Great Britain has taken up the cause of the light women of New Orleans."[42] Instead, the threat of war was "done as an embellishment to the canals which these gentlemen are so industriously digging through this House." There were, in any event, far cheaper and quicker ways to introduce Federal ironclad gunboats on the Great Lakes than bringing them up from the Midwest states or New York through canal extensions that would take years to construct—namely, building them on the spot:

> But suppose Great Britain does declare war; I admit she might send her gunboats in about sixty days into the lakes through the Welland canal. But, in the meantime, ten thousand of the men we are now wasting and destroying could go there and blow up and destroy the Welland canal so that England's gunboats could no more get round the falls than we could. There would be an end to that argument.[43]

Actual events in the Civil War did little to allay the suspicion that such projects, from fortifications to transcontinental railroads, telegraphs and canals to ironclads, were really only about lucrative local contracts—or the expansion of trade interests—and that intricate discussions of a probable war with European powers were deliberately—even dangerously—overplayed. On June 5, R. W. Shufeldt, the U.S. Consul-General at Havana, warned Flag Officer William W. McKean of the East Gulf Squadron at Key West that the "feeling of the reactionists and French in Mexico, is very hostile to us. American interests are now in peril in that country, and there is not an American man of war at Vera Cruz." Less than a month before, Captain L. M. Powell of the old sailing frigate U.S.S. *Potomac* reported ominously before departing Vera Cruz that he had "not seen a sailing vessel of war since I have been among the allied fleet upon this coast."[44] Meanwhile, Flag Officer Chas. H. Bell, commanding the U.S. Pacific Squadron, forwarded a list of British and French naval forces in his vicinity. Among the former were three frigates, four sloops, and two corvettes—all steam powered. "A number of the English vessels on this list were sent from India and the China Seas immediately after the *Trent* affair," Bell observed, "in order to be prepared for hostilities with the United States." Yet given "the present state of the defenses of [Mare Island]," he added, "one-half of this force could command the city of San Francisco and take possession of this yard."[45]

At Nassau, the U.S. Consul reported, the Confederate commerce raider *Oreto* (later commissioned as the C.S.S. *Florida*) was first seized and then released by the British Governor, and was "now about to leave on a privateering cruise, or to attack our gun-boats, without a doubt." Captain Raphael Semmes and his officers, formerly of the raider C.S.S. *Sumter*, were likely to take command. It would be "prudent, therefore, for our cruisers to 'hunt in couples,' for there is a formidable fleet of rebel cruisers here and in this vicinity." The situation was further exacerbated by the presence of "eleven large British steamers," which the Consul excitedly wrote were "all laded with arms" for the South.[46]

The source of all this trouble was Great Britain. Accounts from U.S. diplomats and informants were rapidly increasing of blockade runners fitting out in various British ports. Most of these were accurate, some not, but all of them were described in disturbing detail.[47] Not just arms, munitions, ordnance, and saltpeter were reported as cargoes, but also iron armor plates. On June 21, 1862, the U.S. Consul at London also reported "that the Rebels are having constructed at Sheffield some 60 to 70 marine floating batteries for the destruction of ships in harbors." These would be "about 3 feet long and hardly seen on the surface of the water. . . ."[48] Charles Francis Adams could inform Seward only that pro-Southern British sentiments were based largely on news of the Civil War in America, coming in daily. When the Union's fortunes suffered, literal British ones rose; when Confederate blockade runners were captured, "dismay" was felt at Lloyds, "where many of these had been insured." As a result, the wily American diplomat knew of "nothing that will be of more use on this side of the water than to inspire a salutary fear of our Navy."[49]

This was precisely the solution Ericsson had in mind. As W. L. Barnes, Ericsson's agent in Washington, wrote to Erastus Corning ("a member of Congress and a partner of Winslow in the Albany Iron Works"[50]), "the question of a Superior Iron Clad Navy has taken hold firmly of Capt. Ericsson's mind":

> No man in this Country is more intensely interested in it. He does not like English supremacy and be assured that if his advice is followed we shall energetically push the matter to an acknowledged Conclusion in our favor.[51]

Barnes also discovered from his recent interview in New York that Ericsson secretly authored the article on "Our Iron-Clad Navy" for the *New York Herald* of June 26, which asserted that the "position of the country at the present moment is so intimately connected with the power of our navy" (echoing his historic letter of April 23 to Seward).[52] Much of the credit for the powerful new ironclads under way Ericsson publicly attributed to the Secretary of the Navy and his Assistant.[53] "It has been objected that the Engineer-in-Chief [Isherwood] is not employed in the construction of the new vessels; but Secretary Welles, to the surprise and annoyance of many, has lately been found to entertain very peculiar notions on all matters connected directly with the efficiency of the navy, among which may be attributed that of putting 'the right man in the right place.'" Ericsson the civilian was simply a better-qualified engineer than the Navy Bureau Chief. As a result of this arrangement, Europe would soon "view with astonishment" a "prodigious display of energy and mechanical resources." The national agenda was clear: "The rebels are growing weaker every day; the Union feeling is spreading, and we will be ready to defy all the maritime Powers of Europe combined in less than two months. Napoleon in Mexico may then look out."[54]

Yet the President's own assessment of national, much less naval, aspirations was less than "ironclad." Indeed, the almost heady ambition to invest in continental-scale railroads and canals, in widespread coastal fortifications, and in monitors capable of defending American interests *anywhere*—to challenge British naval supremacy on the high seas as well as along America's own maritime boundaries—only reflected the optimism still existent in the early summer of 1862: that the Civil War might soon be over. Lincoln may have liked to indulge in similar expectations, if not fantasies. The Homestead Act, passed on May 19, 1862, he heartily endorsed. The *promise* of greatness afforded by "that portion of the earth's surface which is owned and inhabited by the people of the United States" was to him logically "well adapted to be the home of one national family; and it is not well adapted for two, or more."[55] But of all people, the President had learned that war was full of harsh surprises. Victory could not be assumed. Moreover, there was a fine line between actively destroying the enemy and merely avoiding defeat.

Lincoln's visit in early May with General McClellan, to discuss the progress of the Peninsula Campaign, did little to reassure him in this regard. By June 28, his "view of the present condition of the War," as he wrote to his closest Cabinet advisor, Secretary of State Seward, was that events had "enabled the enemy to concentrate too much force in Richmond for McClellan to successfully attack." A similar concentration of Union forces would only leave Washington vulnerable to a quicker thrust from Richmond. "Or, if a large part of the Western Army be brought here to McClellan, they will let us have Richmond and retake Tennessee, Kentucky, Missouri, &c." Instead, they should "hold what we have in the West, open the Mississippi, and take Chatanooga [sic] & East Tennessee," while "a reasonable force should, in every event, be kept about Washington for its protection." The North could then continue the mobilization of its vastly superior resources, fielding yet another army "in the shortest possible time," and eventually crush the bulk of Confederate forces in Richmond, carefully held in place by McClellan. If need be, Lincoln pledged, he would "publicly appeal to the country for the new force, were it not that I fear a general panic and stampede would follow—so hard it is to have a thing understood as it really is."[56]

Perhaps it was for this reason the Government found it difficult on July 12 to meet Congress's request for "information in regard to the relations between the United States and foreign powers." Though Seward explained that "the correspondence upon the subject is so voluminous, and the indispensable current of business of [the State Department] is so pressing in proportion to its force,"[57] the fact remained that the Civil War—and the dream of America—demanded first of all the defeat of the Confederacy. Furthermore, the inherent duality of the Civil War—its domestic and foreign imperatives—depended largely upon unforeseeable events that continually shuffled these priorities.

Sure enough, even as Lincoln, Congress, the Navy, the press, and John Ericsson were all determining the best course of Union grand-strategy, the new Confederate general in charge of Richmond's defense, Robert E. Lee, launched a brilliant series of attacks on the besieging Army of the Potomac: the Seven Days' Battles (June 25–July 1). McClellan's loose grip on the war's strategic initiative was suddenly lost. Though Confederate forces suffered more dearly, the siege was lifted, and the Union Army was unquestionably back on the defensive. This in turn only placed more pressure on the Navy, and upon the precarious foreign relations of the United States. "If [McClellan] is not the man," Anne Rodgers anxiously wrote to her husband on July 1, "where are we to look? If we are defeated here England & France will be only too glad of the excuse to be counted in & we shall then be between the upper & the lower millstone."[58]

The next day John Murray Forbes wrote to Fox, enclosing a letter from J. M. Beckwith in Paris, "a shrewd old Democrat long resident in France & well posted up there—a Hater of England & rather a lover of France—which makes his warnings the more valuable." From his perspective, Beckwith found it undeniable "that [the] aristocracy in Europe is arrayed against Democracy in America, and resolved irrevocably to break up the great Republic if possible." The growing strength of the Union Army and Navy had "quickened the instinct of self preservation & revived the alarm of the whole aristocratic class; they now see nothing but danger from the success of the North. . . ." The proverbial iron fist of the European elite, however, would come wrapped in a velvet glove of diplomacy. "They know that . . . offers of friendly mediation will be refused & resisted, but they intend to embrace us with the affectionate hug of a Bear." Beckwith's only consolation was that a foreign war might unite the North and stiffen its determination even more. Napoleon III, in the meantime, was closely watching events in the Civil War, waiting for an opportunity. "The way the Cat jumps depends on the mouse—but the English feel very sure of the Emperor <u>this time</u>." Forbes himself was fairly disgusted with the performance of the Union Army, and the need for even more reinforcements. "You cannot get soldiers now," he wrote Fox, "but there are plenty of mechanics & before you can recruit & drill into value an army of 100,000 men (representing 100 millions per ano) you can get under full headway—& indeed near completion—50 millions worth of Iron cased ship <u>more</u> than now ordered . . ." As far as he was concerned, "these will be worth far more than the 100,000 men—whether for subduing Domestic or preventing Foreign War. The *Monitor* stands us today in as good stead toward Europe as one <u>whole army</u>."[59]

Even Radical Parliamentary Leader John Bright's extraordinary personal attempt to reassure Seward that "Opinion here is quiet on American affairs" following news in Britain of the Union army's reverses came across as weak, ambiguous, and even ominous. English sentiment was "not friendly—but less demonstrative than it was sometime ago." The "richer classes of society," he admitted, tried "to excite our working people to urge the Govt. to do something—but not with much success." The effects of the Union blockade of the

South were a more pressing concern. "There is great & growing distress in this cotton spinning Country, & the coming autumn & winter are looked forward to with apprehension." Bright's polite remark that it "would be a great relief to hear of peace on your continent" only seemed to emphasize the unpleasant truth that peace could be achieved in a variety of ways, through foreign mediation as well as domestic Union victory (or defeat). Still, the insights he offered were valuable. Poor harvest prospects in Britain would mean greater reliance on Northern grain, "which will tend to make our Govt. more peaceably disposed to you." As for the personal character of the British Government itself, Bright thought "our Foreign Minister is well affected to your Govt. tho' he is capricious & not always prudent in what he says." His assessment of Palmerston, though it could be expected, was discomfiting to Lincoln's Cabinet—for the British Prime Minister had "no rule but that which for the moment suits his low ambition."[60]

Now Webb's standing offer to build an indomitable seagoing ironclad, less controversial than Ericsson's, was finally accepted at a cost of $1,250,000.[61] "At the time this decision was made and the vessel commenced," Welles noted in his diary in 1865, "a foreign war was feared. We had a large defensive force, but not as many . . . formidable vessels as we should need in the event of a war with a maritime power."[62] The U.S.S. *Dunderberg*, "Thunder Mountain," represented the changing character of the Civil War in America—and the Union's perspective on foreign affairs.[63]

All this served only to intensify Union ironclad shipbuilding efforts still further. Smith was threatening contractor Charles Whitney that "the time for completing [the twin-casemated ironclad *Keokuk*] is rapidly approaching, and if you are delinquent in this respect, heavy damages will be claimed under the contract."[64] Yet in transmitting progress reports of the ironclad contractors under his supervision to Smith, Francis Gregory found it "very gratifying to know that all are sensible to the importance of their labors in the present crisis, and appear to be governed more by patriotism than selfish considerations."[65] Work on the *Passaic*-class monitors was progressing rapidly. Smith was pleased. The contractors' bills were approved and the next payment installments sent out.[66]

The ever-energetic John Ericsson took an alternative view to Gregory's, however, especially after the Fourth of July. "Our men observed the great festive day of the nation with so much spirit last Friday," he complained to Fox, "that they were unfit for work yesterday [Saturday]." As a result, "we lose three valuable days in succession." Already cracks were beginning to appear in the ironclad construction business. The explosion of Government work available placed a high premium on labor. As far as Ericsson, the contractor, was concerned, "we have not got our men 'in hand' as we had a year ago." Furthermore, the Department's (political) need to balance the contracts for the six original, improved monitors under Ericsson's responsibility around the country was leading to irregularities in production. Relatively inexperienced and poorly equipped Pennsylvania and Delaware firms were failing to meet their deadlines, which only involved delays in other aspects of the vessels' construction. Not taking any chances, Ericsson would build both his seagoing monitors in New York.[67] This was bound to irritate other interested parties.

On July 19 Robert Forbes wrote to Fox from Boston. He had met "several of our principal mechanists & iron workers" and had "very little doubt from what they say, that by a combination of two shops, now doing little, a three tower ship could be got up here. . . ." When Forbes suggested this to Ericsson, he received a "laconic response of yesterday's date," in which "he makes no allusion to doing any thing here beyond machinery & he cautions me specially against promising more for this City than we can carry out." Forbes acknowledged the lack of investment capital "of our machinists" but insisted they were "as good workmen as exist any where in the Country & will do all they can to carry out any thing they undertake. . . ." It would be imprudent for them, moreover, to promise "to do any large work very quick [or] very cheap—unless they can get their pay in the equivalent of gold or silver—it would be suicidal to do so."[68]

Problems with Ericsson's super-monitors began even before the contracts were formally signed.[69] It was "more and more apparent that our Government must lose no time in placing our Navy in condition to combat foreign powers," wrote Griswold, "and I have no doubt we shall be called on to construct the four large ships instead of the two if we desire to take the contract." Barnes and Stimers would attempt to wield their influence at the Department of the Navy, but Lenthall, Isherwood, and other competitors were surely on the lookout. Ericsson's strong arguments previously overdid it; the naval professionals had entrenched, placing pressure of their own upon Fox and Welles. Future efforts, Griswold concluded, "must we think be under cover, as our open efforts might be suspected." Winslow, however, had telegraphed Bushnell "to meet him in New York for the purpose of coming to an understanding in relation to the contract for big ships." Ericsson expected unacceptable demands from Winslow and was preparing to countermand his iron orders with Abbott.[70] There could be no complications. Perhaps Winslow sensed, like Ericsson, the construction disputes that were coming. But for Ericsson it was far too late to turn back. Already there were, as Gregory reported to Smith on July 9, "over 1000 men at work at Greenpoint."[71] "We are pushing ahead the ironclad as fast as possible," Ericsson assured Fox. "A fleet of these vessels afloat at this moment would inspire the nation with fresh life and confidence."[72]

Coincidentally, the same day (July 29, 1862) Palmerston wrote the First Lord of the Admiralty that the "Events of the Civil War in America shew the value of Gun Boats in assisting Troops in a Country intersected by Rivers which communicate with the Sea and are navigable for Gun Boats," namely China, Welles pressed Secretary of War Stanton of the "importance of capturing Vicksburg and keeping open and unobstructed the Mississippi river"—an operation that would require a diversion of "a sufficient land force to cooperate with the Navy in taking and holding the place. . . ."[73] This, Welles assured his colleague, was "a source of regret" for both of them because Vicksburg "keeps our Squadrons unemployed" from other duties.[74]

Army-Navy cooperation was critical, especially in the West— where the most dramatic Union advances of the war had been made (as Lincoln recognized). Corinth, Mississippi, was captured on May 30. Memphis, Tennessee, surrendered June 6, following a climactic, though one-sided, naval battle that morning between Confederate gunboats and Union Flag Officer Charles Henry Davis's force of ironclads and rams, operating out of Cairo, Illinois. As Welles noted in his diary, "the army has fallen in love with the gunboats and wants them in every creek."[75] Farragut had meanwhile run his saltwater blockaders past Vicksburg's upper-bluff batteries to join combined Union forces there. Commander David Dixon Porter also arrived from New Orleans with his flotilla of heavy mortar boats. "It was intended that the Army should supply 6000 men," he privately wrote Fox at the end of June. Instead only 3,500 were supplied, but these he felt were still "quite enough, though, to do the business." But "General [Thomas] Williams objected . . . to landing his troops to assault the main forts, where he would have had a perfect success, with scarcely the loss of a man, as I have since learned." Porter was confident he could "destroy the forts in 24 hours":

> Our mortar practice has been terrible to them, almost every shell falling into their works and killing those who dared to remain there. There is no use, however, in destroying them until the time comes to take possession, as they are nothing but earth works, and the guns can be moved anywhere else.

As a result, "we have gained nothing by going through except to show that the navy is ready to do anything," Porter bitterly complained. "No British fleet of three deckers would ever attempt to pass these forts. The officers here have done it with eggshells."[76] Accomplishing little with his mortar vessels, Porter was sent back to New Orleans, observing Confederate operations along the way. On July 13 he sent a brilliant analysis of these to Farragut, which Welles promptly forward to Stanton.

The situation was not good. Confederate troops, munitions, flour, and cattle from Texas and Louisiana were pouring across the lower Mississippi. Such trafficking was supplying the South from the West and defying the efforts of the Union blockade. New batteries of heavy guns were appearing to protect the new rebel base:

> Up the Red River and Ouachita they have about twenty steamers, some of the largest class. We all know how troublesome they can be made if converted into vessels of war. There is also a fine ram being prepared up the Ouachita, intended to operate against our gunboats in low water, when it can escape into shallow places. My opinion is that it would be better to pounce on them at once, and break them all up.[77]

This would require, however, Federal warships already tied up above and below Vicksburg. Here, General Thomas Williams's army was "frittering away" its time digging a canal to bypass the rebel stronghold. Disease was rampant. As far as Commander Porter was concerned, Union naval forces would be better spent actively policing the Mississippi, whose water levels were rapidly falling in an exceptionally hot summer. If Farragut's deeper-draft steam sloops "don't return down river at once (at least as far as Red River)," he warned, "they will not come down this season."[78]

Porter might have added a final reason for striking quickly. Reports circulated that the Confederate States Navy was rapidly completing another ironclad-ram up the Yazoo River, just north of Vicksburg. "We must seek this great danger before it hunts us," Commander H. H. Bell nervously wrote in his diary in early June.[79]

A reconnaissance in force, consisting of the ironclad-gunboat *Carondelet*, the ram *Queen of the West*, and the paddle-wheel gunboat *Tyler*, finally went in search of the C.S.S. *Arkansas*. But unlike the situation at New Orleans, the Confederates had managed to finish their ironclad just in time. Early on the morning of July 15, the *Arkansas* ran into this probe. Caught off guard, the Union vessels turned about to warn the rest of the combined fleet. A running gun battle ensued in which the *Arkansas* quickly disabled the *Carondelet*, driving her aground, and then chased the remaining Union gunboats into the Mississippi. There her captain, Isaac Brown, "approached the Federal fleet—a forest of masts and smoke-stacks—ships, rams, iron-clads, and other gun-boats on the left side, and ordinary river steamers and bomb-vessels on the right."[80] Due to extensive damage to her smokestack (which reduced her draft and speed), the *Arkansas* could not ram. Instead, she blasted her way through the Union squadrons, which did not have their steam up, inflicting damage in every direction, and receiving pummeling hits in turn. At last the Confederate ironclad reached shelter beneath the guns at Vicksburg, a battered but powerful boost to moral there and across the South. Immediately there was talk of sending her, upon repairs, to retake New Orleans single-handed if need be.[81]

Farragut was outraged. At sunset a sortie was made to sink the *Arkansas* below Vicksburg, but it was driven off under heavy fire in the approaching darkness. An 11-inch shot penetrated the ram's casemate at short range, however, disabling the engine, killing two, and wounding three more. "This single shot caused also a very serious leak," Brown wrote, "destroyed all the contents of the dispensary . . . and, passing through the opposite bulwarks, lodged between the woodwork and the armor."[82] Nevertheless, the mere presence of a single Confederate ironclad had again completely upset Union strategy. Farragut reported to Welles his "deep mortification . . . that, notwithstanding my prediction to the contrary, the iron-clad ram Arkansas has at length made her appearance, and taken us all by the surprise."[83] Davis preferred waiting to attack the *Arkansas* until after she was prepared and moved away from the protection of Vicksburg's guns; Farragut wished to attack before her repairs could be completed. Rising sickness, falling river levels, shrinking coal supplies, uncertainty of army reinforcements against Vicksburg, and the damage to morale by prolonging tensions over the ram were other considerations. At any rate, an ill-coordinated attempt to sink her on July 22 with the new ironclad gunboat U.S.S. *Essex* also proved ineffective.[84] Welles could only assert by telegram three days later that the rebel ironclad "must be destroyed at all hazards," and on August 2 wrote to Farragut "that the escape of this vessel and the attending circumstances have been the cause of serious mortification to the Department and the country. It is an absolute necessity that the neglect or apparent neglect of the squadron on that occasion should be wiped out by the capture or destruction of the *Arkansas*, which I trust will have been effected before this reaches you."[85] By that time, however, Farragut had already withdrawn his fleet to New Orleans in disgust. The army was too sick to stay and moved off to Baton Rouge; and as long as the Confederate ironclad remained before Vicksburg, the city could not be taken. Welles and Stanton might have blamed one another with equal success.[86]

What finally destroyed the *Arkansas* was her own mechanical breakdown. Forced to assist in a Confederate attack on Union forces at Baton Rouge without full repairs, her starboard engine failed—after a 300-mile journey, within sight of Baton Rouge—and the *Arkansas* ran hard aground. As Federal warships approached, the ram was scuttled.

But the lesson of her example was undeniable. The North could not win the war as long as Confederate ironclads could be built in shallow waters and launched to threaten Union gunboats penetrating into the South. Just as the *Monitor* and the *Passaic*-class follow-ons were needed to protect the Atlantic blockade from European threats on the outside and Confederate ones within, so would even lighter-draft ironclads of superior armor-crushing armament and impregnability be needed to bolster Union combined operations in the West.[87] Until then the North was as much on the strategic defensive there as it was again in the East.[88]

There were political side effects as well. "Ram Fever" was growing in the North as newspapers spread reports and rumors of new Confederate ironclads under construction all over the South. "Merrimac No. 2" was ready at Richmond, while the English blockade runner *Fingal* was being converted into a powerful armored ram at Savannah, after delivering a precious supply of arms and munitions. But the Secretary of the Navy correctly surmised it was unlikely these were suitable for offensive operations. "In the mean time the sensationalists will get up exciting alarms and terrify the public into distrust and denunciation of the Navy Department."[89] This was important because public trust in the government was a necessary precondition for public support of the Civil War—one whose nature would soon radically transform, as Welles learned two days before the *Arkansas* burst out onto the Mississippi; Lincoln was ready to issue a preliminary Emancipation Proclamation:

> It was a new departure for the President, for until this time, in all our previous interviews, whenever the question of emancipation or the mitigation of slavery had been in any way alluded to, he had been prompt and emphatic in denouncing any interference by the General Government with the subject. . . . But the reverses before Richmond, and the formidable power and dimensions of the insurrection, which extended through all the Slave States, and had combined most of them in a confederacy to destroy the Union, impelled the Administration to adopt extraordinary measures to preserve the national existence. The slaves, if not armed and disciplined, were in the service of those who were, not only as field laborers and producers, but thousands of them were in [*sic*] upon the armies in the field, employed as waiters and teamsters, and the fortifications and intrenchments [*sic*] were constructed by them.[90]

It was under these circumstances during the summer of 1862 that John Ericsson again addressed a letter to the nation's Chief Executive. The famed engineer-inventor positively endorsed "Mr. Rafael's repeating rifle," which he could authoritatively pronounce was "free from those imperfections which invariably defeat the usefulness of such contrivances." Technology drove tactics, and therefore strategy.

Warfare, in fact, was becoming more efficient. Perhaps attrition could be avoided, if not "radical mobilization":

> The time has come, Mr. President, when our cause will have to be sustained not by numbers, but by superior weapons. By a proper application of mechanical devises alone will you be able with absolute certainty to destroy the enemies of the Union. Such is the inferiority of the Southern States in a mechanical point of view, that it is susceptible of demonstration that, if you apply our mechanical resources to the fullest extent, you can destroy the enemy without enlisting another man.[91]

Ericsson, however, was about to be taken at his word again. As with the *Virginia* at Hampton Roads, the *Arkansas* on the Mississippi only increased public pressure upon the Navy and therefore upon its veritable "Chief of Operations," Fox.[92] As in March, the Assistant Secretary in August turned to Ericsson for help in preventing similar debacles from occurring. But history could not repeat itself exactly; the situation had changed. In March, Ericsson's only preoccupation was with the six *Passaic* monitors, mounting 15-inch guns. Now, in the hot new climate of crisis, he was already committed to providing plans for another four *Passaics,* and two of the huge oceangoing monitors he had dreamed of even before the *Monitor's* ironclad duel with the *Virginia.* Before the end of the month, he would be introducing two new classes of monitors—one for "harbor and river defense," drawing 10 feet with improved speed, and another drawing 6 feet.

By this time, the Assistant Secretary knew how to play on Ericsson's jealousies perfectly, with a mixture of subtlety and candor. Even though Fox informed Ericsson on August 4 that the Department had decided to build "a double turreted wooden Monitor in each Navy Yard like Quintard's vessel" (thereby satisfying even further the bureau's desire for turreted ironclads more of their own design), he casually added that one of the four new ironclads of what would be the *Monadnock* class would feature Ericsson's vibrating-lever engines to directly compare with Isherwood's. This was small compensation for the engineer-inventor's threatened sense of worth, so Fox was prepared to "offer" more:

> I wish somebody of brains would give us a six foot draft boat of great velocity and high pressure for the western waters, impregnable like your boats. We have plenty of 3-inch plating but the Rebels seem to beat us in their *Arkansas.* They have also got an iron clad ready at Richmond and Savannah, and two ready at Charleston, and we are no where.[93]

This applied equally to problems with 15-inch gun manufacture and handling, especially elevation. Dahlgren was still balking at his own lack of control and tacitly willing to leave the onus upon the man behind the monitors, who, he wrote in his diary, "is just the man to be very wrong or very right, when one or the other. . . ."[94] But Fox wrote Ericsson, "I have so much confidence in your scientific skill that I do not permit myself to hesitate with regard to that or the pilot house about which Dahlgren expresses some doubts of its standing a heavy shot." Clearly, the man behind the ships was more important than the man behind their guns. Therefore, Fox "told Dahlgren he must consult with you and if the 15 in. gun cannot be furnished, why then to do the best he can for you." The situation demanded results above and beyond conflicting personalities:

> What we want is an invulnerable vessel with any kind of a gun. We are again in a pinch where another Monitor may strike a blow as important as that of the first creation of your brain. Let every effort be thrown upon *one* boat and call upon the Bureau of Ordnance in time for the guns.[95]

Personal quarrels in many ways determined the course of the Civil War—and Ericsson also knew how to "give" by asking for something in return. "On the subject of a 6 feet draught boat for the Western waters," he therefore replied on Aug. 5, "I wish you had instructed to me the planning of . . . early last spring." Instead, the two oceangoing giants "now keep me hard at it night and day for some time." Ericsson's problems with the Bureau of Ordnance also required attention—or direct intervention from Fox. "Captain Dahlgren's fears that guns could not be obtained in time for our turret fleet have filled me with apprehensions," he confessed. Such a circumstance would also be a "national calamity" because, without 15-inch guns to destroy the enemy in "a single shot," the entire system would fall apart, never mind Dahlgren's recent target tests. "With the XI shell gun it will be the Hampton Roads contest over again." A telegram from Dahlgren, meanwhile, promised that only *one* 15-inch gun would be ready in time for the new monitors. Ericsson was therefore insistent: "Can you not adopt some plan of procuring the big guns for half a dozen foundries at once?"[96]

Fox replied with flattery. "I feel that we should have more of your vessels, nothing that has been presented approaches them in value," he wrote. "The *Galena* and *Ironsides* are the work of a blacksmith; the *Monitor* a piece of delicate, perfect mechanism." This turned to a straightforward appeal:

> Your associates have nearly five millions worth of work, and the public whom we all serve, expect other work to be scattered. For yourself with your patriotic impulses the establishment of your system must be your greatest reward. People incapable of making one of your ships are begging,

beseeching and demanding one. We propose to advertise say for a class of vessels like the big Monitor, Quintard's vessels, and the new Monitors to be built on the Atlantic or Western Waters; will you help us by furnishing drawings &c with the present royalty for the small ones, and say $10,000 each for the big ships? I am most anxious to see Monitors on the Mississippi. . . . Shall we advertise and rely upon you? This seems the only way since we cannot have the entire use of your brains exclusively. I have thought about the matter deeply and have come to the conclusion that your boats only can give us the Mississippi. . . . If you say yes, we will go ahead at once and the credit belongs entirely to you.[97]

Suggested here was not just one but two more distinct classes of monitor ironclad, of 10- and 6-foot drafts. Ericsson would supply the plans, but other contractors would construct them beyond his direct— or even indirect—supervision. This strategy was ambitious and risky because, potentially, the specifications for such complicated vessels would have to be furnished in even greater detail in Ericsson's absence. They would also preferably need to be supplied at once and in greater numbers to separate private firms—and subcontractors—across the country. Nor were the new monitors the only response by the Union Navy to events of the summer. On the same day (Aug. 5) that Fox wrote to Ericsson, Welles announced to Dahlgren that "the Department is about contracting for more double-ended Gunboats, say fifteen," in addition to the four Navy-built, double-turreted ironclads, and a new class of "screw Gunboats."[98] All these shipbuilding efforts would be likely competing against one another for mobilizing limited national resources—especially in terms of manpower.

This last detail was turning into a serious consideration. Even though Ericsson the next day indeed wrote Fox to "advertise as soon as you deem proper for more vessels and count on my assistance, pay or no pay" labor gangs on the *Passaic* monitors could no longer be worked night and day "during this warm season," and double gangs of men were no longer possible. "Such is the pressure produced by the Government work that we cannot fill up our day gangs much less work the double system." How would this affect Ericsson's other pressing concern: the supply of 15-inch guns? "Can you not by employing all the makers at Pittsburgh, West Point and Boston obtain a supply?" he asked. "It will be nothing short of national disgrace if we are forced into protracted contest with the rebel craft when we ought to sink them as soon as engaged."[99]

National conscription only made matters worse, and threatened, as Ericsson wrote to Welles, to "put a stop to the work on the Iron Clad Navy." It would cause half the workmen involved to be lost to the draft, while also "depriving us of the leaders of gangs and hands trained to particular work. . . ." Ericsson had already taken the initiative of preserving this vital, specialized workforce by contacting "the owners of the rolling mills now employed in the manufacture of our Armor and other plating, as also the builders of vessels and machinery, to make out accurate lists of the names of the men employed on the Government work, with a view of obtaining exemption from drafting for these men." This, he informed the Secretary, was respectfully not intended to commit or embarrass the Department:

> It is not for me to urge the imperative necessity of your prompt action in this matter, nor would it become me to set up an argument to prove, that a man drafted to pursue rebels or digging trenches, does not contribute more effectually to the defense of the nation than the toiling laborer who heats and clenches the rivets of the Armor intended to resist hostile shot.

Though it was in fact precisely what Ericsson was arguing, he concluded by pointing out to Welles "that the instant you obtain exemption from [the] military for men employed on the national vessels, new life and vigor will be infused into our building yards. Skilful [*sic*] and good men in great numbers will at once seek work on the Iron Clads."[100] Gregory, too, after reporting to Welles on Aug. 9 "that the Contractors are making every possible exertion to fulfill their obligations in good faith," felt it "proper to call your attention to the consequences a draft of the Militia." Skilled laborers simply could not be replaced. "So great has been the demand, particularly for Iron Workers," Gregory observed, "that the Contractors have not been able at any time to procure as many as they required."[101]

Nevertheless, that August Fox continued with his scheme for building two new classes of monitors. The Navy Department was under stress.[102] Ericsson's answer of Aug. 6 was "a loyal one and such as I counted upon." Fox wasted no time in making out his order: "10 feet gives us the main part of the Mississippi most of the year; to be sure 6 would be better, and I trust you will turn over in your brain a six foot invulnerable 11 knot boat, and we will bring it out so soon as your brain gets a little rest. In the meantime we must have some 10 foot Monitors out west."[103] Even more extraordinary, Ericsson replied he would send "a general plan of a swift and powerful Monitor Ram for the Mississippi, of 10 feet draught" within *two days*. But his efforts could not be single-handed. The Assistant Secretary must procure exemption from the draft of everyone employed building such ironclads. "If you cannot," he warned "the country must then look to its soldiers alone for protection, for a long time to come."[104] Fox was still elated at the level of protection Ericsson was offering. True to his word, the plans for the improved, swift monitor drawing 10 feet arrived within days. To Stimers, Fox wrote:

The advertisement (required by law) will be sent to day, and every shop capable of doing the work, shall have one, both here and on the western waters. I was surprised to find the royalty upon Ericsson's brain was divided amongst associates. We threw work so far as we could, into his hands to reward him for his success, but I should have preferred that the pre-eminent skill which has characterized him should have been devoted directly to our cause. However his answer to my letter and his generous offer without price is noble, and if Congress do not do him justice, the country will.

Fox was also "delighted" that Ericsson was proceeding with the ultra-light draft monitors next. "It is all we require to complete our series." Yet Stimers's concerns that the contracts might be let to unqualified firms promising more than they could deliver, Fox answered, could not be avoided. "We must advertise by law: there is no help for it, but we can confine the work to bona fide workers." He was able to promise, on the other hand, "that the men who are working on boilers &c. for us will be immediately discharged whenever they are drafted."[105]

After meeting with Ericsson again in New York on Aug. 15, Fox reported to Welles that the first improved monitor, the *Passaic,* would be launched on the 30th, followed by another one two weeks later. He expected the third to be ready by the end of October, "a favorable time to go South." In the meantime, Ericsson's work was being "driven all night. Even one inch plates cannot be furnished fast enough."[106] Ericsson could expect comparatively less zeal in return concerning the new monitors' armament. Plenty of reasons existed to move cautiously, Dahlgren argued, even suggesting that Ericsson resort to mounting the longer 15-inch Rodman (Army) guns in the new turrets to save time. This, of course, Ericsson found "impracticable" and too late in any case. Dahlgren then noted the "great difficulty however in procuring the fabrication of such guns at all, and whether they shall prove reliable or not when made, remains to be seen." There was, after all, only one prototype of this caliber in existence. His 11-inch gun was in 1854 "considered too heavy to be allowed as a gun of the Navy— and was not admitted until I went to sea in the Plymouth (1857–1858) and proved practically that the gun was manageable." Could Ericsson "practically prove" a class of ordnance two and half times heavier without a trial? Could manufacturers be persuaded "to encounter the risk" of casting them?[107] The immediate concerns of the Civil War seemed to weigh against their adoption.

What ultimately tipped the scales in favor of procuring 15-inch smoothbores for the monitors, however—despite the difficulties, despite the risks—was the recurring influence of European concerns. On Aug. 4 Frederick Edge, a journalist proclaiming to be an American "heart and soul . . . not merely the correspondent of an English (loyal) newspaper," requested permission to visit the ironclads under construction. Edge told the Assistant Secretary of the Navy exactly what he wanted to hear, exactly when he needed to hear it. "England and France will not interfere, notwithstanding all their talk: their harvests are bad, and, besides, they fear your iron navy. 1863 will see the U.S. the first naval power on the ocean—incontestably."[108] Here was an invaluable opportunity for crucial international publicity, if not propaganda. Perhaps not coincidentally, Ericsson's early April suggestion of *Dictator* for his large "Ocean Monarch" class of monitors was finally approved; his recommended "Protector" for the sister ship was changed to *Puritan* by Fox on Aug. 8.[109] But there was also the danger of revealing technological secrets. Fox deferred the question to Ericsson, whose reaction was mixed. More than anyone else, perhaps, he understood the monitors' propaganda value, but he was also careful not to reveal too many technical details about them. In October he wrote "that it would be highly objectionable at present to make any explanations in public exposing the peculiar construction of our Iron Clads. We imagine that we have got hold of ideas far in advance of England and France and we mean to keep them to ourselves; at any rate until we have crushed out the rebellion."[110] This did not prevent Edge from visiting *New Ironsides* in Philadelphia, which he described as "a noble looking craft, but still I cannot help preferring Ericsson's principle." Having now "found the road" to act "against these infernal rebels and their still worse sympathies and fellow-conspirators in England," he would now do everything in his power to "silence many of the enemies of the government here and put a final stop to all opposition in Europe."[111]

It was in this vein, therefore, that Ericsson wrote on Aug. 29, 1862, that he would "cheerfully incur the expense" of re-attaching the roof of the turret and the pilothouse of his first *Passaic* monitor at his own expense when the first pair of 15-inch guns arrived. "The Nation cannot afford to sacrifice the prestige which will attend a perfectly successful first trial of our system," Ericsson explained to Dahlgren. If the guns for the second monitor were delayed, Ericsson felt it better to "put only one XV inch gun into each," rather than none at all, "well convinced that with only one of the large guns in each vessel we shall be able to destroy all rebel craft[,] inspire a wholesome dread in Rebeldom[,] and prove to foreign powers that we can punish intermeddling."[112] That same day, the second battle of Bull Run (or "Second Manassas") had begun, ending with the defeat of the Union Army of Virginia under General John Pope by General Thomas "Stonewall" Jackson and Lee's combined forces on Aug. 30. On Sept. 5 Lee took advantage of the Federal retreat into Washington's defenses to invade

Maryland, which he hoped would then be "free" to secede also. A campaign on Northern soil would spare the rich Shenandoah Valley of further pillaging, feed the Confederate Army of Northern Virginia on enemy harvests, and force McClellan's Army of the Potomac, back up from the Peninsula, to fight its own desperate battle. A victory on Northern soil would then demoralize the Union still further and encourage European powers to offer mediation on the basis of a permanent breakup of the United States.[113]

Doubt and stress in the Department of the Navy turned to pessimism and panic. As Lee struck out from Virginia, Fox wrote to Stimers that Dahlgren's recent test against an inclined target representing the *Passaic*-class monitor's deck had proven its weakness. It also supported Dahlgren's claims since the battle of Hampton Roads that "30 lbs. of powder makes the 11 in. a terrible weapon." Perhaps Ericsson should accept that the 15-inch guns were unrealistic and unnecessary after all? "Give us two monitors and the *Ironsides*, and we will make Jeff Davis unhappy," Fox dolefully concluded, "though now he seems to have every thing his own way, and darker days are coming."[114] The Union needed a victory, and evidently only the Navy could supply one. But where? Richmond and Vicksburg defied combined Federal arms. There was only one major target city left in the South, of little practical military value but conceivably as important morally, if not strategically, to the Union cause—where the Navy might strike a blow with minimal support from the hapless U.S. Army: Charleston. This was where the great rebellion began, and where British interests most visibly touched the South in the form of blockade running.[115] Seward therefore implored the Navy to attack Charleston, "his remedy for all evils," Fox complained to his wife, Virginia.[116]

Welles had other problems to consider as well. Little was actually known on Confederate ironclad-rams built and under construction at Richmond.[117] On Sept. 3 the commerce-raider C.S.S. *Florida* had dashed past Union blockaders into the safety of Mobile Bay, preparing for a cruise under the protective guns of Fort Morgan. Another British-built Confederate cruiser, the much more formidable "290" (soon to be commissioned the C.S.S. *Alabama*), had slipped out of Liverpool earlier that summer before she could be legally detained by the Foreign Office. Most of her crew were British. By September, Semmes and the *Alabama* were destroying Union merchantmen off the Azores, then grain shipments in the North Atlantic, generating yet another alarm in the North. Welles could only advise New York shippers to arm their vessels courtesy of the Navy Yard.[118] He did not want to materially weaken the blockade by detaching warships fast enough to catch the *Alabama* and her sisters, and powerful enough to sink them when cornered. Though Commodore Charles Wilkes (of *Trent* affair fame) was indeed ordered on Sept. 8 to command a special flying squadron of fast steamers to hunt privateers in the West Indies and the Bahamas, Welles was not prepared to give up the overall strategic initiative of the Civil War "at sea'" to the South.[119] The Navy would absolutely not assume the defense—as the Army too often had. The Union blockade would be magnified, and its special focus would be Nassau.[120] After all, the Secretary of the Navy could not be held entirely responsible when the Confederacy was manifestly aided by Great Britain.

To Secretary of State Seward, therefore, Welles directed his own frustration. "While our officers have been admonished to regard the rights and jurisdiction of neutrals, are the British authorities at Nassau to disregard all neutral obligations without remonstrance on our part?" The United States could not ignore its own dependence upon Great Britain's choice of conduct in the Civil War. Moreover, if strong steps were not taken, the two nations would find themselves at war after all. "The fact that almost the whole of the arms, munitions, and assistance which the rebels have received in the war which they are waging on the Government has come through the neutral British port of Nassau, that a perfect system of violating the blockaders is there in execution, that our officers and people are openly insulted in the streets of that neutral place, while the rebels are encouraged and favored by the officials and the inhabitants, are facts of notoriety," Welles angrily noted, "and I would respectfully urge are calculated, if not checked, to lead to international difficulty."[121]

It was to avoid further internal Navy disputes that Stimers responded to Fox's forecast of "darker days" with his own preference for Dahlgren's 11-inch gun—with 30 pounds of powder—"for present purposes.

"New and untried guns in our new system of vessels which in reality have yet to make their name to the satisfaction of our Naval officers have all along made me anxious," he confessed.[122] Realizing that his own convictions had become perilously isolated, John Ericsson, however, characteristically struck back. "I cannot yet give up the idea of having one big gun in the *Passaic's* turret," he wrote to Fox on Sept. 8, enclosing a copy of his reply to Dahlgren, whose "trial just made fully corroborates my views." This reaction may have seemed strange, but in fact Ericsson set out to counter-discredit Dahlgren before the Assistant Secretary. Hence, Ericsson found the *Passaic*-deck target test "very interesting as it exposes the fallacy of <u>inclined</u> armor," he wrote to Dahlgren:

I hope you will lose no time in making trials that have a direct bearing on the question of the resisting power of the decks of our impregnable fleet. 15° is an angle at which no competent Commander will ever permit his deck to be struck, excepting by spent balls. I need not point out the fact that to be struck at an angle of 15° from a battery of the great altitude of 120 feet, a vessel must be within a distance of 160 yards.[123]

Yet Ericsson was also under enormous stress. "I am not surprised to learn that you are experiencing effects of over effort. . . ." Griswold wrote to him. "No other person could have achieved what you have and lived through it."[124] When Ericsson was reprimanded for not hurrying up work on the *Passaic,* he lashed out at his old colleague, Thomas Rowland of the Continental Iron Works, for not accepting his assistant's request for an explanation for the delay.[125] In the meantime, Fox and Stimers pushed ahead on altering Ericsson's specifications for the new Harbor and River (*Canonicus*)-class monitors, despite his arguments. Deck armor would be increased to 2 inches, reported Stimers, who was also hard at work providing fresh copies of the updated plans to every contractor. A model had been prepared by the Chief Engineer, now General Inspector of the ironclads under construction, while Ericsson busied himself with the *Passaic*-monitors he was building, the *Dictator* and *Puritan,* and a design for an ultra-light-draft monitor drawing 6 feet. "Capt Ericsson and the Admiral [Gregory] are very much disappointed at the prospect of being compelled to send her out without at least one XV inch gun," Stimers added.[126]

The next day, Sept. 13, Stimers notified Gregory that he had established a separate office in New York, next door to Ericsson's residence on Franklin Street, "by renting the whole floor of the second story, which gives two large rooms for drawing and one small one for an office." He had also hired 10 new draftsmen.[127] Any doubt over Stimers's increasing responsibilities—and control—over the newer classes of monitor ironclads was perhaps dispelled when he wrote to Boston contractor Harrison Loring that the "model of the *Canonicus* differs too much from that of the *Nahant* for you to get the plates from the same lines." Accordingly, Stimers—not Ericsson—was "having a general plan made, also models."[128] Fox made sure, however, to remind the ambitious Stimers that "the Admiral [Gregory] superintends every thing now, wood and iron, and all the Engineers who have been reporting to the Bureau, report to him as you do." This would give the new ironclads "one organization," or secular authority, if possible, free from interference but still keeping the Navy in one piece, if not preserving an essential chain of command.[129] Though the order from the Secretary of the Navy made this official on Sept. 12, Gregory reassured Lenthall that "the Department . . . has directed me to observe such instructions as you may be pleased to order from time to time." Likewise, Isherwood was informed that future weekly reports on "vessels building outside Navy Yards, on the Atlantic seaboard, &c."

would be made out to him as well as the Chief of the Bureau of Ship Construction & Repairs. Indeed, for Gregory's duties to "be performed with greater facility" he would need their active cooperation as well.[130]

By this time, the fate of the Union seemed to be "drifting on a troubled sea and God only Knows where," as one Navy Department insider wrote to John Rodgers.[131] Matters again depended on McClellan's Army of the Potomac, which was at last facing against Lee and Jackson's combined forces at Sharpsburg, Maryland, near Antietam Creek. The great battle of Sept. 17 subsequently managed to compel Lee to withdraw back across the Potomac, thereby ending the invasion. But while the Union had not suffered another defeat, neither was it altogether certain it had achieved a clear victory. The Army of Northern Virginia was left intact—and even allowed to escape without Federal pursuit. The war would continue. A dismayed President Lincoln nevertheless saw an opportunity to come forth with his Emancipation Proclamation, which he did on Sept. 22, 1862. The war would become more encompassing.

Fox knew the nation could not afford to wait much longer for the new monitors. How many would *definitely* be ready by Nov. 1? he asked Stimers. "Look at this by comparing them with all past experience, so that our movements may not be defeated by overestimating, as is almost always the case." Furthermore, a more total war would undoubtedly require a wider, more comprehensive spread of Federal monitors. "Capt. E. must not give up the light draft boats," he persisted. "Our series is not complete without them." The Assistant Secretary had already told the Department and "the iron folks here and out West" that advertisements for their construction, based on new plans from the redoubtable John Ericsson, would soon be placed. His message for Ericsson (which he understood Stimers would read to his new neighbor that day) was that Fox had "every confidence" in him to "furnish such plans"—and in fact, could rely on no one else to do so.[132]

But Gregory's report to Lenthall of Sept. 22 revealed a much more restrained optimism compared with those of the summer. According to the various government inspectors, "in general, the progress of the work under construction is satisfactory."[133] Four days later the bubble burst. Welles, reports in hand, wrote directly to Gregory of the "necessity for having half a dozen of these vessels completed by the middle of November, so as to use them during the fair weather which may then be expected, and the great results to be hoped for from their character. . . ." The Admiral in charge must therefore make "extraordinary exertions for their early completion." Rowland should be pressed—hard— "throwing his whole energies into the works, giving daily the influence of his presence among the workmen, especially in the case of the *Catskill*, so far behind hand." The state of the experimental, lightly armored *Keokuk* was even more shocking. No extra hours were put into her construction, despite the "assurances of zeal and perseverance" originally made to the Department by her contractor. Henceforth, the Secretary demanded that weekly reports list the number of workmen employed upon each ironclad, and the amount of overtime work given. By mid-November he specified that the *Passaic, Patapsco, Montauk, Nahant, Catskill, Weehawken,* and *Keokuk* should be sent to sea.[134]

Even as Welles called upon Gregory to lead the ironclad contractors in a renewed sense of patriotic energy, other elements within the Union Navy were anything but optimistic. Captain Percival Drayton was a prime example. "I am quite willing to take the *Passaic* and do what I can to reduce Charleston or any other place that it may be thought proper to attack," he wrote New York naval engineer Charles W. Copeland. "I doubt the fact of any of these vessels being very seaworthy, but some one must decide the point," he added, "and I might as well do it as any one else." Beneath this exterior indifference, however, Drayton was a sharp activist in his own right. The monitors were obviously flawed. "As it seems that a good deal of ballast will be required to bring these vessels down to a proper draft, I think it a great folly that it should not be effected by means of water, which could be removed to lighten the draft in case of getting ashore." He also opined that "the decks will be found to be very easily penetrated, this however can be left for the first action to decide. . . ."[135] Pessimism, like its opposite, was a self-fulfilling prophecy during the Civil War. Fox on the same day questioned Stimers with exasperation why Ericsson would need 100 tons of extra shot in the *Passaic.* "If it is to bring her down, it might as well have gone on the decks, where the system is weak." In the same breath he reminded Stimers that the *Passaic* and her sisters were daily expected. "When Congress adjourned last session, we promised them Charleston on assembling. I am afraid the Monitors will be behind hand."[136]

Two days later, Fox again wrote to Ericsson. Though he was intrigued with the engineer-inventor's most recent suggestion of "Flying Artillery" or "Monitors on shore" (or tanks) for the troubled Union Army, Ericsson "must recollect one thing—your brain is more engaged to us to a certain extent." Virtually in exchange, the Assistant Secretary promised that 15-inch guns were only days away. Could not Ericsson in the meantime "give them a stir-up, there at Greenpoint, so as to enable us to settle the question of iron clads against stone forts, before Congress meets"?[137] Fox also confessed his doubts over the *Passaic* monitors' forward ballast, which he presumed was "unavoidable, or your extraordinary skill and ingenuity would not have been forced to adopt it."[138] This read like a suggestion of error on Ericsson's part, however. Perhaps Fox (if not also Ericsson) was becoming careless as well as nervous. At any rate, Stimers assured him that Ericsson was indeed "hard at the 6 foot vessels, but you know he will never show me a plan until he has worked it out."[139] At this, Fox became only more perturbed—and outspoken—with Stimers.[140]

Ericsson, no longer able to ignore the latest crisis of faith from naval professionals, responded to Fox on Sept. 29. The Union Navy did not have to worry about his ideas for technologically rescuing the Army, since the "great moving cause no longer exists, besides which I am now fairly up to my ears in the construction of the big ships and completion of the small ones, to say nothing of the Shallow water boat." As for proper ballast, this was a matter of careful calculation and choice. Ericsson could quickly change his calculations; but dispensing with ballast at all "would utterly destroy the needed accommodation within the forward part of the vessels," or require "additional time and money." Giving the vessel finer lines would also give it great speed as well as reduce the ballast, but then the Navy would have to "put up with uncomfortable quarters." The choice, of course, was up to Fox, Ericsson challenged—if ballast was such a critical issue. "The best sailing vessels require ballast, why should not also the most comfortable Monitor vessels be allowed to carry it?"[141] Ericsson then summoned Stimers, reading to him his reply to Fox and explaining it with "great force. . . . So much so that I am not certain that we can improve matters at present in these vessels," Stimers wrote to Fox. Evidently, Ericsson also rammed home another vital issue to the young Chief Engineer (as well as redirecting pressure back to the Bureau of Ordnance): the number of *weapons* that would be available, as much as the number of weapons *platforms,* would determine when operations could commence against Charleston. Fifteen-inch guns would unquestionably wreak greater damage against the brickwork of Fort ·Sumter than Dahlgren's preferred 11-inchers. Likewise, the "fewer the number of vessels which carry these guns the less will be the target for the enemy to fire at. Four vessels will carry eight of them. Will you have more than that?"[142]

Ericsson then got to the main issue at stake. "I infer from expressions used by Chief Engineer Stimers at our interview last evening that you attribute the ballasting the *Monitor* fleet to mistake or miscalculations on my part," he wrote to Fox. "Should this inference be correct I can no longer afford to deal with the subject in the playful manner I did in my letter of yesterday":

> I must state then emphatically that not one pound of ballast above what I calculated upon will have to be put into these vessels nor would I dispense with this ballast for the price of the whole fleet. The question of stability of vessels built on the new system is one of serious importance and has engaged more of my attention than any other part of the subject.

Because of the monitors' low freeboard at sea, plunging into waves that washed over the deck, it would "not answer to increase the thickness of the deck and armor indiscriminately without putting weight below to balance the heavy top." Ericsson, unlike Drayton, Fox, or even Stimers, had precalculated the unusual metacentric height of the *Passaic* monitors in direct relation to their sea-keeping abilities, not just their protection against possible enemy fire. He then repeated his argument "that the number of 15 inch guns rather than the number of vessels will decide your success against the Stone forts."[143] Yet implied here was an important tactical oversight. Fox, sharply rebuked, could nevertheless rejoice in the mathematical certainties Ericsson provided—as no one else could—in the Union's gloomy summer of 1862. Charleston *would* fall. How it would fall was another question: were the forts guarding it to be pulverized or bypassed after all? Gone were the discussions of monitors running Confederate gauntlets, or confronting European ironclads. Instead, protection from plunging fire, battering down casemates, and the lightest possible draft had become the new priorities. The problem was whether such a uniquely complicated war could be "solved" as precisely as Ericsson's individual monitor designs, or as systematically as Fox's series of strategic layers.

As much as Union navy leaders could push for action, the war forced them to react to situations beyond their control. Nowhere was this more obvious—and important—than in the threat of hostilities with Great Britain, whether through mediation and intervention, incidents arising from the blockade, or, as the Civil War progressed, escalating Northern anger with British aid to the South. At least with the 15-inch guns in place, enemy ironclads and fortifications would probably be destroyed. But Ericsson could not oversee everything. His efforts would be directed outward, across the Atlantic. Stimers would be left with a continental interior no less crucial in many ways. At the same time, the tactical confusion over how actually to employ Ericsson's *Passaic*-class monitors at Charleston would not guarantee the type of victory Lincoln's administration badly needed. "The greatest misfortune will turn out to be that which we thought was giving the Navy most glory," Du Pont confided to his wife, "its constant protection and saving of the Army instead of following its own sphere. . . ."[144]

Chapter 18

The *Passaic* Crisis

At first, the belated presence of the U.S.S. *New Ironsides* did little to reassure Union naval leaders. Although commissioned on Aug. 21, her trial run from Philadelphia to Hampton Roads proved so unsatisfactory that she was forced to spend another month back in Philadelphia for an emergency refitting. On Oct. 4, 1862, Commodore Smith wrote to her builders, Merrick & Sons, that "$100,000 of the reservations" was being paid by the Navy; "the balance will be held for further trial of the ship, especially in regard to speed." The speed of this ironclad had been guaranteed to be 9.5 knots, and she would draw 15 feet and carry eight days' worth of coal for steaming at that speed.[1] Those attributes, it soon became clear, would never be met. Perhaps this failing was the result of numerous changes made to her while under construction (as with many of the monitors). For the Union's only armored broadside frigate to see service in the Civil War, these included, significantly, the addition of armored bulkheads—sealing off the battery forward and aft to prevent raking fire—an armored pilot-house (foolishly mounted *behind* the smokestack), 4-inch–thick gun-port shutters, and an increase of armament (and therefore carriages, ammunition, and handling crew) from a battery of 9-inch to 11-inch Dahlgrens.[2] Clearly disheartened, Smith showed little mercy to Merrick & Sons. As long as the additions in weight did not affect her draft, the builders of the *New Ironsides* would be deducted $500 pay per day "from contract over time."[3]

By Oct. 6, however, Chief Engineer Stimers reported to Fox that Ericsson's plans for an ultra-light-draft monitor were ready. "Of course," he wrote, "it is quite original differing from all other plans yet proposed and surpassing them all just as much as it differs from them."[4] Two days later Ericsson transmitted the general specifications to Welles—who had finally seen the original *Monitor* in the midst of refitting at the Washington Navy Yard, just three days before.[5] Among other features, each new monitor would have a long wooden-hull overhang over an inner, submerged iron one, staggered twin screws, and two layers of ½-inch plating for deck armor. "The turret, pilot house, turret machinery, blowers, blower engines, Worthington pumps, and impregnable smoke pipe," Ericsson noted, would be "precisely [the same] as the *Passaic* and the other U.S. Gunboats of her class." This precision would make those portions of the new monitor class at least as well protected as the *Canonicus* class. A uniform design would furthermore allow greater ease of construction for new and experienced constructors, who could be supplied with veritable duplicates of existing plans—and thereby save mass-production drafting time. As Ericsson pointed out, "the plans and general specifications thus furnished will no doubt furnish the bidders to make their estimates of cost more particularly since the whole of the turret work is now accurately defined by precise working drawings."[6] Stimers, however, could only write Fox that Ericsson expected him to provide the drawings for the various monitors. Managing ironclad production on a mass scale, involving multiple firms across the country, was an added, unprecedented responsibility. Simple oversights, assumptions, and lack of coordination between bureaus could quickly lead to disaster. Chief Engineer King, Stimers noted to Fox, was in Pittsburgh superintending the construction of two *Canonicus* monitors; "he has now orders to superintend the *Manayunk*, building at Pittsburgh, with its machinery building at Brownsville—50 miles away—and the two vessels *Tippecanoe* and *Catawba* building at Cincinnati, O." Personal rivalries could also come into play. To ease the burden on King, Stimers recommended an associate, Chief Engineer Elbridge Lawton, serving on the frigate U.S.S. *Mississippi*; "but I have an idea that the Chief of the Bureau of Engineering would do nothing which he would consider as favoring in any way Mr. Lawton." Extra superintendents and inspectors would also need extra assistants and draftsmen.[7] In fact, what was needed was a distinct bureau, if not a separate infrastructure.

But Stimers was already presuming too much, and Fox let him know it. The Assistant Secretary had noticed he was openly promising additional compensation to contractors who were already behind schedule. "All my letters to you are unofficial and you must not use them in your official dispatches," Fox reproached. For any monitor that could be ready at Hampton Roads by Nov. 15, the Secretary would probably "remit all forfeitures," and this was a better strategy for urging the builders, if nothing else.[8] He also continued to face doubts over the new monitors and their rapid completion. Drayton, commander of the first *Passaic,* reported that his ship "does not seem to be much further completed than ten days back and I doubt if even now any time can be appointed for her delivery to the yard." Only by making a short trip in the *Passaic* herself, wrote Drayton, would the Assistant Secretary "get a clear idea of the capabilities for sea service of this class, which I doubt your being able to obtain in any other way." Although Drayton himself had never been to sea in a monitor, how could Ericsson possibly assure the Navy of its investment? Worse than being pessimistic, perhaps, Drayton was fatalistic. "The Monitors have undoubtedly many faults but it seems difficult to correct them without falling into others equally bad. . . ."[9] Fox could not ignore his officers' opinions; if possible, he would go to New York and try out the *Passaic* for himself, he informed Stimers. He was not confident about the monitors' ventilation, "which is of the greatest importance," and there were "some other points that I desire to examine carefully." Against the misgivings of his naval professionals, however, Fox had to respectfully weigh Ericsson's assertions to the contrary. The engineer-inventor's bristling explanation of ballast versus top-weights in the *Passaic* was but a recent example. "If such is the case," Fox admitted to Stimers, "of course there is no answer to it."[10]

Still, the matter of ironclads appearing at all, never mind their actual effectiveness, was paramount. "We must have six vessels on the 20th November and we will astonish the world," Fox pressed Stimers. "Time slips away." Though hesitant firms were at last taking on more of the *Canonicus* contracts, some preferred to bid for the light-drafts instead; others demanded more time and money, and how could the Government actually refuse any offer in a period of national emergency? Fox also regarded Ericsson's matter-of-fact observations on light-draft construction as "most admirable but the conclusion is dreadful, viz: that if Delamater was not employed he would produce 3 in 90 days."[11] Gregory could at least report to Lenthall and Isherwood on Oct. 6 that the contractors had noticeably increased their efforts, though these were combined with Stimers's talk of "extra compensation to the Contractors under certain circumstances. . . ."[12] Two days later, the Admiral could also assure Welles that his urgent appeal of Sept. 26 had taken effect: the monitor *Nahant* was launched, with the *Montauk* to follow the next day; *Keokuk* was swarming with an "ample force of men" to complete her.[13] The results themselves seemed encouraging. Having "minutely examined the exterior" of the *Nahant* just before her launch, Stimers let Gregory know he was "proud of her as a specimen of our proficiency in this country in the art of iron ship building."[14]

Flush with this sentiment, Stimers candidly addressed Fox's worries on Oct. 9. The Chief Engineer was "quite grieved" to find he had over-stepped his bounds in his last official report. "Hereafter you may con-sider everything you write me as <u>private</u> and <u>unofficial</u> unless it has your rank attached to the signature and I will make no official reference to any but such letters." As for why contractors could obviously work harder at some moments than others, Stimers reminded Fox that for private indus-try the work was "a matter of business." To "hurry work faster than is ordinarily done by energetic men adds to its cost." The Government-contracted firms would of course secure as many laborers as they needed, provided the Government was willing to pay 50 percent more for them than any other builder. Furthermore, "if you pay this to new hands you must also increase the wage of the old to an equal amount." The same principles applied to materials, especially iron. To get as much as required, as quickly as possible, would simply cost more. "Therefore, if a Military exigency has arisen which makes it important that you have these ships before you can get them by driving them up to the limit, of what may be termed, commercial energy, you must pay an additional sum." How could the Government hold contractors responsible for labor problems that the war—and hence the Government—exacerbated with extraordinary demands? Contracts were made under ideal conditions; and New York was a world away from the front-line environment of Washington. Hence, Stimers advised Fox that "[$5,000] per vessel would make a difference of a month in the time of a ship in the present condi-tion of the *Sangamon* or the *Weehawken*":

> Ericsson has given orders to expend that amount in increased wages upon the power vessel, he cares not whether it will be refunded or not, he will expend it, but at Jersey City they must be satisfied that it will be returned before they will expend it even though they pretend to me that they will do it, and really, you cannot blame them for they could easily ruin themselves if they worked without care of the cost and they do not know as well as Ericsson how much they will be in or out of pocket when all bills are settled.

This was behind Stimers's earlier suggestion to the contractors. If Gregory were instructed to *guarantee* up to $5,000, then night and Sunday work would also (and only) be considered "cast-iron." "Then we could drive matters." The war had forced Lincoln's administration to choose between time and money; and recent events made the fear of its political collapse seem more immediately a matter of time—as a military defeat—rather than money—in the form of national bank-ruptcy. These were tough decisions for a junior officer to make, caught between the opposing needs of two crushing realities—as reflected by the alternative interests of these two groups, the Government and private industry. "I am almost frightened at times when I reflect upon the enormous amounts which are now being expended by the Government under my general inspection," Stimers confided. "I feel like the man who walks the tight rope across a rapid, the slightest deviation from a direct line is immediate ruin, not only in acts of common honesty but also in the advice I give and the suggestions I make to the Government."[15]

In addition, naval professionals were proving quick to detect any imperfections that, however quickly resolved, could still leave a seriously complicated mechanism inoperable. "Today I was made unhappy by learning from Capt. Drayton that the ports of his Iron Clad the *Passaic* are but 17 inches in diameter whilst the 200 pounder for the Turret is 27 inches," Commodore Paulding wrote to Welles on Oct. 15. This was "a discrepancy that Ericsson should have provided for & which to remedy will occasion delay." It seemed unlikely that the ironclads would go south until December, he predicted. "It grieves me that it is so but we are helpless in the hands of the Iron men [though] I believe they are doing all they can."[16] Smith also wrote to Ericsson to only "caution . . . against a failure" regarding his new monitors, whose sea-keeping properties he still did not trust, though by mid-October he had learned to keep a respectable distance.[17] A bigger problem was administrative, he informed Welles. Contractors' bills and payments were made to and from various bureaus including his own (Yards & Docks) and should be consolidated under the Bureau of Ship Construction & Repair.[18]

The Department reacted to these concerns encouragingly, however, continually driving efforts forward—even as the British Cabinet debated mediation in the American Civil War. There were other practical details to attend to, Welles reminded Gregory. Could the *Nahant* be brought to New York to receive her 15-inch gun? How *were* the ordnance arrangements for each of the ironclads coming along? Were pilots familiar with the Southern coast and ports being obtained for the monitors? Was the Admiral even making sure that "enough tallow or slush [was] put on board each of them to slush decks and turrets in action"? Two more *Canonicus* monitors were contracted in the meantime to be put under his superintendence: the *Saugus* and *Oneota*.[19]

On Oct. 24 Ericsson addressed another of Fox's concerns over obstacles to Union success—literally, "the removal of obstructions in the harbor of a certain Southern City." The Assistant Secretary wanted to try underwater explosives, but Ericsson the engineer was dubious. "The removal of piles by the process of explosion is a very tedious one and nearly impracticable under the enemy's guns." Furthermore, the "explosion of powder under water is quite local," he argued, "its effect being remarkably limited owing to the incompressible nature and great specific gravity of water." Against piles Ericsson instead suggested a large wooden raft, heavily armored, and specially designed to be "pushed by one of our Monitors, the process being a continuous butting and backing." Coordinated by their signal lights, two such monitors and their rafts could work in tandem at night, he suggested. "Should any obstructions be met that we cannot remove by the momentum of our 1200 ton vessel and the battering ram, we can employ powder as you propose."[20] Fox was again relieved, enthusiastically replying that "thanks to the extraordinary product of your brain, I consider the attack upon a certain city to resolve itself entirely into a question of Harbor obstructions. No guns at present used by the rebels can penetrate your new Monitors, consequently, be their forts more or less, they do not form an element to deter us from the attack." This, he considered, left only pilings, floating rafts, torpedoes, "and ropes anchored to foul the propellers" as possible southern defenses, and pilings or boons were always subject to natural forces which made them easily pushed apart in deeper waters with swift currents. Dangling ropes bothered him most.[21]

Gregory had meanwhile replied to Welles that the "Ordnance Arrangements for the Vessels are in advance of other matters."[22] On Oct. 17 Drayton had indicated his personal preference for the Parrott "200-pounder" rifle "against forts and ironclads. . . to say nothing of the great advantage to be derived in every case from the smaller opening required for the rifle" straight to Ericsson, who was not disposed to reject the suggestion outright since there were not enough 15-inch guns on hand.[23] The next day (upon Drayton's request) Parrott himself wrote to assure Ericsson that his 8-inch rifle, a 150-pounder, was already furbished with an elevating screw "which works rapidly & with great facility, being managed by the man who also sights the Gun." He had penetrated an inclined target composed of six 1-inch plates with his 100-pounder, firing a 70-pound solid shot with charges of 12, even 14, pounds—a charge he was not prepared to exceed in proportion to the weight of the shot. The 150-pounder admittedly had not tested against armor as well.[24] Still, by Oct. 28, Ericsson was already writing to Captain Wise at the Bureau of Ordnance to inform him "by telegram, if the enclosed plan correctly represents the 200-pound Parrott gun intended for the *Patapsco*. I need not say that the modification which I am now making in the XV in. gun carriage, to receive the 200 pdr. demands perfect accuracy."[25]

Yet how to handle the 15-inch Dahlgren gun within the *Passaic*-class turrets had become another source of contention for the "Bureau of Ericsson." The gunports, originally designed in the uncertain days of spring to accommodate an experimental 13-inch smoothbore, were too small for the barrel of the new 15-inch gun to protrude from. Rather than increase the openings, however, Ericsson saw this development as a further tactical improvement. As long as the 15-inch shot itself could pass through the 17-inch diameter opening, the gun was essentially effective—and protected even more because its muzzle could not be shot off. But could such a massive cannon be fired *inside* a turret? Again, Ericsson's calculated guess said yes, and only awaited a proper test. October 16 arrived, yet where was the 15-inch Dahlgren? "It is indispensable to ascertain at once if my plan is practicable of firing through a small hole without passing the muzzle of the gun through the turret," he complained to Fox.[26] When it finally did arrive and was mounted and duly tested on board the *Passaic* on Oct. 28, the results were controversial, indicative once more of the wider—yet personal—tensions that existed within the Union Navy's ironclad program.

Captain Drayton's report to Rear Admiral Gregory was, perhaps not surprisingly, anything but flattering toward Ericsson and stressed his system's defects. With only a 15-pound blank charge, the 15-inch Dahlgren had filled the turret "with smoke to a degree almost suffocating and which was so for a very disagreeably long period, although the two hatches were off which could not have been the case in action." Under a greater charge and solid shot the smoke was less, "but the concussion such that I should not think that a heavier charge could have been used with safety to the guns crew, it seems that the compressor was not on this occasion properly screwed up, which permitted a recoil that a time prevented further trial, which was also the case with the eleven inch gun which was fired with a solid shot and fifteen pounds of powder." Though Drayton admitted the "trial is not considered as finally settling the question," it had nevertheless satisfied him "that it will not be practicable to use the guns inside of the turret." Rather than write off the idea, Gregory's notational remark on the copy of Drayton's report forwarded to the Bureau of Ordnance stated Drayton's remarks "are premature—arrangements are in progress for the purposes stated."[27]

Ericsson, on the other hand, stressed in his telegram to Fox that the "trial of the fifteen inch Gun yesterday by no means proves that it may not be fired inside of the Port Hole." He was fitting an iron "muzzle piece" around the end of the barrel inside the turret to control the discharge-smoke better. More significant to him, it took only two men to "run the large Gun in and out"—an amazing technical advance in the annals of heavy armaments for warships.[28] The next day, Oct. 30, Ericsson's defensive optimism turned into a virulent counterattack on Drayton and the other scoffers present at the trial, including Commander John Worden of the original *Monitor*. "The trial of Tuesday was made at my request for the sole purpose of firing the large gun <u>without</u> the muzzle piece," he explained to Fox. "It was the first time such an enormous gun had been fired on board of a vessel." As for the noise produced, he pointed out, many experienced witnesses considered it *less* than that associated with an open-air 11-inch Dahlgren firing. "The smoke which entered the turret was heavy but passed down by suction of the blowers in about 10 seconds." The muzzle box would reduce it further. Ericsson vigorously objected to widening the port, "until engineering expedients have been exhausted." Larger portholes would only require larger shutters, or, if the turret was rotated while reloading, increase the chances of shot entering the turret, killing the crew and destroying the guns—which were themselves in precious short supply.[29]

Worse still, Gregory and Stimers had prematurely allowed the press to cover the experimental trial. As a result, wrote Ericsson, "a very damaging account appeared in the [*New York*] *Herald* of yesterday":

> A few more such statements will relieve Jef [*sic*] Davis of his present anxiety about the Iron Clads that threaten his strongholds. Our rivals across the water will also be greatly relieved. Should our guns not be capable of sustaining more than one third of the proper charge demanded by the magnitude of the gun and weight of Shot, it is a misfortune we ought to keep to ourselves.[30]

Ericsson was even more "greatly annoyed" by his critics, if not embarrassed for the country, than he let on. The day before the *Passaic*'s initial 15-inch gun test, an unsigned essay of his appeared in the *New York Herald,* on "American and English Iron-Clads." Here, Ericsson attempted to place the Union's ironclad program in sharper yet broader focus. The historic events at Hampton Roads had succeeded in frightening Great Britain away from all thoughts of troubling the United States. In response, Armstrong had created a gun that could penetrate the armor of the strongest ironclad. "This reassuring fact was forthwith made known through the press, and John Bull took a long breath, quite sure that the Yankees, after all, had not hit upon anything better than the *Warrior.*" But the isolated British targets were misleading, not representative of an American monitor's armor shelf, supported by the full flat deck resting in water. "In return for the attention which our proceedings receive from the English," Ericsson informed *Herald* readers, "we are carefully looking into what they are doing with their iron-clads." *Warrior*'s armor protection scheme was well known, and weak; the 15-inch guns of the new *Passaic* monitors would put the *Warrior* and her sisters on the run, for the *Dictator* to then hunt down on the open ocean. Because the *Dictator* was much more heavily armored on her sides and turret than anything the British were planning, Ericsson concluded there were "substantial reasons for believing the *Dictator* will prove a dictator."[31]

Ericsson's simplistic emphasis on foreign affairs drew some attention away from the period of uneasy calm that followed the bloodbath of Antietam. "But little is being done just at this time by either the Army or Navy, I regret to say," Welles wrote to his son on Nov. 2, 1862. "All the contractors are greatly behind their time in completing & delivering their vessels thereby deranging all plans, and while I perhaps am the person most wronged and disappointed, the country will be very likely to blame me most for delay or neglect."[32] Indeed, it seemed a long time since the Union had achieved any notable successes in the Civil War—and the Congressional elections were at hand in November. Meanwhile, at sea, the C.S.S. *Alabama* was wreaking havoc on Northern commerce. By June 1864 this single Confederate raider had destroyed 65 Union merchantmen worth over $7 million and the U.S.S. *Hatteras*, a converted paddlewheel gunboat (Jan. 11, 1863). Far worse, however, was the indirect damage. In the course of the war, 715 U.S. vessels transferred their flag over to British registry—thereby ending America's growing challenge to British domination of world shipping. For these operations by the Confederate States Navy, Welles also expected the blame to be directed at him, rather than his colleague William Seward, whose policy toward Britain since the *Trent* affair, he felt, was one of "meeting aggression with concession . . . to avoid hostilities, but to throw the labor of the conflict on the Navy if there was to be a war."[33]

Seward's policy was most likely Lincoln's: to avoid a war with European powers if at all possible during the Civil War, while simultaneously preparing for one. In a letter to the U.S. Consul in Vienna, the Secretary of State wrote that the Union would not take direct offense to the French imperial presence in Mexico. Napoleon III had "on the breaking out of the insurrection . . . adopted the then current opinion of European statesmen that the efforts of this government to suppress it would be unsuccessful":

> To this pre-judgment we attribute his agreement with Great Britain to act in concert with her upon international questions which might arise out of the conflict, his practical concession of a belligerent character to the insurgents, his repeated suggestions of accommodations by this government with the insurgents, and his conferences on the subject of a recognition. These proceedings of the Emperor of France have been very injurious to the United States by encouraging and thus prolonging the insurrection.

Yet France and the United States were in a state of peace. "We have not an acre of territory nor a fort which we think France could wisely covet, nor has she any possession that we could accept if she would resign it into our hands." Only a misconception of Union strength and resolve in defeating the Confederacy would lead the Emperor "further in the way of encouragement to the insurgents, whose intrigues in Paris we understand and do not underestimate." What the Union needed, therefore, was *time*—time and victory. Greater strength, and thus renewed European respect for the United States, were inevitable. Until then, the Monroe Doctrine in relation to Mexico was undeniably threatened. The U.S. Government knew, Seward wrote, that an imposed monarchy was not the wish of the people of Mexico, who were influenced by popular opinion in America that revered democratic republicanism:

> The President, moreover, believes that this popular opinion of the United States is just in itself and eminently essential to the progress of civilization on the American continent, which civilization he believes can and will, if left free from European resistance, work harmoniously together with advancing refinement on the other continents. This government believes that all foreign resistance to American civilization, and all attempts to control it, must and will fail before the ceaseless and ever-increasing activity of material, moral, and political forces which peculiarly belong to the American continent.

A French imperial policy in the Western Hemisphere, Seward therefore thought, would "scatter seeds which would be fruitful of jealousies that might ultimately ripen into collisions between France and the United States and other American republics." Though the President was wary of rumors of French intrigues and conspiracies, "he knows, also, that such suspicions will be entertained more or less extensively in this country, and will be magnified in other countries, and . . . that it is out of such suspicions that the fatal web of national animosity is most frequently woven."[34]

The mounting national and international tensions of late 1862 had thus turned the cramped confines of the gun turret of the U.S.S. *Passaic* into a pressure-cooker. Ericsson and his engineers were under close scrutiny by the Navy to make their vaunted machines work as quickly and flawlessly as possible. As a result, the unprecedented challenge of mounting a single 15-inch gun of 22 tons on a single ship, and making it fire in an enclosed space without deafening, concussing, or smoking out the gun crew, had become indicative of the many deeper—and personal—issues at stake. On Nov. 4 Dahlgren demonstrated his desire to at least help Ericsson fix the problem, suggesting not that the experimental 15-inch gun be abandoned (it was far too late for that argument), but that its muzzle be cut into the inner turret wall around the porthole to channel the blast, versus the alternative of fitting a cumbersome smoke-box around it.[35] Yet the day before, Ericsson had already arranged a new test fire. "I was much pleased with my trip on the *Passaic*," wrote one of his guest-observers, Robert Forbes, "though my ears still ring with the concussion produced by the 15 in."[36] The official report of the *Passaic*'s captain, Percival Drayton, was not so politely restrained, nor had his opinions changed. "The conclusion that I came to . . . both from my own observations and the remarks of others is," he wrote to Dahlgren, "that the guns cannot be fired unless the face of the muzzle projects beyond the inner face of the turret."[37]

Another future monitor captain, Daniel Ammen, also expressed his doubts toward Ericsson's plans. Indeed, a new conservative Navy "clique," or cadre, was forming against the ambitious "Monitor People," and Dahlgren was known to be sympathetic. "I understand Mr. Ericsson is now engaged in arranging some kind of stuffing box so as to continue the muzzle of the gun inside," Ammen wrote the Bureau Chief. "[I]n this matter I cannot but subscribe to a general opinion you have frequently expressed to me: that a state of war was a most unfavorable period for experiments." Surely the 11-inch gun, "at the short ranges suggested by the 'Monitors,'" would be very destructive "against bricks and mortar" and wooden vessels, "which was all that was supposed possible for wooden ships" when Dahlgren invented it—before the Civil War. "Now, with a change of vessel and with increased pretension on our part: (that of assailing and battering down casemated works) could you not with advantage increase the weight of metal of the eleven inch gun designed for batteries of iron clad vessels, and use such charges as would destroy 'Warriors' &c. and knock down everything in the shape of forts yet built[?]"[38]

Ericsson, for his part, considered the execution of his ideas inevitable.[39] This included employment of an iron smoke-box around the 15-inch gun. "The experiment is simply a question of strength," he wrote to Fox. "I have employed ½ inch thick plate, not having been able to obtain heavier plate without losing too much time."[40] Time proved decisive, however. On the 15th the efficiency of the box in reducing smoke and concussion was proven enough after three test fires; Stimers then advised removing the muzzle ring to test it still further. The fourth shot ruptured the box.

An added pivotal factor in the ongoing conflict between (at least) the engineers and the naval officers was public opinion. For the *Passaic* trial of the 15th, up the Hudson River, Ericsson had made sure to invite reporters to see the results for themselves "to prevent any more foolish stories about our trial trips, delays, &c.," he wrote to Fox, adding his regret at "not having adopted this course from the beginning." Corrections were already made in the *New York Herald* and the *New York World*, "the best that could be done until our next trial, when nothing will be published that our enemies should not know, and our strong points placed before the country in a proper manner."[41]

But the ruptured smoke-box on the fourth fire only backfired on Ericsson. The ever-critical *New York World* described it as "near shattered to pieces," which drew Ericsson's immediate response. Without the muzzle ring, the outcome, he wrote, had been "precisely as I had previously demonstrated, a considerable increase of pressure within the muzzle box, the effect being that [the] same light bolts which temporarily secured the front plate were broken and the plate bent forward a few inches." "This you will admit," he told the editor of the *New York World*, "is a very different affair from the box being shattered to pieces." The structure of the box was quite strong enough to contain its internal pressures, which the test had "afforded practical data for estimating exactly," and the matter was all but concluded. As a result, "we handle the 420 pound guns with as little discomfort and with more facility than Hull and Perry handled their 40-pounders."[42] More significant, *Harper's Weekly* depicted the *Passaic*'s gun trial at the Palisades, New York, in direct contrast to an illustration, on the same page, of the launch of the British converted ironclad H.M.S. *Caledonia*. American periodicals were accustomed to reprinting the spectacular though distorted images of British warship launches found in the *Illustrated London News* (and later the *Graphic*), which were themselves designed to astound British—and especially foreign—audiences. This time *Harper's* turned British greatness against itself, suggesting the hulking broadside ironclad was nothing more than a Goliath, and the *Passaic* monitor a David:

> It will be seen that the only deviation from the old system adopted thus far by the British Admiralty consists in the plating of their vessels. They are still huge monsters, soaring high above the water, and presenting a target which the most inexperienced gunner could not miss; and which, at a proper distance, a 400-pound ball would penetrate as easily as card-board.[43]

At any rate, General Superintendent Rear Admiral Gregory was satisfied with Ericsson's test fire, reporting to Welles on Nov. 15 that the "certainty of being able to use guns of that large caliber in my opinion [is] fully established."[44] The Secretary, having written to Gregory the same day that it was "very important that the *Passaic* should be at Hampton Roads on Saturday next," congratulated him on the "continuation of the triumph of mechanical skill."[45] To Dahlgren, however, Gregory reported on Nov. 16 that "the arrangements made by Capt. Ericsson . . . were not entirely successful as there was some damage done the box fitted round the port by the concussion. . . ." But he agreed the test was nonetheless *indicative* that Ericsson would "perfect the [arrangements] in such manner as to answer the purpose effectually. . . ."[46]

Drayton's assessment of the same day took Gregory's wavering to the other extreme. Although it was "practicable to fire the gun in the way proposed," he admitted to Dahlgren, it was "at the sacrifice of some convenience in loading and sighting." On the other hand, it would always be easier to drill out a porthole larger than 17 inches than to fill it up. The newspaper reports of the trial were "pretty much false, the fact being that the gun is not fired inside of the turret, but into a chamber attached to it, and in point of fact I have been right and not Mr. Ericsson from the start, as I always told him he could not fire the gun as it was when you were on board. . . ." It was thus Drayton's suggestion to construct a smoke-box, not Ericsson's, and Drayton who urged that it be made strong enough, "which it is difficult to make him do," he added sarcastically, "as his experience as a Swedish Artillery officer has taught him that there is no lateral escape from the muzzle, but that the gas goes straight ahead."[47]

Rodgers noted to his wife this discrepancy of attitudes: "Ericsson says make the box stronger and it will answer completely. Drayton doubts whether it can be made strong enough."[48] Unfortunately, so did one of Ericsson's reporters, who, according to Stimers, "expressed himself quite freely about the Naval Officers and did not show his complete report to the Capt., so that although nothing is published which can be objectionable to the Government there is an apparent discourtesy to a large number of officers which has caused a good deal of feeling and which makes the Admiral, Capt Drayton and Myself regret that we took the responsibility of permitting the reporters to accompany us."[49] Ericsson later attempted to trivialize the affair, yet with an unmistakable air of official denial.[50] Between the press, the Navy, and Ericsson, no one was willing to state openly that there might be a civil-military relations issue over the monitors hanging in the balance.

Chapter 19

Shifting Ironclad Confidence

Again, the wider circumstances of the Civil War put these diverse and often conflicting personal, working relationships into sharp relief. Exactly how would the Union ironclads be used when they were ready? Where would they strike? Or would they be used strictly for coastal and harbor defense? The subsequent discussions of their deployment were a matter of national policy: would the Navy assume the strategic defense with its ironclads or try to regain its initiative with them? When John Rodgers bemoaned his initial refusal to be reassigned to one of the new monitor ironclads—and taken off the stricken *Galena*—his inside contact at the Navy Department assured him on Nov. 6 that "at this moment greater anxiety is felt about the 2nd *Merrimac* [the diminutive casemate ironclad-ram C.S.S. *Richmond*] than upon any other subject connected with the naval operations of the war, not excepting the '290' [the C.S.S. *Alabama*], when she is destroyed or blows herself up."[1] Hampton Roads, Fortress Monroe, and the recaptured base at Norfolk—and perhaps even Washington—were still considered far from secure; the memories of the *Virginia* and the *Arkansas* lingered, even as Rodgers in the *Galena* languished.

That same day, Captain Thomas Turner of the *New Ironsides* was even more fretful. No one seemed to understand the iron gun carriages provided for her powerful battery of sixteen 11-inch Dahlgren smoothbores—neither Dahlgren nor the builders, he complained to Rear Admiral Samuel P. Lee of the North Atlantic Blockading Squadron. Their recoil was so violent as to preclude a sustained fire; at the same time, the gun deck of the broadside ironclad was not large enough to house the crews needed to work such heavy guns with conventional truck and tackle. Until that technical problem was fixed, or lighter ordnance substituted (the latter of which Turner preferred), the *New Ironsides* would guard Hampton Roads with virtually no armament. Her captain, in the meantime, wished his concerns formally reported to the Navy Department "if any disaster should occur in the partially crippled condition of my ship—by which the enemy might inflict serious damage, or escape to the waters of the Chesapeake. . . ."[2]

Even if the Union had an additional ironclad frigate in service, Welles apparently indicated he would like to see it stationed in New York harbor, "ready for sea."[3] The threat of the *Alabama* and other fast, British-built Confederate cruisers always on the horizon had caused considerable alarm in the big eastern port cities. Deputations from the powerful New York Chamber of Commerce and the Governor pressed Welles to allocate at least one of the new ironclads for the permanent defense of their harbors from quick raids or humiliating demands for "tribute."[4] The Boston Board of Trade wrote:

> In view of the recent reckless depredations of the piratical steamer *Alabama*, and her reported near proximity to our bay, and also the apparently well authenticated fact recently made public, that powerful steam rams are now partially constructed in England, to be used by the rebels in an attack on our principal cities on the Northern coast, added to an apprehension (by no means unfounded) that our country may suddenly be involved in a foreign war, it can not be regarded strange that this community should be pervaded by deep solicitude as to the absence of immediate means to make any adequate defense against an attack from either of the sources referred to.

Though there were three forts—Warren, Independence, and Winthrop—ready to accommodate 475 guns, only 153 were in place, "and none of these can be said to be of sufficiently large caliber to make a successful defense against an armor-plated steamship, especially if she should attempt to enter the harbor through Broad Sound." And while this form of defense was the responsibility of the U.S. Army, its resources were obviously stretched, and the necessary ordnance would take added time to procure. It was logical to the Board that, in the meantime, the Navy should fill the gap with a "floating battery." "We are not unaware of the embarrassment which the Government has suffered from the limited means of supplying ordnance in its great emergency, nor would we make the claims of Boston Harbor for protection unduly prominent, but you will pardon us if we suggest that, after a war of twenty months, the harbor of the third commercial city in the Union ought no longer to be allowed by its very weakness to invite the aggression of a desperate enemy." Boston therefore wanted the *Nahant*, which was finishing under Loring.[5] The next day, Welles was even informed by fellow Cabinet member Secretary of the Treasury Salmon P. Chase that the Governor and Port Collector of New York had called upon *him* in "reference to the defenses of that city." Chase could not resist the opportunity of blithely informing Welles that the "duty of providing such defenses on the water belongs appropriately to your Dept.," and that his own could provide two revenue steamers, if need be.[6]

Welles relented to Governor Morgan. Instead of the old sailing frigate *Savannah* (now being used as a training ship), the converted multi-turret ironclad *Roanoke* would be placed under the command of Rear Admiral Paulding for the defense of New York until another armored man-of-war was ready.[7] But when Paulding inadvertently informed Hiram Barney, the New York Collector of Customs, that the *Passaic* was already ordered south, and that the *Roanoke* would not be ready for at least another 60 days, Welles was quickly told that New York City would indeed use the armed revenue steamers to at least act as warning pickets and reassure its citizens "that the naval authorities are ready to perform the duty which they have undertaken of destroying any hostile vessels which may possibly reach the harbor." The next day, Nov. 20, Barney—with Morgan— telegraphed Welles to inform him that they wanted "the *Passaic* [to] remain for the defense of this harbor until the *Montauk* is ready for that service."[8]

As events unfolded, it became clear that the control of Federal ironclads would be pried out of the hands of the Navy Department in Washington, D.C. Moreover, an ironclad allocated for the direct defense of one city would oblige the Navy to allocate an ironclad for every other city that needed one. The question thus arose: were the nation's interests best served locally or not? Welles wasted no time in replying. It was, he acknowledged, "proper at all times to guard against danger, though it may not be imminent." Yet there was "seldom a day when there are not several Naval vessels at New York undergoing repairs," some of which would probably be "ready for instant service." The defenses of New York were, at any rate, "much better provided for . . . so far as the Navy is concerned, than most of the places on our seaboard." Most crucially, the Secretary of the Navy specified:

> This is in no respect a maritime war, and the War Department has doubtless attended to the harbor defenses. It can hardly be expected that the Navy Department should suspend active operations and divert vessels from their destination from merely apprehended dangers, or apprehended omission on the part of the Government or others, in regard to defenses.[9]

When John Forbes wrote from Boston on Nov. 19 that people on the coast were "subject to spasmodic attacks of the Shakes—& just now our public [are] much concerned about the *Alabama*," Fox replied the same day as Welles that he had no doubt such cruisers "can be kept out by our present forts." Besides, the *Alabama* was "doing a better business with less risk than attacking Boston."[10] What Fox had in mind for the monitors was a series of offensive strikes all along the southern coast, starting at Wilmington, then Charleston, possibly at Savannah, and finally sweeping the Union tide of victory back into the Gulf of Mexico, where Farragut was waiting. To Rear Admiral Lee, he almost cavalierly suggested on Nov. 7 that it would be "a grand stroke to take a couple of steamers, tow these vessels down in good weather, and clean out Wilmington and its railroad connections." Indeed, he added: "Perhaps the forts would surrender if you got to the town."[11] In fact, for those "of undaunted courage and great coolness," Fox was even willing to offer $5,000 to any pilot familiar with the harbor, "if they take an ironclad to the town of Wilmington and back."[12] But these plans, he already knew, were reliant upon the Navy's ability to circumvent enemy obstructions, as much as the Union might rely upon them for harbor defense as well. Though Stimers reported to him on Nov. 10 that he had "[t]orpedoes men placed in hand," Gregory had his doubts that the monitors would have the necessary power to batter through obstructions with armored rafts the way Ericsson and Stimers envisaged.[13] Even if the various obstructions could be overcome and the dreaded ropes avoided, would the forts surrender? Would the town?

In any event, troubles continued to plague the *Passaic*. On her two-day maiden voyage to Hampton Roads, her boilers broke down as a result of obviously poor construction and even worse management by her chief engineer. The ship was shuttled back up to the Washington Navy Yard, and Isherwood himself was ordered by Fox to examine the cause. The company Martin Boilers had been recommended by the Bureau Chief. Drayton did not waste time complaining to Rear Admiral Lee about Ericsson's injured ironclad, "owing to bad work and negligence"; meanwhile the Assistant Secretary, always the positive conciliator, assured Lee that, although the "arrival of the *Passaic* was very discouraging," she would quickly be back in service. "We have learned something by the accident. Accident is a good teacher."[14]

Ericsson, however, was anything but satisfied. Even though the *Montauk* was also ready, he was annoyed that she was not being ordered out for duty, "as the several officers found all sorts of things to do." Holes were being drilled into her decks for various fittings, making him uneasy. "One would think from the manner the Monitor fleet is viewed by your officers," he wrote to Fox, "that it must be intended for cruising and not for attacking and destroying the enemy."[15] It was little wonder that Rodgers was nervous about meeting the fiery and reclusive inventor, a sort of great and brooding volcano. "He is said to keep himself aloof from vulgar eyes, much in the manner of the great Mogul; and to offend generally those who gain admittance," he noted to his wife. "I think I can get on without receiving offense as I am neither captious nor touchy."[16] When Loring inquired on Dec. 15 whether Ericsson was sure he had not omitted any extra details for the monitors that the Navy might require, the volcano erupted. Additional fittings were not his responsibility, he exclaimed, but Stimers's. "It is here that in order to please the several officers of the Gunboats I have invented and applied various contrivances such as bits, timber houses, chocks, flag staffs, auxiliary steering gear, holding down gear of hatches, Shot lifters and a variety of other similar contrivances but in no instance have I succeeded in calling forth expressions of approbation." While the Government and general public seemed to appreciate his efforts, nothing had "so far given satisfaction to the commanding officers." Yet Ericsson had responded to their concerns—and the builders'—within days, if not hours, in most cases. "I politely offered the other day to send you a turret sight ready made," he pointed out to Loring, offended; "you have not even noticed my attention." What right did Loring or anyone have, therefore, to suggest any "neglect" on his part? The *Passaic*'s boilers were only the latest example. Ericsson expected more gratitude, respect—and perhaps faith—by then. "I could show you that such herculean [sic] labor as I have performed in relation to the Monitor fleet is not on record in the history of engineering":

> Not one plan have you waited for essential to the prosecution of the work. Matters of detail unconnected with the vessel and machinery yourself and the Government Inspector should have looked after.
>
> I have repeatedly urged your sending some competent person to copy what was doing here if you desired to follow me in every thing. I now again urge this course.
>
> I will at once report the whole case to the Secretary of the Navy as I cannot permit blame to be fastened on me as my reward for almost superhuman exertions during the last seven months.[17]

But when Ericsson did complain to Fox, not Welles, the Assistant Secretary finally boiled over himself. Indeed, he could afford to be more forthright, in one respect, with Ericsson than with his fellow Union officers. It was for Ericsson to remember that Fox, too, was under stress because of the monitor ironclads—from the officers, the contractors, and the bickering at all levels over matters of technical detail that threatened to derail the Union ironclad program unless *someone* proved willing to actually *fix* such problems as they occurred, and *everyone* was kept on track—which was not always a rewarding task:

> Being myself responsible that some twenty are now underway, and knowing that the exigencies of the public service did not permit experiments with the details, I have personally considerable at stake in the matter. It is a stake of reputation which is the greatest one that can be imposed. It is briefly whether I shall be considered an Ass or a very sensible man. I take this risk on these boats most cheerfully, having every confidence that your skill will work out successfully the perfection of all minor details.[18]

Ericsson was again mollified, to some extent, but seems to have missed Fox's wider point. Two weeks later, Ericsson openly acknowledged he was "more and more surprised at the course of this officer [Drayton] who seems bent on prejudicing everybody against the vessel under his command." Not only was Drayton's proclivity for criticism and despair unsuitable for the *Passaic*, it was severely infectious. In a state of civil war, it was perhaps even treasonous. Was this the type of officer the Union needed? In fact, Ericsson was prepared to show "by legal testimony" that it was Drayton who had "called on the Editor of *The [New York] World* and told him that the muzzle box had been torn to pieces and that the idea would prove an utter failure." This was a much weightier indictment than those against Rowland, the "overbearing" builder with his poor choice of foremen, or the various "incompetent" engineers of the monitors— assigned by Isherwood, the "malign" Chief of the Bureau of Steam Engineering. The man behind the monitors threatened to demand the replacement of the captains in command of the nation's most important, high-profile warships—*Ericsson's ironclads:*

> I trust the man may prove to be what you expect, certain it is however that he is discouraged by the slightest difficulty. I have found him on every occasion to give in on the first appearance of trouble. I will try to believe that it is <u>mechanical</u> difficulties alone that appall [sic] him.[19]

Fox again responded diplomatically. It was his job to do so. There was an important distinction to be made between those who operated the ironclads and those who commanded (if not directed) them. Senior engineers in charge of the ships' engines could, should, and would be rather easily replaced if need be. "It is only necessary for you to give us an intimation in time, to have a change instantly made, as in the case of the *Passaic*," Fox confirmed. But the charge against Isherwood was more complicated, and the Assistant Secretary disapproved of "Mr. Stimers putting on to Isherwood's shoulders any 'malign influence' against the Monitor fleet." Isherwood was *not* the mastermind of an anti-monitor conspiracy; one of his bureau's clerks assigned the engineers for the monitors, and these were then under Stimers's supervision, not the Engineer-in-Chief's. Once more, Fox reminded—and reassured— Ericsson: "I have shouldered this fleet, and I doubt if any one can stand in the way provided we are successful, of which I entertain no doubt." Complaints from officers he absolutely liked to hear of "because it teaches a lesson—Pride never does." Bickering, on the other hand, was inexcusable, even dangerous, in the Navy. "Mr. Stimers and Mr. Isherwood belong to a military family, and it is impossible for the former to talk openly about the latter, and the Officers tell me Stimers does, without laying himself liable to be called upon to prove all he says." If Ericsson or Stimers were ever to put Fox's professional loyalties to the test on the basis of patriotism, Fox could assure them both that there was no inherent conflict of his duty. "I have no friend in all this business except those who most earnestly and zealously work to defeat the public enemy," he wrote, "and all those who are banded together to work to the same end, should endeavor to do it with harmony."[20]

Perhaps more significant, the monitors at least had been commissioned, at last were becoming a reality, and already were fulfilling their original primary role. As Rodgers indicated to his wife on 16 December, the *Montauk*'s trial trip, "which [Stephen] Rowan, George Rodgers and I were ordered to witness and take note upon," including the test firing of the 15-inch gun inside the turret, was "very satisfactory." Furthermore, "Capt. Lessoffsky[,] Russian Navy[,] with 2 other Russian officers were on board and very much impressed with the power of the gun."[21] Despite the setbacks and uncertainties of 1862, Rodgers contemplated the New Year with a sense of hope, and this was all that Ericsson, the Department, and Lincoln asked. His new command, the monitor U.S.S. *Weehawken,* already needed a repair just before her departure south. "An accident happened to the machinery, whereby two of the cog wheels for moving the turret were damaged by having some of the teeth broken out," yet this could be easily mended, he wrote. Eager to be off, Rodgers was more than ready "to have a finger in humbling Sumpter [*sic*]." Indeed, the "garrison should be <u>made</u> to surrender without conditions. . . ." Fanaticism and confidence went hand in hand. The Navy still expected victory, and its ironclads were the key:

> When the army takes the city in keeping, every horses [*sic*] head[,] every artillery wagon[,] every ambulance, every caisson, should carry an American Flag in pocket Handerkerchief shape[,] and they should gleam from every window occupied by us like leaves in a forest. Any man who

looks askant at them should be shot[,] every woman imprisoned, every child whipped, and the higher the rank the better.

As for the threat posed by the "Merrimac No. 2" against Hampton Roads, Rodgers thought it possible that "when the iron clads are taken off to some pressing exigency . . . she will pitch in, and strike for Washington." But he would be "pleased" if she attacked before then. "I stood Fort Darling 3½ hours," he assured his wife, "and in less than that time the *Merrimac* will be chips."[22]

Chapter 20

Regaining the Strategic Initiative?

Regaining the strategic initiative during the Civil War had by this time become an international issue for the Union as well. On Dec. 7, even as the Army of the Potomac, under the new command of General Ambrose Burnside, finally began to march against the Army of Northern Virginia—toward Fredericksburg—Secretary of State Seward stressed to the U.S. *Chargé d'Affaires* at St. Petersburg, Bayard Taylor: "Our great expedition assigned to Major General Banks has moved towards its destination, and it will soon be heard from. Our forces are clearing the valley of the Mississippi. Another army is pressing the insurgents in Virginia. Our iron-clad fleet is growing with rapidity, and it will soon reduce the last remaining insurgent port. The principal part of Tennessee is restored." It was the task of all U.S. consuls to constantly assure—and warn—"that any foreign power which thinks this people is ready to divide and destroy itself is mistaken, and that if any such state thinks the Union can be destroyed by interference from any foreign quarter, this belief is even still more erroneous." Taylor likewise replied on Dec. 17 (before news arrived of the repulse of Burnside at Fredericksburg) that "nothing can do us so much damage abroad as inaction, either real or apparent." The intervention crisis following the news of Antietam and the Emancipation Proclamation had temporarily passed, and Taylor hoped "that the restoration of confidence . . . will not again suffer a relapse."[1] The Union had to demonstrate strength as well as resolve—against the Confederacy, and against Europe, if need be. But against the latter, it had to do so tactfully, even politely.

A case in point was the increased effort of Gideon Welles to find and destroy the C.S.S. *Alabama*—which was busily wrecking Yankee prestige as much as its maritime commerce—and to disrupt "Anglo-Rebel" blockade-running operations.[2] Yet the Secretary was also cautioned by the State Department to tread carefully on British neutrality in the process. His instructions to the ever-assertive Rear Admiral Wilkes, hovering with his cruisers outside Bermuda, amounted to a curious mixture of approval and admonition. While the British Governor's complaints against Wilkes were clearly exaggerated and biased, Welles wrote:

> It is desirable that you should cultivate a friendly feeling with other Powers, and while maintaining our rights, to respect the rights of others. We must be careful not to be aggressive. If it is a duty to conciliate other Powers at other times, it is equally so at present. Regretting that the British Colonial authorities should sympathize with the insurgents, and that the proclamation of her Majesty is so little regarded by some of her subjects who are engaged in systematic illicit trade against our authority, and schemes to evade the blockade and aid the insurgents, nevertheless I would have you, while keeping a vigilant watch to detect and seize all vessels that directly or indirectly waging war on this Government, avoid, as far as you well can, entering British ports.[3]

How difficult this must have been for Welles, who within a week had to complain to Seward about ironclad frigates reported to be under construction at Glasgow and Liverpool for the Confederate States Navy.[4] Welles, among others, thought that perhaps the United States should simply outbid Southern agents in Britain and buy up all such belligerent vessels. Fox wrote that this idea was "frequently . . . under discussion, and as a matter of precaution is expensive, as it would involve us in unlimited purchases without entirely curing the evil, since every steamer could not be obtained." The blockade seemed effective enough to stop most runners. In his estimate "not one in twenty have landed a cargo and returned safely to England." The ironclads were another matter. These, he informed John Forbes, should be purchased "if they can be obtained for money. Mr. Welles favors the idea and Mr. Seward simply urges it." How they would keep such a transaction secret from Congress was an additional problem, but a future one. For the Department of the Navy, British-built ironclads for the Confederacy were a long-dreaded nightmare, "deserving instant action at any price, since we have not a port north that can resist an Iron Clad of very moderate power."[5] Forbes added that it was doubtful "as to John Bull allowing any <u>decent</u> people to take them away—but even so far it may be well worth trying—then perhaps some friendly Government—Spain or Portugal may hereafter buy them of us if we fail to get them out while we are Belligerent!"[6] This was also important: the United States might purchase a sea-going ironclad more expensive than the *Dictator* or *Dunderberg*—and never be able to wield that added power against Britain herself someday. What would prevent the Royal Navy from grabbing it up as its own—a donation from the belligerent Yankees, if not the South? Indeed, less than a year later, Lord Palmerston shrewdly urged the First Lord of the Admiralty to purchase the twin "Laird Rams" built at Liverpool for similar reasons:

> Now what I wish you to consider is whether it would not be a good thing to buy these Iron Clad Rams for our Navy; we are short of Iron Clads, and it takes Time to build them, we want a good many more to put us on our proper level with France; here are Two nearly finished, no doubt well built, fast sailors, and fitted as Rams; if you want Two such either in our Dockyards or in a private yard you would not get them till the end of next year, and these will be available before the End of this year. If the Federals get them they will strengthen the Yankees against us if they should be disposed and able next year to execute their threatened vengeance for all the Forbearance we have shewn them; if we get these Ships they will tend to give us Moral as well as maritime strength.[7]

At any rate, Welles had taken the lesson to heart and promptly notified Congress that "the line of policy which the events and the necessities of the period have instituted" made it "obvious that other and vigorous measures should be adopted in order that we may, when circumstances require it, be able to act with effect on the offensive." In order for the U.S Navy to be "formidable abroad as well as at home," Welles continued, it "should have armored vessels of great power and speed and of different construction from any that we now possess as cruisers." The energetic attempts of the South to obtain such ironclads in Great Britain, combined with rising tensions with at least that European Power, meant the Union could not afford to be taken at any disadvantage, anywhere, if possible. Therefore, "We shall require for service in case of a foreign war a class of vessel of this description that will be capable of encountering any enemy and asserting and maintaining our rights in the ocean as well as to assist in guarding our coasts." The Department "for some months past had in view the construction of two or three powerful Steamers of Iron and to be Iron Clad," and these would help enable the Union to take the initiative—in a war which did not exist but nevertheless seemed probable. The nation's "turret boats of the Monitor class" were distinctly for coast and harbor defense. Combined, such an ironclad navy would "go far to render us invulnerable as a naval power, capable of resisting the assaults of any nation and always able to assist and maintain our rights at home and abroad."[8]

Yet there were hitches in this ambitious new naval strategy. As Welles noted, the "cost of the proposed vessels would necessarily be great, so much so that I deem it proper before commencing them that the subject should receive the attention of the Naval Committees and, should they deem it advisable, be submitted to Congress for its sanction and approval." Their ostensible purpose, however, while "taking the offensive" if the United States was "at any time engaged in hostilities with a naval power," was still one of strategic defense, for they "could disperse any blockade that might be attempted"—rather than initiating one of their own. Could not the existing ironclads, especially the monitors, already fulfill that role? This had been the primary justification for their construction the previous December, at the height of the *Trent* crisis. Furthermore, Welles was specifying massive, iron-hulled, sea-going ironclads of the European pattern, which would require at least $12 million in addition to the annual estimate and take several years to build, and which the Northern press was actively campaigning against in preference to American monitors. Was now the time to build such a navy? Could Northern resources even handle such an order, in addition to all those vessels already being built for coastal assault and defense, let alone those for riverine warfare? So far there had been only contract delays, labor shortages, and cost overruns. Would these problems become better or worse as the war progressed? These were questions that undoubtedly occurred to knowing members of Congress, though Welles pointedly neglected to address them. Instead, he resorted to the classic, often unanswerable argument for military expenditure that had failed to convince politicians long before the Civil War:

> To be prepared for war is one means of preventing its occurrence. It is true wisdom to be ready at all times for any emergency, and hence the proposition for a few powerful Steamers, Iron Clad, and each having the properties of Ram of immense power, with a speed of at least sixteen knots.[9]

In fact, Welles had already outlined the Department's vision for the future in his Annual Report to Congress, dated Dec. 1, 1862. Here he asserted that the overriding strategic role of the Navy, the blockade of the South, was maintained almost despite the efforts of Great Britain. "A multitude of island harbors under foreign jurisdiction, looking nearly upon our shores, and affording the most convenient lurking places from which illicit commerce may leap forth to its prohibited destination and purpose, are so closely watched as to render the peril of all such ventures far greater than even their enormous gains when successful." Indeed, this was the ultimate economic logic of the blockade, whose consequent efficiency was proven by "the current price of our southern staples in the great commercial marts of the world, and more especially in the whole industrial and commercial conditions of the insurgent region." Confederate commerce raiders, however, threatened to work their own mercantile damage in return—and this was as much the responsibility of the British as of the insurgents themselves. "How far and to what results this abuse may be carried with impunity to the Government which tolerates it is a matter of grave consideration." The Secretary "alluded to it now and here," he added, "not only from a sense of duty towards our commercial interest and rights, but also by reason of the fact that recent intelligence indicates that still other vessels of a similar character are being fitted out in British ports to deprecate upon our commerce."[10]

Stymied as he was by the quieter protocol of diplomacy in carrying out his duties without openly offending Britain, Welles informed Congress it had been "deemed advisable . . . that we should have a few large-sized armed cruisers, of great speed, for ocean service, as well as of the class of smaller vessels for coastwise service and defensive operations." In this altered perception of Union ironclad strategy, the monitors would "penetrate the inner waters, rivers, harbors, and bayous of our extended double coast," while vessels similar to the *Warrior* would deal with "foreign powers" on their own terms after all. This was the silent, but strong-armed political leverage of naval power at work. The British Empire would respect nothing less. With a rival fleet of American "Warriors" to contend with, it might respect such power even more. Just as Ericsson had promised the previous December that his monitors would serve a vital deterrent function against foreign intervention, the Department's call for high-seas ironclads this year might force the British Government to more strictly observe its own stated neutrality—and stop further blockade runners, raiders, and even ironclads from being built in private British establishments, manned by British subjects, and finding quarter in British colonial ports. As Welles wrote: "The time has arrived when, in order to maintain ourselves and our true position as a nation, we must have a formidable Navy, not only of light draught vessel to guard our extensive and shallow coast, but one that with vessels always ready for the service, and of sufficient size to give them speed, can seek and meet an enemy on the ocean."[11]

Yet "great speed" required "enormous steam power," and for this the United States "must have vessels of the greatest magnitude." Iron construction would therefore also be needed; and to facilitate this a new, Government-owned naval and industrial base would be necessary. "No private establishment can undertake such heavy work as the Government requires for its armor and steam purposes," Welles pointed out. "Possessing advantages that no nation enjoys, we should avail ourselves of them. Our iron and coal are found in the same region, and we have fresh-water rivers in which iron vessels can be docked and kept clean, and from which all enemies can be excluded." The greatest justification for this sweeping program for an entirely new, Government-controlled, naval-industrial infrastructure was, in fact, Welles contended—as did Controller of the Royal Navy, Spencer Robinson, to the Admiralty—the failings of the private sector in meeting the equally radical demands of modern warfare.

Consequently, for the nation-state to wield even more military and naval power, it would need to consolidate the means of that power. National conscription, the legal tender act, the income tax, the constitutionally dubious liberties that the Executive branch of the Government had assumed to prosecute the war successfully against the Rebellion, perhaps even the Emancipation Proclamation—all these were symptoms of the same process, and all were contingent upon the shifting circumstances of the Civil War itself, domestically and internationally.[12] Welles's admonition to Congress about neglecting greater investment in Federal power prior to the outbreak of secession carried a double meaning. Not only was the republic ill prepared for suddenly waging—if not deterring—a great, modern civil war, but perhaps this state of weakness—or a weak State—was intentional:

> Successive Administrations, with a view to the appearance of economy and a show of small expenditure, restricted the estimates for supplies to amounts barely sufficient to keep its few ships afloat.
>
> The war found us literally destitute of materials in our navy-yards, as well as with but few ships to sustain the national integrity. From mistaken economy, or from design, the Government was, in its need, deficient in ships and destitute of material for their construction.[13]

By this reasoning, the Navy Secretary and his Department could hardly be criticized, much less investigated, by Congress in its dealings with private shipbuilders—its procurement policies—or possibly even its operations, either successful or failed, against the Confederate States. Moreover, the victories the U.S. Navy had achieved in the past year, including, above all, the vigorous establishment of a grand blockade of the South, despite the limited means at its disposal, merited praise from the nation. For his part, Welles presented an opinion of the efficiency of the national legislature that was anything but flattering. "The demagogues in Congress disgrace the body and the country," he confided in his diary on Christmas Eve. "Noisy and loud professions, with no useful policy or end, exhibit themselves daily."[14]

But the Secretary's report undercut itself. For the purposes of the Civil War, an ironclad fleet was already being launched, thanks to private industry—and the specter of foreign intervention seemed laid to rest by the small ironclad monitors with their 15-inch ordnance on the one hand, and the faltering yet persistent advances of the Union Army on the other. Despite the chronic lack of preparation for a major modern war—of increasing scope—the Nation and its Executive were by the end of 1862, more powerful than ever before. Did the Navy really need to build oceangoing ironclads matching European enterprises to "insure peace," when, admittedly, smaller coastal versions were already within the capacity of Northern industry to produce?[15]

It was not clear what could trigger a foreign war. Even greater Federal power might actually disrupt peaceful relations with Britain and France by tempting the United States to "bully" them (a common cry even before the Civil War) into compliance with its views on the nature of the terrible war in America, and the justice of the Union cause over the Confederacy's. Welles's personal irritation with the British was only one indication of the complexities of maintaining peace and avoiding war. "It is annoying when we want all our force on blockade duty to be compelled to detach so many of our best craft on the fruitless errand of searching for this wolf from Liverpool," he wrote in his diary concerning the *Alabama*. "We shall, however, have a day of reckoning with Great Britain for these wrongs, and I sometimes think I care not how soon nor in what manner that reckoning comes."[16]

Contrast this sentiment with Lincoln's own, in his Annual Address to Congress, which began with, above all else, the state of the Nation's foreign relations. By June 1862 there were, he wrote, "some grounds to expect that the maritime Powers which, at the beginning of our domestic difficulties, so unwisely and unnecessarily, as we think, recognized the insurgents as a belligerent, would soon recede from that position, which has proved only less injurious to themselves than to our own country." This comment referred to growing cotton shortages and unemployment in textile mills in Britain and France, a result of both the Union blockade and Southern planters' self-imposed embargo at the beginning of the war—"King Cotton's" attempt to openly extort European naval intervention against the United States. But the fortunes of war had once again changed. Though the conflict in America "excited political ambitions and apprehensions which have produced a profound agitation throughout the civilized world," the United States had carefully "attempted no propagandism, and acknowledged no revolution; but we have left to every nation the exclusive conduct and management of its own affairs":

> Our struggle has been, of course, contemplated by foreign nations with reference less to its own merits than to its supposed and often exaggerated effects and consequences resulting to those nations themselves.

Nevertheless, complaint on the part of this Government, even if it were just, would certainly be unwise.[17]

A strong defense was therefore one thing; the threat of attack was another. "I have a single idea of my own about harbor defences," Lincoln expressed in a little-known memorandum of April 1863. "A steam-ram, built so as to sacrifice nearly all capacity for carrying, to those of speed and strength, so as to be able to split any vessel hollow enough in her to carry supplies for a voyage of any distance." Lincoln's notion clearly referred to transatlantic threats. "Such ram, of course could not her self carry supplies for a voyage of considerable distance; and her business would be to guard a particular harbour, as a Bull-dog guards his master's door." Fittingly, Abraham Lincoln's personal approach to influencing "the conduct of men" was to convince a potential enemy "that you are his sincere friend." The way to win over his reason was through his heart. "On the contrary, assume to dictate to his judgment, or to command his action . . . and he will retreat within himself, close all avenues to his head and his heart. . . ." This statement stretched into another of his metaphors, for which he was famous: "though your cause be naked truth itself, transformed into the heaviest lance, harder than steel, and sharper than steel can be made, and though you throw it with more than herculean force and precision, you shall be no more able to pierce him than to penetrate the hard shell of a tortoise with a rye straw." Nothing served Union diplomacy better than a strong Federal military that could demonstrate its power by successfully crushing the South; and for that purpose, blue-water ironclads of the "greatest magnitude," Welles had already assured Congress, could not "nearly approach our shores. . . ."[18]

Surprisingly, even leading professional officers of the Navy were not as keen on the Department's new plan as might be expected. On Dec. 26 a new Ironclad Board composed of (now Rear Admiral) Smith, Commodore Charles Davis (of the original Ironclad Board of 1861), and Isherwood reported on a proposal by Otis Tufts of Boston for an iron-hulled, twin-screwed, armored cruiser, 375 feet long and "to draw no more than 21 feet of water when loaded." According to Tufts, his casemate-ram would take at least $2,800,000 and, ideally, 16 months to construct. With a spar deck amidships at only "4 feet above the loadwater line and the sills of the ports . . . to float 7¼ feet above water," the central inclined casemate itself would be armored with 9 inches of 1-inch plates, backed by wood, and would house "10 XI inch Guns, viz. 4 on each side and one at each end, or two on each side and three at each end; or by enlarging the Vessel by adding 25 feet in length and 2 feet to the beam, Mr. Tufts proposes to carry 10 XV Guns." Though Smith was generally favorable to the idea, commenting that "we have built too many vessels on the same or of similar models and power, without first testing the qualities of one of the class" (i.e., the monitors), he also wished to avoid the same mistake with even grander conceptions. This was the lesson he had taken from 1862. He was aware that the Department had advertised for "proposals to construct three immense ships with heavy Armor; these ships to be capable of carrying and working 10 XV inch Guns of the modern pattern." While the Government might "invite competition by public advertisement for all its vessels built outside of Navy Yards," Smith thought this best only "for Models and Specifications of its own designing" because "no Government would undertake to thus trespass on the rights of a Citizen by adopting his plan by such a course without his consent!" This was thinly veiled criticism of Ericsson's own popularity and influence. Smith would rather "encourage different plans which appear to possess merit, in order to obtain the best by actual practice." Thus, even though the Department's advertised super-ironclads might "prove to excel all other ships in the world, but One such should suffice for the <u>experiment</u>." Caution was the order of the day. Maybe the Navy should not be so eager to plunge into "The Future" any more than it already had. Regardless, Smith pointed out further: "You will be compelled to build docks for these vessels . . . before they can be repaired or even their bottoms examined and cleaned when fouled." The size and strength of an ironclad, like power itself, had practical limits. "It is true that small Vessels cannot be modeled and made buoyant enough to sustain heavy armor and possess the needed speed," Smith observed, "but I say there must be bounds to the dimensions of ships not to be exceeded. What these bounds are experiments must prove."[19]

Toward the end of 1862, Dahlgren's views had also changed. In his masterful Annual Report as Chief of the Bureau of Ordnance—which Welles drew heavily upon for his own—Dahlgren summarized that both "the construction and armament of ships-of-war" were "so unavoidably interwoven that it is impossible to treat or consider either independently of the other, or to form any reliable opinion as to their future course or final shape." Indeed, the age-old competition between offense and defense was "impelled now . . . by existing circumstances with a rapidity beyond all precedent in naval affairs." As Dahlgren recounted for the Secretary, up until the development of shell fire in naval warfare, "the defense had the advantage of the attack, for the broadsides of these vessels, when continued for hours, were seldom able to do more than destroy masts, men, and guns. The instances are very rare of a line-of-battle ship being sunk, or fatally injured in battle by the sole action of shot." Dahlgren's own scholarly exploration had revealed that, aside from the devastation of a Turkish squadron at

Sinope (Nov. 30, 1853) by a Russian squadron armed with Paixhans shell-firing guns, "there was no illustration of the full effect of shells in any of the operations during the Crimean War. . . ." Nevertheless, the French were quick to use iron-armored batteries with success against the Russian forts at Kinburn in 1855, and then followed this up shortly afterward with the first ironclad frigate, the wooden-hulled *Gloire*. This action had set the British Admiralty off in a race, "with a remarkable celerity, quite regardless of expenditure," starting with the iron-hulled H.M.S. *Warrior*. Yet the urgent nature of the European powers' rearmaments against one another made these "gigantic" and "costly" efforts, at best, experiments. Furthermore, "their shores being washed by the deep waters of the ocean," Dahlgren elaborated, their ironclads "must be more than mere floating batteries, and be possessed of the best nautical qualities":

> With the United States the case is, happily, different—the depth of water on the coast being generally adapted to vessels of light or moderate draught, and only a few of our ports are at all accessible to heavy ironclads like those of France or England.
>
> Vessels of the *Monitor* and [*New*] *Ironsides* class are likely to serve present purposes sufficiently well, and to give time to obtain from our own and the experience of others better data than can now be had for advancing to a more perfect order of vessels.

This was Dahlgren's first point in acceptance of the Union's ironclad program, as it already stood: geographical reality. Though the defense in naval warfare seemed to regain the edge with armor plating, few of the leading experts (including himself) were in agreement as to either the best form of armor or "upon the cannon that shall be employed to overcome that resistance." Warship designers, meanwhile, had to accommodate the weights of each to the point "that a vessel with one-half greater capacity than a two or three-decker is so far shorn in height as to leave but one gun-deck, thus becoming a frigate by the general definition. Of course the ordnance is reduced proportionately in number and weight." Offensive and defensive qualities were *concentrating* themselves: armor needed to be thicker, and guns needed to be larger. Nor was there any clear advantage to solid slabs of iron for plating when the fastenings between were just as important—the veritable chinks in the armor—while the "ordnance expert can by no means rejoice in being free of difficulties that puzzle his ingenuity":

> If he acquires power by greater weight, he loses by loss of time in manipulation of the gun and projectile, hence some reduction by slowness of repetition. Then, again, shall he use rifled or smooth-bore, breech or muzzle loaders? Shall he pierce or crush and break bolts and strip off the armor, or shall he even attempt to enter the interior with shells?

At any rate, Dahlgren's own conclusion was that, despite the advent of iron armor plating, no "sea-going ship is considered to be so armored as to be impregnable to artillery." Though Armstrong's vaunted 150-pounder with 50-pound charges had burst after only a fourth round in April, trying to fully pierce the *Warrior* target, both the 13-inch Horsfall smoothbore and a Whitworth rifled gun had unquestionably accomplished the objective. But armor plating also bought time during an engagement for one's own guns to take effect. The duel between the *Monitor* and the *Virginia* was a case in point, subsequently misinterpreted by British authorities—namely Somerset, who had "imputed the default of injury to life or limb in this combat to a lack of power in the artillery which the two vessels carried; which is no doubt true; but it is equally true that no guns of like weight and kind now used in the British Navy would have effected as much under like circumstances." According to Dahlgren, the First Lord of the Admiralty "more nearly approached the present state of the question when he doubted the capacity of plates finally to resist the action of Ordnance; but was in fact overestimating the service to be expected of the Armstrong gun."

In the meantime, Dahlgren's own target tests had actually confirmed Ericsson's belief that laminated armor was a viable, though temporary, substitute for solid plating, and was even "preferable on many accounts . . . and would be altogether if it were not for the increased number of bolts that become requisite, and are the weakness of all such plating." Likewise, iron metallurgy had yet to produce slabs of iron at greater thicknesses with inner welds as strong as thinner plates. Dahlgren's greatest tribute to Ericsson, however, was in stating that "the turret class" was free of many of the inherent weaknesses of heavy, iron-armored sea-going vessels, and were "probably of greater and more certain endurance under severe fire than the ordinary plated vessel." Dahlgren went on to say, "So far they are likely to find the most fitting sphere for their peculiar powers in the less troubled waters of harbors and rivers; though the ability that has devised them may also be able to give a wider scope to their usefulness."

If Dahlgren had finally come around to Ericsson's choice of ironclad design, he also seemed to acknowledge the practical utility of the 15-inch gun. At longer ranges, rifled fire became ineffective, and elongated shells frequently toppled in flight whereas round shot could at least be ricocheted off the water. Against an ironclad, Dahlgren was also convinced from his own testing—and the graphic experience of the *Galena* in action—that smashing was better than penetrating. "So long as the present mode of plating continues, there can be little doubt that it will be most effectively attacked by cracking and bending the iron, starting the bolts, stripping off the armor, and breaking away large portions of the wooden structure within." Though rate of fire was jeopardized by a smoothbore heavier than his own 11-inch gun, Dahlgren had to admit that "it may be conceived that the effects of shells of 330 pounds, and shot of 450 pounds, will be damaging beyond any experience in former battles."[20] Like the monitors themselves, the gun was at worst an experiment and at best the supreme naval weapon afloat.[21]

Culmination and Consequence: "The Fiery Focus"

What happened at Charleston on April 7, 1863? A long-planned—and long-expected—naval attack by the Union's most powerful force of ironclads against the rebel city's combined defenses failed ignominiously. Was it the fault of the men in command or their technology? Though the question is simple enough, the answers, then and now, ultimately blaming one or the other, are not. While the commander in chief, Rear Admiral Samuel Francis Du Pont, faced a difficult task with questionable means ("monitors against forts"), it was probably a misapplication of his popular yet controversial vessels that guaranteed their failure that day. Yet the fault was not entirely his own.

Nearly every naval history of the American Civil War devotes at least a passing analysis to this famous repulse and the infamous controversy that followed, starting with Charles B. Boynton's two-volume *History of the Navy During the Rebellion* (1867), and including most notably Daniel Ammen's *The Atlantic Coast* (1883) and David Dixon Porter's *The Naval History of the Civil War* (1886), all three of which were contemporary and often self-serving; Porter was perpetually at odds with the Navy; Ammen the former commander of the monitor *Patapsco*; and Boynton a well-known and ambitious apologist for the Navy Department. The valuable firsthand accounts that appeared in *Century Magazine*, later codified in the magnificent four-volume *Battles and Leaders of the Civil War* (1887–1888), are also unavoidably tainted, perhaps, with observations between various contributors often directly at odds with one another. Twenty years on, the controversy surrounding the repulse proved as lively as its participants.

Conclusions drawn since then, particularly in Bruce Catton's centennial three-volume history of the Civil War, generally avoid technical dissections of the mass of official records and accounts. The "judgment of history," more properly seasoned, is more willing to condemn the machines in question instead of the personalities. For Kevin J. Weddle, "Du Pont's story is one of the most heartbreaking of the Civil War." In 1851 the Union admiral had "advocated a strategy similar to that later advanced by America's greatest strategist Alfred Thayer Mahan." But following Du Pont's defeat at Charleston, the Navy Department relieved him of his command, and this "was probably preordained the moment he identified the monitors' shortcomings."[1] Here Russell Weigley blamed "the monitors' armament": "with so few guns, the defensive strength of their iron plates was not enough to prevent their vulnerability from exceeding the damage they could inflict on the Charleston forts. The attack failed, and the failure ruined Du Pont's career."[2] In *This People's Navy: The Making of American Sea Power* (1991), Kenneth J. Hagan concurred: "The question was whether well-armored gunships could batter heavy forts into submission."[3] Even the most recent general work, Spencer Tucker's *A Short History of the Civil War at Sea* (2002), notes that "the slow rate of fire rendered the monitors incapable of inflicting, in a short span of time, the sort of damage necessary to reduce shore fortifications," even though he later mentions the inability—or unwillingness—of the lead monitor, U.S.S. *Weehawken*, under Captain John Rodgers, to smash through the obstructions that prevented a dash against Charleston itself, and that "meant the end of Du Pont's plan of running past the point with the heaviest concentration of Confederate firepower."[4]

The common implications here are twofold: monitors were *meant* to overpower fortifications, and therefore the problem was one of means—not ends. A broader analysis is offered in E. Milby Burton's *The Siege of Charleston, 1861–1865* (1970), which emphasizes Confederate intentions to fight "street by street," even if "Du Pont's fleet managed to break through all these obstructions, and if enough ships were still afloat and a landing was effected. . . ."[5] This at once transfers the onus of the debate to the inability of Union naval forces to negotiate the obstructions in the first place, if not also the strategic and political expectation in Washington that the rebel city would surrender if only placed under the guns of Federal ironclads. Indeed, Bern Anderson preferred to blame the "stubborn insistence" of Secretary of the Navy Gideon Welles for the failure of the Union assault, rather than Du Pont, the senior officer in charge.[6] Finally, an excellent article by Robert Erwin Johnson in 1997 sought to analyze the Union repulse at Charleston in terms of "ships versus forts." This angle, however, was possibly misleading. He succeeds in demonstrating "that Admiral Du Pont had no faith in monitors," seemed "not to have made any attempt to gain additional information after 1862" on Charleston's defenses, and formulated an attack "obviously unrealistic because it required that the monitors steam through the first line of obstructions without the means to clear a passage." But he also speculates a greater probability of Union success had the monitors been armed with more rifled ordnance, and this was clearly not the issue.[7]

It was not until late March 1863 that U.S. Senator Charles Sumner could write to his English friend Richard Cobden that the fleet destined to attack Charleston was finally ready. "The delay has been caused by the extent of the preparations," he explained, for "the rebels are confident there," but "so also is our Navy Department."[8] This was reflected by Captain Turner of the broadside ironclad U.S.S. *New Ironsides,* who confirmed to the Chairman of the Union League Defense Committee that the officers and crew of the fleet "detest the conduct of the South from the bottom of our hearts, and pine for the opportunity to punish their infamy—and this feeling especially towards this place steels our hearts. . . ."[9]

But Welles meanwhile had his doubts, particularly with the leadership of the expedition under Du Pont. Though he was a natural choice for command, especially after his relatively easy capture of the vital strategic base for the Atlantic blockade at Port Royal (Nov. 7, 1861), Du Pont was mesmerized by the rapidly growing extent of fortifications ringing Charleston harbor a year later. If an assault was to be made with a lesser degree of firepower than at Port Royal, albeit protected with iron, he would need every monitor available before an attempt could be made. Unfortunately, cautious delays proved it was easier for the South to improvise earthwork fortifications than for the North to manufacture steam-powered ironclads. Technology might favor the Union, but time was on the side of the Confederacy. Moreover, two small rams fashioned in Charleston, the *Chicora* and *Palmetto State,* sortied against Du Pont's wooden blockaders on Jan. 31, 1863. Though they inflicted minimal damage on his ships before returning to the inner harbor, neither could he hope to attack now without ironclads of his own—all of them. Why risk failure? Yet Welles, writing in his diary, confided, "Du Pont is getting as prudent as McClellan, is very careful; all dash, energy, and force are softened under the great responsibility. He has a reputation to preserve instead of one to make."[10]

It was not until noon of April 7 that the *New Ironsides,* the flagship of the Union squadron, finally hoisted the signal to weigh anchor and proceed with Du Pont's pre-arranged order of battle: line ahead, with the monitors *Weehawken, Passaic, Montauk,* and *Patapsco; New Ironsides* at the middle of the formation (to facilitate signaling during the action);

followed by the monitors *Catskill, Nantucket,* and *Nahant;* with the experimental, twin–"fixed-turret" ram U.S.S. *Keokuk* bringing up the rear. The ships were to be navigated between Forts Sumter and Moultrie, firing "when within easy range," to a position "six . . . to eight hundred yards" off Sumter's *northwest* face. "After the reduction of Fort Sumter," Du Pont's plan concluded somewhat vaguely, "it is probable that the next point of attack will be the batteries on Morris Island."[11] Despite the differences in armament, draft, and speed, all of the new ironclads were fairly ponderous and unwieldy, taking the better part of an hour just to jostle into formation. Their local pilots carried perhaps the greatest responsibility of all, steering through treacherous shoals in unfamiliar and novel vessels from crowded armored pilothouses. It was up to them to wait for the morning mists to clear and to time an ebb tide. Running aground here and now could prove fatal; for a squadron in line ahead, it would be worse. The lead monitor, *Weehawken,* commanded by Rodgers, ran into further problems. Specially fitted with a large armored raft at her bow, which Ericsson had provided to destroy channel obstructions, *Weehawken's* anchor became entangled with one of the grappling chains that dangled below the raft. It was not until 1:15 that she was ready again and began slowly steaming up the main ship channel toward the right of Fort Sumter. Time dragged on, as did the ironclads. Their hulls already encumbered with marine growth and "grass," their engines never intended for high speed, they made no more than 4 knots—with difficulty—against the flowing tide and a notorious current.[12]

A Confederate circular of instructions dated more than three months before the attack specified:

> As the enemy approaches, let the distance he will be in passing be accurately estimated by the distance buoys, and the elevation made to correspond, making it too little rather than too great for direct fire. . . .
>
> In the case of wooden vessels, the object will be to hit them near the water line, just abaft the smokestack. In the case of ironclad vessels, to hit the deck or the turrets at the intersection with the deck, and especially to let all the shots strike at once. . . .
>
> The guns of Beauregard battery, Fort Moultrie, Battery Bee, and the eastern, northeastern, and northwestern faces of Fort Sumter will be used to form the first circle of fire to which the enemy must be subjected, the center being a little to the eastward of a line between the forts and midway. Every effort must be made to crush his vessels and repel his attack within this circle, and especially while he is entangled in the obstructions. . . .[13]

At 10 minutes past 2, as the *Weehawken* slowly approached a point directly between Forts Sumter and Moultrie, Rodgers saw "rows of

casks very near together . . . and there was more than one line of
them." Their appearance "was so formidable," he later reported, "that,
upon deliberate judgment I thought it right not to entangle the vessel
in the obstructions which I did not think we could have passed
through, and in which we should have been caught."[14] Before the
obstructions *Weehawken* now hesitated—next to a pre-placed
Confederate ranging buoy, "No. 3," in the middle of the channel.
Moultrie then opened fire. Ranges specified in the various reports are
conflicting but probably stood at 900 yards. *Weehawken* responded,
with both her heavy guns directed against Fort Sumter.

Many accounts have described what happened next. Immediately,
guns from Sumter joined the action, soon to be aided by more distant
fire from batteries Bee, Beauregard, Cumming's Point, Wagner, and Fort
Johnson. It was a sight "that no one who witnessed it will ever forget,"
wrote C. Raymond P. Rodgers, Du Pont's Chief of Staff. "Sublime,
infernal, it seemed as if the fires of hell were turned upon the fleet.
The air seemed full of shot, and as they flew they could be seen as
plainly as a base-ball in one of our games."[15] Soon the *Weehawken*
"was so enveloped in spray from the shot showered at her as to be
completely invisible and people thought we had gone down," John
Rodgers later explained to his wife.[16] Turning to starboard, the
Weehawken threw the rest of the squadron into confusion as the
Passaic and the rest of the ironclads bunched forward to receive similar treatment.[17] *New Ironsides*, even more unwieldy in the tide and
current than the monitors, and burdened by her deeper draft, was
obliged to anchor out of effective range.[18] She managed only a single
broadside that day, while the rest of the Union ironclads, huddled
before the obstructions, could only return a fraction of the enemy's
concentrated fire. Indeed, by 4:30 many of the monitors had suffered
breakdowns, while the *Keokuk* herself was riddled by hits that penetrated her weaker armor protection.[19] The signal to withdraw was
given, and the battered and beaten Union squadron returned to its original anchorage inside the bar to lick its wounds and perhaps renew the
attack the following day. But the *Keokuk* could barely be kept afloat
that night, and on the following morning it finally sank in shallow
water, her two towers peeking just above the surface of the water at
low tide—her guns later salvaged by the Confederates under Du Pont's
nose. At the longest range involved, though representing a far larger
and often stationary target, *New Ironsides* was struck at least
95 times. One of the shots ripped off an external iron port shutter that
was 4 inches thick, and several more penetrated her unarmored
wooden ends, but caused no serious injury.[20]

The damage sustained by the monitors in this contest between forts
and ironclads proved to be much more historically controversial, if not

"critical." According to John Rodgers's report, several heavy shots struck the *Weehawken*'s 5-inch laminated side armor near the same place, shattering it enough to expose the wood backing. *Passaic* was hit by two successive shots near the base of her turret, "which bulged in its plate and beams, and, forcing together the rails on which the XI-inch carriage worked, rendered it wholly useless for the remainder of the action." More serious damage occurred when "a very heavy rifle shot struck the upper edge of the turret, broke all of its eleven plates, and then glancing upward took the pilot house, yet with such force as to make an indentation of 2½ inches, extending nearly the whole length of the shot." The damage to *Nahant*'s pilothouse was also severe; the monitor was pounded 36 times, including 6 times on the pilothouse and another 9 times on the turret, with an alarming number of bolts loosened, broken, and even found lying outside on the deck. Like the *Weehawken,* the *Nahant* was victimized by a chance heavy shot or two at the vulnerable juncture between pilothouse and turret, which proved sufficient to disable its rotation.[21] The *Nantucket,* having been struck a total of "fifty-one times, besides a number of dents by fragments of shells," had her 15-inch gun port stopper jammed. Though some were bent, none of the turret plates were broken. The executive officer assured his commander "the ship is tight and can, if necessary, go into another fight at once, but to do so would, in my opinion, greatly endanger the ship, unless considerable repairs are first given her, there being several places too much weakened to resist a second blow." On the other hand, John Worden, another ironclad battle veteran, acknowledged 14 hits on the *Montauk,* with "no material damage"; the *Catskill* "was struck some twenty times but without any serious injury except one shot upon the forward part of the deck, which broke both plates, the deck planking, and drove down the iron stanchion sustaining this beam about 1 inch, causing the deck to leak"; the *Patapsco*'s commander, Daniel Ammen, reported "47 perceptible blows," but, as with the *Montauk* and the *Catskill,* "no damage was done which disabled her."[22]

The next morning Chief Engineer Stimers, assigned to the ironclad squadron with a corps of specialized mechanics, examined the vessels. Having witnessed the action, he "expected to find . . . at least an approach to the destructive results which had been obtained by the Chief of the Bureau of Ordnance in his experiments against iron targets in the ordnance yard at Washington." Instead, he was "agreeably disappointed" that none of the monitors was actually penetrated, despite the vigorous hammering each received, and reported to Secretary Welles his "firm opinion that the obstructions can be readily passed with the means already provided," but never used, "and that the monitor vessels still retain sufficient enduring powers to enable them to pass all the forts and batteries which may reasonably be expected."[23]

This encouraging assessment infuriated Du Pont. For him the damages spoke for themselves, confirming his own gnawing pessimism, even before the attack, that ironclad monitors were incapable of withstanding sustained enemy fire, never mind their agonizingly slow rate of return fire. Nor could the channel obstructions be overcome in any obvious way. Stimers's own professional position, if not bias, as Chief Engineer was suspect in the matter and therefore regarded by the Rear Admiral as an attempt to undermine his authority. Shortly afterward, Du Pont called for Stimers's court-martial. Stimers was later exonerated after five months of testimonies and cross-examinations. In closing his defense, he labeled the charges made against him as an attempt to "justify a failure by Rear Admiral Du Pont, which had attracted the observation of the world, by condemning as inadequate the instruments which a liberal government had placed in his hands." This comment referred specifically to the armored rafts, armed with a torpedo, that were intended to blast through the obstructions, which none of the monitors' officers were willing to use. John Rodgers concluded that "folly would rise into crime which should carry torpedoes in a rapid tide-way in a somewhat narrow channel, without known buoys, under fire, and with the attention divided amongst a friendly fleet." As for the monitors' condition after their abortive attack on April 7, 1863, Stimers regarded their trial as one of vindication.[24]

Probably the most significant statistic was the number of casualties on board the monitors as a result of their ordeal: one dead and six wounded, all from the *Nahant*—and these were attributed by her commander to the inferior quality of iron used for the armor bolts, since "the other vessels were most of the them struck quite as frequently on the turret, and some of them much more so than the *Nahant,* and yet their loss of bolts has been trifling in comparison. . . ."[25] For Rodgers's wife, Anne, *this* was the critical factor, never mind the controversy. "Hurrah for the ironclads! Hurrah for the ironclads!" she wrote on receiving the news from Charleston. "I have always had strong faith in the Monitors, but I had not dared to hope they would prove so entirely invulnerable."[26]

Yet while their powers of resistance were almost unbelievable against Charleston harbor's outer network of forts, their offensive powers were extremely limited. Official Confederate records list 76 heavy guns that fired a total of 2,209 rounds, which in the opinion of one of the batteries' commanding officers was perhaps "a little too rapid, but I have no doubt that in the end it [served] a good purpose. The storm of shot and bolts which fell around the enemy confused, if it did not appall him."[27] The Union squadron replied with 139 rounds—8 of these from *New Ironsides'* only broadside and 3 from the *Keokuk*. The 14 guns of the seven *Passaic*-class monitors therefore managed only 128 discharges.[28] Accuracy was equivalent:

> About 19% of the fort[s'] rounds hit (520), while the Union forces had a 50% rate of hitting, though their target [Fort Sumter] was certainly larger than the individual ships. The Confederates were helped by pre-placed range markers, since normal gunnery percentages for hits would have been closer to 10% than the 19% achieved.[29]

The damage to Fort Sumter's 5-foot–thick brick casemates was largely superficial, with only five men wounded. As against the monitors, continued hits in the same areas might have produced more serious breaches. "The greatest penetration in good, sound masonry was 3 feet," recalled one of Sumter's captains of artillery, "but everything around was cracked and started more or less. The most severe blow, I think, was about 3 or 4 feet below the crest of the parapet, where two or three balls struck and just loosened everything clear through for a space of about 6 feet in length."[30] But fearing the effect of plunging shot striking the moderately armored decks of his ironclads, Du Pont directed their fire against the fort's upper barbettes (where much of it overshot) rather than at the base, where repeated blasts from 15-inch–caliber shells, each weighing 330 pounds, might have brought down an entire wall.[31]

At any rate, the various reports made to the Union Rear Admiral from the monitor captains on the evening of April 7 convinced him not to renew a strictly naval attack, which, as he expressed in a letter to the Secretary of the Navy the following day, "would have converted a failure into a disaster."[32] The withdrawal from action officially became a repulse. This news traveled slowly back to Washington, where Gideon Welles felt "a yearning, craving desire for tidings from Charleston." Renewed Army and Navy operations in the west against Vicksburg were stalled; bitterness over the new national draft and emancipation was feeding a growing "Peace Party" of Democrats in the North—and the prospect of a war with England loomed larger than ever. "For months my confidence has not increased, and now that the conflict is upon us my disquietude is greater still," he wrote in his diary. "I do not believe the monitors are impregnable, as [Fox] does, under the concentrated fire and immense weight of metal that can be thrown upon them, but it can hardly be otherwise than that some, probably most of them, will pass Sumter. What man can do, our brave fellows will accomplish, but impossibilities cannot be overcome."[33]

Was a Union naval victory at Charleston "impossible"? Certainly to the "brave fellows" in the fleet, or at least the commanding officers, the harbor defenses could *not* be challenged by the means at their disposal—particularly by the monitor ironclads. Individual weight of shell mattered little when a rapid and overwhelming "suppressing" fire was needed to subdue forts. It was a question of matériel.[34] Then again, dashing through the extended gauntlet of the main ship channel, up to the wharves of Charleston, was not Du Pont's intention, despite the popular expectation that this was precisely what he, like Farragut, would do. Nearly a year before, he warned Fox to "think coolly and dispassionately on the *main object*," for unlike the lower Mississippi River approach to New Orleans, or even Mobile Bay, Charleston harbor was a cul-de-sac.[35] There would be no shelter for the ironclads from start to finish. In the absence of a methodical joint Army-Navy siege, a strictly naval incursion would be all or nothing, all at once. Neither the War Department nor the White House had the resources or patience to spare for yet another siege, and Welles was willing to accept heavy losses if the coveted rebel city was nevertheless brought to heel.[36] In that respect, it was a question of *tactics*.

Even assuming some of the ironclads managed to reach the city—with constant motion and the smoke of Confederate gunfire perhaps working to their advantage—they would face a *morale,* if not moral, dilemma. Less than two months before the attack, Fox wrote to Du Pont that "it seems to me very clear that our course is to go in and demand a surrender of the Forts or the alternative of destruction to their city."[37] But there was no guarantee Charleston *would* surrender easily, let alone quickly; and the monitors carried reserves of ammunition barely proportionate to the city's size, if a general bombardment followed a gunfight with the city's waterfront batteries.[38] Perhaps sensing this, Lincoln telegraphed to Welles on April 9 an extract from the Richmond *Whig*, which stated, "[A]t last the hour of trial has come for Charleston. The hour of deliverance or destruction, for no one believes the other alternative, surrender. . . . We predict a Saragossa defense, and that if Charleston is taken it will be only a heap of ruins."[39] Examples throughout the Civil War are mixed on this point of conjecture. General Pierre Gustave Beauregard, in charge of the city's defense, stated he planned to fight "street by street, and house by house" in the event of a landing.[40] Few Federal troops were on hand to actually take possession and hold the city, let alone the forts, against any major counterattack, so the ironclads might have resorted to setting defiant Charleston on fire, before turning to run the long gauntlet back out again: a Pyrrhic raid, not a propaganda victory.[41] It was therefore in the dubious hope that the good citizens of Charleston would acknowledge defeat—if only a few monitors proved impenetrable enough to reach them—that the Lincoln administration was willing to wreck the nation's only coastal ironclad force.[42]

It was a vicious circle of strategic, tactical, and political misccalcu-
lation. Du Pont, increasingly skeptical of the defensive, let alone
offensive, capabilities of the monitors against fortifications, was
nonetheless obliged "to take Charleston." The pressure was far too
great for him to back down now; there was national as well as private professional reputation at stake. To minimize this sense of risk,
the Union Admiral therefore delayed action until every possible
resource was placed at his disposal. The Department of the Navy was
willing to comply, at the cost of depriving every other theater of operation of the armored means of taking more realistic and strategically
valuable prizes—in addition to exposing other vital areas to attack
from new Confederate rams. "You will see that threatened at all points
and at all points continual disaster, all of which is laid solely at the
door of the Secretary," Fox reminded Du Pont before the attack, "yet
he has given you every vessel except *Sangamon,* which against three
Iron Clads of the enemy, guards Hampton Roads, the waters of
the Chesapeake & Washington itself."[43] But this was based in turn on
the understanding that the iron-plated squadron would be used more
as a battering ram than as a siege train against Charleston. For the
Department it was, once again, the quickest, cleanest tactical method
of satisfying a multitude of strategic and political commitments.
Somewhere in the intervening months, between Washington's initial
belief that monitor ironclads could run the gauntlet of Charleston
harbor—that a sensational coup would logically follow this "sublime"
Yankee demonstration of superior technology and moral resolve—
and the growing opinion among the professional officers themselves
that such an enterprise was doomed, even dangerous, victory did in
fact become impossible.

First, by dismissing the idea, but never quite an order, of charging
straight up to Charleston, the monitors were automatically relegated
to a stand-up fight against forts, which some experience already suggested would favor the latter.[44] Yet it was this obvious weakness,
among others, that made the prospect of an even more daring and
extensive test of the monitors' ultimate potential seem ridiculous.
Second, Du Pont's alternative of reducing Fort Sumter to rubble, even
if the obstructions could be negotiated first, played into Confederate
hands perfectly. If Charleston would not surrender directly under the
guns of Union ironclads, how would the destruction of a single fort be
any more decisive? If the entire outer harbor's defenses were to be conquered one at a time before a drive was made upon the city, why start
in the *middle* of a multiple crossfire that everyone knew existed?

Finally, the War Department was unwilling to divert significant
numbers of troops from Mississippi, Tennessee, and Virginia for an
extensive and strictly "political" campaign against Charleston, South

Carolina.[45] Some 12,500 Union soldiers at Port Royal were available for combined operations with the Navy; but bickering among the local generals thwarted the development of any plan to establish a beach-head that could be protected by the fleet and then begin a long-range bombardment against the outer forts by land. Du Pont knew he had no practical alternative left but to run the gauntlet after all. Yet instead of making optimistic preparations to fulfill the Department's wishes, he initiated an ulterior strategy that would minimize the risk to *his* ships, even at the cost of *their* reputation. This included an unwillingness to seriously employ the torpedo rafts the Department furnished for clearing obstructions.

Indeed, the issue of both the obstructions and the monitors dominated the sensational public controversy in the aftermath of the Union naval repulse of April 7. The former laid stress upon the poor tactics chosen by Du Pont. "The ironclads stood very well . . . [against] . . . the slave-mongers at Charleston," wrote Charles Sumner to another English radical and advocate of the Union cause, John Bright. "*The difficulty was in the obstruction of the harbor,* which kept the vessels in the fiery focus. Had these been removed they could have pushed forward."[46] Fox more or less agreed. "He is of a wooden-age, eminent in that, but in an engineering one, behind the times."[47] Du Pont, on the other hand, focused attention on the tools at his disposal. "I think these Monitors are wonderful conceptions," he wrote before the attack, "but oh! the errors of details, which would have been corrected if these men of genius could be induced to pay attention to the people who are to use their tests & inventions."[48] If another attempt was made, Du Pont and the monitor captains later argued, the ironclads might be destroyed, or even worse, be captured by the rebels and used to sweep away the Federal blockade of the eastern seaboard. Foreign intervention would soon follow.[49] By this reasoning, defeat was neatly converted into something more important than victory. Implied here, moreover, was a condemnation by seamen of their civilian Government's huge investment in monitor ironclads—a naive faith in "engineers" and "inventors." What troubled *Scientific American,* however, was "the spirit, if not the exact letter, of the accounts furnished" by the officers of the ironclad squadron.[50] *Harper's Weekly* solemnly reflected:

> Each person draws his own inferences and forms his own opinion of the affair, according to his hopes and views, and the temper of his mind. The most obvious of all inferences is that it insures an indefinite prolongation of the war. Had we destroyed Fort Sumter and occupied Charleston there would have been good ground for expecting the early collapse of the rebellion. As it is, the rebels will of course be encouraged to persevere in their rebellion, while we shall merely renew our preparations

for another and possibly a more successful attack. . . . To a nation fixed
and resolute in its purpose as this is, failure is impossible.[51]

Not surprisingly, an antagonistic London *Times* preferred Du Pont's
analysis of the repulse, and carried it to a different logical extreme:

> Hopes reversed, designs baffled, all efforts made in vain—is there no les-
> son for the North in this stern teaching of events, if passion could read
> them rightly, or if reason were allowed a voice? This naval campaign was
> to retrieve all previous disasters and to avenge them. It has ended in a
> catastrophe more signal than any reverse the North has yet sustained.
> Continual failures are not mere accidents. The object of the North is
> impossible.[52]

When Du Pont insisted that the Navy Department publish his official reports to answer criticism of his actions from the *Baltimore
American*—based, he maintained, on information supplied from Chief
Engineer Stimers—Welles crisply replied, "What public benefit, let
me ask, could be derived from its publicity[?]"[53] As historian James
McPherson writes, the monitors "had been repulsed in a manner that
gave the Union navy a black eye."[54] Now the commanding officer
responsible seemed determined to add insult to injury.

Precious weeks passed. Du Pont refused to back down in his defensive, increasingly political attack upon his superiors, or to venture any
more Navy action against Charleston. Rebellion occurred within his
own ranks, however, when Percival Drayton, the most outspoken of the
monitor captains critical of their own vessels, realized there were more
careers at stake than Du Pont's.[55] On a visit to Washington, he tactfully
regretted the Rear Admiral's "over-sensitive nature" to the Secretary,
suggesting his "morbid infirmity was aggravated by his long continuance on shipboard." As a crowning touch, he offered that the monitors,
even despite their crawling pace, "would have passed the batteries and
reached the wharves of Charleston but for submerged obstructions."[56]
Though Du Pont was rallying powerful connections, Welles finally
relieved him of command on June 3, to be replaced by Rear Admiral
Andrew H. Foote. There was little left to be said: "the Government is
unwilling to relinquish all further efforts upon a place that has been so
conspicuous in this rebellion, and which continues to stimulate treason
and resistance to the Union and Government. . . ."[57]

Even so, political opponents of Lincoln's administration were bound
to exploit another apparent misstep in its conduct of the war. The
resulting Congressional inquiry led to the largest Report of the Secretary
of the Navy ever: "In Relation to Armored Vessels." The big question
was, What were these monitors good for? The answer began with what
the monitors were designed for. The original *Monitor,* according to her
inventor, was intended to "admonish the leaders of the Southern

Rebellion that the batteries on the banks of their rivers will no longer present barriers to the entrance of Union forces." This comment suggested barriers to be *passed through* in the course toward a set objective. The next-generation monitors of the *Passaic* class were to fill the same roles as the original, but on a more ambitious level. They would be armed with even greater guns, themselves protected by even thicker turret armor, making them perfect "weapons platforms." As such, the nature of the monitors' armament should have been self-explanatory to contemporaries: these were ironclad killing machines.[58] Against armor plate, caliber was ultimately more decisive than numbers. By the end of 1863, Welles was responding to a complaint from another monitor captain that "neither the XI inch smooth bore nor the VIII inch rifle can penetrate the armor of the rebel iron clads, and in a contest with them, only the 15 inch gun can be effective, according to the experience derived from the contest between the *Atlanta* and the *Weehawken*. In a contest with sand batteries, broadside vessels are required, so that it is immaterial whether the guns are 15, 11 or 8 inch. Against the exposed masonry of forts we have the testimony of our own officers and the rebels that the 15 inch gun is the most effective."[59] For that matter, the wounds inflicted upon the ironclads at Charleston might have been mortal ones if fewer, though heavier, guns were employed. The only ironclad that was *penetrated* on April 7, 1863, the *Keokuk*, happened to be the only ironclad that was sunk.

Here, therefore, lay the roots of another fateful misconception. Just before news reached him in New York of the great ironclad repulse, Ericsson had confessed:

> . . . I cannot share in your confidence relative to the capture of Charleston. I am so much in the habit of estimating force and resistance that I cannot feel sanguine of success. If you do succeed, it will not be a mechanical consequence of your "marvellous" vessels, but because you are marvellously fortunate. The most I dare hope is that the contest will end without the loss of that prestige which your Iron Clads have conferred on the Nation abroad. . . . A single shot will sink a Ship while a hundred rounds cannot silence a fort.[60]

But this sentiment did not necessarily conflict with Fox's original hope for a strictly naval victory, one that would magnify the importance of the Navy to Congress and free up the large blockading fleet before Charleston for operations elsewhere—including the pursuit of British-built Confederate commerce raiders that were busy wrecking the North's merchant marine (angering powerful New England interests)—and impress foreign powers.[61] It was not surprising, then, that Ericsson referred to the damage reports of the monitors as "trifling," remarking, "[I]t has . . . given me pain to think that our fighting

<u>machines</u> were intrusted [*sic*] to officers who know nothing of mechanics and <u>therefore</u> have no confidence in their vessels."[62] A week before the attack, he wrote to Welles that the monitor captains should be reminded by the Department that "they have entered on a new era, that they are now handling not ships, but floating fighting machines, and that however eminent their seamanship, they cannot afford to disregard the advice of the Engineer."[63]

Welles, for his part, crucially specified to Du Pont's latest successor against Charleston's defenses, Rear Admiral John Dahlgren, that "the Department is disinclined to have its only ironclad squadron incur extreme risks. . . . Other operations of great importance on our southern coast are pending, and in case of a foreign war, which has sometimes seemed imminent, these vessels will be indispensable for immediate use."[64] For while the Union Navy suffered its most embarrassing defeat before the obstructions and beneath the guns of Charleston, the growing probability of the Laird ironclad-rams being built in Liverpool descending upon the Union blockade, if not also Northern ports, in addition to Confederate commerce raiders and blockade runners—built in Britain and routinely sheltered in British ports—had turned Washington's overriding fear of foreign intervention into open threats of a war of retaliation. This "Anglo-Rebel Threat" was now daily referred to in official correspondence and throughout the Northern press. *Harper's Weekly* was graphically "Keeping John Bull's Score" for 1862–1863—*casus belli* greatly in excess of either the American Revolution or the War of 1812—while the *New York Times* suggested a direct connection between "Copperheadism Here and the War-Spirit Abroad." As Chairman of the Senate Foreign Relations Committee, Sumner wrote private letters to his English political contacts who were sympathetic to the Union cause; as time passed, Sumner's letters became increasingly urgent. "Our people are becoming more and more excited, &c., there are many who insist upon war," he wrote to Cobden. "A very important person said to me yesterday—'we are now at war with England, but the hostilities are all on her side.'"[65] Union national resources were mobilizing to undreamed-of levels, marshaling for yet another drive against the Confederacy at Vicksburg, Richmond, and Charleston. Sumner thus wrote, "Our only present anxiety comes from England." Nor was he sure if he could stem the rising tide of revenge. "I hear but one sentiment, whether from the President, his Cabinet, or members of the Senate. . . ." To the Duchess of Argyll (wife of the Lord Privy Seal in Palmerston's Cabinet), Sumner explained:

It has seemed to us an obvious duty of the English government to take the responsibility of enforcing its own statute of neutrality . . . and that it was enough for us to direct attention to the reported fact. Some of our

Cabinet were so strongly of this opinion that they were unwilling that our minister or agents should take any further steps, and insisted that after what had passed the English government should be left to do as they pleased, and we should simply wait the result, it being generally understood that the sailing of the [Laird Rams] would be a declaration of war.[66]

Welles had already begun preparing for the "day of reckoning." Years after the Civil War, he recounted to the Speaker of the House of Representatives the following: "In 1863, during the height of the war, and when the probability of European interference in our domestic strife was imminent, the necessity for a class of fast and formidable Ocean steamers became imperative, partly to intercept the fast blockade runners then recently introduced, but chiefly to enable us, in the event of a war with the great maritime powers, to attack and destroy their commerce." This marked the birth of the *Wampanoag*-class steam sloops, the fastest war steamers of their day, though fraught with engineering compromises that sacrificed strategic range in favor of high speeds requiring the burning of disproportionate amounts of fuel. Unlike the Royal Navy, the United States simply could not rely upon a worldwide network of coaling stations.[67]

Nevertheless, such developments succeeded in alarming Lord Lyons sufficiently to request a naval professional who could thoroughly assess the Union Navy's strengths and gauge its intentions, "for a War with a European Power, and especially a War with Great Britain is a contingency never absent from the minds both of men in power and the Public at large; and some of the measures taken, such as those for the defense of the Northern Ports, have little reference to the present struggle with the Southern States":

It seems, in fact, to be certain that at the commencement of a War with Great Britain the relative positions of the United States and its adversary would be very nearly the reverse of what they would have been if a War had broken out three or even two years ago. Of the two Powers the United States would now be the better prepared for the struggle—the coasts of the United States would present fewer points open to attack— while the means of assailing suddenly our own Ports in the neighbourhood of this Country, and especially Bermuda and the Bahamas, would be in immediate readiness.

The Admiralty responded by sending Captain James G. Goodenough "to obtain accurate and scientific information on points relating to the construction and armaments of Ships and in the manufacture and working of Guns in the United States," while being "most careful to avoid every thing which could justly give umbrage to the Citizens of the United States or be construed into an expression of partiality for either of the contending parties."[68] Yet his reports, submitted in the spring of 1864, only confirmed that "this country is preparing for war against a maritime power by aiming at destroying its commerce and protecting its [own] ports with vessels of a peculiar construction, and by breaking a blockade of any [of] its ports with [the] aid of swift[,] manageable[,] invulnerable vessels."[69]

Whatever deterrence value the Union Navy's ironclad monitors carried in terms of international relations, their importance in sustaining the blockade from within, against Confederate ironclad-rams, was unquestionable. John Rodgers's feelings toward the new men-of-war tended to vary over time as well. He was surprised and then confident in the sea-going qualities of the *Weehawken* on her maiden voyage south, weathering a Cape Hatteras gale while his tow sought shelter. This battering was significant; within a month of the Secretary of the Navy's ambitious 1862 Report to Congress, the U.S.S. *Monitor* foundered in the treacherous waters off Cape Hatteras, North Carolina, infamously labeled the "Graveyard of the Atlantic" since the early sixteenth century.[70] She was on her way south, as part of the first great concentration of Union ironclads against Confederate ports; the planned "dash" on Wilmington had been abandoned in the meantime, probably until the new class of ultra-light-draft monitors might appear to negotiate the Cape Fear River approaches. The next obvious strategic choice was Charleston. So on Dec. 29, as the *Montauk* arrived from Brooklyn Navy Yard, dropping anchor in Hampton Roads, both the *Monitor* and the *Passaic* departed for Beaufort, North Carolina.[71] As part of a now-routine procedure, the ironclads were under tow to conserve fuel. But they were also under careful escort. The *Montauk*, under tow from the wooden paddle-steamer U.S.S. *Connecticut* and under Worden's command, had taken seven days to reach her objective, including two days to readjust the ship's trim because coal consumption steadily brought her down "too much by the head," forward. As her Paymaster, Samuel T. Browne, later described:

> The great interested public knew but little of these vessels; and from steamers, and from all manner of sailing-craft, and from ferry-boats, and from the shore, we were watched with an anxious curiosity that told how the national pulse was beating.
>
> At Sandy Hook the few remaining stanchions that held the lines around the vessel's sides were taken down, and the deck was absolutely clear. From the turret to the flag-staffs, fore and aft, a stout line was rigged, called the "life-line." The turret was "unkeyed," or let down upon its bed of bronze rings, and upon the big rubber band affixed to its base, to make it water-tight. To the extreme bow a heavy iron ring was fixed, and in this was a large shackle, from which two ten-inch hawsers, each one hundred and fifty yards in length, were passed to the steamer

Connecticut, our tow and convoy, one hawser passing to her port, and the other to her starboard quarter. In an hour we were off, steaming seaward.

Among the *Montauk*'s crew was a special passenger, Russian Captain Lessovsky. It was his first chance to join one of the new "Ericsson Monitors" at sea, and as Browne described, "The motion of the ship was very slight, exceedingly buoyant and easy, the rolling not exceeding three to four degrees, and not affecting out filled cups and glasses at the table." This was, however, before the *Montauk* weighed anchor again on Jan. 2, 1863 (when Lessovsky bade his host farewell from shore). The ship soon encountered the tail end of the same fierce gale that had engulfed the *Monitor* and *Passaic* two days before. And this time the *Montauk*'s tow was anything but a lifeline. Though "the vessel was now steadier than we had expected her to be, rising but little to the seas, but rather diving through them, or allowing them to sweep over her," the port hawser eventually parted from the lead ship and threatened to foul the monitor's propeller. Still connected by her starboard line, the *Montauk* was also swung broadside into the dangerous trough of the sea and stood the chance of literally being dragged under by the towing vessel before it could be signaled in time. A brave volunteer was lowered down the side of the turret, secured only by a line around his chest and gripping an ax. Washed several times aft, he eventually struggled to the plunging bow of the monitor and proceeded to hack through the remaining towline. Quickly righting herself, the *Montauk* then steamed for shallower, calmer water. When she finally reached Beaufort the next day, Browne recalled, "We saw the *Passaic* at anchor inside, but no *Monitor* there."[72]

Writing on Jan. 22 to his wife, Rodgers also described a "hard gale" with a "sea about 30 feet high—this to experts expresses a great deal. . . . The weather was fearful and she rode it like a duck."[73] Two months later—and a week before the attack on Charleston—he proudly wrote to his wife that he was still "very well pleased with the *Weehawken* compared with the other monitors." His remarkable vessel featured 12 separate engines, and all of them "work to a charm."[74] However, this love affair between the Captain and his Ship promptly soured when "she" betrayed "him" before Charleston's outer defenses; and by the beginning of May Rodgers was writing to his wife how John Ericsson, "a charlatan, . . . has not made as far as I know a single good engine," and was "suffered to spend millions of public money without experiment to test the soundness of his ideas. . . ."[75]

The situation changed again, however, on June 17, 1863. Encouraged by jubilant reports from Charleston of "feeble monitors" and by the gloominess of the Northern press, the Confederacy dispatched its best ironclad-ram, the *Atlanta,* to recapture Port Royal and scatter the Union blockade. Waiting for her outside Savannah, in Wassaw Sound, were the monitors *Weehawken* and *Nahant.*[76] Four hits and fifteen minutes after the battle started, it was finished, and so was the *Atlanta. Weehawken* did all the shooting before *Nahant* could even get in on the kill. The first hit, a 15-inch cored shot weighing 400 pounds, blasted through the *Atlanta*'s 30° casemate armor at an angle of 50° in line with the keel:

> It broke a hole through the side of the *Atlanta* some four or five feet long, knocked in about a couple of barrels of splinters of wood and iron, wounded a whole gun's crew, and prostrated between forty and fifty men, including those that were wounded. Those who were stunned by the mere concussion remained insensible for some ten minutes. It completely demoralized the crew. They had fancied they were in a secure castle—they found they were in a paper house; and their running below I attribute, in a great degree, to their surprise.[77]

The captain of the *Weehawken* was also more than pleasantly surprised; the Confederate sortie he poignantly described as a "bull's attack upon a locomotive." Here was the soundness, however "cold and calculated," of seapower in a new, machine age. Less than two weeks before his fateful charge against Fort Wagner (June 18, 1863), Union Colonel Robert Gould Shaw of the famous 54th Massachusetts Infantry regiment, visited the U.S.S. *Montauk* off Port Royal. "The officers of the navy have by no means as much confidence in the Monitors as the public at large," he wrote to his wife, "and say they can be of service only against other ironclads, or wooden vessels, and brick-and-mortar walls. Forts of other descriptions, such as fieldworks and sand-batteries [like Wagner], they think would get the better of them." Though Shaw was exposed to the worst anti-Ericsson gossip possible—at the worst time possible—he also visited the captured *Atlanta,* which he described as a "very powerful" though "roughly finished" armorclad which "would have made great havoc in our blockading fleet, if she had got out. . . ." Despite their defects, Shaw concluded that the monitors were "terrible engines, and wonderful in their strength."[78]

The British disagreed. Yankee boasts of the Union's ironclad building program in the face of British naval power had only fostered a sense of defensive skepticism, if not denial, which tended to magnify every perceived weakness or failure—such as the loss of the *Monitor* at sea, or the ironclads' inability to outgun Charleston's fortifications—and minimize everything else.[79] Americans could not ordinarily be trusted at face value, and certainly not when they were engaged in a civil war, rife with propaganda on all sides.[80] When forwarding accounts of the surrender of the *Atlanta* from the Washington, D.C.–based *National Intelligencer* to Earl Russell, Lord Lyons noted the rebel ironclad's description as "not official, but it appears to be minute, and is probably tolerably correct." The Acting British Consul at Savannah echoed Confederate opinion "that the *Atlanta*'s steering apparatus was destroyed by a shot that rendered her helpless and caused her to take ground in the narrow channel, where she lay at the mercy of her antagonist." In other words, it was the Confederates' opinion that, had the *Atlanta* not grounded, the outcome of the engagement might have been different. Still, "it is said the enormous fifteen inch projectiles of the Monitors penetrated the *Atlanta*'s armor with ease."[81]

The London *Times* therefore concluded that the *Atlanta* herself "was not fit to be called an ironclad." The brutal work of the American "430-lb. ball . . . did no more than would have been done as easily by a [British] 68-pound ball. . . ." Royal Navy observer Goodenough was later told "by Admiral Du Pont" that it had "indented and broke all the plating but did not penetrate and having struck a part where the pine backing was not covered with an inner skin of iron, the fine splinters were freely distributed, and disabled by wounds or concussion two entire guns' crews of 17 men each, besides 3 Marines who stood near."[82] On June 27 Chief Engineer and Cartographer Ernest R. Knorr wrote to Rodgers, "You not only took a great weight from many men's mind, but you again gave a lesson to the neutral English aristocracy, which I am sure was very timely. They will be mighty careful now, to trust a fleet near our grave Monitors." The same day, however, the Controller of the Royal Navy, Spencer Robinson, and Edward Reed, his Chief Constructor, informed the Board of Admiralty of their intention to spare none of their draftsmen "to assist Captain Coles" in his designs for a sea-going turret ship. Instead they recommended "that a copy of Sir Alexander Milne's report of the disadvantages attending the Turret system as used in the American Navy be sent to Captain Coles," since "[a]ll the evidence that we can collect on the subject seems to point out that until further trial has been made of the shields, it would not be wise to proceed to construct such vessels except as Floating Batteries." Less than two weeks later, Robinson went further by rejecting an appeal for an extra "50 Blacksmiths and 50 Boilermakers" to hasten the completion of Britain's first turret ship, the converted *Royal Sovereign.* Coles hoped the *Weehawken*'s capture of the *Atlanta* would at least vindicate his preference for the new Armstrong 300-pounders.[83]

The same controversy was repeated the following summer, when the 15-inch Dahlgrens of the *Canonicus*-class U.S.S. *Manhattan* finally compelled the more formidable Confederate casemate-ram *Tennessee* to haul down her flag at the Battle of Mobile Bay (Aug. 5, 1864).[84] "I put one XV in. thro [*sic*] him amidships—and then got a raking position astern, when I shot his steering gear away," wrote *Manhattan*'s commander, J. W. Nicholson, to Fox. Against the *Tennessee*'s side armor of one 1-inch and two 2-inch rolled iron plates, backed by 26.5 inches of heavy yellow pine and oak beams and planking, "[t]hirty-five lbs. [of powder charge] made no impression and even sixty-lbs. only went thro' her once." The London *Times* was quick to suggest "that the casemate of the *Tennessee* was inclined at an angle of 45 degrees, but that condition, as far as our trials have taught us, would not materially affect the issue." The lesson of Mobile Bay, as far as British critics were concerned, was "either the armour of the *Tennessee* was superior to any of the targets which represent our ironclads, or the ordnance of the Federals is inferior to our artillery."[85] This conclusion drew sharp responses from both sides of the Atlantic. "Some respectable engineers have doubted whether inclined armor offered any greater resistance than the same aggregate weight in a vertical position," noted *Scientific American*. "Even if this view is correct, 6 inches at an angle of 45 degrees would be equivalent to $8\frac{1}{2}$ inches in a vertical position. Has the *Times* any record of an $8\frac{1}{2}$-inch target, made up even of 2-inch plates, having been penetrated by cannon shot?" A letter to the editor from Josiah Jones of Liverpool reminded the *Times* that it had in fact endorsed his own "angulated system" of armor both in August 1860 and in 1861. Both the Ordnance Select Committee and the Iron Plate Committee had rejected angled armor schemes, not because of their superior ability to deflect projectiles, but because of their added weight, if practically applied to sea-going, sail-and-steam–powered ironclads.[86] The analysis offered by the new American *Army and Navy Journal* was more comprehensive. "It cannot be doubted that the effect of two or three of these heavy shot, driven with these large charges of powder, at short range, and at nearly right angles to the keel of the ram, would have been fatal":

> We are entitled to conclude that the armor of the latest improved British broadside ironclad, the *Bellerophon*—six inches of iron and ten of wooden backing—could by no means resist a 15-inch shot fired with the service charge and striking at anything approaching a right angle. . . .
>
> But it should not be forgotten that the armor of the *Bellerophon* . . . covers simply the water line and the central portion of the ship where the battery is carried; and the displacement of this vessel is upwards of 7,000 tons, with a draught of about 25 feet. Now, a Monitor iron-clad of about one-quarter this capacity, and one-half the draught, is superior to this craft in every thing else but speed. . . . Those iron-clads which the *Times* has handled so severely, the Monitor *Monadnock* among the rest, are intended for coast and harbor defense. It is not proposed to send these vessels after the *Bellerophons* or *Minotaurs*, but at the same time it may not be prudent to send these unwieldy craft after them.

Our trans-Atlantic cousins are welcome to wring by their sophistical reasoning, whatever conclusions they please from the career of the broadside iron-clad *Tennessee;* but they must use thicker armor, have lighter draught and more manageable vessels, and equip them with more powerful guns, if they expect to meet with success in any act of aggression on our harbors or coasts. . . .

We are surrounded by a wall of iron, within which we intend, unmolested, to develop our national strength.[87]

Conclusion

Great Britain and the United States suffered simultaneous—and inter-related crises—of civil-military relations during the period under examination, though with remarkably different outcomes. Although the public may have overplayed the Victorian ideal of the hero-inventor fighting against the "system," organizations themselves, especially governmental ones such as the British Admiralty or the U.S. Depart-ment of the Navy, cannot be considered victims wholly exploited by crank inventors and greedy entrepreneurs.[1] The truth is that it was not about the individual versus the institution, but about individuals ver-sus other individuals. Cowper Coles made the mistake of attacking Edward Reed as part of an institution, rather than as a rival engineer or shipbuilder. John Ericsson's fame on both sides of the Atlantic only added a measure of personal anxiety to this public campaign, when actions would have spoken much louder than words. Likewise, John Lenthall's and Benjamin Isherwood's complaints of private contractors influencing Fox and Welles could not overcome the fact that Ericsson, the individual truly in question, offered to meet the policy needs of the Navy, established by its civilian leaders, better than they could—or would—do, with their preference for turret ships loosely based on Coles's ideas, the customary deference to British practices only serv-ing to irritate the Navy Department during the Civil War.

The great controversies between Ericsson and various naval officers over the *Passaic*-class monitors were also very much personal struggles that could not, however, be taken personally. It did Ericsson little good to blame "sailors." In addressing their complaints, Ericsson appreciated that only detailed problem-solving would settle matters with Fox and Welles. This would also serve to incriminate his opponents. "Without intending any disrespect to the commander of the *Passaic* [Drayton]," Ericsson thus wrote to Welles on Feb. 8, 1863, "I cannot abstain from calling your attention to his singular custom of drawing on the imagination in order to show what might have happened under certain contingencies, and what dire consequences would have resulted from occurrences which happily did not take place."[2] Ironically enough, Reed and Robinson might have made a similar observation about Coles.

At the beginning of the Civil War, it was not clear to either Great Britain or the United States which was more important, defending one's ports or attacking those of the enemy. Certainly, the *Trent* affair succeeded in confirming the Union Navy's predisposition to concentrate its resources on coastal vessels, and in giving a double meaning to John Ericsson's original "Monitor"-type ironclad. The emphasis of Union ironclads, especially after Hampton Roads, was upon their ship-killing abilities, whether to defend New York Harbor, for example, from British ironclads, to preserve the blockade from more Confederate rams (or European interference), or to help crush the naval defenses of Southern ports. Because of this concentration on coastal operations, the Union Navy succeeded in its choice of strategy—at least as far as the foreign threat was concerned. With various Union ironclad descriptions before him by the beginning of 1863, from American newspapers and Royal Navy officers under Milne's command, Robinson reported to the Board of Admiralty that "there appears to be no novel or important principle elucidated by these constructions." Those that "seem to possess seagoing qualities," particularly the experimental broadside ironclad the U.S.S. *New Ironsides*, "are in no way superior to the French *Gloire* or *Invincible* or the Ships of the *Royal Oak* class." The obvious bulk of the armored Federal warships made them "mere Rafts carrying very few heavy guns propelled at moderate speed, and though perfectly well adapted for the Inland waters of that great Continent, and most formidable as Harbour Defences, are not in any sense sea going Ships of War":

> This is not said with any view of disparaging the Skill and industry which has been displayed in their construction, still less with any intention of undervaluing the enormous defensive power which has thus been developed: a power which I believe renders the Americans practically unassailable in their own waters. . . .
>
> If again, Admiral Milne means that we have not yet an Iron plated Flotilla capable of going into the inland waters, rivers and Harbours of the United States, and when there, able to fight an Action on equal terms with the description of Vessels which will be found awaiting us, he is perfectly right and it will be only necessary to observe that such a proceeding on our part is simply impossible.[3]

Against combined Confederate defenses, however, the Union's preference for coastal ironclads—and especially monitors—entailed important disadvantages. Monitors could not be expected to outgun forts, unless they were given adequate time and army support, or were massed in such numbers as to be instantly irresistible. Even so, no ironclad design was better suited for running gauntlets than the light-draft, low-freeboard, heavily armored monitor. The question, then, revolved around whether simply running a gauntlet successfully would guarantee victory—would compel a determined enemy to surrender. Added to this vexing complication was the simple yet effective countermeasure of obstructions and especially minefields. But if coastal assault ironclads would find these defenses difficult to overcome, sea-going ironclads would most likely have found them all but impossible to negotiate.

The Royal Navy, by contrast, never openly held shallow-draft ironclads to be worthless, whether for defending British ports or attacking those of an enemy. But neither could such vessels be relied upon to openly "command the sea." Maritime or naval war was traditionally acknowledged as best fought on the strategic offensive, with blue-water cruisers taking the initiative, driving a rival back upon his own coastline, bottled up in his own harbors, and thereby leaving the sea lanes open for imperial trade and communications, as well as strategic, waterborne mobility—while depriving the enemy of the same.[4] Superior British imperial resources—financial, industrial, maritime—thus protected, victory was only a matter of time. The relatively "sudden" threat posed by French ironclad frigates necessitated a British reaction obsessed with the sea—not the shoreline. Fortifications, the Defence Committees of 1860 and 1861 insisted, would more properly take care of national defense by "[setting] our fleet free, to operate offensively against the enemy or defensively for the protection of our shores. . . ."[5] Between the taxing demands of building large iron-hulled sea-going ironclads and fortifications, expressly coastal defense ironclads (turret ships on Coles's pattern), though continually endorsed by the Admiralty, were routinely left at the bottom of annual defense estimates.

By the end of 1864, the Controller submitted to the Board of Admiralty the revealing "General Remarks on the Classification, Distribution, and Construction of Armour-plated Ships." Though the dreaded French sea-going ironclad force of 1860 had clearly stalled under its own construction restraints, few of the miscellaneous British ironclads afloat could maneuver as a homogeneous line-of-battle squadron. Nor could the "Class A" broadside ironclads (*Warrior, Black Prince, Achilles, Minotaur,* and *Agincourt* [*Minotaur* class]) "at present be docked out of England," which automatically limited their intended effectiveness *beyond the English Channel;* while "the unprotected extremities of two ships in Class A, and of two in Class C, detract very considerably from their utility as fighting ships." Only with the addition of three more "central-battery" ironclads of the new *Bellerophon* class (pioneered by Reed), and monitors for coast defense, would Britain "not be taken at a disadvantage if forced into a war, with the one exception of the protection to be given to our commerce from privateers and [an] enemy's fast-sailing wooden cruizers."[6] This, coupled with the subsequent, widespread failures of the 110-pounder rifled breech-loading Armstrong guns, implied that Britain remained less protected than expected.[7]

A further problem emerged with this strategy when Great Britain found herself forced by the American Civil War, and particularly the *Trent* affair, to consider how the defense of the Empire and an assault upon Union national defenses was actually to be carried out. In his authoritative, multivolume study *The British Navy: Its Strengths, Resources, and Administration* (1882), Sir Thomas Brassey observed that in 1870 "the failure of the French fleet, owing to the deficiencies of vessels of light draught adapted to coast service, was fresh in the recollection of the maritime world":

> Our own experience in the Baltic campaign, when a powerful fleet of line-of-battle ships and frigates was condemned to inaction for want of gunboats, and the success of the operations against the Confederates conducted by the naval forces of the United States, with a large flotilla of vessels of light draught, seemed to afford conclusive evidence of the necessity for completing our naval *matériel* with a due proportion of vessels adapted for service on the coast.

Nevertheless, Brassey continued, the "view adopted . . . has been that coast service vessels can promptly be improvised and that our efforts should therefore be concentrated in time of peace on those classes of ships the construction of which must necessarily occupy a long period of time." This indeed explained much of the course of the early British ironclad program. But international crises often erupted before even coastal defense vessels could be "improvised." This was the state of both the British and Union navies during the *Trent* affair—though only the latter force adapted itself accordingly. "It is a point to be always borne in mind, that the best ships for coast defence are also the best for coast attack," Brassey concluded, and the "monitor is, *par excellence*, the best type of vessel for the operations of naval warfare on the coast."[8] One wonders how radically different history may have been had Napoleon III originally chosen to concentrate on armored batteries rather than frigates, and had Britain again countered the French initiative appropriately—a question even J. P. Baxter failed to address. Instead, Hampton Roads was seen by Baxter as having "exerted on the building policy of the administration an influence which in one respect may be thought pernicious." Why? Because (in an all-too-often repeated display of historical determinism) "the opportunity for building a high seas ironclad fleet was largely overlooked."[9]

Nearly three-quarters of a century after Baxter, this conjecture is still repeated, often grotesquely. In his highly revisionist (and apologist) account *English Public Opinion and the American Civil War*, Duncan Andrew Campbell declares that "the Royal Navy, with its ocean-going ironclads, was always more than a match for the northern navy." Citing David Paul Crook's *The North, the South and the Powers, 1861–1865*, Campbell assures his readers that "Britain had a marked world lead in armoured warships . . . made for the high seas, whereas the Americans' ships tended to capsize."[10] Captain John Wells, RN, in *The Immortal Warrior: Britain's First and Last Battleship*, offers an interesting appendix of the "*Warrior* in battle" next to French ironclads' strengths and weaknesses, including a comparison of size, tonnage, draft, armor and armament, and speed. But "had either ship [the *Warrior* or *Black Prince*]" been sent to intervene in the American Civil War, "they could have coped quite easily with *Monitor, Merrimac* and any of the Federal frigates." Again no suggestion of evidence is provided in this case; the 1976 *Oxford Companion to Ships and the Sea* refers to John Ericsson's naming of the *Monitor* as a warning to British authorities that "Downing Street, in fact, viewed the *Monitor* with complete indifference, having two years earlier launched the *Warrior*, which could have blown fifty *Monitors* out of the water."[11]

In spite of this tendency in the existing literature, this letter-based narrative has avoided the nuts-and-bolts comparison between Union and British ironclads of the Civil War era that might otherwise be expected. This would have been, as Stanley Sandler suggested, an exceedingly tedious exercise, and probably misleading in any case. Enough of these comparisons abound, from this period in question and ever since, and are more noteworthy for what they tend to overlook. It is pointless to assess a warship's tactical strengths without reference to the wider strategic imperatives that intertwined—and often clashed—with them.[12] As Donald Canney noted:

In the United States, the reflection of these world technological developments was distorted: capital ships such as the revolutionary British *Warrior* of 1860 did not play a significant part, and the emphasis was on light-draft river and coastal vessels—a consequence of the Civil War, a conflict where inland and shoal water warfare was virtually the rule (excepting only the operations of the cruisers on the high seas). An American *Warrior* would have been simply useless in this context, except in the remote possibility of intervention by a European power.

What emerges, however, is that even the Union's coastal ironclads, and especially the monitors, have been previously assessed by a sort of Civil War strategic nearsightedness, a predilection for American self-absorption. It is not the case, as Canney asserted, that "any attempt to compare American and European ironclad fleets of the era is infelicitous: neither fleet could meet the other on common terms."[13] On the contrary, it was precisely because of this historically unique and decisive relationship that the comparison has been made—and not so much on the nuts-and-bolts level, comparing smoothbore gun with rifled, and turret with broadside, but looking beyond the strict confines of the American shoreline; looking outward from a Union perspective, and inward from a British one. After all, if "an American *Warrior* would have been simply useless in this context," how might a British *Warrior* have fared? This was a question that drove much of the Union's ironclad program, especially in the deciding years of 1861–1862, when European intervention was considered far from "remote."

Another notable aspect that has emerged from assessing the comparative strategic and tactical strengths of British and Union ironclad programs of the Civil War era is how Britain and the Union actually assessed each other's ironclads—the perception of power. Ericsson was quick to realize that the monitors, if not also his own public image, served an important propaganda role in sustaining Northern morale, depressing the South's, and warning off Europe.[14] Nor was he alone in this conviction. Imperial Russia, still smarting from the Crimean War and facing renewed Anglo-French opposition to its suppression of the Polish revolt, was the only major European power during the Civil War that expressed unconditional moral support for the Northern States. Both nations recognized a further similarity between Czar Alexander II's freeing of the serfs in 1861 and President Abraham Lincoln's Emancipation Proclamation. When the Czar narrowly escaped assassination on April 16, 1866, Congress passed a joint resolution on May 16 that expressed a deep personal sympathy, especially given the terrible memory of Lincoln's assassination the year before. Gustavus Fox was chosen to personally convey the message to Russia "in a national vessel." For this purpose the Assistant Secretary of the Navy, without hesitation, chose one of the U.S. Navy's newest monitors, the double-turreted, twin-screwed (and Navy-designed) U.S.S. *Miantonomoh.* In fact, he leapt at the opportunity.

Though launched at the New York Navy Yard on Aug. 15, 1863, the wooden-hulled sister of the U.S.S. *Monadnock* was not commissioned until Sept. 18, 1865. This two-year delay reflected the severe labor shortages during the war—followed by drastic cutbacks—as well as delays associated with the incorporation of the latest improvements in these types of ironclads, directly gained from operational and combat experience.[15] She measured 250 feet in length with a wide beam of 50 feet, drawing 12 feet, 8 inches at 3,815 tons.[16] Her propulsion came from twin screws driven by a pair of horizontal back-acting engines of 1,426 total horsepower, giving her a top speed of 9 knots—nothing to boast about, but speed was not considered essential for the services expected. The same could be said for large hulls carrying greater reserves of provisions, ammunition, and most important, coal.

As triumphant as the Union was by the end of the Civil War, professional skepticism on both sides of the Atlantic continued to ebb and flow for and against monitors as successful warships. Though these vessels rode out many storms throughout the Civil War, it was the gale that sank the original prototype on New Year's Eve 1862 that stuck in everyone's mind. Between the periodic boastings—and threats—of the Yankee press against British maritime preeminence, and a Congressional inquiry in 1864 that could find no evidence to censure the Navy Department, Britain's first official naval attaché to Washington, Captain Goodenough, concluded that "altho' not one of them could be sent to sea to cruize against an enemy or for any but a special object involving not more than 48 hours' absence from port, it appears to me that . . . ["as a defensive force"] . . . they would be very valuable."[17] Within a year, even the London *Times* was willing to assert that a "perfect Ironclad is an imperfect seaboat":

> That is the maxim which up to this time might be reasonably propounded as the deduction from all our experience. The best illustration of the doctrine was given by the American Monitors. Probably no fabric ever combined a greater capacity for fighting with a smaller capacity for swimming than Mr. Ericsson's original model.[18]

Joining Fox on the *Miantonomoh* was Goodenough's successor from 1865, Captain John Bythesea.[19] "He has so thoroughly exhausted the field of observation in naval affairs and experimental gunnery in the United States," wrote the new British Minister to the United States, Sir Frederick Bruce, to Earl Clarendon at the Foreign Office, "that independently of the great interest attaching to the trip he is going to take, I think it desirable that Her Majesty's Government should have the opportunity of personal intercourse with him."[20]

Meanwhile in New York, Ericsson saw his personal fame and usefulness to the restored Union gradually eclipsed by 1866. "The Civil and mechanical engineers of America nearly to a man, are my opponents at heart," Ericsson sullenly wrote to Fox in March. "[Y]ou could not <u>now</u> find an orator or an editor of any leading paper who would mention my name in connection with the late struggle, or in connection even with the iron clad navy."[21] Ironically enough, though he had named his original *Monitor* partially to spite "Downing Street" and "the Lords of the Admiralty," Ericsson now sought to gain acceptance of his ideas in Great Britain.[22] John Bourne, a leading English civilian engineer, eagerly acted on his behalf in London:

> There has been great misstatement as to the sea-going properties of the monitors, and I think two parties have been interested in running them down; first, Coles's party, who hope thus to conceal their piracies, and second, the Admiralty people who have been against Coles, and who, to resist him, have been willing to deal a thrust at the turret system.
>
> . . . With all its weakness and faults there is, in public opinion in England, a vast amount of honesty and a sincere desire to do and believe what is right and true; and where such a disposition exists it can never be very difficult to set it right on any topic engaging public attention. . . .
> The body we have to do with is *the engineers*, and once they are set right they will soon be able to set right all the rest.[23]

Subsequently, Ericsson began addressing Bourne's questions on the peculiarities of the low-freeboard monitor system that his critics identified, as well as sending schematics of his huge, single-turret, ocean-going monitor, the U.S.S. *Dictator*. "The Monitor system must no longer be treated as an untried novelty," Ericsson insisted. "Upwards of 50 turret vessels have already been built by one of the shrewdest nations in the world and whole fleets have been doing active service for more than two years of war." Furthermore, the *Monadnock* was already en route to San Francisco via Cape Horn, a distance of 14,000 miles.[24] Bourne's initial interviews with Chief Constructor Reed he reported as favorable. Yet Ericsson was dubious. "To be candid I never felt any surprise at Mr. Reed's dislike to the *Royal Sovereign*," he replied, "but I have been amazed that one so intelligent should fail to see that he has much to fear from the Monitor system. Mr. Reed probably understands that a raking XV inch shot put through the stern of the *Royal Sovereign* would crush the gingerbread work comprising the lower part of Captain Coles [*sic*] four turrets and thus by a single blow cripple the whole concern."[25]

The recourse to British public opinion, however, was a strategy Coles had also attempted, and whose "personal attacks" in the press against Reed's own ironclad designs succeeded only in infuriating the Controller's Department.[26] As the First Naval Lord Sir Frederick Grey observed in May of 1865, Coles was frequently "weak and ill and cannot shake off the impressions that in everything ordered by the Admiralty there is some concealed desire to deprecate his invention."[27] The Admiralty severed its relationship with Coles on Jan. 26, 1866. But this in turn led to Parliament's own sweeping inquiry on "Turret Ships" and a Special Committee that ultimately condemned neither Coles nor the Admiralty, but considered it "desirable that a conclusive trial should be given to the system in a sea-going ship to be armed with *two* turrets. . . ."[28] Ericsson was gleeful of Coles's own trouble with naval professionals and yet approved their decision to *seemingly* reject the idea of a high-freeboard turret ship, as entirely distinct from a monitor.[29] The British press in favor of turret ships might swing American public opinion back in his own favor, while at the same time the Royal Navy would neatly place Coles, his historic rival, "over the fire."[30]

To be sure, leading figures during the American Civil War were in peacetime everywhere fighting to preserve if not perpetuate their status in history. Fox, too, stood much to gain from the *Miantonomoh*. "I think I have rendered the state some service in the last five years, with great opposition to encounter and radical changes to make while a great war was in progress," he wrote to Ericsson:

> . . . [Y]et Congress reduced my pay from $4,000 to $3,500 before the war closed, and I leave next month with not money enough to get home to Portsmouth, N.H. I do not complain; I am perfectly happy, and I would not exchange the victories we have won over *all* our enemies for any wealth. What aid and assistance your brain has been to us I have publicly declared upon all occasions, and I will teach them yet, in Europe, what they fail generally to comprehend, the monitor.[31]

The mission to Russia was thus a perfect opportunity to humiliate old and unrelenting critics everywhere. Fox might even secure a few contracts for U.S.-built monitors with lesser European and South American powers looking for a cheap, reliable system of modern coastal defense.[32]

Finally, there was another, more sweeping agenda at play. When discussing with Ericsson the completion of the *Dictator*'s sister ship, the *Puritan*, with two *20-inch*–caliber smoothbores firing 1,000-pound shot, Fox wrote, "I think she better go to Europe during the Paris fair in 1867—and let the people of Europe see what their Kings would be glad to conceal."[33] This was a common and recurring theme—nationalist propaganda. The first official naval history of the Civil War, published in 1867, spelled it out clearly enough:

> . . . [I]t was for no mere display of national pride or power that the Navy Department ordered the *Miantonomoh* to Europe. The purpose was to show to the people of Europe the power of free institutions. It was to give them visible and tangible proof that the thinking force of a free republic is greater than that of a monarchy when the masses are forced down and held down. . . . .[34]

But cooler and perhaps wiser heads in Washington had their doubts as well. Secretary of the Navy Welles wrote in his diary that

"[President Andrew Johnson], I find, is by no means pleased with the steps that have been undertaken in regard to Fox's going to Russia." Though his Assistant Secretary was "patriotic and true," "he fancies that by going across the Atlantic in the Miantonomah [*sic*] he shall obtain useful celebrity." Encouraged by Secretary of State William H. Seward to display the American flag as never before, Fox, in Welles's opinion, was reflecting a "shambling statesmanship" also seeking to intimidate the French out of Mexico.[35] The United States of America, following its Civil War, had too many political and social concerns of its own for its officers to wield ironclads as a means of settling international, let alone personal, scores.

The *Miantonomoh* steamed from New York Navy Yard to Halifax under sealed orders from the Department on May 6, escorted by the wooden light-draft side-wheel steamers U.S.S. *Augusta* and *Ashuelot*.[36] It took four days for the monitor to reach Halifax, encountering heavy weather, fog, and ice, but her commanding officer, Commander John C. Beaumont, was well pleased with her seakeeping abilities. Coal was the main concern. Fox noted the bunkers were designed to carry 350 tons but really stowed no more than 264. A temporary "crib" was constructed 16 inches off deck to accommodate another 100 tons.[37] From there the American warships headed for St. John's on May 18, and on June 5, maneuvering their way through icebergs, they departed for Queenstown.[38] Ten days and 18 hours later, the squadron arrived safely.

Not surprisingly, the monitor was towed by *Augusta* some 1,100 miles of the distance, "as a matter of convenience and precaution more than necessity," her commander reported, "the *Miantonomoh* consuming a fair proportion of coal":

> I think she could have crossed over alone. The weather was generally very good, the only strong winds being from the westward. Heavy weather does not materially affect the speed or rolling of the monitor, for, while the others vessels were lurching about, and their progress checked by heavy seas, she went along comparatively undisturbed or unchecked.[39]

Fox's official report observed that "head to the sea, she takes over about four feet of solid water, which is broken as it sweeps along the deck, and after reaching the turret it is too much spent to prevent firing the fifteen-inch guns directly ahead."[40] Donald Canney notes here, however, that the monitor was also "fitted with a 3½-foot-high wooden 'breakwater' forward," usefully employed during the *Monadnock*'s voyage to San Francisco.[41] Outward-curved rifle screens on the tops of the turrets also served to help deflect water. "Broadside to sea," Fox continued, " . . . her lee guns could also be worked without difficulty . . . her extreme roll so moderate as not to press her lee guns near the water."[42] This was the unique property of a floating "raft" with an extremely low metacentric height.[43]

These glowing appraisals of the *Miantonomoh*'s seaworthiness and ability to fight in a seaway might be expected from the American officers, but what was Captain Bythesea's assessment?[44] His 1871 testimony, before yet another Parliamentary Ship Design Committee, noted that the weather was almost too fine to fully test the merits of the vessel, "a half gale on the port quarter, a north-westerly wind for two days, but the ship was not head to wind on any occasion" while he was aboard. Though there was "no very heavy sea," waves were rolling "half way up the [forward] turret," which would prohibit fire. Still, water coming onto the deck on the weather side "went off again to windward, a comparatively small portion crossing the deck." When heavy weather was encountered, canvas screens were put over the tops of the turrets to prevent water from entering through the iron gratings—but the canvas was never "washed over with water" and ultimately not needed. Hatches and combings were well waterproofed and of 2-inch–thick iron. Though water might get in through the turret, keyed up 1 inch for rotation, it could only come through the aperture of the turret's central spindle, 8 inches in diameter itself, rather than along the whole circumference of the turret—other than two bottom hatchways for passing up more ammunition. "A couple of wedges and a couple of sledge hammers, one on each side, was sufficient to raise the turret . . . a very good [arrangement]; the wedges were easily knocked out, and the turret could be lowered or raised in five minutes." The ultimate insurance was to have "excessively good pumps, and plenty of them, so that a large quantity of water could be cleared out in a short space of time." To prevent jamming of the turret a 5 × 15–inch iron glacis was fitted around the base, a standard fitting after the Charleston assault three years earlier.[45] Steam power enabled a full rotation, taking around a minute. The passage itself aboard the *Miantonomoh* was, Bythesea admitted, "quite dry." Her ventilation "was exceedingly good," but when the engines were stopped "the lower deck then began to get stuffy and nasty." Still, "there were three pairs of engines to supply air," and "one pair, or even one cylinder, was sufficient to do the duty." Through an armored ventilating shaft on deck, "they sucked the air down, and the foul air went up the turrets." There was also "an arrangement for distributing the air, so that any officer, when in his cabin, could turn a little rose, and have as much air as he liked, or, by closing the rose, the air was turned off." Sickness averaged 3 percent.

Even so, Bythesea concluded, "I think if a vessel is to go to sea, or go from port to port, in all weathers and at short notice, a higher freeboard would be better. The precautions that have to be taken on each occasion that the 'Miantonomoh' goes to sea are very great, and entail a great deal of work, much of which would be obviated by having a higher freeboard." Otherwise, he "saw no necessity for any increased height."[46]

As soon as the U.S.S. *Miantonomoh* entered Queenstown, anchoring between the towering broadside ironclads H.M.S. *Black Prince* and *Achilles*, a fresh storm of public controversy broke over the United Kingdom. The day before her arrival, the Admiralty had carried out an unusual and severe target practice by the Reed-designed central-battery ironclad *Bellerophon*—against the turrets of Coles's converted "cupola ship," the *Royal Sovereign*. Coles was recently reinstated, but not with all of his former influence until more doubts about turrets versus broadsides were addressed in the most practical manner possible. The tests embarrassed everyone involved. Coles was doubted publicly by the Admiralty, which openly questioned the increasingly popular turret principle, even after its widespread application in the American Civil War. The Royal Navy seemed to be at war with itself, and the Admiralty—thanks to Coles—found itself cornered in a civil-military relations crisis with the British press. Ironically, the same issue of the *Illustrated London News* that covered the event also depicted the presence, beyond all expectation, of a Federal monitor in Ireland. Here was American naval and technological prowess—what the Royal Navy considered lunacy—in the face of apparently endless British experiments and uncertainty. Crowds were flocking to Queenstown to take a look, "greatly to the profit of the railway and steamer companies," added the *ILN*.[47]

When the *Miantonomoh* proceeded next to Portsmouth, arriving on Saturday, June 23, the attention of the nation followed her. "A strange vessel, with a strange figure and still stranger name, now lies at Spithead," wrote the London *Times*. "She is a real genuine Monitor, a true specimen of that singular fleet on which the Americans rely for their position on the seas." "As these vessels resemble no other floating things," the *Times* reasoned, "it follows almost inevitably that if the American shipbuilders are right, ours must be wrong, and it is our imperative duty to investigate the subject without prejudice or delay."[48] Nor was it solely a question of seaworthiness. A thorough inspection of the *Miantonomoh* left a *Times* correspondent observing that "as a war machine for close heavy fighting she appears to be perfect." The 15-inch Dahlgren smoothbore was itself at odds with the "best present ship gun [in the Royal Navy], the 12-ton 9-inch rifle, or 250-pounder," while the iron gun carriages and slides "were superior to anything of the kind previously seen in this country. . . . Two men can run the gun in or out with ease, and one man can regulate the compressors."[49] *The Scientific American,* which had battled for years with the opinions of the British *Engineering* journal and *Mechanics' Magazine* on monitors, now quoted them eating their own words.[50] "Everywhere it is our resources, strength, inventions," Fox wrote to Welles from London, "[the Monitor] is a wave of triumph for us all over this country. . . ."[51]

On June 29 the Board of Admiralty, Coles, Bythesea, and Fox traveled to Spithead for a special guided tour of the *Miantonomoh.* "There their Lordships were received by the captains and officers of the United States' ships, under a salute from the *Auguste* [*sic*], which was returned by the flag-ship *Victory*, the American flag hoisted at the main."[52] Up on the hurricane deck between the turrets, with thousands watching from the shore, they witnessed the Dahlgrens in action:

> The first gun fired was charged with a 35-powder, cartridge and a *sabot* live shell, at extreme elevation. The effect was very grand as the vast globe of metal propelled from the mouth of the gun with a deep hoarse roar went hurtling towards on its course until it fell at an estimated distance of about 3,500 yards from the ship.
>
> The second gun was charged with 35lbs. powder, a solid iron shot of 460lb., and fired point blank. If the last shot was grand, as exhibiting the flight of a 15-inch shell, this was more interesting, as exhibiting—what we have as yet made no provision for in rifling our heavy naval artillery—the perfection of *ricochet* firing. The immense ball spun along its course over the surface of the water as truly as the cricketer's ball passes over the smooth green sward towards the wicket.[53]

The 10-inch–thick iron turret armor itself, curved, laminated, break-joint layers of 1-inch plates, the *Times* described as "fixed up together in a circular wall in a manner quite equal to a rolled solid plate of moderate quality, and very superior to any rolled plate that has been but imperfectly welded. In fact, the turrets of the Miantonomoh have been welded throughout their ten separate layers by mechanical means alone, and without subjecting the iron to the renewed action of the furnace and the rolling mill, to, as nearly as possible, a continuity of cohesion equal to that of the best solid or rolled armour in this country."[54]

If the *Times* was duly impressed at first, there was also an element of cautious nitpicking. This was to be expected, since it had vehemently denounced the monitors during most of the Civil War, as well as the very concept of a "United States." But British opinion had since changed to a large degree. Abraham Lincoln the dictator and warmonger was now emancipator of the slaves and cruelly assassinated martyr.[55] The Fenians in Canada had found no sympathy from the U.S. Government. Perhaps more crucially, an angry anti-British press by the end of the

conflict had softened its tone, if only because international "reconcilia-
tion" was more compatible with national Reconstruction than was
"retaliation." Though Congress had authorized a final war loan of $600
million in March 1865, the total debt of the country by November stood
at $2.8 billion.[56] Seward had already outlined this rationale to Adams in
November 1863—the midst of the Civil War:

> [O]ne has only to consider the immense forces of population and indus-
> try existing in the United States to become satisfied that whenever
> peace returns, every source of national wealth now closed will soon be
> made to flow even more freely under the application of labor universally
> free than it did before, while slavery was maintained as a part of the
> industrial economy of the country.
>
> Apprehensions that the aggrandizement of the United States as a
> commercial power can bring any practical inconvenience or danger to
> European States can disturb none but visionary minds. We can never
> be dangerous, unless we are armed. We were never so great, and yet
> never so completely unarmed, as we were when this civil war broke
> out. We were never before so shorn of national prestige as we are now,
> through the operation of domestic faction; yet we have never been so
> strongly armed as we are at this moment, upon land and water. . . . We
> can be only a peaceful nation, if we are left to enjoy our independence
> in the way that our destiny leads us. We can only become a disturber
> of the world's peace by being called into the world to defend that
> independence.[57]

The Fourth of July 1866 thus proved a milestone in Anglo-American
relations. "For the first time," the *Times* reported, "the anniversary of
American independence was . . . celebrated conjointly by the
ships-of-war of England and America in an English port," every
British naval vessel in Portsmouth dressed in colors, flying the Stars
and Stripes at their main-royal-mastheads, with "a national salute of
21 guns . . . fired from all of Her Majesty's ships carrying above
10 guns," as well as the from surrounding fortifications.[58] When Fox
announced plans in London to depart England for Cherbourg, the
Prince of Wales and the Duke of Edinburgh appealed for an opportunity to see the *Miantonomoh* as well. Charles Francis Adams, at the
Court of Saint James, wrote to Seward that "in consequence of this
application [Fox] directed it to return to the mouth of the Thames. . . ."
This, too, was a first, Adams adding with a touch of complaint that
Fox "devolved upon me the duty of superintending the details of the
projected visit . . . a business with which I am little familiar."[59]
   By the time the celebrated *Miantonomoh* quietly departed from
Sheerness on July 16, British public opinion was ready to launch a
direct assault on the state of the Royal Navy, using the American monitor as a convenient battering ram. Within the last week, a new Board

of Admiralty, with Sir John Pakington as First Lord again, was formed. Now was the time for the press, naval professionals led by Coles, and private shipbuilders (namely Lairds) to decisively influence Britain's ironclad-building program. Though one old salt described the *Miantonomoh* in *Punch* as "ugliness personified," the *Times* regarded her as "a very extraordinary and—we wish we could not feel it—a portentous spectacle."[60] In Parliament it was asked why the Navy now seemed to vacillate on ironclads when even land-based rival powers were making every effort to produce them wholesale. If a settled design was the problem, turret ships were the obvious solution. Pakington, formerly in the opposition, could only agree. "We have, I think, already seen enough from what has taken place in foreign nations, as well as from the experiments made by ourselves, to lead us to the conclusion that the time has arrived when experiments should cease and action commence."[61]

Indeed, the summer of 1866 was vibrant with change. Lord Palmerston, the stalwart icon of generations of British imperial power, died the year before, along with the Liberal Coalition Government he held together as Prime Minister in the aftermath of the Crimean War. As much as he represented a tradition of assertive foreign policy, "Old Pam" was the epitome of a domestic conservatism where every man knew his place in society. In this, only his detestation of human slavery was greater than his fear of democratic republics. Now he was gone; the United States had recently passed its ultimate test; his successor, Earl Russell, was open to an extension of the franchise; and William Gladstone announced at Manchester the previous summer he was now politically "unmuzzled." Russell, however, failed to bring Reform through Parliament, resigning the very week the U.S.S. *Miantonomoh* was dazzling guests off Spithead and capturing headlines, and taking Gladstone down with him.[62] At the urgent request of Queen Victoria, Lord Derby did his best with a minority Conservative Government, which Benjamin Disraeli (as Chancellor of the Exchequer) was determined could pass its own Reform Bill through Parliament by appealing to more of the uneducated working masses than even Gladstone and Bright had dared, and by so doing recapture the "natural," deferential heart of British society from the bottom up.[63] The fierce debates between Gladstone and Disraeli in Parliament, however, inspired little confidence with Radical organizations such as the Reform League, quickly galvanizing into a popular force of their own. This political and social anxiety bordered on panic as the first of the great Hyde Park demonstrations—or "riots"—for Reform occurred on July 24, with Adams writing to Seward that "the government prohibition proved utterly powerless."[64] As if this was not enough to rattle sensibilities at Whitehall, news came at the end of July of a great naval battle of ironclads, at Lissa, between warring Italy and Austria. Though none of the combatants were monitors (only one broadside ironclad being sunk, by ramming), the primacy of heavy artillery in naval warfare was manifest, if only because none of the broadsides exchanged were decisive.[65]

Perhaps even more important, there was a sense to the mid-Victorians that events in Europe and the rest of the world, at least as far as the Navy was concerned, were passing them by. The perception was a naturally self-centered one; the Pax was theirs, as was the industrial, scientific, globalizing age. Contingent for, not upon, that peace, prosperity, and progress was the maintenance of British naval supremacy, at the core of which were British warships—Her Majesty's ironclads.[66] Therefore, when the *Times* recounted Fox's offhand boast that "if the experiment could be made without exciting ill-feeling on either side, he would allow the whole ironclad fleet of England to open fire on the Miantonomoh, and continue it for two days, provided that the Miantonomoh might afterwards be allowed to have ten hours' firing at our ships in return," it reflected that however bad things may seem, "something may be done—nay, it must be done, for waste of time is perilous."[67] If the Government seemed "utterly powerless" to control emerging social and political forces, it could at the very least be pushed by liberal middle-class contempt for bureaucratic inefficiency on matters of national—and imperial—security.[68]

If such was the crisis exemplified by the rather successful visit of the U.S.S. *Miantonomoh* to England, how did the Admiralty respond? John Bourne's greatest effort to gain acceptance for "the American System of Turret Ships" was made at the Institution of Naval Architects on March 23, 1866—three months *before* the physical specimen of Ericsson's ideas reached Queenstown. Monitors were based on "the principle of concentration" of armor and armament. Displacement and proportions of vessels being the same, high-freeboard broadside or low-freeboard turret, the monitor would always have the advantage in raw powers of defense and attack, Bourne argued. Reed's response was crucial. On a point of tactics, he preferred a higher freeboard, to "be able to fire down on the deck" of a monitor. Habitability for the crew was perhaps a more practical consideration, "for it is still, I fancy, a question of naval officers to say whether they would like that sort of vessel for sea-going purposes . . . one might not like being locked up for many days together, down below there, with artificial light and artificial ventilation, and without the slightest sight of the heavens or the sea." Bourne regarded this as a "sentimental affliction with which I do not pretend to deal. . . . I should think that any seaman, or naval officer going into action, would upon it as the first condition of excellence, not that his ship had fine cabins, but that she was shot-proof and safe. . . ."[69] Was the British Lion lean, hungry, and ready for a fight, or sleeping comfortably?

Despite Ericsson's doubts of acceptance—perhaps recalling the successful but futile trial of his revolutionary screw-driven *Francis B. Ogden* before the Lords Commissioners of the Admiralty in 1837—Bourne convinced him to offer his services again in January 1866.[70] Following Bourne's lecture in March, however, Ericsson graphically relished how a monitor of equal displacement to Reed's forthcoming double-turret, high-freeboard H.M.S. *Monarch* "would probably settle the contest":

> . . . [T]wo shots put through the *Monarch*'s insufficient side armor would smash the mechanism of the turrets, while the other two would crush the ship's side at the water line. Another discharge from the four [20-inch caliber] 1000-pounders would expedite matters by making chasms of magnificent proportions through which the sea would enter with perfect freedom.[71]

Bourne unwittingly published the letter. "It will bring out the whole strength of the Admiralty against yourself and the Monitor system," Ericsson explained, hanging his words on his long and bitter experience dealing with naval professionals on both sides of the Atlantic.[72] Within days, the Admiralty curtly informed Bourne that Ericsson's services would not be required.[73]

The fact was, months before the arrival of the *Miantonomoh*, the great turret versus broadside debate in Britain had led to the compromise experiment of not just one but two new capital ships, armed with turrets yet fully rigged as *cruisers*. Plans for the *Monarch* were accepted by the Board even as Coles's own proposals were rejected, and then, when public pressure reacted once more, Coles was finally allowed to proceed with what would become the infamous H.M.S. *Captain*—a dangerously low-freeboard, double-turret sailing ironclad that capsized on Sept. 7, 1870, with the loss of 473 officers and men, including Coles.[74]

Still, Reed and, much more influentially, Admiral Spencer Robinson, the Controller of the Navy, put more faith in the recently completed *Bellerophon*, and the even more powerfully armed and armored central-battery ironclad *Hercules*, laid down on Feb. 1, 1866. If good sea-keeping, larger engines, and greater provisions were to be had only with high-freeboard vessels, an armored casemate housing a concentrated main armament conflicted much less with masts and sails than top-deck rotating turrets "liable to jamming." Almost as if to publicly ram home their point, instructions were given for the *Bellerophon* to test-fire on the *Royal Sovereign*, even while Coles finalized plans for the *Captain*—the ironclad which he envisioned would combine the best qualities of the *Warrior* (speed and range) and the *Monitor* (concentrated turret armament and protection).[75]

Emboldened by the popular approval of the *Miantonomoh*, Bourne again tried to "set right" the most important engineer in England: Reed. But the Chief Constructor knew the Admiralty by then already had a full plate, observing to Robinson on July 31, 1866:

> I am unable to concur with the Writer's opinion that 'nothing short of considerably thicker armour and considerably heavier guns than have already been introduced can be of the least avail in maintaining our Maritime position,' because it is certain that the ships now built and building would be of very considerable avail in accomplishing that object if necessity arose.[76]

The major concern for Reed, as always, was not Ericsson, but Coles. If the *Monarch* was bound to be vulnerable at the waterline, so was the *Captain*—at least in comparison with the *Hercules*. Yet realizing that Bourne had attempted to re-introduce Ericsson's services directly to the new First Lord, who was himself assuring Parliament of a proper reaction to the example of the *Miantonomoh*, Reed now preempted the American influence by suggesting an "improved" type of monitor. "The low protected deck, and the artificial Ventilation offer very great advantages, and where a greater height of ship is indispensable for sea-going purposes this may well be obtained by means of that system, raising the guns sufficiently to admit below them a light unplated deck and side for increasing the freeboard, and adding to the accommodation." The new Board could not help but agree. "This design, however," Reed added suggestively, "is for a Cruiser of moderate dimensions, which can only be considered as a War-Ship of the 2nd or 3rd class, adapted to conform as nearly as possible to the Views expressed in Parliament by members of their Lordships' Board." With extra resources placed at his disposal, Reed also promised "the Design of a First Class Ship, suited in my judgment to secure for us that consideration from an enterprising Naval power like the United States, which ships with 7 inch and 6½ inch armour going only 5 feet below the water will not, I fear, command."[77] Reed's "breastwork monitors" for coastal defense thus became the eventual forerunner to the *Devastation*—and beyond that, the modern battleship.[78]

Ericsson was "disgusted" with Reed's proposed modifications to his "sub-aquatic system" of naval warfare. Despite every possible effort, monitors were obviously not going to be adopted by the Royal Navy "without barbarous mutilation."[79] Bourne's rough sketch of Reed's own vision of a perfect man-o'-war was sent the day before the Swedish-American inventor's sixty-third birthday. If there was to be any vindication for his life's greatest achievement, it was to be found in the ultimate triumph of the United States during its greatest crisis, in the historic fame, already legend, of the original *Monitor.* England's destiny was best left to Englishmen, with their own personal battles to fight, win, and lose in the summer of 1866.[80]

Gustavus Fox had reached similar conclusions while in France. An audience with Napoleon III and a visit of the talented architect of the world's first sea-going ironclad, Dupuy de Lôme, proved too intensely political over Russia and Mexico in the first instance and too disinterested over rafts and smoothbores in the second. "The President is very much complimented in England," he wrote to Welles, "but I think it is a matter of small concern what these Governments think of us or our people, our superiority in everything excepting tinsel, epaulettes and medals can only be felt by coming over here."[81]

But their assumptions were based on the idea that what was good for the United States during the Civil War would naturally apply to the strategic and technical concerns of the British Empire, never mind any political ramifications associated with American ingenuity and experience. It simply would not do for pockets of coastal defense ironclads scattered across the globe to constitute the mainstay of British maritime ascendancy. There would always be the vast stretches of open ocean to consider in the event of war. An ironclad that could act as a cruiser was superior for the "command of the sea" to an *Alabama,* even if it could not contend with a sea-going monitor in terms of armor and armament. Such tactical perfection carried a heavy strategic price that outweighed the *possibility* of such an encounter ever taking place. On the other hand, it said little for coastal power projection—another fundamental tenet of naval power. Yet events in history inevitably spoke louder in such matters. There was no direct threat to Britain in 1866. The monarchs of Europe were fighting among themselves; Russia was expanding into Asia, not India; and America was already dismantling its formidable but expensive Navy for obvious reasons of its own. The "wooden walls" of England were never really more effective than when they were planted just over the horizon, at sea. Perhaps this form of protection was ultimately a chimera, especially compared with the hard evidence presented on iron target and ordnance testing grounds, or when public officials could occasionally walk the deck of a high-tech monitor. As long as the illusion of security endured, however, to all those concerned, peace was assured and risk-taking experiments were unnecessary.

An "ugly" American ironclad had at least demonstrated that power was in the eye of the beholder. "Now the *Miantonomah* [sic] has crossed the Atlantic, we shall have to re-construct our Navy after her pattern, to be a match for the Americans," declared *Punch:*

When we are provided with *Miantonomah*s, then, in the unfortunate event of a war between England and the United States, we shall be in a position to cope with the Americans as at present armed. Before that time, they most likely will have provided themselves with torpedo diving-boats and anti-*Miantonomah* steam-rams. Then, but not till then, we shall do the same. Let us hope that war will not break out in the meanwhile.[82]

The *Army and Navy Journal* was more blunt, headlining the "Victory of Monitors." "[The London *Times*] needed only a sight of the Monitor to complete its gradual conversion to a belief in the system which the English press so long ridiculed. And now, like all new converts, it shames the old believers with its zeal." "The Monitors have won," it concluded. "It is plain they do not longer need advocacy."[83]

But what had the monitors won? Where exactly was the victory? More than proving mere technical points in one warship design over another, Fox and Ericsson had at least succeeded in winning not just the confidence of the American public, but the respect of British policymakers as well—a victory in a long, cold war of deterrence at the very heart of the Civil War—not at its borders. It had been clear from the beginning that Palmerston recognized ironclads as powerful new playing pieces on the *realpolitik* chessboard of international diplomacy. As early in the Civil War as June 1861 the British Prime Minister was keen to use them in a show of force against the Union, for "their going could produce no bad Impression here," he wrote to Somerset, "and depend upon it as to Impression in the United States the Yankees will be violent and threatening in Proportion to our local weakness and civil and pacific in Proportion to our increasing local strength."[84] Perhaps Abraham Lincoln referred to the Union's own ironclads as much as its veteran armies when he declared toward the end of the war that "England will live to regret her inimical attitude toward us." The resolution of the *Trent* affair, he recalled, was "a pretty bitter pill to swallow, but I contented myself with believing that England's triumph in the matter would be short-lived, and that after ending our war successfully we would be so powerful that we could call her to account for all the embarrassments she had inflicted upon us."[85] Until Britain could overcome the Union's new coastal defenses, she could not apply the same political leverage with her naval power from early 1862 as she had during late 1861. Even by September 1864, Palmerston complained to Lewis's successor as Secretary of War, Earl de Grey, that no heavy service guns existed in the Navy to "smash and sink the Monitors," which might block control of the St. Lawrence in the event of an Anglo-American conflict.[86] Indeed, Palmerston was obliged to admit to his increasingly frustrated Chancellor of the Exchequer, William Gladstone, not only that "we must keep Pace with France,

America and Russia," and that "the Fleets numerically smaller of the lesser Maritime Powers will tell more effectively than in the olden Time because of their modern Construction," but that "we are as yet unprovided with Cannon of sufficient power. There is little use in firing at an Iron Clad Ship unless you can send your Shot or your Shell through her Armour Plating—and I believe that at present with the exception of some [experimental] Armstrong Guns, and they are few, our Land Batteries and our Ships of War are not provided with guns that will send a shot through Iron Plates."[87] That December, the London *Mechanics' Magazine*, jubilantly quoted by *Scientific American*, announced that "the fleet of experimental iron-clads, of which the *Warrior* is the type, must, if they are to be in a condition to cope with the armor-plated ships of foreign powers, be reconstructed. . . . The remedy is a bitter pill for the Government to swallow; but there is no avoiding it."[88]

British naval supremacy by the mid-nineteenth century was traditionally expected to act as a diplomatic counterweight to the threat posed by the mass armies of continental powers such as France, Russia, and the United States. The rise of a strong navy in any or all of these powers would upset this often less-than-obvious "balance." It was all too easy, perhaps, for a naval power such as Britain to wield her influence in foreign affairs (let alone "defend her interests" worldwide) and to tip the scales in her favor during international crises. The Royal Navy both neutralized the threat posed by invading armies—given the geography of the British Isles—and therefore offered a means for striking soft targets with impunity. Palmerston's informal "chat" with the Austrian ambassador, Count Apponyi, during the Schleswig-Holstein crisis and Prusso-Danish War (1863–1864) stood as a perfect example. Writing to Russell, the Prime Minister recounted "I begged [Apponyi] that nothing I might say should be looked upon as a Threat but only as a frank explanation between Friends on matters which might lead to Disagreements, and with regard to which unless timely explanation were given as to possible consequences of certain Things a Reproach might afterwards be made that timely explanation might have averted disagreeable Results." England favored Denmark; her independence as a State was vital to keeping British access to the Baltic. The British army was admittedly small against Austria's ally, Germany (Prussia), but "with regards to operations by Sea the Positions would be reversed":

> We are strong, Germany is weak and the German Ports in the Baltic, North Sea and Adriatic would be greatly at our command. Speaking for myself personally and for nobody else I must frankly tell him that if an Austrian Squadron were to pass along our Coasts and Ports to into the Baltic to help in any way the German operations against Denmark I

should look upon it as an affront and Insult to England. That I could not
and would not stand such a Thing and that unless in such case a superior British Squadron were to follow with such orders for acting as the
case might require I would not continue to hold My present position:
and such a case would probably lead to collision—that is War—and in
my opinion Germany and especially Austria would be the sufferer in
such a war. I should deeply regret such a result because it is the wish of
England to be well with Austria, but I am confident that I should be
borne out by Public opinion. I again begged that he would not consider
this communication as a Threat, but simply as a friendly reminder of
consequences which might follow a possible course of action.[89]

Palmerston was more frank with Queen Victoria, who vehemently
opposed his stance on Denmark, and who had also opposed his pen-
chant for foreign interference more than once. That "England, the first
and greatest Naval Power," he wrote, "should allow the Austrian fleet
to sail by our shores, and go and conquer and occupy the island capital of a friendly power, towards which we are bound by national interests and Treaty engagements, would be a national disgrace to which
Viscount Palmerston, at least, never would stoop to be a party. It
makes one's blood boil even to think of it; and such an affront England,
whether acting alone or with Allies, ought never to permit."[90] As a
result, continental powers often resented the "Mistress of the Seas,"
and especially Palmerston's rather imperious foreign policies. For the
United States during the Civil War, the *Trent* ultimatum (which
Britain herself considered a response to American "arrogance") was
the final proof of Britain's far-reaching pretentiousness.[91]

No other single military tool of U.S. diplomacy was considered
more efficient—specifically intended to answer British interference in
American affairs—than the ironclad, specifically the U.S.S. *Monitor.*
John Ericsson went even further in describing his own steep personal
sacrifice. Years after the Civil War, he confided to his brother: "My
future, and my success in the world, required that I should not be troubled with children or with a wife who had a full right to live with me."
Fate had taken him instead to America, where it was "the cannon in
the rotary turret at Hampton Roads that tore the fetters from millions
of slaves, and afterward made the French abandon Napoleon's project
in Mexico."[92] In this mid-Victorian recourse to arms—both between
the Northern and Southern states, and internationally—despite
"Progress," despite "Civilization," despite even "Christianity,"
nothing offered a more reliable assurance of victory, it seemed, than a
war machine coolly calculated upon measurable, immutable principles of opposing force and resistance. This was the new equation in
modern conflict. Like Newton's Third Law of Motion, where every
action causes an equal and opposite reaction, aggression had provoked

reaction. Deterrence had led to the development of counter-deterrence. As Henry Adams in London marveled at the brute ascendancy of iron over wood at Hampton Roads, and the contest of iron against iron on the testing grounds at Shoeburyness, he could not help darkly reflecting how "Man has mounted science, and is now run away with it":

> I firmly believe that before many centuries more, science will be the master of man. The engines he will have invented will be beyond his strength to control. Some day science may have the existence of mankind in its power, and the human race commit suicide by blowing up the world.[93]

And yet this only epitomized the evolving character of the American Civil War itself. "Their campaigns combine the costliness of modern expeditions with the carnage of barbarian invasions," commented the London *Times* by the end of 1864. Supporters of the republic (or "Union") and the abolition of slavery were "so possessed with the magnitude of their purposes that they think no price too great to pay for progress."[94] The Union Navy, like its Army, had resorted to awe-inspiring means to achieve increasingly total ends in a truly modern— that is to say, *modernizing*—"contest for national supremacy."

At the same time, however, the fact that such a mechanized iron-clad did not directly threaten Britain's national security, as did the French armored frigates—though it did represent serious challenges to her imperial commitments—was beneficial in more ways than one. "The one great dread of the prime minister, as it regards American affairs," Charles Francis Adams wrote to Seward in late March 1865, "is that of appearing to be bullied." Because monitors constituted more of a defensive deterrence than an offensive threat, "this feeling, shared in some degree by both branches of the English race," and which Adams observed "interposes most of the obstructions in the way of their harmony,"[95] was left to evaporate harmlessly away.

Notes

Introduction

1. Stanley Sandler, *The Emergence of the Modern Capital Ship* (Newark, 1979), 61.

2. See for example *Memorandum by Sir John Burgoyne, on the Defence of Canada—February 1862*, signed John F. Burgoyne, Inspector-General of Fortifications, (British) The National Archives, Kew, London (hereafter "TNA") WO 33/11, and especially *Report on the Defence of Canada and of the British Naval Stations in the North Atlantic; together with Observations on the Defence of New Brunswick, &c.*, and *Report on the Defence of the British Naval Stations in the North Atlantic*, 25-1-1865, by Lieutenant-Colonel William Francis Drummond Jervois, Deputy-Director of Fortifications, TNA/WO/33/15.

3. "Tactics and their partner technology, have meaning for strategy and high policy and often are driven by strategic considerations. With varying success, states try to invest in military technologies that will provide weapons with characteristics most suitable for the protection or advancement of distinctive national interests," Colin S. Gray, *The Leverage of Sea Power: The Strategic Advantage of Navies in War* (New York: The Free Press, 1992), 206–207.

4. James M. McPherson, *Battle Cry of Freedom: The Civil War Era* (New York: Ballantine Books, 1988), viii.

5. Brian Holden Reid, *The American Civil War and the Wars of the Industrial Revolution* (London: Cassell, 1999), 16.

6. McPherson, *Battle Cry of Freedom*, 382.

7. See at least five theses and dissertations on the subject: "The British attitude towards the American Civil War," C. I. Payne (Birmingham, M.A., 1928); "English opinion and the American Civil War," Emily A. Taylor (Leeds, M.A.,

1921); "English public opinion and the American Civil War: a reconsideration," Duncan A. Campbell (Cambridge, Ph.D., 1997); "The relations of Great Britain and America, especially from 1861 to 1866," Edith E. Baker (Birmingham, M.A., 1920); and "Anglo-American foreign relations, 1841–61, with special reference to trans-Isthmian communication," G. A. Edwards (Wales, M.A., 1951).

8. One could incorrectly assume from such articles as "The Naval Strategy of the Civil War" by Bern Anderson (*Military Affairs*; Vol. 26, No. 1, Spring 1962) that the North had no strategy regarding foreign intervention.

9. C. I. Hamilton, *Anglo-French Naval Rivalry 1840–1870* (Oxford: Clarendon Press, 1993).

10. J. P. Taylor, *The Struggle for Mastery in Europe: 1848–1918* (Oxford: Oxford University Press, 1954), 129.

11. Kenneth Bourne, *Britain and the Balance of Power in North America 1815–1908* (London: Longmans, Green and Co. Ltd., 1967), 251. See also Norman. B. Ferris, *The* Trent *Affair: A Diplomatic Crisis* (Knoxville: University of Tennessee Press, 1977) and Gordon H. Warren, *Fountain of Discontent: The* Trent *Affair and Freedom of the Seas* (Boston: Northeastern University Press, 1981).

12. Bourne, *Britain*, 239–240, 273–276, 305–309.

13. By contrast, John Beeler's study of *The Birth of the Battleship: British Capital Ship Design 1870–1881* (London: Chatham Publishing, 2001) purposely fails to mention the *Monitor, Miantonomoh* or any American ironclad as influencing battleship design.

14. James. P. Baxter, *The Introduction of the Ironclad Warship* (Cambridge, MA: Harvard University Press, 1933), 4; also 302–331. Paul H. Silverstone defines the original *Monitor* as at least the "first ironclad warship built without rigging or sails," *Civil War Navies 1855–1883* (Annapolis, MD: Naval Institute Press, 2001), 4.

15. Oscar Parkes, *British Battleships:* Warrior *1860 to* Vanguard *1950, A History of Design, Construction and Armament* (London: Seeley Service & Co., 1970), 44–48.

16. Sandler, *Emergence*, 189.

17. Andrew Lambert, *Battleships in Transition: The Creation of the Steam Battlefleet 1815–1860* (London: Conway Maritime Press, 1984), 85; also 101, 109–111. Hamilton effectively doubts this; *Anglo-French*, 97–98.

18. D. K. Brown, *Warrior to Dreadnought: Warship Development 1860–1905* (London: Chatham Publishing, 1997), 204. See also John F. Beeler, "A One Power Standard? Great Britain and the Balance of Naval Power, 1860–1880," *The Journal of Strategic Studies* (Vol. 15, December 1992, No. 4), 557–560, and Beeler, *Birth of the Battleship*, who states "the manner in which the Board of Admiralty and its technological experts dealt with the financial, technological, strategic and tactical problems confronting them may furnish an instructive example for contemporary ["American"] policy-makers," 12.

19. Andrew Porter (ed.), *The Oxford History of the British Empire: Volume III, The Nineteenth Century* (Oxford: Oxford University Press, 1999), vi, *emphasis mine.*

20. Peter Burroughs, "Imperial Institutions and the Government of Empire," in Porter, *Oxford History,* 170, 323, 341. E. J. Hobsbawm described

Britain as "one whose power rested chiefly on that most commercially-based and trade-minded weapon, a Navy . . ." *Industry and Empire* (Suffolk, UK: Chaucer Press, 1968), 26.

21. Michael Howard, *War in European History* (Oxford: Oxford University Press, 1976), 122–123.

22. See for example, Andrew Lambert, "The Royal Navy, 1856–1914: Deterrence and The Strategy of World Power," in Keith Neilson and Elizabeth Jane Errington (eds.), *Navies and Global Defense: Theories and Strategy* (Westport, CT: Praeger Publishers, 1995), and "Australia, the *Trent* Crisis of 1861, and the Strategy of Imperial Defence," in David Stevens and John Reeve (eds.), *Southern Trident: Strategy, History and the Rise of Australian Naval Power* (Crows Nest, Australia: Allen & Unwin, 2001).

23. Winston Churchill, *A History of the English-Speaking Peoples: Volume Four, The Great Democracies* (New York: Dodd, Mead & Company, 1958), 4: 29–30.

24. May 18, 1851; from George Henry Francis (ed.), *Opinions and Policy of the Right Honourable Viscount Palmerston* (London: Elibron Classics, 2006 reprint from 1852 original), 429–430.

25. Harold and Margaret Sprout, *The Rise of American Naval Power, 1776–1918* (Annapolis, MD: Naval Institute Press, 1990 reprint of Princeton, 1939), 188–189.

26. Bernard Brodie, *Seapower in the Machine Age* (New York: Greenwood Press, 1941; reprinted 1943 by Princeton University Press), 435, 91–92.

27. Robert M. Browning, Jr., *Success Is All That Was Expected: The South Atlantic Blockading Squadron During the Civil War* (Washington, DC: Brassey's Inc., 2002). See also Donald L. Canney, *Lincoln's Navy: The Ships, Men and Organization, 1861–65* (Annapolis, MD: Naval Institute Press, 1998), 195–196, who writes: "This illogic [of attacking Charleston] can only be explained by the 'monitor fever' rampant in the land . . . one of the earliest examples of the 'magic' of technology when applied to war."

28. William C. Emerson also points the significant disparity in manpower requirements, since a "crew of thirty-five manned each gun in the main battery; 25 for the gun itself, and 10 stationed at the tackle for the ports. These latter crew also relieved the side-tacklemen in serving the guns in continuous and rapid fire." "U.S.S. *New Ironsides*: America's First Broadside Ironclad," *Warship* (1993), 27.

29. William H. Roberts, *USS New Ironsides in the Civil War* (Annapolis, MD: Naval Institute Press, 1999), xii. See also Spencer C. Tucker, *A Short History of the Civil War at Sea* (Wilmington, DE: Scholarly Resources Inc., 2002), 61.

30. Roberts, *New Ironsides*, 122, 124.

31. Alfred Thayer Mahan, *Admiral Farragut* (London: Sampson Low, Marston & Company, 1893), 324.

32. Leading diplomatic studies include E. D. Adams, *Great Britain and the American Civil War*, 3 vols. (New York: Russell and Russell, 1925); D. P. Crook, *Diplomacy during the American Civil War* (New York: Wiley, 1975), and *The North, The South, and the Powers, 1861–1865* (Athens: University of Georgia Press, 1987); and Brian Jenkins, *Britain and the War for the Union*, 2 vols. (Montreal: McGill Queen's University Press, 1974). More recent works

include R. J. M. Blackett, *Divided Hearts: Britain and the American Civil War* (Louisiana State University Press, 2001); Dean B. Mahin, *One War at a Time: The International Dimensions of the American Civil War* (Washington DC: Brassey's, 1999); and Robert E. May (ed.), *The Union, the Confederacy, and the Atlantic Rim* (Lafayette, IN: Purdue University Press, 1995).

33. "Presidential Address: No Peace Without Victory, 1861–1865," reprinted in *The American Historical Review*, Vol. 109, No. 1 (February 2004), 1–18. Indeed, as McPherson also points out, "A major goal of Confederate diplomacy in 1861 was to persuade Britain to declare the blockade illegal as a prelude to intervention by the royal navy to protect British trade with the South," *Battle Cry*, 383.

34. Howard Jones, *Union in Peril: The Crisis over British Intervention in the Civil War* (Chapel Hill: University of North Carolina Press, 1992), 110–111. See also 21-1-1861, Lewis to Edward Twisleton, in Gilbert Frankland Lewis (ed.), *Letters of the Right Hon. Sir George Cornewall Lewis* (London: Longmans, Green, and Co., 1870), 390–392.

35. See particularly the *Confidential and other Instructions issued for the guidance of Cruizers on the Coast of America*, 1863 (annotated by Milne and with an attached note from Sir Frederick Grey), dated *Nile*, at Halifax, 12-11-1863 (National Maritime Museum, Milne Papers, Greenwich.)

36. 27-12-1862, Lyons to Milne, Milne Papers, Greenwich.

37. Regis. A. Courtemanche, *No Need of Glory: The British Navy in American Waters 1860–64* (Annapolis, MD: Naval Institute Press, 1977), 175–176.

38. 28-12-1861, Lyons to Milne, Milne Papers, Greenwich. See also John G. Nicolay and John Hay, *Abraham Lincoln: A History*, 10 vols., (New York: The Century Co., 1917), 5: 35–41.

39. Courtemanche, *No Need of Glory*, 176.

40. 11-2-1864, Milne to Board of Admiralty, TNA/ADM 1/5871.

41. 21-8-1863, Russell to Somerset, Somerset Papers Collection, Aylesbury, Buckinghamshire Record Office.

42. Courtemanche, *No Need of Glory*, 153. See also Hamilton, *Anglo-French Naval Rivalry*, 92.

43. London *Times*, 12-3-1864. Given his close relationship with John T. Delane, the editor of the *Times*, the author of this article may in fact be Palmerston, recently under attack along with Russell in Parliament for being "frightened by the bluster of the Federal Government"; Arthur Irwin Dasent (ed.), *John Thadeus Delane, Editor of the 'Times', His Life and Correspondence*, 2 vols. (London: John Murray, 1908), 2: 151–152; Hansard's *Parliamentary Debates*, Third Series, Commencing with the Accession of William IV, Vol. CLXXIII (173), 4-2-1864 to 14-3-1864, 1st Volume of the Session (London: Cornelius Buck, 1864), 14-3-1864, "Neutrality in America," 1917.

44. Journal entry dated 11-8-1862, in Howard K. Beale (ed.), *Diary of Gideon Welles: Secretary of the Navy under Lincoln and Johnson*, 3 vols. (New York: W. W. Norton & Company, Inc., 1960), 1: 79.

45. Georgian navy Admiral George Ballard ruefully noted in his comprehensive study of Britain's "Black Battlefleet of 1870," for example, that "the strategic conception [of coastal defence] which left the initiative in movement

to the enemy . . . retained at least sufficient official acceptance to absorb an annual and appreciable proportion of the national expenditure on new fleet construction," George A. Ballard (G. A. Osborn and N. A. M. Rodger, eds.), *The Black Battlefleet: A Study of the Capital Ship in Transition* (London: Nautical Publishing Co., Lymington & the Society for Nautical Research, Greenwich, 1980), 218; yet Rear Admiral Raja Menon of the Indian Navy has observed that "the exertions of power abroad necessitates the domination of someone else's littoral," Raja Menon, *Maritime Strategy and Continental Wars* (London: Frank Cass Publishers, 1998), 184.

46. See Bourne, *Britain*, 208; 12-7-1864, Gladstone *Memo*, Palmerston Papers, Southampton, 5. See also Greg Marquis, *In Armageddon's Shadow: The Civil War and Canada's Maritime Provinces* (Montreal: McGill-Queen's University Press, 1998.

47. Charles B. Boynton, *The History of the Navy during the Rebellion*, 2 vols. (New York: D. Appleton, 1867–1868), 1: 6.

48. Boynton, *History*, 1: 14–15; also 56–58, 91–92.

49. Paul Kennedy observes "it would be a great error to suppose that it was British naval supremacy alone which [enabled the success of British foreign policy, if not the 'Pax Britannica']; the disinclination of the European nations for war was of equal significance," *The Rise and Fall of British Naval Mastery* (Malabar, Florida, 1982 ed.), 159. This concurs with Gerald S. Graham's analysis, *The Politics of Naval Supremacy: Studies in British Maritime Ascendancy* (Cambridge, UK: Cambridge University Press, 1965), 119–120. For a diverging view see Peter Burroughs, "Defence and Imperial Disunity," in Porter (ed.), *The Oxford History of the British Empire*, 320–345.

50. 4-4-1864, *Hansard*, 431–432.

Chapter 1

1. TNA/ADM 1/5765, 23-2-1861, *Navy Ships Building, &c.: An Account, showing the Expenses incurred on Her Majesty's Ships Building, Converting, Repairing, Fitting, &c., during the Financial Year 1859–60*, lists £1,018,061 expended for "Ships and Vessels building," most of these for sailing ships still converting to screw, either before or after launching. Ironclad ships are not listed.

2. Hamilton, *Anglo-French Naval Rivalry*; see Chapter 3, "Anglo-French Diplomacy and the Transition from the Screw-Liner to the Ironclad, 1854 Onwards."

3. See Andrew Lambert, *Warrior: The World's First Ironclad Then and Now* (London: Conway Maritime Press, 1987), 67–72; D. K. Brown, "Attack and Defence: Developing the Armour of H.M.S. *Warrior*," *Warship*, 40 (October 1986), 265–272.

4. TNA/ADM 1/576, minutes dated 13-1-1861. J. P. Baxter surmises Feb. 13 as the more likely date of this minute, given the reference to a Foreign Office report dated after. *Introduction*, 171.

5. TNA/ADM 1/5765, 13-1-1861; Andrew Lambert, "Politics, Technology and Policy-Making, 1859–1865: Palmerston, Gladstone and the Management of the Ironclad Naval Race," *The Northern Mariner*, Vol. III, No. 3 (July 1998), 9–38.

6. And perhaps unjustifiable; as Oscar Parkes notes, "[Palmerston] was one of Sir Howard Douglas's disciples, and in consequence work on the wooden line-of-battle ships was speeded up so that our old superiority in these could be regained, and a Two-Power standard in them assured by 1861. And this in the face of the knowledge that the French had not laid down a wooden ship-of-the-line since 1855!" *British Battleships*, 14.

7. Especially that of Captain Cowper Phipps Coles, R.N.; see for example *Shot-Proof Gun-Shields as Adapted to Iron-Cased Ships for National Defence, A Lecture on the 29th of June, 1860, at the Royal United Service Institution by Captain Cowper Phipps Coles, R.N.* (Westminster, 1860).

8. Ballard, *Black Battlefleet*, 241, 247; TNA/ADM 1/5774, 10-1-1861.

9. This weakness was presumably compensated by numerous watertight compartments that could be flooded in the case of shell penetration damage. While the *Warrior*, for example, was to gain only (?) 26 inches more draft, the corresponding loss in speed and manageability to such long ironclad ships with their ends flooded made this safeguard extremely unattractive. See Brown, *Warrior to Dreadnought*, 14, for increase in draft. John Wells writes, "Flooding both ends would have admitted 1070 tons of water . . . barely affecting fighting efficiency, although flooding one end might have been awkward." *The Immortal Warrior: Britain's First and Last Battleship* (Emsworth: Kenneth Mason, 1987), 215.

10. TNA/ADM 1/5774, 10-1-1861.

11. Ibid.

12. Parkes, *British Battleships*, 30.

13. Quoted from the London *Times*, March 31, 1862. The debate was intensified by recent news from America of the battle of Hampton Roads (March 8–9).

14. See Bryan Ranft, "The Protection of British Seaborne and the Development of Systematic Planning for War, 1860–1906", in Bryan Ranft (ed.), *Technical Change and British Naval Policy 1860–1939* (New York: Holmes & Meier, 1977), 1–22, who also points out the Admiralty's growing concern for protection of commerce in the age of steam. The conception of Britain's early ironclads as *frigates* might therefore support the notion that these were intended to serve as cruisers as well as in a line of battle; but would they therefore be effective in *either* capacity?

15. See also Halsted's series of lectures on "Iron-Cased Ships," *Journal of the Royal United Service Institution*, Whitehall Yard, V, 1861–1862 (London, 1862), 121–267.

16. 11-6-1862, Palmerston to Somerset, Somerset Papers, Aylesbury. Andrew Lambert describes Somerset himself as having "no concept of naval policy," taking advice "from all manner of amateurs, especially Palmerston." *Warrior*, 28.

17. Brown, *Warrior to Dreadnought*, 15.

18. Baxter seems to have overlooked the fact that the new Controller, Robinson (appointed Feb. 7, 1861), recommended changes "very essential to the efficiency of the Ship to carry a belt of Armour Plating of 4½ inches in thickness right round the Ship in continuation of that which exists at present only for about 200 ft.," only well after the original plans of the ship were approved by the Board and the ship was ordered on April 10, 1861; and that "the Stern of the 'Achilles', designed after that of the 'Warrior' and 'Black

Prince', should be remodelled to resemble that of the 'Royal Oak' class, by which a complete protection can be given to the Rudder head and Steering Apparatus, and greater safety from shot ensured to the Screw." TNA/ADM 1/5802, 31-5-1862; Baxter, *Introduction*, 166–167. Parkes may have repeated this oversight; *British Battleships*, 40.

19. TNA/ADM 1/5774, 2-5-1861.

20. Ibid., 8-5-1861.

21. Hamilton, *Anglo-French*, 92–98.

22. TNA/ADM 1/5774, 8-5-1861.

23. TNA/ADM 1/5840; the report dated March 25, 1862, notes the original estimate price for *Warrior* as £31.5 per ton and the actual cost at £41.67 per ton, while the *Black Prince* contract estimate at £37.25 per ton rose to £39.78. These figures were later adjusted to: *Warrior*, final rate per ton £42.25; *Black Prince*, £41.57. The *Warrior* cost £239; 646.01 (ADM 1/5802, "Iron-Cased Ships—Statement of Cost," 25-3-1862, No. 408). The cost for the improved *Warrior* class, the *Achilles*, laid down on 1-8-1861, was estimated at the time at £354,410 (TNA/ADM 1/5774, "Drawings for Iron-cased Ships"). J. P. Baxter noted a final cost of £444,380 when she was finally completed for sea on Nov. 26, 1864; *Introduction*, 167. *Royal Oak* cost £254,537 according to Parkes, *British Battleships*, 50.

24. TNA/ADM 1/5765, 21-5-1861.

25. Baxter, *Introduction*, 69–91.

26. TNA/ADM 1/5765, 22-5-1861.

27. TNA/ADM 1/5774; on 7-5-1861 Robinson reported to the Admiralty his criticisms of an ironclad fully belted with solid 7-inch iron plating but with no wood backing—plans for which were being prepared for the Russian government by the British iron shipbuilder J. Samuda.

28. Parkes, *British Battleships*, 60.

29. TNA/ADM 1/5765, 23-5-1861.

30. Ibid.

31. TNA/ADM 1/5765, 23-5-1861; "Iron Cased Ships." Dundas's minute is enclosed but undated.

32. See Colin F. Baxter, "The Duke of Somerset and the Creation of the British Ironclad Navy, 1859–1866," *The Mariner's Mirror*, Vol. 66, No. 3 (August 1977), who also suggests that Somerset was averse to "a crash programme" of additional ironclads until both the sea-going qualities of previous classes and the proposed armor configuration could be fully tested; 281–282. Either the French "threat" was urgent or it was not.

33. TNA/ADM 1/5802, 6-5-1862.

34. 12-6-1863, Sir Frederick Grey to Milne, Milne Papers, Greenwich.

Chapter 2

1. See Bernard Semmel, *Liberalism and Naval Strategy: Ideology, Interest, and Sea Power during the Pax Britannica* (London: Allen & Unwin, 1986). Paul Kennedy describes the mid-Victorian attitude as exceedingly content with its laissez-faire prosperity; this made the need for large defense expenditures seem

unnecessary and provocative. *Rise and Fall of the Great Powers: Economic Change and Military Conflict from 1500 to 2000* (London: Fontana Press, 1988), 193–203.

2. Tensions were rife in Parliament and the Cabinet over security *and* retrenchment during this period; *Hansard's Parliamentary Debates*, 166 (London, 1862), March 31, 1862, 263; Phillip Guedalla, *Gladstone and Palmerston: Being the Correspondence of Lord Palmerston with Mr. Gladstone 1851–1865* (London: Victor Gollancz, Ltd., 1928). See also N. A. M. Rodger, "British Naval Thought and Naval Policy, 1820–1890: Strategic Thought in an Era of Technological Change," in Craig L. Symonds (ed.), *New Aspects of Naval History* (Annapolis, MD: Naval Institute Press, 1981), 142–145.

3. From TNA/ADM 1/5765, *Proclamation by the Queen* [on American Civil War neutrality], May 13, 1861.

4. Palmerston observed on the question of a pre-arranged naval arms limitation treaty with France—and the British addendum for twice the number of French ironclads—discussed in Parliament in July 1861: "[T]he Emperor would laugh at us and say 'By all means! I must have 20 or 24 Iron-cased ships—you are quite welcome to have 40 or 48, and I hope you will find the money to build them; but do not expect that I am to sit with my hands crossed till you have done so!'" Parkes, *British Battleships*, 49.

5. Hamilton, *Anglo-French*, 140.

6. Colin Baxter notes Somerset's willingness to continue construction of unarmored wooden line-of-battle ships as well, however, until the future of ironclad vessels became more clear; "The Duke of Somerset," 280.

7. 31-7-1860, Russell to Cobden, Cobden Papers Collection, West Sussex Record Office, Chichester.

8. 2-8-1860, Cobden to Russell, Cobden Papers, Chichester. See also David Newsome, *The Victorian World Picture: Perceptions and Introspections in an Age of Change* (New Brunswick, NJ: Rutgers University Press, 1997), 101–115.

9. TNA/ADM 1-5767, 6-11-1861, enclosed 25-5-1861, Lyons to Milne; TNA/ADM 1/5774, 12-6-1861; TNA/ADM 1/5774, 14-6-1861. The hours reflected increasing pressure to adopt private industry schedules—and productivity—especially for the new dockyard steam factories; see C. I. Hamilton (ed.), *Portsmouth Record Series, Portsmouth Dockyard Papers 1852–1869: From Wood to Iron* (Winchester: Hampshire County Council, 2005), xxvi, nos. 209, 210 (171–172).

10. TNA/ADM 1/5766, 8-7-1861.

11. TNA/ADM 1/5802, 3-12-1862.

12. TNA/ADM 1/5862, *Annual Account of Expense of Ships, 1861–1862*.

13. See Philip Pugh, *The Cost of Seapower: The Influence of Money on Naval Affairs from 1815 to the Present Day* (London: Conway Maritime Press, 1986), 146–151, 259–261.

14. TNA/ADM 1/5774, 31-8-1861.

15. Ibid. Enclosed letter dated 30-8-1861.

16. Ibid. Enclosed bid for tenders dated 5-8-1861.

17. TNA/ADM 1/5774, 5-9-1861.

18. TNA/ADM 1/5774, 11-11-1861.

19. Ibid. Enclosed letter dated 5-11-1861.

20. TNA/ADM 1/5744, 18-11-1861.

21. TNA/ADM 1/5802, 28-3-1862. Enclosed letter from James Campbell of Westwood Baillie to Paget, Admiralty Secretary, dated 26-3-1862.

22. TNA/ADM 1/5802, 6-3-1862. One contemporary civilian authority, at least, felt otherwise, defending the private shipbuilding industry of Britain while attesting that "no man . . . can know the [Royal] dockyard and naval system of this country without being at a loss for words sufficiently scurrilous to convey a proper sense of his indignation." P. Barry, *Dockyard Economy and Naval Power* (London, 1863), xi–xii. The chief points of criticism were the "need" to defend dockyards when private shipyards were more numerous and valuable, lack of more efficient "division of labour" practices in government yards ("unlike those in America and France"), and bureaucratic "redtape," private patronage, and corruption stifling any administrative reform.

23. TNA/ADM 1/5802, 8-5-1862, enclosed letter dated 5-5-1862. The import of this complaint should not be underestimated, since "the credit for laying the foundations of the Clyde warshipbuilding industry belongs to Robert Napier," who had by this time been constructing iron-hulled warships for the Royal Navy for nearly 20 years. The contracts for *Black Prince* and then *Hector* nearly broke Napier, who "never fully recovered from the débácle." Hugh Peebles, *Warshipbuilding on the Clyde: Naval Orders and the Prosperity of the Clyde Shipbuilding Industry, 1889–1939* (Edinburgh, 1987), 8–15.

24. TNA/ADM 1/5802, 8-5-1862. Robinson's reply to the Admiralty is dated 8-5-1862.

25. TNA/ADM 1/5802, 5-5-1862.

26. TNA/ADM 1/5802, 12-3-1862.

27. TNA/ADM 1/5802, 15-5-1862.

28. TNA/ADM 1/5809, 22-7-1862.

29. Ibid.

30. TNA/ADM 1/5809, 10-10-1862, enclosed reports, dated 16- and 25-9-1862.

31. TNA/ADM 1/5802, 26-9-1862; also 2-7-1862, where the Solicitor's enclosed letter dated 3-7-1862 identifies the loophole in the contract: "[T]he Admiralty have no power reserved to them by such Contract to enter and finish the Vessel *until* the period limited by the Contract for *completing* it has expired. There is no penalty for the non-progress of the Work." *Northumberland* was originally laid down by Mare & Co. in October 1861, who found themselves unable to bear the enormous burden of her construction and finally gave up her contract to the newly re-incorporated "Millwall Iron Works & Shipbuilding Company Limited, Millwall" in the spring of 1863 (at "£321,117, instead of £295,295," or £48 instead of £44 per ton). Millwall in turn liquidated from the effort in 1866, at a heavy loss of some £90,000. The Admiralty agreed to pay £8,000 alone to Millwall's shareholders for costs associated with the spectacular month-long failures in even launching such an iron behemoth (mistakenly armor plated while still on the stocks). Though *Northumberland* was finally off her ways on 17-4-1866, the residual stigma of the controversy and litigation that followed was highly reminiscent of the *Great Eastern*

fiasco, which fatally exhausted Isambard Kingdom Brunel in 1859. See TNA/ADM 1/5840, Jan. 2 and April 10, 1863; TNA/ADM 1/5980, 21-5-1866; TNA/ADM 3/272, 14-5-1866 and 3-12-1866; TNA/ADM 1/6017, 6-2-1867. See also Ballard, *Black Battlefleet*, 38–39.

32. TNA/ADM 1/5802, 26-11-1862.

33. Ibid.

34. TNA/ADM 1/5802, 19-11-1862.

35. TNA/ADM 1/5802, 3-12-1862.

36. Even Sir Frederick Grey of the Admiralty was obliged to respond to Vice-Admiral Milne's request for the replacement of ships on his precarious American Station that "we cannot divert our dockyard men from more important work to do what is after all not an absolute necessity"; 4-10-1862, Milne Papers, Greenwich.

37. TNA/ADM 1/5802, 3-12-1862.

38. "British naval supremacy . . . rested both on number of ships and in the possession of bases (many recently acquired) all over the world, and on British industrial superiority. British interests were so much more numerous and widespread than those of other western powers that the Royal Navy became, in effect, the policeman of the globe, carrying the main burden of suppressing piracy and the slave trade. In addition, the Navy became heavily involved in surveying the seas, exploration and scientific research." John B. Hattendorf, R. J. B. Knight, A. W. H. Pearsall, N. A. M. Rodger, and Geoffrey Till (eds.), *British Naval Documents 1204–1960: Navy Records Society* (Aldershot: Scolar Press, 1993), 563.

39. 4-10-1862, Milne Papers, Greenwich.

40. Robinson later defended the broadside ironclads against the criticisms of their own Channel Squadron Commander-in-Chief, Rear-Admiral Sir Sydney Colpoys Dacres, in 1864. In mentioning the capabilities of the *"Prince Consort*-class [*Royal Oak*-class]" at sea, he stated "after seeing the French and Italian Iron-clads, which perform all the service required of them in the Mediterranean, and elsewhere, I have no hesitation in saying that these ships are fully equal to them, and need not shrink from any comparison with any wooden Iron-clads afloat." TNA/ADM 1/5892, 19-11-1864.

Chapter 3

1. TNA/ADM 1/5765, 23-5-1861; "Iron Cased Ships."

2. Baxter, *Introduction*, 102–103, 112, 113–114.

3. Hamilton, *Anglo-French*, 74–78: "[T]he Crimean War at sea, primarily a coastal war, was distinctly peculiar in comparison with the kind of wars the British and French navies were accustomed to, where for the most part the great events had been engagements on the high seas. This peculiar war, and the new naval instruments it gave rise to, for some years closely shaped men's conceptions of future naval wars, even where the supposed opponents were Britain and France themselves." Andrew Lambert speculates that a full-scale naval attack on Cherbourg might have resembled that on Sweaborg (August 8–10, 1855), where a flotilla of heavy mortar vessels, screened by

heavier gunboats and supported by a blockading fleet, would bombard the dockyard and arsenal from extreme range (4,000 yards). "Under the Heel of Britannia: The Bombardment of Sweaborg 9–11 August 1855," in Peter Hore (ed.), *Seapower Ashore: 200 Years of Royal Navy Operations on Land* (London: Chatham, 2001), 96–129.

4. For one of the best accounts of Coles in this period see David B. McGee, "Floating Bodies, Naval Science: Science, Design and the *Captain* Controversy, 1860–1870," unpublished Ph.D. thesis, University of Toronto, 1994.

5. Baxter, *Introduction*, 181–195, 187–188.

6. See Wells, *Immortal Warrior*, 16, 31–32.

7. See 27-9-1864, Welles to Rear-Admiral Francis Gregory and William H. Webb, Welles Papers, LOC. A copy of the contract (dated 3-7-1862) for *Dunderberg*, with design specifications, can be found in RG 45, Entry 464, Box 51. The turrets were removed because her contractor later claimed his inability to handle their unexpected weight (including 15-inch Dahlgren guns and the latest armor improvements), or rising costs in their production associated with wartime labor shortages and delays. Instead, a longer casemate with larger broadside battery, mounting 15-inch guns, was approved by the U.S. Navy; see 16-10-1863, Webb to Fox, Fox Papers, New York, Box 7. A rare early sketch of the American ironclad made by Royal Navy observer Captain James G. Goodenough, dated 8-1-1864, can be found in TNA/ADM 1/5789.

8. TNA/ADM 1/5802, 6-5-1862; enclosed *Specification of Cowper Phipps Coles—Iron-Cased Ships of War* (London: George E. Eyre and William Spottiswoode, Great Seal Patent Office, 1860); see also Baxter, *Introduction*, 189.

9. TNA/ADM 1/5802, 1-4-1862.

10. TNA/ADM 1/5774, 25-2-1861; enclosed letter from Captain Sherard Osborn to the Secretary of the Admiralty, dated 17-11-1860.

11. TNA/ADM 1/5774, 18-7-1861; enclosed letter dated 15-3-1861, Gunner Henry Hubbard to Commander Lambert.

12. Ibid. It is interesting to note the phrasing "weight of shot thrown at a broadside." This may have been referring to the growing likelihood that foreign station vessels might encounter armored ships, where "the continuous fire from a greater number of smaller Guns . . . spread more over the Vessel" would be futile.

13. ADM 1/5774, 2-9-1861. In the summer of 1864, *Gannet* returned home for repairs and refit at Devonport; the Controller then ordered that "she should be armed during her next commission with a heavy gun in midships, and a lighter rifled pivot gun at bow and stern, in place of the eleven 32-pounders with which she was armed during her last commission, and of which ten were 25 cwt. guns only." TNA/ADM 1/5891, 24-8-1864.

14. 24-9-1861, Palmerston to Russell, from Baxter, *Introduction*, 191–192.

15. TNA/ADM 1/5774, 23-10-1861.

16. Ibid. British tests on armor plates indicated both that inclined armor afforded little more protection for the added weight involved with the increased area required by the angle, and that wood support to vertical iron plates helped absorb the shock of impacting shot; see TNA/WO 33/11, 27-3-1862, *Report of the Special Committee appointed to Inquire into the Application of Iron for Defensive Purposes* [Iron Plate Committee], xvi.

17. TNA/ADM 1/5802, 6-5-1862.

18. TNA/ADM 1/5774, 23-10-1861.

Chapter 4

1. TNA/ADM 1/5768, 4-9-1861. See also Thomas Schoonover, "Napoleon Is Coming! Maximilian Is Coming? The International History of the Civil War in the Caribbean Basin," in May, *The Union*, 101–130.

2. TNA/ADM 1/5768, 4-9-1861.

3. During the *Trent* crisis, the Royal Navy was quite aware that without extra coal there could be no operations against the United States, with reinforcing steam colliers delivering at least 10,000 tons to various American and West Indian Station outposts. See TNA/ADM 128/56, 6-12-1861; TNA/ADM 3/269, 6-12-1860; and TNA/ADM 1/5792, 16-12-1861.

4. TNA/ADM 128/56, 14-12-1861.

5. 2-1-1862, Milne to Somerset, Somerset Papers, Aylesbury.

6. 28-12-1861, Russell to Somerset, Somerset Papers, Aylesbury.

7. 5-12-1861, Somerset to Lewis, Somerset Papers, Aylesbury.

8. Bourne, *Britain*, 206–247. See also Kenneth Bourne, "British Preparations for War with the North, 1861–1862," *English Historical Review* 76 (October 1961), 600–632.

9. *List of the Chief Ports on the Federal Coast of the United States, showing the Shipping, Population, Dockyards and Defences as far as known; also how far accessible or vulnerable to an Attack, as far as can be gathered from the Charts. With an approximate Estimate of the Number of Vessels required to blockade the several Ports and Rivers* (London: HMSO, 1861); copy found in Milne Papers, Greenwich. Bourne identifies the author of the report as Captain John Washington, the Admiralty Hydrographer from 1855 to 1862; Bourne, *Britain*, 240. Washington may have based much of his information in turn on the pre–Civil War alarmist pamphlets of Major J. G. Barnard of the U.S. Corps of Engineers, namely *Dangers and Defenses of New York* (New York: D. Van Nostrand, 1859) and *Notes on Sea-Coast Defense* (New York: D. Van Nostrand, 1861), which specified the importance of the new Rodman 15-inch gun in checking the ascendancy of armored batteries over fortifications; on the latter work see pages 27–28, 44–48, 56–60.

10. Milne Papers, Greenwich, *List*, 1. See also Samuel J. Watson, "Knowledge, Interest and the Limits of Military Professionalism: The Discourse on American Coastal Defence, 1815–60," *War in History*, Vol. 5, No. 3 (1998).

11. The *List* also warned that "the blockading ships . . . must be on their guard against torpedos [*sic*], explosion vessels apparently laden with flour, but really with gunpowder, and other atrocious contrivances. The *Ramilies*, while lying here in June 1813, was nearly destroyed by one of these explosion vessels, fitted out by some merchants of New York; fortunately the vessel was not brought alongside, but one officer and 10 men fell victims to it," 5.

12. 24-1-1862, Milne to Somerset, Somerset Papers, Aylesbury.

13. TNA/ADM 1/5787, 31-12-1861.

14. Milne Papers, Greenwich, *List*, 2–3.

15. See Bourne, *Britain*, 237–244. Bourne concluded that "it was almost entirely upon the moral and military effectiveness of the blockade [of the Northern States] that all Great Britain's chances of success seemed to depend," 244.

16. Milne Papers, Greenwich, *List*, 7–8.

17. Wade G. Dudley, *Splintering the Wooden Wall: The British Blockade of the United States, 1812–1815* (Annapolis, MD: U.S. Naval Institute Press, 2003), 134–135.

18. 24-1-1862, Milne to Somerset, Somerset Papers, Aylesbury. See also Milne's forwarded reports on various defects of vessels under his command in TNA/ADM 128/7, 21-3-1862. In contrast, Robinson, the Controller, did not see the need for building any more paddle steamers "for war purposes," or even for continuing to build unarmored screw vessels; TNA/ADM 1/5802, 5-4-1862.

19. See TNA/ADM 1/5787, 29-12-1861; also 17-1-1862, Milne to Grey, Milne Papers, Greenwich.

20. 10-3-1862, Milne to Grey, Milne Papers, Greenwich; also 15-5-1862, Milne to Somerset, Somerset Papers, Aylesbury.

21. 6-12-1861 Palmerston to Somerset; and 28-12-1861, Palmerston to Somerset, Somerset Papers, Aylesbury. See the collection of reports on "New Scheme of Armament for H.M. Ships, in consequence of Introduction of Armstrong Gun," in TNA/ADM 1/5792.

22. Milne Papers, Greenwich, *List*, 9.

23. TNA/ADM 1/5768, 3-12-1861. Lyons also forwarded to Lord Russell at the Foreign Office the Dec. 5 *Daily Globe*'s full reprint of the U.S. Secretary of the Navy's Annual Report to Congress of Dec. 2, 1861, listing three ironclads under construction; TNA/ADM 1/5768, 26-12-1861.

24. Milne Papers, Greenwich, *List*, 10.

25. 28-1-1860, Colonial Office memo, written by T. Frederick Elliot, dissenting from a recent Report on military expenditure on the Colonies; TNA/WO 33-09, 3.

26. February 1860 printed memo, Somerset to Board, TNA/ADM 1/5741, 12.

27. Cowper Phipps Coles, *Shot-Proof Gun-Shields, as Adapted to Iron-Cased Ships for National Defence*, pamphlet reprinted from the *Journal of the Royal United Service Institution*, Vol. 4, 1860, from his lecture dated 29-6-1860 (Westminster: J. B. Nichols and Sons, 1860), 12.

Chapter 5

1. 12-1-1860, *Scientific American*, 25.

2. 36th Congress, 2nd Session, Senate Executive Document No. 1, Vol. 3, *Message from the President of the United States; Report of the Secretary of the Navy*, 1-12-1860, 3–5.

3. J. A. Dahlgren, *Shells and Shell-Guns* (Philadelphia: King & Baird, 1857), 412–415.

4. 1-10-1860, Dahlgren to Magruder, Dahlgren Papers, LOC. See also Dahlgren's report to Magruder, dated 12-12-1860, found in Executive Document No. 34, House of Representatives, 36th Congress, 2nd Session, *Rifled Cannon and the Armament of Ships-of-War*, 25-1-1861, 7–11.

5. 10-12-1860, Dahlgren to Magruder, Dahlgren Papers, LOC; also 4-5-1861, *Scientific American*, 274.

6. 10-12-1860, Dahlgren to Magruder, Dahlgren Papers, LOC. For an early comparative description of the *Gloire* and *Warrior* see *Harper's Weekly*, 9-2-1861, "Revolution in Naval Warfare—Shot-Proof Iron Steamships," 92–93.

7. 11-2-1861, Dahlgren to Grimes; 19-1-1861, Dahlgren to Morse, Dahlgren Papers, LOC. See also Donald L. Canney, *The Old Steam Navy, Volume Two: The Ironclads, 1842–1885* (Annapolis, MD: U.S. Naval Institute Press, 1993), 7.

8. 11-2-1861, Dahlgren to Grimes; 20-2-1861, Dahlgren to McKay, Dahlgren Papers, LOC.

9. Quoted from Baxter, *Introduction*, 242.

10. March 1861, *Blackwood's Edinburgh Magazine*, 311, 316. In addition to improved monitor ironclads, Fox outlined to Rear-Admiral David D. Porter in November 1863 a new building program of "about 30 men-of-war privateers from 2,000 to 3,000 tons and 15 knots speed, so in case with a war with England, we need not roam the ocean, but keep them in the mouth of the English, where their speed will insure their safety." These veritable "Super-*Alabama*s" evolved into the *Wampanoag*-class screw-sloops; the lead ship achieving 17.75 knots in her sea trials of 1868—the fastest warship in the world; 3-11-1863, Fox to Porter, *Official Records of the Union and Confederate Navies in the War of the Rebellion*, 30 vols., (hereafter "*ORN*"), 1: 25, 529–530.

11. Brougham Villiers and W. H. Chesson, *Anglo-American Relations 1861–1865* (London: T. Fisher Unwin: 1919), 30–31; see also James M. McPherson, "'The Whole Family of Man': Lincoln and the Last Best Hope Abroad," in May (ed.) *The Union, the Confederacy and the Atlantic Rim*, 131–158.

12. 16-5-1861, *New York Herald*.

13. 6-7-1861, *Punch*; Herbert Mitgang (ed.), *Edward Dicey's Spectator of America* (Chicago: 1971; reprint of *Six Months in the Federal States*, 1863), 20.

14. 22-6-1861, *Harper's Weekly*, 386.

15. Echoed by the *New York Herald*; for example, 28-6-1861, "Magnificent Future of the United States." For Seward's "foreign war panacea" see Norman B. Ferris, *Desperate Diplomacy: William H. Seward's Foreign Policy* (Knoxville: University of Tennessee Press, 1976), especially 6–13, 60–62, 91–92; also Glyndon G. Van Deusen, *William Henry Seward* (New York: Oxford University Press, 1967), 247–248, 281–282, 292–302; Ephraim Douglas Adams, *Great Britain and the American Civil War*, 2 vols. (New York: Russell & Russell, 1925), 1: 118–119, 124–136, 154–155; Mahin, *One War At a Time*, 5–8, 14, 50–51; and Bourne, *Britain*, 210–214, 254. For a broader, British-based perspective see also George L. Bernstein, "Special Relationship and Appeasement: Liberal Policy Towards America in the Age of Palmerston," *Historical Journal*, Vol. 41, No. 3 (1998), 725–750, especially 742–743. By August 1864 Seward was still convinced that "in the event of such a war, the alliance of Great Britain with the south would reunite this country and impart new vigor to this government," especially since "the American people, even in their present disturbed condition, would accept a war forced upon them by Great Britain less reluctantly than they would have done at any previous period since 1815." Seward to Adams, August 1, 1864, *Diplomatic Correspondence*, No. 1054, 264.

16. Charles Francis Adams, *An Address on the Life, Character and Services of William Henry Seward* (Albany, NY: Weed, Parsons, 1873), 49–50.

17. Executive Document No. 1, 37th Congress, 1st Session, *Message of the President of the United States to the Two Houses of Congress*, July 4, 1861, 1–11. See also Irving H. Bartlett, *The American Mind in the Mid-Nineteenth Century* (London: Routledge & Kegan Paul, 1968), 70–72. Opposed to this were the "pro-monarchy sentiments" of South Carolinians that William Russell confided to John T. Delane, the editor of the *Times*, 16-7-1861; from Martin Crawford (ed.), *William Howard Russell's Civil War: Private Diaries and Letters, 1861–1862* (Athens: University of Georgia Press, 1992), 89.

18. 7-4-1861, Report of the Secretary of the Navy, 90.

19. Report of the Secretary of the Navy, 96. Captain Gustavus Vasa Fox, also the newly appointed Assistant Secretary of the Navy, testified before the Joint Committee on the Conduct of the War on March 19, 1862, that "this matter of iron-clad vessels was brought up by the department a year ago, and Congress was asked for an appropriation of $50,000 in July to test the different kinds of plating, which was refused. We went to the President and he held a meeting at General [Winfield] Scott's office, and we were authorized to go ahead, without waiting for Congress, and make these iron plates. But when we came to call for proposals, which we did without authority from Congress, we ran against this difficulty— that there was a limit to the making of these vessels. There is no preparation for making the plates in this country, except by forging them, which is altogether too slow and tedious for the necessity. There is but one rolling mill in the country that can make the plates by rolling, and that is the one that made the plates for the *Monitor*." *Report of the Joint Committee on the Conduct of the War*, 3 vols., 37th Congress, 3rd Session, 1863, "Monitor and Merrimack," 3: 416.

20. See 24-7-1861, McKay to Smith, and 25-7-1861, Smith to Bushnell, RG 45, Entry 464, Box 49.

21. Formulated by General Winfield Scott at the beginning of the Civil War, the Union's derisively nicknamed "Anaconda" would (too) slowly strangle the Confederate States into submission with a continental-scale blockade, while Union land and naval forces further cut off the South, East from West, by gaining control of the Mississippi River.

22. Quoted from Baxter, *Introduction*, 246.

23. "Of what avail would be the 'steam guard-ships' if attacked on the new system? Alas! for the 'wooden walls' that formerly 'ruled the waves.' The long-range Lancaster gun would scarcely hit the revolving turret once in six hours, and then, six chances to one, its shot and shell would be deflected by the varying angles of the face of the impregnable globe." Quoted by Ericsson from his original proposal in John Ericsson, *Contributions to the Centennial Exhibition* (New York: The Nation Press, 1876), 410–416.

24. 29-8-1861, Ericsson to Lincoln, Ericsson Papers, Philadelphia.

25. 7-9-1861, Bushnell to Delamater, Ericsson Papers, Philadelphia. Lincoln took a keen personal interest in all "high-tech" weapons of the Civil War, including the most sophisticated and expensive of all, the monitors. While his ship was undergoing minor repairs at the Washington Navy Yard in December 1862, Captain Percival Drayton wrote of Lincoln visiting the U.S.S. *Passaic* with Secretary of the Treasury Salmon P. Chase, "the former went everywhere[,] crawled into

places that Gerald or Henry would scarce have ventured in, and gave us a funny story or two in illustration of the incidents of the occasion"; 9-12-1862, Drayton to Lydig. M. Hoyt, *Naval Letters*, 21. The President also visited the original *Monitor* during the height of the Peninsula Campaign; see William Marvel (ed.), *The* Monitor *Chronicles: One Sailor's Account: Today's Campaign to Recover the Civil War Wreck* (New York: Simon & Schuster, 2000), 62–64, 67.

26. William Conant Church, *The Life of John Ericsson*, 2 vols. (New York: Charles Scribner's Sons, 1890), 1: 92–96, 101–109, 117–151.

27. Church, *Life of Ericsson*, 1: 250.

28. 11-9-1861, Bushnell to Ericsson, Ericsson Papers, Philadelphia.

29. Church, *Life of Ericsson*, 1: 253.

30. Curiously, Dahlgren declined to serve on the Board with Commodores Joseph Smith and Hiram Paulding; Baxter, *Introduction*, 247.

31. As Donald Canney observes, however, the Navy's August 7, 1861, advertisement for ironclad submissions specified "not less than ten or over sixteen feet draught of water"; *The Ironclads*, 8–9. Naval constructor Samuel Pook noted there was "an advantage in the use of small vessel for lightness of draught to carry a heavier armament in proportion to their dimensions, and the increased cost of construction"; 12-11-1861, Pook to Smith, RG 45, Entry 464, Box 49.

32. 16-9-1861, Ironclad Board to Welles, RG 45, Letters Rec'd.

33. Ibid.

34. 16-9-1861, Ironclad Board to Welles, Welles Papers, LOC.

35. Ibid.

36. 21-5-1861, Seward to Adams, from George E. Baker (ed.), *The Works of William Seward*, 5 vols. (Boston: Houghton Mifflin, 1884), 5: 244–245; 24-6-1861, Lewis to Sir Edmund Head, from Lewis (ed.), *Letters*, 397–398; Baker (ed.), *Works*, 280–286.

37. James Tertius DeKay, *Monitor: The Story of the Legendary Civil War Ironclad and the Man Whose Invention Changed the Course of History* (Pimlico: Random House, 1999), 73. DeKay deduces Sept. 20 as the date of his initial presentation of Ericsson's monitor model at Welles's house, but this is well after the report of the Ironclad Board itself. September 5 is therefore more likely. See Church, *Life of Ericsson*, 1: 249; Canney, *The Ironclads*, 25. John Murray Forbes also noted to Fox his "original idea with which I have bored you so much & which I broached to the President in *April 61* that the sea belongs to us, & ought to be made our chief dependence for putting down the Rebels & keeping the foreign bull dogs peaceable"; 19-11-1862, Forbes to Fox, Fox Papers, New York, Box 3.

Chapter 6

1. 2-10-1861, Ericsson to Smith, RG 45, Entry 464, AD, Box 49.

2. 4-10-1861, Bushnell to Smith, RG 45, Entry 464, AD, Box 49.

3. 9-10-1861, Winslow to Ericsson, Ericsson Papers, Philadelphia.

4. 25-9-1861, Smith to Ericsson, Ericsson Papers, Philadelphia; 27-9-1861, Ericsson to Smith, RG 45, Entry 464, AD, Box 49.

5. 4-10-1861, Ericsson to Smith; 8-10-1861, Ericsson to Smith, RG 45, Entry 464, AD, Box 49.

6. 18-10-1861, Ericsson to Smith, RG 45, Entry 464, AD, Box 49.

7. 8-10-1861, Ericsson to Smith, RG 45, Entry 464, AD, Box 49.

8. Though "the entire vessel is but a piece of mechanism, built for specific objects," Stimers enthusiastically wrote to Dahlgren, the armament would in some degree still have to be modified for the weapons platform, rather than vice versa. Ericsson and Chief Engineer Stimers preferred the barrels of the 11-inch Dahlgrens eventually assigned to the *Monitor* to be shortened by 18 inches. Since the ironclad was intended for short-range actions, added range would be a secondary concern to easier loading and greater rate of fire. 6-11-1861, Stimers to Dahlgren, Dahlgren Papers, LOC.

9. TNA/ADM 1/5941, 29-3-1865; the enclosed report of the Ordnance Select Committee is dated 27-2-1865.

10. 8-10-1861, Ericsson to Smith, RG 45, Entry 464, AD, Box 49; 11-10-1861, Smith to Harwood, RG 74, Entry 16, Box 4, Letterbook, 10; 13-10-1861, Ericsson to Smith, 12-10-1861; Smith to Ericsson, RG 45, Entry 464, AD, Box 49; 19-10-1861, Smith to Welles, RG 71, Entry 1, Vol. 74, Letterbook, 126–127.

11. 11-10-1861, Smith to Ericsson, Ericsson Papers, Philadelphia.

12. 14-10-1861, Ericsson to Smith; 16-10-1861, Ericsson to Smith, RG 45, Entry 464, AD, Box 49. Ericsson was also worried the plans for the *Monitor* were leaked, but Smith assured him that the "naval architects" in question were, in fact, those of the Bureau of Construction & Repair (namely John Lenthall), 16-10-1861, Smith to Ericsson, Ericsson Papers, Philadelphia.

13. 14-10-1861, Smith to Ericsson, Ericsson Papers, Philadelphia.

14. 16-10-1861, Smith to Ericsson, Ericsson Papers, Philadelphia. Smith later explained to Chief Engineer Alban C. Stimers (recently assigned to superintend for the Navy the *Monitor*'s construction) that he had "pressed the Department so urgently to have the XI inch Dahlgren guns ready that one has been taken off the *Pensacola*, and another, the only one at the Navy Yard. . . . The foundries have been so engaged that new guns could not be made in time." 15-11-1861, Smith to Stimers, RG 45, Entry 464, AD, Box 51.

15. 17-10-1861, Ericsson to Smith, RG 45, Entry 464, AD, Box 49.

16. See 18-10-1861, Ericsson to Smith, RG 45, Entry 464, AD, Box 49.

17. 12-3-1862, *National Intelligencer.*

18. "Necessarily the specification," Ericsson explained to Smith, "considering the novel character of the work, could not be accurate in matters of detail, as it is not until the actual working plan is made out that precision is attained." 23-10-1861, RG 45, Entry 464, AD, Box 49.

19. 18-10-1861, Ericsson to Smith, RG 45, Entry 464, AD, Box 49.

20. 21-10-1861, Bushnell to Smith, RG 45, Entry 464, AD, Box 49; 21-10-1861, Smith to Ericsson, RG 45, Entry 464, AD, Box 51; 26-10-1861, Smith to Ericsson, Ericsson Papers, Philadelphia.

Chapter 7

1. 16-11-1861, Ericsson to Smith, RG 45, Entry 464, AD, Box 49; 18-11-1861, Smith to Ericsson, RG 45, Entry 464, AD, Box 51; 20-11-1861, Ericsson to Smith, RG 45, Entry 464, AD, Box 49.

2. 16-11-1861, *Scientific American*, 313. The "five" ironclads noted, but still unnamed, were the *Monitor, Galena, New Ironsides*, the perpetually incomplete "Stevens Battery," and the recently contracted *E. A. Stevens*, or converted Coast Guard steamer *Naugatuck*. See Canney, *The Ironclads*, 73–74, on the *Naugatuck*.

3. February 1862, *Blackwood's Edinburgh Magazine*, 228.

4. 19-10-1861, *Harper's Weekly*; and 2-11-1861, 690–691. By Dec. 21 *Harper's* was perhaps unconsciously pairing—in the same issue—the graphic specter of European intervention in the form of the Allied fleet appearing over the horizon to punish Mexico (brushing aside the pretensions of the Monroe Doctrine) and Ericsson's "Battery."

5. 7-12-1861, *Punch*, 234.

6. *Blackwood's Edinburgh Magazine*, October 1861, No. DLII, Vol. XC, "Democracy Teaching by Example," 405. See also William Howard Russell's 14-10-1861 letter to Charles Sumner, stating that "in England we are threatened by Americanization [*sic*] which to our islands would be anarchy & ruin, & the troubles in America afford our politicians & writers easy means of dealing deadly blows at Brightism which is often attacked under the guise of the war & the troubles in America," in Crawford, *William Howard Russell's Civil War*, 153–156.

7. Entry dated 6-12-1861; from Crawford, *William Howard Russell's Civil War*, 198.

8. 16-11-1861, *New York Herald*, "The Effect in England of the Naval Victory in South Carolina." This was a forlorn hope in the age of Palmerston; see R. B. McDowell, *British Conservatism 1832–1914* (London: Faber and Faber, 1959), 75–84; Blackett, *Divided Hearts*, 61. W. L. Burn noted that "the unruffled calm" of the mid-Victorian generation "was not deliberately planned or contrived. It was the outcome of a temporary balance of forces; but of forces struggling, pushing, shoving to better their positions. An ant-hill can look very smooth and quiescent from twenty yards away." *The Age of Equipoise: A Study of the Mid-Victorian Generation* (New York: W. W. Norton & Company, 1965), 82.

9. 30-5-1861, Lyons to Malmesbury, from Lord Newton (ed.), *Lord Lyons: A Record of British Diplomacy*, 2 vols. (London: Edward Arnold, 1913), 1:16; 15-8-1861, Minute of Lord Palmerston, 1:48. As Martin Crawford notes in his study *The Anglo-American Crisis of the Mid-Nineteenth Century*, the "*Times's* reaction to Lincoln's inaugural reflected both its current uncertainty over Republican policy and its long-held suspicion of executive weakness in the United States," 91.

10. "A Field Night in the House of Commons," *Atlantic Monthly*, December 1861, Vol. 8, No. 50, 672–673.

11. G. H. L. Le May, *The Victorian Constitution: Conventions, Usages and Contingencies* (London: Duckworth, 1979), 121.

12. Charles Francis Adams, *An Address on the Life, Character and Services of William Henry Seward* (Albany: Weed, Parsons and Company, 1873), 66–67.

13. 6-3-1862, *National Intelligencer*.

14. 26-1-1862, Palmerston to Sulivan, from Kenneth Bourne (ed.), *The Letters of the Third Viscount Palmerston to Laurence and Elizabeth Sulivan*

1804–1863 (London: Royal Historical Society, 1979), 319; quoted from Norman B. Ferris, *The* Trent *Affair: A Diplomatic Crisis* (Knoxville: University of Tennessee Press, 1977), 194, ff. 6; 197–198.

15. 23-11-1862, *New York Herald*.

16. 1-1-1862, Oliver Batcheller to his mother, Batcheller Letters, U.S. Naval Academy.

17. 25-11-1861, John Hooker to Welles, Welles Papers, LOC. 16-12-1861, Barnard to Welles, Welles Papers, LOC. The same proposal and sentiment, from Buffalo, New York, can be found in 16-12-1861, Millard Fillmore to Lincoln, Lincoln Papers, LOC.

18. 21-12-1861, *New York Herald*; Herman Melville, "Donelson" (part of *Battle Pieces*), from Stanton Garner, *The Civil War World of Herman Melville* (Lawrence: University Press of Kansas, 1993), 129; 17-1-1862, Batcheller to his mother, Batcheller Letters, U.S. Naval Academy. Reflecting back on the *Trent* affair in 1864, Lincoln reportedly thought at the time "that if this nation should happen to get well we might want that old grudge against England to stand." Horace Porter, *Campaigning with Grant* (New York: Da Capo Press, 1986; reprint of Century, 1897), 409.

19. 29-12-1861, *New York Herald*. See also Frederic W. Seward, *Reminiscences of a Wartime Statesman and Diplomat, 1830–1915* (New York: G. P. Putnam's Sons, 1916), 188–191.

20. 28-12-1861, *Scientific American*, 407. Some U.S. naval officers were skeptical of this. In the event of an Anglo-American maritime war, "I see we could do nothing," Captain Percival Drayton wrote to Dahlgren. "Steam places [Britain's] navy in a position of superiority that she never has occupied, and has killed Privateering dead dead [*sic*], first because the privateers could not get coal, and next they could never get a prize in when taken. With our imperfect blockade the Sumpter [*sic*] has not succeeded in doing so." 10-1-1862, Drayton to Dahlgren, Dahlgren Papers, LOC.

21. 28-12-1861, *Scientific American*, 407; also 11-1-1862, 18-1-1862, and 25-1-1862.

22. 11-11-1861, Smith to Ericsson, Ericsson Papers, LOC.

23. 7-11-1861, Smith to Bushnell, RG 45, Entry 464, AD, Box 51.

24. 17-11-1861, Welles to son (possibly Tom), Welles Papers, LOC.

25. Gideon Welles, "The Capture and Release of Mason and Slidell," *The Galaxy*, Vol. 7 (May 1873). "What a howl there will be among the rebel press of the South, on account of the settlement of the *Trent* affair," noted the Terre-Haute *Daily Express* of 31-12-1861. "A war between England and the United States would have been a grand diversion in their favor, but now that hope being blasted, they are left to the last, lingering, feeble one, that the South may be able to become a province of England." From Lincoln Papers, LOC.

26. 21-12-1861, John to Anne Rodgers, Rodgers Papers, LOC.

27. Welles, "Capture," 648.

28. 19-12-1861, *Congressional Globe*, 147.

29. 17-12-1861, *Congressional Globe*, 123.

30. Baxter, *Introduction*, 250–252, 263–264, 275–276.

31. 19-12-1861, *Congressional Globe*, 148. Bending thicker armor plates was itself problematic. Heating them for the purpose was a more labor-intensive,

time-consuming, and expensive process, while "cold-bending" them with special heavy presses, according to tests conducted by the British Iron Plate Committee, tended to damage the weld of the plates themselves and weaken their resisting powers. See TNA/WO 33/13, *Transactions and Report of the Special Committee on Iron, 1863* (War Office, 1864), including Secretary Captain A. Harrison, R.A., "Bending Armour Plates," dated 23-5-1863. On Jan. 21, 1862, Samuel Pook wrote to Commodore Smith that the armoring of the *Galena* was "now going on more rapidly than it has at any time before . . . principally because the bars are now all bent and twisted by a wooden lever, instead of being heated and bent, as was first deemed necessary." RG 45, Entry 464, AD, Box 51.The *Monitor*'s 1-inch laminated iron plates could also be cold-bent, and their more concentrated welds were perhaps individually less subject to strain. For a description of the armor plate press for the monitors in *Harper's Weekly* see Canney, *Lincoln's Navy*, 87–88. For an illustration of a British press see the *Illustrated London News*, 10-1-1863, 36. A description of armor plate manufacture at the Continental Iron Works of Thomas F. Rowland, however, given by *Scientific American*, suggested the turret plates of the *Passaic*-class monitors at least were heated and then bent; 8-11-1862, 298.

32. 10-12-1861, Whitney to Smith; 11-12-1861, Smith to Whitney, RG 45, Entry 464, AD, Box 51.

33. At any rate, Smith found recent shavings from the 4½-inch (hammered) plates "made from scraps," being made for the *New Ironsides*, indicated "great toughness and tenacity." 5-12-1861, Smith to Whitney, RG 45, Entry 464, AD, Box 51.

34. See for example 9-12-1861, Joseph G. Totten (U.S. Army Brevet Brigadier General and Colonel of Engineers) to Simon Cameron (Secretary of War), in Executive Document No. 6, House of Representatives, 37th Congress, 2nd Session, *Estimates for Fortifications*, 1–5.

35. 19-12-1861, Executive Document No. 14, House of Representatives, 37th Congress, 2nd Session, *Fortification of the Sea-Coast and Lakes—Message from the President of the United States*, 1–8.

Chapter 8

1. See Baxter, *Introduction*, 279–280.

2. 8-1-1862, *Congressional Globe*, 219–221.

3. Frank M. Bennett, *The Steam Navy of the United States* (Westport, CT: Greenwood Press, reprint of 1896), 280–281, 337–338.

4. 8-1-1862, Griswold to Ericsson, Ericsson Papers, Philadelphia.

5. "I think the wrought iron shot of the Ericsson Battery will smash in her [the *Merrimac*'s] 2¼ inch plates," Smith wrote Ericsson, "provided she can get near enough to hers, whilst the IX inch Shot and shells of the Merrimac will not upset your Turret. Let us have the test as *soon as possible*, for that ship [the *Merrimac*] will be a troublesome customer to our vessels in Hampton Roads," 29-1-1862, Smith to Ericsson, Ericsson Papers, Philadelphia.

6. 8-1-1862, Griswold to Ericsson, Ericsson Papers, Philadelphia.

7. For a more complete look at Fox's career as Assistant Secretary see William J. Sullivan, "Gustavus Vasa Fox and Naval Administration," Catholic University of America, unpublished Ph.D. thesis, 1977.

8. See Baxter, *Introduction*, appendices, 350–360.

9. 31-1-1862, Daniel B. Martin to Smith, RG 19, Entry 61, Box 1.

10. 28-1-1862, Barnard to Fox, Memo, David Dixon Porter Family Papers, LOC.

11. 14-1-1862, Smith to Ericsson, RG 45, Entry 464, AD, Box 51; 4-10-1861, Ericsson to Smith, RG 45, Entry 464, AD, Box 49; 21-1-1862, Stimers to Smith, with Smith's endorsement included, RG 45, Entry 464, AD, Box 51.

12. 13-1-1862, Worden to Smith, *ORN*, ser. 1, vol. 6, 516–517.

13. See William N. Still, Jr., Monitor *Builders: A Historical Study of the Principal Firms and Individuals Involved in the Construction of USS* Monitor (Washington, DC: Department of the Interior, 1988), especially 24–26.

14. 24-1-1862, Stimers to Smith, RG 45, Entry 464, AD, Box 51. The *Monitor* was launched on the morning of Jan. 30, 1862.

15. Reprinted, with Welles's reply in 8-2-1862, *Congressional Globe*, 697.

16. See for example William H. Roberts, "'The Name of Ericsson': Political Engineering in the Union Ironclad Program, 1861–1863", *Journal of Military History*, Vol. 63, No. 4 (1999), reflecting the bitter contemporary suspicions of Captain Thomas Turner of the U.S.S. *New Ironsides*; see 7-5-1863, Turner to John Andrew (Governor Massachusetts), Hamilton Fish Papers, LOC.

17. Parkes, like Baxter, seems to have overlooked this factor in assessing the two designs. H.M.S. *Prince Albert*, Britain's first purpose-built turret ship, indeed "marks an epoch in British naval construction as important as was the appearance of the *Warrior*," yet pound for pound a monitor could safely mount the heaviest ordnance possible—trained by steam—behind the heaviest proportion of armor. Each of *Prince Albert*'s four Coles-turrets required 18 men to rotate by hand, men who were protected not by the turret armor but 4.5 inches of iron backed by teak on the broadside and only ¾-inch plating around the bow and stern. Parkes, *British Battleships*, 46, 71–72; also Baxter, *Introduction*, 326–329.

18. See for example John Niven, *Gideon Welles: Lincoln's Secretary of War* (Baton Rouge, LA, 1994 reprint), 424–425; and David Mindell, *War, Technology, and Experience Aboard the U.S.S.* Monitor (Baltimore: John Hopkins University Press, 2000), 38–41, 115, and 142, where he concludes that "the legend of the *Monitor* emerged from a blend of contemporary reporting, public debate, and historical commemoration." See also the arguments found in the work of William H. Roberts, namely USS New Ironsides *in the Civil War* (Annapolis, MD: Naval Institute Press, 1999) and *Civil War Ironclads: The U.S. Navy and Industrial Mobilization* (Baltimore: John Hopkins University Press, 2002).

19. Still notes that "Charles H. Cramp, who owned extensive shipbuilding facilities in Philadelphia, wrote in his memoirs of a New York 'ring' presumably involving Admiral Gregory and other naval officers responsible for warship construction in the country, as well as influential civilians. He accused the 'ring' of preventing 'the construction of a type of iron clad vessel except monitors,' and of concentrating warship construction, especially armored

vessels, in New York City." Yet most prewar iron shipbuilding, Still continues, was concentrated in New York City. Ericsson's backers, especially John Griswold, did have political influence. "Nevertheless, there is no evidence that a New York ring existed. Of the 27 monitors contracted before 1863, 20 were built outside New York City, and naval officers in Washington, particularly . . . Fox, were most responsible for concentrating on the monitor type." Still, Monitor *Builders,* 29.

20. 8-2-1862, *Congressional Globe,* 697.

21. 20-1-1862, Ericsson to Fox, quoted from Ericsson, *Contributions,* 465–466 (emphasis mine).

22. 8-2-1862, *Congressional Globe,* 697.

23. See for example 4-2-1862, *Congressional Globe,* 620–621.

24. 1-3-1862, Fox to Goldsborough, *ORN,* ser. 1, vol. 6, 624.

25. 24-2-1862, Fox to Porter, Porter Papers, LOC.

26. 21-2-1862, Marston to Welles, RG 45, Entry 15.

27. 12-2-1862, *Congressional Globe,* 762.

28. J. B. Jones, *A Rebel War Clerk's Diary at the Confederate States Capital,* 2 vols. (Philadelphia: J. B. Lippincott & Co., 1866; 1982 Time-Life Books reprint), 1: 93, entry dated 17 November 1861.

29. *Letter Addressed by the Royal Commissioners on National Defences to the Secretary of State for War, Relative to the Proposed Substitution of Iron-Cased Vessels for the Forts at Spithead* (London: George Edward Eyre and William Spottiswoode, 1861), 3–11; see WO 33–10.

30. 23-12-1861, Ericsson to Welles, quoted from Baxter, *Introduction,* "Appendix G," 358–359.

31. Reflected in Alfred T. Mahan's praise of David Farragut "in recognizing that the rage for material advance, though a good thing, carries with it the countervailing disposition to rely upon perfected material rather than upon accomplished warriors to decide the issue of battle," Mahan, *Admiral Farragut,* 286, 324.

Chapter 9

1. As James McPherson points out, this was "more than the navy suffered on any other day of the war" and "a feat no other enemy would accomplish until 1941." *Battle Cry of Freedom,* 176. Donald Canney adds that "the circumstances were extraordinary: the survivors attest to the helplessness of both wooden vessels and their hapless crews in the face of an impersonal and impenetrable iron behemoth. The trauma of 8 March 1862 would haunt the Union navy for the remainder of the war." *Lincoln's Navy,* 218.

2. Beale, *Diary,* 1: 61–67.

3. See 7-4-1862, Mallory to Davis, *ORN,* ser. 1, vol. 7, 43.

4. See Lee's subsequent 9-11-1861 report to Benjamin, *ORN,* ser. 1, vol. 12, 299–300.

5. Fox had written to Lincoln on March 4, however, that the *Monitor's* trials were complete and she was on her way to Hampton Roads; 4-3-1862, Fox to Lincoln, Lincoln Papers, LOC. Confederate President Davis was urged to

use the *Virginia* offensively, up the Potomac if she were lightened enough; 28-2-1862, Douglas F. Forrest to Davis, *ORN*, ser. 1, vol. 7, 737–739.

6. 8-3-1862, telegram, W.D. Whipple, Assistant Adjutant-General to Major-General Wool, *ORN*, ser. 1, vol. 7, 5.

7. *ORN*, ser. 1, vol. 7, 6.

8. *ORN*, ser. 1, vol. 7, 7.

9. 9-3-1862, telegram, Fox to Welles, *ORN*, ser. 1, vol. 7, 7.

10. For the C.S.S. *Virginia*, this consisted of two layers of rolled iron armor plate, each 2 inches thick, angled at 38° and supported by oak and pine. In response to Lincoln's inquiry as to whether the *Virginia* could ascend the Potomac and attack Washington, Dahlgren replied that only a vessel drawing less than 22 feet might reach the city, and that he was mounting his sole 11-inch gun at Giesboro Point to protect the arsenal, at a range of 50 yards from any passing vessel. "Shot of 170 pounds at 50 or 100 yards will be apt to do something." 9-3-1862, telegram, Dahlgren to Lincoln, *ORN*, ser. 1, vol. 7, 76–78.

11. The "performance, power, and capabilities of the *Monitor*," Welles wrote to Worden, "must effect a radical change in naval warfare." What this might involve the Secretary did not specify; he noted only that Worden's vessel with only two guns had repelled "a powerful armored steamer of at least eight guns" and that this action had "excited general admiration and received the applause of the whole country." 15-3-1862, Welles to Worden, *ORN*, ser. 1, vol. 7, 38. Iowa Senator James Grimes asserted he knew "that a great revolution has taken place in our defenses" but did "not know where it is going to end. I believe that it will end in a complete reorganization of our Army and Navy." *Congressional Globe*, 37th Congress, 2nd Session, No. 88, 27-3-1862, 1397.

12. 10-3-1862, Charles W. Homer, Gunner, to Captain G. J. Van Brunt, *ORN*, ser. 1, vol. 7; also 10-3-1862, Brunt to Welles, *ORN*, ser. 1, vol. 7, 11–12. The *Monitor* later reported firing "forty-one solid cast-iron shot in her engagement with the *Merrimack*, equally divided between guns 27 and 28." 16-3-1862, Lieutenant William Jeffers to Goldsborough, *ORN*, ser. 1, vol. 7, 28.

13. Major-General Benjamin Huger, Commander of the Confederate Department of Norfolk, recognized the long-term problem, however: "As the enemy can build such boats faster than we, they could, when so prepared, overcome any place accessible by water. How these powerful machines are to be stopped is a problem I can not solve. At present, in the *Virginia*, we have the advantage; but we can not tell how long this may last." 10-3-1862, Huger to General S. Cooper, Adjutant and Inspector General, *ORN*, ser. 1, vol. 7, 54–55.

14. 9-3-1862, telegram, McClellan to Wool; 10-3-1862, telegram, Wool to McClellan, *ORN*, ser. 1, vol. 7, 75–76, 84.

15. 11-3-1862, telegram, Fox to Welles, *ORN*, ser. 1, vol. 7, 91–92.

16. 11-3-1862, telegram, Fox to Wise, *ORN*, ser. 1, vol. 7, 92.

17. See the original 11-3-1862 telegram, from Fox to Dahlgren, found in the Dahlgren Papers.

18. 11-3-1862, Dahlgren to Fox, *ORN*, ser. 1, vol. 7, 92–93. Both the 15-inch smoothbore gun and a rifled 12-inch were being tested at Fortress Monroe. "Since the recent naval engagement, it is thought that nothing can stop the

Merrimack here except the *Monitor* and the big guns (the 15-inch and 12-inch). General Wool is desirous of having both of these guns mounted on the beach and plenty of ammunition for them as soon as possible." 11-3-1862, T. G. Baylor, First Lieutenant of Ordnance, to Ripley, *ORN*, ser. 1, vol. 7, 93–94. Nicknamed "Floyd," the 15-inch prototype was ordered by Stanton to be renamed the "Lincoln Gun"; 11-3-1862, telegram, Stanton to Wool, *ORN*, ser. 1., vol. 7, 94.

19. 7-3-1862, Dahlgren to Fox, Dahlgren Papers, LOC.

20. 17-3-1862, Dahlgren to Harwood, RG 74, Entry 201, Item 5, Box 2. Dahlgren quickly added, "Of course I would not be understood as wishing to depreciate the high merit of the projector and builder of the Monitor which so astonishingly endured the brunt of the Merrimack's fire." 12-3-1862, telegram, Ericsson to Fox, *ORN*, ser. 1, vol. 7, on aiming at the *Virginia*'s waterline.

21. "Now comes the reign of iron—and cased ships are to take the place of wooden ships and Stone Forts—Battering Rams to stand in lieu of Ordnance," from Dahlgren's curious history-essay, dated "March 8, 1862" but nevertheless finished later. Dahlgren somewhat unfairly comments, "Upon the untried endurances of the *Monitor*, and her timely arrival did depend the tide of events—Two circumstances which in the particular case amounted to Accidents." In another sense, both the *Monitor*'s defensive capabilities and her immediate deployment to Hampton Roads were by design.

22. See 7-10-1861, Dahlgren to Welles, RG 74, Entry 201, Item 5, Box 2, for Dahlgren's proposal to convert the screw-gunboat U.S.S. *Pawnee* with iron plating "not less than 2 inches thick, nor more than 3 inches." This would "extend along the sides of the section where the body of the vessel begins to fall off into the fine lines of the ends, the extremes of the side plating to be connected across the interior by a transverse partition of plating." See Canney, *Lincoln's Navy*, 66–67, for a description of the *Pawnee*, originally armed with four 11-inch pivots but eventually changed to house twelve 9-inch broadside guns. See 16-10-1861, Dahlgren to Harwood, RG 74, Entry 201, Item 5, Box 2, for his suggestion to partially armor double-ender gunboats.

23. 14-3-1862, Ericsson to Fox, Fox Papers, New York, Box 3. "From the new suggestion in Congress on the subject of gunboats," Sargent wrote to Ericsson, "it would seem to me that they have been trying to steal your thunder—and I only hope that they will not spoil it in the Stealing." Only low-freeboard ironclads could protect their machinery from penetrative hits. 7-3-1862, Sargent to Ericsson, Ericsson Papers, LOC; 12-3-1862, telegram, Ericsson to Fox, *ORN*, ser. 1, vol. 7.

24. 9-3-1862, Stimers to Ericsson, *ORN*, ser. 1, vol.7, 26–27.

25. 17-3-1862, Stimers to Smith, *ORN*., ser. 1, vol. 7, 27.

26. 13-3-1862, Lenthall to Welles, RG 19, Entry 50.

27. See the problems Lenthall faced, for example, when trying to procure the 4½-inch plates for the *Roanoke* conversion; 24-6-1862, Lenthall to Welles, RG 45, Letters Rec'd. Thomas Rowland of the Continental Iron Works at Green Point directly complained that the cost of fitting Ericsson's lighter plates bore "no comparison . . . with that of applying 4½ in. plates to the side of a hull, when said plates are obliged to have compound curves. . . ." In his view, "few Engineers in this country have a proper conception of the difficulties to be surmounted, and the expenses which must necessarily be increased,

in cladding the sides of any of our Steam Frigates. . ." See also 1-1-1862, *Scientific American*, 277.

28. 13-3-1862, Ericsson to Fox, Fox Papers, New York, Box 3.

Chapter 10

1. 15-3-1862, Ericsson to Fox, Fox Papers, New York, Box 3.

2. 18-3-1862, Fox to Ericsson, Fox Papers, New York, Box 5.

3. 19-3-1862, Ericsson to Fox, Fox Papers, New York, Box 3.

4. 20-3-1862, Fox to Ericsson, Ericsson Papers, LOC.

5. 22-3-1862, Fox to Ericsson, Ericsson Papers, LOC; 24-3-1862, Fox to Ericsson, Fox Papers, New York, Box 5. Four years later Fox would have his chance for a more polite exchange of strength.

6. 22-3-1862, Ericsson to Fox, Fox Papers, New York, Box 3.

7. 25-3-1862, Dahlgren to Fox; and Ericsson to Fox, Fox Papers, New York, Box 3.

8. 29-3-1862, *Scientific American*, 203. See also Ericsson's quote on page 194. Ericsson wrote to Fox it was his "duty yesterday to kill, if possible, the scheme of building a Monitor for the harbor. I offended several of our great men here, but I feel I have served the country by preventing an imperfect thing from being got up at the moment when the strong arm of the government, directed by skill like your own, is carrying the new system into practice," referring to even more ambitious free-ranging versions; 19-3-1862, Ericsson to Fox, Fox Papers, New York, Box 3.

9. 19-3-1862, Samuel to Sophie Du Pont, from John D. Hayes (ed.), *Samuel Francis Du Pont: A Selection from his Civil War Letters*, 3 vols. (Ithaca:, NY Cornell University Press), 1: 372.

10. 17-3-1862, Morgan to Ericsson, Ericsson Papers, Philadelphia. See also 15-3-1862, S. H. Sweet, Deputy State Engineer and Surveyor, to Commodore Joseph Smith, on possible ironclads for canal transport; and Smith's subsequent telegram inquiry to B. H. Bartol, care of Merrick & Sons, Philadelphia, for building "the wood work of a gunboat two-hundred by forty-eight by twelve feet, in sixty days. Plates can be had in four weeks. Engines in sixty days," 15-3-1862, Smith to Bartol, RG 45, Entry 464, AD, Box 51.

11. 16-3-1862, Welles to son, Welles Papers, LOC. See *Scientific American*'s scathing criticisms of the Navy Department, RG 45, Entry 464, AD, Box 5. The 5-4-1862 issue redirected the attack from the Secretary to his "leading naval architects" and "bad advisors" (i.e., Lenthall and Isherwood).

12. 18-3-1862, *National Intelligencer*, "The Monitor, and Who Built Her."

13. 19-3-1862, Ericsson to Smith, RG 45, Entry 464, Box 51.

14. 27-4-1862, Paulding to Welles, Welles Papers, LOC. Paulding also wrote of his intention to clad the *Roanoke* with five 1-inch–thick plates in anticipation of the *Merrimack*, but gave up the project when told she would carry towers and solid 4½-inch–thick slabs. For Hale's detestation of a naval officer "clique, a sort of mutual admiration society, who made it their special business to puff one another up quite as much as they had to fight an enemy," see

8-7-1862, "Grades of Naval Officers," *Congressional Globe*, 3182. Welles also opposed naval officer cliques, an "evil I have striven to break up, and, with the assistance of Secession, which took off some of the worst cases, have thus far been pretty successful. But there are symptoms of it in the South Atlantic Squadron, though I hope it is not serious"; entry dated 2 October, Beale, *Diary*, 1: 160. For Welles's suspicion of Hale see Beale, *Diary*, 1: 186–187, entry dated 4-12-1862.

15. 13-3-1862, telegram, Meigs to Dahlgren, Dahlgren Papers, LOC.

16. See for example 24-3-1862, Stimers to Ericsson, Ericsson Papers, Philadelphia.

17. Admiral Spencer Robinson rejected plans "[t]o employ steam for raising the guns . . . for running them out, and checking their recoil; and for working the pinions in the circular racks so as to cause the tower to revolve," because "the whole apparatus" was "very complicated." "It seems apparent on inspecting the diagrams that there would be found great deficiency of stability in this system, especially in a seaway; and that it would be very liable to get out of working order"; 8-1-1863, Robinson to Board, "Plans for Cupola Ships, & for Manoeuvring Guns (W. E. Newton)," TNA/ADM 1/5840. Much of the problem with all steam machinery was a matter not of design complexity but of durability of individual parts. See for example 25-11-1862, Isherwood to Welles, RG 45, Letters Rec'd.

18. 17-3-1862, Lenthall and Isherwood to Welles, RG 45, Letters Rec'd.

19. 19-3-1862, Lenthall and Isherwood to Welles, R.G. 19, Entry 50.

20. 25-3-1862, Welles to Hale and Sedgwick, RG 45, Entry 5; and 37th Congress, Senate, Mis. Doc. No. 70, "Letter of the Secretary of the Navy," 1–3. Congress authorized only $25,000 for iron target tests; 3-4-1862, *Congressional Globe*, 1514.

21. 27-3-1862, *Congressional Globe*, 1393–1403. For a detailed description of the Stevens Battery of 1861–1862 see Canney, *The Ironclads*, 12–14.

22. 27-3-1862, *Congressional Globe*, 1393–1403.

23. 28-3-1862, *Congressional Globe*, 1418–1431. See also Baxter, *Introduction*, 211–219.

24. 26-3-1862, Welles to Smith, Lenthall, Isherwood, and Hart (possibly "Hartt"), RG 45, Entry 13; 26-3-1862, Dahlgren to Fox, RG 74, Entry 201, Item 5, Box 2. Smith's report to Welles, dated 9-4-1862, also mentioned engineer Daniel B. Martin as a board member; RG 45, Letters Rec'd.

25. 26-3-1862, Ericsson to Fox, also 28-3-1862, Fox to Ericsson, and 29-3-1862, Ericsson to Fox, Fox Papers, New York, Box 3, 5.

26. 1-4-1862, Ericsson to Fox, Ericsson Papers, Philadelphia.

27. 7-4-1862, Dahlgren to Harwood, RG 74, Entry 201, Item 5, Box 2. Harwood duly informed Welles that any further demands for guns of even greater caliber, etc., would have to be met in turn by "greater space in the turrets or other modifications in the plans of iron clad vessels"; 8-4-1862, Harwood to Welles, RG 45, Letters Rec'd.

28. 1-4-1862, Ericsson to Fox, Ericsson Papers, Philadelphia. There was also apparent confusion as to whether their armament would consist of 15- or 12-inch–caliber guns; see 5-4-1862, Smith to Welles, RG 45, Letters Rec'd.

29. 3-4-1862, Batcheller to his father, Batcheller Letters, U.S. Naval Academy.

30. 8-4-1862, Sargent to Ericsson, Ericsson Papers, LOC.

31. 4-4-1862, Smith to Dunham, RG 45, Entry 464, AD, Box 51.

32. 7-4-1862, Smith to Bushnell, RG 45, Entry 464, AD, Box 51.

33. 3-4-1862, Smith to Charles W. Whitney, RG 45, Entry 464, AD, Box 51.

34. 8-4-1862, Smith to Ericsson, Ericsson Papers, Philadelphia, RG 45, Entry 464, AD, Box 51.

35. 9-4-1862, Smith to Welles, RG 45, Letters Rec'd. Interestingly, Smith later called in Ericsson to assist with the problem of iron carriages and slides for the *New Ironsides'* broadside battery of sixteen 11-inch Dahlgrens; 17-4-1862, Smith to Ericsson, Ericsson Papers, Philadelphia. In 1865 Ericsson was asked to solve the same problem for the broadside battery of 15-inch guns for the U.S.S. *Dunderberg;* see for example 28-7-1865, Captain Percival Drayton to Gregory, RG 19, Entry 1240, Box 2.

36. 9-4-1862, Smith to Welles, RG 45, Letters Rec'd. "It is presumed that any instructions asked of you in constructing a Government boat," Welles wrote to Ericsson, "you will readily give, and on reasonable terms, to facilitate the speedy completion of [Western river] boats for the Navy." The Department did not expect Ericsson to charge a rumored "5 per cent, or $20,000 for each boat," though "[i]t would probably be justified in adopting the specifications your contract furnished, but would not do so without first consulting you and knowing your views, and assuring you of its interest and disposition to act in a liberal spirit towards you in all matters in which you are concerned in these premises." 22-4-1862, Welles to Ericsson, Ericsson Papers, Philadelphia.

37. 14-9-1862, Ericsson to S. B. Ruggles, Lincoln Papers, LOC. The draft of this letter found in the Ericsson Papers, LOC, specifies "put on the Lakes by England."

38. 11-4-1862, Smith to Ericsson, RG 45, Entry 464, AD, Box 51. Smith wrote the same to Whitney the following day; 12-4-1862, Smith to Whitney, RG 45, Entry 464, AD, Box 51.

39. 15-4-1862, Harwood to Welles, RG 45, Letters Rec'd. The idea of 12- as opposed to 15-inch guns may have stemmed from Ericsson himself, given his original "Oregon" gun for the U.S.S. *Princeton*—a banded, muzzle-loaded 12-inch–caliber gun of wrought iron. Oddly enough, on April 28 Dahlgren submitted tracings of a 13-inch gun to Fox, "the dimensions of which will suit the same Turrets as those intended to receive the XV in. guns"; Dahlgren Papers, LOC. "Captain Ericsson does not expect to mount either gun indifferently I suppose," he added four days later, "but to put one class in one Turret and another kind in another turret." If all the turret portholes were bored to fit 13-inch guns, Dahlgren felt, "it may not be difficult to enlarge it for the 15 in." 30-4-1862, Dahlgren to Fox, Fox Papers, New York, Box 3.

40. 15-4-1862, Fox to Ericsson, Fox Papers, New York, Box 5.

41. 15-4-1862, Fox to Ericsson, Fox Papers, New York; 16-4-1862, Ericsson to Fox, Fox Papers, New York.

42. 15-4-1862, Fox to Ericsson, Fox Papers, New York; 21-4-1862, Ericsson to Fox, Fox Papers, New York.

43. 23-4-1862, Ericsson to Seward, Ericsson Papers, Philadelphia. See also Church, *Life of Ericsson*, 2: 5–6.

44. 28-4-1862, Ericsson to Fox, Fox Papers, New York, Box 3.

45. 23-4-1862, 37th Congress, 2nd Session, House of Representatives, Report No. 86, *Permanent Fortifications and Sea-Coast Defenses*, 21. See also 8-4-1862, 37th Congress, 2nd Session, Senate, Executive Document No. 41, *Letter of the Secretary of War, Communicating the Report of Edwin F. Johnson, upon the Defenses of Maine*; and 30-4-1862, Joseph G. Totten to Lincoln, "Defense of the Upper Lakes—Memorandum for the President," Lincoln Papers, LOC. Totten boldly admitted, especially in the wake of the fall of New Orleans, "It is not possible to prevent the passage of vessels into Lake Michigan by means of fortifications, however placed. . . . As we see that fortifications cannot be so placed as to prevent this, resort must be had to floating means."

46. 10-4-1862, *Congressional Globe*, 1622.

Chapter 11

1. 23-4-1862, Fox to Stimers, Fox Papers, New York, Box 5.

2. Still, Smith, for example, had to admit that Ericsson's plan for supporting the new turrets was better than Stimers's; 24-4-1862, Smith to Ericsson, Ericsson Papers, Philadelphia.

3. 23-4-1862, Newton to Ericsson, Ericsson Papers, Philadelphia.

4. Smith finally relayed these, with Stimers's tracings, to Ericsson on April 19, 1862; Smith to Ericsson, RG 45, Entry 464, AD, Box 51.

5. This idea was not adopted, possibly because of the added weight or vulnerability to damage from shots striking across the deck into the protruding armor joint on the opposite side. Ericsson might have replied that simply increasing the thickness of the deck and shelf armor itself was a more practical solution. In his plans for a super oceangoing monitor the deck plating would be *inset* the top height of the side armor; see 19-5-1862, Ericsson to Fox, Fox Papers, New York, Box 3.

6. 23-4-1862, Newton to Ericsson, Ericsson Papers, Philadelphia.

7. 23-4-1862, John to Anne Rodgers, Rodgers Papers, LOC.

8. 23-4-1862, Smith to Whitney, RG 45, Entry 464, AD, Box 51. Smith also later refused the idea of a *Keokuk* target, to test her armor protection; 16-7-1862, Smith to Gregory, RG 45, Entry 464, AD, Box 51.

9. 25-4-1862, John to Anne Rodgers, Rodgers Papers, LOC. The following day he observed, "The *Monitor* is an extraordinary vessel: the sight of her is not much but a visit has a certain sort of a sublime strength revealed." 26-4-1862, John to Anne Rodgers, Rodgers Papers, LOC.

10. 22-4-1862, Welles to Ericsson, and 24-4-1862, Ericsson to Welles, Ericsson Papers, Philadelphia. James B. Eads agreed with Ericsson that "$500 is a small enough fee for each boat under all the circumstances for your valuable invention, and [I] will cheerfully respond to any drafts you may make for the amount. . . . I will only state that in starting the construction of six boats I am not so abundantly supplied with money as I hope to be after receiving something from the Govt. on account of them." 13-6-1862, James B. Eads to Ericsson, Ericsson Papers, Philadelphia. See also 20-6-1862, Eads to Ericsson, Ericsson Papers, LOC,

where Eads remarks, "I think with you that America is about to make all the world wonder. I am thankful for being born in this era." See also 23-7-1862, Eads to Ericsson, and 28-7-1862, Ericsson to Eads, Ericsson Papers, LOC.

11. Ericsson's biographer, William Conant Church, also noted the inventor-engineer's personal belief that science would eradicate warfare by making it too terrible to practice. See, for example, Ericsson's 19-5-1862 endorsement of the Raphael's repeating rifle to Secretary of War Stanton, which in his assessment formed "one of the many strides which mechanical science is now making to render war too destructive . . . to continue the disgrace of civilization. The true friend of human progress will support such inventions." Ericsson Papers, LOC. See also 28-6-1862, W. L. Barnes to Erastus Corning, Welles Papers, LOC: "[Ericsson's] sympathies are hearty & warm with reference to our success as a government," Barnes wrote, "& failure in this respect would be regarded by him as a calamity that concerned the civilization of the world."

12. 24-4-1862, Stimers to Fox, Fox Papers, New York, Box 4.

13. Time would prove him right. See Roberts, *Civil War Ironclads*, especially 147–169.

14. 28-4-1862, Ericsson to Fox, Fox Papers, New York, Box 3. Ericsson's suspicions proved well founded. He was willing to enlarge the 26-foot–interior diameter turret designed to house two 15-inch guns just under 13½ feet in length, if the 20-inch designs Dahlgren provided would not fit. Dahlgren later specified the lengths of his 20-inch guns at 17 feet but peevishly declared Ericsson's turrets were prescribing the limits, not his guns; 6-5-1862, telegram, Wise to Dahlgren, RG 45, Entry 464, AD, Box 49. 7-5-1862, telegram, Fox to Dahlgren, RG 45, Entry 464, AD, Box 49; and 8-5-1862, Dahlgren to Fox, RG 74, Entry 201, Item 5, Box 2. Stimers confided to Fox that "Captain E. is discouraged about getting guns of sufficient magnitude and I believe is about to propose to build them himself"; 7-5-1862, Stimers to Fox, Fox Papers, New York, Box 4.

15. 28-4-1862, Ericsson to Fox, Fox Papers, New York, Box 3. There is every reason to believe that the "four faster monitors" would become the "Harbor and River" monitors of the improved *Canonicus* class. The U.S. Navy went for four more Passaics, nine Canonicus, *and* the sea-going monitor(s).

16. 28-4-1862, Ericsson to Fox, Ericsson Papers, LOC.

17. Ibid. See also 20-3-1862 and 14-8-1862, Fox to Ericsson, Fox Papers, New York, Box 5.

18. 24-4-1862, Ericsson to Welles, Ericsson Papers, Philadelphia.

19. See 24-4-1862, Smith to Welles, RG 71, Entry 1, Vol. 74. The vessel was officially designated "New Ironsides" on May 10, 1862; Welles to Smith, RG 71, Entry 5, Box 423.

20. 28-4-1862, Ericsson to Welles, Ericsson Papers, Philadelphia.

21. 1-5-1862, Fox to Ericsson, Fox Papers, New York, Box 5.

22. 3-5-1862, Ericsson to Welles, Ericsson Papers, LOC.

23. 10-6-1862, Fox to Ericsson, Fox Papers, New York, Box 3.

24. 18-1-1863, "Impregnable Armor," Ericsson Papers, LOC. See also 5-8-1863, Ericsson to Fox, Ericsson Papers, Philadelphia; and 11-3-1864, Ericsson to Wise, Ericsson Papers, Philadelphia.

25. 5-5-1862, Dahlgren to Welles, Welles Papers, LOC. Perhaps Dahlgren was eager to set up his own iron target tests to confirm, above all, the power of his 11-inch gun, thrown into doubt against the C.S.S. *Virginia* at the Battle of Hampton Roads. See 8-5-1862, Dahlgren to Harwood, RG 74, Entry 201, Item 5, Box 2; and 28-5-1862, Targets 5, 6. In arguing for a massive, Government-controlled base for all aspects of ironclad production at League Island, Fox pointed out that "England and France are building enormous works for the manufacture of plates, required in the construction, and armature, of the new class of vessels." Though these were also privately made, they were "subjected to a rigid test that would reject all of our plates." 28-9-1862, Fox to Professor A. D. Bache, Fox Papers, New York, Box 5.

26. 17-1-1863, *Scientific American*, 42–43.

27. 1-5-1862, John to Anne Rodgers, Rodgers Papers, LOC.

28. 9-5-1862, Welles to Hale, RG 45, Entry 5.

29. 16-5-1862, Petition of Citizens of Franklin County, Ohio, RG 233.

30. 3-6-1862, 37th Congress, 2nd Session, House of Representatives, Report No. 114. "We cannot tell how soon the old and haughty nation of England, smarting under the calamities indirectly brought upon apportion of her manufacturers by our blockade of southern ports, may, in the contemplation of her own distresses, forget ours, and league with the guilty men now in rebellion against us," another Representative warned Congress, deliberating the appointment of a board of fortifications; 5-6-1862, *Congressional Globe*, 2590.

31. 10-5-1862, Smith to Welles, Welles Papers, LOC; also RG 45, Letters Rec'd and RG 71, Entry 1.

32. See also Canney, *The Ironclads*, 62–64. Canney states the *Onondaga*'s designer "eliminated the Ericsson monitor overhang and the excessive armor shelf, or hip, of those [*sic*] vessel," though the ship model photograph and ship's plans to which he refers clearly show an overhanging upper shelf over the stern, protecting the rudder and screws.

33. 3-5-1862, Ironclad Board to Welles, RG 45, Letters Rec'd. These would become the four double-turreted monitors of the *Monadnock* class, and then the even larger double-turreted class of four *Kalamazoo* ocean monitors—all of which incorporated wooden hulls, however.

34. *Scientific American* found this premise objectionable. "A very general opinion prevails in the community that it costs the government more to build steamers in the national navy yards than to obtain them from private builders. And it is believed by many persons . . . that any kind of iron work for war vessels, may be furnished by several manufacturers of angle iron, shafting and rolled plates, at less cost than such work can ever be made at any national navy yard." 28-6-1862, *Scientific American*, 404.

35. 13-5-1862, Ironclad Board to Welles, RG 45, Letters Rec'd. In presenting a bond on behalf of the *Puritan*'s builder, Thomas F. Rowland, for construction extras to John Hale, Ericsson made use of "the remarkable fact that the United States have produced a whole fleet of War vessel built on new system and quite successful, without having expended a single dollar in previous experiments. England has expended a greater amount in unsuccessful efforts to produce a powerful gun, than you have paid for a fleet of

12 turret Iron Clads. I allude to the 10 vessels of the *Passaic* class and the *Dictator* & *Puritan*." 3-6-1864, Ericsson to Hale, Ericsson Papers, LOC. See also his letter in the *Army & Navy Journal*, 16-7-1864, 774.

36. Perhaps a contentious point. But the *Warrior* drew even more water than the *Virginia*; and though her armor consisted of a single 4½-inch layer with an inner iron skin, as opposed to two layers of 2-inch plate, both armor schemes were backed by wood and the *Virginia*'s was inclined at 40° to the horizon. *Virginia* carried a smaller battery but all of it was protected; capable of fore, aft, and quarter-angle fire; and at least as powerful as the *Warrior*'s 68-pounder smoothbores and (dangerously ineffective) 110-pounder breech-loading Armstrong rifles. *Virginia*'s rudder and screw were fully protected; *Warrior*'s was not. Finally, the *Warrior* carried a full rig of masts and rigging—valuable for sailing but useless for steaming, and a serious liability in combat. See also the *Charleston Mercury*, 08-9-1862, for flattering comparisons made by visiting French naval officers of the C.S.S. *Virginia* with European variants.

37. 13-5-1862, Ironclad Board to Welles, RG 45, Letters Rec'd.

38. See for example 10-5-1862, Welles to Harwood, RG 74, Entry 16, Box 4. Fox likewise wrote to Ericsson he was "all ready to receive the plans of the big ship, and trust you will hurry it forward before the people change their minds about iron vessels." 13-5-1862, Fox to Ericsson, Fox Papers, New York, Box 5.

39. See 28-6-1862, *Scientific American*, 407.

40. "I have been using every effort to complete the draft of the 20 in. but have been entirely over run," Dahlgren wrote to Fox on May 13. "It is my desire to carry out the views of the Department to the best of my ability. But there is no Royal Road in science, nor should we Republicans desire it to be so." The English now admitted to being rash, and were "deservedly," "predictably" condemning similar U.S. practices. 13-5-1862, Dahlgren to Fox, Fox Papers, New York, Box 3; see also his attached letter to Harwood, dated 13-5-1862, warning of production of larger-caliber smoothbores without further testing, etc.; also found in RG 74, Entry 201, Item 5, Box 2. Ericsson received Fox's telegraphic news of Dahlgren's 20-inch guns "with delight." He could now inform Fox of his plans to construct a 30-foot–outside diameter turret to house them. But Fox cautioned, "Our advance people think it is an entire risk and experiment and so do I, but the times demand it, and I will take the responsibility." 13-5-1862, Ericsson to Fox, Fox Papers, New York, Box 3; 13-5-1862, Fox to Ericsson, Fox Papers, New York, Box 5.

41. 14-5-1862, Ericsson to Fox, Fox Papers, New York, Box 3.

42. The Bureau of Ordnance, for example, could not guarantee the success of all the new ordnance, "in consequence of the deficiency of Officers skilled in the inspection of guns. . . ." It would therefore have to "employ expert civilians for the purpose until skilled assistants can be spared from the service afloat." 12-6-1862, Harwood to Welles, RG 45, Letters Rec'd.

43. 15-5-1862, Fox to Harwood, RG 74, Entry 16, Box 4.

44. 15-5-1862, Fox to Ericsson, Fox Papers, New York, Box 5.

45. 6-5-1862, Ericsson to Fox, Fox Papers, New York, Box 3. Warren Ripley (*Artillery and Ammunition of the Civil War*, New York: Van Nostrand, 1970,

100) quotes Alexander Holley's measurements for the 20-inch Dahlgren (*A Treatise on Ordnance and Armor*, New York: D. Van Nostrand, 1865, 120–121).

46. 16-5-1862, Ericsson to Fox, Fox Papers, New York, Box 3.

47. 18-5-1862, Stimers to Fox, Fox Papers, New York, Box 4.

48. 19-5-1862, Ericsson to Welles, Ericsson Papers, Philadelphia. Ericsson explained his thoughts to Fox the same day in more detail: "a 16 inch ball (weight 550 lbs.) will produce the *greatest effect possible*. . . . As a small ball can be propelled at a greater speed than a large one, the practical question is simply: what size ball will produce a hole or rent so large that it cannot be stopped during action? Whatever that size be, there let us stop, and then go for the greatest possible initial velocity." 19-5-1862, Ericsson to Fox, Fox Papers, New York, Box 3.

49. 19-5-1862, Ericsson to Welles, Ericsson Papers, Philadelphia.

50. 21-5-1862, Fox to Ericsson, Ericsson Papers, LOC. See also 21-5-1862, Welles to Harwood, RG 74, Entry 16, Box 4.

51. 21-5-1862, Smith to Welles, RG 45, Letters Rec'd; 21-5-1862, Welles to Smith, Lenthall, and Isherwood, RG 45, Entry 13.

52. 22-5-1862, Ericsson to Fox, Ericsson Papers, LOC.

53. 30-5-1862, Fox to Robert B. Forbes, Fox Papers, New York, Box 5. Forbes was the "Principal Inspector" for gunboats built in Massachusetts and Maine, assisted by Samuel Pook; see 10-7-1862, "List of Principal and Assistant Inspectors appointed by the Secretary of the Navy to Superintend the Construction of Gun Boats under Contract," addressed to Gregory, RG 19, Entry 1235.

54. 23-5-1862, Smith to Welles, RG 45, Letters Rec'd.

55. Smith went so far as to "perceive no advantages which the Turret affords over a case-mate." To him, the advantage of rotating the guns was more than offset by the disadvantage that "the guns could not be fired on both sides at the same time, which is often important." 3-6-1862, Smith to Welles, RG 45, Letters Rec'd. By the end of 1864, he had not changed his mind, writing Dahlgren that "I fear the Ericsson big ships will prove a failure but I hope not. I am right on the record in regard to them." 1-12-1864, Smith to Dahlgren, Dahlgren Papers, LOC.

56. 4-6-1862, Fox to Stimers, Fox Papers, New York, Box 5.

57. 4-6-1862, Ericsson to Fox, Ericsson Papers, Philadelphia. "My own opinion, as well as those with whom I converse," Fox replied, "is that the thicker plates ought to be used in preference to the thin ones like the *Monitor*." 6-6-1862, Fox to Ericsson, Fox Papers, New York, Box 5.

58. 5-6-1862, Smith to Ericsson, Ericsson Papers, LOC.

59. 6-6-1862, Ericsson to Fox, Fox Papers, New York, Box 3.

60. 6-6-1862, Stimers to Fox, Fox Papers, New York, Box 4.

61. 9-6-1862, Fox to Ericsson, Fox Papers, New York.

62. See 6-6-1862, Fox to Ericsson, Fox Papers, New York, Box 5.

63. 9-6-1862, Stimers to Ericsson, Church, *Life of Ericsson*, 2: 8–9.

64. Indeed, when the U.S.S. *Dictator* finally arrived at the Norfolk Navy Yard, in December 1864, her commander, Commodore John Rodgers, wrote his wife: "We are all ready to move, but detained by the tide. There is not

water enough for this vessel to go to Hampton Roads except at half tide."
Likewise, there was "barely width in the Channel here to allow the vessel to
swing by means of lines at both ends so as to pivot her in the middle of the
channel." 6-12-1864, John to Anne Rodgers, Rodgers Papers, LOC.

65. 10-6-1862, Lenthall and Isherwood to Welles, RG 19, Entry 50.

66. See also Church, *Life of Ericsson*, 2: 10–11.

67. 13-6-1862, Fox to Ericsson, Ericsson Papers, LOC.

68. 15-6-1862, Stimers to Fox, Fox Papers, New York, Box 4. Among other
changes, Stimers pressed Ericsson to adopt Martin (water-tube) boilers in the
oceangoing monitor, with which Ericsson was little familiar; see
9-11-1862, Ericsson to Fox, Fox Papers, New York, Box 3; and RG 74, Entry 22,
Box 1, 17. For example, Stimers's allusion to "interference . . . which could be
construed . . . into defects" may refer to Ericsson's angry responses to Welles
some two weeks earlier over Jeffers's accusations of the *Monitor*'s faulty
ventilation—which was based in no small degree on Stimers's suggestions.

69. Fox, Stimers, Lenthall, and Isherwood argued that the wood beams
would rot, but Ericsson felt they could be treated (or "*kyanized*—impregnated
with a metallic solution to prevent decay"; see Canney, *The Ironclads*, 89)
and would provide a much tighter fit against leaks around the iron bolt heads
associated with the "effect of expansion & contraction of the deck plating";
16-6-1862, Ericsson to Fox, Ericsson Papers, PA. Ericsson later repeated this
to Smith regarding wood or deck beams for the *Passaic*-class monitor
Camanche (to be built in California), citing his experience as "Superintending Engineer of one of the leading English railroads"; 20-6-1862, Ericsson to
Smith, Ericsson Papers, LOC. Stimers later reversed his opinion and strenu-
ously argued for kyanized wood beams for the *Puritan*; enclosed in
12-11-1862, Stimers to Fox, Fox Papers, New York, Box 4. Lenthall seemed
unaware of the procedure even for the *Dictator*; see 23-11-1862, Gregory to
Ericsson, RG 19, Entry 1235.

70. Compare these specifications with those of the finished *Dictator*, as
described by Ericsson in his *Contributions to the Centennial Exhibition*
(1876), 492–497. Total grate surface, for example, he lists as "1,128 square feet,
and the heating surface over 32,000 square feet."

71. Draft, 16-6-1862, Ericsson to Welles, Ericsson Papers, Philadelphia. All
this rather contradicts historian Donald Canney's assertion that the opinions
of the naval professionals "seemed to have had no effect on the outcome"
concerning the design of the *Dictator* and *Puritan* classes; Canney, *The Ironclads*, 89.

72. Draft, 16-6-1862, Ericsson to Welles, Ericsson Papers, Philadelphia.

73. 18-6-1862, Fox to Ericsson, Ericsson Papers, Philadelphia. The official
letter of approval from Welles is dated 23-6-1862 and bears the influence of
Lenthall and Isherwood, who crucially specify, "The beams of the vessel with
two turrets to be of wrought iron"; Welles Papers, LOC.

74. Canney, *The Ironclads*, 126, 129.

75. Beale, *Diary*, 2: 341, entry dated 24-7-1865.

76. See 27-2-1864, *Scientific American*, 131–132.

77. The contract later specified (*Passaic*-pattern) turrets "not less than
twenty-one feet diameter in the clear, and eight feet high . . . the armor-iron

of which shall not be less than eleven inches thick." See the recompiled version made by L. H. Chandler, Lt., U.S.N., dated 26-3-1900, in RG 45, Entry 464, AD, Box 51. Chandler added, "The Chief of the Bureau of Construction and Repair (Rear Admiral Philip Hichborn) states that, according to his recollection, this designed battery and armament was far in excess of what the ship could carry, and that it was given her more with the idea of inspiring fear in the South than in any hope that she could carry it." More likely, Webb sought to inspire fear in Europe—and tantalize the Navy. Indeed, within six months Smith reported to Welles that "Mr. Webb finds that, to enable him to obtain all the objects he had in view in the construction of the Vessel he contracted to build, he must increase the dimensions of the Vessel and the power, and without doing so, he fears, he will fail of obtaining the grand objects desired." 1-12-1862, Smith to Welles, RG 45, Letters Rec'd.

78. However, it did not satisfy Ericsson. "As the side armor of the hull of this shapeless mass of timber averages only 3½ inches in thickness any of our small monitors could send this extraordinary specimen of human genius to the bottom in a few rounds." 27-4-1866, Ericsson to John Bourne, Ericsson Papers, LOC. See Canney's description of this Union ironclad, U.S.S. *Dunderberg; The Ironclads*, 126–129.

79. 19-6-1862, Ericsson to Fox, Fox Papers, New York, Box 3. See also Church, *Life of Ericsson*, 2: 6–7.

80. See Pugh, *Cost of Seapower*, 213–216.

Chapter 12

1. 5-4-1862, *Punch*, 134.

2. 1-4-1862, London *Times*.

3. Ibid. 5-4-1862, *Illustrated London News*, 328.

4. TNA/ADM 1/5802, 17-3-1862. See also Hamilton, *Anglo-French Naval Rivalry*, 89–92.

5. See for example 11-3-1862, Newcastle to Somerset, Somerset Papers, Aylesbury.

6. 5-4-1862, *Illustrated London News*, 328.

7. 31-3-1862, Russell to Palmerston, Palmerston Papers, Southampton.

8. 31-3-1862, London *Times*.

9. See for example Mindell, *War, Technology, and Experience Aboard the U.S.S. Monitor*.

10. 5-4-1862, *Illustrated London News*, 328.

11. 31-3-1862, *Hansard*, 263–272.

12. Ibid., 275–278.

13. 12-4-1862, *Punch*, 143. Little did *Punch* know that the following day Lewis wrote to Somerset he was now "thinking of requesting the Defence Committee to report on the recent action in America, and to state whether it induces them to modify their opinion respecting the Forts at Spithead." 1-4-1862, Lewis to Somerset, Somerset Papers, Aylesbury.

14. 31-3-1862, *Hansard*, 285–286.

15. A fact that delighted the *New York Herald*, 19-4-1862; "The speeches . . . show that they are greatly alarmed at the position in which their country is placed by the issue of the conflict between the *Merrimac* and *Monitor*."

16. Literally, see *Punch*, 3-5-1862, "Peace," and 19-7-1862, "The Old Sentinel."

17. Asa Briggs, *Victorian People: A Reassessment of Persons and Themes 1851–67* (London: Penguin, 1990 reprint of 1955 original), 43, 97–99.

18. 30-10-1864, Cobden to Coles, Cobden Papers, Chichester. Burgoyne was the Inspector-General of Fortifications.

19. Undated, 1862, Cobden to Palmerston, Palmerston Papers, Southampton.

20. 11-1-1862, Somerset to Palmerston, Palmerston Papers, Southampton.

21. Russell was prepared to rank England's naval power *third*, next to France and then the United States; Russell to Somerset, 25-8-1862, Somerset Papers, Aylesbury.

22. 4-4-1862, *Hansard*, 590.

23. 1-4-1862, Somerset to Palmerston, Palmerston Papers, Southampton.

24. 3-4-1862, Lewis to Somerset, Somerset Papers, Aylesbury.

25. 3-4-1862, *Hansard*, 430–431.

26. Ibid. See 7-8-1862, *Return: Navy Dockyards, Ordered 30-6-1862 and 15-7-1862, Parliamentary Papers*. The *Warrior-* and *Minotaur*-class ironclads could only be accommodated in three docks at "High Water Spring Tides": one at Portsmouth, one at Devonport, and one at Keyham. The *Prince Albert* class of iron-hulled, coastal defense turret ship, by comparison, could be accommodated in at least 20.

27. 3-4-1862, *Hansard*, 438–439.

28. 2-4-1862, Hore to Earl Cowley, TNA/FO 27/1436. The French had also apparently slackened the pace of existing ironclad construction; 4-4-1862, Hore to Cowley, TNA/FO 27/1436.

Chapter 13

1. TNA/ADM 1/5802, 11-4-1862; enclosed letter from Coles to Paget dated 31-3-1862.

2. TNA/ADM 1/5802, 11-4-1862.

3. 4-4-1862, *Hansard*, 588–589. See also Michael Stephen Partridge, *Military Planning for the Defense of the United Kingdom, 1814–1870* (New York: Greenwood Press, 1989), 89–92, 100–119.

4. 4-4-1862, *Hansard*, 602–604.

5. See, for example, 27-3-1861, Palmerston to Somerset, Somerset Papers, Aylesbury.

6. 4-4-1862, *Hansard*, 606–610. The War Office Return on "National Defences," for the loan authorized to pay for the forts, listed £574,872 already spent by March 31, 1862, primarily in modernizing existing defenses of Portsmouth and Plymouth, with over £1 million already committed to buying land for fortifications, leaving £316,000 of the £2 million advance; £5,680,000 was estimated for completion. 26-5-1862, *Parliamentary Papers*, 1–3.

7. 4-4-1862, *Hansard*, 612.

8. Ibid., 614–621.

9. 4-4-1862, Charles Francis Adams to Charles Francis Adams Jr., from Worthington Chauncey Ford (ed.), *A Cycle of Adams Letters, 1861–1865,* 2 vols. (Boston: Houghton Mifflin, 1920), 1: 123.

10. Sir George Grey, undated memo, 1862, General Charles Grey Papers, Durham University Library (Archives & Special Collections), Palace Green, Durham.

11. 11-4-1862, *Hansard,* 853.

12. 4-4-1862, *Hansard,* 613–614, 630.

13. Milne meanwhile desired a hauling-up slip for Bermuda, "for effecting repairs of even small class ships which may have touched the ground." Docking and repairing *Warrior* or even *Defence* at Bermuda was currently impossible; TNA/ADM 128/21, 20-4-1862.

14. TNA/ADM 1/5802, 14-4-1862.

15. See TNA/ADM 1/5791, 17-4-1862, Coles to Robinson, and 20-4-1862, Coles to Romaine; Edward J. Reed, *On the Modifications which the Ships of the Royal Navy Have Undergone During the Present Century* (London, 1859), 25.

16. See TNA/ADM 1/5802, 25-4-1862.

17. TNA/ADM 1/5802. 14-4-1862.

18. See 28-4-1862, Somerset to Palmerston, Newcastle's "Remarks upon proposal to introduce a Bill to enable Colonial *Navies* to be formed," and 29-4-1862, Palmerston to Gladstone, Palmerston Papers, Southampton. Palmerston himself felt "a large yearly expenditure for Army and Navy" was "an economical Insurance" against the catastrophe of a French invasion—provoked in turn by weak British national defenses. See also Gladstone to Somerset, 13-12-1864, Somerset Papers Collection, Aylesbury.

19. Quoted from the *Scientific American,* 7-6-1862, 358.

20. See 11-4-1862, London *Times.*

21. Although Robinson, after a publicized visit to Chatham with the First Lord, recommended the armament of the *Achilles* be reduced from 50 to 30 heavy guns, all within the protected portion of the battery, "very essential to the efficiency of the Ship to carry a belt of Armour Plating of 4½-inches in thickness right round the Ship in continuation of that which exists at present only for about 200 ft." TNA/ADM 1/5802, 3-5-1862.

22. See for example "Mr. Rothwell's plan of destroying an Enemy by squirting Vitriol and Naphtha into the Ports," in TNA/ADM 1/5802, 11-4-1862. Somerset quipped to Palmerston he had "letters now advising me to build ships to imitate the scales of the crocodile, the hide of the rhinoceros, the quills of the porcupine, the wings of the beetle, &c., &c." 27-4-1862, Somerset to Palmerston, Palmerston Papers, Southampton; also 22-4-1862, Palmerston to Somerset, Somerset Papers, Aylesbury.

23. 3-5-1862, *Scientific American,* 282. The same page reported "The British Parliament on the Fight in Hampton Roads."

24. TNA/ADM 1/5791, 8-5-1862.

25. 10-5-1862, *Punch,* 191.

26. See TNA/ADM 1/5791, 14-5-1862.

27. 12-5-1862, Coles to John Blackwood, MS 4168, 197–198, National Library of Scotland, Edinburgh.

28. TNA/ADM 1/5802, 17-5-1862.

29. See the various reports included with TNA/ADM 1/5791, 14-5-1862; Robinson's letter is dated 19-5-1862.

Chapter 14

1. 19-5-1862, *Hansard*, 1933–1945.

2. 23-5-1862, Somerset to Palmerston, Palmerston Papers, Southampton. The First Lord also argued "a retrospect of the comparative navies of England and France will prove that from the year 1835 to the year 1859, the naval expenditure of England has increased from 4¼ to 11 millions or 138 per cent; but the naval expenditure of France has increased from 2¼ to 8¼ millions sterling or 274 per cent. So that our rate of increase is only half that of France in naval expenditure." 30-5-1862, Somerset to Palmerston, Palmerston Papers, Southampton.

3. 25-3-1862, William Baynton to Robinson, forwarded to the Board of Admiralty, ADM 1/5802, 21-5-1862.

4. 27-5-1862, Palmerston to Gladstone, Palmerston Papers, Southampton.

5. 1-6-1862, Palmerston to Somerset, Somerset Papers, Aylesbury; 1-6-1862 Somerset to Palmerston, Palmerston Papers, Southampton.

6. 2-6-1862, Somerset to Palmerston, Palmerston Papers, Southampton.

7. 3-6-1862, *Hansard*, 292, 300–302.

8. Ibid., 305–313. "The position of England at sea is defensive to a far greater degree than that of any other country, for she stands alone in the magnitude of the objects she must be ready to defend in all quarters of the globe, and as the French Commission observes, England is vulnerable everywhere." Admiralty publication, 2nd ed., *Admiralty Administration: Its Faults and Its Defaults* (London: Longman, Green, Longman, and Roberts, 1861), 38–39.

9. Ibid., 327–328. See Daniel R. Headrick, "The Tools of Imperialism: Technology and the Expansion of European Colonial Empires in the Nineteenth Century," *Journal of Military History*, Vol. 51, No. 2 (June 1979), 231–263, on how expanding British "commercial and political interests" and naval technology were often mutually supportive; also Robert Kubicek, "British Expansion, Empire, and Technological Change," in Porter, *Oxford History*, 247–269.

10. 3-6-1862, *Hansard*, 328–333.

11. Less than three weeks later, however, Lewis declared in the Parliamentary Committee on Fortifications and Works that "it is the characteristic of our naval and military system, unlike that of many other countries, that it exists exclusively for defensive purposes." 23-6-1862, *Hansard*, 870.

12. 3-6-1862, *Hansard*, 329–393.

13. Entry dated 3-6-1862, Diary (D/22), Palmerston Papers, Southampton.

14. 11-6-1862, Palmerston to Adams, Palmerston Papers, Southampton.

15. 13-6-1862, Russell to Palmerston, Palmerston Papers, Southampton. See also Adams, *Great Britain*, 1: 302–305.

16. 23-6-1862, *Hansard*, 882, 871, 905907.

17. Ibid., 944–953.

18. "Never before had France had a great arsenal and excellent harbour directly facing the Channel and the South Coast of England. Capable of out-fitting, sheltering, and despatching a great invasion fleet, Cherbourg seemed like a knife pointing directly at Britain's jugular." Hamilton, *Anglo-French Naval Rivalry*, 83–84.

19. 9-7-1863, *Hansard*, "Fortifications (Provision for Expenses) Bill," 493.

20. 30-8-1862, *Harper's Weekly*, 546.

21. 5-4-1862, *Scientific American*, 217.

22. June 1862, *Blackwood's Edinburgh Magazine*, 777.

23. Ironically enough, within a week of Coles's confidently expressing to Cobden his opinion that the *Dictator* was a "bad specimen" and "Ericsson a humbug," Robinson informed the Board of Admiralty "that at a recent inter-view Captain Coles informed Sir F. Grey that he wished to avoid the respon-sibility of designing a turret ship as a whole, he not being a naval architect. . . ." 14-11-1864, Coles to Cobden, Cobden Papers, Chichester; and TNA/ADM 1/5892, 10-11-1864. By contrast, as Donald L. Canney observes, "The navy's dependence on John Ericsson for its Civil War ironclad program was over-whelming. And there was no sign that the trend would have slackened had the war been prolonged. Indeed, the only ironclads retained for the postwar serv-ice were the Ericsson turreted vessels." *The Ironclads*, 75.

24. June 1862, *Blackwood's Edinburgh Magazine*, 784.

25. 11-4-1862, Henry Adams to Charles Francis Adams Jr., quoted from Worthington Chauncey Ford (ed.), *A Cycle of Adams Letters 1861–1865*, 2 vols. (Boston: Houghton Mifflin, 1920) 1: 134.

Chapter 15

1. 23-6-1862, *Hansard*, 956.

2. TNA/ADM 1/5791, 19-6-1862.

3. 17-7-1862, Return, "Navy (Iron-Cased Ships, &c.)," Parliamentary Papers.

4. TNA/ADM 1/5802, 2-7-1862

5. TNA/ADM 1/5802, 22-5-1862, and 22-5-1862. Coles's enclosed letter is dated 20-5-1862.

6. TNA/ADM 1/5802, 27-5-1862.

7. TNA/ADM 1/5802, 4-7-1862; Coles's enclosed letter dated 1-7-1862. See 19-3-1862, Lenthall and Isherwood to Welles, RG 45, Letters Rec'd.

8. TNA/ADM 1/5802, 4-7-1862.

9. TNA/ADM 1/5791, 8-7-1862; Robinson's notation remarks dated 10-7-1862.

10. See 18-7-1862, *Hansard*, 505–510.

11. TNA/ADM 1/5791, 22-7-1862.

12. TNA/ADM 1/5802, 26-7-1862.

13. 7-8-1862, Russell to Somerset, Somerset Papers, Aylesbury; 8-8-1862, Somerset to Palmerston, Palmerston Papers, Southampton. Russell specified

at least eight line-of-battle ships for the Mediterranean Station rather than frigates, since "they tell in effect and naval impression far better." Any reduction in manpower would also drop Britain's naval power ranking to third, behind France and then the United States. 25-8-1862, Russell to Somerset, Somerset Papers, Aylesbury.

14. TNA/ADM 3/270, 17-9-1862. At the end of October 1863 the *Royal Oak*-class ironclad frigate H.M.S. *Prince Consort* was nearly swamped on her maiden voyage from Plymouth to Dublin because of her heavy rolling—shipping seas in a gale—and then her only steam pump failed. As with the *Monitor*'s stormy maiden voyage from New York to Hampton Roads, she, too, barely survived the night. See Ballard, *Black Battlefleet*, 115–123; also 14-11-1863, *Illustrated London News*.

15. 17-9-1862, Somerset to Lewis, and 19-9-1862, Lewis to Somerset, Somerset Papers, Aylesbury. See the report of the Iron Plate Committee, dated 24-9-1862, found in TNA/ADM 1/5809.

Chapter 16

1. 25-9-1862, Lewis to Somerset, Somerset Papers, Aylesbury.

2. 5-8-1862, London *Times*; 13-9-1862, *Punch*.

3. 7-10-1862, London *Times*.

4. 18-10-1862, *Punch*.

5. ". . . [U]nless Lord Russell meant War, I think his letters [of 17-1-1863, to Lord Lyons] most unhappy," U.S. Senator Charles Sumner later wrote to Cobden. "I am tempted to tell you how our imperturbable President felt on receiving the Letter about his Proclamation. As he knew nothing of Lord Russell personally and very little opinion as a public man, he was not able to make the apologies for him which I could. And yet it was hard. The case was very bad. I doubt if all history shews an instance of a question of such magnitude being treated with such mingled levity & ignorance. . . ." 26-4-1863, Sumner to Cobden, Cobden Papers, Chichester. See also Beverly Wilson Palmer (ed.), *The Selected Letters of Charles Sumner*, 2 vols. (Boston: Northeastern University Press, 1990), 2: 160–162; Jones, "History and Mythology," 34.

6. Jones, *Union in Peril*, 199; "The emperor noted [to Confederate emissary John Slidell] that Union rejection of the offer would provide 'good reason for recognition' and in an unmistakable reference to the use of force, 'perhaps for more active participation'"; 201.

7. 2-10-1862, Palmerston to Russell, and 2-10-1862, Russell to Palmerston, Palmerston Papers, Southampton. See Robin D. S. Higham, "The Russian Fleet on the Eastern Seaboard, 1863–1864: A Maritime Chronology", *American Neptune*, Vol. 20, No. 1 (January 1960), 49–61. "How would a war with both Russia and the United States affect the price of bread for all classes in England?" asked the *Philadelphia Inquirer*; 3-9-1863. The London *Times* countered that the United States "have too much to do on their own territory for their policy . . . to cause us very lively alarm"; 7-9-1863.

8. 4-10-1862, Russell to Palmerston, Palmerston Papers, Southampton; copy of memo found in Palmerston Papers, Southampton.

9. Jones, *Union in Peril*, 182–186.

10. 25-10-1862, memo in Palmerston Papers, Southampton, 7. Gladstone also "felt an especial contempt for the money-grubbing Northern Yankee tradesmen and farmers," notes one biographer, "and he shared the prejudiced view held generally by the English upper class, that the Southern planters, with their cultivated drawl, were the nearest approach to gentlemen that America could show." Philip Magnus, *Gladstone: A Biography* (London: 2001 reprint of John Murray, 1954), 152–153.

11. 16-10-1862, Somerset to Lewis, and 19-10-1862, Lewis to Somerset, Somerset Papers, Aylesbury. See also Charles S. Williams and Frank J. Merli (eds.), "The *Normandie* Shows the Way: Report of a Voyage from Cherbourg to Vera Cruz, 4 September 1862," *The Mariner's Mirror*, Vol. 54 (1968), 153–162.

12. 18-10-1862, Palmerston to Russell, Palmerston Papers, Southampton.

13. 24-10-1862, and 25-10-1862, Russell to Palmerston, Palmerston Papers, Southampton.

14. 7-11-1862, Secretary of War Sir George C. Lewis, *Recognition of the Independence of the Southern States of the North American Union*, TNA/WO 33/12, 2.

15. August 1864, *Atlantic Monthly*, 245–248. For British working-class issues and the American Civil War see Blackett, *Divided Hearts*; also Jonathan Rose, "Workers' Journals," in J. Don Vann and Rosemary T. VanArsdel (eds.), *Victorian Periodicals and Victorian Society* (Toronto: University of Toronto Press, 1994), 61, 303.

16. This did not include the 10 "armored wooden vessels, (transferred from the War Department)" for service on "Western rivers," but of the total tally of 54 ironclads, 28 were intended for the "Sea-board," and most of these were turreted monitors. *Congressional Globe*, Appendix, Report of the Secretary of the Navy, 1-12-1862, 17–18.

17. 22-11-1862, *Punch*.

18. ". . . [O]wing to difficulties of maintaining communications and other causes," Milne wrote a very intrigued Board of Admiralty, "it is not easy to collect trustworthy information beyond what the Newspapers furnish on this interesting subject, as I am not aware that there were any British Officers, or other authorities at or near the James River, or on the Mississippi, where the only serious actions between Batteries and Iron clad Vessels have as yet taken place." TNA/ADM 1/5788, 26-8-1862.

19. 9-9-1862, London *Times*.

20. TNA/ADM 1/5791, 8-11-1862; see also TNA/ADM 1/5788, 13-11-1862.

21. TNA/ADM 1/5791, 8-11-1862. Captain Ross of H.M.S. *Cadmus* had the opportunity to tour the completed *New Ironsides* at Hampton Roads on Oct. 24, 1862. Though he found the vessel in "good fighting order," he believed a single shot would disable the rudder, which was "just awash," and she was "very difficult to steer when going more than six knots." The armored bulkheads fore and aft, which protected the main battery, Ross considered inadequate; "a vessel getting athwart her stern, and being exposed to the fire of only one 50 pounder [a pivot on the upper deck], would

soon drive in her after bulkhead and rake her gun deck." 25-10-1862, Ross to Milne, enclosed in Milne's 8-11-1862 collection of forwarded reports to the Admiralty, TNA/ADM 1/5788.

22. TNA/ADM 1/5791, 8-11-1862.

23. Printed as Edward J. Reed, *On the Modifications which the Ships of the Royal Navy Have Undergone During the Present Century* (London: Robertson, Brooman, & Co., 1859), 13, 21–22; 5-12-1861, Lewis to Twisleton, from Lewis (ed.), *Letters*, 406.

24. 3-9-1868, Reed to H. L. Corry, in Milne Papers, Greenwich. Ericsson made sure to take Reed's *Our Ironclad Ships* (1869) to task in 1870, comparing the *Bellerophon* with the *Dictator* in similar fashion; 12-2-1870, *Army and Navy Journal*, 397–398.

25. In one of many angry outbursts, Robinson complained to the Board "how utterly untrustworthy and uncalled for are all [Coles's] remarks on what he chooses to call the determined opposition and condemnation of his principle, openly disclosed by Mr. Reed." Rather, the Controller admitted there had been "an opposition to crude and impracticable ideas, which it was right and proper should be offered by those who have the responsibility of spending the Public Money and whose business it is to see that, Ships which can only carry certain weights are not burdened with double the amount their flotation will support." TNA/ADM 1/5840, 20-4-1863.

Chapter 17

1. 9-6-1862, Fox to Ericsson, Fox Papers, New York, Box 5.

2. 6-6-1862, Fox to Forbes, Fox Papers, New York, Box 5. Dahlgren later indicated the wood was backed with an inner skin plate of 1-inch iron; 12-6-1862, Dahlgren to Fox, Fox Papers, New York, Box 3. See also RG 74, Entry 98, "Reports Concerning Target Practice on Iron Plates, 1862–64." For Robert Forbes's long-standing friendship with John Ericsson, see Church, *Life of Ericsson*, 1: 162.

3. 9-6-1862, Fox to Ericsson, Fox Papers, New York, Box 5.

4. 10-6-1862, Ericsson to Fox, Fox Papers, New York, Box 3.

5. RG 74, Entry 98, "Reports Concerning Target Practice", vol. 2, 23.

6. 12-6-1862, Dahlgren to Fox, Fox Papers, New York, Box 3. See also 15-6-1862, Ericsson to Fox, Fox Papers, New York, Box 3, and especially 18-1-1863, Ericsson to Welles, Ericsson Papers, LOC.

7. 27-4-1862, General Order, Fox Papers, New York.

8. Though predicting the forts could not stop a well-executed dash by Union warships, Major General and Army Chief Engineer John G. Barnard proudly noted to Fox afterward that "my forts were harder to take than supposed. . . ." 11-5-1862, Barnard to Fox, Fox Papers, New York, Box 3.

9. 19-5-1862, 37th Congress, 2nd Session, House of Representatives, Executive Document No. 115, *Change of Materials and Construction of Forts*, 6. Although the Congressional resolution of inquiry was made on April 15, Totten's letter to Stanton is dated 10-5-1862, well after the fall of New Orleans.

10. 13-5-1862, Welles to Du Pont, RG 45, Entry 15.

11. See Rodgers's official report, dated 16-5-1862, to Goldsborough, *ORN*, ser. 1, vol. 7, 357–358. See also Executive Officer L. H. Newman's 16-5-1862 report of damages and Corporal of Marines John Mackie's account, 16-5-1862, Fox Papers, New York. Rodgers himself later observed that the iron fragments from the *Galena*'s shattered armor plating "became very formidable grape shot; our principal loss I am convinced was from them." 19-5-1862, John to Anne Rodgers, Rodgers Papers, LOC.

12. 16-5-1862, John to Anne Rodgers; 18-5-1862, Anne to John Rodgers, Rodgers Papers, LOC.

13. 20-5-1862, Stimers to Fox, Fox Papers, New York, Box 4.

14. See 9-2-1862, Jeffers to Goldsborough, *ORN*, ser. 1, vol. 6, 561–563; also 10-2-1862, Jeffers to Commander S. C. Rowan, 611.

15. *ORN*, ser. 1, vol. 7, 352–353.

16. 15-5-1862, Goldsborough to Rodgers, *ORN*, ser. 1, vol. 7, 354–355.

17. Ericsson calculated this distance, based on the degree of the guns' elevation, to be 650 yards, but pointed out that such an angle (6°) worked two ways: plunging Confederate fire could not penetrate the *Monitor*'s deck; 28-6-1862, Ericsson to Fox, Ericsson Papers, LOC.

18. 16-5-1862, Jeffers to Rodgers, *ORN*, ser. 1, vol. 7, 362.

19. 22-5-1862, Jeffers to Goldsborough, *ORN*, ser. 1, vol. 7, 410–413. See also *Report of the Secretary of the Navy in Relation to Armored Vessels*. Significantly, Jeffers omits to mention his own ship's chief engineer, Isaac Newton.

20. 22-5-1862, Jeffers to Goldsborough, *ORN*, ser. 1, vol. 7, 410–413. For further discussion of the effects of the *Monitor*'s forward fire on the pilothouse see 4-10-1862, Jeffers to Dahlgren, Dahlgren Papers, LOC. Jeffers felt, however, that the concussion experienced within the turret from the fire of the 11-inch guns was less than that of 9-inch Dahlgrens fired "on the maindeck of a Frigate."

21. Ibid.

22. 2-6-1862, Welles to Goldsborough, *ORN*, ser. 1, vol. 7, 445.

23. 3-6-1862, Goldsborough to Welles, *ORN*, ser. 1, vol. 7, 448.

24. 3-6-1862, Jeffers to Goldsborough, *ORN*, ser. 1, vol. 7, 449–450.

25. See *Monitor* engineer Isaac Newton's letter to Ericsson of 10-7-1862, Ericsson Papers, Philadelphia, in which he complains that "Jeffers' peculiar characteristic is that he has not an consideration for anyone but himself, so you may well imagine what I have to go through when he in his spacious and comparatively well ventilated cabin growls." In his opinion, it was not the *Monitor* that was to blame—"the hot weather alone brought out her defects"—but "the stupid head powers of the Navy." Commodore Goldsborough in particular was "so thoroughly impregnated with fear of this bugbear [the *Virginia*], that half the Navy was paralysed." Welles later agreed, writing in his journal Goldsborough "had done nothing effective since the frigates were sunk by the Merrimac, nor of himself much before." 10-8-1862, Beale, *Diary*, 1: 73.

26. 28-5-1862, Ericsson to Welles, Ericsson Papers, LOC.

27. 29-5-1862, Ericsson to Welles, Ericsson Papers, LOC.

28. For Gregory's zeal see 9-6-1862, and 11-7-1862, Gregory to Welles, RG 45, Entry 38. For a sense of Smith's alienation see also 19-6-1862, Smith to Ericsson, RG 45, Entry 464, Box 51. When Gregory submitted Stimers and Ericsson's request to install iron stringers in the *Passaic* monitors, Smith replied the Bureau was "of the opinion that any vessel of war requiring extra ballast to trim her is defective in architecture"; 9-7-1862, Gregory to Smith, RG 19, Entry 1235; 12-7-1862, Smith to Gregory, RG 45, Entry 464, AD, Box 51.

29. 21-6-1862, John to Anne Rodgers, Rodgers Papers, LOC; 24-6-1862, Gregory to Smith, RG 19, Entry 1235.

30. 9-6-1862, Welles to Hale, RG 45, Entry 5, Vol. 14.

31. 20-6-1862, *Congressional Globe*. Nevertheless, Welles supplied the report. See 11-7-1862, Smith to Welles, RG 45, Letters Rec'd, and 14-7-1862, 37th Congress, 2nd Session, House of Representatives, Executive Document No. 150, *Contracts Made with Bureaus Connected with the Navy Department*.

32. John Murray Forbes advised Fox not to "wait for Iron plate mills to be Authorized by Congress. There is a natural & I think sound distrust of Government mills for making anything but big guns & even for these the one great argument is 'Dahlgren's executive ability'! Leave him & perhaps Rodman out of the account & I should hesitate about going outside of private mills for these Guns! For Iron plates I have no sort of doubt private mills are sufficient." 2-7-1862, Forbes to Fox, Fox Papers, New York, Box 3. See especially 28-9-1862, Fox to Professor A. D. Bache, Fox Papers, New York, Box 5. See also 4-11-1862, Report of Chief of Bureau of Yards and Docks, 558-60.

33. 13-6-1862, *Congressional Globe*, 2707. See also 19-5-1862, *Congressional Globe*.

34. 12-6-1862, "Pacific Railroad Bill," *Congressional Globe*, 2675-8. E. J. Hobsbawm observes that "the American Civil War, whatever its political origins, was the triumph of the industrialised North over the agrarian South, almost, one might even say, the transfer of the South from the informal empire of Britain (to whose cotton industry it was the economic pendant) into the new major industrial economy of the United States. . . an early if giant step on the road which was in the twentieth century to turn all the Americas from a British to an American economic dependency." *The Age of Capital, 1848–1875* (London: Abacus, 1975), 98. "Britain's apparent industrial supremacy" Graeme M. Holmes likewise observed, "depended to some extent on her ability to maintain such a large share of world markets." *Britain and America: A Comparative Economic History, 1850–1939* (London: David & Charles, 1976), 11; also 19–24.

35. Ibid. 20-11-1862, King of the Belgians to Queen Victoria, from George Earle Buckle (ed.), *The Letters of Queen Victoria, Second Series*, 2 vols. (London: 1926), 1: 48. The *Passaic*-class monitor U.S.S. *Camanche* was dispatched (manufactured but unassembled) to San Francisco to provide added security; see Canney, *The Ironclads*, 77–78.

36. 30-6-1862, "Ship Canal," *Congressional Globe*, 3023–3031. See also 3-6-1862, 37th Congress, 2nd Session, House of Representatives, Report No. 114, *Enlargement of the Locks of the Erie and Oswego Canals*, authored by Blair. The Secretary of the Navy assured him that "nearly forty" naval vessels "now under construction on the Western rivers including the purchased"

could indeed navigate the proposed canals. The Department regarded it of "great importance that the Gun Boats should be able to pass between the Mississippi and the Lakes." 30-6-1862, Welles to Blair, Welles Papers, LOC. Major Joseph Gilbert Totten's 30-4-1862 memo to President Lincoln "On the Defense of the Upper Lakes" specified "when war shall be deemed to be near at hand, armored vessels of great power should be got ready, to take positions that will prevent the escape of similar vessels from all opposite ports." Lincoln Papers Collection, LOC.

37. 30-6-1862, "Ship Canal," *Congressional Globe*, 3023–3031.

38. Ibid.

39. See Hobsbawm, *Industry and Empire*, 130–131, 137–140, 152, 176–186.

40. Alfred Grant, *The American Civil War and the British Press* (London: McFarland & Company, Inc., 2000), 156; Palmerston to Austen Henry Layard, October 20, 1861, from Jasper Ridley, *Lord Palmerston* (London: 1970), 552. Martin Crawford writes, "Although impossible to measure precisely, the impact of the Morrill Tariff on British attitudes toward the United States was certainly much greater than most modern historians have been willing to admit." *Anglo-American*, 93. Palmerston told Charles Francis Adams simply, "We do not like slavery, but we want cotton and we dislike very much your Morrill tariff." James Ford Rhodes, *History of the Civil War, 1861–1865* (New York: 1917), 65. See also Frank Lawrence Owsley, *King Cotton Diplomacy: Foreign Relations of the Confederate States of America* (Chicago: 1959), 191–192; Jones, *Union in Peril*, 34.

41. 9-12-1861, "Annual Report of the Secretary of the Treasury," *Congressional Globe*, 37th Congress, 2nd Session, 24. James McPherson notes that the new Confederate Constitution specifically prohibited protective tariffs, in order to preserve its "Free Trade" export-import relationship with Great Britain. *Ordeal by Fire: The Civil War and Reconstruction* (Boston: 2001), 150. See Allen Salisbury, *The Civil War and the American System: America's Battle with Britain, 1860–1876* (New York: 1978), for an argument that Britain's economic motives for intervention were far more insidious than simply resuming the cotton trade.

42. 30-6-1862, "Ship Canal", *Congressional Globe*, 3023–3031. This referred to Palmerston's well-publicized outrage at Union General Butler's proclamation against further acts by New Orleans women against U.S. officers garrisoned there.

43. 30-6-1862, "Ship Canal," *Congressional Globe*, 3023–3031. Canals and railroads might improve communications and facilitate greater mobility in modern warfare, but battles would still be fought, even if for their preservation or destruction. Ultimately, victory would depend on the ability to muster superior resources on the spot—in this case, opposing shores—for local "command of the sea." Here the United States would have the advantage.

44. 5-6-1862, Shufeldt to Flag-Officer, RG 45, Entry 152; 14-5-1862, Powell to Welles, RG 45, Entry 38. See also Powell's interesting series of reports to the Department of the Navy on Allied naval and military operations against Mexico in *ORN*, ser. 1, vol. 1, 307–391, from Feb. 19 to May 29, 1862.

45. 29-5-1862, Bell to Welles, *ORN*, ser. 1, vol. 1, 392. Bell's flagship, the screw-sloop U.S.S. *Lancaster*, was launched in 1858 but averaged only 6 knots speed, 10 knots maximum. See also 8-9-1862, Dahlgren to Welles, on the lack of heavy naval guns in California, RG 45, Letters Rec'd.

46. 9-6-1862, Samuel Whiting to Commanding Naval Officer, Key West, RG 45, Entry 152. John N. Maffitt, C.S.N., actually took command of the *Oreto*; see Ivan Musicant, *Divided Waters: The Naval History of the Civil War* (New Jersey: Castle Books, 2000), 332–335.

47. Some of the "leads" obtained were outright forgeries and cost the State Department dearly to buy them; see Beale, *Diary*, 1: 175–176, entry dated 18-10-1862, for example.

48. 21-6-1862, F. H. Morse to Seward, RG 45, Entry 152. See also 4-10-1862, Welles to Acting Rear Admiral J. L. Lardner, RG 45, Entry 152, forwarding the U.S. Consul in London's enclosed color drawings of British-built "infernal machines."

49. 12-6-1862, Adams to Seward, RG 45, Entry 152.

50. Baxter, *Introduction*, 278.

51. 28-6-1862, Barnes to Corning, Welles Papers, LOC.

52. 26-6-1862, *New York Herald*.

53. Barnes revealed to Fox the same day that Ericsson had also "written in the strongest terms privately to the editor of the *New York Herald*. "This will probably end the latter's tirade of abuse." 28-6-1862, Barnes to Fox, Fox Papers, New York.

54. 26-6-1862, *New York Herald*.

55. 1-12-1862, Annual Address to Congress, *Congressional Globe*, Appendix. Lincoln was fascinated with the prospect that, given "an average decennial increase of 34.69 per cent," the population of the United States could reach over 251 million by 1930—in direct relation to Europe's—*but only if* "we do not ourselves relinquish the chance by the folly and evils of disunion, or by long and exhausting war springing from the only great element of national discord among us": chattel slavery.

56. 28-6-1862, Lincoln to Seward, Lincoln Papers, LOC. Lincoln called for 300,000 more volunteers, to enlist for three years, on July 3. A month later this unpopular appeal would be amended to nine months.

57. 12-7-1862, 37th Congress, 2nd Session, House of Representatives, Executive Document No. 148, *Relations Between the United States and Foreign Powers*, 1. Seward's enclosed letter to Lincoln is dated 11-7-1862. Dahlgren notes the same day Seward's desire for "a law authorizing the President to issue Letters of Marque, in view of probable foreign trouble." *Memoirs*, 375.

58. 1-7-1862, Anne to John Rodgers, Rodgers Papers, LOC. See also Dahlgren, *Memoirs*, 373, 376–367, who was sympathetic to McClellan.

59. 2-7-1862, J. M. Forbes to Fox, Fox Papers, New York, Box 3. Beckwith's enclosed letter to Forbes is dated Paris, 13-6-1862.

60. 12-7-1862, Bright to Seward, Lincoln Papers, LOC.

61. The contract was set down between Smith and Webb July 3; RG 45, Entry 464, AD, Box 51. Welles authorized Smith to sign on the 17th; RG 71, Entry 5, Box 423.

62. Entry dated 24-7-1865, Beale, *Diary*, 2: 340.

63. Officially named the day after the Battle of Antietam; 18-9-1862, Stimers to Webb, RG 19, Entry 1250.

64. 20-6-1862, Smith to Whitney, RG 45, Entry 464, AD, Box 51.

65. 30-6-1862, Gregory to Smith, RG 19, Entry 1235. See also 30-6-1862, Gregory to Welles, RG 45, Entry 38. Welles informed Commodore Paulding of the New York Navy Yard he could not grant "the workmen full time for the day on which they were permitted to attend the Union meeting in New York." There was no precedent, and it was "not desirable to inaugurate such a system." 23-7-1962, Welles to Paulding, RG 45, Entry 328.

66. 1-7-1862, Smith to Gregory, RG 45, Entry 464, AD, Box 51.

67. 6-7-1862, Ericsson to Fox, Ericsson Papers, LOC. For problems associated with Civil War America's "Building Iron Ships in a Wooden Shipbuilding Culture" see William H. Thiesen, *Industrializing American Shipbuilding: The Transformation of Ship Design and Construction, 1820–1920* (Gainesville: University Press of Florida, 2006), notably 80–139.

68. 19-7-1862, R. B. Forbes to Fox, Part 1, Letterbook, Forbes Papers, LOC. Fox replied with some annoyance, "If our Boston people are going to make terms for gold, they will see the work go to New York and Phila. The last bid for engines from Boston was 40% higher than the two latter places. We have ordered a board to go on and examine the cause of the delay in Carey's engines on board the Housatonic. Somebody is trifling, and whether it is our fault or Carey's I am most anxious to find out." 26-7-1862, Fox to R. B. Forbes, Fox Papers, New York, Box 5.

69. See 2-7-1862, and 14-7-1862, Ericsson to Fox, Ericsson Papers, LOC.

70. 8-7-1862, Griswold to Ericsson, Ericsson Papers, LOC; and 8-7-1862, Ericsson to Griswold, draft telegrams, Ericsson Papers, Philadelphia. Fox had already sounded out Ericsson on prices for two more of his oceangoing monitors after all; 5-7-1862, Fox to Ericsson, Fox Papers, New York, Box 5. Winslow indeed withdrew his support; 23-7-1862, Winslow to Ericsson, Ericsson Papers, LOC.

71. 9-7-1862, Gregory to Smith, RG 19, Entry 1235.

72. 24-7-1862, Ericsson to Fox, Fox Papers, New York, Box 3. Even Commodore Paulding wrote Welles he had "never been so much concerned as I am now." The President should be urged to institute a national draft. "Notwithstanding all the great and the enthusiastic meetings there is an apathy throughout the country and the people will not meet the wants of the government for any bounty that can reasonably be given, and at this time I consider Washington in greater danger than Richmond." 27-7-1862, Paulding to Welles, Welles Papers, LOC.

73. 29-7-1862, Palmerston to Somerset, Somerset Papers, Aylesbury; 29-7-1862, Welles to Stanton, Welles Papers, LOC.

74. 29-7-1862, Welles to Stanton, Welles Papers, LOC.

75. Entry dated 10-10-1862, Beale, *Diary*, 1: 167.

76. 30-6-1862, Porter to Fox, Porter Papers, LOC. S. H. Locket, the Chief Engineer of the Confederate defenses of Vicksburg, later ridiculed the mortars' "steady bombardment . . . even the citizens of the town became so accustomed to it that they went about their daily occupations." "The Defense of Vicksburg," in Robert Underwood Johnson and Clarence Clough Buel (eds.), *Battles and*

Leaders of the Civil War, 4 vols. (Edison: Castle Books, 1956 reprint of 1884–1888 original series), 3: 484.

77. 13-7-1862, Porter to Farragut, *ORN*, ser. 1, vol. 18, 678–681.

78. Ibid.

79. Entry dated 6-6-1862, *ORN*, ser. 1, vol. 18, 708.

80. Isaac Brown, "The Confederate Gun-Boat Arkansas," in Johnson and Buel, *Battles and Leaders*, 3: 575. His official report lists "4 or more ironclad vessels, 2 heavy sloops of war, 4 gunboats, and 7 or 8 rams." 15-7-1862, Brown to Mallory, *ORN*, ser. 1, vol. 19, 64.

81. Ibid. Brown reported 10 killed and 15 wounded on the *Arkansas*; half his remaining crew were exhausted from the overpowering heat of the engine room. For Southern morale, see Confederate Major-General Earl Van Dorn's enthusiastic telegrams to President Jefferson Davis, 15- and 16-7-1862, *ORN*, ser. 1, vol. 19, 65.

82. Brown, "The Confederate Gun-Boat Arkansas"; Johnson and Buel, *Battles and Leaders*, 3: 577. This must have been fired by the steam sloop U.S.S. *Oneida*, which mounted two 11-inch Dahlgren pivots; see 16-7-1862, Commander S. Phillips Lee to Farragut, *ORN*, ser. 1, vol. 19, 27. As Brown described his ironclad later that night, "We are much cut up, out pilot house mashed, and some ugly places through our armor." 15-7-1862, Brown to Flag-Officer William F. Lynch, *ORN*, ser. 1, vol. 19, 70.

83. 17-7-1862, Farragut to Welles, *ORN*, ser. 1, vol. 19, 4.

84. See 17-7-1862, Davis to Farragut, *ORN*, ser. 1, vol. 19, 9–10; 18-7-1862, Farragut to Davis, *ORN*, ser. 1, vol. 19, 13.

85. 25-7-1862, Welles to Farragut and Davis, telegram, *ORN*, ser. 1, vol. 19, 36; 2-8-1862, Welles to Farragut (and Davis), *ORN*, ser. 1, vol. 19, 5–7.

86. Beale, *Diary*, 1: 71–72; also 30-7-1862, Gideon to Mary Welles, Welles Papers, LOC.

87. In Barnard's opinion, however, quantity—and speed of construction—was perhaps more important than quality. "To build a regular iron clad gun boat is a long job," he wrote to Fox. "Might we not, as they did on the Mississippi, and as the Confederates have done [on the James], improvise for this service by simply taking river steamers or our present gun boats and giving the iron shields[?] If the vessel is to be confined to river operations it is not of much consequence that she has not seagoing qualities." 19-7-1862, Barnard to Fox, Fox Papers, New York, Box 3.

88. 19-8-1862, Welles to Farragut, Welles Papers, LOC. Even if Union warships were freed from supporting the Army of the Potomac on the James River to bolster Farragut instead, Welles could only advise Stanton if "Newport News is to be held by the Army . . . that half a dozen 200 lb. Rifled Parrott guns be mounted there, as means to assist in keeping blockaded the Iron Clad vessels now building at Richmond." 29-8-1862, Welles to Stanton, Welles Papers, LOC.

89. 10-8-1862, Beale, *Diary*, 1: 72. "Not but that the Rebels may get up a formidable affair—may injure some of our vessels, and do harm," Welles wrote to his wife. "The child might be born—might crawl into the oven, &c., &c., When the Iron monster crawls into New York harbor, destroys all the shipping, burns the city, the scare will have been consummated. There are a great many people in this world who like to despair with them. . . . It is good

for such to read the sensational articles in the N. York papers." 13-8-1862, Gideon to Mary Welles, Welles Papers, LOC.

90. See Beale, *Diary*, 1: 70–71. Welles and Seward were privately informed of Lincoln's intentions on July 13, and the Cabinet formally on July 22. The prevailing view was to wait until the North achieved a clear battlefield victory before announcing emancipation—otherwise Europe would regard the action as a sign of desperation on the part of the Union. Welles personally favored Emancipation as a weapon of war: "the Rebels themselves had invoked war on the subject of slavery, had appealed to arms, and they must abide the consequences"; entry dated October 1, Beale, *Diary*, 1: 159.

91. 2-8-1862, Ericsson to Lincoln, Lincoln Papers, LOC. The "repeating rifle" was in fact a machine gun. See also Robert V. Bruce, *Lincoln and the Tools of War* (Urbana: University of Illinois Press, 1989), 208–211.

92. See 16-8-1862 and 20-8-1862, Fox to Welles, Welles Papers, LOC; also John D. Hayes, "'Captain Fox—*He* Is the Navy Department,'" *U.S. Naval Institute Proceedings*, Vol. 91, No. 9 (1965).

93. 4-8-1862, Fox to Ericsson, Fox Papers, New York, Box 5.

94. Entry dated 30-7-1862, Dahlgren, *Memoirs*, 377. Dahlgren was also increasingly frustrated with his responsibilities at the Bureau of Ordnance, preferring the glory of a flag-command, which Welles and Fox both opposed despite Dahlgren's close ties with Lincoln; *Memoirs*, 374.

95. 4-8-1862, Fox to Ericsson, Fox Papers, New York, Box 5.

96. 5-8-1862, Ericsson to Fox, Fox Papers, New York, Box 3.

97. 5-8-1862, Fox to Ericsson, Ericsson Papers, Philadelphia.

98. 5-8-1862, Welles to Dahlgren, RG 74, Entry 16.

99. 6-8-1862, Ericsson to Fox, Ericsson Papers, LOC.

100. 7-8-1862, Ericsson to Welles, Ericsson Papers, LOC. See also 20-10-1862, Ericsson to Brigadier-General C. P. Buckingham, Ericsson Papers, LOC, enclosing a list of draftees he wished exempt from the Pennsylvania State militia. "These men are of the greatest importance and without them the rolling mill has had to stop."

101. 9-8-1862, Gregory to Welles, RG 19, Entry 1235.

102. See 13-8-1862, Welles to his wife, and 20-8-1862, Fox to Welles, Welles Papers, LOC.

103. 8-8-1862, Fox to Ericsson, Ericsson Papers, LOC.

104. 9-8-1862, Ericsson to Fox, Fox Papers, New York, Box 3.

105. 13-8-1862, Fox to Stimers, Fox Papers, New York, Box 5.

106. 16-8-1862, and 20-8-1862, Fox to Welles, Welles Papers, LOC.

107. 23-8-1862, Dahlgren to Ericsson, Ericsson Papers, LOC.

108. 4-8-1862, Edge to Fox, Fox Papers, New York, Box 3.

109. 1-4-1862, Ericsson to Fox, draft, Ericsson Papers, Philadelphia; 6-8-1862, Ericsson to Fox, Ericsson Papers, LOC; 8-8-1862, telegram, Ericsson to Fox, Fox Papers, New York, Box 3.

110. 14-8-1862, Fox to Ericsson, Fox Papers, New York, Box 5. 10-10-1862, Ericsson to A. C. Banstan, Ericsson Papers, LOC.

111. 18-8-1862, Edge to Fox, Fox Papers, New York, Box 3. See also 26-12-1862, Edge to Fox, Fox Papers, New York, Box 3.

112. 29-8-1862, Ericsson to Dahlgren, Ericsson Papers, LOC.

113. See McPherson, *Battle Cry of Freedom*, 534–53-5; 3-9-1862, 4-9-1862; also 8-9-1862, Lee to Jefferson Davis, *ORN*, ser. 1, vol. 29, 590–592, 600.

114. 5-9-1862, Fox to Stimers, Fox Papers, New York. See also 1-9-1862, telegram, Dahlgren to Fox, RG 45, Letters Rec'd. Dahlgren himself regarded the *New Ironsides* as "a clumsy attempt at an iron clad." The original *Monitor's* turret, however, he was convinced, "would not long stand battering with XI in. shot," *Memoirs*, 377, 381.

115. See 9-9-1862, Fox to Farragut, *ORN*, ser. 1, vol. 19, 184–185. Fox expected that the "first new monitor will be ready October 1; others will come out during the month. Their first strike must be Charleston, where all the munitions go for the use of the rebels." Mobile would have to wait; Farragut's forces were too weak. "It is a dark time for us just now, and the country asks for another naval victory, but my opinion is that wood has taken risk enough, and that iron will be the next affair."

116. 6-9-1862, Gustavus to Virginia L. Woodbury Fox, Fox Papers, New York, Box 5.

117. 9-9-1862, Welles to Wilkes, Welles Papers, LOC.

118. See for example, 4-9-1862, Welles to Spofford, Tileston, & Co., RG 45, Entry 328.

119. 8-9-1862, Welles to Wilkes, Welles Papers, LOC.

120. See 6-8-1862, Welles to Lardner (commanding the West Gulf Squadron at Key West), Welles Papers, LOC. Both Captain Raphael Semmes of the *Alabama* and the Confederate purchasing agent in Britain, James D. Bulloch, criticized Welles for not stationing cruisers instead off the strategic choke-points of key shipping lanes. Raphael Semmes, *Memoirs of Service Afloat During the War Between the States* (Baton Rouge: Louisiana State University Press, 1996 reprint of 1868), 628–630; James D. Bulloch, *The Secret Service of the Confederate States in Europe* (New York: Random House, 2001, reprint of 1884 original), 193–194. For Nassau's importance see Thomas E. Taylor, *Running the Blockade: A Personal Narrative of Adventures, Risks and Escapes During the American Civil War* (Annapolis, MD: U.S. Naval Institute Press, 1995 reprint of 1896), 22–27.

121. 7-8-1862, Welles to Seward, Welles Papers, LOC.

122. 6-9-1862, Stimers to Fox, Fox Papers, New York.

123. 8-9-1862, Ericsson to Fox, Fox Papers, New York. Ericsson's enclosed letter to Dahlgren is dated 3-9-1862; see also 18-9-1862, Welles to Dahlgren, RG 74, Entry 16, Box 4, and 25-9-1862, Dahlgren to Welles, RG 45, Letters Rec'd.

124. 8-9-1862, Griswold to Ericsson, Ericsson Papers, LOC.

125. 15-9-1862, Ericsson to Rowland, Ericsson Papers, LOC. This came hard on the heels of Rowland's capturing front-page headlines (with a portrait-illustration) of the 6-9-1862 *Harper's Weekly*, as builder of the original *Monitor*, with contracts for the *Onondaga*, *Puritan*, three of the *Passaics*, and three more of their turrets for others. See also 8-11-1862, *Scientific American*, 297.

126. 12-9-1862, Stimers to Fox, Fox Papers, New York, Box 4.

127. 13-9-1862, Stimers to Gregory, RG 19, Entry 1248. Perhaps it was for this reason that Ericsson sought a new address by 1864, having lived there previously for 21 years, moving to No. 36 Beach Street, where he remained until his death on March 8, 1889; see Church, *Life of Ericsson*, 2: 302–303.

128. 17-9-1862, Stimers to Loring, RG 19, Entry 1250.

129. 20-9-1862, Fox to Stimers, Fox Papers, New York, Box 5. Stimers eventually disobeyed this order, with Gregory complaining by the spring of 1864 that Stimers "keeps me as ignorant as he possibly can of his doings—considering himself as the supreme director and dictator in all matters. . . ." 12-4-1864, Gregory to Lenthall, RG 45, Entry 464, AC, Box 30; see also 15-12-1864, Fox to Ericsson, Ericsson Papers, Philadelphia.

130. 15-9-1862, Gregory to Lenthall, and 22-9-1862, Gregory to Isherwood, RG 19, Entry 1235. Isherwood already had power as Chief of the Bureau of Steam Engineering to recommend engineers of his choosing to the Navy Yards, and was aware of which engineers were attending to privately built ironclads. See for example 16-9-1862, Isherwood to Welles, RG 45, Letters Rec'd. Gregory's control was extended to cover *Canonicus*-class monitors to be built in the West, namely Pittsburgh and Cincinnati; see 25-9-1862, Fox to Stimers, Fox Papers, New York, Box 5.

131. 16-9-1862, F. A. Murray to Rodgers, Rodgers Papers, LOC.

132. 20-9-1862, Fox to Stimers, Fox Papers, New York, Box 5.

133. 22-9-1862, Gregory to Lenthall, RG 19, Entry 1235.

134. 26-9-1862, Welles to Gregory, Welles Papers, LOC.

135. Enclosed in 25-9-1862, Drayton to Fox, Fox Papers, New York, Box 3.

136. 25-9-1862, Fox to Stimers, Fox Papers, New York, Box 5.

137. 27-9-1862, Fox to Ericsson, Ericsson Papers, Philadelphia.

138. Ibid.

139. 25-9-1862, Stimers to Fox, RG 19, Entry 1250.

140. 27-9-1862, Fox to Stimers, Fox Papers, New York, Box 5.

141. 29-9-1862, Ericsson to Fox, also 12-12-1862, Ericsson to Fox, Fox Papers, New York, Box 3.

142. 29-9-1862, Stimers to Fox, Fox Papers, New York, Box 4.

143. 30-9-1862, Ericsson to Fox, Ericsson Papers, LOC.

144. 29-8-1862, Samuel to Sophie Du Pont, from Hayes, *Samuel Francis Du Pont*, 2: 207.

Chapter 18

1. 4-10-1862, Smith to Merrick & Sons, RG 45, Entry 464, AD, Box 51.

2. See Roberts, *New Ironsides*, 21–22; 25–26; 29–30; also Canney, *The Ironclads*, 18. Roberts's attempted excuse of "tradition" for the placement of the pilot-house does not make it any less impractical in a steam-powered warship. The designer of *New Ironsides*, Barnabas H. Bartol, had made several critical errors.

3. 4-10-1862, Smith to Merrick & Sons, RG 45, Entry 464, AD, Box 51. The ship was under trial for ninety days after being turned over to the Navy. See Roberts, *New Ironsides*, 37–38. See also 15-10-1862, Smith to Captain Thomas Turner, RG 45, Entry 464, AD, Box 51. *New Ironsides* steered so badly as to prevent any greater speed than 6½ knots because her poorly-designed hull gave little power to the rudder—critically exposed above the waterline

unless the ship was weighted down with extra coal. See also 31-10-1862, Turner to Dahlgren, Dahlgren Papers, LOC.

4. 6-10-1862, Stimers to Fox, Fox Papers, New York.

5. 5-10-1862, Gideon to Virginia Welles, Welles Papers, LOC.

6. 8-10-1862, Ericsson to Welles, Ericsson Papers, LOC, Box 4.

7. 6-10-1862, Stimers to Fox, Fox Papers, New York, Box 4.

8. 8-10-1862, Fox to Stimers, Fox Papers, New York, Box 5.

9. 7-10-1862, Drayton to Fox, Fox Papers, New York, Box 3.

10. 7-10-1862, Fox to Stimers, Fox Papers, New York, Box 5.

11. Ibid. See also 5-10-1862, Ericsson to Fox, Fox Papers, New York, Box 3.

12. 6-10-1862, Gregory to Isherwood; 6-10-1862, Gregory to Lenthall, RG 19, Entry 1235.

13. 8-10-1862, Gregory to Welles, RG 19, Entry 1235.

14. 8-10-1862, Stimers to Gregory, RG 19, Entry 1250.

15. 9-10-1862, Stimers to Fox, Fox Papers, New York. The most detailed study of Stimers's role in the Union ironclad program remains Dana Wegner's "Alban C. Stimers and the Office of the General Inspector of Ironclads, 1862–1864," State University of New York at Oneonta M.A. thesis, 1979; see also William H. Roberts, *Civil War Ironclads: The U.S. Navy and Industrial Mobilization* (Baltimore, MD: The John Hopkins University Press, 2002).

16. 15-10-1862, Paulding to Welles, Welles Papers, LOC.

17. 17-10-1862, Smith to Ericsson, Ericsson Papers, LOC.

18. Welles concurred. 21-10-1862, Smith to Welles, RG 45, Letters Rec'd.; 22-10-1862, Welles to Smith, RG 71, Entry 5, Box 423.

19. 17-10-1862, Welles to Gregory, Welles Papers, LOC.

20. 24-10-1862, Ericsson to Fox, Fox Papers, Box 3.

21. 28-10-1862, Fox to Ericsson, Fox Papers, Box 5.

22. 20-10-1862, Gregory to Welles, RG 19, Entry 1235.

23. 17-10-1862, Drayton to Ericsson, Ericsson Papers, LOC.

24. 18-10-1862, and 21-10-1862, Robert Parrott to Ericsson, Ericsson Papers, LOC.

25. 28-10-1862, Ericsson to Wise, RG 74, Entry 22, Box 1.

26. 16-10-1862, Ericsson to Fox, Ericsson Papers, LOC.

27. 29-10-1862, Drayton to Gregory, RG 74, Entry 22, Box 1.

28. 29-10-1862, telegram, Ericsson to Fox, RG 74, Entry 22, Box 1.

29. 30-10-1862, Ericsson to Fox, Fox Papers, New York, Box 3. Welles still had his doubts, sending Fox, Dahlgren and Smith to New York to witness further tests; see Beale, *Diary*, 1: 179, entry dated 1-11-1862.

30. 30-10-1862, Ericsson to Fox, Fox Papers, New York, Box 3. Welles subsequently reprimanded Gregory about reporters "giving accounts of the trial trips of our new iron clad steamers and making public much information which they should not," citing a General Order of the Department dated April 22, 1862; 1-11-1862, Welles to Gregory, Welles Papers, LOC. See also 12-12-1862, U.S. Navy General Order on secrecy, copy found in RG 45, Entry 328.

31. 27-10-1862, *New York Herald*. See the contemporary description of this monitor in *Scientific American*, 16-8-1862, 106, which also quotes Ericsson's claim that the reinforced iron structure of the ship's prow "will split an iceberg."

32. 2-11-1862, Welles to son, Welles Papers, LOC.

33. 14-10-1862, Beale, *Diary*, 1: 172; also 10-10-1862, 165–166, 13- and 14-10-1862, 170–171. See also 10-10-1862, Seward to Welles, and 15-10-1862, Welles to Seward, Welles Papers, LOC; for the *Alabama* see John M. Taylor, "Defiance: Raphael Semmes of the *Alabama*," in William N. Still, Jr., John M. Taylor and Norman C. Delaney (eds.) *Raiders and Blockaders: The American Civil War Afloat* (London: Brassey's, 1998), 23–34; John M. Browne, "The Duel Between the 'Alabama' and the 'Kearsage'," in Johnson and Buel, *Battles and Leaders*, 4: 625; Bulloch, *The Secret Service*, 193; and Mahin, *One War at Time*, 156–159.

34. 9-10-1862, Seward to J. Lothrop Motley, No. 45, *Diplomatic Correspondence*, 936–938. See also Lynn M. Case and Warren F. Spencer, *The United States and France: Civil War Diplomacy* (Philadelphia: University of Pennsylvania Press, 1970).

35. 4-11-1862, Dahlgren to Ericsson, Ericsson Papers, Philadelphia; also RG 74, Entry 22. Six days later Dahlgren posted Ericsson a model of his proposal as well; 10-4-1862, Dahlgren to Ericsson, Ericsson Papers, Philadelphia. By the end of the month, however, Ericsson was convinced Dahlgren's expedient, in light of recent tests, would prove "insufficient"; see 24-11-1862, Stimers to Fox, and 25-11-1862, Fox to Stimers, Fox Papers, New York, Box 5.

36. 4-11-1862, R. B. Forbes to Ericsson, Forbes Family Papers, LOC.

37. 7-11-1862, Drayton to Dahlgren, RG 74, Entry 22.

38. 9-11-1862, Ammen to Dahlgren, Dahlgren Papers, LOC.

39. Success was also necessary; as Stimers pointed out to Fox, the 15-inch gun would have to utilize charges of more than 40 pounds to be effective against strongly-armored targets, 10-11-1862, Stimers to Fox, Fox Papers, New York, Box 4.

40. 9-11-1862, Ericsson to Fox, Fox Papers, New York, Box 3.

41. Ibid. See also RG 74, Entry 22. Stimers later explained to Fox that, according to Ericsson, "it appeared reports were always obtained someway of such trials and that it would be better to have only such facts as would encourage our own people published than to have all the secrets we desire to keep blazoned forth in an irresponsible report," 20-11-1862, Stimers to Fox, Fox Papers, New York, Box 4.

42. 17-11-1862, Ericsson to editor of *New York World*, Ericsson Papers, LOC. Captain Isaac Hull commanded the frigate U.S.S. *Constitution* in her duel with H.M.S. *Guerriere* (19 August 1812); Oliver Hazard Perry commanded U.S. forces in their victory over the British at the Battle of Lake Erie (10 September 1813).

43. 29-11-1862, "Iron-Clads," *Harper's Weekly*, 758.

44. 15-11-1862, Gregory to Welles, RG 19, Entry 1235.

45. 15-11-1862, Welles to Gregory, RG 45, Entry 15; 17-11-1862, Welles to Gregory, Welles Papers, LOC.

46. 16-11-1862, Gregory to Dahlgren, RG 19, Entry 1235.

47. 16-11-1862, Drayton to Dahlgren, Dahlgren Papers, LOC.

48. 19-11-1862, John to Anne Rodgers, Rodgers Papers, LOC.

49. 20-11-1862, Stimers to Fox, Fox Papers, New York, Box 4.

50. 26-11-1862, Ericsson to Fox, Ericsson Papers, LOC.

Chapter 19

1. 6-11-1862, Murray to Rodgers, Rodgers Papers, LOC.

2. 6-11-1862, Turner to Lee, and 11-11-1862, Dahlgren to Welles, RG 45, Letters Rec'd. See also 2-11-1862, Dahlgren to Welles, RG 45, Letters Rec'd. At any rate, the U.S.S. *Monitor* had returned to Hampton Roads by the 15th.

3. 10-11-1862, David Radly Field to Welles, Welles Papers, LOC.

4. See 16-9-1862, telegram, E. D. Morgan to Welles, *ORN*, ser. 1, vol. 1, 475–476, and 8-11-1862, Morgan to Welles, *ORN* ser. 1, vol. 1, 539.

5. 12-11-1862, Boston Board of Trade to Welles, *ORN*, ser. 1, vol. 1, 542–544. See also the deputation of the Boston Marine Society, 18-11-1862, to Welles, *ORN*, ser. 1, vol. 1, 547–548; and 14-11-1862, C. H. Marshall, Chairman of the New York City Chamber of Commerce, to Welles, requesting commissions to fit out private vessels to capture the *Alabama* "under promise of reward by citizens," *ORN*, ser. 1, vol. 1, 545.

6. 13-11-1862, Chase to Welles, Welles Papers, LOC.

7. See 17-11-1862, Morgan to Welles, Welles Papers, LOC; also *ORN*, ser. 1, vol. 1, 546–547; and 18-11-1862, Welles to Paulding, RG 45, Entry 328.

8. 19-11-1862, Barney to Welles; 20-11-1862, telegram, Morgan and Barney to Welles; *ORN*, ser. 1, vol. 1, 548. Gregory meanwhile reported "a very large force employed" on the *Roanoke*, 22-11-1862, Gregory to Lenthall, RG 19, Entry 1235.

9. 22-11-1862, Welles to Morgan, Welles Papers, LOC.

10. 19-11-1862, John Forbes to Fox; 22-11-1862, Fox to John Forbes; Fox Papers, New York, Box 5.

11. 7-11-1862, Fox to Lee, *ORN* ser. 1, vol. 8, 203–204.

12. 28-11-1862, Fox to George W. Blunt, *ORN*, ser. 1, vol. 8, 237. See also 26-11-1862, Welles to Lieutenant-Colonel Martin Burke, *ORN* ser. 1, vol. 8, 235.

13. 10-11-1862, Stimers to Fox, Fox Papers, New York; 13-11-1862, Gregory to Welles, RG 19, Entry 1235.

14. See 29-11-1862, Drayton to Turner; 3-12-1863, Drayton to Lee; 9-12-1863, Fox to Lee, *ORN*, ser. 1, vol. 8, 243; 269.

15. 10-12-1862, Ericsson to Fox, Fox Papers, New York, Box 3.

16. 7-12-1862, John to Anne Rodgers, Rodgers Papers, LOC.

17. 16-12-1862, Ericsson to Loring, Ericsson Papers, LOC.

18. 16-12-1862, Fox to Ericsson, Fox Papers, New York, Box 5.

19. 30-12-1862, Ericsson to Fox, Fox Papers, New York, Box 3.

20. 30-12-1862, Fox to Ericsson, Fox Papers, New York, Box 5.

21. 16-12-1862, John to Anne Rodgers, Rodgers Papers, LOC.

22. 31-12-1862, John to Anne Rodgers, Rodgers Papers, LOC.

Chapter 20

1. 7-12-1862, Seward to Taylor, and 17-12-1862, Taylor to Seward, *Papers Relating to Foreign Affairs*, 771–773.

2. See for example, 1-12-1862, Welles to Paulding, RG 45, Entry 328.

3. 2-12-1862, Welles to Wilkes, Welles Papers, LOC. See also 15-12-1862, Welles to Wilkes, ibid.

4. 8-12-1862, Welles to Seward, Welles Papers, LOC. See also William E. Geoghegan, Thomas W. Green and Frank J. Merli, "The South's Scottish Sea Monster," *The American Neptune*, Vol. 29, No. 1, (January 1969), 5–29.

5. 9-12-1862, Fox to John M. Forbes, Fox Papers, New York, Box 5. See also Bulloch, *The Secret Service*, 33–34, 262–307.

6. 10-12-1862, John M. Forbes to Fox, Fox Papers, New York, Box 3.

7. 13-9-1863, Palmerston to Somerset, Somerset Papers, Aylesbury. According to J. P. Baxter, "when Fox sent [Ericsson] a plan of one of the Laird rams . . . [he] replied 'such a gingerbread affair must not come near our XV inch bulldogs in their impregnable kennels,'" 26-9-1863, Ericsson to Fox, from Baxter, *Introduction*, 329.

8. 12-12-1862, Welles to Sedgwick and Hale, RG 45, Entry 5.

9. Ibid.

10. 1-12-1862, *Appendix to the Congressional Globe*, 37th Congress, 3rd Session, *Report of the Secretary of the Navy*. For the effects of the Union blockade upon the South see David G. Surdam, *Northern Naval Superiority and the Economics of the American Civil War* (Columbia: University of South Carolina Press, 2001).

11. 1-12-1862, *Report of the Secretary of the Navy*.

12. See for example John Sherman, *Recollections of Forty Years in the House, Senate and Cabinet: An Autobiography*, 2 vols. (Chicago: The Werner Company, 1895), 1: 298.

13. 1-12-1862, *Report of the Secretary of the Navy*.

14. Entry dated 24-12-1862, Beale, *Diary*, 1: 206.

15. Welles makes the point in his journal entry of 26-12-1863 that "a few strong, powerful vessels will conduce to economy because they will deter commercial nations from troubling us, and if not troubled, we need no large and expensive navy," Beale, *Diary*, 1: 496.

16. Ibid, entry dated 29-12-1862, 1: 207. See also David Niven, *Gideon Welles: Lincoln's Secretary of the Navy* (Baton Rouge: Louisiana State University Press, 1994 reprint), for the debate on issuing letters of marque, or state-sanctioned privateering, as another possible diplomatic counter to Great Britain. Though Seward was in favor of the measure, Welles opposed it vehemently; it would forfeit control of the naval war while provoking another— "a serious calamity to us but not less serious to [England]," 448–451.

17. 1-12-1862, Message of the President of the United States. Not long after this, Lincoln did, however, make an address "To the Workingmen of Manchester, England"; that "A fair examination of history has seemed to authorize a belief that the past action and influences of the United States were generally regarded as having been beneficent towards mankind. I have therefore reckoned upon the forbearance of nations," 19-1-1863, from Don E. Fehrenbacher (ed.), *Abraham Lincoln: Speeches and Writings, 1859–1865* (New York: Literary Classics of the United States, Inc., 1989), 431–433; see also James M. McPherson, *Abraham Lincoln and the Second American Revolution* (New York: Oxford University Press, 1990), 28–29, 51–56, 115–118, 135–136, and his chapter, "'The Whole Family of Man': Lincoln and the Last Best Hope Abroad," in May (ed.), *The Union, the Confederacy, and the Atlantic Rim*, 131–158; also Frederick Merk, *Manifest Destiny and*

Mission in American History: A Reinterpretation (Cambridge, MA: Harvard University Press, 1963, 1995 reprint), 261–262. For the cotton embargo of 1861–1862 see Owsley, *King Cotton Diplomacy*, 18–20, 23–42. Needless to say, Earl Russell was revolted by the South's attempt to strong-arm British diplomacy through 'cotton famine' and the threat of a working-class 'Revolution.'

18. 1-12-1862, *Annual Report of the Secretary of the Navy*. 4-4-1863, Abraham Lincoln, "Memorandum Concerning Harbor Defenses," from Roy P. Basler (ed.), *The Collected Works of Abraham Lincoln*, 9 vols. (New Brunswick, NJ: Rutgers University Press, 1953), 6: 163; J. G. Randall, *Lincoln the Liberal Statesman* (London: Eyre & Spottiswoode, 1947), 182. In writing to Queen Victoria on February 1, 1861, expressing condolences for the recent death of Prince Albert, Lincoln carefully noted that the "moral strength" of the "People of the United States" originated from its "kindred relationship" with the "People of Great Britain," despite "our distinct national interests, objects, and aspirations"; from Basler (ed.), *Collected Works*, 5: 117.

19. 26-12-1862, Smith to Welles, RG 45, Letters Rec'd.

20. 22-11-1862, *Congressional Globe* Appendix, *Report of the Secretary of the Navy*, Enclosure No. 5, Report of the Bureau of Ordnance, 709–722.

21. "As far as results can be compared," concluded Alexander Holley in his exhaustive 1865 *Treatise on Ordnance and Armor*, "the simple 15 in. cast-iron ball at a moderate velocity appears to be capable, with much less strain upon the gun, of inflicting much more of the kind of damage under consideration, than the more powerful and costly rifle-bolts, because it wastes less power in local effect . . . the destructive effect of heavy projectiles at low velocities, particularly upon the *Warrior* class of armor, has been seriously underrated, especially in Europe," 178–179; also 152–153, 171. Holley stressed, however, that the 15- or 20-inch shot had to strike at relatively high velocities upon impact—i.e., at close range—to achieve this sort of maximum power. One assumes, as did Ericsson, that a low-freeboard, monitor-type ironclad was best suited for this.

Culmination and Consequence: "The Fiery Focus"

1. Kevin J. Weddle, *Lincoln's Tragic Admiral: The Life of Samuel Francis Du Pont* (Charlottesville: University of Virginia Press, 2005), 213–215.

2. Russell F. Weigley, *The American Way of War: A History of United States Military Strategy and Policy* (Bloomington: Indiana University Press, 1977), 171.

3. Kenneth J. Hagan, *This People's Navy: The Making of American Sea Power* (New York: The Free Press, 1991), 170.

4. Spencer C. Tucker, *A Short History of the Civil War at Sea* (Wilmington, DE: Scholarly Resources, 2002), 94–97. See also Charles M. Robinson III's chapter on "The Charleston Effect" in *Hurricane of Fire: The Union Assault on Fort Fisher* (Annapolis, MD: Naval Institute Press, 1998), 41–50. Probably the best recent treatment of the Union campaign against Charleston can be found in Musicant, *Divided Waters*, 368–408, though it lacks in analytical conclusions what it can boast in a well-researched, stimulating narrative.

5. E. Milby Burton, *The Siege of Charleston, 1861–1865* (Columbia: University of South Carolina Press, 1970), 132, 135–136.

6. Even though he later describes Union naval officers as "realists"; "they were willing to face up to their tasks but they tended to be overawed by the strength of the opposition that they had to contend with," Bern Anderson, "The Naval Strategy of the Civil War," *Military Affairs*, Vol. 26, No. 11 (Spring 1962), 19, 21.

7. Robert Erwin Johnson, "Ships Against Forts: Charleston, 7 April 1863," *The American Neptune*, Vol. 57, No. 2 (Spring 1997), 123–135.

8. Letter dated 24-3-1863, from Beverly Wilson Palmer (ed.), *The Selected Letters of Charles Sumner*, 2 vols. (Boston: Northeastern University Press, 1990), 2: 152–153.

9. 30-3-1863, Turner to Hamilton Fish, Hamilton Fish Papers, LOC.

10. Entry dated 12-3-1863; Beale, *Diary*, 1: 247.

11. "Order of battle and plan of attack upon Charleston, South Carolina," in *Report of the Secretary of the Navy in Relation to Armored Vessels* (Washington, DC: GPO: 1864), 60–61.

12. "These iron bottomed vessels foul in a very remarkable degree. Copper bottomed ones do also," observed John Rodgers, "Grass on the Wabash is I hear a foot long—what must be our condition[?]" 2-6-1863, John to Anne Rodgers, Rodgers Papers, LOC.

13. "Circular of instructions from the commanding general at Charleston, S.C.," 26-12-1862, *ORN*, 1: 14, 102–105.

14. "Report of Captain John Rodgers, commanding United States iron-clad *Weehawken*, April 8, 1863," *Report of the Secretary of the Navy*, 63–64.

15. Rear-Admiral C. R. P. Rodgers, "Du Pont's Attack at Charleston," in Johnson and Buel, *Battles and Leaders*, 4: 37. See also the depiction offered by Major John Johnson, Confederate Engineer-in-charge at Ft. Sumter, quoted in Jack Greene and Allesandro Massignani, *Ironclads at War: The Origin and Development of the Armored Warship, 1854–1891* (Conshohocken, PA: Combined Publishing, 1998), 140–141.

16. 13-4-1863, John to Anne Rodgers, Rodgers Papers, LOC.

17. Henry Kloeppel, serving aboard the monitor U.S.S. *Patapsco*, described how his vessel "stood up [towards the forts] under a most fearful fire[,] the shot & shell fall close and plentiful all around us," and that shot and shell "fell so closely around us as to bury us in the Spray of water, flying up like so many waterspouts, as to spoil their aim and range," April 7, 1863 entry, Diary of H. Henry Kloeppel, LOC, Manuscript Division. See also the detailed account in Alvah F. Hunter (Craig L. Symonds, ed.), *A year on a Monitor and the Destruction of Fort Sumter* (Columbia: University of South Carolina Press, 1987), 47–61.

18. At one point she anchored above an electrically-fired Confederate mine filled with 3,000 pounds of gunpowder. "For ten minutes," Captain Langdon Cheves of the Confederate Army later wrote, "I could not have placed the *Ironsides* more directly over it if I had been allowed to, but the confounded thing, as is usual, would not go off," Roberts, *USS New Ironsides*, 54.

19. *Keokuk* passed in front of the monitor *Nahant* to within 550 yards of Fort Moultrie, where she quickly drew the attention of most of the Confederate

gunners. Her "career," as Donald Canney expresses, "was entirely Hobbesian: short and violent," *The Ironclads*, 73.

20. "Report of Captain T. Turner," 10-4-1863, *Report of the Secretary of the Navy*, 76.

21. *Nahant* temporarily lost control of her pilot house wheel and drifted towards the obstructions under the returning flood tide until a secondary apparatus was engaged. The *Passaic*-class monitors were fitted with three steering wheels, "in case the pilot house should be destroyed in action," 26-11-1862, John Ericsson to Fox, Ericsson Papers, LOC.

22. See the individual battle/damage reports in *ORN*, ser. 1, vol. 14, 10–24. The most serious damage to the ironclads was inflicted by the four 10-inch smoothbore Columbiads and two 7-inch Brooke heavy rifled guns of Fort Sumter and the five 10-inch Columbiads of Battery Bee, near Fort Moultrie; see "Return of guns and mortars at forts and batteries in Charleston Harbor, engaged April 7, 1863," *ORN*, ser. 1, vol. 14, 83.

23. 14-4-1863, "Report of Chief Engineer Stimers, U.S. Navy," *ORN*, ser. 1, vol. 14, 41–42.

24. See "Enclosure No. 2.—Despatch No. 208, 1863," dated 20-4-1863, Rodgers to DuPont, in *Report of the Secretary of the Navy*, 94–96; for Stimers's court-martial see pages 114–170; also Bennett, *The Steam Navy*, 403–422.

25. "Report of Commander Downes, U.S. Navy, commanding U.S.S. *Nahant*, regarding the inferior quality of bolts used in the construction of that vessel," 29-4-1863, *ORN*, ser. 1, vol. 14, 51. Henry Kloeppel agreed, noting in his journal entry of April 7, 1863 that "Nahant was also very mutch [*sic*] injured but not so as to make her unfit for service, her injuries as mostly owing to poor construction, not being put together as strong as the rest of the Monitors. Her bolts in the Turret flying outward, she resembled more a Hedgehog than anything I ever saw," Kloeppel Diary, LOC.

26. 12-4-1863, Anne to John Rodgers, Rodgers Papers, LOC.

27. "Report of the commanding officer of the batteries on Sullivan's Island," 13-4-1863, *ORN*, ser. 1, vol. 14, 101.

28. *Report of the Secretary of the Navy*, 75.

29. Greene and Massignani, *Ironclads in Action*, 143.

30. "Copy of a letter found on the C.S.S. *Atlanta*," 26-4-1863, addressed F. H. Harleston to Lieutenant Thurston, Confederate States Marine Corps, C.S.S. *Atlanta, ORN*, ser. 1, vol. 14, 111.

31. *Civil War Naval Ordnance* (Naval History Division, Navy Department, 1969), 10. See also Warren Ripley, *Artillery and Ammunition of the Civil War* (New York: Van Nostrand Reinhold, 1970), 97–100, 255–257, 370. For damage to Fort Sumter see "Report of Major Echols, C. S. Army," 9-4-1863, *ORN*, ser. 1, vol. 14, 85–95, 95–98; also Rowena Reed, *Combined Operations in the Civil War* (Annapolis, MD: Naval Institute Press, 1978), 294.

32. 8-4-1863, DuPont to Welles, *Official Dispatches and Letters of Rear Admiral Du Pont, U.S. Navy 1846–48, 1861–63* (Wilmington, DE: Ferris Bros., 1883), 441–442. Irritation with their own vessels was manifest even before the attack; see George E. Belknap, "Reminiscent of the 'New Ironsides' off Charleston," *United Service Journal*, January 1879, 63–82, taken from the

"Civil War Pamphlets" collection, Volume 5, U.S. Naval Historical Center Archives, Washington Navy Yard, DC.

33. Entry dated 9-4-1863, Beale, *Diary*, 1: 264–265. Dahlgren likewise described Lincoln on February 14 as "restless about Charleston," Dahlgren, *Memoir*, 388. For the domestic circumstances of the Civil War at this time see McPherson, *Battle Cry of Freedom*, 591–611, 625; also Reed, *Combined Operations*, 280–281.

34. See "Statement of commanding officers of ironclads which participated in the attack on Fort Sumter, in response to newspaper accounts," 24-4-1863, *ORN*, ser. 1, vol. 14, 45–48.

35. Described by DuPont as "a porcupine's hide and quills turned outside in and sewed up at one end," from Reed, *Combined Operations*, 268, ff. 14; Johnson, "Ships Against Forts," 124–125; 31-5-1862, DuPont to Fox, from Robert Means Thompson and Richard Wainwright (eds.), *Confidential Correspondence of Gustavus Vasa Fox, Assistant Secretary of the Navy 1861–1865*, 2 vols. (New York: Books for Libraries Press, 1972), 1: 122–123.

36. See Welles's journal entries dated the April 8th and 10th, 1863 in Beale, *Diary*, 1: 264, 266; also 16-2-1863, Fox to DuPont, *Confidential Correspondence*, 1: 179–180. There were other strategic reasons for a swift capture of Charleston: it would free blockading vessels for service elsewhere; see 31-1-1863, Welles to DuPont, RG 45, Entry 15, Volume I.

37. Fox, ibid. This echoed Gideon Welles's order to DuPont, dated 6-1-1863, to "enter the harbor of Charleston and demand the surrender of all its defenses or suffer the consequences of a refusal," *ORN*, ser. 1, vol. 13, 503.

38. 3-2-1863, Downes to Dahlgren, RG 74, Entry 22, Box No. 1, Volume 1.

39. 9-4-1862, Lincoln to Welles, telegraph, *ORN*, ser. 1, vol. 14, 37. 'Saragossa' refers to the famous defense of the Spanish city during the Peninsula War against French troops, in a protracted siege from 1808–1809.

40. Burton, *The Siege of Charleston*, 144–145. Southerners refused to surrender Fort Sumter five months later, even when it was battered into rubble, and proved willing to set their own city ablaze on 18 February 1865 as they evacuated before the landward approach of Union General William T. Sherman.

41. See Reed, *Combined Operations*, 284–285. Acting Assistant Paymaster Daniel Angell Smith of the U.S.S. *Nahant* promised his sister "we shall burn the city if we cannot capture it," having already listed the Moultrie House Hotel for destruction, 21-10-1863, Daniel Angell Smith Papers, LOC, Manuscript Division, Washington, DC.

42. On the other hand, some reports coming to Union commanders even after the April 7 repulse tended to sustain their belief that putting Charleston under their guns would force a surrender; see for example the "Examination of [Confederate deserter] George L. Shipp," *ORN*, ser. 1, vol. 15, 233.

43. 11-3-1863, Fox to Du Pont, *Confidential Correspondence*. 1: 192.

44. "Du Pont had command of the whole expedition, army and navy,— never was directed even to attack Charleston, but everything was left to his judgment and discretion," 27-2-1864, Fox to Ericsson, Ericsson Papers, LOC.

45. Although as Rowena Reed suggested, "Loss of Charleston in 1863 might have been more fatal to Southern morale than the fall of Vicksburg," "The

Siege of Charleston," in William C. Davis (ed.), *The Image of War 1861–1865*, 6 vols. (New York: Doubleday & Company, Inc., 1983), 4: 166.

46. 12-4-1863, Sumner to Bright, Palmer, *The Selected Letters of Charles Sumner*, 2: 156.

47. 27-2-1864, Fox to Ericsson, Ericsson Papers, LOC.

48. 19-3-1863, DuPont to Fox, *Confidential Correspondence*, 1: 194–195.

49. A notion possibly originating with Captain Percival Drayton, who wrote "I told our admiral the day before the attack, that I did not believe we could do anything that it would make it worth while running the risk of some of our iron clads getting into the enemy's hands," 15-4-1863, Drayton to Alex Hamilton, Jr., *Naval Letters from Captain Percival Drayton, 1861–1865* (New York: New York Public Library, 1906), 35; 8-4-1863, DuPont to Major General D. Hunter, *Official Dispatches*, 439–440; 15-4-1863, DuPont to Welles, *ORN*, ser. 1, vol. 14, 7; 26-4- and 2-5-1863, Rodgers to Anne Rodgers Papers, LOC.; Johnson, "Ships Against Forts," 133–134. By early summer, however, DuPont was apparently willing to dismiss this threat by instead condemning the monitors as "not sea-going or sea-keeping vessels"; their slow speed making them "unfit to chase," while in heavy weather they "could not keep themselves from going ashore," 3-6-1863, DuPont to Welles, *Official Dispatches*, 492–494.

50. 30-5-1863, *Scientific American*, 346.

51. 25-4-1863, "Charleston," *Harper's Weekly*. See also the *New York Herald*, 11-4-1863, which regarded the initial reports—via Richmond newspapers—as suggestive the attack was "intended merely as a feeler of the enemy batteries. . . ."

52. 27-4-1863, London *Times*.

53. 22-4-1863, DuPont to Welles, *Official Dispatches*, 464–472; 15-5-1863, Welles to DuPont, Welles Papers, LOC. See also "The Monitors—Their Conduct, Endurance, and Invulnerability," 26-12-1863, *Army and Navy Journal*, 277.

54. McPherson, *Battle Cry of Freedom*, 646.

55. "Drayton does not know fear, and would fight the devil himself," said Farragut, "but he believes in acting as if the enemy can never be caught unprepared; whereas I believe in judging him by ourselves, and my motto in action . . . is 'L'audace, et encore de l'audace, et toujours de l'audace,' " Mahan, *Admiral Farragut*, 319.

56. Beale, *Diary*, entry dated 8-5-1863; 1: 294–295; also 307, 312. As late as December 19, 1863, a letter to the *Army and Navy Journal* signed "Diving Bell" attested that "the taking of Charleston depends almost entirely upon the Navy, and that the Navy cannot operate without the obstructions are removed . . . . The Navy cannot be blamed for not removing these obstructions. It is a civil engineering problem, and one which the necessities of warfare have never called upon them to study," 259.

57. 3-6-1863, Welles to DuPont, Welles Papers, LOC.

58. "Both classes of vessels were incomparable in their own way, and both classes should have been equally tested; and while perhaps the enemy dreaded the approach of the 'Ironsides' more than the united efforts of half a dozen monitors, the latter, with their 15-inch guns, would probably have made short work of the frigate," Belknap, "Reminiscent of the 'New Ironsides' off Charleston," 79.

59. 2-12-1863, Welles to Commander Thomas Craven, Welles Papers, LOC.

60. 10-4-1862, Ericsson to Fox, Ericsson Papers, Philadelphia.

61. Fox well knew the value of obstructions against ironclads for protecting coastal cities—only they could hope to stop them, 22-11-1862, Fox to J. M. Forbes, Fox Papers, New York, Box 5. The effect of growing U.S. naval power, or superiority, as a stabilizing element in Anglo-American relations during the Civil War was, however, double-edged, *Colburn's United Service Magazine and Naval and Military Journal* (London: Hurst and Blackett, 1863) observing as early as January 1863 that "the rapid, and so far as this war is concerned, unnecessary, increase of the United States Navy is more than an empty boast,—it is a serious threat against the independence of our American Colonies and the naval supremacy of England," Part 1, "The United States, Canada and England," 17–18.

62. 15-4-1863, Ericsson to Fox, Ericsson Papers, LOC.

63. 29-3-1863, Ericsson to Welles, Ericsson Papers, LOC.

64. 9-10-1863, Welles to Dahlgren, Welles Papers, LOC; see also Dahlgren, *Memoir*, 605.

65. 25-4-1863, *Harper's Weekly*, "Keeping John Bull's Score," 272; 6-5-1863, *New York Times*; 16-3-1863, Sumner to Richard Cobden, from Palmer, *The Selected Letters of Charles Sumner*, 2: 150.

66. 7-4-1863, Sumner to John Bright; 21-4-1863, Sumner to Duchess of Argyll, from Edward L. Pierce (ed.), *Memoir and Letters of Charles Sumner*, 2 vols. (London: Sampson Low, Marston and Company, 1893), 2: 131, 136. The two turreted-rams were not seized by British authorities until October 1863, Earl Russell writing to Palmerston "We shall thus test the law, and if we have to pay damages, we have satisfied the opinion which prevails here, as well as in America, that this kind of neutral hostility should not be allowed to go on without some attempt to stop it," 3-9-1863, Russell to Palmerston, Palmerston Papers, Southampton.

67. 18-7-1868, Welles to Schuyler Colfax, RG 45, Entry 5. *Wampanoag's* designer, Benjamin Isherwood, declared "She would obtain a plentiful supply of coal, water, provisions, and other stores from her prizes for an indefinite length of cruising," but this was not necessarily sustained by experience in the Civil War; the C.S.S. *Alabama* was herself cornered in Cherbourg in June 1864 by much-needed repairs; Frank M. Bennett, *The Steam Navy of the United States* (Westport, CT: 1896), 577; 396–400, 535–6, 553–83; see also *The* Wampanoag *Reports: A Few Remarks on the Reports of the Captain and Engineers of the U.S.S.* Wampanoag (New York: 1868); Richard J. West, *Gideon Welles: Lincoln's Navy Department* (New York: 1943), 326; and Edward William Sloan III, *Benjamin Franklin Isherwood—Naval Engineer: The Years as Engineer in Chief, 1861–1869* (Annapolis, MD: 1965).

68. 3-11-1863, Lyons to Russell; 7-12-1863, Secretary to the Admiralty to Goodenough, in TNA/ADM 1/5852. "I don't think the Government here at all desires to pick a quarrel with us or with any European power," Lyons wrote to Russell, "but the better prepared it is, the less manageable it will be," 3-11-1863, Lyons to Russell, from Lord Newton's *Lord Lyons: A Record of British Diplomacy*, 2 vols. (London: Edward Arnold, 1913), 1: 120–121. See also the letter from Lyons to Russell, dated 19-4-1864, 1: 128–129.

69. TNA/ADM 1/5879, "Report on Ships of United States Navy 1864, Capt. J. G. Goodenough, R.N., received in 'M' Dept. 21 October, 1864." Goodenough's enclosed report to Lyons is dated Washington, 12-4-1864.

70. With the loss of 4 officers and 16 of the crew.

71. 29-12-1862, telegram, Lee to Welles, *ORN*, ser. 1, vol. 8, 339.

72. Samuel T. Browne, *First Cruise of the Montauk, Personal Narratives of Events in the War of the Rebellion*, No. 1, Second Series (Providence, RI: The N. Bangs Williams Co., 1880), 15–24.

73. 22-1-1863, John to Anne Rodgers, Rodgers Papers, LOC. Fox wrote to Du Pont the next day that Rodgers's casting off his tow line and deciding to weather the storm was "a great risk, too great, but he has solved a problem that otherwise would have had few backers. The loss of the *Monitor* brought up the 'I told you so' people. Rodgers's courage has extinguished them." Ericsson further noted to Welles that "Not a single leak has been discovered in the hull or at the juncture of the overhang fore or aft," a theory which some historians still suggest accounted for the loss of the *Monitor*—as opposed to improper caulking around the turret base; 23-1-1863, Fox to Du Pont, Fox Papers, New York, Box 5A; 24-1-1863, Ericsson to Welles, Ericsson Papers, LOC; see for example, Robert E. Sheridan, *Iron from the Deep: The Discovery and Recovery of the USS Monitor* (Annapolis, Naval Institute Press, 2004), 32; David Mindell, "Iron Horse, Iron Coffin: Life Aboard the USS *Monitor*," in Harold Holzer and Tim Mulligan (eds.), *The Battle of Hampton Roads: New Perspectives on the USS* Monitor *and CSS* Virginia (New York: Fordham University Press, 2006), 52; Mindell, *War, Technology, and Experience*, 113–115; also Marvel (ed.), *The* Monitor *Chronicles*, 227–236; and deKay, Monitor: *The Story of the Legendary Ironclad*, 215–219.

74. 31-3-1863, John to Anne Rodgers, Rodgers Papers, LOC.

75. 9-5-1863, John to Anne Rodgers, Rodgers Papers, LOC.

76. *ORN*, 1: 14: 265–268; 273–276.

77. "Report of Captain Rodgers, U.S. Navy, commanding U.S.S. *Weehawken*," 17-6-1863, *ORN*, 1: 14, 265–266. This "compound angle" hit of 22 degrees, Ericsson later pointed out, "means that, independent of deflection, the shot must pass through nearly five feet of obstruction,—namely, eleven inches of iron and four feet of wood." The significance of the *Weehawken*'s victory over the *Atlanta* to Ericsson (if not also to much of the nation), however, was that it "proved that the 4½-inch vertical plating of the magnificent *Warrior* of nine thousand tons—the pride of the British Admiralty—would be but slight protection against the 15-inch monitor guns," Captain John Ericsson, "The Early Monitors," in Johnson and Buel, *Battles and Leaders of the Civil War*, 4: 30–31; *Report to the Joint Committee on the Conduct of the War: Heavy Ordnance*, 71; see also Hunter, *A Year on a Monitor*, 77–78, 93.

78. 6-7-1863, Robert to Annie Shaw, quoted from *Letters of Robert Gould Shaw* (Cambridge, UK: Cambridge University Press, 1864), 319–320; also 317.

79. The accounts of British Consul Robert Bunch at Charleston, for example, clearly indicated where the personal preferences of many British officers and officials lay. See Eugene H. Berwanger , *The British Foreign Service and the American Civil War* (University of Kentucky Press, 1994).

80. In reporting to Milne on Union monitors and ironclads, Captain John James Kennedy of H.M.S. *Challenger* noted there were "orders from the United States Government not to allow strangers on board. Admiral Lee refused me permission point blank." Was this a cover-up? "Officers with whom I have conversed inform me that they are dreadful, and that it has been determined to relieve officers and men every six months, that they can only be useful to defend harbours and will then require a steamer to attend them for Officers and me to live on board," 13-7-1863, Kennedy to Milne, TNA/ADM 1/5820. Palmerston saw the American ironclad repulse at Charleston as useful defending his Fortifications Bill; see "Occasions in the Civil War in America in which Forts and Guns have had the best of it against Iron Clad Ships," 24-6-1863, TNA/FO memo, Palmerston Papers, Southampton.

81. 20-6-1863, Lyons to Russell, from TNA/ADM 1/5851; 30-6-1863, TNA/ADM 1/5852.

82. 17-2-1863, London *Times*; 24-1-1864, TNA/ADM 1/5879.

83. 27-6-1863, Knorr to Rodgers, Rodgers Papers, LOC; 27-6-1863, and 10-7-1863, Robinson to Board, TNA/ADM 1/5841; 15-7-1863, Coles to Paget, and 21-7-1863, Coles to Romaine, TNA/ADM 1/5827.

84. See *ORN*, ser. 1, vol. 14: 417-20, 425–428, and 21: 494–496, 531–533.

85. 13-8-1864, Captain James Alden (USS *Richmond*) Report to Rear-Admiral Farragut, reprinted in *Congressional Globe*, "Report of the Secretary of the Navy," 453; 8-8-1864, Nicholson to Fox, Fox Papers, New York, Box 9; 26-9-1864, London *Times*.

86. 29-10-1864, *Scientific American*, 281; 1-10-1864, London *Times*. "By comparing the penetration of the shot," reported Captain Hewlett of the Gunnery Ship H.M.S *Excellent* on the Jones Target, "it appears that at 52° the force is less than one half of what it is against a perpendicular surface," 23-8-1860, forwarded to the War Office 12-9-1860, *Minute* 2126, "Iron plates for the protection of vessels" (Ordnance Select Committee), TNA/WO 9; see also 24-1-1862, TNA/WO 33/11; 9-11-1866, Minute 20,348 "Iron Armour Plates" (Ordnance Select Committee), 837–838, TNA/WO 33/18; also 3-12-1860, Walker to Board of Admiralty ("Designs submitted and reported on about December 1860") TNA/ADM 87/77.

87. 18-3-1865, *Army and Navy Journal*, 473. There was little question over *Confederate* respect for the Union's 15-inch guns. In describing the damage inflicted on the 6-inch iron casemate of the *Virginia II* at Trent's Reach (24 January, 1865) by the double-turreted monitor U.S.S. *Onondaga*, an officer of the C.S.S. *Fredericksburg* declared that "Projectiles of this weight will penetrate any Iron Clad that has ever been built, I believe." The range was 900 yards. 27-2-1865, E. Eggleston to R. Townes, in RG 74, Entry 16, Box 4. See also *ORN*, ser. 1, vol. 11, 670, 693; 12: 190. See also John M. Coski, *Capital Navy: The Men, Ships and Operations of The James River Squadron* (Campbell, CA: Savas Publishing Company, 1996), 206–210; and Paul D. Lockhart, "The Confederate Naval Squadron at Charleston and the Failure of Naval Harbor Defense," *The American Neptune*, Vol. 44, No., 4 (Fall 1984). Confederate General P. T. Beauregard had already condemned the three ironclads under his command at Charleston (*Chicora, Palmetto State*

and *Charleston*) as "incapable of resisting the enemy's XV-inch shots at close quarters . . ." Memo dated 14-11-1863, *ORN*, ser. 1, vol. 15: 695–696.

Conclusion

1. See Andrew Lambert, "The Ship Propeller Company and the Promotion of Screw Propulsion, 1836–1852," in Robert Gardiner (ed.), *The Advent of Steam: The Merchant Steamship before 1900* (London: Conway Maritime Press, 1993), 136–137; also Gideon Welles, "The First Iron-Clad Monitor" in *The Annals of War* (Dayton, OH: Morningside House, Inc., 1988), 17–31; and Church, *Life of Ericsson*, 1: 192. For designing the entire *Passaic*-class of Civil War monitors, Ericsson profited from their contractors's use of his patented lever-engine "one per cent on the contract price," and "3/8 per cent of the contract price" for the *Canonicus*-class; 16-4-1864, Ericsson to Gregory, Ericsson Papers, LOC; also 24-4-1862, Ericsson to Welles, Ericsson Papers, Philadelphia.

2. 8-2-1863, Ericsson to Welles, *Report of the Secretary of the Navy in Relation to Armored Vessels*, 601.

3. TNA/ADM 1/5840, 30-1-1863.

4. Clark G. Reynolds, in *Command of the Sea: The History and Strategy of Maritime Empires* (Malabar, FL, 1983), argues that "Great Powers have evolved to the height of their political prestige and might by becoming imperial nations," and "for *maritime* nations, the navy has been the main strategic arm of the nation's defensive structure, dominating the defensive policies of the home government, maintaining a generally *offensive* stance, and operating mainly on the "blue water" of the high seas," though "the ultimate expression of naval superiority comes when naval power can be projected inland against the vitals of the enemy homeland," 3, 12–13.

5. *Letter Addressed by the Royal Commissioners on National Defences*, 11; see TNA/WO 33/10.

6. 13-12-1864, TNA/ADM 1/5892, 1–5. See also Reed's self-promoting work, *Our Ironclad Ships; Their Qualities, Performances, and Cost* (London, 1869).

7. See the numerous Ordnance Select Committee reports on the subject of failed Armstrong 110-pounders (breech-loading), TNA/WO 33/11 to /16; London *Times*, 30-7-1866, 13-8-1866, and "Warships and Monitors," in *The Nautical Magazine and Naval Chronicle for 1866: A Journal of Papers on Subjects Connected with Maritime Affairs* (London, 1866), December 1866, 675–680.

8. Sir Thomas Brassey, *The British Navy: Its Strength, Resources, and Administration*, 3 vols. (London: Longmans, Green, and Co., 1882–1883), 2: 380–387; also 3: 72.

9. Baxter, *Introduction*, 302.

10. Duncan Andrew Campbell, *English Public Opinion and the American Civil War* (Woodbridge, The Boydell Press, 2003), 241. See also John F. Beeler's remarks in "A One Power Standard? Great Britain and the Balance of Power, 1860–1880," *Journal of Strategic Studies*, vol. 15, no. 4 (December 1992), 558. Crook himself does not offer a comparison between Anglo-American ironclads

other than rightly observing that monitors were "likely to be confined to harbor service and local defense," David Paul Crook, *The North, the South and the Powers, 1861–1865* (New York, John Wiley & Sons, 1974), 186–189. No monitors 'capsized' during the American Civil War; the original prototype foundered in the 'Graveyard of the Atlantic' for reasons still unknown, while the *Weehawken* sank at anchor 6 December, 1863, when the forward hatch was accidentally left open, flooding the vessel (already down by the bow due to inordinate ammunition stowage forward) enough so that the pumps could not be brought into action in time; see *Congressional Globe*, 1863, "Report of the Secretary of the Navy," 248–257; 7-12-1863 letter, unaddressed, Papers of Daniel Angell Smith (Acting Assistant Paymaster, U.S.S. *Nahant*), LOC; 12-12-1863, Ericsson to Welles, Ericsson Papers, LOC. Crucially, what the 'semi-submersible' design lacked was a large reserve of internal *buoyancy*—a point which Oscar Parkes makes, though he might have added submarines have faced the same problem; *British Battleships*, 46.

11. Wells, *The Immortal Warrior*, 240–241; Peter Kemp (ed.), *Oxford Companion to Ships and the Sea* (New York: Oxford University Press, 1976), 555.

12. A flaw endemic to 'strictly' naval history, noted Professor Andrew Lambert in his November 14, 2002 King's College, London Inaugural Address, reprinted in *Historical Research: The Bulletin of the Institute of Historical Research*, vol. 77, no. 196 (May 2004), 274–288.

13. Canney, *The Ironclads*, 1; 9.

14. See, for example, Mindell's thought-provoking analysis in *War, Technology and Experience aboard the USS* Monitor, especially 123–134; and James P. Delgado, "A Symbol of the People: Assessing the Significance of the U.S.S. Monitor," in J. Lee Cox, Jr. and Michael A. Jehle (eds.), *Ironclad Intruder: U.S.S. Monitor* (Philadelphia, PA: Philadelphia Maritime Museum, 1988), 34–40.

15. One reason for delay was the Bureau of Construction's insistence that the turrets be fitted with hand-turning gear; see 12-10-1864, Lenthall to Gregory, RG 19, Entry 1240, Box 1.

16. *Dictionary of American Fighting Ships*, Vol. 3 (Washington, DC: Navy Department, Office of the Chief of Naval Operations, Naval History, 1968), 767–768. Tonnage is 'new tonnage'; old was designated as 1,564.

17. Capt. J. G. Goodenough, "Report on Ships of United States Navy 1864," TNA/ADM 1/5879, 33–34. See also Richard M. Basoco, William E. Geoghegan and Frank J. Merli, eds., "A British View of the Union Navy, 1864: A Report Addressed to Her Majesty's Minister at Washington," *American Neptune* Vol. 27, No. 1 (January 1967), 30–45.

18. 1-11-1865, London *Times*.

19. See 15-5-1866, Bruce to Earl Clarendon, TNA/FO 5/1065; also 1-3-1865, Russell to Somerset, Somerset Papers, Aylesbury. Bythesea's own "Remarks on the U.S. Navy," dated 19-8-1865, can be found in TNA/ADM 1/5954.

20. TNA/FO 5/1065, 15-5-1866, Bruce to Clarendon. See Bythesea's own report on the strength of the U.S. Navy, dated 19-8-1865, in TNA/ADM 1/5954.

21. 22-3-1866, Ericsson to Fox, Ericsson Papers, Philadelphia. See also 17-3-1866, Ericsson to Fox, Fox Papers, New York, Box 11, where he complains

"the time necessary to plan the *Monitor* formed only a fraction of what has been requisite to defend it."

22. Quoted from John Ericsson, *Contributions to the Centennial Exhibition* (New York, 1876), 465–6.

23. 28-2-1865, Bourne to Ericsson, from Church, *Life of John Ericsson*, 2: 80–81.

24. 12-1-1865, Ericsson to Bourne, Ericsson Papers, LOC. For accounts of this voyage see the reports and private letters of Commodore John Rodgers, Rodgers Papers, LOC, containers 11, 12, and 23.

25. 16-1-1866, Ericsson to Bourne, Ericsson Papers, LOC.

26. See 10-1-1866 and 19-1-1866, Robinson to Board of Admiralty, TNA/ADM 1/5980.

27. 25-5-1865, Grey to Captain Cooper Key, National Archives of Scotland (General Register House); GD 51/17/68 (NRA 10188), Private Letterbook of Rear Admiral Sir F. W. Grey, 1861–1866.

28. See 5-2-1866, Robinson to Board, TNA/ADM 1/5980; 11-4-1866, Robinson to Board; *Parliamentary Papers*, 5-3-1866 and 16-4-1866, "Navy (Turret Ships)," "Correspondence between the Admiralty and Captain Cowper Coles, relative to Turret Ships, and Papers relating thereto (in continuation of Parliamentary Paper, No. 87, of Session 1866)," 8.

29. 3-4-1866, Ericsson to Bourne, Ericsson Papers, Philadelphia; see also 27-4-1866, Ericsson to Bourne, Ericsson Papers, LOC.

30. 10-2-1866, Ericsson to Fox, Fox Papers, New York, Box 11. See also 2-3-1866, Ericsson to Fox, ibid. On Coles's claim of turret ship progenitor, see 3-2-1865, Ericsson to Bourne, Ericsson Papers, LOC. Nor was Coles above using Ericsson's advances to further his own; see his letter to Richard Cobden, dated 8-4-1864, regarding the consequences of an action between the *Dictator* and Reed's newest central-battery ironclad, H.M.S. *Bellerophon*, and Cobden's own observation, dated 12-11-1864; Cobden Papers, Chichester.

31. 23-4-1866, Fox to Ericsson, Ericsson Papers, Philadelphia; also Church, *Life of John Ericsson*, 2: 77.

32. See 27-7-1866, Ericsson to Bourne, Ericsson Papers, LOC. Though Ericsson felt it was Fox's due, and stated he would not interfere with his efforts, he could not "imagine that he ever entertained the absurd idea of building anything in the way of ships for the great Mechanical Island Nation." A likely customer might be warring Prussia.

33. 26-1-1866, Fox to Ericsson, Ericsson Papers, LOC.

34. Boynton, *History of the Navy*, 1: 66–67. Boynton expressly intended his history to vindicate the reputation of the monitors at Charleston and "go no further into the history of the 'Old navy' at present than to show that our navy is an original creation, a true outgrowth of American thought," 17-8-1866, Boynton to Welles, Welles Papers, LOC.

35. Journal entries dated 17-, 21- and 23-5-1866; Beale, *Diary*, 2: 509, 512, and 625–626. A letter to *The Scientific American*, 9-6-1866, opposed giving up valuable secrets, gained from hard-fought experience, by sending a monitor to "our great maritime rival," 395–396.

36. Once at sea, *Ashuelot* proceeded separately to Boston to pick up Assistant Secretary Fox and Captain Bythesea, who later joined the rest of the squadron at

St. John's, Newfoundland on the 3rd of June; 4-5-1866, Welles to New York Navy Yard; 4-5-1866, Welles to Commander Alexander Murray, RG 45, Entry 15, Volume I.

37. Undated, suggested improvements for *Miantonomoh*, Fox Papers, New York, Box 11; John D. Champlin, Jr. (ed.), *Narrative of the Mission to Russia, in 1866, of the Hon. Gustavus Vasa Fox, Assistant-Secretary of the Navy, from the journal and Notes of J. F. Loubat* (New York, 1873), 26-8.

38. 5-6-1866, Fox to Welles, Welles Papers, LOC. Fox observed the squadron was "typical of the changes of naval warfare—a monitor, double-ender and converted merchant vessel."

39. 16-6-1866, Murray to Welles, RG 45. Fox's own assessment was more to the point: "The performance of this vessel, her accommodations, ventilation, and light to read below without candles [through overhead rather than bulwark glass scuttles] are all that could be desired and it is only necessary for the Dept to build one for ocean cruising for us to have a sea going cruiser that will perform in a superior manner to any wooden ship. Letting the water over is the true principle: it gives stability, protection and economy of construction . . . . For coast service this class of vessel cannot be surpassed at the present condition of iron clad information. We have not much power in this vessel and space is wasted that ought to have been studied for economy. The third day out from St. Johns I began to suspect that we had not the quantity of coal given to me so the Augusta has given us a tow of a week," 16-6-1866, Fox to Welles, Welles Papers, LOC. Towing appeared to reduce consumption to one ton per hour; 23-7-1867, Murray to Welles, in *Congress Return*, 67, 69–70.

40. Champlin, *Narrative*, 32.

41. Canney, *The Ironclads*, 66–70.

42. Champlin, *Narrative*, 32.

43. Brown, *Warrior to Dreadnought*, 56. "The extreme lurch observed when lying broadside to a heavy sea and moderate gale was seven degrees to windward and four degrees to leeward, mean five and one-half degrees, while the average roll at the same time of the Augusta—a remarkably steady ship—was eighteen degrees, and the Ashuelot twenty-five degrees, both vessels being steadied by sail," Champlin, *Narrative*, 33. See also 21-3-1898, U.S. Senate, Document No. 197, 55th Congress, 2nd Session, "Monitors v. Battle Ships," 4–5. For additional eye-witness European opinions see the 3-12-1866 Report of the Secretary of the Navy, Appendix to the *Congressional Globe*, 39th Congress, 2nd Session, 41.

44. Fox considered rather monumental success a foregone conclusion, writing to Welles on 30-5-1866 "the voyage of the vessel and my report will be a justification of your administration. Europe will give you the endorsement which at present our own people bestow grudgingly," Welles Papers, LOC. In evidence to the 1871 Parliamentary Ship Design Committee, Assistant Constructor Nathaniel Barnaby opined "although the 'Miantonomoh' made passages across the Atlantic, she was the first ship of the kind which had done so, and the officers and men put up with a great deal of inconveniences rather than complain of her. If we were to build such ships as the 'Miantonomoh' and the 'Monadnock,' and send them to sea, we should never hear the last of the complaints about them," *1871 Report of the Committee . . . to Examine the Designs Upon Which Ships of War Have Recently Been Constructed* (London, 1872), 50.

45. Canney, *The Ironclads*, 62, 79–80.

46. *1871 Report of the Committee*, 34–41. See also the copy of Bythesea's report to Earl Clarendon, dated 16-6-1866, including a log account of the *Miantonomoh*'s first crossing, in TNA/ADM 1/5992.

47. 30-6-1866, *The Illustrated London News*, 639–641; 651–653.

48. 27-6-1866, London *Times*.

49. 28-9-1866, London *Times*.

50. 14-7-1866, *The Scientific American*, 34. See also 13-7-1866, Ericsson to Wise, Ericsson Papers, Philadelphia.

51. 29-6-1866, Fox to Welles, Welles Papers, LOC.

52. 30-6-1866, London *Times*.

53. 2-7-1866, London *Times*. See also "Monitors versus Ironclads," in *The Nautical Magazine and Naval Chronicle* (London: Simpkin, Marshall, and Co.), June 1867, 308–309.

54. 2-7-1866, London *Times*. Target tests conducted by the Ordnance Select Committee at Shoeburyness in 1867 seemed to support Ericsson's original calculations, 11-10-1867, Ericsson to Wise, Ericsson Papers, Philadelphia; *Third Report of the Director of Ordnance, being of the year 1867–8* (War Office, 1869), TNA/WO 33/19, 1868, 40–41; 30-10-1868, Report No. 5164, *Abstracts of Proceedings of the Ordnance Select Committee, from 1ˢᵗ October to 7ᵗʰ December, 1868; and of the Department of the Director General of Ordnance from 8ᵗʰ December to 31ˢᵗ December, 1868* (London, 1869), TNA/WO 33/20, 1869, 865.

55. In December 1864 *The Examiner* wrote that "A man of bad character would be incapable of so much mischief," while *Punch* caricatured him as "The Federal Phoenix," burning human freedoms with satisfaction. In its May 6, 1865 issue, however, *Punch* depicted how "Britannia Sympathises with Columbia," a former slave with broken chains weeping nearby. See also Alfred Grant, *The American Civil War and the British Press* (Jefferson, 2000), 179.

56. See Sherman, *Recollections*, 1: 349, 377.

57. 30-11-1863, Seward to Adams, *Diplomatic Correspondence*, No. 771, 1321–1322.

58. 5-7-1866, London *Times*.

59. 14-7-1866, Adams to Seward, No. 1239, *U.S. State Department, Papers Relating to Foreign Affairs, Second Session, Thirty-Ninth Congress, Part I* (Washington, 1866), 149.

60. 14-7-1866, *Punch*, "Venus and Valour," 13; 17-6-1866, London *Times*.

61. *Hansard*, 20-7-1866, "State of the Navy," 1167–1198.

62. Philip Magnus, *Gladstone: A Biography* (London, 1970), 172; see also Thomas Archer, *Gladstone and His Contemporaries*, 4 vols. (London, 1899), 4: 181–183. *Harper's Weekly* declared it was "a foolish injustice which charges Mr. Gladstone with reducing the liberal majority of seventy in the House of Commons to a minority of eleven. He did not do it. The present Parliament was elected upon the cry of Palmerston and anti-Palmerston, not upon any policy or principle. Palmerston carried the day; but he was opposed to Reform, and his policy was merely brag and inaction. He had no political convictions whatever, unless a hearty desire to maintain the existing condition can be called a principle," 21-7-1866, "Mr. Gladstone."

63. See Gertrude Himmelfarb's challenging analysis of Disraeli's appeal to British working class 'political deference' in *Victorian Minds: A Study of Intellectuals in Crisis and Ideologies in Transition* (Chicago: Ivan R. Dee, 1968, 333–392.

64. 26-7-1866, Adams to Seward, No. 1246, *U.S. State Department, Papers Relating to Foreign Affairs*, 156.

65. See Philip Howard Colomb's analysis, "Lessons from Lissa" (delivered 29-4-1867) in the *Journal of the Royal United Service Institution*, Whitehall Yard, XI (London, 1868), 104–126. The Italians had one turret-ship/ram in their fleet, the *Affondatore*, built by Millwall in 1863–1866 and armed with two 300-pounders, but she effected very little during the action.

66. Paul Kennedy writes that "having achieved the pinnacle of worldly success, [they] had nothing to gain and much to lose from changes in that global order. Britain was now a *mature* state, with a built-in interest in preserving existing arrangements," *The Realities Behind Diplomacy: Background Influences on British External Policy, 1865–1980* (London, 1981), 69; Graham, *The Politics of Naval Supremacy*, 96–125. See also Richard Shannon, *The Crisis of Imperialism 1865–1915* (London, 1974), 19–23.

67. 16-7-1866, The London *Times*.

68. Contrast this worried reaction to that on the other side: "We are well satisfied with the fact that we can build the most invulnerable gunboats, and manufacture the most effective artillery, without proving these facts, in time of peace, to the satisfaction of those who may be our enemies, and, in consequence of our own foolish demonstration, be enabled to fight us with our own weapons," 18-8-1866, *The Scientific American*, 119.

69. John Bourne, "On the American System of Turret Ships," 23-3-1866, *Transactions of the Institution of Naval Architects*, Seventh Session, 1866, 131–143.

70. See Church, *Life of Ericsson*, 1: 88–91; 2: 82.

71. 3-4-1866, Ericsson to Bourne, Ericsson Papers, Philadelphia.

72. 11-5-1866, Ericsson to Bourne, Ericsson Papers, Philadelphia.

73. 13-4-1866, William Romaine (Admiralty Secretary) to Bourne, from Church, *Life of Ericsson*, 2: 82–84.

74. Only 17 survived—a loss of life greater than that suffered by the U.S. Navy at Hampton Roads, or by the British at the Battle of Trafalgar; Parkes, *British Battleships*, 142. See Arthur Hawkey, *Black Night Off Finisterre: The Tragic Tale of an Early British Ironclad* (Annapolis, MD: Naval Institute Press, 1999) and David B. McGee, "Floating Bodies, Naval Science: Science, Design and the *Captain* Controversy, 1860-1870," University of Toronto Ph.D. thesis (1994).

75. 25-5-1866, TNA/ADM 3/272.

76. 31-7-1866, Robinson to Board, No. 3205, "Construction of Armour Plated ships," TNA/ADM 1/5981. Reed and Bourne's letters are attached, as well as comments form the Board. See also 14-7-1866, Bourne to Ericsson, Ericsson Papers, Philadelphia.

77. 31-7-1866, Robinson to Board, TNA/ADM 1/5981. These proposals were later codified in the Controller's submission to the Board, *New Designs for Ships*, dated 20-11-1866, TNA/ADM 1/5982.

78. See Reed, *Our Ironclad Ships*, 50–55, 241–242; Parkes, *British Battle-ships*, 166; Brown, *Warrior to Dreadnought*, 56–57; and Sandler *The Emergence of the Modern Capital Ship*. Reed remained skeptical of Ericsson's ideas compared with his own preference for high freeboard, central battery iron-clads; "if we have made a mistake with reference to the introduction into the British Navy of turret-ships, and especially of monitors, that mistake has consisted in adopting them too rapidly, rather than too slowly." The experience of the American Civil War had, in his assessment, given "ample cause for the exercise of prudence and caution in introducing them," *Our Ironclad Ships*, 254.

79. 16-8-1866, Ericsson to Bourne, Ericsson Papers, Philadelphia.

80. See Ericsson's stunning letter to Bourne dated 1-5-1866, in Church, *Life of Ericsson*, 2: 86–88.

81. 5-7-1866, Fox to Welles, Welles Papers, LOC.

82. *Punch*, 28-7-1866, "Ready, Aye Ready," 46.

83. 4-8-1866, *Army and Navy Journal*, 797.

84. 23-6-1861, Palmerston to Somerset, Somerset Papers, Aylesbury.

85. Porter, *Campaigning*, 407–408.

86. 11-9-1864, Palmerston to De Grey, Palmerston Papers, Southampton. Lewis had died on 13-4-1863. The new American Station commander, Vice Admiral Sir James Hope, held little confidence in winning a naval war on the Lakes: "The real question is, can we in the face of the great natural advantages possessed by the Americans, obtain this superiority—and if so would the cost both in men and money not be so great as to render it much more serviceable to the Country to spend it elsewhere. I should view any such attempt as a drain and a most unwise one on the resources of the Country in no degree inferior to that occasioned to Russia by the siege of Sebastopol," Hope to Somerset, 27-12-1864, Somerset Papers, Aylesbury.

87. 19-10-1864, Palmerston to Russell, Palmerston Papers, Southampton.

88. 24-12-1864, *Scientific American*, 26, 402.

89. 15-1-1864, Palmerston to Russell, Grey Papers, Durham. See also Chamberlain, *Pax*, 116–118.

90. 22-2-1864, Palmerston to Victoria, from Buckle, *Letters of Queen Victoria*, 1: 161–163. See also Brian Connell, *Regina v. Palmerston: The Correspondence Between Queen Victoria and Her Foreign and Prime Minister, 1837–1865* (London: Evans Brothers, Ltd., 1962), 349.

91. See for example 14-1-1862, *Congressional Globe*, 333.

92. 27-12-1867, John to Nils Ericsson, from Church, *Life of Ericsson*, 2: 219.

93. 11-4-1862, Henry Adams to Charles Francis Adams, Jr., from Ford, *Cycle of Adams Letters*, 1: 134.

94. 1-11-1864, London *Times*.

95. 30-3-1865, Adams to Seward, *Papers Relating to Foreign Affairs*, 298.

Bibliography

PRIMARY SOURCES

British National Archives (Kew, London)

National Archives, Washington, DC

Private Paper Collections (UK)

Richard Cobden Papers, Chichester, West Sussex Record Office
Cochrane Family Papers, Royal Naval Museum Archives, Portsmouth
General Charles Grey Papers, Durham University Library (Archives & Special
　　Collections) Durham, Palace Green
Palmerston Papers (Henry John Temple, 3rd Viscount), MS 62 ("Broadlands"),
　　University of Southampton, Southampton
Rear Admiral Sir Frederick W. Grey, Private Letterbook, 1861–1866, National
　　Archives of Scotland, Edinburgh, General Register House
Somerset Papers (Edward Adolphus Seymour, 12th Duke of Somerset),
　　Buckinghamshire Record Office, Aylesbury
Vice Admiral Sir Alexander Milne Papers, National Maritime Museum,
　　Greenwich

Private Paper Collections (U.S.)

Oliver Ambrose Batcheller Letters, Manuscript Collection No. 264, U.S.
　　Naval Academy Nimitz Library, Annapolis, MD
Edmund Ross Colhoun Papers, Library of Congress, Manuscript Division,
　　Washington, DC
John A. Dahlgren Papers, Library of Congress, Manuscript Division,
　　Washington, DC

John   Ericsson   Papers,   American-Swedish   Historical   Foundation,
    Philadelphia, PA
John   Ericsson   Papers,   Library   of   Congress,   Manuscript   Division,
    Washington, DC
Forbes Family Papers, Massachusetts Historical Society, Boston, MA (copy in
    Library of Congress, Manuscript Division, Washington, DC)
Hamilton   Fish   Papers,   Library   of   Congress,   Manuscript   Division,
    Washington, DC
Gustavus Vasa Fox Papers, New York Historical Society Library Manuscripts,
    New York, NY
Simon   Palmer   Gillett   Papers,   Library   of   Congress,   Manuscript   Division,
    Washington, DC
Edward   Nealy   Kellogg   Papers,   Library   of   Congress,   Manuscript   Division,
    Washington, DC
H.   Henry   Kloeppel,   Diary,   Library   of   Congress,   Manuscript   Division,
    Washington, DC
Logbook   of   Milo   Lacy,   U.S.   Naval   Historical   Center   Library   Collection,
    Washington, DC
Abraham   Lincoln   Papers,   Library   of   Congress,   Manuscript   Division,
    Washington, DC
Charles H. Loring Papers, Carlisle Army Archive Collections, Carlisle, PA
David Dixon Porter Family Papers, Library of Congress, Manuscript Division,
    Washington, DC
William   Radford   Papers,   Library   of   Congress,   Manuscript   Division,
    Washington, DC
Rodgers Family Papers, Naval Historical Foundation Collection, Library of
    Congress, Manuscript Division, Washington, DC
Cornelius Marius Schoonmaker Papers, Library of Congress, Manuscript
    Division, Washington, DC
Daniel   Angell   Smith   Papers,   Library   of   Congress,   Manuscript   Division,
    Washington, DC
Harrie   Webster   Papers,   Library   of   Congress,   Manuscript   Division,
    Washington, DC
Gideon   Welles   Papers,   Library   of   Congress,   Manuscript   Division,
    Washington, DC

Hansard's Parliamentary Debates

Parliamentary Papers

Session 1861, Paper number 150; 591, "Return of Number of Steam Battle-
    Ships, Iron-cased Ships, Frigates, Corvettes, Sloops, and Gun-Boats,
    March 1859 and 1861"
Session 1861, Paper number 207; 597, "Correspondence between the Admiralty
    and the Contractors who built the Warrior in reference to the Non-fulfilment
    of their Contract within the stipulated Time"
Session 1861, Paper number 347; 637, "Return of the Makers' Names, and Mode
    of Manufacturing the Armour Plates of the Warrior, the Quantities of Iron or
    Armour Plates Condemned, and the Date and Reason of their Condemnation"

Session 1861, Paper number 361; 389, "Return of Iron-cased Ships as to Date of Contract, Time for Completion and Penalties"

Session 1862, Paper number 392; 891, "Return of Number of Proposals or Plans for Shot-Proof Ships received at Admiralty, May 1859–62"

Session 1862, Paper number 68; 895, "Return of Total Cost of the Warrior before being Ready for Sea"

Session 1862, Paper number 432; 887, "Return of Iron-cased Ships and Floating Batteries building or afloat"

Session 1862, Paper number 507; 125, "Return of Number and Area of Basins and Dockyards of Chatham, Deptford, Woolwich, Sheerness, Portsmouth, Devonport, Keyham and Pembroke; Number of Docks capable of admitting Iron-cased Ships"

Session 1862, Paper number 3063; 887, "Correspondence relating to Civil War in U.S.A."

Session 1863, Paper number 83; 301, "Statement relating to the Advantages of Iron and Wood, and the relative Cost of these Materials in the Construction of Ships for Her Majesty's Navy"

Session 1863, Paper number 86; 293, "Return of Iron-cased Floating Batteries, from Date of Launching to March 1862"

Session 1863, Paper number 190; 295, "Return of Cost of Iron-plated Ships fitted for Sea since Warrior"

Session 1864, Paper number 145; 25, "Admiral Kuper's Official Report of Performance of Armstrong Guns in Action at Kagosima"

Session 1864, Paper number 176; 555, "Account of Guns and Munitions of War shipped from port of Liverpool to America, 1861 and 1862"

Session 1864, Paper number 408; 605, "Correspondence from Commander-in-Chief at Devonport, on Inspection of H.M.S. Research"

Session 1865, [Bill] Paper number 51; 189, "Bill to make better provision for Naval Defence of Colonies"

Session 1865, Paper number 156; 553, "Return of Alterations and Repairs on Royal Sovereign and Prince Consort; Estimated Cost of altering Royal Alfred"

Session 1865, Paper number 279; 309, "Report of Admiral Kuper in reference to Armstrong Guns in Action of Simonosaki"

Session 1865, Paper number 307; 321, "Return of Expenses of Armstrong Guns; Number of Armstrong Guns exchanged from Ships of Channel Squadron at Plymouth, May 1864"

Session 1865, Paper number 367; 519, "Return of Iron-plated Ships and Batteries built, building or ordered to be built"

Session 1865, Paper number 3511; 125, "Correspondence arising out of Conflict between Kearsage and Alabama"

Session 1866, Paper number 87; 367, "Report of Admiralty Committee on Turret Ships; Correspondence between Admiralty and Captain Cowper Coles"

Session 1866, Paper number 121; 591, "Return of iron-clads built of Wood, adapted or converted from Wooden Ships in course of Construction built in Royal and Private Yards"

Session 1866, Paper number 416; 217, "Supplementary Estimate of Navy: 1866–67 (Completion of H.M.S. Northumberland)"

Session 1867, Paper number 537; 279, "Return of Armour-clad Ships and Batteries built by Contract for H.M. Service, 1855–67"

Session 1867–68, Paper number 166; 641, "Papers on Progress of Shipbuilding in H.M. Dockyards, 1868–69"

Session 1867–68, Paper number 167; 637, "Return of Number of H.M. Ships on Station, 1847–67"

Session 1867–68, Paper number 283; 773, "Controller's Report on Trials of Warrior, Minotaur and Bellerophon"

Session 1868–69, Paper Number 415; 569, "Return of the Number of Serviceable Rifled Guns and Carriages; Number of Guns required for Fortifications and Iron-clad Ships; Number of Guns under Manufacture at Royal Arsenal at Woolwich"

Session 1877, Paper number 369; 717, "Official Despatches from Rear-Admiral de Horsey reporting Encounter between H.M.S. Shah and Amethyst, and Peruvian Iron-clad Ram Huascar"

1871 Report of the Committee . . . to Examine the Designs Upon Which Ships of War Have Recently Been Constructed—Dissenting Report by Admiral George Elliot and Rear-Admiral A. P. Ryder (London: Harrison and Sons, 1872)

Congressional Globe

Congressional Reports

Executive Documents, 36th Congress, 2nd Session, 1860–1861 (Washington, DC: GPO, 1861)

Ex. Doc. No. 6, Letter of the Secretary of State Transmitting a Report of the Commercial Relations of the United States with Foreign Nations for the Year Ending September 30, 1860

Ex. Doc. No. 43, Rifled Cannon and the Armament of Ships-of-War, Letter from the Secretary of the Navy, January 22, 1861

Ex. Doc. No. 65, Estimate—Armament of Fortifications, &c., Letter from the Secretary of War, February 11, 1861

Miscellaneous Documents of the House of Representatives, 37th Congress, 2nd Session, 1861–1862 (Washington, DC: GPO, 1862)

Misc. Doc. No. 70, Letter of the Secretary of the Navy to the Chairman of the Committee on Naval Affairs of the Senate of the United States, in relation to the construction of iron-clad steamers, &c., 25 March, 1862

Misc. Doc. No. 82, Iron-Clad Ships, Ordnance, &c., &c., Letter from the Secretary of the Navy, March 25, 1862

Executive Documents, 37th Congress, 2nd Session, 1861–1862 (Washington, DC: GPO, 1862)

Ex. Doc. No. 4, Intervention of European Powers in the Affairs of Mexico, Message of the President of the United States, December 9, 1861

Ex. Doc. No. 5, Armed Flotilla on the Western Waters, Communication from the Secretary of War, December 10, 1861

Ex. Doc. No. 6, Estimates for Fortifications, Letter from the Secretary of War, December 10, 1861

Ex. Doc. No. 8 (Senate), Message of the President of the United States Transmitting a Correspondence between the Secretary of State and the authorities of Great and France, in relation to the recent removal of certain citizens of the United States from the British mail-steamer Trent, December 30, 1861

Ex. Doc. No. 14, Fortification of the Sea-Coast and Lakes, Message from the President of the United States, December 17, 1861

Ex. Doc. No. 23, Iron Steam Battery, Letter from the Secretary of the Navy, January 6, 1862

Ex. Doc. No. 41 (Senate), Letter of the Secretary of War Communicating the Report of Edwin F. Johnson, upon the Defences of Maine, April 5, 1862

Ex. Doc. No. 103, Forts and Other Means of Defence, Letter from the Secretary of War, April 18, 1862

Ex. Doc. No. 104, Insurgent Privateers in Foreign Ports, Message from the President of the United States, April 26, 1862

Ex. Doc. No. 115, Change of Materials and Construction of Forts, Letter from the Secretary of War, May 12, 1862

Ex. Doc. No. 128, Enlargement of the Locks of the Erie and Oswego Canals, Message from the President of the United States, June 13, 1862

Ex. Doc. No. 148, Relations Between the United States and Foreign Powers, Message from the President of the United States, July 12, 1862

Ex. Doc. No. 150, Contracts Made with Bureaus Connected with the Navy Department, Letter from the Secretary of the Navy, July 14, 1862

Reports of Committees of the House of Representatives and Courts of Claims, 37th Congress, 2nd Session, 1861–1862 (Washington, DC: GPO, 1862)

Report No. 22, Reciprocity Treaty with Great Britain, February 5, 1862

Report No. 23, Harbor Defences on Great Lakes and Rivers, February 12, 1862

Report No. 86, Permanent Fortifications and Sea-Coast Defences, April 23, 1862

Report No. 114, Enlargement of the Locks of the Erie and Oswego Canals, June 3, 1862

Executive Documents, 37th Congress, 3rd Session, 1862–1863 (Washington, DC: GPO, 1863)

Ex. Doc. No. 15 (Senate), Letter of the Secretary of the Navy Communicating . . . extracts from reports in relation to the accident on board the steam-battery Passaic, January 6, 1863

Reports of Committees of the House of Representatives and Courts of Claims, 37th Congress, 3rd Session, 1862–1863 (Washington, DC: GPO, 1863)

Report No. 4, The Naval Defences of the Great Lakes, January 8, 1863

Report No. 53, Niagara Ship Canal, March 3, 1863

Miscellaneous Documents of the Senate of the United States, 37th Congress, 3rd Session, 1862–1863 (Washington, DC: GPO, 1863)

Mis. Doc. No. 38, Mr. Sumner, Concurrent Resolutions of Congress concerning Foreign Intervention in the existing Rebellion, February 28, 1863

Executive Documents, 38th Congress, 1st Session, 1863–1864 (Washington, DC: GPO, 1864)

Ex. Doc. No. 69, Armored Vessels in the Attack on Charleston, Letter from the Secretary of the Navy, April 11, 1864

Reports of Committees of the House of Representatives and Courts of Claims, 38th Congress, 1st Session, 1863–1864 (Washington, DC: GPO, 1864)

Report No. 39, Reciprocity Treaty, April 1, 1864
Report No. 61, Proposed Improvements to Pass Gunboats from Tide Water to the Northern and Northwestern Lakes, Message from the President of the United States, March 29, 1864
Report No. 100, Sites for Navy Yards, May 12, 1864

Miscellaneous Documents of the Senate of the United States, 38th Congress, 1st Session, 1863–1864 (Washington, DC: GPO, 1864)

Mis. Doc. No. 110, Memorial of The Legislature of Wisconsin in favor of the Fox and Wisconsin rivers, improvement of a ship canal around the Falls of Niagara, and the improvement of the Erie canal, April 27, 1864

Reports of Committees of the House of the Senate, 38th Congress, 2nd Session, 1864–1865 (Washington, DC: GPO, 1865)

Rep. Com. No. 121, Report of the Joint Committee on the Conduct of the War on Heavy Ordnance, February 13, 1865
Rep. Com. No. 123, Report on Claims of Captain John Ericsson, February 16, 1865

Executive Documents, 55th Congress, 2nd Session, 1888–1889 (Washington, DC: GPO, 1889)

Ex. Doc. No. 197 (Senate), "Moses Stuyvesant, Monitors v. Battle Ships," March 21, 1898

Report of the Secretary of the Navy in Relation to Armored Vessels (Washington, DC: GPO, 1864)

Official Records of the Union and Confederate Navies in the War of the Rebellion, 30 vols. (Washington, DC: GPO, 1894–1922)

Official Records of the War of the Rebellion, Union and Confederate Armies, 120 vols. (Washington, DC: GPO, 1880–1901)

PERIODICALS

Army and Navy Journal
Atlantic Monthly
Blackwood's Edinburgh Magazine
Charleston Mercury
Chicago Tribune
Daily Cleveland
Colburn's United Service Journal
Economist
Edinburgh Review
English Nautical Magazine
Harper's Monthly
Harper's Weekly
Illustrated London News
Journal of the Royal United Service Institution
London Engineer
Mechanics' Magazine
National Intelligencer
National Republican
Nautical Magazine
Naval Science
New York Herald
New York Times
New York Tribune
New York World
Philadelphia Inquirer
Punch
Quarterly Review
Saturday Review
Scientific American
(London) Times
Transactions of the Institute of Naval Architects

PUBLISHED COLLECTIONS

George E. Baker (ed.), *The Works of William Seward*, 5 vols. (Boston: Houghton Mifflin and Company, 1884)
Roy P. Basler (ed.), *The Collected Works of Abraham Lincoln*, 9 vols. (New Brunswick, NJ: Rutgers University Press, 1953–1955)

John M. Batten, *Reminiscences of Two Years in the United States Navy* (Lancaster, PA: Inquirer Printing, 1881)

Howard K. Beale (ed.), *Diary of Gideon Welles: Secretary of the Navy under Lincoln and Johnson*, 3 vols. (New York: W. W. Norton & Company, Inc., 1960)

Arthur Benson and Viscount Esher (eds.), *The Letters of Queen Victoria: 1837–1861*, vol. 3 of 9 vols. (London: John Murray, 1907)

Charles Beresford, *The Memoirs of Admiral Lord Charles Beresford*, 2 vols. (London: Methuen & Co. Ltd., 1914)

Hector Bolitho (ed.), *Further Letters of Queen Victoria, From the Archives of the House of Brandenburg-Prussia* (London: Thornton Butterworth, Ltd., 1938)

Kenneth Bourne (ed.), *The Letters of the Third Viscount Palmerston to Laurence and Elizabeth Sulivan, 1804–1863* (London: Royal Historical Society, 1979)

John Bright and James E. Thorold Rogers (eds.), *Speeches on Questions of Public Policy by Richard Cobden, M.P.*, 2 vols. (London: Macmillan and Co., 1870)

George M. Brook, Jr., (ed.), *Ironclads and Big Guns of the Confederacy: The Journal and Letters of John M. Brooke* (Columbia: University of South Carolina Press, 2002)

George Earle Buckle (ed.), *The Letters of Queen Victoria, 1862–1878, Second Series*, 2 vols. (London: John Murray, 1926)

P. H. Colomb (ed.), *Memoirs of Admiral the Right Honble. Sir Astley Cooper Key* (London: Methuen & Co., 1898)

Brian Connell, *Regina vs. Palmerston: The Private Correspondence between Queen Victoria and Her Foreign Minister* (New York: Doubleday & Co., 1961)

Martin Crawford (ed.), *William Howard Russell's Civil War: Private Diaries and Letters, 1861–1862* (Athens: University of Georgia Press, 1992)

Madeleine V. Dahlgren, *Memoir of John A. Dahlgren, Rear Admiral United States Navy, by His Widow* (New York: C. L. Webster, 1891)

Arthur Irwin Dasent (ed.), *John Thadeus Delane, Editor of the 'Times', His Life and Correspondence*, 2 vols. (London: John Murray, 1908)

Naval Letters of Captain Percival Drayton, 1861–1865: Donated to the New York Public Library by Miss Gertrude L. Hoyt (New York, 1906)

Official Dispatches and Letters of Rear Admiral Du Pont, U.S. Navy, 1846–48, 1861–63 (Wilmington, DE: Ferris Bros., 1883)

Don E. Fehrenbacher (ed.), *Abraham Lincoln: Speeches and Writings, 1859–1865* (New York: Literary Classics, Inc., 1989)

Worthington Chauncey Ford (ed.), *A Cycle of Adams Letters, 1861–1865*, 2 vols. (Boston: Houghton Mifflin Company, 1920)

G. P. Gooch (ed.), *The Later Correspondence of Lord John Russell, 1840–1878*, 2 vols. (London: Longmans, Green and Co., 1925)

Victoria Goodenough, *Memoir of Commodore Goodenough, with Extracts from His Letters and Journals*, 3rd ed. (London: C. Kegan Paul & Co., 1878)

Philip Guedalla (ed.), *The Palmerston Papers: Gladstone and Palmerston, being the Correspondence of Lord Palmerston with Mr. Gladstone 1851–1865* (London: Victor Gollancz, Ltd., 1928)

C. I. Hamilton (ed.), *Portsmouth Record Series, Portsmouth Dockyard Papers 1852–1869: From Wood to Iron* (Winchester, UK: Hampshire County Council, 2005)

John D. Hayes (ed.), *Samuel Francis Du Pont: A Selection From His Civil War Letters*, 3 vols. (Ithaca, NY: Cornell Univ. Press, 1969)

Robert Underwood Johnson and Clarence Clough Buel (eds.), *Battles and Leaders of the Civil War*, 4 vols. (Edison, NJ: Castle Books, 1956, reprint of 1884–1888 original series)

William F. Keeler (Robert W. Daly, ed.), *Aboard the USS* Monitor, *1862: The Letters of Acting Paymaster William Frederick Keeler, U.S. Navy, to His Wife, Anna* (Annapolis, MD: U.S. Naval Institute, 1964)

Gilbert Frankland Lewis (ed.), *Letters of the Right Hon. Sir George Cornewall Lewis, Bart. to Various Friends* (London: Longmans, Green, and Co., 1870)

William Marvel (ed.), *The* Monitor *Chronicles: One Sailor's Account— Today's Campaign to Recover the Civil War Wreck* (New York: Simon & Schuster, 2000)

H. C. G. Matthew (ed.), *The Gladstone Diaries*, Volume VI: 1861–1868, 9 vols (Oxford: Oxford University Press, 1978)

William James Morgan, David B. Tyler, Joye L. Leonhart, and Mary F. Loughlin (eds.), *Autobiography of Rear Admiral Charles Wilkes, U.S. Navy 1798–1877* (Washington, DC: GPO, 1978)

Allan Nevins and Milton Halsey Thomas (eds.), *The Diary of George Templeton Strong: The Civil War, 1860–1865* (New York: Octagon Books, 1974)

John Niven (ed.), *The Salmon P. Chase Papers*, Volume 3: Correspondence, 1858–March 1863, 5 vols. (Kent, OH: The Kent State University Press, 1993–1998)

Arthur Otway (ed.), *Autobiography and Journals of Admiral Lord Clarence E. Paget* (London: Chapman & Hall, Ltd., 1896)

Beverly Wilson Palmer (ed.), *The Selected Letters of Charles Sumner*, 2 vols. (Boston: Northeastern University Press, 1990)

Edward L. Pierce (ed.), *Memoir and Letters of Charles Sumner*, 2 vols. (London: Sampson Low, Marston and Company, 1893)

Ernest Rhys (ed.), *Selected Speeches of the Rt. Honble John Bright, M.P., on Public Questions* (London: J. M. Dent & Co., 1907)

Warren Ripley (ed.), *Siege Train: The Journal of a Confederate Artilleryman in the Defense of Charleston* (Columbia: University of South Carolina Press, 1986)

John Earl Russell, *Recollections and Suggestions, 1813–1873* (Boston: Roberts Brothers, 1875, reprint of London, Longmans, Green, 1873)

William Howard Russell (Eugen H. Berwanger, ed.), *My Diary North and South* (Baton Rouge: Louisian State Press, 2001, reprint of Alfred A. Knopf, 1988)

Frederic W. Seward, *Reminiscences of a Wartime Statesman and Diplomat, 1830–1915* (New York: G. P. Putnam's Sons, 1916)

Letters of Robert Gould Shaw, 1861–1863 (Cambridge, MA: University Press, 1864)

John Sherman, *Recollections of Forty Years in the House, Senate and Cabinet: An Autobiography*, 2 vols. (Chicago: The Werner Company, 1895)

John Y. Simon (ed.), *The Papers of Ulysses S. Grant, Volume 13: November 16, 1864–February 20, 1865*, 13 vols. (Carbondale: Southern Illinois University Press, 1985)

Robert M. Thompson and Richard Wainwright (eds.), *Confidential Correspondence of Gustavus V. Fox, Assistant Secretary of the Navy, 1861–1865*, 2 vols. (New York: New World Book Manufacturing, 1918–1919)

Sarah Agnes Wallace and Frances Elma Gillespie (eds.), *The Journal of Benjamin Moran, 1857–1865*, 2 vols. (Chicago: The University of Chicago Press, 1949)

Sydney Eardley-Wilmot, *An Admiral's Memories: Sixty-Five Years Afloat and Ashore* (London: Sampson Low, Marston & Co., Ltd., *ca.* late 1920s)

George Wrottesley, *Life and Correspondence of Field Marshall Sir John Burgoyne*, 2 vols. (London: Richard Bentley & Son, 1873)

SECONDARY WORKS

Charles Francis Adams, Jr., *Charles Francis Adams* (Boston: Houghton-Mifflin, 1900)

Ephraim Douglas Adams, *Great Britain and the American Civil War*, 2 vols. (New York: Russell and Russell, 1925)

Lloyd Ambrosius, *A Crisis of Republicanism: American Politics During The Civil War Era* (Lincoln: University of Nebraska Press, 1990)

Daniel Ammen, *The Navy in the Civil War: The Atlantic Coast* (New York: The Blue & The Gray Press, 1905, reprint of Charles Scribner's Sons, 1898)

_____, *The Old Navy and the New* (Philadelphia: J. B. Lippincott, 1891)

Bern Anderson, *By Sea and by River: The Naval History of the Civil War* (New York: Alfred A. Knopf, 1962)

J. Cutler Andrews, *The North Reports the Civil War* (Pittsburgh: University of Pittsburgh Press, 1955)

Thomas Archer, *William Ewart Gladstone and His Contemporaries, Vol. IV* (London: Gresham Publishing Co., 1899)

John Black Atkins, *The Life of Sir William Howard Russell: The First Special Correspondent*, 2 vols. (London: John Murray, 1911)

Philip S. Bagwell and G. E. Mingay, *Britain and America: A Study of Economic Change, 1850–1939* (London: Routledge & Kegan Paul, 1970)

George A. Ballard (G. A. Osborn and N. A. M. Rodger, eds.), *The Black Battlefleet: A Study of the Capital Ship in Transition* (London: Nautical Publishing Co., Lymington & the Society for Nautical Research, Greenwich, 1980)

K. C. Barnaby, *The Institution of Naval Architects, 1860–1960: An Historical Survey of the Institution's Transactions and Activities over 100 Years* (London: George Allen and Unwin, 1960)

J. G. Barnard, *The Dangers and Defences of New York* (New York: D. Van Nostrand, 1859)

_____, *Notes on Sea-Coast Defence* (New York: D. Van Nostrand, 1861)

_____, *A Report on the Defenses of Washington:* (Washington, DC: GPO, 1871)

James J. Barnes and Patience P. Barnes (eds.), *The American Civil War through British Eyes: Dispatches from British Diplomats*, 2 vols. (London: Caliban Books, 2005)

Patrick Barry, *Dockyard Economy and Naval Power* (London: Sampson Low, Son, and Co., 1863)

_____, *The Dockyards, Shipyards and Marine of France* (London: Simpkin, Marshall, and Co., 1864)

_____, *Shoeburyness and the Guns: A Philosophical Discourse* (London: Sampson Low, Son, and Marston, 1865)

C. J. Bartlett, *Great Britain and Sea Power, 1815–1853* (Oxford: Clarendon Press, 1963)

_____, *Defence and Diplomacy: Great Britain and the Great Powers, 1815–1914* (Manchester, UK: Manchester University Press, 1993)

_____, (ed.), *Britain Pre-Eminent: Studies in British World Influence in the Nineteenth Century* (London: Macmillan and Co., Ltd, 1969)

Irving H. Bartlett, *The American Mind in the Mid-Nineteenth Century* (London: Routledge & Kegan Paul, 1968)

Marshall J. Bastable, *Arms and the State: Sir William Armstrong and the Remaking of British Naval Power, 1854–1914* (Burlington, VT: Ashgate, 2004)

James Phinney Baxter 3rd, *The Introduction of the Ironclad Warship* (Cambridge, MA: Harvard University Press, 1933)

Ian F. W. Beckett, *The War Correspondents: The American Civil War* (London: Grange Books, 1997 ed.; original 1993)

John F. Beeler, *British Naval Policy in the Gladstone-Disraeli Era, 1866–1880* (Stanford, CA: Stanford University Press, 1997)

_____, *Birth of the Battleship: British Capital Ship Design, 1870–1881* (London: Caxton Publishing 2003, reprint of Chatham Publishing, 2001)

Herbert C. F. Bell, *Lord Palmerston*, 2 vols. (Hamden, CT: Archon Books, 1966, reprint of London, Longmans Green & Co., 1936)

Frank M. Bennett, *The Steam Navy of the United States* (Pittsburgh, PA: W. T. Nicholson Press, 1896)

_____, *The* Monitor *and the Navy under Steam* (Boston: Houghton, Mifflin and Co., 1900)

George Bennett (ed.), *The Concept of Empire: Burke to Attlee, 1774–1947* (London: Adam and Charles Black, 1967)

Eugene H. Berwanger, *The British Foreign Service and the American Civil War* (Lexington: The University Press of Kentucky Press, 1994)

Geoffrey Best, *Mid-Victorian Britain, 1851–75* (London: Fontana Press, 1971)

John Bigelow, *France and the Confederate Navy (1862–1868): An International Episode* (New York: Bergman Publishers, 1968 reprint of 1888 original)

R. J. M. Blackett, *Divided Hearts: Britain and the American Civil War* (Baton Rouge: Louisiana State University 2001)

Kenneth Bourne (ed.), *The Foreign Policy of Victorian England, 1830–1902* (Oxford: Clarendon Press, 1970)

_____, *Britain and the Balance of Power in North America, 1815–1908* (London: Longmans, Green and Co. Ltd., 1967)

Charles B. Boynton, *The Navies of England, France, America and Russia, Being an Extract from a Work on English and French Neutrality, and The Anglo-French Alliance* (New York: John F. Trow, 1865, reprinted in 1866 by C. F. Vent & Co. as *The Four Great Powers*)

_____, *The History of the Navy During the Rebellion*, 2 vols. (New York: D. Appleton & Co., 1867–68)

James C. Bradford (ed.), *Captains of the Old Steam Navy: Makers of the American Naval Tradition, 1840–1880* (Annapolis, MD: Naval Institute Press, 1986)

J. D. Brandt, *Gunnery Catechism, as Applied to the Service of Naval Ordnance* (New York: D. Van Nostrand, 1865)

Thomas Brassey, *The British Navy: Its Strength, Resources, and Administration,* 6 vols. (London: Longmans, Green, and Co., 1882–83)

Asa Briggs, *Victorian Cities* (Harmondsworth, UK: Penguin Books Ltd., 1982 reprint of Odhams Press, 1963 original)

_____, *Victorian People* (Chicago: University of Chicago Press, 1970)

John Henry Briggs (Lady Briggs, ed.), *Naval Administrations, 1827 to 1892: The Experience of 65 Years* (London: Sampson Low, Marston & Company, 1897)

Bernard Brodie, *Sea Power in the Machine Age* (Princeton, NJ: Princeton University Press, 1941)

David K. Brown, *Before the Ironclad: Development of Ship Design, Propulsion and Armament in the Royal Navy, 1815–1860* (London: Conway Maritime Press, 1990)

_____, *Warrior to Dreadnought: Warship Development, 1860–1905* (London: Chatham Publishing, 1997)

Charles Orde Browne, *Armour, and Its Attack by Artillery* (London: Dulau & Co., 1887)

Samuel T. Browne, *First Cruise of the* Montauk—*Soldiers and Sailors Historical Society of Rhode Island—Personal Narratives of Events in the War of the Rebellion* (Providence, RI: N. Bangs Williams Co., 1880)

Robert S. Browning, III, *Two If By Sea: The Development of American Coastal Defence Policy* (Westport, CT: Greenwood Publishing, 1983)

Robert M. Browning, Jr., *From Cape Charles to Cape Fear: The North Atlantic Blockading Squadron During the Civil War* (Tuscaloosa: University of Alabama Press, 1993)

_____, *Success Is All That Was Expected: The South Atlantic Blockading Squadron During the Civil War* (Washington, DC: Brassey's Inc., 2002)

Robert V. Bruce, *Lincoln and the Tools of War* (Chicago: University of Illinois Press, 1989)

Samuel W. Bryant, *The Sea and the States: A Maritime History of the American People* (New York: Thomas Y. Crowell, 1947)

James D. Bulloch, *The Secret Service of the Confederate States in Europe, or How the Confederate Cruisers Were Equipped,* 2 vols. (London: Richard Bentley & Son, 1883, reprint of New York: Sagamore/Thomas Yoseloff, 1959)

W. L. Burn, *The Age of Equipoise; A Study of the Mid-Victorian Generation* (New York: W. W. Norton & Company, Inc., 1964)

Amos Burton, *A Journal of the Cruise of the U.S. Ship Susquehanna* (New York: Edward O. Jenkins, 1863)

David H. Burton (ed.), *American History—British Historians* (Chicago: Nelson-Hall, 1978)

E. Milby Burton, *The Siege of Charleston, 1861–1865* (Columbia: University of South Carolina Press, 1970)

Hans Busk, *The Navies of the World; Their Present State and Future Capabilities* (London: Routledge, Warnes, and Routledge, 1859)

Ian Buxton, *Big Gun Monitors: The History of the Design, Construction and Operation of the Royal Navy's Monitors* (Annapolis, MD: Naval Institute Press, 1978)

James Cable, *The Political Influence of Naval Force in Naval History* (London: Macmillan Press, Ltd., 1998)

Charles S. Campbell, *The Transformation of American Foreign Relations, 1865–1900* (New York: Harper Colophon Books, 1976)

Duncan Andrew Campbell, *English Public Opinion and the American Civil War* (Woodbridge: The Boydell Press, 2003)

Eugene B. Canfield, *Civil War Naval Ordnance* (Washington: Navy Department, Naval History Division, 1969)

Donald L. Canney, *The Old Steam Navy, Volume Two: The Ironclads, 1842–1885* (Annapolis, MD: Naval Institute Press, 1993)

———, *Lincoln's Navy: The Ships, Men and Organization, 1861–65* (Annapolis, MD: Naval Institute Press, 1998)

Richard J. Carwardine, *Lincoln* (Edinburgh, UK: Pearson Education Limited, 2003)

Lynn M. Case and Warren F. Spencer, *The United States and France: Civil War Diplomacy* (Philadelphia: University of Pennsylvania Press, 1970)

Bruce Catton (James M. McPherson, ed.), *The American Heritage New History of The Civil War* (New York: Viking Penguin, 1996, reprint of 1960 original)

Algernon Cecil, *British Foreign Secretaries, 1807–1916: Studies in Personality and Policy* (London: G. Bell and Sons, Ltd., 1927)

Muriel E. Chamberlain, *'Pax Britannica'? British Foreign Policy, 1789–1914* (Harlow, UK: Longman Group UK Limited, 1988)

———, *Lord Palmerston* (Washington, DC: Catholic University Press, 1988)

John D. Champlin, Jr. (ed.), *Narrative of the Mission to Russia, in 1866, of the Hon. Gustavus Vasa Fox, Assistant-Secretary of the Navy, from the journal and Notes of J. F. Loubat* (New York: D. Appleton and Company, 1873)

Winston S. Churchill, *A History of the English-Speaking Peoples: The Great Democracies* (New York: Dodd, Mead & Company, 1958)

William Conant Church, *The Life of John Ericsson*, 2 vols. (New York: Charles Scribner's Sons, 1890)

William Laird Clowes, *The Royal Navy: A History from the Earliest Times to 1900, Volume VII* (London: Chatham Publishing, 1997, first published by Sampson Low, Marston and Company, 1903)

William B. Coger (ed.), *New Interpretations in Naval History: Selected Papers from the Twelfth Naval History Symposium, Held at the United States Naval Academy, 26–27 October 1995* (Annapolis, MD: Naval Institute Press, 1997)

Paolo E. Coletta (ed.), *American Secretaries of the Navy*, 2 vols. (Annapolis, MD: Naval Institute Press, 1980)

Julian Corbett, *Some Principles of Maritime Strategy* (London: Longman, Green & Co., 1911)

John M. Coski, *Capital Navy: The Men, Ships and Operations of The James River Squadron* (Campbell, CA: Savas Publishing Company, 1996)

Regis A. Courtemanche, *No Need of Glory: The British Navy in American Waters, 1860–64* (Annapolis, MD: Naval Institute Press, 1977)

J. Lee Cox, Jr. and Michael A. Jehle (eds.), *Ironclad Intruder: U.S.S. Monitor* (Philadelphia: Philadelphia: Maritime Museum, 1988)

Martin Crawford, *The Anglo-American Crisis of the Mid-Nineteenth Century: The* Times *and America* (Athens: The University of Georgia Press, 1987)

David Paul Crook, *The North, the South, and the Powers, 1861–65* (New York: John Wiley & Sons, Inc., 1974)

_____, *Diplomacy During the American Civil War* (New York: John Wiley & Sons, Inc., 1975)

John A. Dahlgren, *Shells and Shell-Guns* (Philadelphia: King & Baird, 1857)

Lance E. Davis and Robert A. Huttenback, *Mammon and the Pursuit of Empire: The Political Economy of British Imperialism, 1860–1912* (Cambridge, UK: Cambridge University Press, 1988)

William C. Davis (ed.), *The Image of War: 1861–1865*, 6 vols. (New York: Doubleday & Company, Inc., 1981–1984)

James Tertius DeKay, Monitor: *The Story of the Legendary Civil War Ironclad and the Man Whose Invention Changed the Course of History* (Pimlico, UK: Random House, 1999)

Ludwell Denny, *America Conquers Britain: A Record of Economic War* (New York: Alfred A. Knopf, 1930)

Edward Dicey (Herbert Mitgang, ed.), *Spectator of America* (Chicago: Quadrangle Books, 1971, reprint of *Six Months in the Federal States*, London: Macmillan and Co., 1863)

Conrad Dixon, *Ships of the Victorian Navy* (Southampton, UK: Society for Nautical Research/Ashford Press, 1987)

David Dougan, *The Great Gun-Maker: The Story of Lord Armstrong* (Newcastle, UK: Frank Graham, 1971)

Howard Douglas, *On Naval Warfare with Steam* (London: John Murray, Albemarle Street, 1858)

_____, *A Treatise on Naval Gunnery*, 5th ed.(London: John Murray, 1860)

Wade G. Dudley, *Splintering the Wooden Wall: The British Blockade of the United States, 1812–1815* (Annapolis, MD: 2003)

Henry A. Du Pont, *Rear-Admiral Samuel Francis Du Pont, United States Navy: A Biography* (New York: National Americana Society)

James B. Eads, *System of Naval Defences* (New York: D. Van Nostrand, 1868)

C. C. Eldridge (ed.), *British Imperialism in the Nineteenth Century* (London: Macmillan Publishers, Ltd., 1984)

John Englander (ed.), *Britain & America: Studies in Comparative History 1760–1970* (New Haven, CT: Yale University Press, 1997)

John Ericsson, *Contributions to the Centennial Exhibition* (New York: Nation Press, 1876)

David Evans, *Building the Steam Navy: Dockyards, Technology and the Creation of the Victorian Battle Fleet, 1830–1906* (London: Conway Maritime Press, 2004)

William Fairburn, *Treatise on Iron Shipbuilding: Its History and Progress* (London, 1865)

Loyall Farragut, *The Life of David Glasgow Farragut, First Admiral of the United States Navy, Embodying His Journal and Letters, by his son, Loyall Farragut* (New York: Appleton and Co., 1879)

Norman. B. Ferris, *The Trent Affair* (Knoxville: University of Tennessee Press, 1977)

E. Gardiner Fishbourne, *Our Ironclads and Merchant Ships* (London: E. & F. N., 1874)

Philip S. Foner, *British Labor and the American Civil War* (New York: Holmes & Meier, 1981)

Charles Stuart Forbes, *A Standing Navy: Its Necessity and Organisation* (London: John Murray, 1861)

William M. Fowler, *Under Two Flags: The American Navy in the Civil War* (New York: Norton, 1990)

George Henry Francis (ed.), *Opinions and Policy of the Right Honourable Viscount Palmerston* (London: Elibron Classics, 2006 reprint of 1852 original)

Arthur Fremantle, *Three Months in the Southern States* (London: William Blackwood and Sons, 1863)

Robert Gardiner (ed.), *Conway's History of the Ship Series—The Advent of Steam: The Merchant Steamship Before 1900* (London: Conway Maritime Press, 1993)

_____(ed.) *Conway's History of the Ship Series—Steam, Steel & Shellfire: The Steam Warship, 1815–1905* (London: Conway Maritime Press, 1992)

Stanton Garner, *The Civil War World of Herman Melville* (Lawrence: University Press of Kansas, 1993)

Quincy A. Gillmore, *Engineer and Artillery Operations against the Defences of Charleston Harbour in 1863* (New York: D. Van Nostrand, 1865)

_____, *Supplementary Report on Operations Against Charleston* (New York: D. Van Nostrand, 1868)

Jan Glete, *Navies and Nations: Warships, Navies and State Building in Europe and America, 1500–1860*, 2 vols. (Stockholm: Coronet Books, Inc., 1993)

James Goldrick and John B. Hattendorf (eds.), *Mahan is Not Enough: The Proceedings of a Conference on the Works of Sir Julian Corbett and Admiral Sir Herbert Richmond* (Newport, RI: Naval War College Press, 1993)

Barry M. Gough, *The Royal Navy and the Northwest Coast of North America, 1810–1914: A Study of British Maritime Ascendancy* (Vancouver: University of British Columbia Press, 1971)

G. S. Graham, *The Politics of Naval Supremacy: Studies in British Maritime Ascendancy* (London: Cambridge University Press, 1965)

Alfred Grant, *The American Civil War and the British Press* (Jefferson, NC: McFarland & Co., Inc., 2000)

Colin S. Gray, *The Leverage of Sea Power: The Strategic Advantage of Navies in War* (New York: The Free Press, 1992)

Jack Greene and Alessandro Massignani, *Ironclads at War: The Origin and Development of the Armored Warship, 1854–1891* (Conshohocken, PA: Combined Publishing, 1998)

Eric Grove (ed.), *Great Battles of the Royal Navy: As Commemorated in the Gunroom, Britannia Royal Naval College, Dartmouth* (Surrey, UK: Armstrong and Armour Press, 1994)

Philip Guedalla, *Palmerston* (London: Hodder and Stoughton, 1926)

J. M. Haas, *A Management Odyssey: The Royal Dockyards, 1714–1914* (Lanham, MD: University Press of America, 1994)

Kurt Hackemer, *The U.S. Navy and the Origins of the Military-Industrial Complex, 1847–1883* (Annapolis, MD: Naval Institute Press, 2001)

Kenneth J. Hagan, *This People's Navy: The Making of American Sea Power* (New York: The Free Press, 1991)

_____ (ed.), *In Peace and War: Interpretations of American Naval History, 1775–1984* (London: Greenwood Press, 1984)

C. I. Hamilton, *Anglo-French Naval Rivalry, 1840–1870* (Oxford: Clarendon Press, 1993)

Charles Hamley, *Fleets and Navies* (London: William Blackwood and Sons, 1860)

Frank Hardie, *The Political Influence of Queen Victoria, 1861–1901* (London: Frank Cass & Co. Ltd., 1963)

Jerry Harlowe, *Monitors: The Men, Machines and Mystique* (Gettysburg, PA: Thomas Publications, 2001)

Richard Harwell (ed.), *A Confederate Marine: A Sketch of Henry Lea Graves with Excerpts from the Graves Family Correspondence, 1861–1865* (Tuscaloosa, AL: Confederate Publishing Company, 1963)

John B. Hattendorf, R.J.B. Knight, A.W.H. Pearsall, N. A. M. Rodger, and Geoffrey Till (eds.), *British Naval Documents, 1204–1960* (Aldershot, UK: Scolar Press for the Navy Records Society, 1993)

Arthur Hawkey, *Black Night Off Finisterre: The Tragic Tale of an Early British Ironclad* (Annapolis, MD: Naval Institute Press, 1999)

P. C. Headley, *The Miner Boy and His Monitor, or The Career and Achievements of John Ericsson* (New York: William H. Appleton, 1865)

F. J. C. Hearnshaw (ed.), *The Political Principles of Some Notable Prime Ministers of the Nineteenth Century* (London: Macmillan and Co., 1926)

Emanuel Hertz (ed.), *Lincoln Talks: A Biography in Anecdote* (New York: Viking Press, 1939)

William B. Hesseltine, *Lincoln and the War Governors* (New York: Alfred A. Knopf, 1948)

Martin Hewitt (ed.), *Age of Equipoise? Reassessing Mid-Victorian Britain* (Aldershot, UK: Ashgate Publishing Group, 2000)

Christopher Hibbert, *The Illustrated London News: Social History of Victorian Britain* (London: Book Club Associates, 1976)

Jim Dan Hill (ed.), *The Civil War Sketchbook of Charles Ellery Stedman: Surgeon, United States Navy* (San Rafael, CA: Presidio Press, 1976)

Richard Hill, *War at Sea in the Ironclad Age* (London: Cassell, 2000)

Gertrude Himmelfarb, *Victorian Minds: A Study of Intellectuals in Crisis and Ideologies in Transition* (Chicago: Ivan R. Dee, 1968)

E. J. Hobsbawm, *The Pelican Economic History of Britain Volume 3: Industry and Empire* (Harmondsworth, UK: Penguin Books, Ltd., 1969, reprint of Weidenfeld & Nicolson, 1968)

_____, *The Age of Capital, 1848–1875* (London: Abacus, 1975)

Ian V. Hogg, *Coast Defences of England and Wales, 1856–1956* (Newton Abbot, UK: David & Charles Publishers, 1974)

Ian Hogg and John Batchelor, *Naval Gun* (Poole, UK: Blanford Press, 1978)

Alexander L. Holley, *A Treatise on Ordnance and Armor* (New York: D. Van Nostrand, 1865)

Harold Holzer and Tim Mulligan (eds.), *The Battle of Hampton Roads: New Perspectives on the USS* Monitor *and CSS* Virginia (New York: Fordham University Press, 2006)

Peter Hore (ed.), *Seapower Ashore: 200 Years of Royal Navy Operations on Land* (London: Chatham Publishing, 2001)

Michael Howard, *War in European History* (Oxford: Oxford University Press, 1976)

Stephen Howarth, *To Shining Sea: A History of the United States Navy, 1775–1991* (New York: Random House, 1991)

Richard Humble, *Before the Dreadnought: The Royal Navy from Nelson to Fisher* (London: Macdonald & Jane's Publishers, Ltd., 1976)

Alvah F. Hunter (Craig L. Symonds, ed.), *A Year on a Monitor and the Destruction of Fort Sumter* (Columbia: University of South Carolina Press, 1987)

Fred T. Jane, *The British Battle-Fleet: Its Inception and Growth throughout the Centuries*, Introduction by Anthony Preston (London: Conway Maritime Press, UK: 1997, reprint from London; S.W. Partridge & Co., Ltd., 1912)

Brian Jenkins, *Britain and the War for the Union*, 2 vols. (Montreal: McGill-Queen's University Press, 1974)

Roy Jenkins, *Gladstone* (London: Macmillan Publishing, 1995)

T. A. Jenkins, *The Liberal Ascendancy, 1830–1886* (London: Macmillan Press, Ltd., 1994)

John Johnson, *The Defense of Charleston Harbor, Including Fort Sumter and Adjacent Islands, 1863–1865* (Charleston, SC: Walker, Evans and Cogswell, 1890)

Robert Erwin Johnson, *Rear Admiral John Rodgers, 1812–1882* (Annapolis, MD: United States Naval Institute, 1967)

Howard Jones, *Union in Peril: The Crisis over British Intervention in the Civil War* (Chapel Hill: University of North Carolina Press, 1992)

J. B. Jones, *A Rebel War Clerk's Diary at the Confederate States Capital*, 2 vols. (Philadelphia: J. B. Lippincott & Co., 1866; 1982, Time-Life books reprint)

Virgil C. Jones, *The Civil War at Sea*, 3 vols. (New York: Holt, Rhinehart, & Winston, 1960–62)

Wilbur Devereux Jones, *The Confederate Rams at Birkenhead: A Chapter in Anglo-American Relations* (Tuscaloosa, AL: Confederate Publishing Co., 1961)

_____, *The American Problem in British Diplomacy, 1841–61* (Athens: University of Georgia Press, 1974)

Donaldson Jordan and Edwin J. Pratt, *Europe and the American Civil War* (Boston: Houghton Mifflin Company, 1931)

Gerald B. Kauvar and Gerald C. Sorensen (eds.), *The Victorian Mind* (London: Cassell & Company, 1969)

Paul Kennedy, *The Rise and Fall of British Naval Mastery* (Malabar, FL: Robert E. Krieger Publishing Company, 1982, reprint of Harold Ober, 1976)

_____, *The Realities Behind Diplomacy: Background Influences on British External Policy, 1865–1980* (London: George Allen & Unwin, 1981)

_____, *The Rise and Fall of the Great Powers: Economic Change and Military Conflict from 1500 to 2000* (London: Fontana Press, 1988)

J. W. King, *The Warships of Europe* (London: Griffin and Co., 1878)

David F. Krein, *The Last Palmerston Government* (Ames: Iowa State University Press, 1978)

Benjamin W. Labaree, William M. Fowler, Jr., Edward W. Sloan, John B. Hattendorf, Jeffrey J. Safford, and Andrew W. German (eds.), *America and the Sea: A Maritime History; The American Maritime Library: Volume XV* (Mystic, CT: Mystic Seaport, 1998)

Roy C. Laible (ed.), *Ballistic Materials and Penetration Mechanics* (New York: Elsevier Scientific Publishing Company, 1980)

Andrew Lambert, *Battleships in Transition: The Creation of the Steam Battlefleet, 1815–1860* (London: Conway Maritime Press, 1984)

_____, *Warrior: The World's First Ironclad Then and Now* (London: Conway Maritime Press, Ltd., 1987)

_____, *The Crimean War: British Grand Strategy against Russia, 1853–56* (Manchester, UK: Manchester University Press, 1991, reprint of 1990 original)

G. H. L. Le May, *The Victorian Constitution: Conventions, Usages and Contingencies* (London: Duckworth, 1979)

Charles L. Lewis, *Admiral Franklin Buchanan, Fearless Man of Action* (Baltimore, MD: Norman, Remington, 1929)

Emanuel Raymond Lewis, *Sea Coast Fortifications of the United States: An Introductory History* (Annapolis, MD: Naval Institute Press, 1979, reprint of Smithsonian, 1970)

Mary P. Livingston (ed.), *A Civil War Marine at Sea: The Diary of Medal of Honor Recipient Miles M. Oviatt* (Shippensburg, PA: White Mane Books, 1998)

Jay Luvaas, *The Military Legacy of the Civil War: The European Inheritance* (Lawrence: University Press of Kansas, 1988, reprint of University of Chicago Press, 1959)

Clarence E. Macartney, *Mr. Lincoln's Admirals* (New York: Funk & Wagnalls, 1956)

Robert MacBride, *Civil War Ironclads: The Dawn of Naval Armor* (Philadelphia: Chilton, 1962)

Philip Magnus, *Gladstone: A Biography* (London: John Murray, 1970, reprint of 1954 original)

Alfred Thayer Mahan, *Admiral Farragut* (New York: D. Appleton, 1897)

_____, *The Influence of Seapower Upon History, 1660–1783* (New York: Hill and Wang, American Century Series, 1957, reprint of 1890 original)

_____, *Naval Strategy Compared and Contrasted with the Principles and Practice of Military Operations on Land* (Boston: Little, Brown, 1911)

Dean B. Mahin, *One War at a Time: The International Dimensions of the American Civil War* (Washington: DC: Brassey's, 1999)

Curt von Maltzahn, *Naval Warfare: Its Historical Development from the Age of the Great Geographical Discoveries to the Present Time* (London: Longmans, Green, and Co., 1908)

Greg Marquis, *In Armageddon's Shadow: The Civil War and Canada's Maritime Provinces* (Montreal: McGill-Queen's University Press, 1998)

Ian Marshall, *Armored Ships: The Ships, Their Settings, and the Ascendancy That They Sustained for 80 Years* (Charlottesville, VA: Howell Press, Inc., 1993)

———, *Ironclads and Paddlers* (Charlottesville, VA: Howell Press, Inc., 1993)

B. Kingsley Martin, *The Triumph of Lord Palmerston: A Study of Public Opinion in England Before the Crimean War* (London: George Allen & Unwin Ltd., 1924)

Robert E. May (ed.), *The Union, the Confederacy, and the Atlantic Rim* (West Lafayette, IN: Purdue University Press, 1995)

R. B. McDowell, *British Conservatism, 1832–1914* (London: Faber and Faber, 1959)

Peter McKenzie, *W. G. Armstrong: The Life and Times of Sir William George Armstrong, Baron Armstrong of Cragside* (Newcastle, UK: Longhirst Press, 1983)

William H. McNeill, *The Pursuit of Power: Technology, Armed Force, and Society since A.D. 1000* (Chicago: University of Chicago Press, 1982)

James M. McPherson, *Battle Cry of Freedom: The Civil War Era* (New York: Ballantine Books, 1988)

———, *Abraham Lincoln and the Second American Revolution* (Oxford: Oxford University Press, 1990)

Maurice Melton, *The Confederate Ironclads* (New York: Thomas Yoseloff, 1968)

Raja Menon, *Maritime Strategy and Continental Wars* (London: Frank Cass Publishers, 1998)

Frederick Merk, *Manifest Destiny and Mission in American History: A Reinterpretation* (Cambridge, MA: Harvard University Press, 1995, reprint of 1963 original)

Frank J. Merli, *Great Britain and the Confederate Navy, 1861–1865* (Bloomington: Indiana University Press, 1970)

———, David M. Fahey (ed.), *The Alabama, British Neutrality, and the American Civil War* (Bloomington: Indiana University Press, 2004)

James M. Merrill, *The Rebel Shore: The Story of Union Sea Power in the Civil War* (Boston: Little, Brown and Company, 1957)

Edward M. Miller, *U.S.S. Monitor: The Ship That Launched A Modern Navy* (Annapolis, MD: Leeward Publications, Inc., 1978)

David A. Mindell, *War, Technology, and Experience aboard the U.S.S. Monitor* (Baltimore, MD: John Hopkins University Press, 2000)

Charles L. C. Miner, *The Real Lincoln: From the Testimony of His Contemporaries* (Harrisonburg, VA: Sprinkle Publications, 1992, reprint from Everett Waddey Co., 1904)

Jay Monaghan, *Diplomat in Carpet Slippers: Abraham Lincoln Deals with Foreign Affairs* (New York: Bobbs-Merrill, 1945)

John Morley, *The Life of Richard Cobden*, 2 vols. (London: Chapman and Hall, 1881)

F. Darrell Munsell, *The Unfortunate Duke: Henry Pelham, Fifth Duke of Newcastle, 1811–1864* (Columbia: University of Missouri Press, 1985)

Ivan Musicant, *Divided Waters: The Naval History of the Civil War* (Edison, NJ: Castle Books, 2000, reprint of 1995 original)

Mark E. Neely, Jr., *The Union Divided: Party Conflict in the Civil War North* (Cambridge, MA: Harvard University Press, 2002)

David Newsome, *The Victorian World Picture: Perceptions and Introspections in an Age of Change* (New Brunswick, NJ: Rutgers University Press, 1997)

Lord Newton, *Lord Lyons: A Record of British Diplomacy*, 2 vols. (London: Edward Arnold, 1913)

John G. Nicolay and John Hay, *Abraham Lincoln: A History*, 10 vols. (New York: The Century Co., 1917)

John Niven, *Gideon Welles: Lincoln's Secretary of the Navy* (Baton Rouge: Louisiana State Press, 1973)

Frank Lawrence Owsley, *King Cotton Diplomacy: Foreign Relations of the Confederate States of America* (Chicago: 1959)

Peter Padfield, *Rule Britannia: The Victorian and Edwardian Navy* (London: Pimlico, 2002, reprint of Routledge & Kegan Paul Ltd., 1981)

John C. Paget, *Naval Powers and Their Policies* (London: Longmans and Co., 1876)

Philip Shaw Paludan, *"A People's Contest": The Union and Civil War, 1861–1865* (New York: Harper & Row, Publishers, 1988)

Foxhall A. Parker, *Squadron Tactics Under Steam* (New York: D. Van Nostrand, 1864)

Oscar Parkes, *British Battleships, 'Warrior' 1860 to 'Vanguard' 1950: A History of Design, Construction and Armament* (London: Seeley Service & Co., Ltd., 1970)

Jonathan Parry, *The Rise and Fall of Liberal Government in Victorian Britain* (New Haven, CT: Yale University Press, 1993)

Michael Stephen Partridge, *Military Planning for the Defence of the United Kingdom, 1814–1870* (New York: Greenwood Press, 1989)

Charles Oscar Paullin, *Paullin's History of Naval Administration, 1775–1911* (Annapolis, MD: Naval Institute Press, 1968)

A. W. H. Pearsall, C. I. Hamilton, and Andrew Lambert (eds.), *Publications of the Navy Record Society, Vol. 131, British Naval Documents 1204–1960* (Aldershot, UK: Scolar Press, 1993)

Hugh B. Peebles, *Warshipbuilding on the Clyde: Naval Orders and the Prosperity of the Clyde Shipbuilding Industry, 1889–1939* (Edinburgh, UK: John Donald Publishers, Ltd., 1987)

Geoffrey Penn, *Up Funnel, Down Screw: The Story of the Naval Engineer* (London: Hollis & Carter, 1955)

Harold L. Peterson, *Notes on Ordnance of the American Civil War, 1861–1865* (Washington: American Ordnance Assn., 1959)

Andrew Porter (ed.), *The Oxford History of the British Empire: The Nineteenth Century* (Oxford: Oxford University Press, 1999)

David D. Porter, *Naval History of the Civil War* (Secaucus, NJ: Castle, 1984, reprint of Sherman, 1886)

Horace Porter, *Campaigning with Grant* (New York: Da Capo Press, 1986, reprint of Century, 1897)

Anthony Preston and John Major, *'Send a Gunboat': A Study of the Gunboat and Its Role in British Policy, 1854–1904* (London: Longmans, Green and Co. Ltd., 1967)

Philip Pugh, *The Cost of Seapower: The Influence of Money on Naval Affairs from 1815 to the Present Day* (London: Conway Maritime Press, 1986)

J. G. Randall, *Lincoln the Liberal Statesman* (London: Eyre & Spottiswoode, 1947)

Bryan Ranft (ed.), *Technical Change and British Naval Policy, 1860–1939* (London: Morrison & Gibb, Ltd., 1977)

E. J. Reed, *Our Iron-Clad Ships: Their Qualities, Performances, and Cost* (London: John Murray, 1869)

———, *Shipbuilding in Iron and Steel* (London: John Murray, 1869)

———, *Our Naval Coast Defences* (London: John Murray, 1871)

Rowena Reed, *Combined Operations in the Civil War* (Annapolis, MD: Naval Institute Press, 1978)

Brian Holden Reid, *The American Civil War and the Wars of the Industrial Revolution* (London: Cassell, 1999)

Clark G. Reynolds, *Command of the Sea: The History and Strategy of Maritime Empires*, 2 vols. (Malabar, FL: Robert E. Krieger Publishing Company, 1983, reprint of William Morrow & Company, 1974)

Allen Thorndike Rice (ed.), *Reminiscences of Abraham Lincoln by Distinguished Men of His Time* (New York: North American Review, 1888)

Jasper Ridley, *Lord Palmerston* (London: Constable & Co. Ltd, 1970)

Dennis J. Ringle, *Life in Mr. Lincoln's Navy* (Annapolis, MD: Naval Institute Press, 1998)

Warren Ripley, *Artillery and Ammunition of the Civil War* (New York: Van Nostrand Reinhold Co., 1970)

William H. Roberts, *USS* New Ironsides *in the Civil War* (Annapolis, MD: Naval Institute Press, 1999)

———, *Civil War Ironclads: The U.S. Navy and Industrial Mobilization* (Baltimore, MD: The John Hopkins University Press, 2002)

———, *Now for the Contest: Coastal and Oceanic Naval Operations in the Civil War* (Lincoln: University of Nebraska Press, 2004)

N. A. M. Rodger, *The Admiralty* (Lavenham, UK: Terence Dalton Ltd., 1979)

Theodore Ropp (Stephen S. Roberts, ed.), *The Development of a Modern Navy: French Naval Policy, 1871–1904* (Annapolis, MD: Naval Institute Press, 1987)

John Scott Russell, *The Fleet of the Future: Iron or Wood?* (London: Longman, Green, Longman and Roberts, 1861)

Allen Salisbury, *The Civil War and the American System: America's Battle with Britain, 1860–1876* (New York: Campaigner Publications, Inc., 1978)

Stanley Sandler, *The Emergence of the Modern Capital Ship* (Newark, DE: University of Delaware Press, 1979)

Andrew Saunders, *English Heritage Book of Channel Defences* (London: B. T. Batsford, 1997)

Robert J. Schneller, Jr., *A Quest for Glory: A Biography of Rear Admiral John A. Dahlgren* (Annapolis, MD: Naval Institute Press, 1996)

Donald Mackenzie Schurman, *The Education of a Navy: The Development of British Naval Strategic Thought, 1867–1914* (London: Cassell, 1965)

———(John F. Beeler, ed.), *Imperial Defence, 1868–1887* (London: Frank Cass & Co., 2000)

G. R. Searle, *Morality and the Market in Victorian Britain* (Oxford: Clarendon Press, 1998)

Bernard Semmel, *Democracy versus Empire: The Jamaica Riots of 1865 and the Governor Eyre Controversy* (New York: Doubleday Anchor Books, 1962, reprint 1969)

————, *Liberalism and Naval Strategy: Ideology, Interest, and Sea Power During the Pax Britannica* (London: Allen & Unwin, Inc., 1986)

Richard Shannon, *Gladstone, Volume 1: 1809–1865* (London: Hamish Hamilton, 1982)

————, *The Crisis of Imperialism, 1865–1915* (London: Paladin Books, 1979, reprint of 1974 original)

Belle Becker Sideman and Lillian Friedman (eds.), *Europe Looks at the Civil War* (New York: Orion Press, 1962, reprint of 1960 original)

Paul H. Silverstone, *Warships of the Civil War Navies* (Annapolis, MD: Naval Institute Press, 1989)

Edward Simpson, *A Treatise on Ordnance and Naval Gunnery: Compiled and arranged as a Text-Book for the U.S. Naval Academy* (New York: D. Van Nostrand, 1863)

Edward William Sloan III, *Benjamin Franklin Isherwood, Naval Engineer* (Annapolis, MD: Naval Institute Press, 1965)

Lawrence Sondhaus, *Naval Warfare, 1815–1914* (London: Routledge, 2001)

Warren F. Spencer, *The Confederate Navy in Europe* (Tuscaloosa: The University of Alabama Press, 1983)

Harold and Margaret Sprout, *The Rise of American Naval Power* (Princeton, NJ: Naval Institute Press, 1939, 1990, with an Introduction by Kenneth Hagan)

E. D. Steele, *Palmerston and Liberalism, 1855–1865* (Cambridge, UK: Cambridge University Press, 1991)

William N. Still, Jr., *Confederate Shipbuilding* (Athens: University of Georgia Press, 1969)

————, *Iron Afloat*: The Story of the Confederate Armorclads (Nashville, TN: Vanderbilt University Press, 1971)

————, *American Seapower in the Old World: The United States Navy in European Waters, 1865–1917* (Westport, CT: Greenwood Press, 1980)

————, *Monitor Builders: A Historical Study of the Principal Firms and Individuals Involved in the Construction of U.S.S. Monitor* (Washington, DC: National Maritime Initiative, National Park Service, Department of the Interior, 1988)

William N. Still, Jr., John M. Taylor, and Norman C. Delaney, *Raiders and Blockaders: The American Civil War Afloat* (Washington, DC: Brassey's Inc., 1998)

David G. Surdam, *Northern Naval Superiority and the Economics of the American Civil War* (Columbia: University of South Carolina Press, 2001)

A. J. P. Taylor, *The Struggle for Mastery in Europe: 1848–1918* (Oxford: Oxford University Press, 1954)

Thomas E. Taylor, *Running the Blockade: A Personal Narrative of Adventures, Risks and Escapes During the American Civil War* (Annapolis, MD: Naval Institute Press, 1995 reprint of 1896)

William H. Thiesen, *Industrializing American Shipbuilding: The Transformation of Ship Design and Construction, 1820–1920* (Gainesville: University Press of Florida, 2006)

Geoffrey Till (ed.), *Seapower: Theory and Practice* (Ilford, UK: Frank Cass & Co. Ltd, 1994)

Daniel Todd and Michael Lindberg, *Navies and Shipbuilding Industries: The Strained Symbiosis* (Westport, CT: Greenwood Publishing Group, 1996)

Herbert Henry Todd, *The Building of the Confederate States Navy in Europe* (Nashville: Tennessee Joint Universities Libraries, 1941)

George Macaulay Trevelyan, *The Life of John Bright* (Boston: Houghton Mifflin Company, 1914)

Spencer Tucker, *Arming the Fleet: U.S. Navy Ordnance in the Muzzle-Loading Era* (Annapolis, MD: Naval Institute Press, 1989)

———, *The Handbook of 19th Century Naval Warfare* (Stroud, UK: Sutton Publishing, 2000)

———, *A Short History of the Civil War at Sea* (Wilmington, DE: Scholarly Resources, Inc, 2002)

Hugh Tulloch, *The Debate on the American Civil War Era* (Manchester, UK: Manchester University Press, 1999)

Glyndon G. Van Deusen, *William Henry Seward* (New York: Oxford University Press, 1967)

Sheldon Vanauken, *The Glittering Illusion: English Sympathy for the Southern Confederacy* (Washington, DC: Regnery Gateway, 1989)

Brougham Villiers and W. H. Chesson, *Anglo-American Relations, 1861–1865* (London: T. Fisher Unwin, 1919)

John Vincent, *The Formation of the British Liberal Party, 1857–1868* (London: Penguin Books, 1972, reprint of Constable, 1966)

Gordon H. Warren, *Fountain of Discontent: The* Trent *Affair and Freedom of the Seas* (Boston: Northeastern University Press, 1981)

Richard H. Webber, *Monitors of the U.S. Navy, 1861–1937* (Washington, DC: Naval History Division, Navy Department, 1969)

Kevin J. Weddle, *Lincoln's Tragic Admiral: The Life of Samuel Francis Du Pont* (Charlottesville: University of Virginia Press, 2005)

Russell F. Weigley, *The American Way of War: A History of United States Military Strategy and Policy* (Bloomington: Indiana University Press, 1977, reprint of Macmillan Publishing, 1973)

Stanley Weintraub, *Disraeli: A Biography* (London: Hamish Hamilton, 1993)

John Wells, *The Immortal Warrior: Britain's First and Last Battleship* (Emsworth, UK: Kenneth Mason, 1987)

Richard S. West, Jr., *Gideon Welles, Lincoln's Navy Department* (New York: Bobbs-Merrill Co., 1943)

———, *The Second Admiral: A Life of David Dixon Porter, 1813–1891* (New York: Coward-McCann, 1937)

Francis Brown Wheeler, *John F. Winslow, L.L.D. and the* Monitor (New York: Poughkeepsie, 1893)

Ruth White, *Yankee From Sweden: The Dream and the Reality in the Days of John Ericsson* (New York: Henry Holt and Company, 1960)

Roger Willcock, *Bulwark of Empire: Bermuda's Fortified Naval Base 1860–1920* (Princeton, NJ: Roger Willcock, 1962)

John Wilkinson, *The Narrative of a Blockade-Runner* (New York: Sheldon & Company, 1877)

H. W. Wilson, *Ironclads in Action: A Sketch of Naval Warfare from 1855 to 1895 With Some Account of the Development of the Battleship in England*, 2 vols., 5th ed.(London: Sampson Low, Marston & Co., 1897)

_____, *Battleships in Action*, 2 vols. (London: Conway Maritime Press, 1995, reprint from Sampson Low, Marston & Co., 1926)

Stephen R. Wise, *Lifeline of the Confederacy: Blockade Running During the Civil War* (Columbia: University of South Carolina Press, 1988)

_____, *Gate of Hell: Campaign for Charleston Harbor, 1863* (Columbia: University of South Carolina Press, 1994)

Anthony Wood, *Nineteenth Century Britain, 1815–1914* (Harlow, UK: Longman Group, Ltd., 1982, reprint of 1960 original)

Llewellyn Woodward, *The Oxford History of England: The Age of Reform, 1815–1870* (Oxford: Clarendon Press, 1962, reprint of 1938 original)

ARTICLES

John D. Allen, "Born Forty Years Too Soon," *The American Neptune*, Vol. 22, No. 4 (October 1962)

Dean C. Allard, "Naval Technology During the American Civil War," *The American Neptune*, Vol. 49, No. 2 (Spring 1989)

Francis J. Allen, "*Roanoke*: A Civil War Battleship," *Warship*, No. 35 (July 1985)

Bern Anderson, "The Naval Strategy of the Civil War," *Military Affairs*, Vol. 26, No.1 (Spring 1962)

Neil Ashcroft, "British Trade with the Confederacy and the Effectiveness of Union Maritime Strategy During the Civil War," *International Journal of Maritime History*, Vol. 10, No. 2 (December, 1998)

John Bach, "The Imperial Defense of the Pacific Ocean in the Mid-Nineteenth Century: Ships and Bases," *The American Neptune*, Vol. 32, No. 4 (October 1972)

Pascal Barras, "The Royal Navy and the Role of Seapower in Global Politics, 1856–1871," in Anthony Preston (ed.), *Warship 2001–2002* (London: Conway Maritime Press, 2001)

C. J. Bartlett, "The Mid-Victorian Reappraisal of Naval Policy," in Kenneth Bourne and D. C. Watts (eds.), *Studies in International History: Essays Presented to W. Norton Medlicott* (Hamden: Archon Books, 1967)

Richard M. Basoco, William E. Geoghegan, and Frank J. Merli (eds.), "A British View of the Union Navy, 1864: A Report Addressed to Her Majesty's Minister at Washington:," *The American Neptune*, Vol. 27, No. 1 (January 1967),

K. Jack Bauer, "Naval Shipbuilding Programs 1794–1860," *Military Affairs*, Vol. 29, No. 1 (Spring 1965)

Colin F. Baxter, "The Duke of Somerset and the Creation of the British Ironclad Navy, 1859–1866," *The Mariner's Mirror*, Vol. 66, No. 3 (August 1977)

James P. Baxter III, "The British Government and Neutral Rights, 1861–1865," *The American Historical Review*, Vol. 34, No. 1 (October 1928)

John F. Beeler, "A One Power Standard? Great Britain and the Balance of Naval Power, 1860–1880," *Journal of Strategic Studies*, Vol. 15, No. 4 (December 1992)

George E. Belknap, "Reminiscent of the 'New Ironsides' off Charleston," *The United Service*, Vol. 1 (January 1879)

George L. Bernstein "Special Relationship and Appeasement: Liberal Policy Towards America in the Age of Palmerston," *The Historical Journal*, Vol. 41, No. 3 (1998)

John Bourne, "Ships of War," *Proceedings of the Institution of Civil Engineers* 26 (1866–1867)

Kenneth Bourne, "British Preparations for War with the North, 1861–1862," *English Historical Review*, Vol. 76 (October 1961)

Edgar M. Branch, *American Literature*, "Major Perry and the Monitor," *Camanche*: An Early Mark Twain Speech, Vol. 39, Issue 2 (May 1967)

Bernard Brodie, "Military Demonstration and Disclosure of New Weapons," *World Politics*, Vol. 5, No. 3 (April 1953)

David K. Brown, "Introduction of the Screw Propeller into the Royal Navy," *Warship*, No. 1, January 1977

———, "Technical Topics: Roughness and Fouling," *Warship*, No. 12, October 1979

———, "Technical Topics: Where the Power Goes," *Warship*, No. 16, October 1980

———, "Attack and Defence," Parts 1–2, *Warship*, Nos. 18 and 21, 1981–1982

———, "Developing the Armour of HMS *Warrior*, *Warship*, No. 40, October 1986

———, "H.M.S. *Warrior*—The Design Aspects," Royal Institution of Naval Architects, 129, (Spring 1986)

———, "Wood, Sail, and Cannonballs to Steel, Steam, and Shells, 1815–1895," in J. R. Hill (ed.), *The Oxford Illustrated History of the Royal Navy* (London: BCA, 1995)

Franklin Buchanan, "The Confederate States Navy," in Ben La Bree (ed.), *The Confederate Soldier in the Civil War* (Louisville, KY: Prentice Press, 1897)

Lance C. Buhl, "'Mariners and Machines: Resistance to Technological Change in the American Navy, 1865–1869," *The Journal of American History*, Vol. 61, No. 3 (December 1974)

Donald L. Canney, "The Union Navy During the Civil War, 1861–65," *Warship*, 1995

Martin P. Claussen, "Peace Factors in Anglo-American Relations, 1861–1865," *Mississippi Valley Historical Review*, Vol. 26, No. 4 (March, 1940)

W. F. Durand, "John Ericsson: Navies of Commerce," in John Lord (ed.), *Beacon Lights of History*, vol. 14 (New York: James Clarke and Co., 1902)

R. B. Ely, "This Filthy Ironpot," *American Heritage*, Vol. 19, No. 2 (1968)

William C. Emerson, "U.S.S. *New Ironsides*: America's First Broadside Iron-clad," *Warship*, 1993

John Ericsson, "The Monitors," *The Century Magazine*, Vol. 31, No. 2 (December 1885)

D. Evans, "The Royal Navy and the Development of Mobile Logistics 1851–1894," *The Mariner's Mirror*, Vol. 83, No. 3 (August 1997)

Howard J. Fuller, " 'The Whole Character of Maritime Life': British Reactions to the U.S.S. *Monitor* and the American Ironclad Experience," *The Mariner's Mirror*, Vol. 88, No. 3 (August 2002)

―――, " 'This Country Now Occupies the Vantage Ground': Understanding John Ericsson's Monitors and the American Union's War Against British Naval Supremacy," *The American Neptune*, Vol. 62, No. 1 (Winter 2002)

E. G. Garrison, "Three Ironclad Warships—The Archaeology of Industrial Process and Historical Myth, *Historical Archaeology*, Vol. 29, No. 4 (1995)

William E. Geoghegan, Thomas W. Green and Frank J. Merli, "The South's Scottish Sea Monster," *The American Neptune*, Vol. 29, No. 1, (January 1969)

Norman A. Graebner, "Northern Diplomacy and European Neutrality," in David Donald (ed.), *Why the North Won the Civil War* (New York: Collier, 1962)

Daniel G. Harris, "The Swedish Monitors," *Warship*, 1994

John D. Hayes, " 'Captain Fox—*He* is the Navy Department,' " *U.S. Naval Institute Proceedings*, Vol. 91, No. 9 (1965)

Daniel R. Headrick, "The Tools of Imperialism: Technology and the Expansion of European Colonial Empires in the Nineteenth Century," *The Journal of Modern History*, Vol. 51, No. 2 (June 1979)

William Ray Heitzmann, "The Ironclad *Weehawken* in the Civil War," *The American Neptune*, Vol. 42, No. 3 (July 1982)

Robin D. S. Higham, "The Russian Fleet on the Eastern Seaboard, 1863–1864: A Maritime Chronology," *The American Neptune*, 20, No. 1 (January 1960)

S. W. Jackman, "Admiral Wilkes Visits Bermuda During the Civil War," *The American Neptune*, Vol. 24, No. 3 (July 1964)

Mark F. Jenkins, "The Technology of the Ironclads," *Naval Gazette*, Vol. 2, No. 6, and Vol. 3, No. 1 (1998)

Robert Erwin Johnson, "Investment by Sea: The Civil War Blockade," *The American Neptune*, Vol. 32, No. 1 (January 1972)

―――, "Ships Against Forts: Charleston, 7 April 1863," *The American Neptune*, Vol. 57, No. 2 (Spring 1997)

Frank Joseph, "A Strategic Reassessment: Ironclads at Hampton Roads," *Command Magazine*, 45 (October 1977)

Klari Kingston, "Gunboat Liberalism? Palmerston, Europe and 1848," *History Today*, Vol. 47, No. 2 (February 1997)

Andrew Lambert, "The Royal Navy, 1856–1914: Deterrence and The Strategy of World Power," in Keith Neilson and Elizabeth Jane Errington (eds.), *Navies and Global Defense: Theories and Strategy* (Westport, CT: Praeger Publishers, 1995)

―――, "The Shield of Empire, 1815–1895," in J. R. Hill (ed.), *The Oxford Illustrated History of the Royal Navy* (London: BCA, 1995)

_____, "History, Strategy, and Doctrine: Sir John Knox Laughton and the Education of the Royal Navy," in William B. Cogar (ed.), *New Interpretations in Naval History: Selected Papers from the Twelfth Naval History Symposium* (Annapolis, MD: Naval Institute Press, 1997)

_____, "Politics, Technology and Policy-Making, 1859–1865: Palmerston, Gladstone and the Management of the Ironclad Naval Race," *The Northern Mariner*, Vol. 3, No. 3 (July 1998)

_____, "Australia, the *Trent* Crisis of 1861, and the Strategy of Imperial Defence," in David Stevens and John Reeve (eds.), *Southern Trident: Strategy, History and the Rise of Australian Naval Power* (Crows Nest, Australia: Allen & Unwin, 2001)

_____, "Laughton's Legacy: Naval History at King's College, London," *Historical Research*, Vol. 77, No. 196 (May 2004)

_____, "Economic Power, Technological Advantage, and Imperial Strength: Britain as a Unique Global Power, 1860–1890," *International Journal of Naval History* (www.ijnhonline.org), Vol. 5, No. 2 (August 2006)

Leo B. Levy, "Hawthorne, Melville, and the *Monitor*," *American Literature*, Vol. 37, No. 1 (March 1965)

Paul D. Lockhart, "The Confederate Naval Squadron at Charleston and the Failure of Naval Harbor Defense," *The American Neptune*, Vol. 44, No. 4 (Fall 1984)

Charles W. Maccord, "Ericsson and His 'Monitor,'" *The North American Review*, Vol. 149, No. 395 (October 1889)

Douglas H. Maynard, "Plotting the Escape of the *Alabama*," *The Journal of Southern History*, Vol. 20, No. 2 (May 1954)

_____, "The Forbes-Aspinwall Mission," *The Mississippi Valley Historical Review*, Vol. 45, No. 1 (June 1958)

James M. McPherson, "Presidential Address: No Peace Without Victory, 1861–1865," *The American Historical Review*, Vol. 109, No. 1 (February 2004)

Philip Melvin, "Stephen Russell Mallory, Southern Naval Statesman," *The Journal of Southern History*, Vol. 10, Issue 2 (May 1944)

John D. Milligan, "From Theory to Application: The Emergence of the American Ironclad War Vessel," *Military Affairs*, Vol. 48, No. 3 (July 1984)

Walter Millis, "The Iron Sea Elephants," *The American Neptune*, Vol. 10, No. 1 (January 1950)

Robert W. Neeser, "The Department of the Navy," *The American Political Science Review*, Vol. 11, No. 1 (February 1917)

John Niven, "Gideon Welles and Naval Administration During the Civil War," *The American Neptune*, Vol. 35, No. 1 (January 1975)

Nathan Okun, "Armor and its Application to Warships," *Warship International*, Vol. 15, No. 4 (1978)

Philip Ransom Osborn, "The American Monitors," *U.S. Naval Institute Proceedings*, Vol. 63, No. 408 (1937)

Harriet Chappell Owsley, "Henry Shelton Sanford and Federal Surveillance Abroad, 1861–1865," *The Mississippi Valley Historical Review*, Vol. 48, No. 2 (September 1961)

Charles Oscar Paullin, "President Lincoln and the Navy," *The American Historical Review*, Vol. 14, No. 2 (January 1909)

John D. Pelzer, "Liverpool and the American Civil War," *History Today*, Vol. 40, No. 3 (March 1990)

Arnold A. Putnam, "The Introduction of the Revolving Turret," *The American Neptune*, No. 56, No. 2 (Spring 1996)

———, "*Rolf Krake*: Europe's First turreted Ironclad," *The Mariner's Mirror*, Vol. 84, No. 1 (February 1998)

Bryan Ranft, "Parliamentary Debate, Economic Vulnerability and British Naval Expansion, 1860–1905," in Lawrence Freedman, Paul Hayes, and Robert O'Neill (eds.), *War, Strategy, and International Politics: Essays in Honour of Sir Michael Howard* (Oxford: Clarendon Press, 1992)

E. J. Reed, "State of the British Navy"; "The Ironclad Reconstruction of the Navy," *Quarterly Review*, Vol. 134 (1873)

Rowena Reed, "The Siege of Charleston," in William C. Davis (ed.), *The Image of War 1861–1865*, 6 vols. (New York: Doubleday & Company, Inc., 1983), 4

Stephen S. Roberts, "The French Coast Defense Ship *Rochambeau*," *Warship International*, Vol. 30, No. 4 (1993)

William H. Roberts, "The Neglected Ironclad: A Design and Constructural Analysis of the U.S.S. *New Ironsides*," *Warship International*, Vol. 26, No. 2 (1989)

———, "'Thunder Mountain'—The Ironclad Ram *Dunderberg*," *Warship International*, Vol. 30, No. 4 (1993)

———, "'The Name of Ericsson': Political Engineering in the Union Ironclad Program, 1861–1863," *Journal of Military History*, Vol. 63, No. 4 (1999)

———, "'The Sudden Destruction of Bright Hopes': Union Shipbuilding Management, 1862–1865," in Randy Carol Balano and Craig L. Symonds (eds.), *New Interpretations in Naval History* (Annapolis, MD: Naval Institute Press, 2001)

Robert Spencer Robinson, "England as a Naval Power," *The Nineteenth Century*, No. 37 (March 1880)

N. A. M. Rodger, "British Naval Thought and Naval Policy, 1820–1890: Strategic Thought in an Era of Technological Change," in Craig L. Symonds (ed.), *New Aspects of Naval History* (Annapolis, MD: U.S. Naval Institute, 1981)

Stanley Sandler, "A Navy in Decay: Some Strategic Technological Results of Disarmament, 1865–69 in the U.S. Navy," *Military Affairs*, Vol. 35, No. 4 (December 1971)

———, "The Day of the Ram," *Military Affairs*, Vol. 40, No. 4 (December 1976)

———, "The Royal Navy's Coastal Craze: Technological Results of Strategic Confusion in the Early Ironclad Era," *The American Neptune*, Vol. 51, No. 3 (Summer 1991)

Brooks D. Simpson, "Olive Branch and Sword: Union War-Making in the American Civil War," in David K. Adams and Cornelis A. Van Minnen (eds.), *Aspects of War in American History* (Keele, UK: Keele University Press, 1997)

Edward Simpson, "The Monitor *Passaic*," *The United Service*, Vol. 2 (April 1880)

_____, "Ironclads," in *Hammersly's Naval Encyclopedia* (Philadelphia: L. R. Hamersly & Co., 1881)

Ernest F. Slaymarker, "The Armament of HMS *Warrior*," parts 1–3, *Warship*, No. 37, (January 1986); No. 38 (April 1986); No. 39 (July 1986)

William N. Still, Jr., "Confederate Naval Strategy: The Ironclad," *The Journal of Southern History*, Vol. 27, No. 3 (August 1961)

_____, "*Monitor* Companies: A Study of the Major Firms That Built the U.S.S. *Monitor*," *The American Neptune*, Vol. 48, No. 2 (Spring 1988)

Richard H. Thompson, "The Rise and Fall of the Monitor 1862–1973," *The Mariner's Mirror*, Vol. 60, No. 3 (August 1974)

Spencer C. Tucker, "The Stevens Ironclad Battery," *The American Neptune*, Vol. 51, No. 1 (Winter 1991)

W. C. B. Tunstall, "Imperial Defence, 1815–1870," in J. Holland Rose, A. P. Newton, and E. A. Benians (eds.), *The Cambridge History of the British Empire* (Cambridge, UK: Cambridge University Press, 1940)

Edward W. Very, "The Development of Armor for Naval Use," *Proceedings of the United States Naval Institute*, Vol. IX, No. 3, 1883

Samuel J. Watson, "Knowledge, Interest and the Limits of Military Professionalism: The Discourse on American Coastal Defence, 1815–60," *War in History*, Vol. 5, No. 3 (1998)

Donald B. Webster, Jr., "Rodman's Great Guns," *Ordnance* (July-August 1962)

Kevin J. Weddle, "'There Should Be No Bungling About this Blockade': The Blockade Board of 1861 and the Making of Union Naval Strategy," *The International Journal of Naval History*, Vol. 1, No. 1, (April 2002)

Gideon Welles, "The Capture and Release of Mason and Slidell," *The Galaxy*, Vol. 7 (May 1873)

Arnold Whitridge, "The *Alabama*, 1862–1864: A Crisis in Anglo-American Relations," *History Today* (March 1955)

THESES

Colin F. Baxter, "Admiralty Problems During the Second Palmerston Administration, 1859–1865," University of Georgia Ph.D. Thesis (1965)

Martin S. Crawford, "The Times and America 1850–1865: A Study in the Anglo-American Relationship," Oxford University Ph.D. thesis (1979)

T. S. Good, "The British Parliament & the American Civil War," Durham University M.A. thesis (1993)

T. Keiser, "The English Press and the American Civil War," Reading University Ph.D. thesis (1971)

John S. Kinross, "The Palmerston Forts in the South West: Why Were They Built?" Exeter University M.A. thesis (1995)

David B. McGee, "Floating Bodies, Naval Science: Science, Design and the *Captain* Controversy, 1860–1870," University of Toronto Ph.D. thesis (1994)

Robert John Schneller, "The Contentious Innovator: A Biography of Rear Admiral John A. Dahlgren U.S.N. (1809–1870): Generational Conflict, Ordnance Technology," Duke University Ph.D. thesis (1991)

William J. Sullivan, "Gustavus Fox and Naval Administration, 1861–1866," Catholic University Ph.D. thesis (1977)

Dana Wegner, "Alban C. Stimers and the Office of the General Inspector of Ironclads, 1862–1864," State University of New York at Oneonta M.A. thesis, 1979

Index

About the Author

HOWARD J. FULLER is Senior Lecturer of War Studies in the Department of History as well as a Core Member of the History and Governance Research Institute (HAGRI) Conflict Studies Research Group at the University of Wolverhampton. He specializes in Anglo-American nineteenth-century history, particularly the American Civil War and the British Empire.